ATTACKS ON THE PRESS
in **2001**

On the cover: A camera-shy police officer,
Macedonia, March 21, 2001.
(AP Photo/Dimitri Messinis)

D1403019

330 Seventh Avenue, 12th floor, New York, N.Y. 10001

Phone: (212)465-1004 Fax: (212)465-9568 e-mail: info@cpj.org

Web site: www.cpj.org

Founded in 1981, the Committee to Protect Journalists responds to attacks on the press everywhere in the world. CPJ documents more than 600 cases every year and takes action on behalf of journalists and their news organizations without regard to political ideology. Join CPJ and help promote press freedom by defending the people who report the news. To maintain its independence, CPJ accepts no government funding. We depend entirely on the support of corporations, foundations, and individuals.

The Associated Press, IDT, Lexis-Nexis, and Reuters provided electronic news and Internet services that were used to conduct research for this report.

  REUTERS

Editor: Richard McGill Murphy
Deputy Editor: Amanda Watson-Boles
Associate Editor: Trenton Daniel
Design: FTK Media LLC
Desktop Publishing: Cynthia Gibson

Attacks on the Press in 2001: A Worldwide Survey by the Committee to Protect Journalists
ISSN: 1078-3334
ISBN: 0-944823-21-1

PREFACE

by Anne Garrels

ON NOVEMBER 19, 2001, I WAS AT THE BORDER negotiating with officials to get across into Afghanistan. There was suddenly an unexplained problem, yet journalists arriving from Afghanistan said they had no trouble along the way. I was frustrated.

None of us knew that a caravan of our colleagues had just been attacked on a deserted stretch of highway between Jalalabad and Kabul, a few hours away. Gunmen forced four foreign journalists and an Afghan guide from two of the lead cars. One of the drivers described how his passengers were pushed down to the riverbank and shot dead. He said the gunmen claimed to be members of the Taliban militia, though their identity has never been confirmed.

"I saw the gunmen using stones," said an interpreter who also escaped. "I heard the sound of Kalashnikovs three or four times."

The slain journalists were Harry Burton, 33, an Australian television cameraman for Reuters; Azizizulla Haidari, also 33, a Pakistani photographer for Reuters; Julio Fuentes, 46, a journalist from *El Mundo* newspaper in Madrid, and Maria Grazia Cutuli, 39, a reporter for *Corriere della Serra* newspaper in Milan.

I made it to Jalalabad shortly before Thanksgiving. A dozen or so journalists who had survived the attack organized a dinner. Collecting the ingredients for this traditional meal took on a new meaning, as well as providing sanity amid madness. Everyone at the hotel, no matter what his or her nationality, was invited.

Pamela Constable of *The Washington Post* raised a glass to her dead friends. Many of us hadn't known the four journalists, but we knew what they had been doing, and why they were in Afghanistan, and we knew that any one of us could have been receiving this unwanted and untimely tribute.

The next day I made the same journey from Jalalabad to Kabul on a public bus. There had been a lot of discussion about organizing another convoy, this time armed, but I decided any convoy was a bad idea. I would be safer alone, I figured—it was my choice. Along the road, the Afghan passengers pointed out the place where the murders had taken place. My trip was uneventful, and had I not known about the murders I would have thought it was a starkly beautiful place. There was nothing to distinguish this curve of rock from any other.

An Italian journalist has since placed a plaque at the Spin Gar hotel, from where the four journalists set off on their last reporting trip. No one will ever leave that hotel again with such innocence.

The lawlessness and chaos in Afghanistan have presented both a challenge and a threat to hundreds of journalists covering a conflict that involves shifting alliances and widespread banditry. Eight journalists were killed there in the line of duty last year. More than ever before in my career, I have received praise and sympathy for working in Afghanistan. Yet Afghanistan is only the most high profile of many dangerous places where journalists work worldwide.

And most of the journalists killed around the world last year were not covering combat. As CPJ executive director Ann Cooper has said, we should also remember "that journalists around the world who uncovered corrupt illegal acts and graft at high levels of power were murdered with impunity." There are no plaques for them.

Then there are those who have not been killed, thank God, but who endure relentless persecution, prosecution, and psychological pressure. Day in and day out, Georgian journalist Akaki Gogichaishvili and his team from the investigative television program "Sixty Minutes" report on illegal activities and official corruption, despite constant threats of arrest and worse. He does not have to go to a front line to face a minefield. I can go home. He is at home.

Advised by CPJ staffers about Gogichaishvili's situation, I stopped by to see him in his cramped offices while on a reporting trip to Tbilisi. CPJ cannot provide bodyguards, but Gogichaishvili says the support and publicity CPJ has provided at key moments are what he needs to carry on, for now.

For me as a journalist, the good news is seeing new colleagues emerge around the world like Akaki Gogichaishvili in Georgia. But as formerly totalitarian states, especially in the former Soviet Union, begin to allow press freedom, there is a rise in abuses which if not lethal are certainly frightening, and highly dangerous to these emerging democracies.

In the wake of September 11, many governments may be tempted to use the threat of terrorism as a pretext to crack down on a prying, inconvenient press. If they do, CPJ will be there to make a fuss—we owe that to our colleagues around the world.

Anne Garrels is a CPJ board member and a foreign correspondent for National Public Radio. She has covered the former Soviet Union, before and after the collapse of communism, and has reported on the Gulf War, as well as the conflicts in Bosnia, Kosovo, Chechnya, and, most recently, Afghanistan.

| TABLE OF CONTENTS |

p. 2   p. 16   p. 25   p. 597

In **Sierra Leone**, journalist Abdul Karim Karoma was threatened after reporting that a former government official had been seen begging for food at restaurants. [See page 77]

In 2001, the **United States** jailed free-lance writer Vanessa Leggett on contempt-of-court charges, joining **Cuba** as the only other country in the Western Hemisphere to imprison journalists for their work. Leggett is believed to have been jailed longer than any other journalist in U.S. history. [See pages 182, 202]

A **Nigerian** judge jailed two journalists for covering proceedings in her courtroom, promising that they would "have plenty to write about" after being locked up with accused criminals. [See page 72]

In **Venezuela**, agents detained lawyer and columnist Pablo Aure Sánchez for writing in the daily *El Nacional* that "we imagine [the military] parading...in multi-colored panties," referring to a campaign in which women's underwear (in a variety of festive hues) was delivered anonymously to military officers to insult their manhood. [See page 205]

Liberia's Ministry of Information, Culture, and Tourism issued a May 27 statement declaring that "no more surprise visits to Liberia by foreign journalists will be allowed." [See page 64]

Chinese journalist Jiang Weiping was sentenced to eight years in prison for reporting on corruption, while one of the officials implicated in his article was promoted to provincial governor. [See page 321]

In communist **China**, publications can even be penalized for being too Marxist. One prominent leftist monthly was closed after sharply criticizing the president's call for capitalists to join the Communist Party. [See page 270]

In a government crackdown against political dissent, **Eritrean** authorities suspended all the country's privately owned newspapers until further notice. [See page 53]

After September 11, officials in **Benin, China, Liberia**, the **Palestinian Authority Territories**, and the **United States** used the crisis to censor media outlets. [See pages 94, 327, 126, 523, and 202]

In December 2001, the Internal Affairs Ministry of **Ukraine** authorized journalists covering sensitive topics, such as corruption, to carry guns with rubber bullets. [See page 403]

In **Iran**, the government closed or suspended 20 newspapers and publications in 2001. [See page 477]

In **Iraq**, it is a criminal offense to be found in possession of a satellite dish. [See page 479]

The **Yemeni** Supreme Court upheld a sentence of 80 lashes against a former newspaper editor, a punishment that was only avoided when the plaintiff dropped the suit. [See page 500]

A journalist with the state television network in **Rwanda** was suspended for two weeks for airing images of President Paul Kagame perspiring heavily. [See page 138]

INTRODUCTION

by Ann Cooper

IN THE WAKE OF SEPTEMBER 11, 2001, journalists around the world faced a press freedom crisis that was truly global in scope.

In the first days and weeks after the terrorist attacks on New York City and Washington, D.C., governments across the globe—in China, Benin, the Palestinian Authority Territories, and the United States—took actions to curb reporting on the assault and its aftermath. While the world focused on Manhattan and Kabul, leaders in Eritrea and Zimbabwe seized the moment, launching crackdowns to silence all independent media.

And in Afghanistan itself, where hundreds of journalists deployed to cover the "war on terrorism," reporters and photographers were assaulted, censored, and even murdered. In 16 deadly November days, eight journalists were killed in Afghanistan, pushing the year's worldwide total to 37.

The 2001 death toll was up dramatically from the 24 who died a year earlier, and it was the worst since the first half of the 1990s, when dozens of journalists died during conflicts in Algeria, Bosnia, and Tajikistan. The toll is just one of the year's grim statistics and stories:

- After four years of steady decline, the number of journalists in prison jumped nearly 50 percent—from 81 in 2000 to 118 in 2001. More than two-thirds of that alarming increase came from little-noticed crackdowns in Eritrea and Nepal, carried out after September 11. China, already the world's leading jailer of journalists, arrested eight more, ending the year with a total of 35 journalists behind bars.
- Invoking "national security," governments around the world sought new restrictions on the press or unleashed new intimidation. As justification, some cited U.S. actions after September 11, such as the State Department's attempt to censor a Voice of America interview with Taliban leader Mullah Omar. "If the most celebrated democracies in the world won't allow their national interests to be tampered with, we will not allow it, too," said Zimbabwean information minister Jonathan Moyo. Then he denounced as "terrorists" the country's independent journalists, who have endured violence, jail, and torture at the hands of the state.
- The United States and Israel ignited press freedom controversies by bombing two media outlets. Al-Jazeera's bureau in Kabul was bombed in November by the United States as part of its attack on Taliban territories. In a letter to Al-Jazeera, the Pentagon offered no apology to the Arabic-language satellite television station and called its building "a known al-Qaeda facility," referring to the Taliban-supported terrorist group blamed for the September 11 attacks. Israel was equally unrepentant for its December bombing and bulldozing of Voice of Palestine's radio facilities in the West Bank. In January 2002, Israel struck again, this time destroying

the Palestinian Broadcasting Corporation building in Ramallah. International humanitarian law prohibits deliberate attacks on civilian facilities unless they are used for military purposes.

These incidents represent major setbacks for press freedom, but is the damage permanent? Some international experts suggest that the war on terrorism, which is likely to continue for years, signals an end to the era of human rights—the post–Cold War period when building democracy and respect for fundamental liberties became central foreign policy objectives.

A decade ago, the collapse of authoritarian communist regimes brought an explosion of press freedom around the world. More recently, the gains have slowed, with key indicators of press abuse tending to rise and fall each year in concert with conflicts around the world. In 1994, for example, wars in the Balkans, Rwanda, and Algeria sent the death toll soaring to 72, while 173 journalists languished in jail—74 of them in a single country, Turkey, which harshly suppressed reporting on Kurdish separatists. As the conflict in Turkey has abated, the number of journalists in jail has declined, though 13 remained there at the end of 2001, a record surpassed only by China and Nepal. Burma, another perennial offender, held 12 journalists at year's end.

The conflict in Afghanistan and the larger war on terrorism have already taken a toll on press freedom, but it seems premature to draw conclusions about a long-term impact. In the two decades since CPJ's 1981 founding, press freedom has become a worldwide movement, supported not just by international organizations such as CPJ but also by dozens of grassroots journalists' groups around the world. The press freedom gains achieved by all of them form a crucial bulwark against more general human rights violations.

Despite the conflict in Afghanistan, there were important gains in 2001, even in countries with some of the worst press freedom histories. Yugoslavia's independent journalists, scrappy survivors of Slobodan Milosevic's ruthless dictatorship, breathed easier, if not completely freely, for the first time in a decade. In 2001, Syrians finally read independent newspapers—the first published outside of state control in nearly 40 years. And formal censorship was lifted in Sri Lanka, although other pressures remain.

Some of the year's other positive developments affirmed our conviction that documenting and publicizing press freedom violations can force recalcitrant countries to take action. CPJ's Africa program conducted intensive advocacy on Ethiopia prior to a fact-finding mission in September, with the result that seven journalists were released from prison; at year's end, only one journalist remained in an Ethiopian jail. Meanwhile, two CPJ International Press Freedom awardees, in prison when their awards were announced in 1999 and 2000, were each released in 2001, before serving out their full sentences. Jesús Joel Díaz Hernández, the 1999 awardee from Cuba, was freed after serving half of his four-year sentence, while 2000 awardee Mashallah Shamsolvaezin was spared a year of his 30-month sentence when Iran freed him in September.

These releases are powerful evidence that even the most hard-line opponents of press freedom are not immune to international pressure. (Cuba and Iran were both on CPJ's 2001 Ten Worst Enemies of the Press list.) By documenting and publicizing abuses against journalists around the world, CPJ tries to ensure that those who would suppress critical reporting will only attract greater scrutiny.

This strategy applies both to governments and nonstate actors who violate press freedom, such as the guerrillas in Colombia and the kidnappers who took *Wall Street Journal* reporter Daniel Pearl in January 2002. As this book went to press in late February, CPJ learned that Pearl had been killed. This cruel and pointless murder served no purpose, political or otherwise. Pearl's killers gained nothing, not even publicity for their views.

An important question, though, is whether the international spotlight will continue to shine as brightly on press freedom violations in the post–September 11 world. Will Western governments—many of which have frequently denounced press freedom abuses since the Cold War era ended—now be more reluctant to speak up?

The war on terrorism, for example, gives Uzbekistan a new strategic importance because of its border with Afghanistan. Will that make democracies turn a blind eye to Uzbekistan's undemocratic regime of prior censorship and its dubious distinction as the region's leading jailer of journalists?

Does Russia's enthusiasm for the new war mean the West will forgive President Vladimir Putin's wily tactics for wresting control of private broadcasting, and his military's fierce intimidation of journalists who dare report on the army's human rights abuses in Chechnya?

And in exchange for China's support of the war, will the international community be silent about its imprisonment of journalists such as 2001 CPJ International Press Freedom awardee Jiang Weiping? Jiang exposed sensational abuses by a local official after the government encouraged reporters to help ferret out official corruption. But taking the government at its word earned him eight years in prison, while the powerful, corrupt official won a promotion.

Jailing journalists is a highly effective means of stifling dissent or unwelcome questions, so the international community must continue to make it costly for those countries that do imprison their journalists. But there are signs that the political cost has declined somewhat since the war on terror was declared; the crackdowns that left 11 in prison in Eritrea and 17 in Nepal, for example, were carried out swiftly and with little international outcry.

An American example in 2001 could embolden leaders in countries eager to suppress reporting. For the first time in CPJ's 20-year history, a U.S. journalist is included on the annual imprisoned list. Houston-based free-lancer Vanessa Leggett spent more than five months in jail for refusing to turn over her research to a grand jury. (Leggett was finally released on January 4, 2002).

In a letter sent to U.S. attorney general John Ashcroft in August, CPJ noted that, "By detaining Vanessa Leggett, the U.S. government is effectively reducing the stigma associated with the jailing of journalists. This sends exactly the wrong signal to authoritarian governments, who may now show even less restraint in using state power to restrict press freedom."

It is no exaggeration that the United States, with its First Amendment and its fiercely competitive media, is the world's press freedom beacon. While the government does attempt to influence the work of U.S. journalists, they are in a strong position to resist such pressure.

But in 2001, when the U.S. government complained about Al-Jazeera's coverage of the war on terror and urged American networks to censor tapes of al-Qaeda leader Osama bin Laden, other governments took careful note, and their journalists watched in alarm. While no U.S. journalists suffered reprisals from those actions, President Putin's spokesperson in Russia said that the stern talk from U.S. officials just might make a good model for new restrictions on Russia's media.

In response, one journalist lamented, "Here in Russia the authorities are always most eager to borrow from the worst elements of western experience."

Ann Cooper is the executive director of the Committee to Protect Journalists. Before joining CPJ in 1998, she was a foreign correspondent for National Public Radio for nine years, serving as bureau chief in Moscow and Johannesburg.

THE MYANMAR TIMES

& BUSINESS REVIEW

Myanmar's first international weekly journal

Stairway to Nirvana

ing architecture with the man behind the entrance to our most famous landma

CPJ

Spotlight

JOURNALISM REMAINED AN EMBATTLED PROFESSION in many countries last year, nowhere more so than **Burma** (*page 2*), where one of the world's most repressive dictatorships does its best to ensure that local newpapers carry anything but news. In **Colombia** (*page 16*), feared paramilitary leader Carlos Castaño enjoys the media spotlight when he isn't having journalists killed. And in **Syria** (*page 25*), hopes that the press would revive after the death of strongman Hafez al-Assad have proved premature under his son and heir.

Newsstand, Rangoon, 2001.

by A. Lin Neumann

BURMA
Under Pressure

How Burmese journalism survives in one of the world's most repressive regimes.

ANGOON—The most surprising thing about the Burmese press is that it still exists. Governed repressively since 1962 and currently under military rule, Burma is by far the most information-starved country in Southeast Asia. And yet the press refuses to die.

In most cases, the identities of Burmese individuals and publications have been disguised. This was necessary to protect CPJ sources from loss of livelihood or even imprisonment.

The ruling junta enforces obligatory and capricious censorship at every turn. A host of topics are off-limits, from heavy rainstorms to local politics, losing soccer matches to details of the World Trade Center attacks. But there is a strong literary tradition in Burma, and many living journalists and writers remember past freedoms and dream of better days to come.

At the end of 2001, there were 12 journalists jailed for their work in Burma, according to CPJ research. The writers and editors who are still allowed to work must contend with a vast web of regulation and censorship imposed in the name of national security. Despite these challenges, certain courageous journalists within Burma and in the overseas Burmese community still manage to report the facts about their appalling government.

On a recent visit to Burma, CPJ found surprising good humor and energy in a situation that would drive most reporters to despair. CPJ's correspondent was welcomed by dozens of local journalists. Many had suffered harassment and jail time for their work. They risked their freedom just by talking to an international human rights organization.

"Never mind, we are used to the threats," said a retired newspaper editor who has spent years in prison during the last four decades. "If you haven't been in jail you haven't been a reporter here."

The impasse

Modern Burma is deadlocked between pro-democracy forces on one side and the military regime on the other. Given strict censorship and government control over news content, it is virtually impossible for the Burmese people to engage in a frank national dialogue about their future.

In 2001, for example, the local press barely commented on closed-door talks—the first since 1994—between the regime and opposition leader Daw Aung San Suu Kyi. The United Nations–brokered negotiations were widely covered everywhere except Burma. "We have no idea about this," said one local journalist. "The talks cannot be discussed."

The press restrictions put Suu Kyi herself at a marked disadvantage. If she hammers out a secret power-sharing deal with the junta, she and her allies will merely be perpetuating the undemocratic practices of the past 40 years. But government officials clearly fear that any crack in the façade of repression could lead to a reprise of the 1988 democratic uprising, which was brutally crushed by the current junta. Hence the general ban on domestic press coverage of the negotiations

For the first time in years, however, state newspapers have been permitted to mention Suu Kyi without attaching ritual insults to her name. The official *New Light of Myanmar*, for example, no longer refers to Suu Kyi as an "evil tool of foreign interests."

The Myanmar Times, a new English-language weekly that is pitched mainly at foreign readers and maintains close links with Burmese military intelligence, has even been allowed to cover the releases of some political prisoners and the reopening of offices of Suu Kyi's political party, the National League for Democracy. Operating outside the direct control of the Ministry of Information, the paper has been billed as evidence that the junta is becoming more tolerant of independent political speech.

That is not the case. Most Burmese read neither the *The Myanmar Times* nor the handful of imported English-language publications available in Rangoon. For the vast majority of Burma's people, the talks are just another rumor in the wind. They fear that the government is only raising expectations in order to undermine the opposition even further. "If we see some reality, then we will believe," said the editor of one magazine.

Past and present

For a time, starting with independence from Britain in 1948 and ending when the military seized power in 1962, Burma enjoyed a fair measure of press freedom. Literary journals, mass market dailies, and political party newspapers competed freely for readers. It was a tumultuous period in which competing ideologies vied for popular support.

Photo: A. Lin Neumann

In those days, Rangoon was a prosperous and fairly cosmopolitan Southeast Asian capital. Everything changed in 1962, when General Ne Win seized power and imposed the "Burmese Road to Socialism," a policy designed to isolate the country from outside

Heroic art, Rangoon.

influences. One of his first moves was to nationalize all newspapers and establish a Press Scrutiny Board to impose strict censorship on all forms of information. The board remains fully active today.

The current junta has made a few cosmetic changes since it seized power in 1988, notably by changing its name, in 1997, from the sinister-sounding State Law and Order Restoration Council (SLORC) to the State Peace and Development Council (SPDC). A public relations offensive of sorts has been underway since then, largely directed by the Office of Strategic Studies (OSS), a think tank run by Lt. Gen. Khin Nyunt, head of military intelligence and effectively the junta's third-ranking member. But the repressive mechanism remains essentially unchanged, and efforts to paint a picture of economic vitality under the new dispensation have not prospered.

In March 2001, Khin Nyunt explained the regime's press policy to an audience of Information Ministry staffers. "The staff should know the importance of the news value in line with the time and condition," said the general, according to the *New Light of Myanmar*. "As the staff...are experienced persons in the journalism field, they have the ability to differentiate between the news which will benefit the nation and the people and the news which will have a bad effect on the nation and the people."

In practice, of course, this means that the regime sets the agenda, determines most news content, and only allows "safe" subjects to pass the censors. As a result, local journalists are reduced to writing tame lifestyle and business features for a range of anodyne weekly journals and monthly magazines.

Occasionally, some try to push the envelope by inserting veiled political references into their copy. When their efforts are censored, they often pass manuscripts around to one another or share banned magazines they have managed to save from the scrap heap. "If we stop trying, there will soon be no journalism in Burma," said an editor at a business magazine.

A retired journalist who spent long years in prison, sacrificing health and career in the process, went out of his way to assist CPJ in meeting some of his colleagues and friends, a risky proposition in Burma. "I do this because this is what I can do," he whispered. "They won't let me write."

A younger journalist with a university degree in urban planning spent a long day driving CPJ's reporter around Rangoon. "I want to show you what they've done to our people," he explained as we passed through the drab outskirts of the city. About an hour outside the city center, he stopped at one of the "satellite towns" constructed after the anti-government uprising of 1988 as a way of emptying central Rangoon of the urban workers who helped swell the ranks of demonstrators. "There are no hospitals out here, few schools," he said, adding that the inhabitants had been forcibly relocated. "There are very few factories and

"We cannot write about any bad news and we must be careful about everything political. That does not leave very much for us to publish."

people have to queue for hours for buses into the city. People are sad. There is a lot of drinking."

Could he ever write about this? "I do," he said as we drove slowly through the fetid squalor of a cramped shantytown carved out of a rice field. "In my private journal. I come here sometimes to talk with the people, but it is very dangerous for them to speak with outsiders. Anyway, it will never be published." Meanwhile, he makes his living writing for a teen fashion magazine.

Streets of terror

In 1988 there was a popular uprising against the semi-socialist dictatorship of General Ne Win. The streets were filled with thousands of young demonstrators calling for democracy. The

A Burmese lifestyle magazine.

demonstrators formed street committees to try and govern a capital that had seemingly been abandoned by its government. Official buildings had been ransacked and the bureaucracy was at a

"If you haven't been in jail you haven't been a reporter here."

standstill. Even customs and immigration officials were scarcely at their posts.

Numerous unofficial papers began appearing in mid-August as the uprising gathered steam and the military largely retreated behind closed gates. Even the doctrinaire state press joined the upheaval and started printing lively and uncensored reports.

Amid the chaos, a quiet lady named Daw Aung San Suu Kyi returned from England to the country of her birth. The daughter of the country's assassinated independence hero, Gen. Aung San, she quickly became a symbol swept up in the struggle for change.

But instead of negotiating with the emerging democracy movement, another set of generals seized power. On September 18, the coup leaders announced the formation of a new junta called the State Law and Order Restoration Council (SLORC)[1] to replace Ne Win's failed socialist regime. A maelstrom of killing ensued over the following days as machine guns swept the streets of protesters, leaving thousands of corpses in their wake.

The underground and independent newspapers were immediately closed following the coup. Many of the journalists involved in Burma's brief flirtation with press freedom fled to exile in neighboring Thailand or joined the underground resistance. Others were rounded up and jailed in the months and years following the crackdown. There was no independent Burmese press left to follow the story, and international media were largely transfixed by the Seoul Olympics.

Fast forward

More than thirteen years later, Rangoon remains a city out of time. The stunning Shwedagon Pagoda complex still glistens magically in the sun and the charmingly faded British colonial skyline has changed little. A handful of new buildings rose in the mid 1990s to herald Burma's planned debut as an Asian economic tiger. A few new hotels were built or refurbished to cater to a tourist wave that never landed. The splendid century-old Strand Hotel, which was a shadow of its Victorian grandeur in 1988, has been restored to its original glory. But the occupancy? "None sir," said the bellman with a sad nod of the head. "No guests this week, sir." The elegant lobby bar only buzzes when the small diplomatic community gathers to swap rumors on Friday evening.

---

[1]. The SLORC changed the official name of the country from Burma to Myanmar after seizing power. But many observers, CPJ included, respect the wishes of many Burmese and continue to use the country's traditional English name. While Ne Win was replaced, it is widely believed that he continues to wield substantial influence behind the scenes.

The freewheeling media debates of 1988 are long gone. They have been replaced by state newspapers such as the *New Light of Myanmar*, whose pages bristle with dour headlines about how Secretary Number One of the ruling junta met with the Fisheries Secretary to discuss the prawn industry. Opinion pages are frequently given over to multi-part diatribes against foreign reporters whose coverage is allegedly part of an elaborate global plot to besmirch the good name of the country.

Other matters of national importance are also off limits. In the mid-1990s, the government conducted a sustained military offensive against several insurgent ethnic minority forces based in northern Burma. The local press ignored the story completely until the regime announced a series of negotiated settlements with purported minority representatives.

Burma is a global center for the narcotics trade, but the problem is not covered except for government pronouncements. Former warlord Khun Sa is wanted for drug trafficking outside Burma. He is said to live in Rangoon, but the fact cannot be mentioned in the domestic press. A severe AIDS crisis is spreading rapidly, according to international experts, but there is little independent reporting allowed on the issue and all domestic coverage must follow the lead of the government. The issue of forced labor, which made Burma a virtual pariah state in the eyes of the International

The Myanmar Times, a pet project of the current military regime.

Labor Organization (ILO), is rarely a subject for media discussion, even though the junta is now allowing ILO representatives to monitor the issue.

Outside information

There is no public Internet access in Burma, apart from a handful of expensive e-mail accounts that pass through a central military server where messages can be delayed for hours while the censors read them. Fax machines must be licensed, and it can take years to obtain a permit to carry a cellular phone. State television is a joke. Satellite television is available in foreign homes and hotels, but few Burmese can afford it.

Tattered copies of foreign newsmagazines are sold as virtual contraband from street stalls. For a premium, passing motorists can also buy smuggled week-old copies of the *Bangkok Post* and the *Nation*, both English dailies from neighboring Thailand. The papers are hawked by skittish newsboys who keep a watchful eye out for the police.

Ordinary people depend on Burmese-language broadcasts beamed into the country by Radio Free Asia, the VOA, the BBC, and the Democratic Voice of Burma, a dissident news service based in Norway. Hungry for news, people keep track of the world on tiny short wave receivers, hiding them from authorities and listening only in the privacy of their homes.

Foreign journalists are generally barred from living in Burma. The international press corps in Rangoon consists of a single correspondent from the Chinese state news agency Xinhua. Foreign reporters must apply for special journalist visas to enter the country, along with a "Permit to Conduct Journalistic Activities." The rules change unpredictably and there are no access guarantees.

In recent months, perhaps because of the ongoing talks with Suu Kyi, some foreign correspondents have found it easier to enter Burma. The PR-savvy OSS has organized press junkets to Burma in order to promote tourism and publicize the regime's drug control efforts. But all visiting reporters are followed and monitored by intelligence agents and it is almost impossible to interview Suu Kyi, who has been under house arrest for years.

International journalists who write negative stories about Burma can be banned indefinitely. Bertil Lintner, a Thailand-based Swedish reporter for the *Far Eastern Economic Review*, has been unable to visit for fifteen years, although he is an internationally respected authority on Burma who has published several books on the country. A number of other Bangkok-based foreign correspondents are unable to obtain visas, perhaps because the regime thinks they know too much.

The September 11 terrorist attacks were ignored by Burmese state television and only mentioned in passing by government newspapers.

Reporters who please the regime, on the other hand, have special access. "It is not a fair system," said Aung Zaw, editor of the Burmese exile magazine *The Irrawaddy*, which is published in Thailand. "The government rewards the foreign journalists they like and punishes those who are too critical."

For years, much of the information from inside Burma has come from foreign embassies whose staffers can field phone calls from reporters abroad with relative security. International wire services must otherwise rely on Burmese stringers who operate under constant scrutiny. Wary of talking openly to CPJ for fear of government reprisals, a number of these reporters say they are regularly called in for questioning when their agencies run stories that are too critical of the regime.

"It is a constant dance," said one stringer. "We have to be very careful." The reporters must frequently disguise their sources and plead ignorance on stories they write, especially when they cover human rights issues or anything concerning Aung San Suu Kyi. Overseas news editors sometimes change bylines on sensitive stories or add a Bangkok dateline in order to protect their colleagues inside Burma.

Several Burmese stringers told CPJ that they can work sources inside the military government but must be very careful how they report the information. "Up there, among...the generals, there is difference of opinion," said one wire agency stringer. "Sometimes we can get stories from them."

Burmese censors are extremely wary of bad news. The September 11 attacks were ignored by state television and only mentioned in passing by government newspapers. Police confiscated contraband videotapes of CNN's September 11 coverage and threatened vendors with arrest. Even the news of junta leader Than Shwe's letter of condolence to the United States was delayed by several days.

When the national soccer team was eliminated from the regional Tiger Cup tournament in the early rounds in late 2000, the official censorship board quietly ordered newspapers to refrain from reporting the results. "We just enjoyed the trip. They wouldn't let us do any work," said a reporter who covered the tournament, which was held in Thailand.

Others are less relaxed about the restrictions. "To me it is mental genocide. They are not killing the Burmese people physically but they are killing our ability to think," said Pe Thet Nee, the editor of the Burmese Independent News Agency (BINA), a small exile news service that covers Burmese politics from Thailand. "It is a tragedy."

Voices of power

Private publications operate under a Byzantine regulatory framework. To obtain a publishing license, which can be revoked at any time, they must pay stiff fees (as well as bribes) to government agencies such as the Department of the Navy and the Drug Control Board. The licensing agencies generally appoint officials as nominal chief editors.

All four of Burma's daily newspapers are published by the News and Periodicals Enterprise (NPE), a division of the Information Ministry. These dull rags are almost exclusively vehicles for government propaganda. In addition, some 50 private weekly and monthly magazines are allowed to exist under strict government supervision. It is a corrupt, Kafkaesque system in which journalists must do constant battle with the regime.

Photo: A. Lin Neumann

Burma boasts many newspapers with little news.

"The censorship board has told us we must not write about AIDS, corruption, education, or the situation of students," said the editor of a monthly magazine whose publishing license is held by a government ministry. "We also cannot write about any bad news and we must be careful about everything political. That does not leave very much for us to publish."

BORDERLAND

In Thailand, exiled Burmese journalists struggle to report on their own country.

Mae Sot, Thailand—The Burma Border Press Club is in session tonight at an empty, dimly lit Chinese restaurant in this dusty trading town near the Burmese border. At the table, six reporters are eagerly discussing their work.

These journalists, five men and one woman, most of them former political activists exiled now in Thailand, are stringers for wire agencies and Burmese language short-wave radio services. They cover ongoing ethnic rebellions along the border, as well as the thousands of Burmese refugees inside Thailand. The task is daunting.

Some 100 Burmese exiles are now working as journalists along the Thai-Burmese border. Their reports form the basis for news items that are then beamed back into Burma by the BBC, VOA, Radio Free Asia, and the Oslo-based Democratic Voice of Burma, via short-wave radio.

It is illegal and dangerous for these journalists to enter Burma. If they sneak in, they face possible arrest. Burmese military intelligence agents are believed to operate inside Thai border towns and refugee camps. Thai military intelligence agents routinely monitor the activities of these journalists, checking their papers, milking them for information, and sometimes threatening them with deportation.

Exiled Burmese political leaders also exert pressure on reporters, trying to enforce their own version of political correctness on coverage of news from across the border. "We have to be afraid of the Thai authorities, the Burmese authorities and the rebel authorities," says Win Myint, a BBC stringer based in Mae Sot.

These émigré reporters are among the very few news professionals who are able to obtain reasonably accurate information about the ethnic insurgencies inside Burma. The reporters interview Burmese refugees, migrant workers, and traders who move between the two countries. Occasionally, they even take daring jaunts across the border.

Exiled Burmese journalists are denied both Thai passports and political refugee status. Thai authorities tolerate the Burmese journalists but refuse to grant them legal status for fear of offending the Burmese junta. During periods of political tension—as in 2000, when a band of Burmese rebels attacked a Thai hospital and briefly took the staff hostage—the journalists face harassment and possible deportation.

The English-language magazine *The Irrawaddy* has built an international reputation since it began about 10 years ago as a newsletter produced in the Thai

The only substantial change in censorship policy has been the gradual elimination, in the late 1990s, of the practice of inking out offending pages or ripping out whole sections of magazines. But the current system is hardly an improvement. Under laws dating back to the 1960s, each edition of every publication must be submitted in advance to the Press Scrutiny Board, an agency of the powerful Ministry of Information. If the censors object to any portion of a story, the entire layout must be redone to remove the offending material.

Even after the censors have cleared the magazine, they must review all changes again after printing. Magazines must frequently scrap entire print runs living room of its editor, Aung Zaw. Now operating out of a substantial office in the northern Thai city of Chiang Mai, *The Irrawaddy* hopes to become an independent national news magazine in Burma once the military regime is gone. "Our goal is always to go back home," said Aung Zaw, a one-time student activist who fled to Thailand following the 1988 pro-democracy uprising.

Other exile publications have a narrower focus. The Shan Herald Agency for News (SHAN), for example, grew out of the struggle for independence inside the Shan State in northern Burma. When Khun Sa, a drug lord who was the main Shan military leader, struck a deal with the Burmese junta in 1996, many other Shan who remained committed to the independence struggle were forced into exile.

Relying on informants inside the Shan State, SHAN puts out *Independence*, a monthly magazine that focuses on Shan community issues, including the surviving Shan rebel groups. "Outside of our community, people know very little about the Shan," said Khun Sai, the editor of *Independence*. "We want to increase awareness. We believe that in order to become free and democratic, we need a free press."

Similar publications cover the Karen community inside Burma, the only ethnic group that has not yet struck a deal with the junta. There are also newsletters tied to the National League for Democracy, Aung San Suu Kyi's opposition political party, and to exiled student groups. The National Coalition Government of the Union of Burma, a shadow government in exile with links to the political opposition, puts out its own newsletters.

Most of these groups try to distribute their publications inside Burma, although just being caught reading one of these newsletters can result in a lengthy jail sentence. *Independence*, which publishes in both Burmese and Shan, claims to circulate 500 of its 2,000 copies a month inside the country, but editors say it is risky even to get the paper across the border.

The publications must patch their funding together from international donors whose priorities are constantly shifting. Most publications operate on a hand to mouth basis. It is tough work, performed by dedicated reporters, most of whom could seek an easier life by applying for political asylum in the West.

"We have no place to go," said VOA stringer Aye Aye Mar, one of the few women journalists working on the border. "But we are here to be journalists and we want to work on the border. We want to stay as close as we can to our country."

—A. Lin Neumann

because of last-minute objections from the censors. All this creates a powerful incentive toward self-censorship.

The censorship process is also said to be rife with bribery. Censors must often be bribed to clear each new edition for publication. Publishers say they must also turn over up to 20 percent of each print run to the censors, who sell them on the street. One editor told CPJ that his magazine and others even had to pick up the tab for a Press Scrutiny Board holiday junket in 2000. "Even without the political problems, they are making money from us," said the publisher of a beauty magazine. "Every time we turn around we have to pay."

Corruption and censorship notwithstanding, some outside observers see the emergence of semi-independent publications as a hopeful sign. "Burma is in transition from being...one of the most closed societies in the world," said historian and Burma-watcher Martin Smith, who notes that business publications have "found a niche that didn't exist before."

Typically inoffensive Burmese magazine covers.

It is difficult to sustain even such tempered optimism in conversation with journalists inside the country. Two monthly business publications, *Dana* (Prosperity) and *Myanmar Dana* were launched in the 1990s as part of the regime's drive to privatize state-owned industries and attract foreign investors. These publications are qualitatively among the best in Rangoon, but they operate within very narrow confines. "If we could report what we know, that would be one thing, but we can't," said one staffer.

Under the radar

The July 2001 issue of a journal called *Sabai Phyu* (White Jasmine) featured a cover quote from the Western social theorist Edward de Bono: "You can analyze the past, but you must design the future. Otherwise it may be no better than the past." One editor said the quote probably escaped censorship only because the censors didn't understand what it meant. The editor of a fashion magazine told CPJ that the list of banned topics he had encountered included everything from deposed dictators such as Slobodan Milosevic of Yugoslavia and Suharto of Indonesia to floods, plane crashes, and train wrecks. Staffers knew not to write anything even remotely critical about the Association of Southeast Asian Nations (ASEAN), the ten-member regional alliance that Burma joined in 1997. "We are encouraged, though, to write anything bad about Thailand," said the editor, noting that the two countries are currently embroiled in a border dispute. "But that could also change."

The board even spiked a local film critic's review of *The Man in the Iron Mask*. Why? Because he quoted the Musketeer slogan, "One for all and all for one!" The censors apparently decided that "one" referred to Aung San Suu Kyi and "all" to the Burmese people.

Tin Maung Than, the editor of the journal, *Thintbawa* (Your Life), fled into exile with his family in late 2000. Tin Maung Than got into trouble for circulating photocopies of a speech by a government official who criticized Burma's economic policies. The military also watched him closely because he was once associated with Suu Kyi's opposition political party, an affiliation he gave up many years ago to concentrate on writing. "Real journalism is not possible in Burma," he told CPJ. "We have to say everything in general terms and let the readers feel the meaning for themselves."

Not much has changed since Tin Maung Than's departure. During CPJ's visit to Rangoon, one magazine was forced to delay publication after censors objected to a personal memoir that ran under the headline "Foolish Father, Foolish Daughter."

"They don't like the word 'foolish,'" explained the author of the story. "They think it shows disrespect for authority."

Burmese journalists are allowed to write about money.

No bad news

In June 2001, a dam broke near Wundwin township, about 100 miles south of the city of Mandalay in central Burma. The barrier had silted over and become unstable due to poor maintenance and unusually heavy rains. When it finally gave way, some 200 villages were flooded. As many as 1,000 people died, some of them bitten by poisonous snakes that had been swept along by the deluge.

International media reported the bare details of the disaster, but Burmese journalists mostly avoided it. However, one enterprising local reporter thought he had found a way to slip past the censors and into the story.

He went to the flood area with his camera and notebook and documented relief efforts organized by the local people. "I took the angle that the Burmese people help one another in times of crisis and natural disaster," the reporter recalled. "I didn't say anything about the reason for the dam breaking or the maintenance problem." Instead, he played up a spontaneous flood relief donation drive launched in Mandalay to help the victims and reflected on the Buddhist devotion that such charity implied.

His editor showed me the layout that was sent to the censors. It was a 16-page photo essay, with dramatic pictures of the flood's aftermath and quotes from survivors, a disaster story straight out of Journalism 101. But the public will never read it. "They censored it. I never got an explanation," the writer said. That month,

"State newspapers feature dour headlines about how Secretary Number One met with the Fisheries Secretary to discuss the prawn industry."

Photo: A. Lin Neumann

News vendor relaxing in Rangoon, 2001.

the magazine went to press 16 pages short of its normal length. And today, the censored article exists only in a handful of page proofs that were printed prior to the censor's decision.

"It is so silly," said an editor. "What country does not have floods, accidents, natural disasters, conflicts? Yet they tell us that the image of the nation will suffer if we report these things."

More equal than others

In March 2000, *The Myanmar Times* opened for business. The weekly English language paper features snazzy graphics and good paper. It is published by an Australian entrepreneur named Ross Dunkley, who prepared for the job by serving as managing director of the *Vietnam Investment Review*, one of the first private magazines in that heavily censored country.

With good color separation, quality paper, and a slick layout, *The Myanmar Times* is unlike any other publication sold on the streets of Rangoon. But the US$2 cover price is more than four times the cost of any other weekly journal and well beyond the means of most Burmese readers. A recently launched Burmese language version is also expensive in local terms.

The Myanmar Times is exempt from many of the rules that govern other publications in Rangoon, a fact that annoys its competitors no end. For example, the *Times* is the only Burmese paper to have carried fairly straight coverage of the ongoing talks between Aung San Suu Kyi and members of the ruling junta. On occasion, Suu Kyi's picture even appears on the inside pages of the paper. *The Myanmar Times* is also the only local paper to have mentioned recent releases of political prisoners and to have noted that the International Labor Organization recently accused the Burmese military of using forced labor in rural areas.

Dunkley plugs his new weekly as the first "truly free press" in recent Burmese history. In fact, Dunkley's enterprise is the brainchild of intelligence chief Lt.-Gen.

Khin Nyunt, Secretary Number One of the ruling junta, and members of the Office of Strategic Studies (OSS), the government think tank over which he presides. Earlier this year, the *Times* even carried a rare interview with Khin Nyunt.

The Myanmar Times is a key part of Khin Nyunt's strategy to rehabilitate the battered international image of the military junta, says *The Review's* Bertil Lintner, who has covered Burmese affairs for 20 years. Lintner and other analysts believe that Khin Nyunt disagrees with the Information Ministry's heavy-handed approach to propaganda. An influential OSS officer named Col. Thein Swe is frequently quoted in *The Myanmar Times* and appears to be actively involved in running the paper. When the *Times* was launched, Thein Swe told *Asiaweek* that the paper would be "different, more flexible" than other papers.

For his part, Dunkley downplays his paper's obvious closeness to the regime. "Officially we go through military scrutiny, but the reality is that we have an amicable dialogue, and 95 percent [of the paper] is not subject to censorship," Dunkley told Agence France-Presse earlier this year. "I just report the facts," he added.

When reached by phone in Rangoon, Dunkley refused to speak with a CPJ reporter. He referred all questions to an assistant who subsequently could not be reached despite repeated calls.

The cost

The net effect of years of isolation and censorship has been to starve the Burmese people of news access that is taken for granted in most countries. By comparison, even China is an open society despite its heavy-handed system of media control.

As the world moves ever faster toward a more open global information society, the people of Burma are stuck in the past. Many of the social and political problems that plague Burma—ethnic tensions, rampant corruption, poverty—are worsened by the lack of information and debate on the issues. The regime apparently fears that any media liberalization could provoke a political transition in which it would risk loss of power and subsequent reprisals.

Whatever happens to the current regime, one lasting legacy of military rule will be the generals' steadfast opposition to press freedom. For almost 40 years, ever since Ne Win staged his coup in 1962, the country has been run as the parochial playground of whatever band of officers is in power, with the result that not only the financial capital but also the intellectual capital of the country has been depleted. It will be a long time in recovery.

"If we were allowed to, we could set up newspapers tomorrow because we have the presses," said a frail former editor who once spent seven years in solitary confinement because of his newspaper work. "But where would we find the journalists? I am one of the last...who remembers what it was like to have real newspapers in this country." ■

A. Lin Neumann is CPJ's Asia program consultant, based in Bangkok, Thailand. He was one of only four foreign journalists in Rangoon when the pro-democracy uprising was brutally crushed in September 1988.

Paramilitary leader
Carlos Castaño in
northern Colombia,
February 26, 2001.

COLOMBIA
by Frank Smyth
Bad Press

This Colombian warlord cultivates journalists. He also murders them. For Carlos Castaño, it's all about image.

BOGOTÁ—ON MAY 3, 2001, CPJ named Colombian paramilitary leader Carlos Castaño to its annual list of the Ten Worst Enemies of the Press. Six weeks later, a reporter from the Paris daily *Le Monde* caught up with Castaño in northern Colombia and asked how he felt about the distinction.

"I would like to assure you that I have always respected the freedom and subjectivity of the press," said the leader of the United Self-Defense Forces of Colombia (AUC), Colombia's leading right-wing paramilitary organization. "But I have never accepted that journalism can become an arm at the service of one of the actors of the conflict. Over the course of its existence the AUC has executed two local journalists who were in fact guerrillas." He no longer remembered their names.

Since 1999, in fact, forces under Castaño's command have been linked to the murders of at least four journalists, the abduction and rape of one reporter, and threats against many others, according to CPJ research. "Against the violent backdrop of Colombia's escalating civil war, in which all sides have targeted journalists, Carlos Castaño stands out as a ruthless enemy of the press," CPJ's citation noted.

This self-confessed murderer of journalists is now turning to the local press in an effort to rehabilitate his image in Colombia. To that end, Castaño has launched a uniquely Colombian public relations campaign, seemingly modeled after tactics employed by legendary drug lord Pablo Escobar. Not unlike Escobar, Castaño's strategy combines a charm offensive with forthright acknowledgements of the AUC's use of terror.

While Escobar attacked journalists who favored his extradition to the United States to face drug trafficking charges, Castaño attacks any journalist whom he suspects of cooperating or even sympathizing with Colombia's left-wing rebels. In 2001, Castaño admitted that he had murdered journalists and tried to bomb a newspaper for its alleged communist sympathies. He has been implicated in many other attacks on the press in recent years.

In November 2000, Castaño granted an exclusive interview to the Bogotá weekly *Semana*. The reporter asked whether Castaño thought he deserved to be compared to the late Escobar. "There is no way you can compare me with a monster like that," replied Castaño. "While he sought to destroy the country, I intend to save it."

Old war

Eleven years after the fall of the Berlin Wall, the Cold War remains hot in Colombia. The U.S.-backed Colombian military has been fighting against various Marxist guerrilla organizations (see sidebar) for nearly forty years. The army frequently collaborates with private paramilitary groups, including the AUC, which the Colombian government has outlawed. In 2000, Human Rights Watch reported that half of the army's 18 brigades were sharing intelligence and other resources with rightist paramilitary groups, most of them under Castaño's command.

Since the 1980s, both right-wing paramilitaries and left-wing guerrillas have increasingly been supported by profits from Colombia's burgeoning trade in illegal drugs.

Carlos Castaño is Colombia's top paramilitary leader as well as the country's leading fugitive. He is currently wanted on multiple murder, kidnapping, and arms trafficking charges dating back to 1988. He is also "a major drug trafficker," according to the U.S. Drug Enforcement Administration (DEA). Last April, U.S. ambassador to Colombia Anne W. Patterson told the Bogotá newspaper *El Espectador* that if Castaño is involved in drug trafficking, "and we think he is," the United States might one day seek to prosecute him in the United States.

Childhood memories

In 1981, when Carlos Castaño was 15 years old, his father was kidnapped and murdered by leftist guerrillas. At 23, he allegedly participated in a series of massacres of banana pickers in northwestern Colombia. Also known as "Monoleche" (Milkwhite) because of his fair complexion, Carlos allegedly killed at the side of his brother Fidel, and both brothers joined Colombia's first national paramilitary organization, "Death to Kidnappers" (MAS).

According to DEA documents, MAS was founded in 1981 by Escobar's Medellín cartel. But the Castaño brothers and Escobar later fell out. Fidel Castaño became chief of operations for a paramilitary strike force called "Los Pepes" (People Persecuted by Pablo Escobar). Following Fidel's mysterious 1994 disappearance in northern Colombia, Carlos emerged as Colombia's leading anti-communist militant.

Three years later, Carlos Castaño unified a number of regional rightist groups to form a national paramilitary organization called the United Self-Defense Forces of Colombia (AUC). In 1997, Castaño admits, he ordered the massacre of 49 peasants in rural Mapiripán, eastern Colombia. Since then, Castaño and his allies have committed about 80 percent of Colombia's human rights abuses, according to Human Rights Watch. The Colombian Defense Ministry reports that rightist paramilitaries carried out three-fourths of the country's massacres last year.

"Guerrillas, whether in uniform or civilian clothes, remain a legitimate military objective," Castaño said on camera on March 1, 2000, when he showed his face to Colombians and others for the first time. "I know this violates international humanitarian law."

On May 30, 2001, Castaño issued a cryptic online communiqué announcing his resignation as military commander of the outlawed AUC. Days later, he announced that he was forming a nonviolent political organization, linked to the AUC, that would seek legal recognition in Colombia (none was granted). And he continued to grant interviews.

AUC meets the press

Journalists have figured prominently among Castaño's victims. In January 1999, for example, Castaño repeatedly threatened Alfredo Molano Bravo of the Bogotá newspaper *El Espectador* after Molano wrote a story about anti-communist paramilitary groups and their ties to Colombian drug traffickers.

In June 1999, AUC members threatened Carlos Pulgarín, a reporter for Bogotá's largest daily, *El Tiempo*, after Pulgarín wrote an article about paramilitary assassinations of indigenous activists. Pulgarín fled to Peru, where his movements were apparently monitored; he later received telephone threats in Lima.

Photo: AP/El Tiempo

The late Pablo Escobar, former boss of the Medellín drug cartel, is shown with his wife and son in this undated photograph. Escobar's widow and her 21-year-old son were arrested in Buenos Aires on November 16, 1999.

On September 16, 1999, two assassins on a motorcycle shot and killed Guzmán Quintero Torres, editor of the northern Colombian daily *El Pilón*. Quintero was investigating several AUC-linked murders at the time, including the 1998 slaying of television journalist Amparo Leonor Jiménez Pallares, who was killed after she reported that local paramilitary forces had murdered peasants.

On September 9, 2000, AUC paramilitaries abducted and killed a rural community leader named Carlos José Restrepo Rocha, who ran two small regional publications. AUC fliers were left next to Restrepo Rocha's bullet-ridden corpse, but the motive for this particular murder remains unclear. Later that year, AUC members threatened Eduardo Luque Díaz, of the daily *La Nación*, at his office and home, demanding that he reveal the whereabouts of a family he had mentioned in a story.

On April 27, 2001, Flavio Bedoya, a southwestern Colombia correspondent for the Communist Party weekly *La Voz*, was murdered. Colleagues believed the murder was linked to a series of highly critical reports that Bedoya had published in *La Voz* since the beginning of April about collusion between the security forces and outlawed right-wing paramilitary gangs in southern Nariño Department.

One month after Bedoya's death, the AUC tried unsuccessfully to bomb the Bogotá offices of *La Voz*. Castaño took responsibility for the incident a few days later.

On October 31, 2000, rural community radio station director Juan Camilo Restrepo Guerra was summoned to a meeting by rightist paramilitaries who were apparently incensed by his sharp criticisms of the local administration. Restrepo Guerra's brother drove him on a motorcycle to the rendezvous site. The paramilitaries shot Restrepo Guerra dead in front of his brother, who has since declined to testify and has gone into hiding.

Journalists who choose to remain in Colombia despite Castaño's intimidation privately admit that they censor their own reports to protect themselves and their families. "Of course I censor myself," said one threatened journalist who elected to stay. "You have to tell the story, but there are some things I can't include."

Carrot and stick

Although journalists all over Colombia have been threatened and attacked for daring to criticize the AUC, Castaño has also used the press to launch a PR offensive. The formerly reclusive leader has "gained public visibility in the national and international media with disconcerting ease," according to a March 2001 report by the United Nations human rights office in Colombia.

"Carlos Castaño, Colombia's fugitive paramilitary leader, unleashed a national stir when he stepped from the shadows and submitted to a ninety-minute, one-on-one interview, televised on March 1 [2000]," wrote then-U.S. Ambassador Curtis W. Kamman in a recently declassified U.S. embassy cable. "The 35-year-old Castaño appeared intelligent, articulate, well-poised, and, above all, very charismatic."

Photo: AP

Nearly one in five Colombian adults watched at least half the program, about the same percentage that supports Castaño, according to opinion polls. Since that first television appearance, Castaño has made himself freely available to both domestic and foreign reporters.

The Garzón murder

While Castaño has been linked to numerous attacks on the press, he currently faces just one criminal charge over an attack on a journalist. The charge, aggravated homicide, relates to the 1999 murder of Colombian television host Jaime Garzón. According to the official charge sheet, Castaño ordered Garzón's murder because of the journalist's role in negotiating the release of hostages held by leftist guerrillas.

The 39-year-old Garzón was a morning news host for the Caracol network and a regular columnist for the weekly magazine *Cambio*. But Garzón was best known for his work as a television comedian who used humor to criticize all factions in the civil conflict. He specialized in uncannily accurate impersonations of Colombian officials and other notables and was so popular across

Journalist, entertainer, and activist Jaime Garzón, shot dead in Bogotá, August 13, 1999.

Colombia that in 1997, then-presidential candidate Andrés Pastrana Arango appeared live with other candidates on his TV show.

Garzón regularly traded on his stature as a well-respected broadcaster to negotiate for the release of victims of guerrilla kidnappings. He also served on an independent commission that mediated between the government and the leftist guerrillas of the National Liberation Army (ELN).

Two points emerge clearly from the Garzón case. First, some of Colombia's most dangerous criminals work for Carlos Castaño; and second, not even famous and well-connected journalists are safe from him.

On August 10, 1999, Garzón heard that Castaño was planning to kill him. The news was conveyed by a Colombian senator named Piedad Córdoba, who chaired

KILLING THE MESSENGERS
Colombia's leftist guerillas also pose a serious threat to press freedom.

Carlos Castaño is by no means the only threat to the embattled Colombian press. The country's two main leftist guerrilla organizations, the ELN and the FARC, have both threatened and kidnapped dozens of journalists in recent years.

The FARC kidnapped seven journalists in October 1999 and held them for five days. *El Tiempo* editor Francisco Santos (who was once kidnapped by Pablo Escobar) has also been threatened by the FARC and is now living in Spain. And RCN television correspondent Claudia Gurisatti received FARC threats last year after the station aired her interview with Castaño. Both Santos and Gurisatti have since fled into exile.

There are indications that FARC was responsible for the December 13, 2000, killing of radio station director Alfredo Abad López, according to reliable Colombian sources. Abad was the director of Voz de la Selva (Voice of the Jungle), an affiliate of the national Caracol radio network in the southern Colombian city of Florencia. Just before his death, Abad had conducted an on-air discussion on whether the government should renew its grant of a Switzerland-sized chunk of territory to the FARC. A majority of the callers apparently opposed renewal.

The FARC has also been linked to the July 6 killing of José Duviel Vásquez Arias, who took over as news director of Voz de la Selva after Abad was murdered. Vásquez's last broadcasts dealt with an AUC communiqué announcing changes in local leadership and promising to refrain from kidnapping and extortion.

On May 23, 2001, FARC guerrillas briefly detained three employees of the Medellín daily *El Colombiano*, according to the Colombian press freedom organization FLIP (Fundación para la Libertad de Prensa). Correspondent Gustavo Gallo Machado, photographer Donaldo de Jesús Zuluaga Velilla, and driver Ramón Morales were held for several hours, and their vehicle was damaged. That same day, FLIP reported, an urban faction of the ELN distributed a pamphlet directed at all Colombian journalists, who were warned to avoid partiality.

—*Frank Smyth*

the Senate's human rights committee at the time. In late 1998, Castaño's men kidnapped Córdoba and held her for nine months. During that time, Castaño told Córdoba that Garzón was on his list of targets. Castaño read her excerpts from what he said were transcripts of Garzón's private telephone conversations. He claimed that the transcripts proved Garzón was really a guerrilla.

After Córdoba was released in June 1999, she told Garzón that Castaño was planning to eliminate him. During the second week of August, Garzón learned that Castaño had ordered him killed by the end of that week. On August 10, desperate to get in touch with Castaño, Garzón visited La Modelo prison, a maximum-security installation in Bogotá where several important AUC figures are incarcerated.

According to the charge sheet, Garzón met with Ángel Custodio Gaitán Mahecha, also known as "The Baker," and with Jhon Jairo Velásquez Vásquez, also known as "Popeye." Velásquez was an early 1990s Escobar loyalist who later transferred his allegiance to the AUC. Both were well-connected members of the Colombian underworld.

Gaitán used his cell phone to call Castaño. He handed the phone to Garzón, who

Castaño, Colombia's paramilitary kingpin, is currently wanted on multiple murder, kidnapping, and arms trafficking charges dating back to 1988.

pleaded with Castaño to spare his life. Castaño called Garzón a "son of a bitch" who supported the guerrillas and added that he was a coward who didn't have the guts to meet him face to face. Before hanging up, the two men arranged to meet the following Saturday, August 14.

On August 13, a motorcycle-riding gunman shot Garzón dead at a traffic light just four blocks from his office. A few hours later, Castaño himself called Garzón's radio show and denied responsibility on the air. Velásquez and Gaitán also claim they had nothing to do with Garzón's death.

The gunman who shot Garzón allegedly belonged to a criminal band known as La Terraza. In the past, La Terraza carried out attacks for the late Pablo Escobar. However, Castaño admits he has hired La Terraza to carry out a number of crimes in recent years, including kidnappings. The official government charge sheet accuses him of hiring La Terraza to kill Garzón.

On August 3, 2000, three months after Castaño was formally charged with Garzón's murder, he invited seven La Terraza leaders to a meeting in northern Colombia. Authorities later discovered all seven of their corpses near a local road. Meanwhile, Castaño issued a communiqué saying that the AUC had executed them for giving leaders like him a bad name.

Three months later, several young men who claimed to be La Terraza members surfaced in Medellín. Wearing masks, they taped a television interview in which they claimed to have committed many kidnappings and murders on behalf of the AUC,

Photo: AP/Ariana Cabillos

Investigative reporter Jineth Bedoya with bodyguard, December 22, 2000.

including the Garzón assassination. During the interview, they claimed that Castaño was planning to kill them and their families with the help of local police and military forces. Castaño did not deny the accusation. In March 2001, he told *El Tiempo* that only one or two members of the band were still alive.

War on *El Espectador*

On May 24, 2000, a suspected AUC militant tried to abduct Ignacio Gómez, an investigative reporter with *El Espectador*, in downtown Bogotá. The man who failed to trick Gómez into boarding a "taxi" that day matched the composite sketch of an AUC suspect in the massacre of 49 peasant farmers at Mapiripán in 1997.

Gómez had just published a story that documented the Colombian Army's collaboration with the AUC in the Mapiripán massacre. That same day, Gómez found an envelope with his name stenciled on it in his mailbox at work. The envelope contained a photocopy of a recent article by Jineth Bedoya, one of his colleagues at *El Espectador*.

Bedoya had reported that La Modelo prison guards were allowing AUC inmates to keep guns in their cells even after clashes between them and other inmates that left 25 prisoners dead, 18 wounded, and an undetermined number missing, according to a United Nations report on the incident.

Bedoya and her editor, Jorge Cardona, received identical envelopes. An hour and a half later, Bedoya's telephone rang. Gaitán was calling from his cell in La Modelo. He offered Bedoya the opportunity to interview him at the prison at 10:00 a.m. the next day. He promised the 25-year-old reporter an exclusive and asked her to come alone.

Cardona insisted on accompanying Bedoya and on bringing a photographer. The three *El Espectador* journalists arrived at La Modelo shortly before 10:00 a.m. on May 25. Prison guards told them to wait.

The visitors waiting area is just inside the entrance to La Modelo, although many visitors prefer to wait in the street just outside the entrance. Cardona and the photographer walked to a nearby concession stand to buy sodas, leaving Bedoya standing in front of the prison entrance. She stayed within view and earshot of the waiting area in case the guards cleared them to enter the jail.

Bedoya disappeared during the few minutes it took her colleagues to buy the sodas and return to the prison entrance. The prison guards claimed they had seen nothing.

At 8 p.m., the police reported that Bedoya had been admitted to a police medical clinic in the city of Villavicencio, a three-hour drive from La Modelo. A taxi driver found her lying with her hands tied in a garbage dump on the outskirts of town. She had been drugged, brutally beaten, and sexually assaulted. Bedoya was found in a state of nervous collapse but eventually recovered from the attack and returned to work at *El Espectador.*

Photo: AP

Paramilitary troops train in the mountains of northern Colombia, April 7, 2001.

During the assault, the men told her in graphic detail about all the other journalists whom they planned to kill, including her colleague Gómez. They did not explain why they chose to free her. A week later, Gómez fled to the United States.

No suspects have been charged in the attack on Bedoya. Gaitán and Velásquez both denied any role in her abduction, as do La Modelo prison authorities.

In a June 2000 interview with *El Tiempo,* Castaño also disclaimed responsibility for Bedoya's ordeal. He acknowledged that Gaitán was his subordinate, but claimed that Gaitán had assured him he was not involved.

On the evening of September 7, 2001, Gaitán was murdered in a prison called La Picota. He was apparently killed by leftist guerrilla inmates in retaliation for the previous year's jailhouse massacre at La Modelo.

The hunt for Castaño

Since the death of Pablo Escobar, no Colombian has terrorized so many members of the Colombian press, to say nothing of Colombian society in general. Carlos Castaño's extraordinary assault against local journalists comes as the Colombian government is receiving a record amount of U.S. aid. On September 10, as U.S. secretary of state Colin Powell was about to leave on a visit to Colombia, the State Department formally designated the AUC as a terrorist organization.

Yet U.S.-backed Colombian forces have so far been powerless to stop Castaño. As a result, he has enjoyed complete impunity for his crimes. The Attorney General's Office was the only Colombian law enforcement agency that even tried to pursue Castaño. Earlier in 2001, its civilian agents launched a series of raids against the AUC. But they complained of working without the support of the military or other government bodies. "In this struggle...the Attorney General's Office has been alone," chief investigator Pablo Elías González told *El Tiempo* in June 2000.

At that time, the AUC had just kidnapped seven members of González's staff while they were exhuming the corpse of an alleged AUC victim in Cesar State. All seven investigators remain missing and are presumed dead at the hands of Castaño's men. ■

Frank Smyth is an investigative reporter and CPJ's Washington representative.

Syrian men mourn
the death of President
Hafez al-Assad,
June 13, 2000.

SYRIA
Stop Signs
by Joel Campagna

Syria's press showed signs of life after Bashar al-Assad succeeded his iron-fisted father last year, but the thaw proved fleeting.

DAMASCUS—Sitting in a smoky downtown coffee shop, Syrian journalist Saleh (not his real name) instinctively redirects the conversation when he senses the waiter lingering a little too long in the vicinity. "So, how is your stay in Damascus?" he asks blandly. When the waiter disappears into the next room, Saleh continues his original, more serious train of thought.

"I don't think things will revert to the old way, but to a funny or false opening," he whispers. "The president says there's an opening with the press, but this is laughable when you consider the new papers." Beginning in 2001, Syria's press—and more generally its civil society—showed signs of emerging from a deep slumber after three decades of harsh authoritarian rule under Hafez al-Assad. His death in June 2000 sparked hope that his son and successor, 35-year-old Bashar al-Assad, a Western-trained opthalmologist and computer aficionado, would ease the Syrian police state's viselike grip on society and promote political and economic reforms.

In the initial months of his presidency, Syria's press seemed to benefit from the more relaxed new atmosphere. State-controlled papers displayed unusual flair, publishing relatively lively discussions of democracy and political reform. Meanwhile, Syria saw the launch of its first independent newspapers in four decades.

More than a year later, press reforms have slowed to a trickle following a government backlash. State-owned papers have reverted to their docile old ways. And while the existence of independent publications represents a marked change from the past, local observers complain that they lack true grit. Saleh's cynicism reflects the sentiments of many reform-minded Syrian journalists and intellectuals who hoped for rapid reform under Bashar. To them, last year's "opening," or infitah, is a clear case of style over substance.

Syrian residents visit Hafez al-Assad's mausoleum in Qardaha, June 14, 2000.

Photo: AP/Martin Gnedt

Open-and-shut

Hafez al-Assad led one of the most authoritarian regimes in the Middle East. Accordingly, its media was one of the most highly censored in the region.

Syria boasted a lively independent press in the nearly two decades after independence from France in 1946. Despite frequent bouts of censorship after military coups and during the 1958-1961 union with Egypt, the Syrian media was a model for the Arab world. After the Baath Party coup of 1963, however, the incoming government banned all independent papers. When Hafez al-Assad seized power in 1970, he extended the Baath regime's total control over the press while successfully stifling all opposition to his rule.

Under Assad, the Syrian press was dominated by the state-run dailies *Al-Thawra*, *Al-Baath*, and *Tishreen*. Like state-controlled radio and television at the time, the papers were tame, tedious, and laden with paeans to Assad. Syrian censorship often extended beyond its borders to Lebanon—where Syrian troops were stationed beginning in 1976—and to the foreign media, where local and even exiled dissidents muted their criticisms of the Assad regime out of a well-founded fear of reprisals.

After years of repression, a wave of optimism hit Syria when Bashar al-Assad assumed the presidency in July 2000. Bashar's reformist credentials were boosted by the highly publicized anti-corruption campaign that he ran in the last years of his father's rule. Moreover, he was identified with the younger and more

While the existence of privately owned publications represents a marked changed from the past, local observers complain that the new independent papers lack true grit.

liberal generation of Arab rulers who succeeded their fathers in countries such as Morocco, Jordan and Bahrain.

In his inaugural address, Bashar called for greater openness in the media: "Our educational, cultural and media institutions must be reformed and modernized in a manner that ... renounce[s] the mentality of introversion and negativity." Bashar then released some 600 political prisoners. The normally rigid state-controlled press began to feature cautious discussions of reform and democracy. The government allowed pro-regime political parties to launch newspapers, and Bashar licensed the country's first privately owned newspaper in nearly 40 years. Meanwhile, Internet use started to expand as Bashar, formerly the head of the Syrian Computer Society, promised 200,000 public connections by 2001.

All the while, intellectuals and interested citizens made increasingly bold calls for greater freedom and respect for human rights. During the summer of 2000, informal political discussion groups, or salons, sprouted up in the living rooms of intellectuals across the country. And in January 2001, a maverick parliamentarian named Riad al-Seif announced plans to launch an independent political party.

Soon after Bashar's inauguration, he replaced the heads of the major print and broadcast media. At the same time, he ordered the media to eschew garish honorifics such as "eternal guide" when referring to him—a common practice during his late father's rule.

Other officials declared the need for a media that would function as a watchdog over the government. "We want the media to be the fourth [estate] in the country," said newly appointed state television and radio director Fayez al-Sayegh in August 2000. "All government bodies are being told to open their doors and let everybody see the truth to serve the public interest." Many repressive regimes pay lip service to the idea of an independent press while forbidding independent journalism in practice, but these statements carried more weight at a time when a degree of political reform seemed within reach.

By September, signs of life were seen not in the Syrian press but in neighboring Lebanon, where some 20,000 Syrian troops are stationed and where Syria is the dominant power broker. Emboldened by Assad's moves, 99 domestic and exiled Syrian intellectuals published a petition in the daily Lebanese newspaper *Al-Safir* urging political reform and calling on the government to respect basic human rights, including freedom of expression and the press. The Syrian government took no action against the authors, although local media completely ignored the petition and foreign Arab newspapers that covered the story were banned.

The "Statement of the 99," as the document later became known, was the most prominent of a trickle of bold articles published by local and exiled dissidents in pan-Arab and Lebanese media in 2001. It catalyzed a small but growing reformist movement and later helped embolden Syria's state-controlled press. "After the prisoner releases, people began to speak out. An opening was encouraged," Saleh said. "Then there was the Statement of the 99 and a storm broke out."

In early October, the official daily *Al-Thawra* published economist and reform advocate Aref Dalila's unusually critical analysis of the state-run Syrian economy. Dalila lashed out at corruption and blamed the government for two decades of

Bashar al-Assad, though well intentioned in his drive for reform, ran into stiff resistance from entrenched interests in the regime.

economic stagnation. In subsequent months, *Al-Thawra* featured articles by former political prisoners and intellectuals who were previously barred from writing in the papers. These authors began cautiously debating sensitive issues such as the financial accountability of government.

While provocative, the articles were not revolutionary by any standard and did not challenge the authority of the regime or the Baath party. Their tone and substance, however, were a marked departure from the past. "I submitted my first article and didn't think they would publish it," Dalila told CPJ in May. "There was a desire after the president's speech to...allow alternative opinions."

In January 2001, one thousand intellectuals and citizens published a second declaration in pan-Arab and Lebanese newspapers, very similar to the "Statement of the 99." And once again, the Bashar government showed restraint. Although

Syrian newspapers did not run the petition, the authorities also did not censor foreign papers that published it.

Backlash

In the early morning hours of January 30, 2001, unidentified thugs assaulted writer Nabil Suleiman, the host of an intellectual salon, in the city of Lattakia. The incident occurred while Suleiman was on his way home, just hours after Information Minister Adnan Omran launched a blistering verbal attack against intellectuals and civil-society activists. Among other things, Omran accused Syrian reformists of taking money from foreign embassies.

A few days later, on February 8, in his first major interview since taking office, Bashar told the London-based daily *Al-Sharq al-Awsat* that "the

Photo: AP/Hussein Malla

Syrian intellectuals at a political salon in Damascus, October 2, 2001.

government will stand firmly against any work that might cause harm to the public interest." Recalling the police-state rhetoric of his father's era, Bashar denounced unnamed Syrians who he claimed had "relations with foreign channels." He charged that the salons did not represent all of Syrian society and cautioned against overzealous reform.

Before long, the salons were suspended. Following Assad's lead, government officials issued a volley of acerbic comments about the civil society movement. Baath leaders reasserted their authority over the party's rank and file members. The chill quickly reached the press.

Bashar in a corner

At the near-empty Havana Café in downtown Damascus, former journalist Radwan (not his real name) sits over a steaming glass of mint tea. "Now the local press is back to where it was," he says glumly. "They cover the president and all his actions. The talk now is about modernization and development, whatever that means."

Indeed, the main state newspapers contain little of interest. Last year's mildly critical discussions of democracy and reform are gone. Instead, the pages of *Al-Thawra* are dominated by fawning coverage of the president, numbing stories about the activities of government ministers, and vociferous criticism of Israel.

Local journalists argue that Bashar al-Assad, though well intentioned in his drive for reform, ran into stiff resistance from entrenched interests in the regime. This so-called Old Guard, consisting of Hafez al-Assad's inner circle and the powerful intelligence apparatus that has run the country for decades (while allegedly amassing vast personal wealth), felt threatened by change and applied pressure to slow the quick pace of reform.

Now the regime focuses on economic reform and modernization. In the press, there is little or no substantive discussion of political reform. "When Bashar came to power people expected him to introduce many changes. They were wrong," one Damascus-based Western diplomat commented. "He has many handicaps: no career in the party, army, or the security services. I think he wants to change, but...he has no recipe so the easiest thing is to continue in the path of his father for the time being."

Many Syrian journalists and intellectuals are convinced that the seeds of change have already been planted, however. Critics of the state express themselves in the pages of Lebanese and pan-Arab newspapers or on satellite channels such as Qatar's popular Al-Jazeera. And they are still doing so without official reprisal.

Although the Syrian press is still highly restricted under Bashar, there is less of the pervasive fear seen under his father's regime. "The people have energy and haven't stopped speaking and being active," Aref Dalila says. "People now have a desire and zeal for change and dialogue."

Because the Bashar government has generally tolerated criticism from media outside its borders, Syrians writing in the pan-Arab press have been able to operate with a modicum of freedom. In an ominous recent development, however, dissident and former political prisoner Riad al-Turk was arrested on September 1, apparently as the result of a talk that he gave at a Damascus salon. Two leading pan-Arab newspapers published Al-Turk's remarks, which constituted his first political appearance after 17 years in prison.

Photo: Joel Campagna

Ali Farzat, cartoonist and publisher, with his satirical weekly *Al-Domari*.

The Lamplighter

Ali Farzat is one of the Arab world's preeminent cartoonists; he cuts an avuncular figure as he puffs on his cigar in the small apartment-office that houses his new weekly satirical paper, *Al-Domari* (The Lamplighter). Farzat speaks of his shock when Al-Domari's maiden issue, published in February 2001, sold all its 25,000 copies in a matter of hours. He was forced to rush back to the printer and print a second run, which was gobbled up with similar alacrity.

Al-Domari's 20-plus pages of cartoons and humorous articles put a sarcastic spin on social, political, and cultural issues in Syria. The articles are written in colloquial Syrian Arabic and poke fun at corruption, bureaucracy, quality of life issues, and the occasional unscrupulous official. By Syrian standards, this constitutes highly aggressive journalism.

Like Farzat's cartoons, which make oblique references to sensitive topics such as dictatorship, corruption, and human rights without identifying a particular country or person, Al-Domari's political criticisms are usually indirect. The paper's job, Farzat says, is to monitor the government, Parliament, and society at large. "We're not interested in people but in what people do," he adds. "We're against personal libel."

The paper has already gotten a rise out of readers. Every day, Farzat says, people come to the office with complaints about a certain article or cartoon. Sometimes, even government ministers stop in to vent their displeasure.

But Farzat's incremental approach has frustrated some readers who are eager for serious and hard-hitting journalism. While they acknowledge that the mere existence of a paper like *Al-Domari* is a significant improvement on the tightly controlled press of just a year earlier, they want more. "*Al-Domari* is dealing with small issues in a very small way," said Radwan. "Maybe it talks about problems with the streets not being clean or criticizes a minister, but it does not tackle real problems."

Issues unaddressed by *Al-Domari* include the regime, democracy and human rights, and the actions of high-level officials and the security services. As a result, the paper

Photo: AP/Bassem Tellawi

Syrians read about Ariel Sharon's Israeli election victory at a Damascus newsstand, February 7, 2001.

is no longer difficult to find on Syrian newsstands, according to many local sources.

Even so, Farzat appears to have ruffled some official feathers. By late June, the authorities were already censoring the paper. According to press reports, officials ordered Farzat to cut two articles from a recent issue, along with a cartoon said to defame the government of Prime Minister Mohammad Mustapha Miro. "We had obtained permission for a satirical newspaper and suddenly we are forbidden from criticizing," Farzat told Agence France-Presse.

Join the party

For the most part, new pro-regime party newspapers such as *Sawt al-Shaab* and *Al-Wahdawi* are devoid of any critical edge. Both are highly deferential to the regime and full of praise for the president, sometimes even more so than official papers.

In May 2001, an offshoot of the Syrian Communist Party launched the newspaper *Al-Nour*. Although the paper is said to be an improvement on the other party papers (particularly in its cultural pages) it too avoids substantive criticism of the government.

A local human rights organization has launched a magazine, and a new financial newspaper has started publishing. Some applications have been denied, however, and the government is clearly not prepared to tolerate a serious opposition or independent newspaper.

"I don't think Syria will follow the Jordanian, Moroccan, or Egyptian models for the press," said Subhi Hadidi, a Syrian expatriate journalist who writes for the London-based *Al-Quds al-Arabi.* "They will be happy with half-measures."

Across the border

In the meantime, many of the bolder Syrian journalists write for the Lebanese and pan-Arab press. As early as 1999, papers such as the Beirut daily *Al-Nahar,* with its top-notch weekly cultural supplement, and the influential London daily *Al-Hayat,* published notably daring dissident opinions in essays or interviews with released political prisoners. An alternative Syrian press of sorts has emerged in these papers, as well as on Al-Jazeera and other regional satellite television channels, where intellectuals and journalists have carried out vigorous debates about democracy, political reform, and human rights.

In recent months, *Al-Nahar* published a powerful interview with Faraj Bayraqdar, a poet and former political prisoner, who talked about his torture in the notorious Tadmor Prison, located in Syria's eastern desert. *Al-Nahar* ran a similarly frank interview with former imprisoned journalist Nizar Nayyouf. Meanwhile, the London-based Arab press has run critical columns by other dissidents and former prisoners.

But foreign media cannot replace substantive local news coverage. "We can't publish all of our opinions in [the foreign press]," said Aref Dalila. "They only publish individual pieces and do not deal with issues in a complete way." Moreover, the recent arrests of al-Turk and other dissidents could have a dampening effect on Syrians who write for the pan-Arab press.

Back home

Bashar al-Assad's first year in power has been marked by mixed official signals about the future of the press. Despite a series of significant initial steps, a degree of uncertainty now exists among journalists and intellectuals. And while the pace of press reform has slowed, the public's appetite for serious journalism has been whetted.

"You cannot launch a serious dialogue about the main issues in economic, social, political, and cultural life in Syria without the press," said Dalila. "If the situation continues like this it will be very bad...You need the media for reform. It plays a large role. The people want a new media."

For the moment, Syrians will have to settle for Bashar's incremental infitah, while hoping that the Old Guard will not insist on crackdowns that could send Syria back to Hafez-al-Assad-style authoritarianism. ∎

Joel Campagna is CPJ's senior program coordinator, covering the Middle East and North Africa. He spent two weeks in Syria in late April and early May 2001 conducting the research for this article. **Hani Sabra,** CPJ's Middle East research associate, provided research assistance and translations. This report was first published on CPJ's Web site in September 2001.

OVERVIEW: AFRICA

by Yves Sorokobi

SILENCE REIGNED SUPREME IN ERITREA, where the entire independent press was under a government ban and 11 journalists languished in jail at year's end. Clamorous, deadly power struggles raged in Zimbabwe over land and access to information, and in Burundi over ethnicity and control of state resources. South Africa, Senegal, and Benin remained relatively liberal from a press freedom perspective, while corruption and fear pervaded newsrooms in Mozambique and Togo.

Almost a decade into the continent-wide democratization process, independent journalism has emerged as a powerful force capable of rooting out entrenched dictatorships and educating the masses about the responsibilities of elected governments. Consequently, leaders across the continent have devised new ways to deal with journalists who refuse to be silenced.

Some, like Robert Mugabe of Zimbabwe, have advanced harsh new laws to keep out foreign media and increase state control of the local press. Others, such as President Isaias Afeworki of Eritrea and Charles Taylor of Liberia, have used illegal means to suppress independent criticism of their governments.

In 2001, no journalists were killed in Africa because of their work, despite continuing armed conflicts in the Democratic Republic of Congo, Angola, and Somalia. But much of the fighting was low intensity, visiting less destruction on civilian populations and generating less media scrutiny than in the past.

Southern Africa was by far the continent's most troubled region. On October 12, CPJ wrote to President Bakili Muluzi of Malawi, in his capacity as chairman of the Southern African Development Community (SADC), to highlight the region's alarming pattern of state harassment and censorship of the media. The letter drew particular attention to Zimbabwe, where an unprecedented press freedom crisis erupted last year.

The Mugabe government of Zimbabwe, fearing defeat in elections planned for March 2002, has been linked with bomb attacks and other violence against news reporters.

On May 3, CPJ placed President Mugabe on its list of the Ten Worst Enemies of the Press. Mugabe was southern Africa's fiercest oppressor last year, but he was by no means the only regional leader to turn on his country's press.

In Swaziland, King Mswati III was only convinced to withdraw the obnoxious Decree No 2, which made criticism of the royal family and state officials a seditious offense, after Western powers threatened him with economic sanctions.

In Malawi, ruling party thugs beat news reporters, seized copies of private papers, and scared newspaper vendors off the streets. Even in relatively liberal Tanzania, police suppressed coverage of ethnic tensions while the Information

Yves Sorokobi is the Africa program coordinator at CPJ. **Adam Posluns** and **Wacuka Mungai** are the Africa program researchers at CPJ. They contributed substantially to the research and writing of this section. CPJ's mission to Ethiopia was partly funded by the **Freedom Forum**.

Ministry banned a dozen publications for allegedly spreading AIDS due to their "pornographic content."

Last year's greatest disappointment was Mozambique, whose once-vibrant independent press grew afraid to speak out after the murder of the country's leading journalist, Carlos Cardoso, in November 2000. In July, a CPJ investigative team found that Mozambican journalists are terrified at the possible consequences of reporting aggressively on the country's numerous banking scandals, press scrutiny of which may well have led to the murder of Cardoso.

In Namibia, Zambia, and Angola, long-serving leaders restricted independent news media "in the national interest." At year's end, there was a showdown between journalists and government in Botswana, where a Zimbabwe-style Mass Media Communications Bill was up for debate. And in November, the SADC unveiled controversial plans to establish a southern African accreditation system for journalists, to be administered by appointees from regional governments.

In June, CPJ began aggressively reporting on Eritrea's rough treatment of local journalists, revealing a tiny, highly dedicated private press and a militaristic regime fiercely bent on crushing it. In September, as international criticism of Afeworki's dictatorship mounted, authorities simply outlawed the private press, jailed a dozen reporters, and forced others into exile.

In contrast, conditions for Ethiopian journalists improved slightly in 2001. Since CPJ completed a mission to Ethiopia in October, Prime Minister Meles Zenawi made small but significant concessions to the private press, even though the country's harsh press laws stood unchanged and at least one reporter was in jail at year's end.

In all, 15 journalists and media workers were in jail in Africa as of December 31. The countries that jailed journalists were: Eritrea (11), Ethiopia (1), Rwanda (1), the Comoros Islands (1) and the DRC (1). Although no West African reporters were jailed at year's end, historically liberal countries such as Senegal and Mali renewed old patterns of media repression. In 2001, government interference with the flow of information increased markedly in Togo, where longtime despot Gnassingbé Eyadema seemed more willing than ever to crush dissent.

While attempts to topple Côte d'Ivoire's current government prompted it to detain reporters, no leader proved as volatile as Liberian strongman Charles Taylor.

As the United Nations prepared a sanctions regime against Liberia as a way to curb Taylor's criminal activities, Liberian authorities jailed reporters for "espionage," suspended news media for unpaid taxes, imposed strict regulations on foreign media, and imposed a news blackout on an ongoing rebellion in the north of the country. For his efforts, President Taylor was added to CPJ's list of the Ten Worst Enemies of the Press.

Journalists in Guinea also faced increasingly muscular government censorship, while Sierra Leone, where 15 journalists have been killed since 1997, was relatively calm as the civil war wound down and the United Nations moved in to prosecute war crimes. Meanwhile, the year-old Economic Community of West African States (ECOWAS) Court of Justice, sitting in Lagos, Nigeria, adopted rules of procedure allowing it to challenge press freedom abuses and other human rights violations by member states.

Political and media life in the East African Community (EAC) was relatively uneventful last year. In central Africa, meanwhile, the new DRC government, led by Joseph Kabila since the murder of his father, Laurent-Désiré Kabila, remained the region's main violator of press freedom, although press conditions have improved there overall.

In Gabon, President Omar Bongo toughened his grip on power by outlawing critical media outlets. President Ange-Felix Patassé of the Central African Republic used a state investigation into an abortive coup to clamp down on a private press that was already polarized along ethnic lines.

In May, the shared perception that journalists in many central African countries face similar challenges inspired journalists to create the Central African Media Organization (OMAC), based in the DRC capital, Kinshasa, and led by 2000 CPJ International Press Freedom awardee Modeste Mutinga.

According to the African Development Bank (ADB), about 200 African regimes were violently removed from power between 1963 and 2000. Only one African head of state lost an election between 1960 and 1989. In contrast, 12 leaders lost elections between 1990 and 1999. Both the ADB and the World Bank acknowledge the important role that independent media have played in this new trend of peaceful political transitions. But Africa's journalists, raised in societies where illiteracy is high and where many leaders squander public resources on weapons and personal follies, still need professional training along with backgrounds in public health, international trade, law, and other key disciplines.

Several African news organizations expanded their operations to other countries last year. In January, South Africa's African Broadcast Network began beaming its signal into Ghana, Kenya, Uganda, Nigeria, Tanzania, Zambia, and Zimbabwe.

In December, TV Africa, a joint venture of the International Finance Corporation (IFC) and the African Media Group (AMG), started broadcasting free programs to more than 110 million viewers through a network of 39 affiliates operating in 23 African countries. ■

ANGOLA

ANGOLA'S RULERS REMAINED POWERLESS TO REMEDY longstanding woes such as appalling child mortality and rampant corruption, but government troops meddled in civil wars in the two Congos and carried out bloody forays into Zambia, allegedly in search of fighters from the rebel UNITA organization.

As the country's basic social indicators sink ever lower on the global scale, a broad-based civil society movement has emerged, supported by leading clergymen and journalists. In 2001, the ruling Popular Movement for the Liberation of Angola (MPLA) responded by tightening its hold on the state media, which employs 80 percent of Angolan media workers and includes the country's only daily, *Jornal de Angola*, the wire service ANGOP, and a nationwide television and radio network.

Over the course of 2001, Angolan authorities fired journalists from state media for alleged "excessive transparency," banned radio programs because they "went against the government," and restricted the movements of outspoken independent reporters such as Gilberto Neto of the newspaper *Folha 8*.

At year's end, opposition parties, of which there are more than 100 in a country of 12 million people, continued to slam President José Eduardo dos Santos' decision to hold general elections in late 2002, a timetable deemed unrealistic because of the violence related to ongoing civil war. Dos Santos said he would not run but stuck to his schedule, relying on the Army's drive to recruit 15,000 new soldiers and secure peace on the battlefield before the election.

But signs were scarce that Angola's 26-year-old conflict would end anytime soon. The United Nations and the so-called Troika of Observer Countries (Russia, Portugal, and the United States), charged with monitoring implementation of the 1994 Lusaka peace accord, made vigorous efforts to isolate UNITA.

On May 4, Vice Minister for Social Communications Manuel Augusto visited CPJ's New York offices for a meeting with staff and board members. Augusto said that a draconian draft press law proposed in late 2000 and slammed by CPJ and others was still being rewritten.

Augusto said the government had received dozens of expert comments on the draft law, which would be evaluated by a special commission of lawmakers, lawyers and journalists to be appointed by President dos Santos. The commission would be given a deadline to study the draft law and the submissions and send a revised draft to the government. At year's end, Angolan authorities had still not begun this process.

During the meeting with Augusto, CPJ reiterated concerns about the vulnerability of journalists working in Angola's war-torn provincial regions. In response, Augusto blamed the journalists themselves for the problems they faced, saying they needed more training and better professional ethics, an argument commonly used by Angolan authorities to divert attention from their repressive actions.

Two months later, on July 9, a group of nine reporters in the northern province of Kwanza-Norte issued a statement denouncing local officials who had accused them of being unpatriotic and had threatened them with jail or worse. The signatories included reporters from both sides of the political divide, including Silvino Fortunato and Afonso Garcia of the official ANGOP news agency and Andre Mussamo of *Folha 8*.

Coverage of the civil war proved equally tricky for foreign correspondents on assignment in Angola. In early April, Portugal protested the Angolan government's decision to bar seven Portuguese journalists from reporting on a hostage crisis in the remote northern enclave of Cabinda, near the border with Congo. Two Cabinda-based separatist groups, FLEC-FAC and FLEC-Renovada, had taken a dozen Portuguese men hostage weeks earlier.

Unmoved, Angolan officials retorted that the Portuguese journalists had merely been "advised" to leave because Angolan troops could no longer guarantee their safety in the region.

As in past years, Radio Ecclesia, a Catholic Church-owned station known for its political independence, suffered repeated harassment last year. Ecclesia's main tormentors were the state media, which accused the station of plotting subversion against the MPLA. On July 9, Radio Ecclesia suspended all news programming, airing only religious music and a recorded message that urged listeners to pray. This followed a vicious slander campaign spearheaded by *Jornal de Angola*. The Catholic station resumed normal programming on July 11, saying that the 48-hour interruption was due to "internal restructuring."

On July 18, the Angolan Journalists Union (SJA) condemned the "terror campaign" against Ecclesia and other independent media, and accused state media of fostering a "climate of political intolerance."

At year's end, disturbing new information emerged about the June 5, 1998, murder of Simao Roberto, an outspoken *Jornal de Angola* columnist who was shot dead as he returned from an assignment at the presidential palace. According to reports in *Folha 8*, three men arrested two weeks after the killing only confessed to the crime under duress.

Suspect Raul Paulo Agostinho told *Folha 8* that police had detained him and two friends in connection with a car accident. Agostinho said that four days after their arrest, one of the other suspects was taken from his cell, tortured, and then shot dead. (Police later claimed that the suspect was trying to escape.) After that, Agostinho said he quickly confessed to a crime that he never committed.

BENIN

IN MARCH, PRESIDENT MATHIEU KEREKOU won a second term in office by a landslide amid allegations of fraud from the opposition. Press coverage of the candidates became a major issue in the months preceding the vote.

In an early January television address, Timothé Adanlin, head of the High Authority for Audio-Visual Communications (HAAC), cautioned reporters against distortion of facts and other unethical practices during the electoral campaign.

The HAAC, Benin's official media regulator, set out strict rules for all broadcasters during the campaign period, limiting the amount of airtime allocated to each party on the public broadcast network. It also prohibited campaign-related briefings by press spokesmen for government officials or ministries. The HAAC claimed that both measures were taken in the interest of fairness and transparency during the election campaigns.

However, the HAAC faced criticism from some quarters. The Communist Party of Benin protested Adanlin's admonitions, saying they were an attempt to "muzzle the press" during an important period of national debate.

These strict regulations notwithstanding, Benin's media covered the election vigorously. While many found the coverage comprehensive and analytical, an August report by the independent Media Ethics Observatory (ODEM) found that most leading dailies supported President Kerekou's re-election. Local journalists admitted that despite the HAAC's attempts to ensure fairness, candidates and their parties were able to influence press coverage with bribes.

The local press has come a long way since the last elections were held in 1996. Though figures vary, Benin now has as many as 18 independent dailies and 40 magazines. Since a liberal broadcasting law was passed in 1997, about a dozen private radio stations and two television stations have begun operations. The lively independent press, known for its diversity and for its informed criticism of state officials, is admired across West Africa.

Though authorities have generally been tolerant of criticism from the media, a law passed in 1997 makes libel a criminal offence punishable with jail time. Print journalists are also challenged by high printing costs, poor distribution services outside urban areas, and low literacy rates. Most journalists receive very low salaries, and many are not paid at all, making them susceptible to bribes.

In an effort to address this problem, the government has offered 300 million CFA francs (US$411,900) in aid to the private media every year since 1997.

BOTSWANA

BOTSWANA IS GENERALLY CONSIDERED A MODEL OF PEACE and stability in southern Africa, and its press, though relatively small, is vibrant and outspoken. Relations between the government and the press were strained this past year, however, as officials tried to influence editorial policy and cooperated less with independent journalists.

In early May, all government offices were ordered to stop advertising in two independent weeklies—*The Guardian* and *The Midweek Sun*—following the publication of articles that accused Vice President Ian Khama of abusing his authority.

The government is the largest advertiser in local publications. Fearing the loss of vital revenues from the state and from private companies that follow its lead, the papers' editors filed suit against the government. In late September, in what was celebrated as a victory for press freedom throughout southern Africa, a High Court judge ruled the advertising ban unconstitutional, arguing that by applying unfair financial pressure on *The Guardian* and *The Midweek Sun*, the authorities were violating their right to freedom of expression.

In late November, the government presented a draft Mass Media Communications Bill to a group of journalists and media professionals. The proposed legislation is almost identical to a 1997 bill that was later shelved under pressure from local press organizations. It seeks to establish a press council whose principal appointments would be made by the government. Botswanan journalists say that such official control would pose a threat to journalists who criticize the government.

The media bill gives police the right to seize publications that violate its provisions, which include the requirement that all journalists obtain government accreditation before reporting in Botswana. The bill was still pending at year's end.

Officials frequently lambasted the independent press last year, accusing it of sensationalism and fuelling ethnic tensions. In October, a High Court judge brought a civil defamation suit against the private weekly *Mmegi*, seeking an unprecedented 5 million pula (US$853,000) in damages. *Mmegi*'s editors feared the massive fine would bankrupt the paper, or land them in jail if they could not afford to pay it. In November, the judge ruled for the plaintiff but reduced the damages to 250,000 pula (US$42,650). At press time, *Mmegi*'s editors were trying to negotiate a still lower settlement.

In late April, Chris Bishop, head of news and current affairs at the official Botswana Television (BTV), abruptly quit his post to protest alleged government interference in the station's editorial policy and programming. Bishop, who claimed to have been repeatedly threatened by state officials, left the station after the authorities blocked the broadcast of a feature documentary on Marietta Bosch, a South African woman who was executed in early April after a Botswanan court convicted her of murder.

BURKINA FASO

THE PEOPLE OF BURKINA FASO HAVE GROWN USED TO President Blaise Compaoré's broken promises to respect the law. So on March 30, after the president opened the "National Day of Forgiveness" with an extraordinary apology for all crimes committed by his government, hundreds of people took to the streets to demand justice, not apologies.

The demonstrations included local journalists with grievances ranging from the unsolved December 1998 murder of editor Norbert Zongo to yet another empty Compaoré promise to reform the country's press laws.

The president's act of contrition was apparently inspired by the results of an inquiry into official crimes committed since Compaoré shot his way to power more than 13 years ago. In late February, a government-appointed council of elders called on the authorities to soothe public anger that had been mounting since the murder of Zongo, editor of *L'independant.*

The council of elders cited over 170 specific crimes allegedly perpetrated by the regime, and asked President Compaoré to "assume all responsibility on behalf of the state" and ask the nation for forgiveness.

"At this solemn moment, in my position as president of Burkina Faso, I ask for forgiveness and express deep regret for torture, crimes, injustices, bullying and other wrongs," Compaoré told his countrymen. The president announced the creation of a "compensation fund" for families of victims of political violence. He also pledged to make March 30 an annual "day of remembrance, human rights and promotion of democracy."

Critics dismissed the apology as a government bid to evade its responsibilities under the law, and events last year appeared to validate this view. In early February, Warrant Officer Marcel Kafando of the infamous Presidential Guard Regiment (RSP) was indicted for the murder of Zongo. But the indictment only prompted further claims that the regime was obstructing justice.

In January, another RSP serviceman considered a serious suspect in the Zongo case was found dead in a prison cell where he was serving a 20-year term for the murder of David Ouedraogo, the chauffeur of President Compaoré's brother François. Ouedraogo was tortured to death in 1998 for allegedly stealing money from his employer.

Zongo was investigating the chauffeur's death until December 13, 1998, when unknown individuals fired several automatic rifle bursts at his car, killing him and three passengers.

Authorities said the RSP prisoner died "after a long illness" but did not elaborate.

When asked to disclose the evidence against Warrant Officer Kafando, the state prosecutor said that the indictment resulted from "contradictions noted in [Kafando's] alibi for December 12 and 13 of 1998." Few believed the prosecutor.

On April 30, police raided the National Press Center in the capital, Ouagadougou, and arrested a dozen journalists, students, and others who had gathered to reflect on challenges posed by new developments in the Zongo affair. They were released a few hours later.

CPJ protested delays in the Zongo case in a March 29 letter to President Compaoré. On April 4, CPJ released a detailed account of the Zongo affair, called "Refuse To Forget."

In some ways, the Zongo controversy has helped Burkina Faso's embattled press. In a joint statement released on May 3, World Press Freedom Day, the Burkina Faso Association of Journalists (AJB), the Media Freedom League, the Movement for Human and People's Rights (MBDHP) and the National Media Observatory (ONAP) noted that "repression against the media has become less barbaric" in Burkina Faso ever since Zongo's death.

If the situation had indeed improved, the statement added, it was thanks to the determination of journalists and others in the democracy and human rights movement, and not to the good will of the Compaoré regime.

BURUNDI

ON APRIL 18, TROOPS LOYAL TO PRESIDENT PIERRE BUYOYA, a member of the Tutsi ethnic group, dislodged hardline Tutsi soldiers calling themselves the Patriotic Youth Front from Radio Burundi. In an act reminiscent of African coups during the 1970s and 1980s, the rebels had occupied the station and aired a statement announcing Buyoya's overthrow.

The rebels were apparently protesting a power sharing agreement signed in August 2000 between President Buyoya's administration, 10 Tutsi-based parties, and seven ethnic Hutu-based opposition parties, which was expected to end Burundi's civil war.

The dissident soldiers only occupied the state radio station, even though dozens of private and community stations have emerged in the war-plagued nation since the early 1990s. Although the government had often been at odds with non-state broadcasters prior to the coup, officials used the private radio stations to counter the rebel message, reassure the population, and coordinate the deployment of loyalist troops.

The implications of the independent media's role in crushing the coup were not lost on Burundians, as President Buyoya praised private stations for offering a counter-balance to extremist opinions in the country.

While Burundi seemed relatively calm at year's end, the picture was rather grim in early 2001, with peace talks deadlocked and recurrent gun battles raging in and around the capital, Bujumbura. On May 15, general exhaustion with the endless political intrigues associated with the civil war prompted the state-run Radio Burundi to castigate both the government and the opposition for failing to restore peace.

In an unusually outspoken editorial, the state radio station chided "a political class that has failed in the vital mission" of ending the conflict, according to the Panafrican News Agency (PANA). "The stalemate can no longer continue," the station warned, adding that the fate of the country's political class would be determined by the success or failure of the peace talks.

Although the majority of Burundians are ethnic Hutus, Tutsis have controlled the armed forces, the government, and much of the economy since independence from Belgium in 1962. This situation fueled the ethnic hatred that caused the civil war. The toll of the eight-year war is staggering: 200,000 dead; 600,000 internally displaced persons; and 400,000 refugees scattered in neighboring countries, the Committee for Refugees reported in October.

In April, President Buyoya launched a national security task force to develop internal security mechanisms and announced a three-year plan to build houses and other basic infrastructure for 1.2 million Burundians affected by the war. But Burundian journalists remained skeptical that the government, short of cash and grappling with a 40 percent drop in the production of coffee—Burundi's main resource—would fulfill its promises.

The widespread cynicism did not deter the authorities, however. On July 23, peace negotiation facilitator Nelson Mandela, former president of South Africa, announced that the various parties had agreed on a three-year transition process, to begin November 1. Outside Burundi, many analysts dismissed the accord as no more than a façade. But the local press, worn out by years of war, seemed to welcome the plan, urging the deeply divided Hutu and Tutsi ethnic groups to join forces and end the killing.

A new private broadcaster called Radio Publique Africaine (RPA) was particularly influential in advocating ethnic reconciliation, an ideal that station management put into practice by hiring both Hutu and Tutsi staffers. RPA struck a national chord, quickly becoming the country's most listened-to station.

In late October, the transitional assembly adopted a provisional constitution with reasonable safeguards for basic rights, including freedom of speech and the press. And on November 1, a Tutsi-dominated interim government led by President Buyoya was installed with a three-year mandate for national reconciliation and reconstruction.

The main, Hutu-dominated rebel groups, the Force for the Defense of Democracy (FDD) and the National Liberation Force (FNL), both boycotted the negotiations that produced the new constitution, under which Hutu and Tutsi are supposed to alternate control of the government every three years. But most political parties did join the talks, raising hopes that real peace was a possibility.

CAMEROON

COMPARED TO PREVIOUS YEARS, the government of President Paul Biya seemed less keen to abuse the local press in 2001. In February, officials scrapped the value-added tax on imported media equipment and multimedia goods and services. Two months later, in June, the state television and radio network RTC allowed the BBC World Service to broadcast news on the FM band in the capital, Yaoundé. In September, the agreement was extended to include Cameroon's second city, Douala, and the town of Bamenda in the English-speaking southwestern province.

Cameroon's "Anglophone problem" dominated political life last year. The former German, then British, then French colony started independent life as a federation of autonomous provinces. In May 1972, Cameroon became a "united republic." In 1982, President Biya removed the word "united" from the country's official name. Since then, the Southern Cameroon National Council (SCNC) has been agitating for the English-speaking southwestern provinces to secede. The SCNC's cause is backed by a number of local media outlets, notably Radio Buea and *Postwatch Magazine.*

The government continued to suppress all political opposition last year. In March, officials harassed newspapers that ran stories about the February disappearance of nine youths during an opposition rally in a Yaoundé suburb. At year's end, the scandal threatened to ruin President Biya's efforts to regain the confidence of the people, who have a poor opinion of their leader almost two decades since he rose to power, according to opinion polls.

The Biya regime has been under particular pressure to show respect for basic rights since the World Bank gave the go-ahead for the 600-mile Chad-Cameroon oil pipeline project, expected to flush billions of dollars into Cameroon. As a result, public relations ranked high among government priorities last year.

In June, authorities paid journalist lbert Mukong US$137,000 in damages for detaining him without warrant in 1988 and again in 1990, and for banning his book, *Prisoner Without a Crime*. Mukong, who took his case to the United Nations Human Rights Committee in 1994, benefited from the legal expertise of ARTICLE 19, the London-based anti-censorship group.

As the Anglophone problem persisted into the second half of the year, authorities detained and interrogated half a dozen reporters who had reported on alleged defense secrets or the state's uneven response to the SCNC's struggle. In January, as the Franco-African Summit was opening in Yaoundé, police officers raided the Bamenda-based *Postwatch Magazine*, impounded several dozen copies of the magazine, and interrogated publisher Ntemfac Aloysius Nchwete Ofege for a piece deemed irreverent toward French policies in Africa.

CENTRAL AFRICAN REPUBLIC

PRESIDENT ANGE-FÉLIX PATASSÉ SPENT MUCH OF THE YEAR cracking down on coup plotters as the media, clustered in the capital, Bangui, struggled to cope with harsh economic realities and a breakdown in the rule of law.

In December 2000, President Patassé warned local journalists their "leisure time" was over. On February 4, 2001, police arrested and tortured Aboukary Tembeley, a writer for *Journal des Droits de L'Homme*, for publishing an opinion poll showing that most citizens favored Patassé's resignation.

Political and social tensions, deemed "explosive" in January by United Nations Secretary General Kofi Annan, had been simmering since the withdrawal of most U.N. peacekeepers in March 2000. Dissatisfaction among civil servants, coupled with recurrent showdowns between government and opposition forces, erupted in a May 28 coup attempt during which transmitters for the national radio station were destroyed.

Private and community radio stations stayed off the air for days, with the exception of the Swiss-funded Radio N'Deke Luka, which was noted for its fair and balanced journalism. The newspaper distribution network, greatly affected by the mayhem, was still recovering at year's end.

In early July, Radio N'Deke Luka's star presenter, Tita Samba Sollet, was questioned by a state commission set up to probe the failed putsch after soldiers found weapons in a bus adorned with the words "n'deke luka" (bird of good omen). The commission cleared Sollet and the station of any wrongdoing. Radio N'Deke Luka then threatened to sue anyone making unauthorized use of the name, which it shares with many bars, bus services and grocery stores.

The coup attempt, led by former president Gen. Andre Kolingba, was crushed with the help of foreign mercenaries. It was followed by weeks of bloody reprisals, fueled by ethnic rhetoric, that caused many journalists from General Kolingba's Yakoma tribe to seek refuge abroad. They include Samba Ferdinand of *Le Démocrate*; Fouquet-Kpolodo of *L'Avenir*; and Bambou Faustin of the weekly *Collines de Bas Oubangui*.

The post-coup trauma among journalists was so severe that even members of President Patassé's Sara ethnic group toned down their criticisms of the regime. The few who dared speak out against the violence, such as editor Maka Gbossokotto of *Le Citoyen*, were quickly silenced with death threats.

On December 7, state media workers issued a joint statement asking the government to let them do their job without fear of reprisals. The statement lambasted "political censors" who it claimed had eroded even the "smallest margin for free speech" available to journalists. The government journalists also stressed that their allegiance was to the people of the poor and unstable nation, and not to the Patassé regime, which has consistently limited freedom of expression to the president's cronies.

CHAD

PRESIDENT IDRISS DEBY BEGAN THE YEAR WITH BAD NEWS. On January 2, the rebel Movement for Democracy and Justice (MDJT) announced that it had killed the head of Deby's security team, General Kerim Nassour, and his aide, Colonel Fadoul Allamine. The next day, Deby was heard on state radio pleading with the MDJT to end the standoff in the northern Tibesti region, which he said kept foreign investors away from Chad. But fighting only intensified.

Meanwhile, Chad's independent press geared up to cover the May 20 presidential election amid mounting criticism of their ethics and lack of training. Ironically, most of the vitriol came from the state press, which was itself attacked for favoring Deby's Rally of Democratic Forces (RFDT).

State and independent journalists were still at each other's throats in early February, when a court in the capital, N'Djamena, sentenced Mickael Didama of the independent weekly *Le Temps* to a suspended six-month jail term. The ruling related to a December 2000 story accusing General Mahammat Ali Abdallah, a nephew of President Deby, of plotting several coup attempts.

Around that time, the World Bank appointed an International Advisory Group (IAG) on the planned 600-mile oil pipeline between Chad and Cameroon. Among other duties, the Bank said the IAG would work on reducing poverty in Chad and tracking government use of revenues generated by the oil project. The bank's announcement caused much nervousness among officials, journalists told CPJ, as it bolstered popular demands for an unbiased commission to probe corruption in this desert nation where radical Islam is rapidly becoming a political force.

In early April, President Deby dismissed all ministers from the National Union for Development and Renewal (UNDR) from his coalition government after the party endorsed Agriculture Minister Saleh Kebzabo as its candidate. Then on April 17, a month before the elections, the official High Council on Communications (HCC) barred all non-state radio stations from airing "programs of a political nature," threatening to suspend delinquent stations.

Predictably, Deby made short work of his opponents, raking in 67 percent of the first round ballots. The vote was followed by weeks of violent unrest nationwide. Several members of the state electoral commission resigned in protest prior to Deby's landslide and his opponents, citing massive fraud, have vowed to contest the results in court.

The election was also marred by the expulsion from Chad of two observers from Côte d'Ivoire and of Roger-Francois Hubert, a reporter with the Ivorian daily *Le Belier*, on the ground that they had no official clearance.

COMOROS

MEDIATORS FROM THE ORGANIZATION OF AFRICAN UNITY (OAU) tried to broker a peace plan for the three-island Islamic republic starting in January, after members of the self-styled parliament of the breakaway island of Anjouan asked Colonel Said Abeid, the island's military leader, to relinquish power.

Anxious to prevent bloodletting, OAU mediators brokered a unity agreement that military rulers and politicians signed on February 17. The signatories agreed to draft a new constitution that would include the rights to free speech and freedom of the press.

In early March, the publisher of *La Gazette des Comores*, Allaoui Said Omar, was summoned to court for alleged libel of Mahamoud Mradabi, a leader of the Shawiri political party. Mradabi later dropped the case after an unprecedented wave of criticism from local journalists and members of the Comoran diaspora, many of whom expressed their views on an Internet discussion forum run by the bimonthly *Comores-Infos*.

In mid-April, two other papers, *Al-Watan* and *La Gazette des Comores*, also went online, followed in August by *Mayotte-Hebdo* and *Wewu*.

August 9 saw the country's 19th coup attempt in the 25 years since independence. Soldiers on Anjouan toppled Colonel Said Abeid, the military leader. Six weeks later, shooting broke out on Anjouan after the new military junta chose one of its members, Mohamed Bacar, as head of state.

Disgruntled soldiers occupied the premises of Radio Anjouan and inflicted minor damage on the facility to protest alleged neglect by superior officers. On December 19, six people were killed when French mercenaries, acting on behalf of former interior minister Achirafi Said Hachim, raided Comoros' other separatist island, Moheli, in a foiled bid to overthrow its government. That brought the total number of attempted coups to 20.

On October 11, Cheikh Ali Cassim, head of the private radio station Tropic FM, was freed after fourteen months in jail. Arrested in August 2000, Cassim was charged with illegal possession of firearms. Prosecutors provided no evidence to support the charge, but the military government insisted that Cassim had planned to kill former strongman Colonel Azali Assoumani.

The prosecution's case fell apart on June 7, when Cassim's lawyers arrived for a court hearing in the capital, Moroni, to find that the charge sheet was blank and the state's main witness had not shown up. Comoran journalists have long argued that Cassim was jailed to intimidate the independent-minded Tropic FM.

A month after Cassim's release, the junta arrested Izdine Abdou Salam, director of Radio Karthala, for airing allegedly defamatory political commentary. He still languished in a Moroni jail at year's end, weeks after 75 percent of voters chose a new constitution that ended the secessionist crisis (Anjouan and Moheli seceded unilaterally in 1997). Adopted on December 22, the new constitution grants the islands of Grande Comore, Anjouan and Moheli greater autonomy in a redefined federal state.

CONGO

CONDITIONS FOR CONGOLESE JOURNALISTS IMPROVED SLIGHTLY last year, even though the harsh 1996 Press Law remained on the books. In the main, President Denis Sassou Nguesso's unity government found it expedient to tolerate frequently caustic press criticism.

On January 13, however, authorities jailed Richard Ntsana of the opposition newspaper *Le Flambeau* and accused him of causing "confusion about state institutions." *Le Flambeau* was banned until Ntsana's release a month later.

In late 1999, Congo's decade-long ethnic civil war ended with a peace accord, although President Nguesso's victorious Mbochi tribe dominates national affairs. In March and April, all-party talks were held in the capital, Brazzaville, to negotiate conditions for a constitutional democracy. The local press fractured along ethnic lines during the conflict but since then has reportedly grown more professional in its hiring and reporting practices.

The public television network, refurbished in 2000 with Chinese funding, ran smoothly, although critics charge that its pro-government bias lingers. State radio got better reviews, but the president's personally owned Radio Liberté dominated the airwaves while avoiding sensitive topics such as corruption, HIV/AIDS, and the surging crime rate.

In June, the International Monetary Fund (IMF) cautioned Congo about widespread official corruption, threatening that the poverty-ridden, oil-rich country might lose its eligibility for debt relief under the Highly Indebted Poor Countries (HIPC) scheme. In late August, President Nguesso reinforced this message in his Independence Day address, saying the time had come for officials to stop "siphoning public funds."

On June 20, the Voice of America returned to Brazzaville's FM band, four years after the U.S. government network pulled out of Congo due to the civil war. A week later, President Nguesso opened a workshop of journalists from

Francophone countries and vowed to pressure parliament to pass a new law that would make defamation a civil, instead of criminal, offense. This had not happened by year's end.

However, the transitional parliament did adopt a draft constitution that won cautious praise for its liberal provisions on press freedom.

CÔTE D'IVOIRE (IVORY COAST)

ON JANUARY 8, PRESIDENT LAURENT GBAGBO'S GOVERNMENT thwarted an attempted coup by mercenaries whom the ruling Popular Front (FPI) accused of being in the pay of Burkina Faso and other countries bordering Côte d'Ivoire.

The rebels occupied the compound of the official RTI broadcasting network and aired communiqués saying that the elected government had been overthrown.

Government troops then shelled the RTI compound, ransacked studios, and destroyed broadcasting equipment. Thirty-one rebels were arrested after an hour-long shoot-out.

In the wake of the botched coup, authorities launched a crackdown against former government and Army officials and journalists perceived to be hostile to the Gbagbo regime. The government particularly targeted supporters of the opposition Rally of Republicans (RDR), whose leader, Allassane Ouattara, fled abroad, citing security concerns.

Several local journalists suffered harsh reprisals for allegedly propagandizing on behalf of the RDR. Police harassed others for their non-Ivorian descent or for being Muslim northerners in a country ruled since independence by southern Christians.

On January 13, local newspapers reported that "unidentified persons" had ransacked the home of Meite Sindou, editor of the pro-RDR daily *Le Patriote*. On February 10, police raided the printing press of *Le Jour*, an Abidjan daily known for its strongly independent stance. The officers, who claimed to be acting on an anonymous phone tip, forced a security guard to lie prone while they searched the premises for "arms and mercenaries." They found nothing.

And despite President Gbagbo's insistence that "no journalist [would] be imprisoned" by his administration, Sindou and four other staffers from *Le Patriote* were prosecuted for "inciting people to rebellion" in the wake of the failed January 8 coup.

The incitement charges were later dropped. But on May 10, Sindou and *Le Patriote* publisher Patrice Lenonhin became the first journalists to be convicted of work-related crimes under President Gbagbo. Charged with defamation for reporting on alleged corruption and embezzlement at a local nongovernmental organization called the Human Rights League (LIDHO), both men received suspended three-month jail terms.

The case against Sindou and *Le Patriote*, often described more as a feisty political pamphlet than a newspaper, moved the Press Freedom and Media Ethics

Observatory (OLPED), a local media watchdog group, to urge a public boycott of allegedly "non-credible" papers.

OLPED issued the statement on May 3, World Press Freedom Day. Journalists of all political persuasions responded by accusing OLPED of unethical behavior. However, OLPED's take on Ivorian media ethics drew strong support from President Gbagbo and Prime Minister Affi N'Guessan. Speaking to a gathering of media professionals, N'Guessan asserted that Côte d'Ivoire needed an "appeased media" rather than an "arsonist" one, claiming that allegedly biased news reports had caused "75 percent" of the political turmoil leading to the January 8 coup attempt.

In response, local journalists charged that the government was itself creating instability by bullying the press and keeping it underdeveloped through outdated laws that criminalize the practice of journalism.

In a separate incident, widespread xenophobia and anti-immigrant feelings are believed to have inspired the April 12 suspension of *Solidarité Paalga*, a bimonthly catering to immigrants from Burkina Faso. The National Press Commission, which banned the paper for allegedly flouting regulations for the operation of print media, lifted the suspension order on May 3 following an active protest campaign by local journalists.

The second half of the year was quieter, as the government took steps to liberalize the state media. In June, officials announced the creation of an independent broadcasting authority (private radio stations were first licensed in 1990). In July, the government solicited private investment in the state-owned Fraternité Matin newspaper group.

The government also said that RTI would be streamlined to make it more competitive with private broadcasters and with the Voice of America, which in August obtained approval for an FM relay station in Abidjan.

Meanwhile, the Gbagbo administration released a number of political detainees and won back the favor of international lenders. In October, the government initiated reconciliation talks with opposition parties. The effort succeeded beyond expectations. RDR leader Ouattara and former president Henri Konan Bedie, who was toppled in a December 1999 military coup, returned home in late November and resumed political activities.

DEMOCRATIC REPUBLIC OF CONGO

DURING THE FOUR YEARS THAT HE RULED THE DEMOCRATIC REPUBLIC OF CONGO, President Laurent-Désiré Kabila compiled one of Africa's worst press freedom records. On January 4, 2001, the last three journalists jailed by Kabila were released on the president's personal orders. Two weeks later, Kabila was assassinated.

According to Congolese journalists, Kabila's murder by a disgruntled security aide followed a rift between the late leader and his top army chiefs over the prosecution of a war against rebels backed by Rwanda and Uganda. Labeled Africa's first world war, the 4-year-old conflict involves six African governments, three major rebel movements, and a host of smaller armed opposition groups, all of which have contributed to the erosion of press freedom and other civil liberties in the DRC.

Laurent-Désiré Kabila was succeeded by his son, Joseph, who inherited not only a seemingly intractable conflict but also a staggering legacy of human rights abuses. Although Joseph Kabila promised respect for civil liberties and encouraged opposition political activities, he appeared uncomfortable with the outspokenness of local media, particularly during the surge of political violence during the transition period.

In early February, the Kinshasa regime rounded up and shot a dozen Lebanese businessmen accused of involvement in a conspiracy to kill Laurent-Désiré Kabila. Gen. Eddie Kapend, an influential cabinet member who seemed to have taken charge of the government just after Kabila's death, was also placed under arrest and later executed. Journalists covering the events were harassed by the authorities, or even jailed.

On February 28, police picked up Kasongo Kilembwe of the satirical weekly *Pot-Pourri* for publishing a cartoon lampooning the new president. Kilembwe was never charged; he was released on March 22. In mid-February, a police squad raided Victoire Square in the capital, Kinshasa, and arrested half a dozen newspaper vendors who were selling copies of the private weekly *Alerte Plus*. The issue contained allegations that 16 top military officers had been arrested in connection with the murder of Kabila *père*.

Congolese police also harassed foreign journalists. On February 17, soldiers roughed up and robbed Khan Jooneed from the Montreal daily *La Presse*. Two days earlier, Egyptian journalist Yehia Ghanem, South African bureau chief for the Cairo daily *Al Ahram*, was detained for questioning.

Stung by widespread international criticism of the DRC's press freedom and human rights record, the new authorities agreed to shut down "all detention centers that are not answerable to the public prosecutor's offices." The announcement was a victory for the local press freedom group Journalists En Danger (JED), which had lobbied for the closure of the detention centers because they were often used to confine independent journalists, many of whom were mistreated while in jail. (*Pot-Pourri*'s Guy Kasongo Kilembwe was held in one such center after his February 28 arrest.)

While the civil war devastated the DRC's economy, it somehow led to an unparalleled proliferation of private and community radio and television stations, many of them associated with various Congolese rebel groups or political factions. Despite President Joseph Kabila's promise to improve relations with opposition parties, the Kinshasa authorities remained highly sensitive about any positive news coverage of opposition figures.

In April, after the private RAGA television aired a trailer announcing the broadcast of an interview with opposition leader Etienne Tshisekedi, authorities raided the station and confiscated the videotape, which remained in government custody at year's end.

On May 21, Minister of Communications and Press Kikaya bin Karubi announced that eight community radio and television stations in Lower Congo Province would be banned as of June 30. The minister claimed the stations were "not operating in accordance with Law 96-002 of June 1996, which regulates the exercise of the media in the DRC."

According to the Congolese Association of Community Radio Stations (ARCO), the minister demanded that each of the broadcasters pay US$5,000 in overdue registration fees. ARCO insisted that all the stations had already paid US$2,500 each to the Ministry of Posts, Telephones and Telecommunications, which allocates frequencies.

On July 22, as the argument intensified, Communications Minister bin Karubi defended the new registration fee structure and denounced what he described as "the anarchic occupation of the audio-visual space by private and religious radio and television stations, which air demoralizing programs all day long and programs that incite young people and women to debauchery, and idleness by promising low-cost pleasures, joy and miracles."

The minister promised to pass new regulations requiring that the signals of such programs be scrambled, but the rules had still not been made public as of December 31.

Meanwhile, on August 8, the leadership of the Rwandan-backed Congolese Rally for Democracy (RCD) rebel forces, which control the northeastern Kivu region, lifted a two-year ban on the community station Radio Maendeleo in the town of Bukavu. RCD officials pulled the plug on Radio Maendeleo in July 1999 to silence the station's coverage of the rebel group's rampant human rights abuses in the region.

In the government-controlled south, meanwhile, Communications Minister bin Karubi issued an October 13 decree reversing the forced nationalization of the private radio and television stations RTKM and Canal Kin.

The late Laurent-Désiré Kabila nationalized both stations in 2000. (Government authorities charged at the time that the stations were built with public funds embezzled under the late dictator Mobutu Sese Seko, who was deposed in May 1997). RTKM is the property of Aubin Ngongo Luwowo, an exiled former official under Mobutu, while Canal Kin belongs to Jean-Pierre Bemba, leader of the Uganda-backed Movement for the Liberation of Congo (MLC), which controls large swathes of territory in the northeast.

In an effort to get political mileage out of a visit by U.N. secretary general Kofi Annan to the rebel-controlled northeastern town of Kisangani in late August, the Rwandan-backed Congolese Rally for Democracy (RCD-Goma) invited journalists from Kinshasa to visit Kisangani as well as other towns in the region where there have been persistent reports of massive human rights abuses.

The rebels said the visit would allow journalists living in government-controlled areas "to see for themselves the reality of the situation in the region" under their control.

ERITREA

THE ERITREAN GOVERNMENT BANNED THE ENTIRE INDEPENDENT PRESS last year, as part of a crackdown on political dissent in the tiny Red Sea nation.

In early August, a dozen senior officials and other members of the ruling elite signed a public letter criticizing President Isaias Afeworki's dictatorial rule. The letter followed a lengthy internal debate about human rights, democracy, and the conduct of the debilitating war with Ethiopia, which claimed the lives of 19,000 Eritreans.

The letter sparked a full-blown political crisis, involving defections, the resignations or dismissals of top officials, and the jailing of government critics and journalists. General elections planned for December 2001 were postponed, with little explanation, to sometime in 2002.

While the political alienation of many top officials and citizens was hardly a secret in the capital, Asmara, there was little advance warning of the crisis that erupted in early September. Even today, President Afeworki enjoys a certain prestige for leading the liberation struggle against Ethiopia that led to independence 10 years ago. According to *The Economist*, the chief complaint against Afeworki is the lack of accountability in his government. "The government is still called 'transitional,' but looks pretty well entrenched," the magazine noted.

At least 10 journalists were arrested during the crackdown; all remained in government custody at year's end. Most of them were picked up around September 18, after state radio announced a blanket ban on independent publications. Their bank accounts and other assets were frozen or confiscated and their relatives were denied the right to visit them.

According to sources in the capital, Asmara, six other journalists have managed to flee abroad. At least two more have been missing since their arrests in September, and a third since July 2000.

Eritrean authorities offered various justifications for jailing independent journalists and banning newspapers, accusing them, variously, of draft evasion, threatening national security, and failing to observe licensing requirements. But it seemed apparent that the crackdown was motivated by political anxiety ahead of the December elections.

CPJ made this argument in a December 3 letter to President Afeworki, who did not respond. However, previous CPJ letters and statements on the crackdown drew angry replies from government officials and members of the Eritrean diaspora.

In a June 7 letter to Justice Minister Foazia Hashim, CPJ requested information about the whereabouts of 15 independent journalists alleged to have been jailed or conscripted. Hashim replied on June 11, claiming that five of the 15 journalists were free and working for local publications, while the remaining 10 were "performing their obligations in the National Service Program."

On June 13, CPJ representatives met with Girma Asmeron, the Eritrean ambassador to the United States. During the meeting, Ambassador Asmeron stated that Eritrea was "moving toward a constitutional democracy, and the press laws are going to be revised and improved after that process is completed."

On July 10, Eritrean journalists from the state and private press met with Ethiopian colleagues as part of an innovative, U.N.-sponsored effort to end the war of words that continued to rage between their two countries, seven months after the end of active hostilities in the disputed border region. They met on a bridge over the Mereb River, which separates the two countries, and talked about using information to promote reconciliation.

The journalists pledged to create an atmosphere conducive to bringing their nations to mutual understanding and cooperation. But while Ethiopian journalists enjoyed at least some increased freedom last year, the Eritrean media literally ceased to exist.

Eritrean authorities consistently rejected international criticism of the crackdown. After CPJ released a news alert about the July 25 police kidnapping of Mattewos Habteab, editor of the independent newspaper *Meqaleh*, Ambassador Asmeron wrote that CPJ was "trying to guide the policy of the Eritrean government" by "distributing baseless accusations" from its New York headquarters. Habteab was freed in early September. Upon his release, the journalist confirmed that he had indeed been in police custody. He was re-arrested on September 19.

In March, Eritrean officials criticized a Reuters report titled "Eritrean troops threaten Ethiopia peace." Asmara claimed the report, which summarized a March 7 statement by U.N. secretary-general Kofi Annan, was "inflammatory, false and biased." And on at least one occasion last year, President Afeworki personally summoned and rebuked an Eritrea-based foreign reporter (who asked to remain anonymous) over an article that the president claimed was "inaccurate" and "against Eritrea."

Italian ambassador Antonio Bandini was thrown out of the country on October 1, after he protested the arrests of dissidents and the ban on the private press. Italy then expelled Eritrea's representative in Rome (the two traditional allies normalized diplomatic relations a month later).

On October 11, authorities arrested two Eritrean employees of the U.S. embassy in Asmara for allegedly translating "sensitive" official documents and reports in the local press, the United Nations' Integrated Regional Information Network (IRIN) reported. And on October 15, the Afeworki government accused a number of Western countries of a "concerted effort" to criticize Eritrea after the U.S. and several European Union countries objected to the degradation of human rights in the country.

ETHIOPIA

THE GOVERNMENT OF PRIME MINISTER MELES ZENAWI is no longer Africa's foremost jailer of journalists, but severe structural and legal difficulties still impaired the growth of the independent press. Ethiopia's rulers held one journalist in prison at year's end, while seven others were freed in the course of the year.

The freed journalists included Garuma Bekele, Tesfaye Deressa and Solomon Nemera, from the defunct Oromo-language weekly *Urji*. All three were jailed in October 1997 for criticizing "ethnic federalism," Ethiopia's contradictory state ideology. All three fled abroad upon their release on June 1.

Ethnic federalism, a doctrine enshrined in the Ethiopian Constitution, empowers ethnic groups to secede. But it also authorizes the state to crack down on separatists and other critics. In recent years, more than 60 Ethiopian journalists have been jailed and about a dozen publications put out of business for lambasting the official philosophy.

Although the ruling Ethiopian People's Revolutionary Democratic Front (EPRDF) is a multi-ethnic coalition, real power rests firmly with Zenawi's own minority Tigray People's Liberation Front (TPLF), which introduced ethnic federalism after toppling a Marxist regime in 1991.

In early 2001, the EPRDF government announced that it was abandoning ethnic federalism in favor of "revolutionary democracy," although the constitution was not amended. Many observers, including local journalists, argued that the shift was merely cosmetic.

On February 13, authorities in the remote northwestern state of Benishangul-Gumuz jailed Befekadu Moreda, editor of the newspaper *Tomar*, over a story on the secessionist demands of the local Berta people. Befekadu was released on bail after two weeks, half of which he spent on a hunger strike to protest his detention.

The fall issue of CPJ's biannual magazine *Dangerous Assignments* magazine featured "A Letter From Ethiopia," a harrowing prison diary by Bizunesh Debebe, former editor of the newspaper *Zegabi* and one of Ethiopia's few female journalists. Debebe has spent most of the last three years in jail on various work-related charges, most related to her articles about the government's oppression of the southern Oromo people. At press time, Debebe was out of jail but faced another court hearing in March 2002.

In March, long-standing tensions within the TPLF exploded into a full-fledged power struggle between moderates loyal to Zenawi and hardliners who apparently opposed Ethiopia's December 2000 peace treaty with Eritrea. The crisis fueled the Zenawi government's normal hostility toward the independent press, which covered the politicking aggressively.

On March 26, Zenawi was quoted as saying that the splinter group "posed a grave danger to the country." Soon after, the government launched a major crackdown, which lasted for months, arresting over 140 party and state officials, opposition and human rights activists, university lecturers, and businessmen on charges of corruption.

On March 28, the Amharic daily *Eletawi Addis* folded after just eight months in circulation, leaving 150 journalists and other staff members jobless. The paper's publisher shut it down after a row with editor-in-chief Solomon

Abate. Informed sources told CPJ that the publisher, who has close ties to the ruling elite, clashed with Abate over *Eletawi Addis'* aggressive coverage of the crackdown.

Abate later told the BBC that he and his staff "took it as immoral and unethical to remain silent." The publisher, for his part, argued that the paper was supposed to concentrate on social issues, rather than dwelling on politics.

In late April, Addis Ababa University students rioted to protest the police presence on their campus. Government officials dismissed the riots as an uprising of "hoodlums and lumpen." Meanwhile, local police moved aggressively to restore order. At least 38 people died in the unrest and police detained over 2,300 students.

Sixty newspaper vendors were arrested on April 20, a move that temporarily halted the circulation of most local private papers.

In June, as the crackdown escalated, security forces sealed the offices of *The Daily Monitor* newspaper and arrested publisher Fitsum Zeab Asgedom for alleged improper financial dealings.

In early October, CPJ completed a 10-day fact-finding mission in Ethiopia with a visit to jailed journalist Tamirate Zuma at the Kerchele Penitentiary in Addis Ababa. At year's end, Zuma was the only journalist jailed for his work in Ethiopia. He was convicted on various charges, including defamation and inciting the public to rebellion.

CPJ also met with senior government officials, opposition and human rights activists, as well as with journalists from both the state and private press. In the course of the mission, CPJ urged authorities to release Zuma and to repeal restrictive clauses in the Press Proclamation No. 34/1992, under which journalists can be jailed on vague charges such as criminal defamation, incitement to violence, or spreading false information. CPJ also insisted the private media must be given access to government information.

Toward the end of the CPJ mission, Zenawi told lawmakers that "responsible and constructive" private newspapers would henceforth have access to official information and briefings. Zenawi, who in the past has dismissed local independent newspapers as the "gutter press," said that the non-state press could perform a constructive role in developing a democratic culture in Ethiopia.

Since then, officials have apparently been trying to win the confidence of independent journalists, whose main representative body, the Ethiopian Free Press Journalists Association (EFJA) remained wary of the government's actual intent.

Meanwhile, CPJ remained concerned about the status of some 30 Ethiopian journalists and media workers who fled to Kenya over the past three years to avoid prosecution for press offenses at home. Most of them have been granted refugee status and have been living in private accommodations in the capital, Nairobi.

The local office of the UNHCR, which has jurisdiction over their cases, has been trying to force the journalists into the Kakuma Refugee Camp outside

Nairobi, where Ethiopian government operatives are apparently active. The journalists have so far refused to move into the camp, citing security concerns.

In early December, CPJ wrote to the UNHCR in Nairobi arguing that the journalists had a legitimate fear of persecution and should not be sent to the Kakuma Refugee Camp. The agency had not yet replied at year's end.

GABON

WITH CONFOUNDING EASE, PRESIDENT OMAR BONGO MAINTAINED his smooth-talking, iron-fisted rule by suppressing critical media voices via the Penal Code and by simply purchasing good press. In January, the president appropriated 500 million francs (US$690,000) to support private media outlets, causing reporters to engage in embarrassing public squabbles over how to divvy up the bounty.

Throughout the year, the National Communications Council (CNC), a state institution mandated to promote press freedom and ensure quality journalism, presided over a devastated media landscape. Since 1998, the CNC has been using licensing regulations to trim the number of private radio stations. There are still a few apolitical private and community radio stations in Gabon, and opposition newspapers appear regularly. But local journalists say self-censorship is more pervasive than ever.

The state broadcasting network, which includes two radio and two television stations, remains the preserve of the ruling Democratic Party. And harsh defamation laws continue to impair investigative journalism. (A more liberal press law was drafted in 1999 but has yet to clear parliament.)

Gabonese press freedom took another hit in February, when the satirical weekly *La Griffe* and its supplement *Gris Gris*, both consistent thorns in President Bongo's side, were banned by the CNC for the third time in two years. *La Griffe*'s publisher, Michel Ongoundou, and the paper's editor, Raphaël Ntoutoume, were both ordered to quit journalism. The CNC justified its decision by claiming that articles published in the two papers "bordered on provocation against the President."

In the weeks before the banning, *La Griffe* was taken to court twice, first by President Bongo and his wife, and later by the president's sister-in-law, Gisèle Opra. All three claimed to have been defamed in several articles. Their cases were still in court at year's end.

After relocating to Paris in May, Ougoundou launched *Gris Gris International*, another satirical paper. In October, authorities banned its distribution in Gabon. Government officials gave no reason for this move, but the government daily *L'Union* editorialized that press freedom must have "some limits."

Not to be outdone, Prime Minister Jean François Ntoutoume Emane castigated the "appalling, disrespectful attitude" of news outlets such as *Gris Gris International* that had the audacity, he said, to speculate on prospects for political change in the oil-rich nation. The prime minister's reaction reflected a common mindset in Gabon, where public expressions of unconditional support for President Bongo are often rewarded with cash-filled envelopes.

In search of global support as the very existence of the press appeared increasingly at risk, Gabon's Association of Free and Independent Publishers joined the World Association of Newspapers in November.

During the December parliamentary elections, a record 82 percent of Libreville residents declined to vote and 56 percent of the eligible voters in other parts of the country also elected to stay home. The ruling Democratic Party won with 80 percent of seats in the National Assembly. The president's son, Ali Bongo, raked in 100 percent of the vote in Bongoville, his father's native village.

Opposition leader Pierre Louis Agondjo Okawe of the Progress Party was moved to complain that Gabon had returned to the one-party system, while other opposition candidates attacked the state media for not covering their campaign tours.

THE GAMBIA

THROUGHOUT THE YEAR, GAMBIAN JOURNALISTS FEARED that authoritarian president Yahya Jammeh and his ruling Alliance for Patriotic Reorientation and Construction (APRC) would deal harshly with journalists ahead of the October presidential elections. To the surprise of many, these fears proved misplaced. However, repression resumed soon after President Jammeh won reelection. One journalist was subsequently arrested and tortured.

During the official campaign season, Independent Electoral Commission rules required state radio and television to give five minutes' airtime per day to each presidential candidate, and to allocate equal coverage to each party's rallies. In early October, the Gambia Press Union adopted a code of conduct for journalists covering the elections. As a result, the presidential election campaign saw some of the most balanced political coverage in the country's history.

Yet independent journalists complained that the president and the APRC dominated state media in the months preceding the campaign season, with almost no coverage of opposition activities.

The influence of the APRC went well beyond manipulating state media for its own ends. In June, ten editors from the *Daily Observer*, the country's only independent daily, resigned their posts in protest over alleged management interference with the paper's editorial policies. The journalists, who included editor-in-chief Paschal Eze, claimed their resignation was prompted by a management ban on all stories relating to a prominent opposition politician who was fiercely critical of the APRC.

The *Daily Observer*'s managing director, Buba Baldeh, is an active APRC member. The *Daily Observer*, once respected for its fair and balanced journalism, has been widely criticized for pro-government bias since its purchase by an APRC stalwart in 1999.

Gambian officials often complain that the independent media lacks objectivity and is aligned with opposition parties. In July, apparently believing their own rhetoric and fearful of growing popular support for the opposition before the elections, officials summoned several foreign diplomats and accused them of sponsoring the independent press. When questioned about the meeting, the secretary of state for foreign affairs claimed the APRC was not out to muzzle the press, but was merely reacting to its distorted political coverage.

In July, Jammeh lifted a ban on the opposition party that he had toppled in his 1994 coup. He went on to win elections international observers considered free and fair. After the election, however, the Jammeh government reverted to its repressive tactics. Authorities responded to allegations of electoral fraud by arresting numerous opposition and civil society activists, complaining that the opposition was trying to spoil the happy mood after the president's victory.

Among the detainees was Alhagie Mbye, a senior reporter for the local newspaper *The Independent*. Mbye was arrested for filing a story to the London-based *West Africa Magazine* alleging that thousands of non-citizens had been illegally registered in order to vote for Jammeh. The National Intelligence Agency (NIA) detained Mbye for eight days and tortured him in reprisal for his story. (The NIA had previously detained Mbye for three days in August after he published an article about an alleged coup attempt.)

Since Gambian journalists work with scant resources and have meager incomes, independent reporters feared that the government would use burdensome tax arrears to harass its critics during the election. After the election, NIA officials used this pretext to arrest the owners of the only independent radio stations in the Gambia that broadcast news—Baboucar Gaye of Citizen FM and George Christensen of Radio 1 FM. Citizen FM was forced to stop broadcasting after Gaye was unable to pay the station's back taxes.

Citizen FM, which frequently criticized the APRC, was one of the most popular stations in the country from its inception in 1995, primarily because of the regular newscasts in the local Wollof and Mandinka languages that it broadcast to a largely illiterate population. But the station has suffered unremitting official harassment. Citizen FM was off the air for nearly two years starting in 1998, when the government closed the station's offices and seized all its equipment after accusing Gaye of operating without a license. Gambian journalists believe the government is determined to silence Citizen FM permanently.

On the bright side, Gambian journalists appeared to have effectively quashed the draconian National Media Commission Bill of 1999. The bill would have established a regulatory commission chaired by a presidential appointee. The commission could have punished offending journalists with heavy fines and prison sentences.

When a copy of the bill was leaked to the press early in the year, journalists and media organizations launched vigorous protests, prompting the government to withdraw it from parliamentary consideration.

GHANA

AFTER JOHN AGYEKUM KUFUOR WAS SWORN IN as Ghana's new president in January, he promised to make defamation a civil and not a criminal offense. On July 27, Ghana's parliament unanimously repealed the country's criminal libel and sedition laws, including clauses governing sedition and defamation of the president. Also scrapped were laws granting the president discretionary power to ban news outlets. As a result, all pending legal cases filed under the repealed sections were dropped.

In February, the court reopened a 1996 case against Kofi Coomson of the *Ghanaian Chronicle*, Eben Quarcoo, formerly of the *Free Press,* and Tommy Thompson of Tommy Thompson Books, Ltd. All three men were charged with "making false publications likely to injure the reputation of the state," under section 185 of the Criminal Code, for alleging that the government of the time was involved in drug and arms smuggling. The case was finally dropped after the July amendment of the criminal libel and sedition laws.

In March, Seidu Paakuna Adamu, a minister in the government of former President Jerry Rawlings and a stalwart of the National Democratic Congress (NDC) party, attributed his party's poor showing in the presidential elections to its antagonistic relationship with the independent media. Radical NDC members had pledged to keep criminal libel laws on the books if the NDC candidate won the presidential contest.

By contrast, President Kufuor seemed determined to cultivate an open and accessible image. In April, the president marked the first 100 days of his administration with a press conference featuring a free question-and-answer session with reporters—a first for Ghana. Kufuor promised to make such meetings a regular feature of his time in office.

After the libel law was repealed, the National Media Commission (NMC) and the Ethics Committee of the Ghana Journalists Association assumed responsibility for monitoring the country's media. The NMC is one of several statutory bodies created by the 1992 Constitution. The first cases to be heard involved allegations of bribe-taking by journalists, as well as cases brought by individuals who felt they had been defamed in newspaper articles.

Other issues brought before the NMC and the Ethics Committee related mainly to the perceived lack of professionalism in the media. This led to calls for better pay for journalists to reduce their susceptibility to corruption. Meanwhile, the Ghana Journalists Association also came out with a code of ethics to guide the operations of its members.

GUINEA

THE POPULAR OPPOSITION LEADER ALPHA CONDE WAS RELEASED in late March, after serving three years of a five-year sentence for allegedly endangering national security. Conde's release raised expectations that political change was coming to Guinea. But President Lassana Conté, who has ruled the country for nearly two decades, saw matters differently, plotting tirelessly to strengthen his grip on power.

In late November, parliamentary elections scheduled for the following month were postponed for "logistical and political reasons." Two weeks earlier, a national referendum extended the president's term from five to seven years and scrapped term limits. Only 20 percent of registered voters took part in the referendum. Some opposition activists, impatient with President Conté's maneuvers, urged citizens to engage in armed struggle.

The Conté government, civilian in appearance but military at its core, arrested and jailed two journalists who had reported on corruption, cowing many others. Police, who frequently rough up reporters, assaulted at least one press photographer at a rally in the capital, Conakry.

Poor working conditions and low salaries continued to take a toll on reporters' morale. Citing government harassment, three journalists fled Guinea in 2001, including Georges Leonard Sagno of the bi-monthly *Le Dauphin*.

At year's end, Guinea remained on a war footing along its border with Sierra Leone and Liberia. Rebels from both countries have reportedly crossed into Guinea only to be bombed into retreat by Guinea's superior air force, a tactic that caused numerous civilian casualties. In March, Human Rights Watch denounced Guinea's indiscriminate use of force against civilians after Guinean troops raided Sierra Leonean villages along the border in search of rebels from Sierra Leone's notorious Revolutionary United Front (RUF).

The Liberian government also claimed that Guinea had killed civilians in Liberian villages along the border. The situation remained tense at year's end, as other West African countries considered sending at least a thousand peacekeeping troops to protect civilian populations.

On September 19, local journalists set up an independent ethics monitoring body, the Media Ethics Observatory, which the government dismissed as insufficient to improve local journalistic practices.

GUINEA-BISSAU

THE GOVERNMENT OF GUINEA-BISSAU remained paralyzed for most of the year following a split in the governing coalition that left the ruling Social Renewal Party (PRS) in the minority amid widespread allegations of official corruption and mismanagement. Unable to create stability in the country, President Kumba Yala resorted to an increasingly dictatorial style that pitted his administration against the legislature, the judiciary, and the press.

As tensions between the PRS and opposition parties mounted throughout the year, officials became less tolerant of aggressive press coverage. In early March, following the arrest of two journalists from the independent daily *Diario de Bissau*, Assistant State Prosecutor Genésio de Carvalho threatened to start prosecuting journalists and warned the press to practice self-censorship. In response, some 30 journalists signed a petition denouncing censorship and the arbitrary arrest of media workers, and appealed to the government to respect the laws governing their profession.

The statement was not well received. On March 30, Air Force brigadier general Melciades Lopes Fernandes burst into the studios of the independent Radio Bombolom during a debate on the fate of over 100 soldiers who had been held in detention without charge following a November 2000 coup attempt. The general accused the station of fomenting civil war and said the broadcaster would become an early military target in such an event.

As President Yala became more isolated and autocratic, antagonism grew between the PRS and the private press, particularly *Diario de Bissau*. Joao de Barros, publisher and director of the paper, and senior reporter Athizar Mendes were arrested in June after they reported on corruption in the ruling party. After his release, de Barros said that Yala had personally called him into his office and accused the press of causing civil unrest by publishing biased articles. The president then threatened to beat him up, de Barros said.

In early September, former prime minister Caetano Ntchama, whom Yala appointed attorney general, went to the offices of the private Radio Pidjiquiti to demand the tapes from a program aired earlier that day. On the program, *Diario de Bissau* journalists questioned the motives behind the recent appointment, claiming that Ntchama had been an incompetent prime minister.

At the end of the summer, the Supreme Court declared unconstitutional the president's decision to expel members of the Ahmadiyya Islamic sect, whom he had accused of causing instability. Over the next two months, Yala went on a rampage. The president sacked four Supreme Court judges for alleged corruption, vowed to replace the majority of the country's civil servants with members of his own party, and threatened to shoot any politician who tried to use the army against him.

In late October, Attorney General Ntchama banned *Diario de Bissau* and *Gazeta de Noticias*, Guinea-Bissau's only private newspapers, because of their critical coverage of these scandals. Ntchama accused the two papers of a "continuing practice of criminal activity which was a potential cause of irreparable damage, as it attempted to undermine the nation's independence, integrity and national unity."

Sources in Guinea-Bissau reported that Ntchama also threatened to close Radio Bombolom and Radio Pidjiquiti, the country's only private radio stations. Local journalists suspect that the tremendous popularity of these two stations in Guinea-Bissau, where only half of the population is literate, and their importance as sources of information to government officials, explained why they were spared the same fate as the two newspapers.

Because state journalists practiced a high degree of self-censorship and rarely questioned government policies, they mostly escaped such persecution. Due to the country's faltering economy, however, state journalists often went unpaid. In

February, staffers from the national radio and television stations went on strike, demanding better working conditions and months of salary arrears.

KENYA

CONTINUING A TREND THAT BEGAN IN 2000, high-ranking politicians and legislators—led by President Daniel arap Moi—brought several libel and defamation suits against the press last year. The judiciary responded by awarding record libel damages, introducing bankruptcy as a possible tool to silence critical media.

In July, President Moi and senior cabinet minister Nicholas Biwott filed a lawsuit against former U.S. ambassador to Kenya, Smith Hempstone, alleging that he had portrayed them as murderers in a 1997 memoir called *The Rogue Ambassador*. Kenya's largest and most influential independent newspaper, *The Daily Nation*, announced plans to serialize the book, but Biwott was granted an injunction on August 21 that forbade the paper from publishing any excerpts until the case was heard.

Moi and Biwott also sued a local bookstore chain, which was forced to remove the books from its shelves. A few days later, Moi's son also sued the *Daily Nation* for libel and successfully blocked the paper from publishing any stories about him until the libel case was heard. As of year's end, all these cases remained in court.

In October, the government announced controversial proposed amendments to the Book and Newspaper Act and the Film and Stage Plays Act. The bill, a revised and harsher version of a bill that was introduced and then shelved last year, sought to increase the publisher's bond one hundred-fold, from the current 10,000 shillings (US$ 127) to 1 million shillings (US$ 12,722). As in the previous year's bill, publishers that failed to post this bond would face fines totaling 1 million shillings (US$ 12,722), a three-year jail sentence, or both. Repeat offenders could be jailed for five years and banned permanently from publishing.

A disturbing new provision would make it an offense to sell or distribute any book or newspaper without first depositing a copy with the Registrar of Societies. Offenders would risk a fine of 20,000 shillings (US$254), a maximum of six months jail, or both. It was unclear whether this clause would require newspapers to submit copies to the registrar prior to publication.

Attorney General Amos Wako failed to attend Parliament on December 5, when he was due to move the bill, and still had not presented it before the House's Christmas recess on December 13. Although some took this to mean that the bill had been shelved, Wako indicated that he would re-introduce it when Parliament reconvened in March, but invited media owners, journalists and the Kenya Union of Journalists to comment on the bill.

The country's increasingly popular leisure publications, locally referred to as the "gutter press," caused consternation among the country's elite by publishing sensational, sex-filled articles about well-known personalities. There were allegations that some editors of these publications routinely extorted money from politicians in exchange for keeping their names out of the magazines. Politicians and even members of the judiciary used these allegations to justify both the draconian media bill and exorbitant libel awards against the mainstream media.

LIBERIA

PRESIDENT CHARLES TAYLOR REMAINS THE SINGLE GREATEST THREAT to press freedom in Liberia. As global pressure mounted on his government to improve its bleak human rights record, Taylor responded with his usual mix of paranoia and brutality, jailing reporters for "espionage," shutting down newspapers for unpaid taxes and imposing a news blackout on an armed rebellion in northern Lofa County. On May 3, CPJ included Taylor on its annual list of the Ten Worst Enemies of the Press. (See page 597.)

Early in the year, a United Nations Panel of Experts found "unequivocal and overwhelming evidence" that Liberia has been actively supporting Sierra Leone's notorious Revolutionary United Front (RUF) rebels. The panel's report charged that, "President Charles Taylor is actively involved in...international criminal activities." The panel recommended international sanctions against Liberia.

In response, the Taylor regime announced a "new policy of disengagement" from Sierra Leone on January 12, and agreed to help disarm its RUF partners, who terrorized Sierra Leone during a decade of civil war. On January 18, however, the Liberian government released a white paper titled, "Motive and Opportunity for U.N. Panel of Experts Recommended Sanctions Against Liberia." Said to be the work of presidential spokesperson Reginald Goodridge, the document contained an abridged chronology of Taylor's rise to power and discussed his strained relations with the world community. The paper suggested that Taylor was the victim of a vast international conspiracy.

On February 21, police picked up four reporters from *The News* and charged them with espionage. The detentions came in reprisal for a story on government spending on helicopter repairs, Christmas cards, and souvenirs. The four were jailed for over a month and freed only after vocal protests from the local press community and after they agreed to send Taylor a letter of apology. While they were in prison, however, *The News* was shut down for unpaid taxes.

Authorities seized equipment from three other newspapers, the *New National*, *The Analyst*, and *Monrovia Guardian*, on similar grounds. *The News* resumed publication on March 7, while the three other papers continued to publish, though with great difficulties. In May, police seized *The Analyst*'s remaining equipment, silencing it for another month.

Meanwhile President Taylor was reported as saying, without apparent irony, that "there is freedom of the press [in Liberia] and it will grow. There are no journalists or political prisoners in jail like in other African countries."

On March 7, the U.N. Security Council imposed an arms embargo on Liberia. The sanctions also affected the sale of diamonds from Liberia and the foreign travel of some 130 senior Liberian officials. The Security Council hoped the restrictions would help secure peace in Sierra Leone, where the Liberian government has been arming the RUF in exchange for diamonds. Liberia's rulers were given a two-month grace period in which to prove that they did not in fact maintain ties with the RUF.

Flustered, the Taylor government accused foreign media of pursuing a "massive negative media agenda" against Liberia, "so as to justify pending U.N. sanctions against it," according to Radio Liberia International, a Taylor mouthpiece. The regime also denounced allegedly "inflammatory and libelous articles" in the press advocating the imposition of sanctions, which were ultimately implemented, as Liberia proved unable to counter the U.N. charges.

On May 25, Taylor's obsession with conspiracy theories inspired his information minister to set new guidelines for foreign reporters visiting Liberia. An official press release stated that the new rules were intended to "minimize the impact of anti-government propaganda" allegedly fueled by foreign reporters and publications such as *Newsweek* magazine and the London *Daily Telegraph*.

The Taylor regime argued that the restrictions would prevent negative coverage of Liberia by dissuading "surprise visits by foreign journalists." Henceforth, all foreign reporters wishing to visit Liberia were instructed to send a letter of intent at least 72 hours prior to departure. In addition, the release said, Liberian security agents would conduct background checks on all applicants. Foreign media were advised to heed the guidelines or face serious consequences.

Local reporters also got their own set of new rules. In April, after fighting erupted in Lofa County, the government announced that all news reports on the violence and other national security issues would have to be cleared by Information Ministry censors prior to publication or broadcast. The new censorship regime was ostensibly designed to block "disinformation that could cause doubt and panic in the public," according to Agence France-Presse. Liberian journalists protested, to little avail, that the rule was unconstitutional because the government had not declared a state of emergency.

As the war escalated in Lofa County, President Taylor pursued carrot-and-stick diplomacy aimed at both real and perceived foes. In late July, he offered a general amnesty to all exiles charged with treason in Liberia and to the rebels in Lofa. But few dared to accept the offer, which followed a July 2 ban on short wave broadcasting by the Catholic Church–owned Radio Veritas, the only private station to reach all corners of Liberia with unbiased news about the war. Taylor's own Radio Liberia International is now the only national broadcast outlet.

In November, the continued erosion of basic freedoms prompted the Press Union of Liberia (PUL) to resume publication of the monthly press watchdog magazine *Media Line* after a three-year hiatus. In a statement, the PUL declared that *Media Line* would keep watch on the authorities, promote the welfare of journalists, and lobby for better salaries and working conditions. Days after *Media Line* reappeared, police shut down *The News* and the *Monrovia Guardian* for the second time in 10 months. They also arrested Wilson Tarpeh, an executive at *The News*.

Liberian officials claimed that the papers had refused to pay back taxes, but many doubted the justification. Tarpeh was freed on November 25, and both newspapers resumed publication in early December. But their tax arrears remained unpaid at year's end, leaving President Taylor with a pretext for future harassment.

MALAWI

OFFICIALS AND RULING PARTY SUPPORTERS INTENSIFIED A CAMPAIGN of intimidation against critical voices in Malawi following revelations of widespread government corruption and amid growing speculation that President Bakili Muluzi would run for an unconstitutional third term in office.

Members of opposition parties are often denied coverage in the state media, which is almost entirely controlled by the ruling United Democratic Front (UDF). In March, the local chapter of the Media Institute of Southern African (MISA) criticized the overwhelming pro-UDF bias in the state-owned media, saying it set a poor standard for Malawian journalism in general.

Authorities used every means at their disposal to silence media outlets that reported unfavorably on the UDF or that covered public scandals. Police frequently arrested journalists on specious charges. In early February, six reporters for the independent *Daily Times* were arrested and charged with "publishing false news likely to cause public alarm" after they reported on a series of killings in the southern district of Chiradzulu. Martines Namingah, editor of the independent *Dispatch*, and Kalera Mhango, the newspaper's printer, were arrested on similar charges in late May following a series of articles about corruption and power struggles within the UDF.

Deputy Inspector General of Police Joseph Aironi admitted that the *Dispatch* articles had not in fact caused any unrest but claimed they had the potential to do so, according to The Associated Press. Aironi added that Malawi's constitutional press freedom guarantees did not protect offending journalists.

In early January, following news reports alleging that former finance minister Cassim Chilumpha had been involved in corrupt activities before President Muluzi dismissed him from the Cabinet in 2000, Chilumpha obtained an injunction restraining the press from implying that he was corrupt. When *Daily Times* journalists reported that the former minister had been given a chance to defend himself in front of parliament, Chilumpha tried to get them jailed for contempt of court.

In September, Chilumpha became chairman of the board of directors of Blantyre Printing and Publishing Company, which owns the *Daily Times*. Chilumpha's appointment followed the installation of a pro-UDF board at the company. Local journalists believe that the sacking of *Daily Times* editor Mike Kamwendo in early December was motivated by the new board's distaste for the paper's aggressive coverage of government affairs.

Officials also tried to silence critical news organizations by draining their economic resources. The independent, Lilongwe-based *Chronicle* newspaper was forced to contend with several pending libel suits last year, all of them filed in 2000 by President Muluzi, government ministers, and the Reserve Bank of Malawi. The *Chronicle* staff believes that the plaintiffs will not actually go to court, and that their true intention is to bankrupt the paper with legal costs.

Malawian authorities also targeted printers for harassment. In December, Design Printers refused to print an edition of *The Chronicle* that contained an article about the death in police custody of local reggae star and government critic Evison Matafale. Design Printers administrative manager Billy Chimimba, said that because Malawian law did not protect printers of controversial material, he decided he could not afford to print *The Chronicle*.

Malawian journalists faced numerous threats and physical attacks from ruling party supporters last year, especially from the youth group that calls itself the "Young Democrats." There was a concentration of such attacks around the time of the Southern African Development Community (SADC) summit in Blantyre in August. African Eye News Service correspondent Brian Ligomeka and *People's Eye* editor Chinyeke Tembo were both assaulted by UDF supporters around the time of the summit because they had published critical articles about Malawi's political climate. John Saini, publisher of the independent magazine *Pride*, received death threats while covering the SADC conference because of his paper's unfavorable reporting on the government.

Vendors who sold copies of newspapers that were critical of the government were frequently harassed; on several occasions, UDF supporters attacked the vendors or burned copies of their newspapers. There were also reports of opposition party supporters attacking journalists in response to media criticism.

Though President Muluzi was elected the new chairman of SADC at the conference, he was silent regarding these attacks on the press. The Panafrican News Agency reported that during a political rally in September, Muluzi was outspoken about what he described as Malawi's improved press freedom record, saying that journalists were free to write whatever they wanted. But just a month earlier, Muluzi berated "biased" news organizations in a speech, claiming they did not deserve to exist because they were "out to distort and frame the presidents and their governments in all sorts of negative aspects."

MALI

ALTHOUGH MALI'S PRESS LAWS INCLUDE punitive presumption-of-guilt standards, the media environment is reasonably liberal compared with many other African countries. Mali also has a strikingly diverse press corps, with about 40 private newspapers, some in French and others in vernacular languages, and about 100 radio stations, one fifth of them unlicensed.

Mali's only television network is state-run, however, and the government has failed to implement a licensing regime that was included in a progressive broadcasting law passed nine years ago. The Internet is still in its infancy, mainly because landline telephone service is erratic.

On March 26, Malians commemorated the 10th anniversary of the popular uprising that brought down dictator Moussa Traoré in 1991. Meanwhile, at least five politicians from the ruling party announced they would challenge President Alpha Oumar Konar in the presidential elections scheduled for 2002.

In July, the government eliminated jail as a penalty for ordinary libel, although libel is still classified as a criminal offense. Reporters convicted of "offenses" against the head of state, ministers, or public institutions now face three to 12 months in jail, down from six months to five years.

Meanwhile, aggrieved officials and citizens continued to settle personal scores with journalists. On July 25, three men kidnapped and roughed up Abdoulaye Ladji Guindo of the weekly *Liberté* for an article denouncing corruption in the sugar industry.

Guindo was abducted a few months after attending a seminar on the use of investigative journalism to combat corruption, which has evidently reached troubling proportions in Malian society. In March, a Bamako judge grilled Communications Minister Ascofaré Ouleymatou Tamboura, who is suspected of stealing money allocated for the expansion of the state telecommunications company, SONATEL.

Western donors, who have consistently praised Konaré, were concerned when the president announced plans for a referendum to grant himself total immunity from prosecution. Under popular pressure, Konar cancelled the referendum in late November. Opposition leaders, for their part, spent the year warning against ballot fraud during next year's vote.

MOZAMBIQUE

PRESIDENT JOAQUIM CHISSANO, RESTRICTED BY CONSTITUTIONAL TERM LIMITS, announced that he would not seek reelection in 2004. This was unusual in southern Africa, where leaders such as Frederick Chiluba of Zambia and Sam Nujoma of Namibia have indulged in constitutional manipulation in an attempt to stay in power.

After Chissano announced his intention to retire from politics, so-called modernist and traditionalist factions within the ruling FRELIMO party began jockeying over the succession. The modernists are led by Prime Minister Pascoal Mocumbi, a former economist. Armando Guebuza, a nationalist who is unpopular with foreign donors, leads the traditionalist camp. Anxious to keep Mozambique on good terms with the IMF and the World Bank, Chissano is said to favor Mocumbi.

But like many top FRELIMO officials, Mocumbi has been shadowed by allegations of corruption and worse. In late November 2000, Mocumbi allegedly pressured Carlos Cardoso, editor of the daily investigative newsletter *Metical*, to drop a story he was investigating "for the country's sake." The meeting allegedly took place on November 17, 2000, just five days before Cardoso was gunned down three blocks from his paper's office.

Before his death, Cardoso was investigating corruption scandals that may have reached the highest levels of the ruling elite. President Chissano has vowed that justice will be done in the Cardoso case, but few journalists believe him. In July, Mozambican journalists told a visiting CPJ delegation in the capital, Maputo, that Cardoso's murder had left them too frightened to cover sensitive stories, particularly those involving corruption.

The delegation included CPJ board member Clarence Page, a columnist for the *Chicago Tribune*; CPJ deputy director Joel Simon; CPJ Africa program coordinator Yves Sorokobi; South African journalist Phillip van Niekerk; and Mozambican journalist Fernando Lima. During their four-day visit, the delegation members met with reporters, police, and senior government officials.

Mozambican authorities say they have made significant progress in their investigation into Cardoso's murder. Two brothers from a prominent banking family, one of their business partners, and three alleged gunmen are in jail on charges of conspiring to murder Cardoso. Yet few in Mozambique are satisfied. The government's account is full of holes and inconsistencies, ranging from the number of hit men (variously, between one and three) to the alleged motive. The government says the bankers killed Cardoso because of his reporting on a 1996 scandal at a local bank called BCM.

CPJ has determined that Cardoso was not actively investigating the four-year-old BCM scandal at the time that he was killed, but was instead probing a newer and even larger scandal at another financial institution called Banco Austral. A senior manager at Banco Austral was murdered in August, a crime that Mozambican authorities have suggested is linked to the Cardoso killing.

Cardoso was also looking into questionable real estate deals in Maputo. Just a few days before he was killed he faxed a list of pointed questions to a prominent local businessman who chaired Banco Austral and was also involved in local land development projects. Yet government investigators interviewed by CPJ insisted that Cardoso's murder was solely related to his reporting on the BCM affair.

Metical was a subscriber-only faxed newsletter that set new standards for investigative journalism in impoverished, formerly Marxist Mozambique. Many questions clouded *Metical*'s prospects for survival without Cardoso. But the paper continued to break important stories, earning more hostility from the political and business elite. In March, businessman Nympine Chissano, President Chissano's son, filed criminal defamation charges against the paper and its chief reporter, Marcelo Mosse.

The younger Chissano is seeking damages worth US$80,000 in connection with a February 21 article alleging that he was briefly detained in South Africa around February 15 on unspecified charges. Nympine Chissano's lawyer rejected the story, saying his client "never transported cocaine or other substances forbidden by law inside or outside the country," according to AIM, the official news service.

Interestingly, the *Metical* story made no mention of cocaine or any other controlled substance (although other news reports did). It seemed clear that *Metical* had been singled out because of its aggressive coverage of the Maputo business community, of which Nympine Chissano is a prominent member. Court hearings have been postponed several times. In the worst-case scenario, the court could bankrupt *Metical*, now the property of Cardoso's two underage children, and jail Marcelo Mosse. Under pressure, *Metical* closed down on December 27.

NAMIBIA

JOURNALISTS AND PRESS FREEDOM ADVOCATES from around the world attended a UNESCO conference on press freedom held in the Namibian capital, Windhoek, on May 3, World Press Freedom Day. The conference celebrated the 10th anniversary of the Windhoek Declaration, which affirmed that a free and pluralistic press is essential for democratic government.

In a statement read to the assembled delegates in his absence, President Sam Nujoma accused the African press of irresponsibility. Demands for more press freedom, the president charged, were often driven by the desire to "unscrupulously engage in sensationalism, misinformation, falsifications, and lies in order to sell their products and build untouchable empires." The public would be better served, Nujoma argued, if the press concentrated on conveying information from the government to the people.

Meanwhile, the government cautioned all foreign journalists attending the May 3 celebration against reporting on any events outside of the UNESCO conference itself, saying they would have to apply for work permits in order to do so. Under Namibian law, foreign journalists must apply for accreditation at least one month in advance of their arrival and state the purpose of their proposed visit.

Nujoma's personal mistrust of journalists is reflected in official policy toward the independent press in Namibia. On March 23, the government ordered all its offices and agencies to stop buying advertising in *The Namibian*, the country's largest daily. The ruling South West African People's Organization (SWAPO) made no attempt to hide the fact that the ban was imposed in reprisal for the paper's critical coverage of the government.

Two months later, Nujoma ordered all government agencies to cancel their subscriptions to *The Namibian*. At the time, a SWAPO official told *The Namibian* that the advertising ban was inadequate, and that the authorities believed the added restriction would "teach the paper a lesson."

On September 25, the government moved a new defense bill in the National Assembly that allowed the government to restrict a great deal of information on "national security" grounds. The bill was widely criticized by journalists and press freedom organizations. Among other restrictions, the bill would penalize disclosure of all "unauthorized information" and prohibit all photography of military premises and installations.

As justification for the proposed restrictions, Defense Minister Erkki

Nghimtina said that the media were not sufficiently security conscious. Namibian journalists countered that "national security" was a vague term and that the bill gave the government far too much latitude to restrict important public information. The bill was still pending at press time.

Private interests also used the legal system to restrict information last year. In October, for example, the private Olthaver and List company obtained a court gag order against four news organizations, preventing them from quoting from a statement by the National Farm Workers Union alleging that the company was criminally liable for the death of one of its workers.

State media continued to show strong bias in favor of the ruling SWAPO. In October, when callers to the popular radio show "Free Voice" began criticizing government plans to build an airport near President Nujoma's home village of Okahao, the Namibian Broadcasting Corporation (NBC) banned the program from airing what it called "political campaigning." Two weeks later, "Free Voice" began insisting that callers state their names, addresses and phone numbers before speaking on air.

NIGER

TWO YEARS AGO, NIGER'S MEDIA OMBUDSMAN judged the local press healthy. In 2001, that assessment seemed optimistic at best. Journalists in this vast, impoverished country remained at odds with the administration of President Mamadou Tandja.

In January, three local media rights groups accused public authorities of "suffocating the press." The Niger Press Association (ANEPI), the Reporters' Network for Human Rights (RJDH), and the Union of Private Press Journalists (UJPN) said in a joint statement that colleagues who criticized the government faced threats, illegal arrest, and rigged court cases, and that preventive detention was a common means of censorship.

The statement urged authorities to respect the principles of democracy and obey Niger's constitution and laws. But Niger's unimpressed officials kept on filing criminal charges against media outlets that accused them of corruption.

In May, President Tandja filed charges against the independent newspaper *Mat-Info* for printing allegedly false information about his health. The case was dropped on May 18, but it had created a useful precedent for other senior officials with grievances against the press.

Corruption, meanwhile, continued to take a serious toll on the country's meager finances. In April, for example, Kenya's *East African* daily reported that Niger had spent almost US$60,000 on toilet paper rolls for five senior members of parliament from the governing coalition.

To no avail, opposition leaders called for an investigation into the management of public funds. They were equally unsuccessful in urging President Tandja to order a state probe into the April 1999 assassination of former president Ibrahim Bare Mainassara.

However, the opposition was instrumental in launching Parliament's own radio station. Billed as "a radio [station] for the expression of democracy," La Voix de l'Hemicycle (The Voice of the National Assembly) went on the air April 24.

On May 3, World Press Freedom Day, the three leading media rights groups (ANEPI, RJDH and UJPN) asked the state to contribute US$1.8 million to a media development fund. The government declined, citing earlier donations and an expensive military campaign to disarm ethnic Tuareg and Toubou rebels, still active along the border with Libya despite a 1997 amnesty law that was supposed to integrate the rebels into military and civil service.

On October 19, after a Niamey court sentenced publisher Abdoulaye Tiémogo of Le Canard Enchaîné to six months in jail for allegedly defaming agriculture minister Wassalké Boukari, the government argued that prison would improve Tiémogo's ethics. (Boukari was also awarded US$6,700 in damages.)

Tiémogo was finally released on December 7, four days after the entire private press corps walked out to protest Finance Law 2002, a new tax regime that imposes heavy levies on private news outfits. In addition to an annual registration fee of US$220, private media owners must now pay the Industrial and Commercial Profit Tax, the Value-added Tax, and a so-called Initiation Tax.

Under pressure, the government agreed to apply the new law only to news outlets with more than US$12,000 in capital. Even so, Finance Law 2002 bodes ill for the future of independent journalism in Niger.

NIGERIA

MIRRORING THE LARGER SOCIETY, the Nigerian media were severely fractured along ethnic and regional lines in 2001, although mainstream news outlets remained economically robust, dynamic, and politically outspoken.

Throughout the year, a host of new publications hit newsstands, many of them in local languages. In the Christian-dominated south, private radio and television stations expanded their national coverage. In contrast, deadly religious uprisings hampered the growth of media outlets in the Islam-influenced north. Religious fundamentalism in the northern states not only strengthened the local Islamic legal system, which imposes severe penalties for alleged press offenses, but also raised the specter of secession in this historically unstable federal republic.

The mystery surrounding the death of Dele Giwa, the founding editor of the Lagos-based weekly Newswatch, continued to make headlines 15 years after a parcel bomb killed him. Giwa's death dominated the final hearings of the Human Rights Violations Commission, popularly known as the Oputa Panel. The panel was created by President Olusegun Obasanjo to investigate human rights abuses committed under the military regimes that ruled Nigeria from 1966 to 1998. Its mandate was to determine whether those abuses resulted from "deliberate state policy or the policy of any of its organs or institutions."

The Oputa Panel began conducting hearings in 2000, all of them carried live by several Nigerian broadcasters. The result was a highly charged national debate over democracy and government accountability.

Three formerly jailed journalists appeared before the Oputa Panel and recounted their experiences in detention: Kunle Ajibade of *The News* and Ben Charles Obi and George Mba of *Tell*, both of whom had been convicted and sentenced to 25 years in jail for their alleged involvement in a phantom 1995 coup plot to overthrow Nigeria's former dictator the late Gen. Sani Abacha.

Summonses to appear before the Oputa Panel were also sent to members of the public, current, and former government and army officials, including President Obasanjo, and three former military heads of state. Although Obasanjo testified twice in person and appealed to all three of the country's former military strongmen to do the same, they consistently refused.

Public pressure was particularly intense in the case of Gen. Ibrahim Babangida, who ruled Nigeria at the time of Giwa's assassination and allegedly masterminded the murder. But General Babangida was still refusing to testify when the Oputa Panel wrapped up its work in October.

President Obasanjo's appearance before the Oputa Panel seemed to usher in a new culture of openness and respect for human rights in official circles. But Obasanjo upset Nigerian journalists when he declared that news professionals had "continued to demonstrate lack of control and responsibility in some of their reports. They call it press freedom, but I think sometimes it is press anarchy." In July, Obasanjo filed criminal defamation charges against Nnamdi Onyenua, editor of the weekly, Lagos-based magazine *Glamour Trends*. Onyenua was detained for 11 days and was only released after the president's lawyers dropped the charges.

On the other hand, Obasanjo often courted Nigeria's fiercely outspoken media. In June, the Obasanjo government sponsored a National Media Tour, in which 75 journalists from print and electronic media traveled to all 36 states to meet local authorities and inspect federal development projects. In several states, local governors and other officials used the platform offered by the Media Tour to lambaste journalists for their perceived sensationalism, ethnic favoritism, and regional biases.

The Media Tour elicited mixed reactions among both journalists and officials. Some journalists labeled it a money-wasting ploy, while others dismissed the tour as an Obasanjo public relations scheme ahead of general elections planned for 2003.

But the government did not try to interfere directly with the media, and several newspapers and broadcasters made their debuts in an already competitive market. Numerous new English-language and vernacular papers, both state- and privately owned, were launched. In July, African Independent Television (AIT) went on the air, breaking the decades-long monopoly of the official Nigeria Television Authority.

The former capital, Lagos, remained an important base for foreign media covering West Africa. In May, CNN opened a full-time bureau there.

Meanwhile, the Voice of Nigeria (VON), the country's external broadcasting service and one of only a few such services in Africa, announced plans to establish six new bureaus in Nigeria, as well as external bureaus in the United States, Europe, and other African countries. In October, VON purchased three new shortwave transmitters. The station, which has links to eight other broadcasters in South Africa, Sudan, Sierra Leone, and Kenya, currently airs programs in two local and four foreign languages, including English, French, Arabic, and Kiswahili.

Several special interest radio and television stations were also launched or about to begin operations. Zamfara, one of the northern states that adopted the Islamic legal system, known as sharia, announced plans to create a television station called Voice of Islam. In September, supporters of independence for the former breakaway Biafra region launched Voice of Biafra International in an effort to revive their cause.

Despite the dynamism and increasing freedom of the Nigerian press, journalists must still contend with harsh laws and regulations. In addition to criminal defamation, journalists must contend with Decree 60, a 1999 law that created the government-appointed Press Council. Decree 60 also mandates state accreditation of journalists. In order to be accredited, all journalists must have received professional training from an "approved institution."

Late in the year, in an attempt at self-regulation, the Nigerian Union of Journalists introduced a nationwide registration system. Also, a much debated Freedom of Information Bill, for which Nigerian journalists have vigorously campaigned, received overwhelming popular support at a series of public hearings in October. The bill would enshrine the right of access to information or records kept by government agencies and private bodies carrying out public functions.

Journalists used their influence to focus attention on serious societal problems such as domestic violence, HIV/AIDS, and gender discrimination in the work force. In May, Journalists Against Aids, an advocacy organization founded in 1997, opened a media and resource center devoted to providing information on HIV/AIDS and reproductive health issues. The organization also launched a Web site intended to improve the quality and accuracy of reporting on HIV/AIDS in the Nigerian media.

RWANDA

PRESIDENT PAUL KAGAME SURPRISED HIS OWN CABINET in December when he refused to sign a contentious media bill that prescribed the death penalty for journalists found guilty of inciting genocide.

Lawmakers passed the bill in September, citing the macabre role that certain Rwandan media outlets played in promoting and orchestrating the 1994 massacre of more than 800,000 ethnic Tutsis and moderate Hutus by Hutu extremists. The bill also prescribed lifetime imprisonment for reporters convicted of stirring ethnic hatred, even in cases where mass slaughter does not ensue.

The bill also proposed that foreign reporters found guilty of inciting genocide be banned from Rwanda and that prosecutors be given the authority to compel journalists to reveal confidential sources. The bill was presented by a Legal Reform Commission mandated to review all existing laws as part of a general overhaul of the Rwandan political system prior to national elections scheduled for 2003.

Officials claimed the bill was intended to foster a professional and responsible media. But Rwandan journalists voiced shock and outrage at its content, complaining that the Ministry of Local Government and Social Affairs, which drafted the bill, did not properly consult with them.

Although he had originally supported the bill, President Kagame ultimately changed his position, arguing that Rwanda needed genocide laws that addressed the roots of the problem.

Long ruled by Hutu or Tutsi leaders whose cabinets were packed with relatives and whose ideologies were firmly rooted in ethnicity, Rwanda has since July 1994 been under a unity government made up of five parties. Real power is firmly in Tutsi hands, however.

In March, the ruling coalition won by a landslide in municipal elections. Half of Rwanda's 8 million people cast ballots, a turnout President Kagamé hailed as a "significant step for democratization." Independent journalists were more reserved in their assessments. Many said the ruling coalition's overwhelming victory mirrored at best the government's unwillingness to open the political arena to opposition voices.

In February, the government suspended two Hutu-dominated parties for allegedly "organizing and participating" in the 1994 genocide. In June, authorities banned former president Pasteur Bizimungu's Democratic Party for Renewal (PDR) just days after its official launch.

The Kagame government claimed the PDR was bent on "destabilizing the country." That argument prompted contentious public debate, which in turn brought restrictions on the press. On December 31, for example, police arrested Amiel Nkuliza, a reporter for the newspaper Le *Partisan* who had questioned the circumstances surrounding the December 26 murder of Gratien Munyarubuga, a PDR co-founder. Nkuliza was released on January 3 without charges.

All year long, Rwandan officials bullied state media and harassed independent journalists who accused them of overstating the genocide issue for their own gains. In this intensely Catholic country, reporters also got in trouble for writing bluntly about religious matters, particularly in relation to the president.

In April, state television producer Gerard Mbanda was suspended without pay for airing footage of President Kagame being shown a passage in the Bible. CPJ sources said the footage could have been construed as suggesting that Kagame could not read the Bible without help.

Meanwhile, controversy mounted over the rights of detainees at the International Criminal Tribunal for Rwanda (ICTR), a U.N. court sitting in Tanzania that prosecutes alleged perpetrators of the 1994 genocide. Passions flared after an ICTR security team searched the cell of Hassan Ngeze, former editor of the defunct extremist Hutu paper *Kangura,* and seized materials that Ngeze had posted on an unauthorized Web site devoted to his defense. Ngeze claimed that "vital defense documents" were also taken from his cell, a charge the ICTR dismissed as baseless.

Ngeze is on trial for genocide and other crimes against humanity. He is alleged to have fueled the mass killings with virulent editorials and articles in *Kangura.* Ferdinand Nahimana, former director of Radio Television Libre des Mille Collines (RTLM), and Jean-Bosco Barayagwiza, a founding member of RTLM, are being tried on similar charges in what has become known as the ICTR's "media trial."

In early April, a witness testified that Faustin Rucogoza, Rwanda's minister of information at the time of the genocide, had warned RTLM officials on at least two occasions against broadcasting material that could incite ethnic hatred.

The witness, identified only as "G.O." for security reasons, said the first meeting took place in November 1993, and the second on February 10, 1994, when the genocide was in full swing. Testifying for the prosecution, Belgian journalist and Rwanda expert Colette Braeckmann said that former Prime Minister Agathe Uwilingiyimana had also expressed worries about RTLM's broadcasts in November 1993.

Witness G.O., who monitored RTLM broadcasts for the state, testified that the station blamed all of Rwanda's woes on Tutsis and repeatedly aired the Ten Hutu Commandments, a set of edicts first published in Hassan Ngeze's *Kangura* that banned all social interaction between Hutus and Tutsis. After the Commandments were read on RTLM, Hutu men started murdering their Tutsi wives, and children from mixed marriages bludgeoned their Tutsi mothers to death, G.O. said.

RTLM's ghoulish role in Rwandan history has not deterred authorities from seeking to encourage the development of local broadcasting. In June, the semi-official *New Times* reported that the government might license more private radio stations. Also in June, the government granted the Voice of America a license to broadcast on the FM band in the capital, Kigali.

SENEGAL

Conditions for local reporters in Senegal have worsened since the March 2000 election of President Abdulaye Wade. A fiery opposition leader for four decades before his rise to power, Wade had cultivated good relations with the media, which he rallied behind his Democratic Party with promises to scrap repressive clauses from the press law.

However, Senegal's reputation as a model for press freedom in Africa has taken several blows under Wade's administration. Although the colonial-era press law prescribes jail terms for "publishing false information," "discrediting the state," "inciting the population to disorder," and "insulting the Head of State," Wade's predecessors generally refrained from using the law against the outspoken Senegalese media, which has grown to include 17 radio stations, eight daily newspapers, and four dozen other periodicals, according to the latest official count.

Wade not only failed to repeal the obnoxious press law clauses, he also announced that there were "limits" to press freedom. He made the statement as his government began peace negotiations with rebels in the Casamance region in December 2000. On at least five occasions since Wade took office, his government has detained journalists and pressured them to reveal confidential sources. Though most of these cases were not brought to trial, journalists were alarmed by the harassment, given that the Penal Code, under which the burden of proof rests with the accused, could force them to compromise sources in their own defense.

President Wade's alliance with a powerful Muslim sect called the Mourides caused much hand wringing among local columnists, many of whom warned that Senegal's secular state could be in jeopardy. At year's end, police were still trying to find the perpetrator of an early October arson attack against the offices of the private Wal Fadjri media group, which includes a radio station called Walf FM, and the daily newspaper *Wal Fadjri*. Senegalese journalists suspect the attack related to scathing remarks about Wade's Mouride connections made by Sidy Lamine Niasse, the host of the controversial Wollof-language radio show "Religion and Current Affairs," which airs weekly on Walf FM.

The press has received some support from the new government. In the run-up to legislative elections in April, President Wade granted local media 300 million CFA (US$411,900), supplementing a press support fund set up by the previous government, to enable journalists to cover the 21-day election campaign. The government has also increased funding for the prestigious, Dakar-based Center for Media Studies (CESTI). To date, CESTI has trained nearly 800 journalists from several French-speaking African countries.

Costs for newsprint are high in Senegal and advertising is hard to come by, obliging publications to generate about 80 percent of their revenue through the sale of newspapers. This has led to the emergence of a fast-expanding tabloid press, known as the "press of the masses," sparking heated debates on media ethics. In September, the Dakar tabloid *Tract* published scandalous photographs that allegedly showed Prime Minister Madior Boye in a compromising situation. *Tract*'s publisher later admitted that the pictures had been manipulated.

SIERRA LEONE

FOR THE FIRST TIME SINCE 1996, NO JOURNALIST WAS KILLED IN SIERRA LEONE last year, a welcome development in a country that had earned the dubious distinction of being the most dangerous country in Africa for journalists.

However, journalists were threatened by former rebels and government officials alike. In September, seven members of the independent press received bizarre, identical letters signed by a so-called danger squad that threatened to kill them for being "enemies of the state." CPJ sources in Freetown linked the threat to outspoken opinion pieces on President Ahmed Tejan Kabbah's decision to postpone general elections from December 2001 to May 2002.

Meanwhile, the Independent Media Commission, established by an act of parliament to register newspapers, magazines, and radio and television stations and to advise the minister of information on media issues, started operating last year. In December, the commission updated publication licenses for 21 existing newspapers. But the publications still need approval from the registrar general and income tax department, which had not been granted at press time.

The commission's mandate includes arbitrating libel cases and other complaints of journalistic misconduct. In this capacity, the cash-strapped commission was busy even before its official launch. By June, it had already received complaints from three former and present cabinet ministers against Freetown publications.

In addition, journalists faced accusations of corruption and bribery throughout the year, with several complainants questioning the media's ethics. For their part, news professionals have voiced worries about the Commission's independence, given that the head of state appoints its members.

Meanwhile, the United Nations authorized a war crimes tribunal for Sierra Leone, after a May agreement between the rebel Revolutionary United Front (RUF) and the pro-government Civil Defense Force (CDF) militia to begin disarming and reintegrating their fighters into society.

The tribunal will prosecute the alleged ringleaders of the country's decade-long civil war, which was marked by exceptional brutality that included targeting journalists for assassination. In all, 15 journalists were murdered in Sierra Leone between 1997 and 2000. Thirteen of them were killed by the RUF, infamous for cutting off the limbs of government supporters at the behest of its controversial leader, Foday Sankoh, who is currently in prison.

SOMALIA

THE SO-CALLED FAILED STATE SYNDROME HAMPERED EFFORTS to reunite Somalia, wracked by inter-clan warfare since 1991. Although the year began with news that the economy was slowly recovering, it ended with a bleak United Nations assessment that Somalia was on the brink of an economic collapse unmatched in its modern history.

The grim forecast was issued a month after the United States reportedly started contemplating an attack against the desert nation, which is alleged to harbor Al Qaeda terrorists. American suspicions have focused mostly on the Somali-based Islamist organization Al-Ittihad al-Islami. Somalia's Transitional National Government (TNG), whose control does not extend beyond the capital, Mogadishu, has strenuously denied any link with terrorists.

News of U.S. military activities in the region has also renewed worldwide media interest in Somalia. Ironically, this comes just a few months after the U.N. Security Council voted to exempt reporters and aid workers in Somalia from wearing flak jackets and helmets, nine years after it imposed the requirement.

Somali journalists, caught in the middle, struggled to report objectively on the country's violent clan politics and on allegations of Islamist terror cells in their midst. They also grappled with mounting insecurities about the future of journalism in the country.

In November, Somalia lost most of its communication links with the outside world when the U.S. government shut down the Al-Barakaat banking and telecommunications firm for its alleged part in bin Laden's terrorist network. Al Barakaat Communications was Somalia's largest employer until its abrupt demise. It had a telephone and Internet subscriber base of 45,000, including the self-declared autonomous region of Puntland in the northeast and the self-declared republic of Somaliland in the northwest.

On January 13, Abdirihman Nur Mohamed Diinar, a reporter for the popular radio and television station HornAfrik, was appointed press secretary to President Abdiqassim Salad Hassan.

On February 17, President Hassan opened the second session of the Transitional National Assembly before a large audience of local reporters. However, the journalists were only allowed to cover the opening and closing sessions. A parliamentary spokesperson conducted press briefings on the other sessions.

On May 3, World Press Freedom Day, a Libyan delegation visited Mogadishu to assess the feasibility of setting up a radio and television station for the TNG, twenty years after state-run Somali Radio and Television was destroyed in the civil war.

The plans bore fruit on August 23, when the TNG launched Radio Mogadishu–Voice of the Somali Republic, Mogadishu's sixth news radio station. Today, an estimated two-dozen privately owned radio and television outlets operate in Somalia. Some are clan-based, and one operates clandestinely.

Political and media life in Somaliland was relatively uneventful last year. Puntland, on the other hand, was by far the most volatile region of Somalia. On February 6, Puntland authorities freed Abdishakuur Yusuf Ali, editor of the newspaper *War-Ogaal*. Ali was arrested on February 2, allegedly for supporting the Mogadishu government, along with Ahmed Kismaayo, editor of *Riyaq*. At year's end, there was still no confirmation of Kismaayo's release.

While still trampling on reporters' rights, the Puntland authorities nevertheless allowed the region's first private FM radio station to begin broadcasting on June 20. Officials at the station later announced plans to open a television station in October (CPJ could not verify the launch of the TV station due to communications problems following the demise of Al Barakaat).

In early July, a messy power struggle erupted between Puntland president Colonel Abdullahi Yusuf, who refused to leave office at the end of his term, and Chief Justice Yusuf Haji Nur, who claimed to be the "legitimate authority" in the breakaway region. Armed fighting broke out and continued until mid-November when the Puntland legislature elected a third local leader, Jama Ali Jama, as president. During the mayhem, all sides harassed and detained journalists for "publishing false information" and threatened to kill reporters who criticized them.

Back in Mogadishu, clan politics unfolded in their usual unpredictable way.

On March 21, faction leaders opposed to the TNG formed the Somali Reconciliation and Restoration Council (SRRC) with the blessings of the Puntland regime, ostensibly to "lead the nation towards national unity." As splinter groups bound by clan loyalty and Islam continued to challenge the TNG's authority, the government grew touchier about Western influences on the content of local media.

On June 7, for example, Attorney General Ilyas Hasan Mahmud threatened to punish the broadcaster HornAfrik for "propagating Christianity" after the station aired BBC programs with some Christian content.

As the year drew to a close, Somalia's warring factions gathered in the Kenyan town of Nakuru for peace talks. On December 24, after weeks of formal and informal meetings, all sides signed a peace deal designed to firm up the TNG's legitimacy while granting clan leaders a voice in the political process.

SOUTH AFRICA

WHILE THE SOUTH AFRICAN MEDIA IS WIDELY RESPECTED throughout the continent, the South African government's attitude to press freedom is riddled with contradictions. On one hand, the Promotion of Access to Information Act, which went into effect in March, granted citizens access to any personal information held by the state and private entities. The authorities also posted public records on the Internet.

On the other hand, apartheid-era laws give the state power to subpoena reporters and compel them to reveal sources. In August, lawmakers debated a new bill that would allow security organs to eavesdrop on cellular communications and intercept electronic messages.

If passed, the Interception and Monitoring Bill will empower law enforcement and intelligence agencies to "establish, equip, operate and maintain monitoring centers" to tap electronic and cellular communication, in some cases without warrant. Authorities say they need the law to fight organized crime.

Journalists were wary of this argument, claiming that the law would compromise the confidentiality of their e-mail and cell phone exchanges with sources. At year's end, the bill was still with Parliament's justice committee, which had amended it so that a judge's order would be required to conduct wiretaps and obtain telephone records.

In September, the Cabinet approved the Electronic Communications and Transactions Bill, which empowers the authorities to access private citizens' e-mail messages.

Other new bills and statutory bodies were equally controversial. The Media Diversity and Development Agency (MDDA) was set up by the government to "increase access to the media for all citizens," develop community radio stations and newsletters, and ensure a racial balance in newsrooms. South African press groups complained that the MDDA's mandate gives the agency sweeping powers of investigation, lobbying and intervention.

But the MDDA has its supporters as well. The Media Workers Association of South Africa, for one, claimed that racism pervaded the country's newsrooms, which it said needed constant monitoring to ensure South Africa's commitment to diversity.

Investigative journalists were busy last year, and their stories led to the dismissal of more than 30 government employees for corruption. The media's aggressive hunt for corrupt officials further strained relations with the ruling African National Congress (ANC), which often accused journalists of racism.

But no subject busied reporters as much as the trial of members of PAGAD (People Against Gangsterism and Drugs), a vigilante group charged with the brutal murder of a suspected Cape Town gangster in 1996. Three reporters who witnessed the killing were subpoenaed to testify and to provide unpublished photos of PAGAD members who lynched the gangster and set his corpse on fire. The reporters were subpoenaed under Section 205 of the Criminal Procedure Act, which allows the state to investigate journalists' sources and seize any information relating to a crime.

Lawyers for the journalists successfully challenged the subpoenas; none of them testified, and no photos were handed over.

In another startling case, the police charged the *Sunday Times* with "interfering with police work" for publishing a December 9 photograph of a suspect in the murder of Marike de Klerk, the ex-wife of former president F.W. de Klerk. The paper was charged under Section 69 of the 1995 Police Act, which prohibits taking and publishing pictures of people connected to a crime. No ruling was available at year's end.

SWAZILAND

ABSOLUTE RULER KING MSWATI III LEARNED JUST HOW SMALL the global village can be when he signed a June 22 media decree that was immediately denounced by human rights organizations and governments worldwide.

Decree No. 2 made it a seditious offense, punishable with a 10-year jail term, to "impersonate, insult, ridicule, or put into contempt" the king, tribal chiefs, and state officials. The decree allowed the banning of publications without appeal, removed bail for a number of press offenses, and raised penalties for libel. It also upheld a ban on the political opposition and the suspension of the Swazi Constitution, both in place since 1973.

The king's decree marked a climax in his government's protracted face-off with the kingdom's small independent press. The confrontation began in early 2000, after authorities shut down the entire state-owned press for criticizing the Swazi police. (The papers resumed publishing in February 2001 with an entirely new staff).

As international criticism of Swaziland's press freedom record mounted, the government launched a satellite news television channel, Channel S, ostensibly to counter perceptions that the king was quashing democracy and violating human rights. Channel S was supposed to air in 17 countries.

In late July, a CPJ delegate visited the Swazi capital, Mbabane, and met with journalists from the independent press, members of the political opposition, and labor leaders. Managers and journalists from the state media declined to be interviewed, saying that their "hands [were] tied."

CPJ found that tensions between the state and private media have sharpened since economist Sibusiso Dlamini became prime minister five years ago. For example, the Swazi National Association of Journalists (SNAJ) has only 70 members, although the state media employs over 140 media workers. Members of the independent press say their public sector colleagues have been instructed to avoid professional groups not sanctioned by the authorities.

Prime Minister Dlamini is effectively the "editor-in-chief" of all state and pro-government newspapers. He presides over a weekly gathering of editors and vets stories before they are printed. Local journalists told CPJ that it was nearly impossible to investigate sensitive issues because their requests for government-held information are routinely channeled through a daunting bureaucratic maze.

On March 2, local BBC stringer Thulani Mthethwa and others launched a new weekly magazine called *Guardian* and announced that they intended to cover palace intrigues, until then an untouchable subject for Swazi journalists. In its second issue, *Guardian* covered rumors that King Mswati was in ill health, having been poisoned by one of his many wives. Other articles reported on the royal family's efforts to throttle civic organizations. Two days later, on May 4, the state registrar of newspapers suspended the *Guardian*, claiming the magazine had not been properly registered. The authorities also banned the monthly magazine *The Nation* after it ran similar reports.

In mid-May, Parliament threatened to revive the oppressive Media Council Bill, which had been shelved in 1997. And after the High Court lifted the ban on *The Nation* in late May, Prime Minister Dlamini hastened to re-impose it on state security grounds. King Mswati pitched his ill-advised Decree No. 2 as a definitive solution to the crisis in late June. But the government withdrew the decree on July 24, sealing an important victory for the press and for Swazi democracy.

Independent observers concur that pressure from the United Sates, whose trade agreements with Swaziland keep the tiny kingdom afloat, forced the king to scrap Decree No. 2.

The ban on *The Nation* was finally lifted in late June, after editors brokered a gentlemen's agreement with the authorities. In late August, the High Court allowed the *Guardian* to resume publishing. Swazi officials promptly appealed the ruling; the parties were still negotiating a settlement at year's end.

In November, senior police officials threatened three Swazi stringers for foreign media with harsh reprisals if they wrote negative reports about the king. The three are BBC stringer Mthethwa, Lunga Masuku of African Eye News, and Bheki Matsebula of *Sowetan Sunday World*.

Also in November, lawmakers endorsed a proposal to fine journalists over

US$1,000 if they misrepresent any parliamentary debate. But King Mswati seemed to have adopted a more tolerant attitude by year's end. In early December, The Mouth That Never Lies, as the king is also known, commissioned a 15-member team to draft a new, more liberal constitution within the next 18 months.

TANZANIA

IN JUNE, THE GOVERNMENT OF PRESIDENT BENJAMIN WILLIAM MKAPA published a review of its media policy, outlining proposed changes to existing media laws. The document expressed the government's commitment to press freedom and to providing quality education and training for journalists. But it applied only to the mainland and excluded the island of Zanzibar.

Under Tanzania's two-tier constitutional structure, adopted after mainland Tanganyika and Zanzibar merged to create the United Republic of Tanzania, the mainland and Zanzibar generally have separate media policies. Zanzibar's media policy is more restrictive than that of the mainland.

In particular, the island's Registration of News Agents, Newspapers and Books Act provides for mandatory licensing of journalists and state monitoring of the private press. Under this law, unlicensed journalists may not collect or disseminate information on or about the island. In addition, licensed journalists must "promote national policies... and maintain harmony in the society."

Mainland Tanzania boasts a number of independent newspapers, published in English and Kiswahili. They have been criticized for their timidity in tackling issues such as corruption and government mismanagement. The mainland also has 20 private radio stations, although the Broadcasting Services Act restricts their broadcasting range to only 25 percent of the country. Most private stations are concentrated on urban areas. Only the state-owned Radio Tanzania and Televisheni ya Taifa are licensed to cover the entire country.

Unlike the mainland, Zanzibar has no private newspapers or broadcasters. Although the Zanzibar Broadcasting Commission was established in 1997 to regulate private broadcast outlets, none has been licensed so far.

In 2001, as in previous years, the mainland's media laws were used to muzzle press coverage of sensitive issues. The Newspaper Registration Act of 1976, which grants authorities powers to register or ban newspapers, was used in July to shut down nine publications and suspend three others for reports and photographs deemed "contrary to national ethics and [which] encourage promiscuous behavior." The move came a month after President Mkapa announced a crackdown on pornography in print and online.

Meanwhile, the Tanzanian town of Arusha continued to host the International Criminal Tribunal for Rwanda. Three Rwandan media figures (Hassan Ngeze, Ferdinand Nahimana and Jean Bosco Barayagwiza) are facing genocide-related charges for allegedly helping to incite the 1994 slaughter of more than 800,000 ethnic Tutsis and moderate ethnic Hutus by Hutu extremists in Rwanda.

TOGO

FOLLOWING WIDESPREAD ALLEGATIONS OF HUMAN RIGHTS ABUSES in Togo, President Gnassingbé Eyadema and the ruling Rassemblement du Peuple Togolais (RPT) struggled all year to prove their commitment to democracy, promising parliamentary elections that were ultimately postponed until 2002 for "technical reasons." Desperate to improve its international image while retaining a tight grip on power, RPT authorities used a harsh press code and dubious interpretations of the constitution to crack down on journalists and opposition leaders.

Most Togolese newspapers openly back either the RPT or opposition parties, leaving little room for independent journalism. Financial pressures allegedly lead journalists of all political persuasions to accept bribes from politicians and businessmen. Though the opposition press is outspoken in its criticism of authorities, it is confined for the most part to the capital, Lomé.

Togolese journalists engaged in a fierce debate over an Amnesty International report that accused their government of carrying out hundreds of extra-judicial killings after the 1998 presidential elections. Pro-government newspapers accused opposition leaders of conspiring with Amnesty to tarnish the country's image. Opposition newspapers demanded that the RPT admit responsibility for the alleged violations.

In a March address at United Nations offices in Geneva, Prime Minister Agbeyome Kodjo falsely claimed that independent Togolese journalists had unanimously denied there was any truth to the Amnesty report. Earlier that month, in what was perceived as an implicit warning against writing on the topic, Kodjo asked a gathering of independent journalists whether they had personally seen the dead bodies. Many of the reporters present admitted they had not. Kodjo apparently based his claim on this discussion.

The Togolese Private Press Publishers Association (ATEPP) issued a statement accusing the prime minister of "seeking to take advantage of the private press." In early June, Lucien Messan, editor of the independent newspaper *Le Combat du Peuple,* was sentenced to 18 months in prison for forgery after he signed the ATEPP statement using the technically inaccurate title of "publication director." Independent journalists believe that Messan's conviction was intended to intimidate the free press ahead of the parliamentary elections.

Authorities were generally sensitive about press coverage of the country's poor human rights record. The church-owned Jeunesse Espoir Radio was shut down in January when it announced a mass for Sylvanus Olympio, the country's first president, killed in a 1963 coup led by the current president. And police seized entire print runs of the independent papers *Le Regard* and *Le Reporter de Temps Nouveaux* when they published articles about political violence in past years.

Chris Steele-Perkins, a photojournalist with the German magazine *Der Spiegel,* had his film confiscated in July while he was working on a story about child labor in the region.

Reporting on Togo's rampant official corruption landed several journalists in jail and resulted in more newspaper seizures. Opposition journalists received harsher treatment than their pro-government colleagues. In October, Alphonse Nevame Klu, director of the pro-opposition newspaper *Nouvel Echo*, was jailed for reporting on graft. So were Abdoul-Ganoiu Bawa and Rigobert Bassadou, of the pro-government *Echos d'Afrique*. But while Bawa and Bassadou were released shortly after their arrests, Klu was detained for more than two weeks.

In spite of the government's attempt to control broadcast media through the High Authority for Audio-visual Communications (HAAC), pirate radio stations have flourished in Lomé. After licensing four new radio stations in early January, most of which broadcast religious and commercial content, HAAC President Georges Combevi Agbodjan vowed to "end the anarchic proliferation" of unlicensed stations. Agbodjan added that "freedom of expression…is not in danger in Togo so long as private radio stations strictly adhere to HAAC regulations."

UGANDA

DESPITE A STIFF CHALLENGE FROM HIS FORMER PROTÉGÉ Kiiza Besigye, President Yoweri Museveni was reelected in March, fifteen years after he pioneered Uganda's controversial "no party" political system.

During the heated election campaign, there were allegations that the president's office had tried to "vet" articles and columns in *New Vision,* a government daily. The paper denied the charge, although one of its writers stopped his column for the duration of the campaign, citing interference.

Uganda's independent press is healthy and operates largely unfettered. With more than 30 private stations in operation and another 100 applicant broadcasters granted licenses, Uganda now has the largest number of radio stations in East Africa. The country boasts the region's first community radio station run by women. Radio stations played an important role in the elections, airing regular call-in and talk shows with the candidates.

The state radio network was noted for its generally fair and balanced political coverage. Though limited by low literacy rates, print media also covered the elections actively. The pages of Uganda's two leading newspapers, *New Vision* and the independent *Monitor*, were filled with incisive political debates. In October, the *Monitor* launched *Ngoma*, a new Luganda-language paper, to compete with *New Vision*'s Lugoma-language *Bukedde. New Vision* also publishes three other papers in local languages: *Orumuri (*Runyankole*), Rupiny* (Luo), and *Etop (*Ateso*).

In August, the government promised to repeal the unpopular Press and Journalists Statute of 1995 and the Electronic Media Statute of 1996, and replace them with the 2001 Media Bill, a promise still unfulfilled at year's end. The 1995 statute, which established the Media Council and the National Institute of Journalists of Uganda (NIJU), requires every news professional to have a university degree in journalism.

Ugandan journalists have asked that the NIJU be scrapped and its functions transferred to an independent, non-statutory body. But the draft legislation, still awaiting parliamentary debate, sets up a new Media Commission empowered to censor publications of "pornographic matters and obscene materials," neither of which is clearly defined in the bill.

Arguments about pornography have been a national fixture due to the popularity of so-called leisure publications. In October, the editor, deputy editor, and ten other staff members of the tabloid newspaper *Red Pepper* were charged with "trafficking in obscene publications" after the tabloid ran a picture of teenagers apparently having sex on the beach during a school outing. The picture caused considerable outrage among the public, with religious groups and even some journalists calling for more oversight of the media.

The issue of media registration, long a bone of contention, surfaced again when the Media Council was unable to identify the owners of *The Message*, a weekly whose editors and staff vanished after being sued for defamation by the Ugandan YMCA.

In June, the National Association of Broadcasters lobbied parliament to reduce annual license fees for radio and television stations. Journalists argued that relief was warranted because private media outlets already pay a 17 percent value-added tax on advertising revenues. Additionally, private radio stations pay the Ugandan Communications Commission an annual fee of 1 million Ugandan shillings (US$570) while television stations pay 6.5 million shillings (US$3,710). In addition, the Media Council charges news outlets 600,000 shillings (US$342) each time it hears a case against them. Parliament agreed to put a hold on these levies, pending further consultations.

Heightened security concerns in the aftermath of the September 11 terrorist attacks on New York and Washington led the presidential press office to ban all videos, still cameras and tape recorders from presidential functions. In late September, Parliament started debate on a controversial Suppression of Terrorism Bill that included dangerously vague definitions of "terrorist" and "terrorism." The bill would also allow the government to monitor any suspect's communications, including letters, phone calls and e-mails. The possible implications for Ugandan journalists, who routinely cover rebel groups that the government describes as "terrorists," are as yet unclear.

ZAMBIA

INCUMBENT PRESIDENT FREDERICK CHILUBA FAILED TO CONVINCE Zambians that he should be allowed to run for an unconstitutional third term in the December 2001 general elections. Political controversies surrounding the elections dominated media headlines in Zambia all year long. Mounting tensions between the ruling Movement for Multiparty Democracy (MMD) and the opposition were mirrored in the editorial polarization of state and private media.

As the government tightened its control over state media in the run-up to the elections, the independent press became more strident in its criticism of the MMD and incurred the wrath of ruling party officials. Increased MMD oversight over government media was heralded by the May 9 appointment of Vernon Mwaanga as minister of information and broadcasting services. Mwaanga took office claiming to be unaware of any political interference in state media.

Less than two weeks later, Mwaanga dissolved the boards of the state-funded *Times of Zambia*, the *Zambia Daily Mail*, the Zambia National Broadcasting Corporation (ZNBC), and the Zambia Printing Company, ostensibly to "restore the sense of responsibility and accountable journalism."

In late June, Mwaanga announced that he would "not tolerate any nonsense from the private media from now onwards." He accused independent journalists of "unprofessional reporting, gutter reporting and rumor mongering." In mid-August, Mwaanga ordered the closure of Radio Phoenix, the country's most popular independent broadcaster. Though Mwaanga claimed that the station was closed for failing to pay back taxes, journalists said the tax arrears were a pretext to keep critics of the government from airing their views on the station's live call-in programs. Radio Phoenix was allowed back on the air in late September.

The Zambia National Broadcasting Corporation (ZNBC), the country's most important media outlet, was also the most heavily criticized state media organization. In late August, the fear of giving the opposition a platform apparently prompted the ZNBC to cancel a live debate designed to educate voters on election issues. The debate was sponsored by Coalition 2001, a consortium of civil society groups. The debate was only aired after the sponsor obtained a court injunction against the ZNBC.

The ZNBC successfully pulled the plug on a live televised debate among the presidential candidates on the eve of elections. Zambian sources believe the debate was cancelled because of MMD fears that their candidate, Levi Mwanawasa, would not perform well. Though the debate sponsors obtained an injunction preventing the ZNBC from interfering with the broadcast, the station still aired an interview with President Chiluba in its place.

Zambia's independent media played a major role in mobilizing public opposition to President Chiluba's bid for a third term by keeping the issue at center stage until Chiluba was forced to withdraw his candidacy.

Ruling party cadres made every attempt to silence Chiluba's critics. In early April, the *Zambia Daily Mail* threatened legal action against third-term opponents who had reprinted and circulated thousands of copies of a 1998 article from the paper's sister publication, the *Sunday Mail*. The article quoted Chiluba urging fellow party members to look for his successor, as he would not run for another term in office.

At around the same time, the opposition United Party for National Development began running an ad on Radio Phoenix re-playing a 1996 interview with Chiluba in which he pledged to honor the constitution and leave office after his second term. And in May, the offices of the Catholic

Church–owned Radio Icengelo were set ablaze. Station staff suspected that the arson attack was in reprisal for their opposition to a Chiluba third term.

Authorities were particularly sensitive to press coverage of rampant official corruption. In late July, two editors of the *Zambia Daily Mail* were suspended for six months after an article in the paper described Home Affairs Minister Peter Machungwa, who was being investigated for corruption and abuse of office, as "disgraced." *Post* editor Fred M'membe, reporter Bivan Saluseki, and two former MMD politicians were charged with "defaming the Head of State" after the fiercely anti-Chiluba newspaper alleged that the president was involved in a US$4 million graft scheme.

Despite all the harassment, journalists at the *Post* and *Monitor* could take some consolation in the fact that the heated political climate increased their sales, which had been declining for years. (Because of their critical stance toward the government, neither publication receives state advertising.)

One positive development last year was the publication of a draft of the long-awaited Freedom of Information Act. The act is designed to allow the media and the public efficient access to public documents. Though the government invited comments, there was no movement on the draft by year's end. In a related development, the National Assembly acquired a radio transmitter in late October, allowing for the live broadcast of parliamentary debates.

ZIMBABWE

PRESIDENT ROBERT MUGABE WAS NAMED TO CPJ'S LIST OF THE TEN WORST ENEMIES of the press in 2001. (See page 597.) Backed by his volatile minister of information and publicity, Jonathan Moyo, Mugabe harangued, insulted, threatened, and intimidated journalists throughout the year. Mugabe, his unpopularity growing at home, found himself increasingly isolated on the world stage as well, with his government threatened with sanctions from the European Union and expulsion from the Commonwealth.

As weary citizens braced themselves for elections in March 2002, Zimbabwe was torn by unprecedented social unrest. While journalists put themselves in harm's way to cover demonstrations, fuel and food shortages, and lawless takeovers of commercial farms, their government introduced harshly restrictive press legislation, expelled foreign correspondents, and accused independent journalists of "terrorism." Adding insult to injury, both Mugabe and Moyo filed defamation suits against independent newspapers last year.

Marauding "war veterans" were busy throughout the year, not only invading farms and intimidating political opponents of the government, but also menacing members of the independent media. The "veterans," most of them too young to have fought in the war of independence that ended two decades ago, routinely issued death threats against journalists, harassed vendors and destroyed copies of newspapers.

Earlier in the year, with the seeming collusion of the authorities, the "veterans" declared much of the country a "no-go" zone for the independent press. Journalists risked beatings or worse if they traveled to rural areas, and were largely restricted to covering the capital, Harare, and other large towns. As a result, the state-owned media largely controlled information in and from the countryside.

No case of press harassment was more shocking than the January 28 bomb attack on the printing press of the independent *Daily News* in Harare. It was the second bombing that the newspaper had suffered in less than a year. The attack came just a day after Moyo claimed that the *Daily News* posed a security risk to the nation and threatened to silence the paper "once and for all." In November CPJ awarded its International Press Freedom Award to Geoff Nyarota, editor-in-chief of the *Daily News*.

In February, the government expelled two foreign journalists, ostensibly because their work permits had expired. Soon after, the Department of Information and Publicity announced a freeze on new permits until a new accreditation system could be put in place. In June, the government imposed new restrictions on foreign journalists, requiring them to apply for accreditation a month before arriving in the country.

The government announced that it would not accept applications from foreign journalists already in the country, who would have to leave Zimbabwe and reapply from their own countries. The move was initially justified as a way of forcing foreign media companies to employ more Zimbabwean citizens. Later in the year, however, Moyo's ministry suspended the accreditation of all BBC correspondents covering Zimbabwe. Moyo accused the BBC and other foreign media companies of colluding with Zimbabwe's independent media and opposition politicians to discredit the government and incite violence.

The state's strained relationship with the press took a bizarre turn in August, when the independent *Standard* newspaper published a so-called hit list that was allegedly compiled by the Zimbabwe police and by the Central Intelligence Organization, which oversees internal security. The list featured several outspoken journalists.

Prompted by this dire situation, a delegation from CPJ visited Harare in July to meet with journalists and learn more about conditions in the country. The delegation met with over 60 journalists and expressed CPJ's commitment to supporting the Zimbabwean press.

In November, the state-owned *Herald* newspaper quoted an unnamed government official who accused six journalists based in Zimbabwe of participating in "terrorist" activities.

"Terrorism" and "national security" became recurring motifs after the September 11 attacks on New York and Washington, D.C., with Moyo declaring that the United States and Great Britain had reacted to the attacks by limiting press freedoms in the name of national security. "If the most celebrated democracies in the world won't allow their national interests to be tampered with, we will not allow it, too," he said.

The controversial Broadcasting Act, first introduced as a temporary measure in 2000, was reintroduced and made law in April, even though the Supreme Court ruled it unconstitutional and a parliamentary committee declared it illegal. The act, which created a new state-controlled Broadcasting Authority, states that only Zimbabwean citizens are eligible for broadcast licenses.

The act also gives the minister of information and publicity sole authority to grant broadcast licenses and to impose additional conditions on a licensee beyond the set regulations. It provides for only one additional signal carrier to exist in the country in addition to the state-owned Zimbabwe Broadcasting Corporation, and empowers both carriers to decline to transmit programming from a licensed broadcaster.

The Public Order and Security Bill (POSB), intended to replace the notorious Law and Order Maintenance Act (LOMA), was finally re-introduced in November. Although the POSB had originally been presented for Mugabe's signature in 2000, he refused to sign the bill because it was less far-reaching than he would have liked.

The revised bill nominally dealt with security issues relating to terrorism and treason. But according to a report in *The Herald*, it also imposes fines and imprisonment for making or publishing statements deemed "prejudicial to the state," or likely to create "hostility toward the president." Mugabe signed the bill in late January 2002. It came into force on January 22 through an official proclamation.

The highly anticipated Access to Information and Protection of Privacy Bill was approved for parliamentary debate before any of its provisions were made public. The initial draft bill would have required all journalists to be licensed by a state Media Commission, which would maintain a register of all journalists in the country. Only Zimbabwean citizens with journalism degrees would qualify.

The draft bill contained several other alarming provisions—for instance, that journalists could be fined or jailed if found to have "spread rumors, falsehoods or cause alarm and despondency under the guise of authentic reports."

Following protests from journalists, regional leaders, and members of the international community as well as members of Zimbabwe's Parliament— including some from the ruling party—a watered down version was finally passed on January 31, 2002. The new amendments were modest, however, extending media ownership to citizens or permanent residents, or to corporate bodies with citizens or permanent residents as the majority shareholders.

They further provided for citizens or permanent residents to be accredited as journalists, with a new provision that would permit foreign journalists to be accredited for a limited period.

Local and foreign journalists—including members of the newly formed Zimbabwe Foreign Correspondents Association—vowed to challenge the law in the Supreme Court, and to ignore the new requirements. ■

| CASES TABLE OF CONTENTS |

ANGOLA

June 9

"Ponto de Vista"
`CENSORED`

Authorities in the eastern Angola town of Lunda-Norte banned the popular radio show "Ponto de Vista" (Point of View), which aired on Emissora Provincial da Lunda-Norte, a local affiliate of the Angolan state radio network.

Sources in Angola said that on June 6, the provincial director for social communications, Manuel Cambinda, told the program's host, Olavito de Assunção, that the program would be taken off the air for being "against the government." The program remained banned at year's end.

June 27

Tulimeyo Kaapanda, NBC
`HARASSED`
Patric Mettler, NBC
`HARASSED`

Mettler and Kaapanda, reporters for the official Namibian Broadcasting Corporation (NBC), and unarmed members of the Namibian police's Special Field Force were taken hostage for four hours by Angolan soldiers at the border between Namibia and Angola.

The NBC crew was filming a feature on car theft in the region when five soldiers arrested them and accused them of crossing the border illegally. The soldiers also confiscated the journalists' car and cameras.

After negotiations between the crew, the Angolan soldiers, and the Namibian border patrol, the group was freed. The confiscated tape was returned to the journalists several days later.

July 7

Gilberto Neto, *Folha 8*
`HARASSED, CENSORED`

Neto, a journalist for the independent weekly *Folha 8*, was arrested at the airport in the northern province of Malanje, according to sources in Luanda. Neto was traveling with Phillipe Lebillon, a researcher from the London-based Overseas Development Institute, who was also arrested.

As soon as local authorities discovered the presence of a *Folha 8* reporter and a foreigner in the province, they assigned security agents to follow them, Angolan sources reported. The two had been in Malanje for five days researching local economic effects of the Angolan civil war.

On July 6, Malanje governor Flávio Fernandes's spokesperson told Neto and Lebillon that they were prohibited from continuing their work because they had not received authorization from the governor.

Two police officers escorted Neto and Lebillon on the airplane back to Luanda, where they were handed over to the National Directorate of Criminal Investigation (DNIC). The two were interrogated for an hour and accused of traveling illegally to Malanje. The police confiscated their passports, Neto's press accreditation, and several pieces of equipment, including a tape recorder, a camera, notebooks and film.

Neto expressed concern over the confiscation of his equipment, Angolan sources reported. His documents included the names of the people he had interviewed in the province, and Neto said he feared for their security.

JULY 10

Alexandre Cose, Radio Ecclésia
CENSORED

Officials barred Alexandre Cose, a reporter for the independent station Radio Ecclésia, from covering the government's forced evacuation of some 13,000 families from the Boavista district of Luanda. Cose was denied access to a camp in Viana, a town approximately 30 kilometers (18.6 miles) outside Luanda where Boavista residents have been relocated.

Radio Ecclésia claimed that Cose was singled out because he worked for the independent media, noting that a journalist from the state media was allowed to enter the Viana camp.

JULY 12

Justin Pearce, BBC
HARASSED
Rafael Marques, free-lancer
HARASSED

Authorities in Angola detained journalist and human rights activist Rafael Marques for approximately one hour, according to Angolan sources.

Marques was covering the government's forced relocation of residents from the Boavista district of Luanda to a camp in the town of Viana, approximately 30 kilometers (18.6 miles) outside Luanda. During the previous week, the government had forced some 13,000 Boavista families to relocate.

Marques, along with other journalists, followed a delegation

comprising parliamentarians, members of the residents' association, and the lawyer representing the Boavista residents to the settlement.

At around 5:30 p.m., police officers prevented Marques and BBC correspondent Justin Pearce from photographing and interviewing the residents. The officers then took Marques into custody and drove him to the local police station, where he was interrogated by the station chief and accused of "agitating" in the camp. Although Pearce was not detained, police initially tried to stop him from reporting the incident to the BBC.

Authorities let Marques go after approximately one hour, following a phone call from the local administrator requesting the journalist's release.

Police harassed Marques and Pearce on two other occasions in the previous week while they attempted to cover the Boavista relocation.

According to Pearce, on the morning of July 8, police confiscated Marques' digital camera while he was trying to photograph the evacuation of Boavista from a hilltop above the scene. Though the officer returned the camera, he kept the diskette containing the photographs. When the two journalists descended the hill into the residential area, where they intended to conduct interviews, they were confronted by a man who both journalists believe was a plainclothes police officer. He threatened to harm them physically if they persisted in covering the evacuation.

Though the two journalists were able to interview residents without interference on July 11, authorities prevented them from doing so the following day. According to the Media

Institute of Southern Africa, an officer for the Ministry of Social Reinsertion told the journalists that she had strict orders not to allow any journalist to talk to the residents, take pictures, or even walk around the area without a special permit from the government.

BENIN

JANUARY 18

Joel Gbegan, Golfe FM
ATTACKED
Laurent Akobi, *La Cloche*
ATTACKED

Police assaulted Gbegan, a reporter for Golfe FM, and Akobi, a reporter for the daily *La Cloche*, in the town of Abomey Calavi, some 112 kilometers (70 miles) outside Benin's capital, Cotonou.

The incident occurred as riot police dispersed a student protest. The police claimed they mistook the journalists for student demonstrators.

"They grabbed me by the belt and beat me,"Gbegan told Agence France-Presse. "Then they seized my work equipment and my journalist identification papers and trampled on them."

Gbegan and Akobi were released after police realized they were journalists. However, the Union of Private Press Reporters condemned the assault. The next day, several journalists boycotted a press briefing by Information Minister Gaston Zossou.

SEPTEMBER 28

Patrick Adjamonsi, *L'Aurore*
HARASSED

Titus Folly, *L'Aurore*
HARASSED

Adjamonsi and Folly, respectively the publisher and editor-in-chief of the independent daily *L'Aurore*, were detained by police over a September 27 article by Adjamonsi alleging that Osama bin Laden's terrorist network had connections in Benin.

A secretary who worked at *L'Aurore* was also detained.

Adjamonsi's piece also alleged that U.S. intelligence services were investigating Benin in the wake of the September 11 attacks in New York City and Washington, D.C.

On September 28, the Benin Cabinet held an extraordinary meeting to discuss the controversial article. That same day, according to Agence France-Presse (AFP), the government issued a statement condemning the article and asking the Beninese press to avoid publishing stories that "tarnish the image of the country." The statement also criticized the local press for its allegedly lax journalistic ethics.

Government ministers further called on the High Authority for Audio-Visual Communications (HAAC), the official regulatory body for the media, to take action against the newspaper, the United Nations Integrated Regional Information Network reported.

Also on September 28, *L'Aurore* printed a retraction of the story, saying that Benin was not in any way involved in the terrorist attacks, AFP reported. That same evening, however, police detained Folly and the secretary for questioning. Both were released after a few hours.

On the morning of September 29,

police arrested Adjamonsi at his home and took him to the police station, where he was questioned about the article for four hours and then released.

Later that day, the HAAC issued a statement condemning the paper and its publisher for their allegations. Sources in Cotonou told CPJ that no further disciplinary action was taken against *L'Aurore* and that the paper came out on schedule the following week.

On December 3, the HAAC announced that Adjamonsi's press accreditation would be withdrawn, and that *L'Aurore* would be excluded from receiving any state aid. The Beninese government distributes 300 million CFA francs (US$407,301) every year among the private media.

The local journalists association condemned the HAAC's decision, calling it arbitrary and unconstitutional, and vowed to fight to restore their colleague's rights.

BURUNDI

MARCH 10

Jean-Pierre Aimé Harerimana, Reuters.
`HARASSED`
Jacqueline Segahungu, RCA
`HARASSED`
Léon Masengo, Bonesha FM
`ATTACKED, HARASSED`

Police barred three journalists from attending an opposition press conference held at the airport in the Burundian capital, Bujumbura. One journalist was physically attacked.

The three journalists were Reuters cameraman Harerimana; Segahungu, a reporter for the state broadcaster Radio Centre-Afrique; and Masengo, a

reporter for Bonesha FM, a private station based in Bujumbura.

Police stopped the three reporters some 14 kilometers (about nine miles) from the airport, where Epitace Bayaganakandi, a presidential candidate for the opposition coalition of ethnic Tutsi parties known as G6, had scheduled a press conference marking his return to the country.

Although Masengo, Segahungu, and Harerimana all presented valid press credentials, the police denied them access to the airport and beat up Masengo. Segahungu and Harerimana managed to escape unharmed.

MARCH 12

Gabriel Nikundana, Bonesha FM
`IMPRISONED`
Abbas Mbazumutima, Bonesha FM
`IMPRISONED`

Nikundana, a journalist for the Bujumbura independent radio station Bonesha FM, was arrested at his home by state security agents and taken to their headquarters. He was held for 48 hours and then charged with violating the Burundian Press Law.

On March 15, Abbas Mbazumutima, chief editor at Bonesha FM, was also arrested and taken to state security headquarters. He was charged with violating Article 44 of the press law, which prohibits the dissemination of "information inciting civil disobedience or serving as propaganda for enemies of the Burundian nation during a time of war."

Earlier in March, Bonesha FM aired an interview with the spokesman of the rebel National Liberation Front, Anicet Ntawukiganayo. The interview had been conducted two weeks earlier while the rebels occupied the outskirts of Bujumbura.

Following the protests of several local and international human rights and media groups, Nikundana and Mbazumutima were released on March 16 after paying fines of 100,000 Burundian francs (US$100) each. The charges against them were dropped.

OCTOBER 19

Alexis Sinduhije, Radio Publique Africaine
ATTACKED, HARASSED

Sinduhije, director of the private broadcaster Radio Publique Africaine, was detained for a day and beaten in the offices of the Special Investigations Bureau in the capital, Bujumbura.

Authorities took offense at an interview the journalist had conducted with South African military peacekeepers, whose arrival in war-plagued Burundi that same day was supposed to be kept quiet.

The South Africans reportedly came to ensure the safety of ethnic Hutus who had agreed to return from exile to participate in peace talks with the ethnic Tutsi-led government. As in neighboring Rwanda, Burundian Tutsis and Hutus have been fighting a civil war for decades.

After he was released on payment of a 20,000 Burundian Franc (US$25) fine, Sinduhije told local reporters that police officers had insulted and beaten him during his detention. The officers claimed he had violated official instructions that the South African presence not be publicized without prior government sanction.

Sinduhije later dropped plans to file a complaint against the police, according to local journalists.

CAMEROON

JANUARY 17

Ntemfac Aloysius Nchwete Ofege,
Postwatch
HARASSED
Postwatch
CENSORED

Just as the Franco-African Summit was opening in the capital, Yaoundé, police officers in the southern town of Bamenda raided the newsroom of the English-language publication *Postwatch Magazine* and impounded at least 100 copies of the paper.

Waving a search warrant, the officers told *Postwatch Magazine* staff that they had come to seize "incriminating" evidence against Ofege, the paper's publisher, who was taken in custody.

The raid apparently came in reprisal for an article attacking France's Africa policy.

Ofege was interrogated for more than two hours and then charged with sedition. Police released him but warned that he would be called in for further questioning.

Ofege and his *Postwatch Magazine* actively support the Southern Cameroon National Council, which is agitating for greater autonomy and independence for Cameroon's English-speaking provinces.

JULY 30

Ahman Mana, *Mutations*
IMPRISONED
Mutations
HARASSED

About 20 armed police officers cordoned off the editorial headquarters of the independent thrice-weekly

Mutations, based in Cameroon's capital, Yaoundé. The officers said they were looking for Ahman Mana, the paper's publisher, who they claimed had published copies of presidential decrees that contained "military secrets."

The decrees, signed on July 26 by longtime president Paul Biya, related to the government's planned modernization and rejuvenation of military forces at a time when military morale was said to be very low.

The government daily, *Cameroon Tribune*, also published the decrees but suffered no consequences.

Mana was not in his office at the time of the police raid, which lasted more than five hours and ended only after the intervention of Celestin Lingo, head of Cameroon's Union of Journalists.

When Mana responded to a police summons the next day, officials took him into custody and held him incommunicado until August 3. He was released without charge.

During his time in detention, officials pressured Mana to identify the source who gave him the decrees. Mana later told reporters that he had refused to divulge his sources, citing provisions in Cameroon's press law that guarantee source confidentiality.

AUGUST 20

Remy Ngono, Radio Television Siantou
ATTACKED

Ngono, head of the popular private broadcaster Radio Television Siantou (RTS), was arrested by police officers on his way home from a party in Cameroon's capital, Yaoundé. The journalist, who also hosts the popular satirical talk show "Coup Franc" on RTS, was taken to Yaoundé's central police station, where officers beat him repeatedly before releasing him early the next day.

Local journalists say Ngono was attacked because he frequently criticized the Cameroonian police, accusing them of corruption and links to organized crime. No formal charges were filed against the journalist.

AUGUST 22

Georges Baongla, *Le Dementi*
IMPRISONED

Baongla, a journalist with the independent weekly *Le Dementi* in the capital, Yaoundé, was arrested by police for "publishing false news" after he reported that Minister of the Economy and Finances Michel Meva'a M'Eboutou was implicated in an embezzlement scheme.

Police demanded that the journalist reveal his sources, despite the country's press law, which protects journalists from such coercion.

Following protests by local and regional human rights groups, authorities switched the charges against Baongla to "breach of trust." They then claimed the journalist was being detained for failing to repay US$695 that a nephew of Minister M'Eboutou had allegedly loaned him a few months before.

Baongla denied ever receiving the loan. He was released on August 25.

OCTOBER 1

Jean Marc Soboth, *La Nouvelle Expression*
HARASSED

Police summoned Soboth, editor of

the private thrice-weekly paper *La Nouvelle Expression*, and pressured him to name the sources for a September 24 article.

Soboth's piece chastised government efforts to curtail freedom of movement in Cameroon's English-speaking provinces ahead of the 40th anniversary of the country's reunification, a political achievement still challenged by militant groups in those provinces.

Soboth reportedly cited excerpts from confidential correspondence between the office of Deputy Defense Minister Rémy Ze Meka and police forces in the English-speaking provinces instructing officers to use force to break up anti-government demonstrations, and to monitor individuals perceived to be "subversive agitators."

Authorities accused Soboth and *La Nouvelle Expression* of revealing a "defense secret" by publishing the correspondence and have insisted that the editor reveal his sources or face legal action. But Soboth declined to do so, arguing that 1990 media legislation allows journalists to protect their sources.

Soboth was released that same day without charge.

DECEMBER 8

Djenga Mondo, Magic FM
ATTACKED
Magic FM reporter Mondo was beaten by members of President Paul Biya's security service after he approached the head of state for an impromptu interview at a meeting of Central African heads of state in Cameroon's capital, Youndé.

The security agents threatened to arrest Mondo, but he was released after the intervention of Edgar Alain Mebe Ngo'o, a top presidential aide.

CENTRAL AFRICAN REPUBLIC

FEBRUARY 14

Aboukary Tembeley, *Journal des Droits de l'Homme*
IMPRISONED
Tembeley, who writes for the occasional Bangui-based publication *Journal des Droits de L'Homme,* was severely beaten at national police headquarters, where he had gone to answer a summons received a day earlier.

The attack came during an hour-long interrogation about a survey he had published in early February stating that 173 of 200 respondents favored the resignation of President Ange-Felix Patasse.

Tembeley lapsed into a coma after being savagely beaten during the course of the interrogation, Amnesty International reported. He was then taken to a cell at the headquarters of the Gendarmerie Nationale, also known as Camp PK12, where he was again beaten and then denied medical care. Tembeley was held for three weeks.

The journalist, who suffers from a chronic heart condition, appeared in court on February 19. He was charged with inciting hatred and violence against a democratically elected institution, as well as with actions that compromise public security and lead to serious political troubles.

Sources present at the hearing said court officials declined to take

Tembeley to a state-run hospital and asked him to cover his own medical expenses. He was then sent back to his prison cell.

A fiery critic of the government, Tembeley is also president of the Human Rights Defence Movement (MDDH). His detention contravenes Article 15 of the CAR's Law No. 98.006 on freedom of communication, which stipulates that journalists have the right to freely investigate all facts which are in the public interest and to bring forward for discussion all actions and declarations of all public and private institutions.

Le Journal des Droits de l'Homme was launched in 1997 and runs general news and reports about MDDH's human rights monitoring activities.

Tembeley was tried and convicted on March 5. He was sentenced to two months in jail without parole and fined US$215 for publishing a newspaper without a license. On March 6, President Ange-Felix Patasse pardoned Tembeley and ordered his release.

CHAD

APRIL 17

All community radio stations
CENSORED

Chad's High Council on Communications (HCC) barred all private radio stations from airing "political debates" or "programs of a political nature" in the weeks before the May 20 presidential elections.

The state-operated HCC threatened to suspend stations that did not comply with its instructions. To CPJ's knowledge, HCC officials had not

previously interfered with broadcast programming in Chad.

Except for the national radio network, all of Chad's radio broadcasters are so-called community stations, meaning they broadcast within a 300-kilometer (180-mile) range.

COMOROS

AUGUST 2

Allaoui Said Omar, *La Gazette des Comores*
HARASSED, LEGAL ACTION
Omar Badaoui, *La Gazette des Comores*
HARASSED, LEGAL ACTION

Omar, publisher of the private weekly *La Gazette des Comores*, and his reporter Badaoui were summoned to the central police station in Moroni, the capital of Comoros, for questioning.

Police summoned the two journalists after Badaoui reported that high-level members of the military government of Colonel Azali Assoumani had been implicated by a police inquiry into a ring of currency counterfeiters.

According to CPJ sources, two high-ranking officials on the president's staff were later fired after police provided strong evidence linking them to the counterfeiting scheme.

Omar and Badaoui were detained for more than five hours while police pressured them to reveal their sources, which both journalists refused to do. The police recorded their statements and promised to contact them at a future date.

In late October, the two journalists were convicted of defamation and sentenced to suspended six-month jail terms.

NOVEMBER 13

Izdine Abdou Salam, Radio Karthala
`IMPRISONED`

Salam, director of programming and a host for the private Radio Karthala, was detained and interrogated by police officers in the capital, Moroni. A journalist contacted by CPJ said the arrest came after participants in a call-in show hosted by Salam made statements that authorities claim defamed ruling officials.

The show, aired during the week of November 5, focused on a constitutional referendum planned for late December. Many callers harshly attacked provisions included in the proposed referendum text.

The charges against Salam are not known, but he remained in prison as of December 31, more than a month after his arrest. Police also seized tapes of the offending broadcast.

CONGO

JANUARY 13

Richard Ntsana, Le Flambeau
`IMPRISONED`
Le Flambeau
`CENSORED`

Ntsana, publisher of the Brazzaville weekly *Le Flambeau*, a pro-opposition publication, was jailed for more than two weeks over an article that appeared in his newspaper on January 8.

The article in question quoted an open letter by former president Pascal Lissouba that called on the population to mobilize to defeat the dictator, a reference to Lissouba's successor, Denis Sassou-Nguesso. Police claimed that the

article had created confusion about the state institutions.

On the evening of the arrest, authorities also suspended *Le Flambeau* as a protective measure in order "to guarantee public order, social peace and the respect of [state] institutions."

Lissouba and his entire government were forced into exile in 1997 after Sassou-Nguesso staged the country's eighth coup in three decades, declared himself head of state, and proceeded to crush his political opponents. Sassou-Nguesso had previously ruled the country for 13 years before losing Congo's first multiparty elections in 1992.

Ntsana was released in early February, and his newspaper resumed publication in late February.

CÔTE D'IVOIRE (IVORY COAST)

JANUARY 17

Muhamed Junior Ouattara, Agence France-Presse
`IMPRISONED`

Agence France-Presse (AFP) reporter Ouattara was arrested by four plainclothes police officers at the entrance of AFP's office building in dowtown Abidjan, the capital of Côte d'Ivoire.

Police suspected Ouattara of involvement in a failed January 8 coup attempt that resulted in the deaths of several people, including two pro-government soldiers and a dozen rebels.

The officers roughed up several AFP journalists before handcuffing Ouattara and shoving him into an unmarked car. The award-winning reporter was then driven to the Abidjan offices of the police counter-espionage unit (DST) where he was interrogated about phone calls he received from a rebel leader on the night of the coup.

On 18 January, Ouattara's lawyer was prevented from entering the DST building, in violation of Côte d'Ivoire's criminal procedure code. AFP sources in Abidjan said the rebels had called the agency to air their grievances and later called Ouattara at his home to provide further insight into their motivation, which they expected the journalist to publish in an article.

Ouattara was released without charges on January 22. CPJ protested Ouattara's detention in a February 15 letter to President Laurent Gbagbo.

FEBRUARY 10

Le Jour
`ATTACKED`

As many as 30 armed men and three uniformed police officers broke into the printing press that produces the independent Abidjan daily *Le Jour*. As a police helicopter hovered over the factory, the intruders forced a security guard to lie prone while they searched the premises.

The intruders claimed to be law-enforcement officers acting on an anonymous tip, but they did not have a search warrant, Agence France-Presse reported.

After their 30-minute search failed to produce anything suspicious, the intruders accused *Le Jour* administrative director Biamari Coulibaly, who was not present at the time, of recruiting mercenaries and purchasing arms in preparation for a coup.

According to the paper's editor, Abdoulaye Sangare, the men threatened to kill Coulibaly when they found him. They also claimed that pictures of Coulibaly had been circulated to police stations across the country.

CPJ protested the raid in a February 15 letter to President Laurent Gbagbo.

MAY 8

Meite Sindou, *Le Patriote*
`LEGAL ACTION`
Patrice Lénonhin, *Le Patriote*
`LEGAL ACTION`

Sindou and Lénonhin, editor and publisher, respectively, of the privately owned opposition daily *Le Patriote*, were convicted of criminal defamation and sentenced in absentia to a suspended three-month jail term and a US$150 fine each.

The sentences followed a complaint filed by Martin Bléou, head of Côte D'Ivoire's leading human rights group, LIDHO, over a June 2000 report that Bléou had US$155,000 stashed in a Swiss bank account. *Le Patriote* alleged that the money was a payoff from the government of Henri Konan Bedie, who was overthrown in a military coup in December 1999.

Because the journalists were not present at the hearing, they heard of the decision through local papers, which are required by law to publicize any court ruling against the media.

APRIL 12

Solidarité Paalga
`CENSORED`

The National Press Council (CNP) suspended the publication of *Solidarité*

Paalga, a bimonthly that caters to immigrants from Burkina Faso. The CNP said the bimonthly violated Ivoirian press laws because its publisher was not Ivoirian, had ignored so-called legal deposit requirements, and employed unaccredited journalists.

The publisher, Nicolas Sahouidi, claimed that he identified himself as a citizen of Burkina Faso when he applied for a license to publish, and that the license was granted.

He also said that the paper had complied with the legal deposit requirements, which compel print publications to deposit three archival copies of each issue with the CNP.

Sahouidi admitted that no one on his staff was an accredited journalist. But he argued that under the local press law, an adaptation of France's 1881 Press Code, a journalist is defined as any person who collects and distributes information and who draws their main source of income from this occupation.

The CNP lifted the suspension order on May 3, after its members met with Sahouidi.

DEMOCRATIC REPUBLIC OF CONGO

FEBRUARY 15

Jean-Luc Kinyongo Saleh, *Vision*
IMPRISONED

Police officers arrested Saleh, editor and publisher of the biweekly newspaper *Vision*, at the paper's offices. He was held for three days at Kinshasa's main pretrial detention center before being moved to an undisclosed location.

Local sources linked Saleh's arrest to the publication of "Denis Kalume Numbi, Virtual Prime Minister," an opinion piece for the February 8 edition of *Vision* in which Saleh accused Interior Minister Gatan Kakudji of supporting his ostentatious lifestyle with public funds.

The journalist managed to escape from prison in late February and has been in hiding ever since.

On March 16, he was tried in absentia and sentenced to immediate arrest and four months' imprisonment, reportedly for defamation. The Congolese High Court also ordered him to pay US$2,500 in damages to Kakudji.

Jean Kabongo, a lawyer for *Vision*, called the sentencing of Saleh a political affair and charged that neither Saleh nor the newspaper were informed of any hearings before the sentence was issued, according to local sources.

FEBRUARY 13

Clovis Kaddah, *L'Alarme*
ATTACKED

Four plainclothes police officers invaded the home of Kaddah, editor of the semiweekly Kinshasa publication *L'Alarme*. Kaddah had been tipped off about the raid and hid until the officers left.

The armed men remained on the premises for more than 12 hours, harassing and robbing Kaddah's relatives and visitors.

The journalist, whose paper had recently been accused of publishing without a license, was said to have been singled out because of a February 12 *L'Alarme* interview with Honor Ngbanda, former special security counselor to the late Congolese president Mobutu Sese Seko.

In the interview, Ngbanda raised questions about the official biography of President Joseph Kabila, who replaced his father, Laurent-Désiré Kabila, after the latter was murdered in mid-January.

The interview originally appeared in the Paris-based magazine *Jeune Afrique Economie*.

FEBRUARY 28

Guy Kasongo Kilembwe, *Pot-Pourri*
IMPRISONED

Kilembwe, editor of the satirical weekly *Pot-Pourri*, was arrested for allegedly insulting President Joseph Kabila. No charges were filed.

Police claimed that the February 23 edition of *Pot-Pourri* contained an unflattering, insulting caricature of Kabila. During Kilembwe's interrogation, the police claimed that *Pot-Pourri* had demonstrated hatred of a number of state officials, including the president.

Kilembwe was released without charge on March 22, after signing a statement in which he promised "never again [to] write articles that are hostile to" the regime in power in Kinshasa. He was also ordered to submit a written apology to the government.

MARCH 30

Washington Lutumba, *Le Potentiel*
IMPRISONED
Jules-César Mayimbi, *Forum*
IMPRISONED

Congolese National Police officers detained Lutumba, a correspondent for the Kinshasa daily *Le Potentiel*, over a March 15 article in which he reported that some 45 tons of tainted wheat flour unfit for human consumption were being sold in the towns of Boma, Moanda, and Banana, in the Lower Congo Province.

On April 5, police arrested Mayimbi, Matadi correspondent for the private Kinshasa daily *Forum*, after he filed a report that quoted eyewitness accounts to confirm Lutumba's allegations.

The two journalists were taken into custody following a complaint by Boulangerie Joseph, a chain of bakeries headquartered in the neighboring Republic of the Congo, claiming that the articles had negatively affected its business and reputation. Both Lutumba and Mayimba had suggested that Boulangerie Joseph was responsible for delivering the tainted wheat to local markets, and that it should therefore be held accountable.

Lutumba and Mayimba were held on criminal defamation charges at the central prison in Matadi, capital of the Lower Congo Province. They were both released on May 18 pending further investigations.

On May 28, the Matadi court convicted them as charged and sentenced them each to a 45-day jail term and a US$70 fine. However, they were given credit for time served in pretrial detention and then released.

APRIL 23

Kasongo Mukishi, *L'Avenir*
ATTACKED

Mukishi, who writes on human rights issues for the daily *L'Avenir*, was manhandled by Dido Kitungwa, director of the notorious Kokolo Penitentiary and Reeducation Center, in the capital, Kinshasa.

At the time of the incident, Mukishi was attending a legal clinic for prison inmates given by the Congolese Bar Association's human rights committee.

Kitungwa assaulted Mukishi while the journalist was interviewing inmates about the abuses they had endured in prison. The enraged official then ordered prison guards to hold the journalist hostage until he agreed to hand over his notebook.

Several visiting lawyers intervened with Kitungwa, who eventually released Mukishi after cautioning the journalist against negative reporting.

APRIL 29

RAGA TV
CENSORED

Officials from President Joseph Kabila's office confiscated the videotape of an interview that the private television station RAGA TV had conducted with an opposition leader.

On April 24, RAGA TV interviewed Etienne Tshisekedi wa Mulumba, president of the opposition Union for Democracy and Social Progress.
The interview was scheduled to air on April 29.

According to the Kinshasa-based press freedom organization Journaliste en Danger (JED), Tshisekedi said during the interview that he did not recognize Joseph Kabila as the legitimate president of the Democratic Republic of Congo.

Sources in Kinshasa told CPJ that Congolese National Police agents prevented journalists from covering the exiled Tshisekedi's April 23 arrival at

Kinshasa/N'Dhili International Airport. Some 20 journalists were locked in a hangar until Tshisekedi's procession had left the airport.

JED reported that the confiscated interview tape was being held by a high-level official in the president's office and that it had been shown to Minister of Communication Kikaya bin Karubi. By year's end, the tape had still not been returned and the program had not been broadcast.

MAY 10

La Libre Afrique
CENSORED

La Libre Afrique, a controversial Kinshasa-based weekly, was banned by Information Minister Kikaya Bin Karubi. Its two supplements, *Le Derby* and the satirical leaflet *Incognito*, were also banned.

Citing a provision in the June 1996 Press Law, Minister Bin Karubi claimed that publisher Freddy Loseke Lisumbu La Yayenga had acquired his publication license fraudulently, and that his papers did not mention their printer's address, a legal requirement.

The minister also questioned Loseke's journalistic ethics.

Local sources concurred that the ban resulted from an editorial in *La Libre Afrique* criticizing the Zimbabwean army, an ally of the Congolese government in its war against rebels backed by Rwanda, Uganda, and Burundi.

The editorial accused Zimbabwean troops of spreading AIDS and failing to recapture any Congo territory currently controlled by rebels or foreign forces opposed to the regime of Congolese president Joseph Kabila. The paper also complained that, at US$20 a day, Zimbabwean troops were far better paid than Congolese soldiers.

The United Nations Integrated Regional Information Network quoted a Zimbabwean military spokesperson as saying that he had "heard about the story" and had "handed the matter to the Ministry of Information." Minister Bin Karubi, a former ambassador to Zimbabwe, denied that he had acted under pressure from higher authorities, according to the local press freedom advocacy group Journaliste en Danger.

Congolese journalists contacted by CPJ pointed out that the minister's decision contravened the Congolese Press Law, which states that only the High Court can ban publications, while the Ministry of Information can only ban specific issues of publications.

Loseke continued publishing *La Libre Afrique* in defiance of the ban. No official reaction had been reported by year's end.

MAY 30

Freddy Loseke, *La Libre Afrique*
IMPRISONED

Loseke, publisher of *La Libre Afrique*, was convicted of defaming Belgian businessman Vincent Jullet, manager of the private aviation company WaltAir, and Sony Kafuta, a pastor of the Christian congregation Arme de L'Eternel (God's Army).

In April, *La Libre Afrique* reported that Jullet had used unfair means to smother his competition in the local aviation industry. In a May 15 story, the paper reported that Kafuta owed

US$400 to a local mechanic for repair work done on his car, and US$1,000 more in unspecified debts.

The article also charged that after the mechanic asked Kafuta to pay for the car repairs, the clergyman claimed to be a relative of a prominent government official and threatened the mechanic with legal action.

On September 17, a Kinsasha court found Loseke guilty of defaming Jullet and sentenced him to serve 12 months in prison without parole. The court also convicted Loseke of defaming Kafuta and sentenced him to a prison term of five months, of which three months were suspended.

Loseke's legal team appealed the ruling, but he was unconditionally released on November 6, before the appeal could be heard. The release was apparently ordered by Justice Minister Ngele Masudi, according to the DRC-based Journaliste En Danger.

JUNE 14

Joachim Diana Gikupa, *L'Avenir*
IMPRISONED

Agents from the National Information Agency (ANR), a state investigative unit, arrested Gikupa, publication director for the Kinshasa daily *L'Avenir*. According to Gikupa's colleagues, ANR agents called the paper's office to invite him to a "press consultation." The journalist left his office soon after to meet the agents at their downtown Kinshasa headquarters.

On Friday, June 15, the ANR confirmed that it was detaining Gikupa. The agency said the detention resulted from Gikupa's June 8 article about attempts by some of President Joseph

Kabila's advisers to prevent a prominent member of the late president Mobutu Sese Seko's regime from holding a press conference.

L'Avenir also a published a copy of a signed note by Professor Théophile Bemba Fundu, President Joseph Kabila's cabinet director, to support journalist Gikupa's allegations.

The letter was handwritten on Office of the President letterhead and was addressed to "Mister Administrator." Fundu asked the addressee to "take all possible measures" to ensure that the press conference did not take place "as it risks causing a further drop in the head of state's political standing." (ANR agents claimed the letter was a forgery.)

Gukupa was released without charge on June 22.

JULY 26

Pierre Kapepa, *Le Moniteur*
IMPRISONED
Rigobert Kwakala Kashama, *Le Moniteur*
IMPRISONED
Marcel Guy Mujanayi, *Le Moniteur*
IMPRISONED
Kinshasa police arrested Mujanayi, a reporter for the private twice-weekly newspaper *Le Moniteur*, and Kashama and Kapeka, the paper's publisher and associate publisher, respectively.

The arrests came after *Le Moniteur* published a number of articles criticizing the Congolese Air Authority (RVA) and its director.

No charges were filed against Mujanayi, who wrote the stories. He was released on July 30.

According to the police, the 1996

Congolese Press Law mandates that newspaper owners are responsible for offenses committed by journalists they employ. No formal charges were filed, but sources in Kinshasa say police accused Kashama and Kapeka of inciting Mujanayi to defame the RVA and its director.

The publishers were unconditionally released on the afternoon of August 2.

AUGUST 6

François Mada Mbulungu, *La Manchette*
IMPRISONED
Mbulungu, publisher of the Kinshasa twice-weekly newspaper *La Manchette*, was held for two days in an underground cell at the Office of the Public Prosecutor in Gombe, an upscale district of the Congolese capital, Kinshasa.

The journalist had responded to a summons in connection with two stories he wrote in a July edition of *La Manchette*.

According to the local press freedom group Journaliste En Danger, authorities accused Mbulungu of making "libellous accusations" against Ashur Satar, president of the Lebanese community in the DRC, for writing that DRC-based Lebanese were sabotaging the local economy.

Mbulungu was also accused of defaming M. Kamanda, the financial administrator of the government's Office of Maritime Freight, over an article in which he alleged financial impropriety at the office.

Mbulungu was never formally charged and was unconditionally released on August 8.

OCTOBER 9

Kainda Kalenga, *La Fregate*
LEGAL ACTION

Kalenga, publisher of the weekly *La Fregate*, was picked up by police at his residence in Lubumbashi, the capital of Congo's Katanga Province. The officers said they were acting on orders from the Lubumbashi High Court Prosecutor's Office.

Kalenga is charged with defaming Belgian businessman Malta Forrest, owner of the Forrest Group, who claims that an October 3 article in *La Fregate* ruined his reputation by accusing his son of being a racist.

The report also railed against the local court's failure to probe alleged criminal activity by the Forrests, including widespread charges that Congolese employees of the Forrest Group were being paid less than their Belgian or white colleagues for equal work.

No trial date has been set, and Kalenga was released three days later.

OCTOBER 10

Crispin Kalala Mpotoyi, Debout Kasai
IMPRISONED
Debout Kasai
CENSORED

Mpotoyi, director of the private television station Debout Kasai, was arrested at his office and charged with defamation.

The journalist was released three days later after posting a US$500 bail.

Officials accused Mpotoyi of defaming political and military authorities in the Kasai region, as well as managers of the diamond mining firms MIBA and Sengamines.

The accusation stemmed from comments that Mpotoyi made on his Tshiluba-language weekly television program, "Diamant Dia Kasai" (Diamonds of Kasai).

The program, which was banned soon after Mpotoyi's October 13 release, was popular among Kasai residents for its unabashed criticisms of what they view as systematic looting of the region's mineral resources. Mpotoyi had reportedly complained that revenues from diamond sales did not benefit the people of Kasai, most of whom live in squalid conditions without drinking water or electricity.

OCTOBER 31

Kisanga Yenge, *Les Coulisses*
IMPRISONED

Rebels from the Congolese Rally for Democracy arrested Yenge, a reporter for the private weekly *Les Coulisses*, in the northern town of Kisangani. He was held in the town's Department of Security and Intelligence building in connection with an article in which he denounced a local vice governor for allegedly misappropriating textiles.

Yenge's friends and relatives were not allowed to visit him in detention. The journalist was released on November 3.

NOVEMBER 8

Gilbert Kasanda Kabala, Agence Congolaise de Presse
IMPRISONED

Police in Kananga, the capital of Congo's Western Kasai Province, arrested Kabala, the local correspondent for the official news service Agence

Congolaise de Presse, at his office and drove him to the regional police headquarters.

Kabala's employer later confirmed the journalist's arrest, saying Kabala was accused of defaming the Kananga police force in a report about seven police officers who allegedly raped a local woman.

Kabala was released on November 10.

DECEMBER 31

Guy Kasongo Kilembwe, *Pot-Pourri*
IMPRISONED

Kilembwe, editor-in-chief of the Kinshasa-based satirical newspaper *Pot-Pourri*, was arrested by Special Services agents and taken to the State Security Court in Kinshasa. He was charged with "threatening state security" and "insulting the person of the head of state" and was detained for 48 hours. Vicky Bolingola, the newsroom secretary, was also arrested and detained on the same charges.

The State Security Court's prosecutor released both on January 3, 2002. No official reason was given for their sudden release.

DJIBOUTI

JANUARY 15

Daher Ahmed Farah, *Le Renouveau*
IMPRISONED
Le Renouveau
CENSORED

Police detained Farah, editor of the opposition weekly *Le Renouveau*, at his home in Djibouti. He was taken to the Public Prosecutor's Office, charged with

defamation and distributing false news, and then released.

The arrest came after Djibouti police commissioner Daher Ismal Kahin filed a complaint over a January 11 *Le Renouveau* article that criticized him for ordering the destruction of the capital's largest market. (Kahin claimed that the market had become a refuge for thieves and other criminals.)

Le Renouveau supports the opposition Democratic Renewal Party, of which Farah is also the leader. The paper was suspended while police investigated the commissioner's complaint.

ERITREA

JULY 25

Mattewos Habteab, *MeQaleh*
IMPRISONED

Habteab, editor-in-chief of the private Tigrigna-language newspaper *MeQaleh*, was kidnapped by security forces in the capital, Asmara. Eritrean journalists contacted by CPJ said Habteab had received a conscription notice from the Defense Ministry days prior to his disappearance.

Noting that soccer players, artists, singers, and musicians are exempt from military service, *MeQaleh* published a July 26 editorial calling on the Eritrean government not to conscript independent journalists.

Echoing *MeQaleh*, CPJ sources in Asmara believe that consription is being used to punish independent journalists who criticize the regime of President Isaias Afeworki.

Habteab was released on September 3. CPJ published an alert about the case on August 6.

All private newspapers
CENSORED

Eritrean authorities suspended all the country's privately owned newspapers until further notice, the state radio station announced.

Newspapers affected by the suspension order included *Meqaleh*, *Setit*, *Tiganay*, *Zemen*, *Wintana*, *Admas*, *Keste Debena*, and *Mana*.

It is unclear what prompted the decision, but sources in Asmara saw the move as an attempt by President Isaias Afeworki's government to suppress independent news coverage of an ongoing state crackdown on opponents of the People's Front for Democracy and Justice, the party that has ruled Eritrea since independence from Ethiopia in 1991.

According to Eritrea's ambassador to the United States, however, the papers were suspended for failing to comply with media licensing requirements under the country's press laws. Embassy officials said authorities had warned the publishers several times before the suspension order. Ambassador Girma Asmeron said the papers would remain suspended while authorities investigate their current licenses. "This procedure will be transparent and in accordance with the laws of the country," he said.

Yet Ali Abdu, the head of the state television network, told the BBC that the newspapers had been suspended "in the interest of national unity after being given ample time to correct their mistakes." The so-called mistakes amount to publishing critical letters about the government's crackdown on political dissent, the BBC reported.

The government-owned daily newspaper, *Hadas Eritrea*, is now the only publication allowed in the country.

CPJ published an alert about the suspension order on September 20.

Medhanie Haile, Keste Debena
IMPRISONED
Yusuf Mohamed Ali, *Tsigenay*
IMPRISONED
Mattewos Habteab, *Meqaleh,*
IMPRISONED
Temesken Ghebreyesus, Keste Debena
IMPRISONED
Amanuel Asrat, *Zemen,*
IMPRISONED
Fesshaye Yohannes, *Setit*
IMPRISONED
Said Abdelkader, *Admas*
IMPRISONED
Selamyinghes Beyene, *Meqaleh,*
IMPRISONED
Dawit Habtemichael, *Meqaleh,*
IMPRISONED
Seyoum Fsehaye, free-lance
IMPRISONED

Beginning September 18, 2001, Eritrean security forces arrested at least 10 local journalists. Two others fled the country. The arrests came less than a week after authorities abruptly closed all privately owned newspapers, allegedly to safeguard national unity in the face of growing political turmoil in the tiny Horn of Africa nation.

International news reports quoted presidential adviser Yemane Gebremeskel as saying that the journalists could have been arrested for avoiding military service. Sources in Asmara, however, say that at least two of the detained journalists, free-lance photographer Fsehaye and Mohamed, editor of *Tsigenay*, were legally exempt from national service. Fsehaye is reportedly exempt since he is an independence war veteran; while Mohamed is apparently well over the maximum age for military service.

All these journalists remained in government custody as of December 31.

CPJ sources in Asmara maintain that the suspension and subsequent arrests of independent journalists were part of a full-scale government effort to suppress political dissent in advance of December elections, which the government canceled without explanation.

ETHIOPIA

Tilahun Bekele, *Fetash*
IMPRISONED

Police arrested Bekele, editor of the defunct Amharic-language weekly *Fetash*, for failing to post bail in a criminal defamation case stemming from an article of his that had appeared more than five years earlier in another Amharic-language weekly, *Maebel*.

On January 31, the Fifth Criminal Bench of the High Court in the capital, Addis Ababa, ordered Bekele to post bail of US$625 or face detention until his trial, which was then scheduled for April 9. Unable to settle the bail requirement, Bekele was arrested and jailed at the Kerchele Penitentiary in the capital, Addis Ababa.

Bekele was released from prison on April 9, after a second judge voided the bail requirement.

The journalist had been accused of fabricating "a report that stands against...the basic position of the Ethiopian Orthodox Church and thus defames the whole establishment,"

according to court documents obtained by CPJ's local sources.

The 1,000-year-old Orthodox Church, the most powerful religious organization in Ethiopia, has close links to top leaders in the ruling Ethiopian Peoples' Revolutionary Democratic Front.

In addition to the criminal defamation charge, Bekele faced separate charges under Ethiopia's restrictive Press Proclamation of 1992 after he alleged in a 1998 *Fetash* article that the U.S. Central Intelligence Agency had financed an Ethiopian mineral water company that sold contaminated water.

Bekele was arrested on this charge in September 1998. He remained in prison until the Ethiopian Free Press Journalists Association secured his bail in October 2000, with the help of CPJ and other international press freedom organizations. The case was ultimately dismissed.

Befekadu Moreda, *Tomar*
IMPRISONED

Police arrested Moreda, editor of the Amharic-language weekly *Tomar*, in his office and took him to the Addis Ababa Police Station, where he was detained for four days before being removed to the remote district of Benishangul. He was held there for 10 days and then freed on bail.

The arrest apparently came in response to a January 31 article in *Tomar* that reported on the secessionist demands of the Berta people in Benishangul District. CPJ sources in Addis Ababa said the editor was charged with violating the Press Proclamation by publishing an article that could incite people to violence. The same sources also reported that the Benishangul governor phoned Moreda after the article appeared and asked him to reveal his sources, and that the journalist refused.

To protest his detention, Moreda began a hunger strike on February 16. On the morning of February 17, security officers moved the journalist to Benishangul, about 800 kilometers (480 miles) from Addis Ababa, making it virtually impossible for his family, friends, and lawyer to visit him in jail.

Moreda appeared before a district court in Benishangul on February 22, when he was again asked to reveal his sources. The journalist refused, citing a provision in the 1992 Ethiopian Press Proclamation that guarantees confidentiality of sources and emphasizing that freedom of the press is protected by the Ethiopian Constitution.

CPJ protested the editor's imprisonment in a February 26 letter to Prime Minister Meles Zenawi.

On February 27, Moreda was released on bail by the police commissioner of Benishangul. Although the charges were still pending at press time, authorities did not pursue the case.

MARCH 16

Likune Engida, *Dagmawi Wenchife*
LEGAL ACTION

Engida, publisher and editor of the private Amharic weekly *Dagmawi Wenchife*, was charged with disseminating false information and criminally defaming the Commercial Bank of Ethiopia. He was released the same day after posting bail of 1,000 birr

(US$120). A second hearing was scheduled for May 8.

The charges stemmed from a January 3 *Dagmawi Wenchife* report that the bank had lost as much as one billion birr (US$120 million) because of computer problems related to the date change over the new year.

Because of increases in printing costs, *Dagmawi Wenchife* was forced to stop production shortly after Engida's arrest. The paper started appearing again in early March.

At the end of the year, the case had not progressed in court.

APRIL 21

Seifu Mekonnen, *Mebrek*
IMPRISONED

Police secretly detained Mekonnen, a reporter for *Mebrek*, an Amharic-language weekly based in Addis Ababa, and held him for five days without filing charges.

The police questioned Mekonnen about his alleged involvement in a recent spate of anti-government rioting, as well as his ties to a local human rights group, according to the journalist.

Mekonnen disappeared shortly after the Ethiopian Human Rights Council held a press conference to dispute government charges that the council, along with opposition parties and the independent press, had incited students and others in Addis Ababa to riot against the presence of police on local campuses. When Mekonnen's name did not appear on an official list of detainees, his relatives alerted the local press.

Police also arrested some 60 newspaper vendors on April 20, effectively halting the circulation of most local private papers. The majority of the vendors were released on April 22 after signing statements in which they agreed to cease working for an indefinite period, the Ethiopian Free Press Journalists' Association reported.

At least 38 people were killed during two days of street confrontations between protesters and police forces. Several thousand people were held for questioning afterward.

Mekonnen reappeared five days after he was reported missing. He said that he had been in police custody the entire time.

On April 23, CPJ circulated an alert about the case.

APRIL 27

Nita Bhalla, BBC
HARASSED
Zelalem Gemechu, Voice of America
HARASSED

Bhalla, a correspondent for the BBC, and Gemechu, a stringer for the Voice of America, were harassed by police while covering riots in Addis Ababa.

Bhalla was attacked while photographing police antiriot officers beating women and children. One of the officers rushed toward her and snatched her camera, which he damaged beyond repair. She was briefly manhandled and warned against portraying Ethiopia "in this way," the BBC said. Her translator was also roughed up but suffered no serious injuries.

That same day, Gemechu told CPJ, he was tailed by police officers after they saw him recording audiotape of the riot. The next day, an unnamed police officer confiscated Gemechu's recording gear while he was taping the

forcible evacuation of the university by security forces.

The two-day wave of riots, sparked by student opposition to police presence on local campuses, reportedly caused the deaths of at least 38 people. It also disrupted the circulation of local newspapers, whose roadside vendors were among the more than 2,000 people rounded up for questioning.

MAY 2

Daniel Gezzahegne, *Moged*
IMPRISONED

Gezzahegne, deputy editor of the Amharic weekly *Moged*, was arrested after answering a summons to appear in court on defamation charges stemming from an article published nearly three years ago in the now-defunct Amharic weekly *Gemenna*, which he edited at the time. The article alleged widespread corruption among officials of the Ethiopian Orthodox Church in the northern province of Gonder.

Police charged that Gezzahegne had ignored several previous summonses, but the journalist claimed to have received only one, on May 1.

At a hearing on May 4, the court set bail at 5,000 birr (US$600). Unable to raise the money, Gezzahegne was remanded to Kerchele Prison in Addis Ababa pending the resumption of hearings in October. He posted bail and was released on May 25.

The charges were still pending at year's end.

MAY 25

Tamirate Zuma, *Atkurot*
IMPRISONED

Zuma, former publisher and editor-in-chief of the defunct Amharic-language weekly *Atkurot*, was arrested and imprisoned on charges of failing to pay a publishing license fee, inciting violence or rebellion, and defamation. All three are crimes under the Ethiopian Press Proclamation.

The first charge stemmed from a licensing requirement. Strapped for cash, Zuma was unable to pay the fee to renew his annual publishing license. In the second case, Zuma is accused of inciting people to violence or rebellion, a charge resulting from a recent *Atkurot* article that quoted an interview from the U.S.-based magazine *Ethiopian Review*. In it, a former official in dictator Mengistu Haile Mariam's Derg regime, Gen. Haile Meles, predicted the imminent overthrow of the current Ethiopian People's Revolutionary Democratic Front government.

The third case is a defamation charge resulting from an *Atkurot* article that reported on financial mismanagement at a government-owned leather factory. As of December 31, Zuma remained in jail. In October, a CPJ delegation visited the journalist during a fact-finding mission to Ethiopia.

JUNE 1

Tsegaie Ayalew, *Genanaw*
IMPRISONED

Ayalew, editor of the Amharic weekly *Genanaw*, was arrested and imprisoned on a charge of defamation. The charge resulted from a two-year-old *Genanaw* article about a corruption scandal at the Ethiopian Electric Power Corporation.

Ayalew remained in jail until early July, when he managed to post bail of 500 birr (US$60). His case was still pending at year's end.

JUNE 26

Yoftahe Tsegaye, *Kicker*
IMPRISONED

Tsegaye, editor-in-chief of the weekly sports newspaper *Kicker*, was sentenced to one month in prison after being charged with publishing and distributing a newspaper without renewing his press license.

Ethiopian sources said that Tsegaye could not afford to pay the license renewal fee. He was released at the end of July.

JULY 11

Lubaba Said, *Tarik*
IMPRISONED, LEGAL ACTION

Said, editor-in-chief of the independent Amharic weekly *Tarik*, was jailed at Addis Ababa Prison because she was unable to post bail of 1,000 birr (US$130). She faced criminal charges over two articles that appeared in *Tarik* almost two years ago alleging that government security personnel had abandoned their posts.

According to the Ethiopian Free Press Journalists Association, prosecutors charged that "by publishing such articles [Said] disseminated fabricated news at the national level that could have negative psychological effects on members of the Defence Army and cause disturbances in the minds of the people."

Said was released on July 20 after posting bail. Her trial was then adjourned until September, but no further developments had been reported by year's end.

JULY 4

Berhan Hailu, *Wogahta*
IMPRISONED
Merid Zelleke, *Satanaw*
IMPRISONED
Mengistu Wolde Selassie, *Moged*
IMPRISONED
Leykun Ingida, *Dagim Wonchif*
IMPRISONED
Henock Alemayhu, *Medina*
HARASSED
Daniel Abraha, *Netsanet*
HARASSED
Tilahun Bekele, *Netsebrak*
HARASSED

On or around July 4, police in the capital, Addis Ababa, arrested seven independent newspaper editors after they ran stories about the foreign minister's possible defection from Prime Minister Meles Zenawi's faction of the Tigray People's Liberation Front (TPLF).

The story originated on an Ethiopian Web site, ethiopiancommentator.com. *Wogahta*, a new Tigrigna-language Sunday weekly, was the first print publication to pick up the story. *Wogahta*'s article, titled "Where Are You Mr. Mesfin? You Are Not in Your Office," speculated that Foreign Minister Seyoum Mesfin had quit to join a splinter group of the TPLF.

Zenawi's TPLF is one of several parties in the ruling Ethiopian People's Revolutionary Democratic Front coalition.

Wogahta's report was based on the fact that Mesfin had not been seen in his office for several days, during which time the minister's house was surrounded by security guards. Though the paper speculated that the guards were there to protect Mesfin against Zenawi's agents,

local sources said that guards were assigned to the homes of all Cabinet ministers after the May 12 assassination of Intelligence and Security Chief Kinfe Gebre-Medhin, a close ally of Zenawi.

The other six newspapers published similar stories in the following days, most of them lifting their content from the *Woghata* story.

Ingida, who was the first to be called in, was questioned and then released on 5,000 birr bail (US$650). (In Ethiopia, police can demand bail for the release of suspects even before formal charges have been brought against them.) Police considered Ingida's offense less serious since the article in *Dagim Wonchif* was more contextual and contained less serious allegations.

Zelleke and Selassie were held in police custody until July 13, an exceptionally long detention in such a case. Hailu was detained for 48 hours after her interrogation. Alemayhu was released after questioning on 3,000 birr (US$400) bail. Abraha and Bekele were released on bails of 5,000 birr each.

Shortly after the stories appeared, Mesfin was interviewed by government media. The minister denied the reports and verified that he was still in office and with Zenawi's TPLF.

By year's end, no formal charges had been filed against any of the editors involved in the case.

OCTOBER 31

Ato Behailu Desalegn, *Capital*
LEGAL ACTION

Desalegn, editor of the English-language business weekly *Capital*, was summoned to the headquarters of the Criminal Investigation Division in the capital, Addis Ababa, and charged with criminal defamation. He was released hours later after posting bail of 2000 birr (US$230).

The charges stemmed from an October 28 *Capital* story about the advertising campaign of a local company called Moha Soft Drinks.

Authorities claim the article caused financial losses to Moha Soft Drinks because customers became wary of its products after reading the story.

The Ethiopian Free Press Journalists Association strongly protested the charges against Desalegn.

NOVEMBER 26

Tilahun Bekele, *Maebel*
LEGAL ACTION

Bekele, former editor of the Ahmaric-language weekly *Maebel* and currently editor of the weekly *Netsebrak*, was sentenced to one year in jail for criminal defamation.

The presiding judge admonished Bekele and then ordered his release. The judge released the journalist because he had already spent two years in jail for failing to post bail in connection with the same case.

Crown Mineral Water filed the suit after an October 1996 article in *Maebel* alleging poor hygienic standards at the company's refineries.

GABON

FEBRUARY 15

La Griffe
CENSORED
Le Gri-Gri
CENSORED

Michel Ongoundou, *La Griffe*
CENSORED
Raphaël Ntoutoume, *Le Gri-Gri*
CENSORED

The Libreville satirical weekly *La Griffe* and its monthly supplement, *Le Gri-Gri*, were banned, and their respective editors, Ongoundou and Ntoutoume, were ordered to cease practicing journalism temporarily after the state-run National Council on Communication ruled that a series of articles in *La Griffe* bordered on provocation against the head of state.

La Griffe was previously banned in August 1998, following the conviction of one its reporters in a defamation case. It was reinstated in February 1999, only to be banned again on March 17, 1999, on the unsubstantiated charge that its editor did not reside in Gabon. It resumed publication in October 2000.

In January, the paper was again dragged to court, first by President Omar Bongo and his wife, and later by the president's sister-in-law, Gisèle Opra. All claimed to have been defamed in several articles.

La Griffe had accused Opra of illegal real estate deals. The presidential couple reportedly took offense at a piece that mocked Bongo's book, *Blanc Comme Nègre* (White As Black), which *La Griffe* attacked for praising France's controversial colonial legacy in Africa.

In early May, CPJ learned that the paper's staff had relocated to Paris, where they are planning to relaunch the weekly with a pan-African focus.

OCTOBER 18

Le Gris-Gris International
CENSORED

Gabon's government ordered Sogapresse, a state-owned newspaper distributor, to block all shipments of the Paris-based *Le Gris-Gris International*, a satirical monthly published by exiled Gabonese journalists.

A week before the order, Sogapresse had ordered more copies than usual from France, apparently to satisfy a growing demand.

But on October 18, Police Commissioner Jean-Claude Labouba summoned Sogapresse's executives to his office in the capital, Libreville, and asked them to stop distributing *Le Gris-Gris International.*

Acting without a warrant, squads of Criminal Investigation Department officers seized all copies of the newspaper at newsstands and other locations throughout Libreville. The officers later told reporters they were acting on orders from the Ministry of the Interior.

Le Gris-Gris International is the latest avatar of the Libreville-based satirical weekly *Le Gris-Gris*, which was banned earlier in the year, along with *La Griffe*, another weekly that tends to be highly critical of President Omar Bongo.

After the publishers for the two banned publications were barred from practicing journalism in Gabon, they relocated to Paris, where they began publishing *Le Gris-Gris International.*

THE GAMBIA

MARCH 13

Alieu Badara Ceesay, *Daily Observer*
HARASSED

Pa Modou Bojang, *Daily Observer*
HARASSED
Ousman Bah, *Independent*
HARASSED
Lamarana Jallow, *Independent*
HARASSED

Ceesay and Bojang, of the independent *Daily Observer*, and Bah and Jallow, of the *Independent*, were harassed by police officers on the outskirts of Banjul while trying to cover a protest against fuel price hikes.

The police seized and broke Ceesay's camera. Bojang's press card was temporarily confiscated. An officer confiscated Bah's notebook. Jallow's camera was opened and his film destroyed.

JUNE 11

Modou Thomas, Radio 1 FM
HARASSED

National Intelligence Agency officers detained radio journalist Thomas in the town of Basse, where he was covering the Fifth National Youth Conference and Festival. The journalist was interrogated for several hours and then released.

Thomas was apparently detained for reporting that the Ministry of Youth and Sports, which sponsored the conference, had not provided sufficient lodging and food for all the participants.

Thomas was detained shortly after Radio 1 FM aired his report from Basse. The officers threatened Thomas, saying they had been "hearing things about him."

On June 14, Thomas was again briefly detained for questioning by officers in the capital, Banjul.

OCTOBER 29

Baboucar Gaye, Citizen FM
HARASSED

Gaye, owner of the independent radio station Citizen FM, was arrested by National Intelligence Agency (NIA) officers, who came to the station's office and demanded to see copies of Citizen's registration papers.

After looking at the documents, the agents asked for the station's income tax returns, which Gaye had not yet received from the Income Tax Department. The officers then arrested him and took him to the police station. There, they told the journalist that Citizen owed US$9,000 in taxes, and that the station would not be allowed to broadcast until the arrears had been paid.

When Gaye protested, the NIA agents said he would have to pay half the amount before disputing the arrears. He called the station and told them to stop broadcasting immediately, which they did.

Gaye, who still disputes the sum quoted by the NIA, alleged that the station was targeted for announcing its intention to announce the results of the October 18 presidential election. According to Gambian law, the electoral commission must be the first body to announce election results.

Gaye was held for four hours and then released. By December 31, he had paid off half the amount the government said he owed, but Citizen still remained off the air. At press time, Gaye was awaiting an "assessment" from the Income Tax Department to determine the exact amount he would have to pay before his taxes were officially up to date.

NOVEMBER 21

Alhagie Mbye, *The Independent*
IMPRISONED

Mbye, a senior reporter with the private daily *The Independent*, was arrested at his home by officers of Gambia's notorious Intelligence Agency (NIA) and taken to NIA headquarters in the capital, Banjul.

The arrest came days after the London-based *West Africa Magazine* published an article by Mbye about allegedly massive fraud during the October 18 presidential elections, which incumbent president Yahya Jammeh won amid vocal protests and boycotts by opposition and civil society groups.

Mbye's article charged that thousands of noncitizens, mostly from neighboring Senegal, were given Gambian citizenship for the sole purpose of garnering more votes for President Jammeh.

Although Gambian law allows a maximum 72-hour detention without charge, Mbye had still not been formally accused of any crime four days later.

The journalist, who claimed that NIA agents tortured him during his detention, was released eight days later. He was never formally charged.

GUINEA

FEBRUARY 14

Aboubacar Sakho, *Le Nouvel Observateur*
IMPRISONED

Sakho, publisher of the Conakry weekly *Le Nouvel Observateur*, was sentenced to 10 months in prison and

117

fined US$7,000 by the Court of First Instance in Conakry after Justice Minister Abou Camara brought criminal defamation charges against him.

The minister's complaint stemmed from a January 15 article in which *Le Nouvel Observateur* argued that Camara had exceeded his authority by dismissing several magistrates.

After the court ruling was pronounced, Sakho was handcuffed and driven to the central prison in Conakry, where he was beaten by other inmates, a local source told CPJ.

The journalist was unconditionally released a month later.

MAY 8

Tibou Camara, *L'Observateur*
IMPRISONED

Camara, publisher of the private weekly *L'Observateur*, was picked up by police at his newspaper's office in Conakry. According to eyewitnesses, the officers beat him brutally and then took him to Conakry's central prison.

Earlier, Camara had refused to respond to a court decision demanding that he pay a 1 million Guinean francs (US$524) fine or face six months in jail in connection with a defamation charge.

On April 24, the Conakry High Court sentenced Camara and five other journalists from *L'Observateur* in absentia to prison terms and/or heavy fines after Malick Sankhon, a Ministry of Tourism official, claimed that an article in the weekly had defamed him. The story accused Sankhon of trying to kidnap Camara, whose paper had been very critical of the official.

Most other *L'Observateur* journalists, whom police sought because

the incriminating article was bylined "The Newsroom" and not a single author, went into hiding, causing the paper to stop publishing briefly.

On May 12, President Lassana Conté ordered the release of Camara, the author of what some sources describe as a book of praises about Conté, an army colonel who has ruled Guinea harshly for the past decade while dragging the country into a costly border war with Liberia and Sierra Leone.

DECEMBER 4

Mamadou Cellou Diallo, *Le Lynx*
ATTACKED

Diallo, a photojournalist with the private weekly *Le Lynx*, was brutally beaten by officers from the Police Special Protection and Intervention Brigade (BSPI) in the capital, Conakry.

Local sources said a BSPI commander known as Lieutenant Camara ordered the officers to assault Diallo after he photographed Camara at a student rally at Conakry University.

On December 11, Diallo's newspaper filed a complaint against Camara for "blows and injuries." In his complaint, Diallo claimed that the officers who beat him also stole his wristwatch and about US$55 he was carrying in his wallet. No further developments in the case had been reported at press time.

GUINEA-BISSAU

JANUARY 27

Babacar Tcherno Dole, Radio Nacional da Guinea-Bissau
IMPRISONED

Police arrested Tcherno Dole, a

newscaster with the state-run Radio Nacional da Guinea-Bissau, and grilled him for several hours after he incorrectly reported that thenorthwestern town of Sao Domingos was about to be invaded by Senegalese separatists.

Tcherno Dole announced that heavily armed members of the Casamance separatist movement were about to occupy Sao Domingos to further their fight against the Senegalese government and its ally, Guinea-Bissau.

The announcement caused panic in Sao Domingos, normally a quiet provincial town on the border with the southern Senegalese province of Casamance, where a secessionist guerrilla movement has been fighting the Dakar regime, and occasionally the Guinea-Bissau army, for more than two decades.

Gunshots were indeed heard near Sao Domingos on the day of Tcherno Dole's broadcast, but Guinea-Bissau police claimed they were exchanged between rival factions of the rebel group, the Movement of the Casamance Democratic Forces.

Tcherno Dole apologized for his report and was released a day after his arrest, local sources said.

FEBRUARY 15

Athizar Mendes, *Diario de Bissau*
`HARASSED`

Mendes, a reporter for the private weekly *Diario de Bissau*; an unidentified photographer for the newspaper; and their driver were arrested by state security officers who objected to their investigation into police harassment of two local diplomats.

The two journalists were interrogated

and their equipment was confiscated. All three men were detained overnight and released the next day.

On March 8, after the deputy public prosecutor threatened legal action against the local press, some 30 journalists signed a petition against censorship and the arbitrary detention of journalists in Guinea-Bissau.

MARCH 30

Radio Bombolom
`THREATENED`
Guinea-Bissau media
`THREATENED`

An Air Force general stormed into the studios of the private radio station Bombolom FM during a live discussion about the fate of some 100 soldiers accused of participating in a November 2000 coup attempt.

The officer, Brig. Gen. Melciades Lopes Fernandes, claimed the station's programming could incite a civil war and said that the military would not tolerate it, according to journalists in Bissau. He added that in the event of a war, Radio Bombolom would be the first target to be bombed. After the incident, the director of the station suspended broadcasts for the rest of the day, according to local sources.

On March 31, the state-owned Radio-Television of Guinea-Bissau broadcast a debate in which military officers urged local journalists to stop meddling in military affairs.

On April 2, the opposition African Party for the Independence of Guinea-Bissau and the Cape Verde Islands accused the military of trying to gag the press. The country's parliament unanimously condemned the threats.

JUNE 17

Joao de Barros, *Diario de Bissau*
HARASSED
Athizar Mendes, *Diario de Bissau*
HARASSED

Security agents detained de Barros, owner and director of the private daily *Diario de Bissau*, and Mendes, a reporter for the newspaper.

The two were arrested after *Diario* published a June 15 article that accused President Kumba Yala of heading a network of corrupt civil servants who embezzled public funds by claiming false expenses and adding fictitious names to official travel forms.

On June 15, de Barros told a local radio station that after the article was published, a flustered President Yala summoned him to his office and threatened him with arrest and a beating. Yala denied the *Diario* allegations and castigated the press for its alleged bias.

De Barros and Mendes were released without charge on June 18.

OCTOBER 26

Diario de Bissau
CENSORED
Gazeta de Noticias
CENSORED
Joao de Barros, *Diario de Bissau*
HARASSED

Diario de Bissau and *Gazeta de Noticias*, the only two private newspapers in the country, were shut down on the orders of Attorney General Caetano Ntchama.

Ntchama originally closed the two publications for operating without a license. However, he later accused the

newspapers of a "continuing practice of criminal activity which was a potential cause of irreparable damage, as it attempted to undermine the nation's independence, integrity and national unity," according to the Portuguese news agency LUSA.

Journalists in Guinea Bissau claimed the closures were in reprisal for the newspapers' critical coverage of the government. The closures came after President Kumba Yala fired three Supreme Court judges for corruption and threatened to fire more than half the country's civil servants, also for corruption, and replace them with members of his own party.

On November 14, Joao de Barros, publication director of *Diario de Bissau*, was arrested and briefly detained at police headquarters. After the closure of his newspaper, de Barros was required to report to court every 15 days. He was apparently arrested for failing to comply with this order.

KENYA

APRIL 25

Royal Media Service
HARASSED, LEGAL ACTION

Police officers stormed the Nairobi offices of Citizen FM and Citizen TV, destroying and vandalizing property, including broadcasting equipment.

S.K. Macharia, the proprietor of Royal Media Services (RMS), which owns both stations, was arrested and charged with establishing and using radio communication equipment in violation of his broadcast license and the Kenya Communications Act of 1998.

Citizen FM's license permitted the station to erect television and radio transmitters in Limuru, on the outskirts of Nairobi. However, Macharia moved one transmitter to his home in a Nairobi suburb and another to his offices in downtown Nairobi, which violated the terms of his broadcasting license and the rules of the Communications Commission of Kenya (CCK) governing transmitters. Citizen was ordered off the air and forbidden from broadcasting. The police confiscated all the equipment.

Macharia was taken to the Criminal Investigation Department for interrogation and then taken to court, where he was charged with using a radio communication apparatus that violated his license. He was released on bond of Kenyan shillings 500,000 (US$6,670) pending trial on April 29.

The following day, Macharia filed a civil suit against Telkom Kenya, the CCK, the Kenya Broadcasting Corporation, and the attorney general. Royal Media's lawyers also tried to add the police to the list of persons named in the suit, which sought to compel the CCK and the police to return the confiscated equipment, to prevent them from interfering further with Citizen FM and Citizen TV, and to permit the two stations to resume broadcasting.

Macharia's lawyers further claimed that the regulations requiring media owners to obtain permits to relocate equipment were published after the raid on Citizen's offices and therefore did not apply to his case.

Royal Media lawyers argued that police and the CCK used a fraudulent search warrant to raid the station's offices, because in their application for the warrant they failed to disclose the existence of a 2000 High Court order that blocked the commission and its agents from interfering with Royal Media Services Limited.

On August 20, Citizen lost its bid to resume broadcasting. At the same time, High Court judge Alnashir Visram ruled that the CCK's search warrants had been executed according to law, and that there was no evidence that the commission used excessive force.

In a 98-page ruling, the judge found that RMS and Macharia "attempted to legalize unlawful acts through extra-judiciary means" by providing the court with a false statement that claimed the CCK was notified that RMS was going to transfer the broadcasting equipment. He said that even if such a notice existed, it would not absolve Royal Media Service from complying with its statutory obligations under the Communications Act. Vishram dismissed the suit with costs.

On August 29, Macharia filed an appeal asking that all Royal Media equipment be returned to him. The appeal had not been heard by year's end, but a pending case from 1995, in which the Customs and Excise Department seized broadcasting equipment from Royal Media, was finally settled in the company's favor.

By the middle of January, test signals from Citizen FM were being broadcast in Nairobi, although the station was still not legally permitted to go back on the air.

MAY 23

Chris Omollo, *Nation*
ATTACKED

Omollo, a photographer with the *Nation* newspaper, was attacked by police officers while covering a police raid on bars in Nairobi West, a suburb of the capital city.

Officers demanded to know why the journalist was taking pictures and began beating him with their guns. Despite orders from the police squad chief to leave Omollo alone, about 20 officers continued to insult and hit him.

The journalist was bruised, his camera was damaged, and some money was taken from his wallet. His driver was also assaulted in the attack. Omollo reported the incident to police authorities in Nairobi.

JUNE 28

Jackson Orina, free-lancer
ATTACKED

Orina, a free-lance photojournalist, was covering a political rally in Kitale, Western Kenya, for *The Daily Nation* when he was attacked by a mob of supporters from Kenya's ruling party, KANU.

At the end of the rally, Elijah Mwangale, a KANU member who had organized the event, and his agents distributed money to the participants. When Orina began photographing the ensuing scramble for the cash, he was attacked by Mwangale's supporters.

AUGUST 21

Daily Nation
LEGAL ACTION

Minister for Trade and Industry Nicholas Biwott, a top aide to President Daniel arap Moi, won a court injunction blocking *The Daily Nation* from publishing excerpts of *Rogue Ambassador*, the memoirs of former U.S. ambassador to Kenya Smith Hempstone.

In the book, Hempstone alleges that President Daniel arap Moi personally ordered the murder of then-foreign minister Robert Ouko, beat him, and then watched as Biwott shot Ouko. On July 30, Moi and Biwott sued Hempstone for libel and sought to stop the publication, distribution, and sale of the book or any material that refers to the Ouko murder allegations.

Initially, Moi had threatened *The Daily Nation* following a full-page advertisement in the August 20 edition of the paper that read in part: "President Moi and Minister Nicholas Biwott want the High Court to stop its sale. What does it contain? How much does it reveal about the country's most powerful politicians and government?" However, only Biwott filed a case against the paper.

Biwott's lawyers won the injunction, and, although the paper had already published some brief quotes from the book in which Hempstone calls Moi "ruthless, short-tempered, arrogant and self-promoting," the editors said they would comply with the ruling.

On September 4, 2001, a high court in Nairobi extended an interim injunction restraining Text Book Centre from further distributing the book. Commissioner of Assize Jeanne Gacheche also blocked the bookseller's agents and servants from further circulating or selling copies of the book.

The court also extended an order barring the Nation Media Group from publishing parts of the book in *The Daily Nation*. The case was still pending at year's end.

Nation Media Group
LEGAL ACTION

The Nation Media group, which publishes *The Daily Nation*, *Sunday Nation*, *The East African*, *Taifa Leo*, and *Taifa Jumapili*, was barred by the High Court from publishing articles about Jonathan Toroitich Moi, son of President Daniel arap Moi.

High Court Judge Kasanga Mulwa ordered the group not to publish stories on the president's son until the conclusion of his libel case against *The Daily Nation*.

That suit stemmed from an August 20 article in *The Daily Nation* titled "Firm Sues Moi's Son Over Prime Land," which described a landmark lawsuit filed against the Kenyan government in the Common Market for Eastern and Southern Africa (COMESA) Court of Justice.

The article said that the lawsuit, the first filed against a government in the Lusaka-based court, was brought by a Kenyan-incorporated firm, Coastal Aquaculture Ltd., which seeks more than 80 million Kenyan shillings (US$1million) in damages and loss of earnings following the government's compulsory acquisition of part of the company's 13,000 hectares of land in the Tana River Delta, Kilifi District.

The Kenyan Government took over the land, claiming it should be an environmental preserve. However, part of the area was subdivided and reallocated to 16 companies, several of which, the suit alleges, are owned by Jonathan Moi.

At an August 22 press conference, from which *Daily Nation* journalists were expelled, Jonathan Moi denied having been given land in the delta.

The Daily Nation did not contest the injunction, and by year's end there had been no new developments in the libel case.

LIBERIA

FEBRUARY 21

Joseph Bartuah, *The News*
IMPRISONED, LEGAL ACTION
Abdullah Dukuly, *The News*
IMPRISONED, LEGAL ACTION
James Dalieh, *The News*
IMPRISONED, LEGAL ACTION
Bobby Tapson, *The News*
IMPRISONED, LEGAL ACTION

Police in Monrovia arrested Bartuah, managing editor of the independent Monrovia daily *The News*, editor-in-chief Dukuly, news editor Dalieh, and reporter Tapson and charged them with espionage.

The charges apparently came in reprisal for a February 21 story that questioned government spending on helicopter repairs, Christmas cards, and souvenirs. The journalists were jailed for more than a month, while *The News* was issued crippling bills for back taxes.

Acting on a writ issued by the Monrovia City Court, police came to the newspaper's offices at 3 p.m. and arrested Tapson, author of the offending article. Later that day, they arrested Bartuah, Dukuly, and Dalieh.

According to *The News*, authorities claimed that Tapson's article contained national security information and was published in order to weaken Liberia in the event of a military or diplomatic confrontation with unnamed "foreign powers." The four journalists were charged with espionage and denied bail because espionage is a capital offense.

After the February 28 bail hearing, the court recessed until March 5, when it said it would issue its judgment. But in what appeared to be a pre-emptive move, prosecutors moved on March 2 to transfer the case to a higher court, which required the journalists' lawyers to file a new motion for bail.

On March 13, the higher court denied bail, claiming that the article had disclosed information that was useful to rebels, another nonbailable offense.

The four journalists were released from jail on Friday March 30, when the government dropped all charges following an appeal by the Press Union of Liberia and an apology issued by the journalists.

APRIL 17

Sam Howard, BBC
HARASSED

Howard, a stringer for the BBC, was detained by security officers and then threatened by Defense Minister Daniel Chea, according to local sources.

On April 16, Howard commented live for the BBC on the recent killing of Liberia's youth and sports minister, François Massaquoi. Dissidents fighting to overthrow the Taylor regime in the northern area of Lofa claimed responsibility for the murder.

During his BBC appearance, Howard said that "one who rides on the back of a lion ends up in the stomach," insinuating that Taylor or his government may have been involved in the murder.

A day after Howard's BBC appearance, Lewis Browne, an aide to President Taylor, told a local radio

program that the government would not tolerate bad publicity. Shortly thereafter, security officers picked up Howard and brought him before Defense Minister Daniel Chea for questioning. Local sources told CPJ that the minister threatened Howard.

Howard was released later that day.

APRIL 27

All News Organizations
CENSORED

The Liberian Ministry of Information ordered journalists covering national security issues, including civil strife in the north of the country, to clear their stories with the ministry before publication or broadcast.

According to the PanAfrican News Agency, the ministry order stated that "any agency or individual who conveys information to the public that could lead to confusion or panic in the country would bear full responsibility for the source or basis of such information."

Information Minister Reginald Goodridge said the order was meant to prevent "disinformation that could cause doubt and panic in the public," according to Agence France-Presse. Journalists in Monrovia complained the new rules would constitute prior censorship and charged that, since the government had not declared a state of emergency, the orders violated their constitutional right to freedom of expression.

MAY 25

All foreign journalists
HARASSED

The Ministry of Information issued new guidelines for foreign journalists visiting Liberia. The release claimed that the guidelines were designed to minimize the impact of anti-government propaganda by certain foreign correspondents and news organizations.

The release singled out journalists from *Newsweek* and London's *Daily Telegraph* who, it said, recently showed up in Monrovia without advance notice, demanded accreditation and went on to publish negative articles that have further damaged the image of Liberia. The statement then declared that no more surprise visits to Liberia by foreign journalists will be allowed.

The new guidelines require news organizations to write a letter on behalf of their foreign correspondents. Foreign journalists seeking entry into Liberia will have to give notice at least 72 hours before their arrival.

In addition, the new guidelines institute a 24-hour waiting period before accreditation is granted. Finally, they give the Information Ministry the right to conduct background checks on all foreign journalists and to reject their requests for accreditation if their credentials are not bona fide.

Liberia's international image had already taken a serious hit on May 7, when the United Nations imposed sanctions against the country in response to reports accusing President Taylor of trafficking in diamonds from rebel-held territories in neighboring Sierra Leone.

JULY 2

Radio Veritas
CENSORED

The Catholic Church-owned station Radio Veritas was banned from broadcasting on shortwave radio. That left KISS FM and Radio Liberia International, both part of President Charles Taylor's Liberia Communications Network, as the only stations airing political news countrywide.

Radio Veritas continued broadcasting on an FM frequency that only covers the capital, Monrovia.

At the time of the announcement, Radio Veritas was experiencing technical problems that prevented it from broadcasting, but the station's management continued to pay fees to air programs on both FM and shortwave frequencies. While Radio Veritas was off the air, station management received a letter from Minister of Post and Telecommunications Emma Wuor stating that only "short-wave stations in active operation at the moment" would be allowed to operate in Liberia for the time being.

Information Minister Reginald Goodridge said that by airing political programming, Radio Veritas had violated its permit, which only allowed the station to broadcast religious shows. Radio Veritas aired several shows critical of Taylor's government, including the controversial program "Topical Issues."

On 20 August, the Catholic Church sued the state to restore the station's broadcasting rights, accusing the government of violating the Liberian Constitution, which guarantees freedom of expression.

On September 4, government attorneys filed a motion to dismiss the lawsuit, arguing that only the

Supreme Court had jurisdiction in constitutional matters.

By years' end, the case had still not been resolved, and Veritas broadcasts were still limited to Monrovia. On January 10, President Charles Taylor conceded that "opposition complaints about not having access to shortwave transmitters are legitimate concerns" but maintained that "broadcasting on shortwave is not a right, but a privilege."

AUGUST 20

Sam Dean, *Monrovia Guardian*
IMPRISONED

Dean, editor of the independent daily *Monrovia Guardian*, was arrested by police and taken to police headquarters, where he was charged with "criminal malevolence."

Dean's arrest followed the publication, around August 17, of a *Guardian* article reporting that Police Chief Paul Mulbah had been summoned to the House of Representatives for questioning after a female parliamentarian was assaulted in the Monrovia suburb of Gardenville. The article, titled "Police Director Wanted," claimed that the House wished to ask Mulbah why police had failed to arrest the perpetrators of the attack.

Sources in Monrovia said that police were upset by the story's headline, and that Mulbah went to the Press Union of Liberia (PUL) and complained of the *Guardian*'s "sensationalism" and "misleading" reports. The PUL called Dean in for questioning regarding the police chief's complaints, but the editor refused to go, claiming that he had done nothing wrong.

On August 20, the *Guardian*

reproduced the same article and asked the public, "What's wrong with this headline?" Sources say this infuriated the police, who shortly thereafter arrested Dean in the paper's offices.

Dean was detained for 71 hours, according to local news sources, longer than the 48 hours mandated by law. He was released after he wrote an apology to the police for the article, and all charges against him were dropped.

Meanwhile, the *Guardian* withdrew from the PUL in protest, saying that the paper had done nothing wrong. The PUL now says that in order for the paper to rejoin the union, it will have to apologize for its withdrawal.

SEPTEMBER 17

T-Max Jlateh, DC 101.1
HARASSED
DC 101.1
CENSORED

Jlateh, host of the popular call-in show "DC-Talk" at the Monrovia-based radio station DC 101.1, was arrested for airing listener comments that celebrated the September 11 terrorist attacks against the United States.

Police raided the studios of DC 101.1, one of Liberia's last surviving independent broadcasters, and arrested Jlateh midway through his show. The officers evacuated the staff and effectively closed down the station before taking Jlateh back to police headquarters. They presented no warrant for their actions.

DC 101.1 was allowed to reopen after a few hours. Police detained Jlateh throughout the night and did not release him until about 2:00 p.m.

on September 18, according to CPJ sources in Monrovia.

Jlateh's arrest came after several people called in to the show and spoke harshly about the United States. Some of them apparently rejoiced at the terrorist attacks on the World Trade Center in New York City and the Pentagon in Washington, D.C.

Although many callers expressed sympathy for the victims of the attacks, others claimed that the United States was the chief sponsor of terrorism in the world and that it deserved the attacks for imposing sanctions on Liberia earlier this year.

The raid followed a government threat to arrest and prosecute anyone found buying or selling photographs of Osama bin Laden, the prime suspect in the September 11 attacks.

CPJ protested Jlateh's arrest in a September 20 letter to Liberian president Charles G. Taylor.

NOVEMBER 20

The News
HARASSED
Guardian
HARASSED
Wilson Tarpeh, *The News*
IMPRISONED

Police officers entered the newsroom of the independent daily *The News*, a fiery critic of Liberian president Charles Taylor, and ordered journalists and others to leave the building immediately. The officers did not provide a warrant for their action, sources said.

At about the same time, similar action was taken against the daily *Guardian*, another thorn in the president's side.

Police claimed to act at the behest of the Ministry of Finance, which had allegedly determined that both papers owed the government large sums in unpaid taxes. Later that same day, police arrested Tarpeh, chairman of *The News'* editorial board.

Tarpeh was taken to police headquarters in Monrovia and later moved to the National Security Agency offices for interrogation. He remained there until his release on November 25. He was never charged with any crime; police later said his detention was an "invitation" to assist in the probe into the tax matter.

The News and *Guardian* both resumed publication on December 4, after the Press Union of Liberia vigorously protested the harassment of the two publications.

MALAWI

FEBRUARY 12

Mike Kamwendo, *Daily Times*
HARASSED
Wallace Mposa, *Daily Times*
HARASSED
Limbani Moya, *Daily Times*
HARASSED
Mabvuto Banda, *Daily Times*
HARASSED
MacDonald Chapalapata, *Daily Times*
HARASSED
Peter Makossah, *Daily Times*
HARASSED

Six journalists from the independent *Daily Times* were arrested by police in the town of Blantyre after the newspaper reported on serial murders in the southern district of Chiradzulu. The six detainees included editors Kamwendo and Mposa and reporters Moya, Banda, Chapalapata, and Makossah.

The article, which was written by Makossah, quoted a traditional chief who linked the recent killings of eight men to the serial killings of eight women during a three-month period in 2000. The chief said that the manner in which the eight men died resembled the earlier murders, for which two men had already been sentenced to death.

The journalists were held for several hours and then released. Mposa, Moya, and Chapalapata were issued warnings, while Kamwendo, Banda, and Makossah were charged with publishing false news. According to *The Nation* newspaper, Police Commissioner Milward Chikwamba said the journalists were arrested because the story was false and the work of alarmists.

On March 22, President Bakili Muluzi ordered police to drop all charges against the three journalists.

MAY 25

Kalera Mhango, Karora Printers and Publishing House
LEGAL ACTION
Martines Namingah, *Dispatch*
LEGAL ACTION
Namingah, the editor of the independent *Dispatch*, and Mhango, owner of Karora Printers and Publishing House, the paper's printer, were charged with "publishing false information likely to cause public fear and alarm" in connection with a series of articles about President Bakili Muluzi that appeared in *Dispatch* on May 23.

The first article alleged that President Muluzi feared the opposition party would impeach him during the June parliamentary session. Another story, quoting former transport minister Brown Mpinganjira, insinuated that the president was the most corrupt person in the country. The third story outlined charges that the National Intelligence Bureau was spying on members of parliament from the ruling United Democratic Front party who were suspected of sympathizing with an opposition group.

After a police search, Mhango and Namingah surrendered to officers on May 25 and 26, respectively. They were released on bail after a brief court appearance on May 26.

The police said they would call the journalists to court again "when the state was ready." As this book went to press, the journalists had not been summoned, although the charges had not been formally dropped.

In a related development, police arrested four vendors on May 25 for selling copies of *Dispatch*. They were released on a 5,000 kwacha (US$66.78) bail a few days later but were not formally charged.

AUGUST 12

Brian Ligomeka, Africa Eye News Service
ATTACKED
Ligomeka, correspondent for the South Africa–based Africa Eye News Service and an editor at the Malawian weekly *Mirror* newspaper, was attacked by seven men at Chileka airport in Blantyre, where he was covering the arrival of the Angolan delegation to a Southern African Development Community (SADC) heads-of-state meeting.

The *Mirror* is published by former cabinet minister Brown Mpinganjira, who is now a vocal member of the opposition.

The men, who all wore badges accrediting them to the SADC, surrounded Ligomeka on the runway and dragged him into some bushes near the parking lot, where they beat him up. The ringleader, who identified himself as "Sam Zimba," accused Ligomeka of bad-mouthing Malawian president Bakili Muluzi and Zimbabwean president Robert Mugabe. "You have been embarrassing us," Zimba said. "We've been looking for you for a long time."

Zimba's badge designated him as an accredited SADC "official." Ligomeka said he recognized Zimba as a member of the ruling party's youth cadre, commonly referred to as "the untouchables."

According to Ligomeka, Zimba was previously accused of burning a car belonging to a member of the opposition.

A policeman witnessed the beatings and drove Ligomeka to the Chileka airport police station, where he was held in "safe custody."

The police instructed him to return on Monday to record a statement and file a complaint. When he returned, one police officer recorded the statement but the senior officer refused to approve it, saying the police needed to investigate the matter first.

Later that day, Ligomeka received three anonymous phone calls from individuals who said they weren't through with him yet.

SEPTEMBER 1

The Chronicle
LEGAL ACTION

Robert Jamieson, *The Chronicle*
LEGAL ACTION
Christopher Jimu, *The Chronicle*
LEGAL ACTION

During the first week of September, the Leasing and Finance Company of Malawi (LFC), one of the country's major finance companies, filed a criminal defamation suit against Robert Jamieson and Christopher Jimu, respectively editor-in-chief and reporter for the independent, Lilongwe-based *Chronicle*.

The suit stemmed from an article and editorial comment published in the May 28-June 3, 2001 edition of *The Chronicle*. The article, titled "Criminal Probe on LFC Possible," reported that the director of public prosecution (DPP) had launched a criminal investigation against the LFC, which was alleged to have illegally appropriated ownership documents for a private vehicle.

The editorial, titled "Integrity," urged the DPP to conduct a rigorous investigation.

On September 18, both journalists entered a not-guilty plea. Their case was still pending at year's end.

Defamation is still a criminal offense in Malawi and carries a maximum prison sentence of three years. Complainants can also choose to file a civil defamation suit and seek monetary damages.

The Chronicle is currently facing a number of civil defamation suits in addition to the LFC criminal suit. These suits have been filed by President Bakili Muluzi, several Cabinet ministers, and other government officials acting in their private capacity, as well as by the Reserve Bank of Malawi. *Chronicle* staff believe that the complainants do not intend to follow through on their lawsuits, and that their actual intention is to try to bankrupt the paper with legal costs.

Chinyeke Tembo, *People's Eye*
ATTACKED

Tembo, editor of the anti-government weekly newspaper *People's Eye*, based in Blantyre, was pulled out of a minibus and beaten by a group of government supporters. Police later charged the journalist with publishing false news.

Tembo was traveling in a public bus toward Limbe, Blantyre's business district, when a group of ruling United Democratic Front (UDF) party supporters accused him of writing anti-UDF propaganda and began to manhandle him. The bus driver was forced to stop, whereupon the assailants dragged the journalist off the bus and started beating him in the road.

Paramilitary police officers intervened and took the journalist to police headquarters. The UDF supporters followed the officers to the station, where the attackers claimed that they had assaulted Tembo for writing false news about President Muluzi and the UDF government. Instead of investigating the assault, the police then started interrogating Tembo about his newspaper, local sources said.

Police then charged Tembo with "publishing false news likely to cause alarm." According to sources in Malawi, the charges came in response to the August 13 special edition of *People's Eye*, which contained a critical appraisal of Malawi's political climate.

Tembo intended the publication to reach African leaders who were attending the Southern African Development Community Summit that began on August 12 in Blantyre. When the special edition was published, ruling-party youth confiscated and burned copies of it and attacked news vendors selling it.

Tembo was held for four hours before Blantyre civil rights lawyer Viva Nyimba managed to bail him out. The journalist suffered minor injuries from the attack. By year's end, Tembo had not been indicted; sources in Malawi said it was unlikely that police would follow through on the charges.

People's Eye is known for criticizing the ruling UDF. The paper has strong links to the National Democratic Alliance, an opposition group headed by Brown Mpinganira, a former UDF minister of public works and transport.

The Chronicle
CENSORED

The latest edition of the independent, Lilongwe-based *Chronicle* did not appear on newsstands because the paper's printer, Design Printers, refused to print the issue.

Chronicle editor Rob Jamieson told CPJ that Design objected to an article about the controversy surrounding the death of Malawian reggae star and outspoken government critic Evison Matafale, who died in police custody after he was picked up for allegedly writing a seditious letter to President Bakili Muluzi.

Design apparently said it would only print the current issue of *The Chronicle* if Jamieson replaced the offending article.

Design Printers administrative manager Billy Chimimba told the Media Institute of Southern Africa that the company reserved the right to refuse to print its clients' materials. Chimimba added that Malawi's laws do not protect them if they print controversial materials, and that printers have been arrested for doing so.

The Chronicle then suspended publication while it looked for an alternate printer.

DECEMBER 20

Thomas Chafunya, *Daily Times*
`HARASSED`
Lazarus Nedi, *Daily Times*
`HARASSED`

Senior business reporter Chifunya, and photographer Nedi, of the independent *Daily Times*, were harassed while trying to cover violent clashes between police and vendors on the streets of Limbe, just outside Blantyre.

On December 20, the street vendors broke an agreement with the Blantyre City Assembly to operate in designated areas only, deciding instead to sell their wares in the more lucrative main city streets. Police arrived on the scene and attempted to remove the vendors, who put up a fight.

Junior police officers detained Chifunya and Nedi at the scene while the two were covering the clashes, saying that the journalists did not have permission to report on the event. The police then demanded that the journalists hand over the diskettes from the digital camera they had used to photograph the confrontation.

When the journalists refused, the angry police officers took them to a

senior officer nearby for questioning. Though the senior officer allowed the journalists to go, he cautioned them against continuing their coverage of the clashes. The junior officers continued to harass the journalists, demanding they surrender their camera, for 15 minutes before finally allowing them to leave.

MALI

MAY 22

Sidiki Konaté, ORTM
`IMPRISONED`

Konaté, head of the Office of Radio and Television in Mali (ORTM), was convicted of criminal defamation by a court in the town of Segou, some 80 miles north of the capital, Bamako.

The Autonomous Union of the Magistracy filed charges against both ORTM and the mayor of Bamako, Ibrahima N'Diaye, after a March 26 television show in which the mayor accused Malian magistrates of being corrupt and inefficient.

Konaté was sentenced to a month in prison and a US$1,350 fine. The mayor received a 30-day jail sentence and a US$4,000 fine.

Malian press and human rights organizations condemned the decision, as did CPJ in a May 22 statement.

Shortly after Konaté was sentenced, the union withdrew its complaint and closed the case.

JULY 25

Alboulaye Ladji Guindo, *Liberté*
`ATTACKED`

Guindo, publisher of the Bamako-based private weekly *Liberté*, was kidnapped by three men and held for several hours, during which time he was threatened and roughed up.

According to Guindo, the abduction came in reprisal for an editorial in that week's issue of *Liberté* in which he denounced allegedly illegal schemes used by local businessmen to corner the sugar market. The article implicated Amadou Djigué, a prominent Bamako entrepreneur whose Djigué-SA company is one of Mali's biggest sugar suppliers.

Guindo, who claimed that Djigué's son was one of the kidnappers, was held for several hours at Djigué-SA headquarters, where the men bombarded him with angry questions, punctuated with death threats, about the editorial.

Guindo told Agence France-Presse that he had no doubt that Amadou Djigué masterminded the attack. He later filed a formal complaint accusing Djigué of kidnapping and torture, but no progress had been reported in the case as of December 31.

SEPTEMBER 26

Joan Baxter, BBC
HARASSED
Said Penda, BBC
HARASSED

Baxter, a correspondent for the BBC English Radio and Television Service, and Penda, a correspondent for the BBC French Radio Service, were arrested and detained by Republican Guard officials in downtown Bamako.

The two journalists had gone to the center of Bamako's market district to cover merchant protests against the erection of a new barrier around the U.S. embassy. U.S. officials ordered the construction of the barrier after the September 11 terrorist attacks in New York City and Washington, D.C.

Merchants objected to the plan, saying it would force them to move and would greatly diminish their sales. They also complained that the United States offered them no compensation for having to relocate their businesses.

At around 1:00 p.m., when Baxter and Penda approached merchants at the scene, Republican Guard officials stopped the journalists and confiscated their equipment. Embassy officials protested the arrests, telling the officers that such action was not part of their instructions.

Nevertheless, officers detained Baxter and Penda in front of the embassy for three hours without charge before taking them to the central police station. Once there, authorities interrogated the journalists for an hour to determine whether they had authorization to report on the "tense" situation around the embassy.

After police recorded Baxter and Penda's personal information, they returned the seized equipment and released them unconditionally.

MOZAMBIQUE

MARCH 3

Marcelo Mosse, *Metical*
LEGAL ACTION
Metical
LEGAL ACTION

Businessman Nympine Chissano, son of President Joaquim Chissano, filed charges against Mosse and *Metical* over a February 21 article reporting that Nympine was briefly detained in South

Africa around February 15 on unspecified charges.

In a written denial sent to *Metical*, Nympine Chissano's lawyer threatened legal action against the newspaper, declaring that his client was not detained and had "never transported cocaine or other substances forbidden by law inside or outside the country," according to AIM, the Mozambican state news service.

However, all sources interviewed by CPJ concur that the *Metical* story did not mention cocaine or any other illegal substances. That allegation first appeared in the Johannesburg *Mail and Guardian* under the byline of a South African journalist. Mosse later repeated the allegation in the Portuguese weekly *Expresso*, for which he is the correspondent in Mozambique.

Nympine Chissano is seeking damages of US$80,000 from Mosse and *Metical*, said CPJ sources in Maputo.

Metical was owned by its founder and first editor, Carlos Cardoso. After Cardoso's murder in November 2000, the paper became the property of his two underage children, Ibo and Milena, who are represented by their mother, Nina Berg. In the worst-case scenario, the court could jail Mosse and bankrupt the Cardoso family.

Under pressure, *Metical* closed in late December 2001, a year after Cardoso was murdered, gangland style, three blocks from the paper's offices. The case was still pending at year's end.

NOVEMBER 1

Jose Arlindo, TVM
ATTACKED

Arlindo, a cameraman with the state-run Mozambican Television network (TVM), was attacked in the northern town of Nampula, where the opposition RENAMO party was holding a meeting. RENAMO security agents assaulted the journalist, as well as law enforcement officers.

The incident occurred outside the meeting's venue, where a group of dissident party members were holding a rally protesting the softening of RENAMO's party line. (Until the early 1990s, RENAMO was a notoriously brutal guerrilla group that South Africa's apartheid regime backed against the ruling FRELIMO party, which supported the anti-apartheid struggle.)

RENAMO security guards attacked Arlindo after party official Ossufo Quitine asked that no pictures be taken of the demonstration. The security men also attempted to confiscate Arlindo's equipment.

The Mozambican Journalists Union condemned the attack, as did RENAMO leader Afonso Dhlakama.

NAMIBIA

FEBRUARY 2

The Namibian
LEGAL ACTION
Republikein 2000
LEGAL ACTION

Judge President Pio Teek filed contempt of court charges against the independent daily *The Namibian*, the Afrikaans-language daily *Republikein 2000* (also known as *Die Republikein*), and the Namibian Society of Advocates.

The charges stemmed from comments the three organizations made regarding two cases over which

Teek was presiding. The first case concerned the government's planned deportation of Jose Domingos Sikunda, the former representative of the rebel National Union for the Total Independence of Angola (UNITA) in Namibia, for allegedly threatening state security.

The second case concerned contempt of court charges filed against Home Affairs Minister Jerry Ekandjo for disobeying an October 24, 2000, court ruling that ordered Sikunda's immediate release from detention.

Both cases were proceeding slowly, and by early December, Judge Teek had not enforced the court order directing Sikunda's release.

In a December 1, 2000, editorial, *The Namibian* called for speedy judgment in both cases and criticized Teek's refusal to implement the previous court order, saying the judge's inaction violated the constitution and eroded the rule of law. In a December 4 editorial, *Republikein 2000* also criticized Teek's conduct, while the Society of Advocates said that there was no possible justification for Teek's behavior.

Teek filed the contempt of court charges with the Prosecutor General's Office in January, 2001, while a hearing was being conducted into his role in the two cases.

Teek then recused himself from both cases, claiming that his credibility had been irreparably damaged by all the public criticism. Teek accused the three organizations of "the highest order of gross interference and intimidation in Namibian legal history," according to the Media Institute of Southern Africa.

The judges who took over the case found Ekandjo guilty of contempt.

Sikunda was released from prison shortly thereafter. Prosecutor General Heyman said that police continued to investigate the cases against the two newspapers and the Society of Advocates, but none had been formally indicted at press time.

OCTOBER 12

Max Hamata, *The Namibian*
HARASSED

Hamata, a reporter for the national daily *The Namibian*, was detained and charged with "interfering with police duties" while trying to visit Geoffrey Mwilima, a former member of Parliament and a treason suspect, at the Roman Catholic Hospital in the capital, Windhoek.

In 2000, Mwilima was tortured and beaten by police. Hamata was investigating whether Mwilima was transferred from the Grootfontein Military Base to the hospital in Windhoek as a result of further torture.

When Hamata arrived at the hospital, two plainclothes detectives stopped him as he entered Mwilima's room. Hamata demanded to see a superior officer to get permission to speak to the patient. He waited outside for the officer to return with his superior. When neither of them came back, Hamata entered the room, this time with a camera around his neck.

The second detective, who remained outside the door, thought Hamata had taken a picture without permission and demanded that Hamata hand over the film. The journalist refused to give the officer his digital camera. The detective then radioed for his commander and armed reinforcements, who arrived and escorted the journalist to the Police Charge Office.

Hamata was charged with "interfering with police duties." The charges were withdrawn on October 15.

NIGER

OCTOBER 19

Abdoulaye Tiemogo, *Le Canard Dechainé*
IMPRISONED, LEGAL ACTION

Tiemogo, publisher of the independent satirical weekly *Le Canard Dechainé*, was convicted of defamation in a Niamey court.

The charges against Tiemogo were brought by Minister of Agriculture Wassalke Boukari and stem from an article that appeared in *Le Canard Dechainé* in September. The article alleged that Boukari was involved in the embezzlement of more than 3 billion CFA ($US4 million) from the fraudulent sale of gold prospecting permits in the Komabangou area of western Niger, and that he had personally embezzled 200 million CFA (US$280,000).

Several public officials had already been arrested in connection with the gold permit scandal and were awaiting trial at the time.

After the story was published in *Le Canard Dechainé*, it was picked up by several other newspapers, local sources said.

Tiemogo was sentenced to six months in prison and ordered to pay a fine and damages amounting to 5.1 million CFA (US$7,200). He was remanded to prison directly after the trial.

In separate statements, two

journalists associations in Niger, the Union of Private Journalists of Niger and the Niger Association of Independent Editors, condemned the conviction of Tiemogo and demanded that press violations be decriminalized.

Tiemogo was released from prison on December 7, when Boukari decided to drop the charges against him.

NIGERIA

MARCH 6

Sam Chindah, *The Tide*
HARASSED
Rosemary Nwisi, *The Post Express*
HARASSED

Two journalists, Chindah of *The Tide* and Nwisi of *The Post Express*, were briefly detained on orders of Port Harcourt chief magistrate C.I. Nwankwo, who insisted that they required special authorization to cover proceedings in her courtroom. The judge also ordered the temporary confiscation of their professional equipment.

The two journalists arrived in Nwankwo's courtroom in the middle of a hearing. A few minutes later, the judge ordered police to arrest them, saying they would have plenty to write about after being locked up with accused criminals. The reporters were released after the day's court session, although Chindah's equipment was not immediately returned. He was asked to collect it the next day.

APRIL 3

Tade Adesungboye, *Punch*
ATTACKED

Adesungboye, a photographer for the independent Lagos daily *Punch*, was assaulted by security operatives inside the Lagos High Court.

The photographer was at the courthouse to cover the trial of Aminu Mohammed, who had been charged with the attempted murder of Chief Abraham Adesanya, a pro-democracy activist and leader of the ethnic Yoruba organization Afenifere.

After Adesungboye took a picture, he was grabbed by security officers and beaten. The officers also seized his camera and removed the film.

The most senior of the security guards who assaulted Adesungboye claimed that the photographer was beaten for photographing a suspect without permission.

Dayo Omotosho, *Comet*
CENSORED

Omotosho, the state bureau chief for the Lagos-based *Comet* newspaper, was barred from covering the government of Oyo State, in the southwestern part of Nigeria. State officials also demanded that the newspaper name another correspondent to the beat.

Lagos newspapers reported that the ban came in reprisal for an April 2 article in which Omotosho reported that state governor Alhaji Lam Adesina and his wife, Saratu, had snubbed the wife of Vice President Alhaja Titi Abubakar during the wedding of the governor's son.

APRIL 23

Okon Sam, *Pioneer*
ATTACKED

Sam, a reporter for the newspaper *Pioneer*, was assaulted by security

guards from President Olusegun Obasanjo's entourage.

The reporter was at the International Conference Center in Abuja to cover a meeting of the ruling People's Democratic Party. He had just approached the main gate of the center and was trying to enter when a security guard stopped him.

Although Sam was wearing his press identity card on his chest, the security guard denied him entry. When the journalist attempted to prove that he was accredited to cover the event, the guard punched him and beat him with his gun.

Sam sustained a dislocated arm and head injuries. His tape recorder was damaged and his clothes were torn. He was hospitalized with internal bleeding.

JUNE 8

Nnamdi Onyenua, *Glamour Trends*
IMPRISONED, LEGAL ACTION

Armed police officers entered the offices of Millennium Communications, which publishes the magazine *Glamour Trends*, fired their guns in the air to disperse employees, then took Onyenua into custody and drove him to the Nigerian capital, Abuja, under heavy police escort.

Onyenua's arrest came after the magazine published a story on June 6 alleging that President Olusegun Obasanjo received $1 million in allowances for each trip he took abroad, and that as of May 30, 2001, he had amassed a personal fortune of US$58 million.

The independent newspaper *This Day* reported that shortly after the article appeared, the Office of the Inspector

General of Police received a letter from the president stating that the allegation could not be substantiated and that the magazine had thus "committed an offence punishable under section 392 of the Penal Code Law."

According to CPJ sources in Nigeria, Onyenua remained in police custody pending an investigation. Though Nigerian law mandates that no prisoner can be held more than 24 hours without a formal charge, Onyenua was not arraigned until June 19. He was released on bail on or around June 21 and charged with publishing false information and defaming the president.

His case was due to be heard on November 8, 2001, at the Abuja Magistrate Court. The case was still unresolved at year's end.

JULY 4

Aminu Abubakar, Agence France-Presse
THREATENED, CENSORED

Abubakar, the Agence France-Presse (AFP) correspondent for Kano State in northern Nigeria, was harassed by a group of Christian youths in the town of Tafawa Balewa, Bauchi State.

Abubakar went to Tafawa Balewa on July 3 to cover violent confrontations between Christians and Muslims, which became frequent after the introduction of Islamic law (Sharia) in the state last spring. Tafawa Balewa is a small, predominantly Christian town in the predominantly Muslim state. Most of the recent violence there has been perpetrated by Christians against Muslims.

While Abubakar was interviewing people on the street, members of the Christian youth organization Youth of Zar closed in on him and threatened to kill him. They then forced the journalist to tear up his notebook. Shortly thereafter, police surrounded Abubakar and escorted him out of the town.

The AFP bureau in Lagos said Abubakar most likely was harassed because he is a Muslim. The new AFP correspondent in Tafawa Balewa, who is Christian, has not encountered any harassment. However, AFP also said that local authorities were anxious both to play down the violence and to prevent the media from reporting on it. According to AFP, authorities fear that coverage of the incidents could lead to reprisals in other areas of the state.

By mid-July, most Muslims had been driven out of Tafawa Balewa. Citing local medical sources, the AFP said 461 bodies had been buried in the area, all victims of sectarian violence.

JULY 25

Tunde Adesola, *The Punch*
ATTACKED
The Punch
ATTACKED

More than 1,000 students from Adekunle Ajasin University in Ondo State twice attacked *The Punch* newspaper office in the state capital, Akure, and threatened to lynch local correspondent Tunde Adesola.

The students, who raided the office on July 25 and 26, were angered by two recent *Punch* articles, titled "Adefarati Advises Students on use of English" and "Polish your English, Advises Adefarati." Both articles reported on State Governor Adebayo Adefarati's admonition to university students to improve their English.

The students vandalized the office

and destroyed copies of the newspaper. Governor Adefarati and the Nigerian Union of Journalists both condemned the attack.

OCTOBER 5

Simon Materi, CNN
ATTACKED

Materi, a cameraman for CNN, was attacked in the city of Kaduna, capital of Kaduna State in northern Nigeria. Materi was filming outside a mosque for a story on Christian-Muslim tensions in the region when he was assaulted by an angry mob.

Village elders rescued the journalist, drove him away from the scene, and briefly sheltered him before he left for Lagos.

RWANDA

APRIL 12

Gerard Mbanda, ORINFOR
CENSORED

Mbanda, a veteran television news producer for the state-operated Office de l'Information du Rwanda (ORINFOR) media network, was suspended for two weeks without pay for airing images of a profusely perspiring President Paul Kagame.

Sources in the Rwandan capital, Kigali, speculated that the suspension may also have been related to broadcast footage in which Kagame was being shown a passage in the Bible. They said that in heavily Catholic Rwanda, those images could have been construed as suggesting that Kagame was incapable of reading the Bible without help.

ORINFOR runs all publicly funded news operations in the country, including Radio Rwanda, one television station, and two newspapers.

DECEMBER 31

Amiel Nkuliza, *Le Partisan*
IMPRISONED

Police detained Nkuliza, a journalist with *Le Partisan* newspaper, and questioned him about his reporting on the murder of Gratien Munyarubuga, a founder of the opposition Democratic Party for Renewal-Ubuyanja, and his stories about the Democratic Republican Movement party. He was released on January 3, 2002.

SENEGAL

MARCH 5

Cheikh Dieng, *Wal Fadjiri*
ATTACKED

Dieng, a political correspondent for the private Dakar daily *Wal Fadjiri*, was roughed up by supporters of Bèye Baldé, the mayor of Velingara, a town in southern Senegal.

An irate crowd gathered in front of Dieng's home after *Wal Fadjiri* published his article on alleged infighting within the mayor's entourage. The journalist was briefly manhandled when he came out of his home to investigate the commotion.

Dieng, who in the past had complained of threats from the mayor's supporters, sustained minor bruises during the assault. It remains unclear whether or not the mayor, a member of President Abdoulaye Wade's ruling Democratic Party, ordered the assault on Dieng.

APRIL 16

Moussa Diop, *Sud Quotidien*
ATTACKED

Supporters of the ruling Democratic
Party (PDS) in the rural southern town
of Velingara hurled stones and shouted
obscenities at Diop, a local
correspondent for the Dakar daily *Sud
Quotidien*, as he was on his way to
interview a town official.

The assailants apparently had close
links to the town's PDS mayor, Bèye
Baldé. The journalist escaped unharmed,
but the windows of his car were
shattered by stones.

Diop told reporters that the assault
may have been linked to his coverage of
infighting within the local chapter of the
PDS. President Abdoulaye Wade, who
was visiting the area, reportedly
promised to pay for repairs to the
journalist's car.

JULY 10

Alioune Fall, *Le Matin*
HARASSED

Fall, editor-in-chief of the
independent daily *Le Matin*, was
detained for questioning at the Division
of Criminal Investigation (DIC).

He was apprehended by DIC agents
following the publication of an article in
that day's edition of *Le Matin* about the
investigation into a recent riot at
Dakar's Central Prison. The article
reported that several prisoners had
escaped due to official negligence.

Police were particularly upset,
Senegalese sources said, because the
article mentioned that the inquiry into
the riot had been assigned to the
gendarmerie instead of to the police.

There has historically been a strong
rivalry between the two services.

While he was in detention, DIC
officers tried to get Fall to reveal his
sources, but the journalist refused. He
was released after 24 hours.

On August 17, Fall was summoned to
court, where the public prosecutor
charged him with publishing false
information, a criminal offense. Local
sources said Fall pleaded not guilty and
maintained the story was accurate. The
case was ongoing at year's end.

DECEMBER 10

Babacar Ndiaye, Agence de Presse
Sénégalaise
HARASSED
Diatta, Sud-FM
HARASSED

Ndiaye, a reporter for the state-
owned Agence de Presse Sénégalaise
(APS), and another journalist known
only as Diatta, from the private radio
station Sud-FM, were harassed by police
officers while covering a rally in Thiès,
70 kilometers (43 miles) from the
capital, Dakar.

Former Senegalese peacekeepers with
the United Nations Mission in the
Democratic Republic of the Congo
called the demonstration to demand
their salaries from the Senegalese
government. The police had reportedly
received orders to keep out the press.

SIERRA LEONE

JANUARY 25

Abdul Karim Koroma, *Independent
Observer*
THREATENED

Karoma, a reporter for the daily *Independent Observer*, received threatening telephone calls after he reported that a former National Provisional Ruling Council chairman, Valentine Strasser, had been seen begging for food at Freetown restaurants.

After the article appeared, Karoma's newspaper received a phone call from former members of a disbanded paramilitary group called the West Side Boys, who threatened to attack Karoma and other journalists at the newspaper. Karoma's colleagues said that the former head of the West Side Boys, John Johnson, alias Junior Lion, was known to be friendly with Strasser.

When the newspaper ran a story about the calls in the next day's issue, the same people telephoned again to say they were prepared to carry out their threats.

FEBRUARY 5

Pius Foray, *The Democrat*
HARASSED

Police detained Pius Foray, owner and editor of the independent Freetown daily *The Democrat*, after his newspaper ran a story suggesting that President Ahmad Tejan Kabbah feared for his life.

The February 5 article, written by Foray, alleged that President Kabbah had become apprehensive after the January 16 assassination of Congolese president Laurent-Désiré Kabila and the Sierra Leonean government's subsequent decision to postpone general elections. As a result, Kabbah reportedly rotated his security regiment and fired one of his guards because he was a relative of former president Joseph Momoh's wife.

Journalists at *The Democrat* said Criminal Investigation Division officers obtained an advance copy of the news story and a search warrant before arriving at the newspaper's offices to arrest Foray. They drove Foray to police headquarters, where he was interrogated by police inspector general Keith Biddle. Biddle pressured the editor to reveal his sources for the article, but Foray refused on professional grounds. Police released the journalist four hours later.

SEPTEMBER 25

David Tam Baryoh, Center for Media, Education and Technology
THREATENED
Jonathan Leigh, *Independent Observer*
THREATENED
Paul Kamara, *For di People*
THREATENED
Chernor Ojuko Sesay, *The Pool*
THREATENED
Philip Neville, *Standard Times*
THREATENED
Richie Olu Gordon, *Peep*
THREATENED
Pios Foray, *The Democrat*
THREATENED

Seven local journalists, all longtime critics of the government, received identical anonymous death threats.

The seven journalists included: Baryoh, head of the Center for Media, Education, and Technology; Leigh, editor of the *Independent Observer*; Kamara, founding editor of *For di People*; Sesay of *The Pool*; Neville of *Standard Times*; Gordon of *Peep*; and Foray of *The Democrat*.

CPJ obtained a copy of one letter, postmarked September 14 and signed by an otherwise unidentified "Danger

Squad." Titled, "Warning: Journalists' Hit List," the document named all seven journalists. "All must die before elections, all these journalists are enemies of the state," it said.

CPJ sources in Freetown believe that the journalists were threatened for criticizing the government's decision to postpone presidential and parliamentary elections. The elections were scheduled for December 2001 but have now been put off until May 2002.

In a press release issued on September 22, the seven journalists said they reported the matter to the deputy inspector general of police. The release added: "We wish to believe that unlike other police investigations in the country, this one [will] not die a natural death."

In early October, the Sierra Leonean government issued a press statement denying any involvement in the letters. Authorities also accused the seven journalists of attempting to win international sympathy by publicizing unsubstantiated news of threats against them.

SOMALIA

February 21

Abdishakur Yusuf, *War Ogaal*
IMPRISONED

Yusuf, editor of the weekly *War Ogaal*, was arrested in Bosaso, in Somalia's self-declared autonomous Puntland region, after the newspaper reported that two alleged lesbians had been sentenced to death for unnatural behavior.

According to the United Nations Integrated Regional Information

Network, Yusuf was released on April 1 and was considering suing local authorities for unlawful detention. The newspaper, which ceased publication during Yusuf's incarceration, hit newsstands again around April 7.

May 19

Bashir Mohamed Abdi, free-lancer
IMPRISONED

Free-lance journalist Abdi was arrested and detained in the Bay Region capital, Baidoa, by members of the Rahanwein Resistance Army (RRA), a militia that controls both the Bay and Bikol regions of Somalia.

Sources at HornAfrik Radio and TV in Mogadishu told CPJ that the RRA had accused Abdi several times of sending information to local newspapers and radio stations without the army's knowledge. The journalist was released on May 26.

August 27

Bile Mahmud Qabowsade, *Yool*
HARASSED
Muhammad Sa'id Kashawito, *Sooyal*
HARASSED

Police in the self-declared autonomous region of Puntland arrested Qabowsale, editor of the private newspaper *Yool*, and Kashawito, editor of the private newspaper *Sooyal*, for allegedly "publishing false information." They were released more than 24 hours later.

The editors were arrested in Bosaso, the commercial capital of Puntland, after both papers ran a story about a woman who had been raped by burglars.

A local prosecutor apparently

ordered the arrests on the grounds that the story had damaged the reputation of his district. While in custody, the two editors were asked to run retractions. Both stood by their story.

Qabowsade also claimed that several bullets were fired at his car, which was damaged, but that no one was hurt. He and Kashawito are now considering legal action against the regional administration.

At year's end, CPJ was unable to verify whether the editors had proceeded with the lawsuit. This was because the U.S. government had severed telephone and e-mail communications to Somalia as part of its global war on terrorism.

SOUTH AFRICA

MAY 4

Benny Gool, *Cape Times*
LEGAL ACTION
Arie Roussouw, *Die Burger*
LEGAL ACTION
Christo Lötter, *Die Burger*
LEGAL ACTION

Gool, a photographer for the daily *Cape Times*, was issued a second subpoena to testify in the murder trial of members of the vigilante group People Against Gangsterism And Drugs (PAGAD).

Gool was one of several Cape Town journalists, including Roussouw and Lötter, who witnessed the 1996 murder of Rashaad Staggie, a Cape Town drug dealer, by PAGAD militants. Gool's pictures of the murder were widely published.

An earlier subpoena was withdrawn after *Cape Times* management reached

an agreement with the state attorney's office. Gool refused to testify after receiving the second subpoena, arguing that as a journalist he should not be seen to take sides in the case. Gool also claimed that his life would be in danger if he took the stand.

Since May 1998, seven witnesses in PAGAD-related cases have been murdered, according to the Freedom of Expression Institute in Johannesburg.

The Directorate of Public Prosecution threatened to jail Gool for up to two years. On May 15, however, a judge in Cape Town refused to issue a warrant for his arrest.

On June 21, Lötter and Roussouw moved successfully to have the subpoenas set aside.

Gool's subpoena violated an agreement between the South African National Editors' Forum, the Department of Justice, and the Department of Safety and Security, under which authorities agreed not to force journalists to testify without prior consultation.

However, Section 205 of the Criminal Procedure Act states, "A magistrate may, upon the request of the Attorney-General, require the attendance before him or any other magistrate, for examination by the attorney-general or a public prosecutor... of any person who is likely to give material or relevant information as to any alleged offence."

JUNE 13

All media
CENSORED

Public Prosecutor Selby Baqwa banned all press coverage of court hearings about a questionable US$6.3 million arms procurement deal by the South African government.

Baqwa's office was investigating allegations of wrongdoing in the awarding of arms contracts to Swedish, German, British, French, and Italian manufacturers.

Baqwa cited Section 118(a) of the Defense Act of 1957, which requires that media outlets obtain the minister of defense's permission to publish information regarding certain aspects of the Defense Force.

The ruling notably affected the publicly funded South Africa Broadcasting Corporation and the private station E-TV, both of which have sued the government over the constitutionality of Section 118(a). Meanwhile, the South African Freedom of Expression Institute called the ban unacceptable.

Baqwa also cited Section 11 of the Armaments Development and Production Act of 1968, which prohibits unwarranted disclosure of information relating to the acquisition of weapons by the government. The public prosecutor further expressed concerns that news cameras in the courtroom might intimidate witnesses and prevent them from testifying to the full extent of their knowledge.

SWAZILAND

MAY 4

The Guardian
LEGAL ACTION
The Nation
LEGAL ACTION

The government announced that all newspapers that had not been registered under the Books and Newspapers Act of 1963 would be closed.

Any publication that was not registered but had been in existence for more than five years would have two weeks to register. All others would have to close down completely and then apply for registration.

Also on May 4, the independent newspaper *The Guardian*, which started as an online publication in 2000 and launched as a print newspaper the following year, received a hand-delivered letter from the government stating that the publication was not registered and would have to cease production immediately. According to *Guardian* management, however, the paper had obtained a publication license and had deposited a bond with a bank.

That same day, police impounded all copies of *The Guardian* at the South African border (the paper is printed in Middleburg, South Africa.) The copies were transported to police headquarters in Mbabane.

Guardian lawyers filed an urgent application with Chief Justice Stanley Sapire seeking the release of the impounded papers and an injunction against the police to stop them from confiscating any further copies.

Sapire reserved judgment until early Saturday morning. Attorney General Phesheya Dlamini then banned both *The Guardian* and the independent monthly *The Nation*. Dlamini invoked Section 3 of the Proscribed Publications Act of 1968, which gives the attorney general authority to ban publications that do not conform to "Swazi morality and ideals."

Both *The Guardian* and *The Nation* have been outspoken in their criticism of the monarchy, particularly King Mswati III, who rules his kingdom by decree. On May 2, Thulani Mthethwa, editor of the Guardian, was picked up by police from his office, driven to police headquarters, and questioned about his paper's coverage of the royal family (see May 2 case).

On May 18, the ban on *The Nation* was lifted after a Mbabane court ruled the ban unconstitutional. The court also ordered the government to cover the newspaper's legal costs.

On May 22, Swazi police confiscated more than 5,000 copies of *The Nation* from the publication's premises and from retail stores in Manzini and Mbabane, Swaziland's two main cities.

On May 23, the two newspapers were again banned through a legal notice in which Dlamini stated that both were operating illegally and were "prejudicial to the interests of public order."

On Friday June 1, the ban on *The Nation* was lifted after an informal meeting between the attorney general and a senior representative of *The Nation*. According to *The Nation*, Dlamini did not request concessions from the publication and seemed to be acting out of embarrassment at the negative publicity generated by the government's campaign against the independent press.

The Guardian, meanwhile, won its first legal round against the government when Chief Justice Sapire ordered the state to file an affidavit explaining why the publication had been proscribed and why the legal notice banning the publication should not be set aside.

On June 7, Sapire ruled that the government's affidavit was not convincing. By then, *The Guardian* had been out of circulation for two months, although the Internet version, which was unaffected by the ban, continued to appear.

On August 31, High Court judge J. Annandale declared Dlamini's notice "invalid," allowing *The Guardian* to resume publication. In early November, the government appealed the ruling. The dispute remained unresolved at year's end.

OCTOBER 19

Hulasizwe Mkhabela, *Times of Swaziland*
ATTACKED

Mkhabela, a photographer at the *Times of Swaziland*, was assaulted and beaten by police officers in Manzini, Swaziland's largest town. The journalist was covering a press conference held by leaders of the Federation of Trade Unions and the outlawed Democratic Alliance (SDA).

Mkhabela was attacked after he took pictures of the officers' heavy-handed treatment of reporters at the scene. Many journalists were threatened by officers, while others were forcibly dragged out of the conference hall. Mkhabela was beaten with a stick before he managed to escape.

Political parties are illegal in Swaziland. One of the country's leading reformist politicians, SDA head Mario Masuku, was arrested and jailed earlier in the month on sedition charges. Security forces often harass journalists covering the SDA and other opposition groups.

Mkabela filed a formal complaint against the police, but the case remained unresolved at year's end.

TANZANIA

JULY 24

Tafrani
CENSORED
Chachandu
CENSORED
Mizengwe
CENSORED
Maraha
CENSORED
Cheko
CENSORED
Zungu
CENSORED
Kombora
CENSORED
Mama Huruma
CENSORED
Kula Vitu
CENSORED
Uroda kwa Foleni
CENSORED
Simulizi Kutoka Chumbani
CENSORED
Penzi Kikohozi
CENSORED

Tanzanian officials banned nine Swahili-language weeklies and suspended three tabloids for allegedly thwarting the government's HIV-AIDS prevention program by publishing reports and photographs deemed by authorities to be "contrary to national ethics and encourage[d] promiscuous behaviour."

On July 27, the Dar-es-Salam newspaper *The Guardian* quoted Minister of State for Information and

Policy Omar Ramadhan Mapuri as saying that the government remained committed to press freedom, but that it would not hesitate to ban or suspend publications that violated rules and regulations pertaining to public safety or the national interest.

"Publishing pictures of half-naked persons seen making love promotes amorous behaviour and frustrates the move by the government and the society to fight against the killer disease AIDS," the minister explained.

The weekly tabloids *Cheko*, accused of relentlessly publishing pictures of semi-nude women, and *Zungu* were suspended for six months. Another tabloid, *Kombora*, was banned for one year. Other outlawed publications included *Mama Huruma*, *Tafrani*, *Chachandu*, *Mizengwe*, *Maraha*, *Kula Vitu*, *Penzi Kikohozi*, *Uroda kwa Foleni*, and *Simulizi Kutoka Chumbani*.

All 12 publications remained banned at year's end.

AUGUST 22

Erick Nampesya, BBC
HARASSED
Dismas Ayuke, *Majira*
HARASSED
Richard Mgamba, *The East African*
HARASSED

Three journalists were arrested in the village of Nyamongo, allegedly on the orders of Tarime district commissioner Pascal Mabiti.

The three journalists were Nampesya, local correspondent for the BBC; Ayuke, a reporter with the Kiswahili-language daily paper *Majira*; and Mugamba, a reporter with the weekly *East African*.

The journalists had traveled to Tarime District in the Mara Region to investigate reports that 50 victims of ethnic clashes had secretly been buried in a mass grave. The district has seen ongoing strife between two ethnic clans, fueled by disputes over land boundaries, access to gold mines, and the cultivation of marijuana.

Mabiti confirmed the arrests but denied that he had ordered them.

On August 27, Mwanza Press Club chairman Abubakar Karsan said police had confirmed the arrests but had declined to specify charges or provide additional details.

The journalists were detained for two days and accused of "entering a restricted area." According to sources in Tanzania, district commissioners have the power to restrict access to areas under their jurisdiction, and Mabiti had previously forbidden people from visiting the conflict areas without his permission. The journalists were never charged, and no further action had been taken as of the end of December.

AUGUST 30

Saidi Msonda, *Nipashe*
HARASSED
Athumani Hamisi, *Nipashe*
HARASSED
Cassian Malima, *Mtanzania*
HARASSED
Florian Kaijage, DTV
HARASSED
Hussein Idd, DTV
HARASSED
Deus Ngowi, *Mwananchi*
HARASSED

George Marato, Independent Television (ITV)
HARASSED
Hamad Kitumbo, ITV
HARASSED
Samson Chacha, *Mwananchi*
HARASSED

Nine Tanzanian journalists were arrested on their way to the village of Kubiterere, where they were reporting on clashes between the Waanchari and Walyanchoka clans in the Mara region.

The journalists wanted to verify unconfirmed reports about the extent of the violence, which local residents claimed had killed several people, driven thousands of others into exile in Kenya, and destroyed more than 400 homes.

The journalists were held for five hours and then released.

TOGO

JANUARY 13

Jeunesse Espoir Radio
CENSORED

Soldiers sent by the local prefecture sealed the premises of Jeunesse Espoir Radio, a low-wattage radio station owned by the Catholic Church, after it announced that a memorial mass would be held for Sylanus Olympio, the country's first president, who was killed in a coup on January 13, 1963.

President Gnassingbe Eyadema led the coup and seized power for himself in 1967.

Jeunesse Espoir Radio is owned by the Mission of Tabligbo and based in the Diocese of Aneho in southern Togo. The station remained closed at year's end, and it appeared unlikely that it would reopen.

MARCH 27

Le Regard
CENSORED

Police raided newsstands in the Togolese capital, Lomé, and seized more than 3,000 copies of the pro-opposition weekly *Le Regard*, according to the paper's publisher. The seizure apparently resulted from an article alleging that the Togolese government had declined the European Union's offer to help fund legislative elections scheduled for October.

Interior Minister General Sizing Walla said the seizure of *Le Regard* was justified by the country's new press laws, a collection of vague and often contradictory statutes that empower his ministry to ban or seize any publication whose content it finds objectionable.

MAY 23

Lucien Messan, Le Combat du Peuple
IMPRISONED, LEGAL ACTION

Messan, editor of the independent weekly *Le Combat du Peuple* and one of Togo's most senior journalists, presented himself at a Lomé police station after receiving a summons.

Police told Messan that Interior Minister General Sizing Walla was charging him with fraud and then transferred the journalist to Lomé civil prison, where he was detained pending trial.

Messan mistakenly used an incorrect title when he signed a statement from the Togolese Private Press Publishers Association to the United Nations denouncing Prime Minister Agbeyome Kodjo's false statements about the Togolese private press to the United

Nations. Messan identified himself as "publication director" of *Le Combat du Peuple* rather than as "editor-in-chief."

Due to an earlier conviction relating to his work, Messan is legally barred from holding the title of "director," a position his son now occupies at the paper.

On June 5, Messan was convicted of fraud and sentenced to 18 months in prison, with six months suspended. It is widely believed that Messan's conviction came in reprisal for his critical reporting on the ruling Rassemblement du Peuple Togolais party and was meant to intimidate the press during the run-up to October parliamentary elections.

To protest Messan's conviction, 13 independent Togolese newspapers stopped publishing from June 12-15, according to local sources. The editorial staff of two government newspapers also called for a presidential pardon in the case.

President Eyadéma subsequently pardoned Messan, who was released from prison on October 28.

OCTOBER 13

Alphonse Nevame Klu, Nouvel Echo
IMPRISONED

Klu, director of the private weekly *Nouvel Echo*, was detained and placed in police custody after he responded to a summons from the Ministry of the Interior.

Klu's detention stemmed from an article in *Nouvel Echo* alleging that a government official was hiding several billion CFA francs in his basement. The police accused Klu of "distributing false news" and demanded that he reveal his sources.

During his detention, the journalist allegedly admitted that the article was based on unconfirmed rumors. At the behest of the minister of the interior, Klu then published a retraction of the story, which was also broadcast on public radio and television.

Local journalists suspected that authorities wrote Klu's retraction for him, and that he was given the choice between signing it or remaining in jail.

On October 26, Klu was transferred to a civil prison in the capital, Lomé, where he was released on October 30. No formal charges were brought against him.

OCTOBER 29

Abdoul-Ganiou Bawa, *Echos d'Afrique*
HARASSED
Rigobert Bassadou, *Echos d'Afrique*
HARASSED

Bawa and Bassadou, publisher and editor, respectively, of the private weekly *Echos d'Afrique*, were arrested and jailed in the Togolese capital, Lomé.

Police accused them of printing "false news" that "undermined the honor and dignity" of the police chief in the town of Dankpen.

A September 26 *Echos d'Afrique* article reported that the official in question had been bribed 1,130,000 CFA francs (US$1,520) to ignore the illegal sale of teak wood originally destined for the restoration of a town bridge. The weekly also asked Togo's state-appointed Anti-Corruption Commission to probe the accusation.

Bassadou was released the next day. Bawa was released on November 2. The charges against them were dropped.

Motion d'Information
CENSORED

Togolese police seized most copies of the October 29 issue of the pro-opposition weekly *Motion d'Information*, which contained an article reporting on graft allegations against members of President Gnassingbé Eyadéma's regime.

The paper estimated that the Eyadéma administration had stolen more than 1 billion CFA francs (about US$1.36 million), citing recent findings by the country's Anti-Corruption Commission.

Interior Ministry officials justified the seizure under a legal provision added to the country's Press Code in January 2000.

NOVEMBER 29

Radio Victoire
CENSORED

Togo's High Authority for Audiovisual Communications (HAAC) ordered the private station Radio Victoire, which is based in the capital, Lomé, to suspend its two most popular political shows, "Revue de Presse" (Press Review) and "Vice-Versa," until further notice.

In a letter to Radio Victoire, the HAAC claimed that both programs had aired "impassioned and defamatory statements that discredit Togo's constitutional and administrative authorities."

Journalists at Radio Victoire attributed the move to their reports on President Gnassingbé Eyadema's latest trip to France, where he had lied about Togo's disastrous human rights situation when asked about it.

The two programs remained off the air at year's end.

DECEMBER 4

Le Regard
CENSORED

On the orders of the interior minister, authorities seized all copies of that week's edition of *Le Regard*, an independent weekly with close ties to the Togolese opposition.

The seizure likely resulted from an article about the December 1991 putsch that overthrew the transitional government of Prime Minister Joseph Koffigoh and put President Gnassingbé Eyadéma back in power.

The article, which originally ran in 1996 and was reprinted in the seized edition, included eyewitness testimony of the events from one of Koffigoh's guards.

The Interior Ministry provided no justification for the seizure.

UGANDA

JUNE 15

Amlan Tumusime, Radio Hoima FM
ATTACKED

Tumusime, deputy news editor for Radio Hoima FM, was assaulted by Matayo Kyaligonza, a parliamentary candidate in the constituency of Buhaguzi, Hoima District. The assault was meant to preempt the broadcast of a critical news report about Kyaligonza.

The report concerned the disruption of a rally held in the village of Kirisha for Kyaligonza's political opponent, Tom Kyabulwenda. A group of soldiers who backed Kyaligonza, led by a

Lieutenant Colonel Kaganda, allegedly dispersed the crowd in the presence of police officers.

As Tumusime was about to air the report, Kyaligonza and a group of soldiers entered the studio office and warned him not to broadcast the story. When Tumusime refused, Kyaligonza struck him in the head and chest. Sources in Kampala say that Tumusime was later taken to a private clinic and treated for his injuries.

According to the independent *Monitor* newspaper, Kyaligonza claimed that he was not in Hoima District on Friday. But police reports confirmed both the disruption of the rally and the assault on Tumusime.

The government-owned daily *The New Vision* reported that Kyaligonza, who is the current Buhaguzi MP and a former army brigadier, is known for his short fuse. Last March, *The New Vision* reported that he assaulted Dr. Christine Mwebesa, the MP for Kabale, on the floor of Parliament when she disagreed with his position on the election of district women representatives.

Mwebesa apparently fought back, and the two exchanged blows for two minutes. Later, both MPs claimed that the argument amounted only to name-calling and finger-pointing.

SEPTEMBER 27

Dr. Abdul Ndifuna, Thriller publications
LEGAL ACTION

Ndifuna, director of Thriller Publications Limited, was arrested in Kampala and charged with trafficking obscene publications. Ndifuna denied the charges and was released on a 150,000 shilling bond (US$86), with a 300,000 shilling surety (US$172).

The Buganda Road Court prosecutor, Rachael Wandeka, said Ndifuna's publication, Thriller, had published pornographic pictures and writings on several occasions, thus allegedly corrupting the morals of the country. Ndifuna pleaded guilty to the charges and voluntarily closed the publication.

OCTOBER 2

Red Pepper
`HARASSED, LEGAL ACTION, CENSORED`
Richard Tusiime, *Red Pepper*
`LEGAL ACTION`
James Mujuni, *Red Pepper*
`LEGAL ACTION`
Martin Mpoya, *Red Pepper*
`LEGAL ACTION`
John Musinguzi, *Red Pepper*
`HARASSED`
Herbert Mwesigwa, *Red Pepper*
`HARASSED`
Irene Kiconco, *Red Pepper*
`HARASSED`
Fatuma Nakaiza, *Red Pepper*
`HARASSED`
Maureen Karamagi, *Red Pepper*
`HARASSED`
Carol Tushabe, *Red Pepper*
`HARASSED`
Arinaitwe Rugyendo, *Red Pepper*
`HARASSED`
Amon Turyamubona, *Red Pepper*
`HARASSED`

Police raided the offices of the Kampala-based tabloid newspaper *Red Pepper* and held editor Tusiime and eight other staff members for questioning. Staff writers Musinguzi and Mwesigwa and student interns Kiconco, Nakaiza, Karamagi, and Tushabe were questioned and released.

Tusiime, business manager Mujuni, and circulation manager Mpoya were taken to the Buganda Road Court and charged with six counts of "publishing, possessing and trafficking obscene material for trade purposes with intent to corrupt public morals." The charges carry a maximum two year sentence.

Police and Criminal Investigation Department (CID) officers also confiscated photographs and 24 back copies of the publication.

The charges stemmed from the magazine's September 21 cover, which caused considerable public outrage by featuring a photograph of teenagers apparently having sexual intercourse on a beach during a school outing.

Tusiime, Mujuni, and Mpoya were released on separate cash bails of 250,000 shillings (US$143) and separate noncash bonds of 2 million shillings (US$1,142). They were also required to report to CID headquarters every week until their court hearing on November 16.

On October 20, police arrested *Red Pepper* deputy editor Rugyendo and photographer Turyamubona on the same charges. They were released on a bond of 250,000 shillings(US$143), with a noncash bail of 200,000 shillings (US$114).

At the November 16 hearing, the prosecution said it had not completed its investigations. The case was rescheduled for February 20. Meanwhile, *Red Pepper* continued to appear on newsstands.

At a court hearing on Friday, December 14, Tusiime was rearrested on new obscenity charges in connection with other provocative photographs *Red*

Pepper had run in subsequent issues. He spent the weekend in jail. The new charges were also scheduled to be heard on February 20.

Red Pepper was launched in June 2001 as a political magazine. However, the publication gradually incorporated more salacious fare.

OCTOBER 8

New Vision
ATTACKED
Orumuri
ATTACKED

During the morning of October 8, hundreds of students attacked and vandalized the Mbarara bureau offices of the government-owned daily *New Vision* and its sister Runyankole-language weekly *Orumuri*.

The students, all from Alliance High School in the southwestern town of Mbarara, were angered by a story in the latest edition of *Orumuri* titled "200 Students of Alliance Dismissed Because of Pregnancy."

During the riots, the students attacked news vendors and tore up their copies of *New Vision*, *Orumuri*, and *Bukedde*, a Kampala-based Luganda-language paper affiliated with *New Vision*, as well as other newspapers.

The students stormed the *New Vision* and *Orumuri* offices, shattering windowpanes, damaging office equipment, scattering files, and breaking the windows of a car belonging to the newspapers. The students also tried to storm the studios of Radio West, a private station that had covered the *Orumuri* story in one of its broadcasts.

Police later dispersed the rioters.

ZAMBIA

MAY 27

Radio Icengelo
ATTACKED

A fire destroyed parts of the Catholic Church–owned Radio Icengelo, consuming official documents, office equipment, and furniture, and disrupted the station's electricity supply. The station was back on the air two days later, on May 29.

Police investigations found that the fire was set deliberately. Radio Icengelo staffers suspect that the arson was in retaliation for Radio Icengelo's opposition to Zambian president Frederick Chiluba's bid for an unconstitutional third term.

The fire followed a number of recent attacks on Father Vas Miha, a member of the radio station's administration; the stoning of another Radio Icengelo administrator, Father Daka, by government cadres who surrounded his residence; and repeated telephone threats to "silence the radio station."

JULY 9

Ernest Mwape, *The Post*
HARASSED

Mwape, a free-lance journalist and correspondent for *The Post* newspaper, was arrested on July 9 and charged with criminal libel by police in Mpika, a town in the northern province of Zambia.

His arrest stemmed from a story in the June 6 edition of *The Post*, in which Mwape reported that Mpika district administrator (DA) Mulenga Sapuni had reprimanded Mpika police chief Boaz Njolomba for failing to provide him with adequate police protection during a riot by secondary school students, resulting in extensive damage to Sapuni's house and car.

According to Mwape's article, Sapuni further criticized the police for providing security protection for the residence of the district education officer (DEO) home, even though the position of DEO is junior to that of DA.

On June 22, Mwape was picked up for questioning about the article and warned that he would be arrested after the police finished investigating. The police demanded that Mwape either apologize for the article or issue a retraction, both of which he refused to do.

Meanwhile, Njolamba denied that the events described in the article had ever taken place.

When the Zambia Independent Media Association (ZIMA) telephoned Njolamba to protest Mwape's harassment, the officer claimed that Mwape had defamed the police, justifying a criminal libel charge.

According to the police, Mwape was arrested on July 9 and released on his own recognizance that same day. On July 12, all charges against him were dropped.

According to ZIMA, no charges were ever officially filed against Mwape. The police could not have taken the matter to court because they never obtained permission to prosecute from the Director of Public Prosecutions, as required by law. In short, the charges had no legal merit.

JULY 25

Bivan Saluseki, *The Post*
LEGAL ACTION
Amos Malupenga, *The Post*
LEGAL ACTION
Fred M'Membe, *The Post*
LEGAL ACTION

Saluseki, a reporter at the independent newspaper *The Post*, was charged with defaming the president after a July 16th story quoted opposition politician and former minister of labor Edith Nawakwi as saying that "the president allowed ministers to steal and then shared with them."

The piece was headlined, "Chiluba is a thief, charges Nawakwi."

Police summoned Saluseki, held him for three hours, and accused him of "defaming the president."

On July 19, police visited *The Post* offices to ask Saluseki, deputy news editor Amos Malupenga, and editor Fred M'Membe to report to the police station to answer charges stemming from Saluseki's article. M'Membe refused to cooperate, but Malupenga went to the station and recorded a statement.

On August 22, Saluseki, Nawakwi, and M'Membe were formally indicted on charges of defaming the president, which carries a maximum penalty of three years in jail. All three pleaded not guilty. The trial was set to commence on September 5 but was repeatedly postponed. The trial had not yet begun at press time.

AUGUST 2

Amos Malupenga, *The Post*
HARASSED

Police issued a "warn and caution" statement to Amos Malupenga, the deputy news editor of *The Post*, for an article in that day's edition in which he accused President Frederick Chiluba of having "stolen and shattered to pieces Zambia's dream." The article quoted critical statements about Chiluba from former deputy finance minister Newton Ng'uni, who was also "warned and cautioned."

On August 9, Zambia's director of public prosecutions, Mukelebai Mukelebai, ordered police to halt criminal proceedings against Malupenga and Ng'uni. Mukelebai found that Malupenga's article was not defamatory but merely expressed a "personal political opinion," Zambian sources said.

Malupenga had already been "warned and cautioned" two months earlier over an article quoting a former MMD official who criticized some of Chiluba's policies.

AUGUST 21

Fred M'membe, *The Post*
HARASSED, LEGAL ACTION

M'membe, editor-in-chief of the independent Zambian daily *The Post*, was arrested and charged with criminal defamation of the head of state, an offense under Article 69 of Zambia's Penal Code. He was released after posting bail.

The charges stemmed from an article and an editorial in the August 17 edition of *The Post*. Both alleged that President Frederick Chiluba was involved in a US$4 million graft scheme.

Dipak Patel, a member of the opposition party Forum for Democracy and Development (FDD) who was quoted in the article, was charged along with M'membe.

Police arrested and charged M'membe when he arrived at the Lusaka Central Police Station in response to a summons that his lawyer, Mutembo N'Chito, had received the previous day.

M'membe was accompanied by *Post* reporter Bivan Saluseki and FDD politician Edith Nawakwi, who had already been charged with defaming the president over a July *Post* article that also accused President Chiluba and members of his cabinet being involved in various graft schemes.

Police had originally arrested and charged M'membe on August 18, but a magistrate ordered the editor released a few hours later on a technicality.

Police went to M'membe's home seeking to re-arrest him that same evening, but he was out of town attending a family funeral, according to sources at *The Post*. Zambian sources said police fired shots in the vicinity of the editor's house in order to frighten his children.

M'membe appeared in court on August 22 in connection with the charges against Saluseki and Nawakwi. He was indicted along with the other two on the same charges. CPJ issued an alert about the case on August 21.

More than 2,000 Zambians in Lusaka signed a petition protesting the legal action against M'membe and Patel. Another hearing was scheduled for January 2002, but no additional information on the case was available at press time.

Coalition 2001
CENSORED

The state-owned Zambian National

Broadcasting Corporation (ZNBC) prevented the broadcast of a live television program, titled "Defining Quality Leadership," which had been scheduled to air at 9:00 p.m. that evening.

The program, one of a 13-part series on election issues, was sponsored by Coalition 2001, a group of non-governmental organizations (NGOs). All 13 parts, scheduled to air in advance of the December 27 general elections, were to provide viewers with information on the electoral process and party platforms.

The August 27 show was to feature five panelists, including three NGO representatives and two politicians: Dr. Akashambatwa Mbikusita Lewanika, former president of the Agenda for Zambia Party and Love Mtesa, publicity secretary for the United Party for National Development.

According to Ngande Mwanajiti, chairman of the NGO Afronet, shortly before the program was to begin, ZNBC director of programs Mwansa Kapeya canceled the broadcast, saying that the show's topic should be changed. Kapeya later informed Mwanajiti that the program would air on September 1 only if the two politicians were excluded from the panel.

Mwanajiti and the coalition refused to exclude Lewanika and Mtesa, and the program was hastily canceled.

On September 3, the Lusaka High Court granted an injunction restraining ZNBC from interfering with the program, which finally aired on September 10.

NOVEMBER 10

Kunda Kunda, Radio Icengelo
ATTACKED

Radio Icengelo
ATTACKED

Radio announcer Kunda was attacked by a mob of nearly 30 ruling Movement for Multiparty Democracy (MMD) supporters during a live broadcast.

Kunda, an announcer at the Catholic Church-owned Radio Icengelo in the town of Kitwe, was interviewing Michael Sata, a former government minister and ex-national secretary of the MMD who is now president of the opposition Patriotic Front.

During the interview, Sata criticized then-president Frederick Chiluba's government. Following his remarks, a crowd of angry MMD supporters forced their way past a guard and into the station's studio, where they assaulted Kunda, Sata, and an associate. Police then arrived on the scene and ended the fracas.

During their assault, the MMD assailants damaged station equipment worth about 1.5 million kwachas (US$400), according to local sources. Sata and the other two victims were treated at a local hospital.

ZIMBABWE

JANUARY 10

Tsvangirai Mukwazhi, *The Daily News*
HARASSED

Mukhwazi, a photographer with the independent, Harare-based *Daily News,* was accosted by prison and police officers outside the Norton Magistrate's Court. At the time of the incident, Mukhwazi was attempting to photograph Anges Rusike, a leader of the government-sponsored movement to take over Zimbabwe's white-owned farms.

The officers grabbed Mukhwazhi's camera and exposed the film after he refused to surrender the camera. They also threatened to arrest him. Norton court magistrate Elizabeth Chaponda immediately criticized the officers, saying that she would not tolerate such "lawlessness."

Mukwazhi filed a complaint with the police. On February 14, three of the prison officers who had assaulted him were convicted of malicious injury to property and ordered to either replace the film they destroyed or spend 20 days in prison.

JANUARY 23

Julius Zava, *Daily News*
`ATTACKED`
Daily News
`ATTACKED`

Daily News reporter Zava was attacked by supporters of the ruling Zimbabwe African National Union-Patriotic Front (ZANU-PF).

More than 500 ZANU-PF supporters marched on the offices of the independent paper *Daily News* to protest its coverage of the death of Laurent-Désiré Kabila, former president of the Democratic Republic of Congo (DRC).

The newspaper had claimed that Kabila's death would be good for Zimbabwe, arguing that the country had suffered economic damage by supporting Kabila in the DRC's civil war.

The protesters broke windows and then attacked Zava, whom they recognized as a *Daily News* journalist. Zava was kicked to the ground but eventually managed to free himself and flee.

JANUARY 26

Mark Chavunduka, *The Standard*
`HARASSED`

Chavunduka, editor of the independent weekly *Standard*, was summoned to police headquarters for questioning about an October 2000 story which reported that an opposition politician had filed a civil suit against President Robert Mugabe in the United States over state-sponsored violence during the 2000 parliamentary elections.

Chavunduka initially ignored the police requests, but finally presented himself on January 29. Police recorded his statement and told him he would be charged with criminal defamation.

At year's end, authorities had still not pursued the case.

JANUARY 28

Daily News
`ATTACKED`

Shortly after Information Minister Jonathan Moyo described the independent *Daily News* as a threat to national security, bombs exploded at its printing presses in the Zimbabwean capital, Harare.

On January 27, Moyo threatened to silence the paper for allegedly posing a security risk to the nation.

The next morning at around 1:30 a.m., armed men overpowered the six-man security detail at the *Daily News* printing press. Explosives were scattered inside the building; they detonated about 15 minutes later, causing material damage estimated by CPJ sources at US$2 million. No one was hurt in the blast.

The Authentic MDC, a previously unknown group, claimed responsibility for the bombing in a handwritten note found at the scene of the explosion, according to news reports. The note criticized the *Daily News* for siding with the "racist white minority" in the opposition Movement for Democratic Change (MDC).

CPJ protested the bomb attack in a January 29 letter to President Robert Mugabe, noting that the *Daily News* editorial offices were also bombed in April 2000.

JANUARY 29

The Herald
CENSORED

Angry youths attacked vendors selling the state-owned newspaper *The Herald* in the town of Chitungwiza. The youths were protesting a bomb attack against the printing press of the independent *Daily News* the day before (see January 28 case).

The protesters declared a de facto ban on *The Herald* and threatened to attack anyone who brought copies into the area.

Also in Chitungwiza, on January 27, a *Herald* distribution van driver was assaulted by more than 150 people believed to be supporters of the opposition Movement for Democratic Change. The rioters burned nearly 4,000 copies of the paper.

An unspecified number of copies of *The Herald* were also destroyed in nearby Karoi and Harare.

FEBRUARY 15

Mercedes Sayagues, *Mail and Guardian*
EXPELLED

Sayagues, Harare correspondent for the South African weekly *Mail and Guardian*, was ordered to leave the country within 24 hours, according *The Herald*, a government-owned newspaper. The decision to expel Sayagues came after authorities announced a clampdown on permits for foreign journalists working in Zimbabwe.

Officials said no extensions of work permits for foreign correspondents would be allowed until the newly created Department of Information and Publicity, which replaced the Ministry of Information, had developed a new system for accrediting journalists.

Authorities set no deadline for finalizing the new accreditation regime.

Sayagues is a citizen of Uruguay who had been working in Zimbabwe since 1992. Her last Temporary Employment Permit (TEP), the annual document allowing her to work in the country as a foreign correspondent, expired on December 31, 2000 but the government had given her an interim extension valid until February 26. On February 14, Sayagues left Harare on a visit to South Africa, where she learned from local news reports that Zimbabwean authorities had decided not to renew her work permit, and to expel her within 24 hours. She was never officially notified of this decision.

Sayagues had written extensively about corruption in the government, and had documented torture and human rights abuses perpetrated by the ruling ZANU-PF party of President Robert Mugabe.

In addition to the new rules freezing work permits for foreign journalists, Zimbabwean officials announced their intention to introduce measures banning foreign investment in the local media.

On Tuesday February 20, The Herald reported that the government had banned Sayagues and the BBC's Joseph Winter from ever entering Zimbabwe again. According to the report, the Chief Immigration Officer, Elasto Mugwadi confirmed that Sayagues and Winter were "prohibited immigrants" who had "compromised their positions" as journalists.

Mugwadi added that their organizations were free to send other people to fill their positions. This followed government allegations that Sayagues was working as a UNITA agent during her stay in Zimbabwe.

On July 16, Sayagues filed a legal challenge with the High Court of Zimbabwe, arguing that her deportation was illegal. But the case appeared to have stalled as of December 27, as Zimbabwe geared up for presidential election scheduled for March 2002.

APRIL 1

Pedzisai Ruhanya, *Daily News*
HARASSED

Ruhanya, a reporter for the independent, Harare-based *Daily News*, was barred from covering a meeting of the ruling Zimbabwe African National Union-Patriotic Front (ZANU-PF).

As Ruhanya entered the meeting, he was stopped by two self-described war veterans who recognized him as a *Daily News* reporter. They accused him of spying for the opposition Movement for Democratic Change party and for the National Constitutional Assembly, a coalition of civic groups.

The war veterans manhandled the

reporter and confiscated his press card. According to journalists at the *Daily News*, the veterans also tried to intimidate Ruhanya into resigning from the newspaper.

APRIL 3

Zimbabwe Independent
LEGAL ACTION

Jonathan Moyo, the minister of state for information and publicity, sought to have the *Zimbabwe Independent* barred from covering his upcoming trial on embezzlement charges brought by the Ford Foundation.

Moyo's complaint alleged that the *Independent*'s coverage had defamed him. The judge directed the newspaper to "show cause why it should not be stopped from publishing stories" about the lawsuit. The complaint cited *Independent* reporter Dumisani Muleya as the first respondent. The editor of the paper, Iden Wetherell, and its publishers are cited as the second and third respondents, respectively.

On April 17, Justice Moses Chinhengo dismissed the case after ruling that the *Independent* was within its rights to report on the fraud allegations pending against Moyo.

APRIL 4

Geoff Nyarota, *Daily News*
LEGAL ACTION
Sandra Nyaira, *Daily News*
LEGAL ACTION
Julius Zava, *Daily News*
LEGAL ACTION

Daily News editor Nyarota and two of his reporters, Nyaira and Zava, were charged with criminal defamation of

President Robert Mugabe and parliamentary speaker Emmerson Mnangagwa. All three journalists denied the charges in statements recorded at a police station in the capital, Harare.

The charges arose from *Daily News* stories, published in November and December 2000, that linked Mugabe and Mnangagwa to payments made by Air Harbour Technologies in order to secure a contract to build a new international airport in Harare.

The three journalists were charged under the Law and Order Maintenance Act. No trial date had been set as of December 31.

JUNE 6

"Talk to the Nation"
CENSORED

The weekly television chat show "Talk to the Nation" was banned after only three broadcasts because callers criticized President Robert Mugabe on the air.

Zimbabwe Broadcasting Corporation (ZBC) chairman Gideon Gono wrote to the show's sponsor saying that the live phone-in television program had been canceled for "policy" reasons. The program was sponsored by a pro-government civic organization, the National Development Assembly (NDA).

Independent journalists in Zimbabwe charge that ZBC managers pulled the plug on "Talk to the Nation" because callers had openly criticized the government and asked for President Mugabe's resignation. The cancellation came immediately after the program aired a heated exchange over Zimbabwe's economy between an opposition lawmaker and a member of Parliament from the ruling ZANU-PF party.

Callers also criticized the Zimbabwean government over the country's disastrous economic situation.

In a June 6 article in the independent *Daily News*, NDA official Kindness Paradza was quoted as saying, "I do not know the reason for the action, but the best person to ask is Jonathan Moyo."

Moyo, who was once a professor of political science and a frequent contributor to local and international publications, has been Zimbabwe's information minister since June 2000. In this capacity, he has frequently clashed with the country's small independent press. Critics allege that the order to cancel "Talk to the Nation" came from his office.

JUNE 12

Tsvangirai Mukwazhi, *Daily News*
HARASSED

Mukwazhi, a photographer for the independent, Harare-based *Daily News*, was arrested and taken to Harare's central police station, where he was charged with conduct likely to breach the peace.

At the time of his arrest, Mukwazhi was taking pictures of students protesting a government decision to increase enrollment fees for the next university term.

The police confiscated Mukwazhi's equipment and forced him to pay a fine. He was then released.

JULY 19

Patrick Mwale, *Daily News*
HARASSED

Muchaneta Manyengavana, *Financial Gazette*
HARASSED

Mwale, a reporter for the independent *Daily News*, and Manyengavana, a reporter for the independent weekly *Financial Gazette*, were ejected from a land resettlement meeting by Manicaland provincial governor Oppar Muchinguri.

The two journalists were sent to cover the meeting, which included government officials and so-called war veterans, in Mutare, the capital of Manicaland Province. When the journalists arrived, Muchinguri informed them that they needed to leave because government officials were going to discuss sensitive issues.

The two were apparently singled out as reporters from independent newspapers, since journalists from state media outlets such as the Zimbabwe Broadcasting Corporation, the Zimbabwe Inter Africa News Agency, and *The Herald* were allowed to stay.

According to the *Daily News*, as the journalists left the meeting, several war veterans approached them in a threatening manner. Muchinguri intervened immediately and ensured that the journalists were able to leave the building without further harassment.

Daily News
LEGAL ACTION

The independent *Daily News* was forbidden from publishing further reports on the assets and property of Ibbo Mandaza, editor of the *Zimbabwe Mirror*, an independent weekly that tends to support the government of President Robert Mugabe.

On July 6, the *Daily News* published a front-page story about Mandaza's vast land holdings, accompanied by an aerial photograph of property. The newspaper reported that Mandaza had refused to disclose how he was able to acquire the land.

According to Mandaza's lawyer, James Tomana, the *Daily News* story was tantamount to an invasion of his client's privacy. Tomana also said that his client was considering instituting defamation proceedings because the paper allegedly implied that Mandaza had acquired his properties by embezzling funds from the Southern Africa Regional Institute of Policy Studies, of which Mandaza is the executive director.

JULY 25

BBC
CENSORED

On July 25, the Department of Information and Publicity suspended the accreditation of all BBC correspondents in Zimbabwe.

In a letter to the BBC bureau chief in Johannesburg, Information Minister Jonathan Moyo said the suspension resulted from the BBC journalists' "deliberately unethical and unprofessional conduct" and their attempts to "give a false impression that there is no rule of law in Zimbabwe."

The suspension came in the wake of BBC reporter Rageh Omaar's coverage of the official opening of Parliament by President Robert Mugabe on July 24. Omaar reported that Mugabe "vowed to continue with the forcible acquisition of white farmlands."

In his letter, Moyo maintained that "those words were nowhere in the

President's speech," and that Mugabe had "made it clear that land would be acquired as it had been, in terms of the laws of Zimbabwe." In his letter Moyo stated, "There is a world of difference between 'forcible acquisition' and 'lawful acquisition.'"

Moyo's letter also alleged "unprofessional and unethical collusion" between the BBC and Iden Wetherell, the editor of the *Zimbabwe Independent*. In April, Moyo sued the *Zimbabwe Independent* and Wetherell in an attempt to prevent them from reporting on embezzlement charges filed against Moyo in Kenya by the Ford Foundation. The court ruled in favor of Wetherell and the newspaper.

The BBC stood by Omaar's story.

AUGUST 15

Geoff Nyarota, *Daily News*
LEGAL ACTION, HARASSED
John Gambanga, *Daily News*
LEGAL ACTION, HARASSED
Bill Saidi, *Daily News*
LEGAL ACTION, HARASSED
Sam Munyavi, *Daily News*
LEGAL ACTION, HARASSED

At 12:15 a.m., police arrested *Daily News* editor-in-chief Nyarota at his home in Harare. The police detained *Daily News* reporter Munyavi, editor Gambanga, and assistant editor Saidi. All four journalists were taken to the Central Police Station in Harare.

Nyarota and Saidi were charged with "publishing false information likely to cause alarm or despondency in the public" under Section 50, (2)(a) of the draconian Law and Order Maintenance Act (LOMA), according to CPJ sources at *The Daily News*. The charge carries a

maximum prison sentence of seven years.

The arrests of the *Daily News* journalists followed an article by Munyavi, published the day before, reporting that police vehicles had been used in the looting of white farms in Mhangura, a town in Zimbabwe's West Province. Officers from the Law and Order Division of the Harare police visited the newsroom at around 8 a.m. on August 14 to protest the story.

The four journalists were released on the evening of August 15 after their lawyers argued that the charges were unconstitutional.

The next day, the four journalists were called back to the police station. Nyarota was interrogated again. Police then charged all four journalists with "publishing subversive material" under Section 44 of LOMA.

On August 15, CPJ published an alert about the arrests. A CPJ delegation visited Harare from July 11 to 14 to assess press freedom conditions during the run-up to next year's general elections. The delegation, which included board member Clarence Page, deputy director Joel Simon, and Africa program coordinator Yves Sorokobi, met with dozens of journalists from various media.

The charges were still pending at year's end.

AUGUST 21

Wallace Chuma, *Zimbabwe Mirror*
HARASSED
Constantine Chimakure, *Zimbabwe Mirror*
HARASSED

On August 21, Harare police summoned news editor Wallace

Chuma and reporter Constantine Chimakure of the independent weekly *Zimbabwe Mirror* to record a "warn and caution" statement.

Authorities questioned the two journalists for about an hour in connection with an August 17 article titled "War Vets Forced Us to Loot— Farm Workers." The article reported on complaints by agricultural workers in Mashonaland West Province that police were helping so-called independence war veterans to orchestrate attacks on local farms.

Police told Chuma and Chimakure that they faced charges of "publishing materials likely to cause alarm and despondency" under the draconian Law and Order Maintenance Act.

However, the charges were not pursued. Zimbabwean sources speculated that *Mirror* editor Ibbo Mandaza may have used his connections with government officials to get the charges dropped.

AUGUST 22

Mark Chavunduka, *The Standard*
HARASSED

Chavunduka, editor of the independent weekly *The Standard*, was called into Harare Central Police Station to record a so-called warn and caution statement. According to sources at *The Standard*, the summons came in response to an August 19 *Standard* article that was reprinted from the London-based *Sunday Times*.

The story, titled "Paranoid Mugabe Dines With Ghost," reported that President Robert Mugabe felt haunted by the ghost of a leader in the independence movement who died in a suspicious car accident more than 20 years ago. According to the article, many Zimbabweans believe that Mugabe was linked to the death of Josiah Tongogara, a charismatic guerrilla leader who was widely expected to win the 1980 presidential election.

Police told Chavunduka, who was accompanied to the station by *Standard* lawyer Innocent Chagonda, that he faced criminal defamation charges and would be summoned to court if the attorney general decided to prosecute. Police declined to name the complainant but stated categorically that it was neither President Robert Mugabe nor Information Minister Jonathan Moyo.

According to an article that appeared in *The Standard* on August 19, Chavunduka's name appeared, along with those of several other journalists, on a "hit list" compiled by the law and order section of the Zimbabwe Police and the Central Intelligence Organization ahead of the 2002 presidential election. Details surrounding the alleged hit list were murky, however, and CPJ was unable to verify its existence.

AUGUST 27

Mduduzi Mathuthu, *Daily News*
ATTACKED

Mathuthu, correspondent for the independent *Daily News* in the northern city of Bulawayo, was attacked by supporters of the ruling Zimbabwe African National Unity Patriotic Front (ZANU-PF).

Mathuthu was covering a confrontation between a local farmer and ZANU-PF supporters, including several so-called war veterans. When the

ZANU-PF contingent recognized the journalist, they began beating him with clubs and ax handles.

During the assault, Mathuthu was accused of writing negative stories about Zimbabwe's controversial policy of forcibly redistributing white-owned land to black farmers. Although police were present, they did not intervene.

Mathuthu managed to escape when several farmers came to his aid and surrounded him, allowing him to get to a car and drive away. He reported the incident to the police and later sought treatment for chest pains and a cut above his eye.

SEPTEMBER 8

Mduduzi Mathuthu, *Daily News*
`HARASSED`
Loughty Dube, *Zimbabwe Independent*
`HARASSED`

Mathuthu, a correspondent for the independent *Daily News*, and Dube, a reporter for the *Zimbabwe Independent*, were arrested by police in the northern city of Bulawayo and detained for an hour.

The two journalists had gone to Bulawayo Central Police Station to get information on the arrest of three bodyguards of David Coltart, an MP for the opposition Movement for Democratic Change. The bodyguards had been arrested for allegedly possessing a two-way radio without a proper license.

The journalists arrived at the police station in the evening and immediately asked to speak to the chief inspector. According to Zimbabwean sources, when the inspector met with the journalists, he accused them of

trespassing on private property and told them they were under arrest.

Police then confiscated the journalists' press cards in what local sources say was an attempt to curtail their coverage of the mayoral and ward elections. Officials later returned the press cards.

SEPTEMBER 17

Mduduzi Mathuthu, *Daily News*
`ATTACKED`
Collin Chiwanza, *Daily News*
`ATTACKED`
Urgina Mauluka, *Daily News*
`ATTACKED`

Reporters Mathuthu and Chiwanza and photographer Mauluka, all of the independent *Daily News*, and their driver were assaulted by so-called war veterans in Hwedza, a town southeast of the capital, Harare.

The three journalists went to a farm in Hwedza to cover the story of two war veterans who had recently died in clashes with white farmers. Near the farm, they were stopped at a checkpoint manned by war veterans.

In an attempt to avert trouble, Chiwanza told the men at the checkpoint that he and his colleagues worked for the state-owned *Herald*. Though all three reporters were allowed to enter the farm, they were soon asked for identification and recognized as reporters for the *Daily News*.

Several war veterans then converged on the journalists and their driver, accusing them of being British or opposition Movement for Democratic Change agents, and began beating them severely.

Though police were present at the

scene, a soldier from the Zimbabwean army who had been sent to protect the farm stopped the assault by threatening the assailants with his gun. The three journalists and the driver suffered from minor injuries. During the melee, the war veterans confiscated the reporters' equipment.

Sources in Harare said the *Daily News* journalists were apparently singled out, since journalists from the state-owned *Herald* newspaper and from the state-owned Zimbabwe Broadcasting Corporation were not harassed. Sources also reported that some of the state journalists and a number of war veterans arrived at the scene in government vehicles.

Police eventually returned the journalists' equipment, but not the money that had been in their wallets.

NOVEMBER 8

Geoff Nyarota, *The Daily News*
HARASSED, LEGAL ACTION
Wilf Mbanga, *The Daily News*
HARASSED, LEGAL ACTION

Shortly after 6:00 a.m., plainclothes police officers picked up Nyarota, editor of *The Daily News*, Zimbabwe's only independent daily newspaper, and Wilf Mbanga, the former chief executive officer of the Associated Newspapers of Zimbabwe (ANZ), the company that publishes the newspaper, from their homes in Harare and took them to the headquarters of the Criminal Investigation Department (CID).

Neither man was informed of the charges against him, local sources said.

The arrests apparently stemmed from a dispute regarding ANZ's legal registration forms. Authorities alleged that the company filed a fraudulent license application to the Zimbabwe Investment Center. The allegation was based on the fact that ANZ had listed its former company name as "Motley Investment," a nonexistent entity.

Sources at *The Daily News*, however, say the mistake was a clerical error made by the consulting company that filed the application on behalf of ANZ. The name of the former company should have been listed as "Motley Trading," in which Nyarota and Mbanga were the major shareholders.

Although the consultants issued documents confirming the error to the *Daily News*' lawyers, authorities continued to detain Nyarota and Mbanga.

Nyarota and Mbanga were also accused of contravening the terms of their license, which was allegedly for a weekly publication.

Though the newspaper's lawyers submitted an urgent application for their release, Nyarota and Mbanga spent the night in jail. The next morning, both men appeared before a judge and were charged with fraud. They were released on bail of 10,000 Zimbabwean dollars each (approximately US$187) and were due to appear in court again on November 28, at which time they were to surrender all of their travel documents.

The Media Institute of Southern Africa reported on November 19 that a Harare judge had dismissed the charges against Nyarota and Mbanga. According to sources at the *Daily News*, the bail requirements for Nyarota and Mbanga were withdrawn, and their bail money was refunded.

NOVEMBER 30

Cyrus Nhara, Artvak Productions
ATTACKED
The Daily News
ATTACKED
Financial Gazette
ATTACKED
The Zimbabwe Independent
ATTACKED

Nhara, a photographer for the local news agency Artvak Productions, was assaulted by a mob of pro-government demonstrators outside the Munhumutapa Building, which houses the president's office, in the capital, Harare.

The same assailants, many of whom appeared to be drunk, later attacked the offices of the independent *Daily News*, smashing windows and ripping up several hundred copies of the paper. They then proceeded to the building housing the private weekly *Financial Gazette* before ending their rampage at the weekly *Zimbabwe Independent*, whose facilities were also damaged.

Nhara was beaten with fists, bottles, and sticks. He sustained bruises on his face and only managed to escape by jumping on to a moving car. Attackers, who also stripped him of his shoes and glasses, destroyed his film of the demonstrations. ■

OVERVIEW: THE AMERICAS

by Marylene Smeets

AGAINST A BACKDROP OF TROUBLED ECONOMIES AND DEMOCRACIES, the Americas saw an increase in violent and verbal attacks against journalists during 2001.

The number of journalists murdered in the region has grown, with 11 killed for their work in 2001, compared to seven in 2000 and six in 1999. The violence is also occurring in more countries across the region. Notably, in Costa Rica—long considered one of Latin America's freest and most democratic countries—the assassination of Parmenio Medina Pérez was the first murder documented by CPJ in that country's recent history.

Medina's killing proved an anomaly in other ways: As the outspoken producer and host of a radio program in Costa Rica's capital, San José, Medina was the only Latin American journalist killed in a major city in 2001.

Since the late 1990s, CPJ research has shown that provincial journalists in Latin America face the greatest risks. In the past, high-profile journalists in large cities were usually targeted. Today, provincial journalists bear the brunt of killings and non-lethal violence. In Colombia's escalating civil conflict, the three journalists killed in reprisal for their work all came from the provinces, as did the three who were killed for their work in 2000.

The growth of grassroots and local press freedom organizations, which have brought threats against provincial journalists into the spotlight, may account for part of those findings. But vocal protests against murders of well-known journalists are widely deemed to have lessened the violence in large cities.

Although determined advocacy has raised the political cost of attacking journalists, some leaders did not hesitate to lash out against the media when confronted by falling popularity and rising socioeconomic woes. In Venezuela, President Hugo Chávez Frías referred to the Venezuelan press as "anti-social communications media" and publicly threatened to expel foreigners who criticize the country. Because his followers have often taken the president's words at face value, Chávez's anti-press rhetoric created a climate conducive to violent attacks on the media.

In Haiti, President Jean-Bertrand Aristide launched a "zero tolerance" anti-crime campaign in June, implying that street criminals caught red-handed could be summarily punished without trial. A deputy from the president's party later

Marylene Smeets is the Americas program coordinator at CPJ. **Sauro González Rodríguez** is CPJ's Americas program researcher; he did extensive research and writing for this section. Bogotá-based free-lance journalist **Michael Easterbrook** and **Trenton Daniel**, a former Reuters correspondent in Haiti and staff writer for *The Haitian Times* who is currently a New York-based journalist, also contributed to the report. **Cécile Hambye** helped in the research. **The Robert R. McCormick Tribune Foundation** provided substantial support toward CPJ's work in the Americas in 2001. **The Tinker Foundation** is supporting CPJ's campaign to eliminate criminal defamation in the Americas.

announced that the policy should be applied to Brignolle Lindor, news director of the private station Radio Echo 2000. Lindor had already received numerous threats from local authorities for inviting members of the opposition coalition to appear on his show. He was subsequently hacked to death by a machete-wielding mob of ruling-party supporters.

In violence-plagued Haiti, the year ended with an attempted coup that opposition parties maintain was a pretext to crush dissent. Hundreds of government supporters armed with machetes and guns accosted and threatened at least a dozen journalists. Aristide partisans attacked radio stations and vehicles belonging to private news organizations. As a result, at least 15 journalists left the country and as many as 40 went into hiding, according to international press reports.

Despite these daunting challenges, the Latin American press can pride itself in its effective advocacy for legal reform. Many proposals for legal reform presented by Latin American press groups concerned lack of access to government information, widely reported to be a major obstacle to reporting in the region.

The press association Sindicato de Periodistas del Paraguay, for instance, helped draft an access to information law after protests led to the repeal of a more limited government-supported version. And after protests caused the repeal of disastrous legislation in 2000, Panama passed an access to information law proposed by the international nongovernmental organization Transparency International.

Regional protections for freedom of expression also expanded in 2001. The Inter-American Court of Human Rights and the Inter-American Commission on Human Rights, both part of the Organization of American States, handed down rulings that demonstrated that freedom of expression has become a priority. For the first time in a press freedom case, the court issued a "provisional measure"—usually only handed down in cases of "extreme gravity...to avoid irreparable damage," according to inter-American law—ordering Costa Rican judges to stay a previous ruling on a defamation case while it moves through the Inter-American System.

Commission officials highlighted press freedom issues during a visit to Panama and received complaints from Argentina, Colombia, and Venezuela, among others. Journalists throughout the hemisphere seemed to realize that they could seek redress through the Inter-American System, rather than being subjugated to the repressive whims of their national courts.

However, some countries, such as Venezuela, have been reluctant to follow the system's orders. Moreover, criminal defamation suits remained a bane of journalists' work, sometimes despite the reform of defamation laws. Many officials still use any available legal means to stifle press criticism. The tendency in Latin America for protecting honor and reputation at all costs may take at least another generation to die out.

Despite the onerous criminal defamation provisions, only two journalists in the region were jailed at year's end. In the United States, free-lancer Vanessa

Leggett was imprisoned for refusing to turn over research materials about a 1997 murder. Leggett chose jail in order to protect the confidentiality of her sources. After spending five months in jail—reportedly longer than any other journalist in U.S. history—Leggett was freed on January 4, 2002. In Cuba, Bernardo Rogelio Arévalo Padrón remained in jail for insulting President Fidel Castro Ruz and other officials.

In general, government officials seem to have found that jailing journalists is simply too politically costly. Instead, they issued suspended prison sentences and ordered journalists to pay enormous damages. The situation is particularly egregious in Panama, where an estimated one-third of all journalists are currently facing criminal defamation suits.

Some governments and corporations retaliated against the press by doling out advertising in a discriminatory fashion, a tactic that was especially effective because of the economic recession. The potentially crippling threat of losing ad revenues prompted some media outlets to avoid exposing corporate and government wrongdoing.

The combination of a slowing economy and the often-disappointing performance of state institutions—many of which are rife with corruption—has led to a declining support for democracy in the region. According to the *Financial Times*, a study by the private, Santiago, Chile–based Corporación Latinobarómetro found that, "Latin Americans have more faith in the Roman Catholic Church, television, and the armed forces—in that order—than in their respective presidents, police, and judiciary."

While Latin American journalists have actively covered corruption, some are also involved in it. Complaints about corrupt reporters have been heard in countries across the continent; low salaries are often to blame.

The September 11 terrorist attacks on the United States had unexpected repercussions on the U.S. press, which is well protected legally and used to working with little government interference. U.S. media organizations had to push the government to provide access to information about the war on terrorism, while National Security Adviser Condoleezza Rice asked television executives to use caution when airing tapes of Osama bin Laden.

The U.S. influence was felt globally as well. U.S. secretary of state Colin Powell asked Qatar government officials to rein in the Qatar-based satellite television station Al-Jazeera because of what the United States saw as the station's anti-American bias. ■

ANTIGUA AND BARBUDA

THE FAMILY OF PRIME MINISTER LESTER B. BIRD has long dominated Antigua and Barbuda's broadcast media, but the outcome of a four-year court battle that forced Bird's government to allow a private radio station to broadcast has driven a wedge in the family's monopoly.

Winston and Samuel Derrick, editor and publisher, respectively, of *The Daily Observer*, intended to crack that monopoly in 1996 when they created the independent station Observer Radio. But the government shut it down the day after the station began broadcasting. After winning a November 2000 appeal from the Privy Council in the United Kingdom, which acts as the final appellate court for countries within the British Commonwealth, the Derrick brothers were finally able to open their station on April 15, 2001. Observer Radio, which airs many call-in shows, quickly became immensely popular; estimates say that 75 to 80 percent of the country's radio listeners tune in to the station.

The Derrick brothers reported significant government harassment. Samuel Derrick told CPJ that government officials often stop by the radio station to tell the brothers that their station will be closed. Recently, the government began broadcasting one of its shows on a frequency close to the one used by Observer Radio; since the government station has a more powerful transmitter, Observer Radio's signal is often disrupted. "They try to drown us out," Derrick remarked. "Other than publicize it, there's not much we can do."

State and Bird family–owned broadcast media are playing catch-up to Radio Observer, conducting their own talk shows and creating the opportunity for more criticism and dissent. Meanwhile, the opposition United Progressive Party obtained radio and television licenses this year, though it had not yet begun broadcasting at press time.

Print media, which have also suffered under the Bird government, won several decisive battles in 2001. In January, the Supreme Court of the Organization of Eastern Caribbean States lifted two injunctions against the weekly *Outlet*, according to the paper's publisher, Tim Hector. Under one of the injunctions, requested by Minister of Health and Home Affairs Sam Aymer, *Outlet* was barred from referring to any reports it had published about an embezzlement scandal involving the minister. *Outlet* was served the other injunction in the early 1990s after it reported on medical malpractice.

Justice was also served in the case of two top editors, Louis Daniel and Horace Helps, who were fired from the newspaper *The Antigua Sun* just before the 1999 poll that re-elected Prime Minister Bird. The paper, owned by a close associate of Bird's, R. Allen Stanford, fired the journalists when they staged a sick-out to protest heavy-handed editorial control. A court ordered Stanford to pay Daniel and Helps a total of 72,000 Eastern Caribbean Dollars (US$27,000). The owner appealed the ruling, but the journalists' lawyer, Harold Lovell, told CPJ that Stanford filed the appeal late, and the court refused to consider it. Stanford paid Daniel and Helps on August 3, according to Lovell.

ARGENTINA

WHILE ARGENTINA FELL DEEPER INTO ECONOMIC CRISIS DURING 2001, and President Fernando de la Rúa resigned in disgrace as a result, the media worked largely unhindered. But the worsening economy hurt advertising and sales, and the Supreme Court dealt damaging blows to press freedom.

2001 was Argentina's fourth year of recession, and the country saw widespread street protests and strikes against austerity measures aimed at erasing the country's budget deficit. The International Monetary Fund (IMF) provided a US$8 billion bailout in August, but by year's end, the fund withheld a US$1.26 billion loan installment. At press time, Argentina had defaulted on its foreign debts and had devalued its peso.

On May 1, Economy Minister Domingo Cavallo imposed a 21 percent value-added tax (VAT) on all media sales, according to Gabriel Matijas, manager of the publishers' association Asociación de Entidades Periodísticas Argentinas. Matijas told CPJ that before May 1, print media were only required to pay VAT on advertising revenues. Since the new tax would have bankrupted many media outlets—especially smaller ones in the provinces—the government halved the tax and allowed publishers to reduce their social security payments in an equal amount to what they paid in VAT taxes.

Few attacks on press freedom occurred in 2001, a fact attributable to Argentina's vibrant and combative media, which publicized attempted restrictions with gusto. Yet the press was powerless against the Supreme Court, which is stocked with supporters of former president Carlos Saúl Menem. On November 20, the Supreme Court threw out charges against Menem, who had been under house arrest since June on accusations of illegal arms trafficking with Ecuador and Croatia—a scandal that was uncovered by the media. In its widely criticized ruling, the court took the opportunity to warn other judges against the pressure of public opinion, "whether spontaneously formed or oriented by the media."

The Supreme Court handed Menem another victory on September 25 in a case against the newsmagazine *NOTICIAS*. The court ruled that the weekly had violated Menem's right to privacy by reporting on his extramarital relationship with a former schoolteacher. Besides requiring the newsmagazine to pay Menem 60,000 pesos (US$60,000), the Supreme Court ordered *NOTICIAS* to publish the judgment.

On November 15, Horacio Verbitsky and Eduardo Bertoni, secretary-general and legal adviser, respectively, of the Argentine press freedom organization PERIODISTAS, presented the *NOTICIAS* case to the Inter-American Commission on Human Rights (IACHR) in Washington, D.C. Accompanied by CPJ board member and *Chicago Tribune* columnist Clarence Page and World Press Freedom Committee executive director Marilyn Greene, Verbitsky and Bertoni presented a 68-page complaint to IACHR executive secretary Santiago A. Canton on behalf of PERIODISTAS and *NOTICIAS* asking the IACHR to suspend the verdict while the commission examines the case. At year's end, the commission was studying the case.

Verbitsky was in the United States to receive one of CPJ's 2001 International Press Freedom Awards for his pathbreaking reporting and his efforts to fight for a better legal framework for press freedom.

A bill designed to rid Argentine law of criminal defamation statutes was signed by then-president Adolfo Rodríguez Saá on December 27 and is currently awaiting congressional approval. After the IACHR negotiated a friendly settlement in 1999 between PERIODISTAS and the Argentine government relating to several criminal defamation cases, PERIODISTAS developed the legislation, which introduces and codifies the "actual malice" and neutral reporting standards.

Under the "actual malice" standards, first articulated by the U.S. Supreme Court in the 1964 case *New York Times Co. vs. Sullivan*, plaintiffs must prove not only that the published information is false, but also that journalists knew or should have known it was false at the time of publication. The neutral reporting standard, already accepted by the Argentine Supreme Court in a 1986 case, holds that plaintiffs may not sue journalists for accurately reproducing information from an explicitly mentioned source. While the new law only outlaws criminal defamation in the case of public figures, it provides significant additional protections for Argentine journalists.

On August 23, 2001, the Supreme Court confirmed its 1986 decision on neutral reporting standards. The ruling upheld a lower court decision rejecting former army major Arnaldo Luis Bruno's lawsuit against the daily *La Nación* over an article that linked him to the 1992 bombing of the Israeli embassy in Buenos Aires.

In the investigation into the 1999 murder of Ricardo Gangeme, publisher and editor of the weekly magazine *El Informador Chubutense*, three jailed suspects were released on September 21 because they had spent two years in prison without being brought to trial, according to Juan Carlos Rojas, deputy editor of *La Jornada*, a daily that Gangeme edited until 1998. No trial date had been set at year's end, Rojas said.

BOLIVIA

ON AUGUST 6, FORMER MILITARY DICTATOR HUGO BANZER, who was suffering from advanced cancer, resigned his post as president and handed over power to Vice President Jorge Quiroga Ramírez, who will head the government for the remainder of the five-year presidential term, which ends in August 2002.

Despite widespread social and political unrest, the Bolivian press did not face significant impediments to covering the news. Quiroga Ramírez's new government took no active steps to curtail press freedom.

Bolivia is a landlocked country with a poorly developed communications infrastructure. Nearly 40 percent of its 8.3 million inhabitants live in rural areas, according to World Bank data, making newspaper distribution difficult. However, local journalists say that high rates of poverty and illiteracy are the main reasons for low newspaper circulation. This renders the press vulnerable to pressure from a small pool of advertisers.

Media outlets that support the government benefit from generous state advertising, while opposition or critical media must survive on scanty private advertising. Some media outlets are bankrolled by politicians and businessmen who use them to advance their own interests. Bolivia's entrepreneurial class is small, and most media owners have close personal connections throughout the business community. As a result, journalists find it difficult to write about corporate malfeasance.

The Bolivian army, which has often wielded excessive force against landless peasants, coca growers, and miners protesting government policies, has occasionally cracked down on the media. On September 27, soldiers fired at six journalists who were covering coca growers' protests in Chapare, a tropical region in central Bolivia. The journalists, who intended to interview an army commander, were traveling down a road leading to a military camp when soldiers fired without warning. One of the journalists' guides was killed in the attack.

Juan Carlos Encinas, 39, a free-lance reporter in the small town of Catavi in La Paz Department, died on July 29 of wounds sustained while covering a fight between two mining cooperatives that were vying for control of a limestone quarry outside the town.

Investigative journalists often draw the ire of public officials. In August, Luis Roberto Landívar Roca, a parliamentary deputy from the small opposition party New Republican Force, launched a smear campaign against Carlos Mesa and Amalia Pando, of the television station PAT, who were covering a corruption scandal involving Landívar. He publicly accused the journalists of embezzlement and murder, respectively. In addition, he published the allegations in advertisements in several papers and funded the publication of a tract aimed at tarnishing Pando's image.

According to Bolivian journalist Roger Cortés Hurtado, authoritarian traditions and attitudes that still permeate government bureaucracy hinder reporting. With no legal obligation to release information to the public, government agencies remain secretive about issues of clear public interest, such as budgets and public finances.

Journalists in Bolivia must have a university degree in journalism and be registered in the National Registry of Journalists. Though enforcement is lax, penalties are potentially severe and include imprisonment. In 1985, the Inter-American Court of Human Rights in Costa Rica ruled that mandatory licensing of journalists violates the American Convention on Human Rights.

BRAZIL

SUSTAINED MEDIA COVERAGE OF CORRUPTION DURING 2001 helped increase pressure on powerful Congress members and other government officials, several of whom were forced to resign amid accusations of misconduct and embezzlement.

In February, the weekly *ISTOÉ* reported that taped conversations between federal prosecutors and Senator Antônio Carlos Magalhães, who was president of the Congress at the time, revealed that Magalhães knew how senators had voted in a June 2000 secret ballot to impeach Senator Luiz Estevão. Later, it emerged that Magalhães and Senator José Roberto Arruda, leader of President Fernando Henrique Cardoso's ruling coalition in the Senate, had acquired the secret voting records from an employee in the Senate's voting registry. In May, the two senators resigned before the Senate Ethics Committee could expel them for violating Congress' secret balloting system.

Also in May, Minister of National Integration Fernando Bezerra resigned after the weekly magazine *Veja* disclosed that a mining company in which he had invested received millions in public funds despite failing to meet contractual obligations with a government agency under his control. The press also gave sustained coverage to former Senate president Jader Barbalho, who resigned after the Supreme Federal Court (STF), the nation's highest court, lifted his parliamentary immunity and gave officials investigating corruption allegations access to his financial records.

In a troubling development, the judiciary increasingly used prior censorship under the guise of protecting privacy and honor. In one high-profile case in July, a judge banned the Rio de Janeiro daily *O Globo* from publishing transcripts of taped phone conversations that allegedly showed Rio de Janeiro State governor Anthony Garotinho authorizing a bribe. Other papers subsequently published the content of the recorded conversations.

In another case, a judge ordered the confiscation of the July 21 issue of the Rio Grande do Sul State weekly *Tribuna Popular* after it reported on corruption charges against a local mayor.

Media outlets have also suffered disproportionate monetary damages in civil lawsuits. *DEBATE*, a São Paulo State weekly, faces possible bankruptcy after its owner was ordered to pay US$150,000 in damages in a 1995 defamation lawsuit. While the award was lowered somewhat in successive appeals, higher courts have upheld the ruling. The case is still moving through the appellate process.

Brazilian journalists continue to face harassment and violence for their work. In late February, police summoned Nilson Mariano and Altair Nobre, journalist and editor, respectively, for the Porto Alegre daily *Zero Hora*, and ordered them to disclose their sources for an article about a local police chief. Although the Brazilian Constitution guarantees the protection of sources, the journalists were warned that failure to comply could result in prosecution for false testimony, but they remained silent.

In mid-August, journalist Mário Coelho de Almeida Filho was shot and killed the day before he was to testify in a criminal defamation lawsuit. The police official in charge of the murder investigation believes it was a contract killing, but it is not clear whether the journalist was killed for his reporting. CPJ continues to follow developments in the case. At least four Brazilian journalists have been killed because of their work since 1996, according to CPJ research. In most of these killings, the crimes remain unsolved, and those responsible have gone unpunished.

In August, the Associação Nacional de Jornais (ANJ), an association of newspaper publishers, disclosed the results of a survey on the credibility of the Brazilian media. The survey revealed that newspapers were the second most trusted institution in Brazil, behind the Catholic Church. TV stations and radio stations came in fourth and fifth, respectively, behind Protestant churches. The federal government, Congress, and political parties lagged far behind. While the press celebrated the survey's findings, critics pointed out that the percentage of people who said they trusted the papers the most (15 percent) was very low.

An October ruling suspended Decree-Law 972, issued under military rulers in 1969, which required citizens to hold a university diploma in journalism before registering as a journalist with the Ministry of Labor. In 1985, the Costa Rica–based Inter-American Court of Human Rights ruled that mandatory licensing of journalists violates the American Convention on Human Rights.

According to the ANJ, a bill to reform the 1967 Press Law remains stalled in the Chamber of Deputies. Troubling provisions in the legislation would impose enormous fines for defamation and make media owners liable for unlimited damages. If the bill becomes law, small media outlets could be bankrupted by a single defamation case. The Senate is currently considering another bill that would prohibit public officials from leaking information to the press that could damage the reputation, honor, or privacy of any person currently under investigation.

CANADA

PRESS FREEDOM IS GENERALLY RESPECTED IN CANADA, and CPJ does not routinely monitor conditions in the country. However, police harassment of journalists covering demonstrations; investigations into past violent attacks against journalists; and proposed anti-terrorism legislation were all issues of concern last year.

Continuing a trend seen in 2000, police harassed journalists covering protests. Several were detained during the April 20-22 Summit of the Americas in Quebec City, including Charles East, a U.S. photographer for the Sipa Agency covering the summit for *Time* magazine who was arrested on April 20 and held for three days. Police reportedly mistook the journalist, who was accredited and wearing a helmet that identified him as a member of the press, for a demonstrator who had thrown stones at an officer. Photographer Louise Bilodeau of the Stock and Clix agencies and the magazine *L'actualité* was briefly arrested on April 21, according to the Paris-based press freedom organization Reporters sans frontières.

Canadian Journalists for Free Expression (CJFE) reported that on June 24, Royal Canadian Mounted Police (RCMP) officers confiscated video footage and other material from Todd Lamirande, correspondent of the Aboriginal Peoples Television Network in Kamloops, British Columbia. Lamirande was covering a protest against the development of a ski resort that turned into a clash between the protesters and local supporters of the project. After the journalist refused to hand over his footage, RCMP officers seized Lamirande's vehicle with all its contents, including his videotapes. The officers kept the tapes until they had made copies, CJFE said.

A disturbing episode occurred in British Columbia on November 25, when RCMP officers apparently posed as a film crew to capture an escaped convict who had given media interviews while on the loose. According to various press reports, the fugitive was led to believe he was meeting a film crew that was doing a documentary on his life.

There were several developments during the year in the investigation of the September 13, 2000, shooting of journalist Michel Auger. A veteran crime reporter with the French-language daily *Le Journal de Montréal*, Auger had investigated the Hell's Angels motorcycle gang and the local Mafia. On May 30, a couple was arrested for allegedly providing the gang with confidential information about the journalist. Auger, who has fully recovered from the attack, told CPJ that the two suspects are scheduled to appear in court in early 2002. Meanwhile, Michel Vezina, who was arrested in November 2000 and charged with supplying the pistol used in the shooting, was sentenced on September 28 to almost five years in prison.

Alarm over increased biker-gang intimidation led the Canadian government to pass a last-minute amendment to anti-gang legislation that mandates severe penalties for violence, surveillance, threats, or harassment against journalists, Auger said.

But journalist organizations expressed alarm at anti-terrorist legislation passed by both Canada's House of Commons and the Senate. CJFE has harshly criticized a section allowing law enforcement officials to hold investigative hearings aimed at preventing terrorist acts, noting that journalists who contact known or suspected terrorists for information could be compelled to testify about conversations with them.

Another worrisome section proposes allowing the Defense Department's Communications Security Establishment to monitor communications between Canadians and foreign entities. CJFE contends that the new law is far too broad and will leave journalists who contact foreign sources unable to assure them confidentiality.

Violence against the press is relatively rare in Canada. As in the United States, however, immigrant journalists face special risks. The November 1998 killing of Tara Singh Hayer, publisher of Canada's largest and oldest Punjabi-language weekly *Indo-Canadian Times*, remains unsolved. Hayer, who was an outspoken critic of Sikh fundamentalist violence both in Canada and India, was left partially paralyzed after a previous assassination attempt.

In October 2000, the RCMP arrested two men in connection with the 1985 bombing of Air India Flight 182, which killed 329 people. One of the two, Ajaib Singh Bagri, was also charged with the attempted murder of Hayer. On April 10 of this year, the British Columbia Court of Appeal upheld a decision denying Bagri bail. The trial will likely begin in September 2002.

CJFE and the writers' group PEN Canada reported that Tahir Aslam Gora, editor and publisher of the Urdu-language weekly *Watan*, has been threatened by several extremist members of the Toronto Muslim community since early 2001, when Gora wrote a piece about Muslim women's rights.

CHILE

AFTER YEARS OF WRANGLING, Chile's Congress finally passed a press law repealing some of the country's most draconian defamation and libel statutes. There has been intense international pressure to rid Chile's legal system of its severe restrictions on the press. But local media also credit President Ricardo Lagos with reviving the reforms, which were stalled by officials hesitant to relinquish laws that shielded them from criticism.

The law scratched certain provisions of Chile's infamous State Security Law of 1958, including Article 6b, which criminalized insulting high officials. The bill also repealed Article 16, which authorized the suspension of publications and broadcasts, as well as the immediate confiscation of publications deemed offensive, and Article 17, which extended criminal liability to the editors and printers of offending publications. Historically, military courts have heard defamation cases brought by members of the military against civilians; the new legislation repealed that provision.

The law also repealed the 1967 Law on Publicity Abuses, which empowered judges to ban press coverage of court proceedings. While that was a positive step, the repeal also restricted journalists' right to report on a person's private life. Journalists who do so can now be prosecuted under the Penal Code, according to J. Ignacio Correa Amunátegui, vice president of the lawyers' association Asociación de Abogados por las Libertades Públicas. Legislation to review these onerous provisions is stalled in Congress, Correa said.

In addition, the new legislation keeps "disrespect" as an offense under the Penal Code and imposes criminal liability for libel and slander. The law also gives the government the power to determine who is and isn't a journalist. And while legislation guarantees the right to protect sources, it restricts that right to "recognized" journalists, journalism students doing an internship, recent journalism graduates from accredited universities, publishers, editors, and foreign correspondents. The law also specifies that one must have a journalism degree in order to work as a spokesperson or journalist for state institutions.

The passage of the new press law finally resolved one of Chile's most notorious defamation suits. Alejandra Matus, who was sued in 1999 and fled her country after her muckraking exposé of the Chilean judiciary, *The Black Book of Chilean Justice*, was banned under the State Security Law, was able to return to

Chile without risking arrest. Her book was also allowed to circulate freely.

But Matus' case remains pending before the Washington, D.C.–based Inter-American Commission on Human Rights (IACHR), while several criminal defamation laws remain on the books in Chile. On March 23, CPJ submitted an amicus curiae brief to the commission supporting Matus' complaint. The brief urged the commission to recommend that Chile repeal the offending State Security Law articles, which were soon after eliminated as part of press law reforms, and also recommended that Chile adopt an "actual malice" standard for all defamation cases involving public officials or public figures.

The State Defense Council (CDE) asked that Paula Afani, of the daily *La Tercera*, be sentenced to five years in prison for allegedly violating the 1995 Drugs Law with a 1999 article on a government investigation into drug trafficking and money laundering. Afani was also charged under the now repealed Law on Publicity Abuses for publishing parts of the secret criminal dossier of the investigation. In early January, Afani learned that she had been acquitted on the first charge. However, the CDE appealed the decision and also filed a writ with the Supreme Court, Afani told CPJ.

The fact that only a few companies—notably COPESA and El Mercurio—own print media outlets remains a significant problem. The Internet news site *El Mostrador.cl* (www.elmostrador.cl), whose 2000 launch shook up the largely conservative media scene, weathered a tough year and in November was forced to begin charging users' fees. In a sense, *El Mostrador* was a victim of its own success. According to one CPJ source, the publication's daring reports forced the mainstream media to follow suit; because they have better resources, the mainstream press now scoops the publication that had consistently scooped it in 2000.

Meanwhile, stories that touch on the interests of media owners remain off-limits. Said one editor, "If some businessmen get into the media business, it's because they want to make sure of two things: gain public influence and avoid, at any cost, stories unfavorable to their economic interests."

COLOMBIA

THE COLOMBIAN PRESS REMAINED IN THE CROSS FIRE of an escalating, decades-old civil conflict pitting two major leftist guerrilla groups against the Colombian army and right-wing paramilitary forces. While peace negotiations slowly moved forward at the beginning of 2002, the conflict continued to take a deadly toll on journalists and sent many into hiding. At least three journalists were killed for their work in 2001. CPJ continues to investigate the deaths of five others whose murders may have been professionally related.

Attacks against Colombian journalists came from many sources. The paramilitary United Self-Defense Forces of Colombia (AUC) was presumed to be behind the April 27 killing of Flavio Bedoya, a regional correspondent for the Bogotá-based Communist Party newspaper *Voz*. One of the weekly's senior correspondents linked the murder to a series of highly critical reports by Bedoya about collusion between security forces and the paramilitaries. Less than a month after Bedoya's death, the AUC tried unsuccessfully to bomb the Bogotá offices of *Voz*. AUC leader Carlos Castaño took responsibility for the attempt a few days later.

In May, CPJ named Castaño one of CPJ's Top Ten Enemies of the Press. (See page 597.) "Even against the violent backdrop of Colombia's escalating civil war, in which all sides have targeted journalists," CPJ wrote, "Carlos Castaño stands out as a ruthless enemy of the press." A journalist from the Paris daily *Le Monde* asked the paramilitary leader how he felt about the dubious distinction. Castaño, who resigned in late spring of 2001 as the AUC's military commander to focus on the group's political affairs, responded, "I would like to assure you that I have always respected the freedom and subjectivity of the press." He added, "Over the course of its existence the AUC has executed two local journalists who were in fact guerrillas."

Meanwhile, Colombia's largest guerrilla movement, the Revolutionary Armed Forces of Colombia (FARC), was implicated in the July 6 murder of José Duviel Vásquez Arias, one of three journalists from radio station La Voz de la Selva (The Voice of the Jungle) who were assassinated during a seven-month period.

The station is based in Caquetá, a department that has seen heavy fighting and is home to part of the Switzerland-sized swath of land the government ceded to FARC in order to spur peace negotiations. Vásquez's colleague who witnessed the killing, Omar Orlando García Garzón, was threatened after he described the killer to authorities; he and his family went into exile. Earlier in the year, another La Voz de la Selva journalist, Alvaro Dussán, denounced FARC threats and then fled the country, according to the Fundación para la Libertad de Prensa (FLIP), a local press freedom organization that became a member of the International Freedom of Expression Exchange this year.

In the third murder, two unidentified attackers shot and killed radio journalist Jorge Enrique Urbano Sánchez on July 8 while he was celebrating his 55th birthday with friends in a park in the coastal city of Buenaventura. Urbano apparently devoted his final radio broadcast to denouncing a local criminal gang called "Tumba Puertas" (Knock Down Doors). Before his murder, he had received death threats that he attributed to his public campaign to relocate street vendors and remove drug addicts from the park.

The Interior Ministry's Program for the Protection of Journalists and Social Communicators, established in 2000, has helped a number of journalists escape threatening situations. Different institutions and organizations collaborate with the program, but its budget is apparently limited.

Journalists who need to leave the country typically do not have time to look for viable long-term solutions abroad and often only speak Spanish. To accommodate them, CPJ collaborated with FLIP and the Peruvian press freedom organization IPYS to create a safe house in Lima where journalists can stay while looking for long-term solutions. IPYS executive director Ricardo

Uceda and CPJ Americas program coordinator Marylene Smeets made this agreement with Elizabeth Vargas of FLIP during an August visit to Bogotá.

In 2001, controversy erupted over government pressure on television networks to censor reporting on the civil war. The planned broadcast of an April 10 interview that TV anchor Claudia Gurisatti conducted with Castaño was suspended after government officials called RCN Televisión, the network that broadcasts her program. President Andrés Pastrana Arango's press secretary, Samuel Salazar, acknowledged the calls, saying that some government officials worried that the broadcast would jeopardize the safety of peace commissioner Camilo Gómez Alzate whom Castaño had, during the interview, threatened to kidnap. The government has reportedly met many times with the owners of Colombian media groups to request that they refrain from broadcasting or publishing developments about the peace process.

On October 23, the autonomous regulatory National Television Commission (CNTV) proposed banning television broadcasts of violent images and statements from the warring parties in the civil conflict or criminal organizations. Press reports quoted CNTV director Sergio Quiroz as saying, "the censorship . . . aims to make a contribution to the process to normalize and search for peace, security, and tranquility in the country." The proposal generated a controversy, and President Pastrana intervened, suggesting instead a system of "self-regulation."

Although many journalists continue to speak out in spite of the dangers, increasing violence combined with the impunity surrounding attacks has, understandably, induced some degree of self-censorship.

Worsening economic conditions led to a drop in advertising revenue in 2001, causing problems for various media outlets. Meanwhile, in September, *El Espectador*, a daily with a proud tradition of fearless reporting whose publisher, Guillermo Cano, was killed in 1986 by drug cartel hit men, succumbed to Colombia's economic crisis and became a weekly, though it still appears daily on the Internet at www.elespectador.com.

(See special report on page 16.)

COSTA RICA

COSTA RICA, A COUNTRY LONG REGARDED AS ONE OF THE FREEST and most democratic in Latin America, was profoundly shocked by the July 7 murder of veteran journalist Parmenio Medina Pérez—the first assassination of a journalist in the country's recent history.

Unknown assailants shot Medina, producer and host of the weekly radio program "La Patada" (The Kick), three times at close range. His program had often denounced official corruption and earned the journalist numerous threats. Two months before his murder, Medina received death threats in connection with accusations he made on air about fiscal improprieties at a local Catholic radio station, and unknown attackers fired bullets at his house. Twenty minutes after Medina's murder, one of his colleagues at "The Kick" received an anonymous call saying he would be the next victim. The station that carried Medina's program, Radio Monumental, received threatening calls for months, the station's news coordinator told CPJ.

The public demanded justice, and the murder investigation began swiftly. However, it did not produce major results. Soon, a veil of secrecy covered the endeavor. In August, a consortium of individuals and civil society organizations launched the Frente Ciudadano contra la Impunidad (Citizens' Front Against Impunity) to pressure authorities to solve the case.

On January 7—exactly six months after the murder—the San José–based daily *La Nación* quoted a Frente coordinator, Albino Vargas, as saying, "We're convinced there are political, business, and religious influences that are interfering so the truth about the crime won't surface." According to the same article, the Organization of Judicial Investigation, Costa Rica's law enforcement agency, said that even though more than 100 people have been interviewed and many leads have been discarded, no details can be disclosed because the matter remains under investigation.

The impunity surrounding the murder further contributed to its devastating effect on Costa Rican journalists, who now fear violence in reprisal for their work. According to a June survey by *La Nación*, 55 percent of the 97 journalists polled said they had received some kind of threat during their careers. Though some threats were physical, most journalists were threatened with defamation suits.

Medina's murder boosted efforts to reform Costa Rica's antiquated media laws. Two days after the murder, two deputies presented plans to the Legislative Assembly to create a commission mandated to investigate the laws, according to Fernando Guier, a lawyer and columnist for *La Nación*.

On July 23, a group of editors presented a proposal to revise the press laws. One of several currently pending before the Legislative Assembly, the editors' proposal is considered to be the most comprehensive. For defamation cases, it introduces the "actual malice" standard, which requires plaintiffs to prove not only that the published information is false, but also that the journalists knew or should have known it was false at the time of publication. The legislation encodes the neutral reporting standard, which says that journalists cannot be sued for accurately reproducing information from an explicitly mentioned source. The proposal also provides for the protection of journalists' sources.

The Legislative Assembly's press freedom committee convened several times, hearing editors, representatives of the journalists' association Colegio de Periodistas, Supreme Court justices, and legal scholars. But no agreement had been reached by year's end. Only one of the proposed changes was accepted—the elimination of the crime of disrespect, a little-used provision that imposes prison terms of up to two years for offending the honor of a government official

In an unprecedented decision, the Inter-American Court of Human Rights issued provisional measures on September 7 ordering Costa Rican authorities to stay certain sections of a 1999 defamation verdict against the daily *La Nación* and one of its reporters, Mauricio Herrera Ulloa. Decisions of the court are legally binding on Costa Rica and other countries that have accepted the court's jurisdiction.

In November 1999, a Costa Rican Penal Court convicted Herrera Ulloa of criminal defamation and ordered him to pay damages to former diplomat Félix Przedborski based on 1995 articles that cited European press reports alleging corruption by Przedborski. After the Costa Rican Supreme Court rejected *La Nación*'s appeal, the journalist filed a petition with the Inter-American Commission on Human Rights, which ordered the Penal Court to stay its ruling while the commission studied the case. The court refused, so the commission filed a complaint with the Inter-American Court, which issued a stay. At press time, the commission was still studying the case.

On December 26, Costa Rica's Supreme Electoral Tribunal issued a controversial split decision ordering the privately owned television station Teletica Canal 7 to invite all 13 presidential candidates to appear on a scheduled debate, rather than the top four contenders as the station had originally planned. Pilar Cisneros, co-director of the channel's news department, told CPJ that the station appealed to the Supreme Court, which on January 3 refused to hear the case on the grounds that it was an electoral matter. The channel aired the debate between the top candidates as planned on January 7 and followed with January 8 and 9 debates between remaining contenders. Cisneros announced that Teletica Canal 7 would appeal the case to the Inter-American Commission on Human Rights.

CUBA

DURING 2001, CUBAN AUTHORITIES CONTINUED TO WIELD an assortment of repressive tools to silence independent journalism: harassment and intimidation; prison terms and threats of prosecution; detention; disruption of phone communications; and restrictions on the freedom of movement, among others. In May 2001, for the seventh straight year, CPJ named President Fidel Castro Ruz to its annual list of the Ten Worst Enemies of the Press. (See page 597.)

Nonetheless, independent journalists founded the journalists' association Sociedad de Periodistas Manuel Márquez Sterling (SPMMS). The association, which does not accept funding from any government, hopes to promote freedom of expression, train independent journalists, defend journalistic ethics, and provide moral and financial support to its members. Predictably, state security agents targeted the SPMMS, banning it from giving training courses and harassing some of its members in their homes.

Meanwhile, the international community increasingly recognized the important work of the independent media in Cuba. In early April, independent Cuban journalists and European parliamentarians met to discuss press freedom issues during the 105th Inter-Parliamentary Union Conference, held in Havana.

According to Cuban journalist Raúl Rivero, the independent press "cannot publish in their own country, does not have access to official information, and lives under the pressure of decrees, provisions and laws that allow the Cuban government to jail them with the appearance of legality."

Because the government controls all mass media and restricts Internet access, independent journalists struggle to transmit news reports abroad. Operators from the state telephone monopoly, ETECSA, frequently refuse to connect their international calls. Likewise, the government routinely taps journalists' phones, disconnects their phone service, or cuts off international calls. In mid-February, for instance, the government disconnected the phone number of the independent news agency CubaPress for at least 20 days.

In other cases, the government has denied exit permits to journalists who have already obtained a foreign visa to travel to other countries. Some journalists invited abroad are allowed to leave Cuba only if they promise never to return. In September, the SPMMS issued a statement demanding that five journalists who had been granted political asylum be allowed to leave Cuba, but at year's end, they remained in the country.

Three imprisoned journalists were released in 2001. On January 17, Jesús Joel Díaz Hernández—who was subjected to a sham trial in 1999 and convicted of "dangerousness," a crime unknown outside Cuba—was released after being imprisoned for two years because of his work. He was held in degrading conditions and denied even the limited rights guaranteed by Cuban law. In 1999, CPJ honored Díaz Hernández with an International Press Freedom Award. After his release, he returned to work as the executive director of the independent news agency Cooperativa Avileña de Periodistas Independientes, but the state security agency continues to harass him.

CubaPress correspondent Manuel Antonio González Castellanos was freed on February 26 after serving the bulk of his 31-month sentence for "disrespecting" President Castro. During his imprisonment, González Castellanos was placed in a punishment cell for at least 10 days. Though he suffered from a severe cold and lost considerable weight, authorities denied him proper medical care.

Journalist and labor activist José Orlando González Bridón was released on November 22 after serving 11 months and seven days in prison for distributing "false information" in an article about a bungled murder case.

But journalist Bernardo Arévalo Padrón remains imprisoned. He has been jailed since 1997 for "disrespecting" Castro and another Cuban State Council member, Carlos Lage. The charges stemmed from a series of interviews Arévalo Padrón gave in late 1997 to Miami-based radio stations in which he alleged that while Cuban farmers starved, helicopters were taking fresh meat from the countryside to the dinner tables of President Castro, Lage, and other Communist Party officials. The journalist continues to be held in a labor camp despite being eligible for parole, and his health has suffered as a result of his prolonged imprisonment.

Foreign correspondents did not escape government pressures during 2001. In January, President Castro accused several foreign journalists of spreading "lies and insults against the Revolution." He also hinted that in retaliation, the government might consider closing entire news bureaus rather than expelling the offending reporters. As a result, accused British journalist Pascal Fletcher, a reporter for Reuters, was relocated to Venezuela in order to keep Reuters from losing its license.

Independent Cuban journalists can count on their colleagues abroad to use the Web to disseminate information. The online daily *Encuentro en la red* (www.cubaencuentro.com)—launched by a group of Madrid-based Cuban exiles that also publishes the popular quarterly magazine *Encuentro de la cultura cubana*—celebrated its first anniversary in December. The daily showcases the best of the independent Cuban press and provides a forum for debate between Cubans on the island and abroad. Throughout 2001, the government media continued to lash out against the magazine and the Web site, branding them a tool of the U.S. government and Miami-based right-wing exiles.

DOMINICAN REPUBLIC

DOMINICAN PRESIDENT HIPÓLITO MEJÍA has received mixed reviews for his policy toward the press since he took office in August 2000. Although Dominican journalists are generally free to express their views, and the government does not officially restrict the press, journalists have complained of government attempts to influence coverage.

President Mejía, with his blunt and sometimes confrontational style, has used insulting language when referring to journalists and editors who criticize his administration. In late June, the Santo Domingo daily *El Caribe* reported that Mejía's government had diverted funds from public works programs to buy buses for a public transportation plan. Mejía said of the story, "That is a lie. That's only in the mind of Bernardo Vega [*El Caribe*'s editor], one of those idiots who writes things that are not true," according to the daily *Listín Diario*.

In an August 17 interview with the Santo Domingo daily *Última Hora*, José Tejada Gómez, then-president of the journalists' association Colegio Dominicano de Periodistas (CDP), noted that Mejía's insults were common, and that his first year in office was marked by "constant conflicts" with journalists.

According to the CDP, signs of government intolerance toward the press abound. In late June, Darío Medrano and Ramón Carmona, reporter and cameraman, respectively, for U.S.-based Univisión TV network and the Santo Domingo TV channel Color Visión-Canal 9, were threatened, allegedly by government officials, for their coverage of nationwide street protests against a government-imposed economic adjustment package.

Gen. Luis Rodríguez Florimón, of the National Police, meanwhile, warned in early August that he would monitor radio and TV programs and threatened to jail anybody who criticized or offended the president. The general did not carry out his threats, but his words were typical of the government's hard-line reactions to criticism.

Dominican journalists have also complained about low salaries and job instability, which makes them vulnerable to bribery and other economic pressures.

Investigations into the May 1994 disappearance of columnist and academic Narciso González remained stalled at year's end. González, a harsh critic of the Dominican government and military, "disappeared"—allegedly at the hands of the military—after he publicly criticized the tainted elections that brought former president Joaquín Balaguer to power. Although former members of the military and the police have been interrogated, no one has been charged in the case, which the Inter-American Commission on Human Rights took under review in 1998.

The bill to amend the 1962 Law of Expression and Dissemination of Thought, also known as Law 6132, was passed by the Senate on July 18 after being submitted by President Mejía in September 2000. Drafted by local press organizations, newspaper executives, and media law specialists, the legislation widens access to information and provides for civil penalties in cases of defamation. The Chamber of Deputies' Justice Committee was considering the bill at press time.

ECUADOR

IN GENERAL, PRESS FREEDOM IS RESPECTED IN ECUADOR, but journalists complained that government officials continue to blame the media for the country's problems, including rampant corruption.

Throughout much of the year, President Gustavo Noboa sparred with the press over its critical coverage of his administration's failure to handle a rash of failing private banks—a crisis that cost Ecuadoran taxpayers and account holders hundreds of millions of dollars.

In January, Noboa issued a communiqué asking the media to observe "balance when providing information" and to maintain "full identification with the democratic system." In July, Noboa accused the press of trying "to give us a bad international reputation that is difficult for me to overcome in [my] travels abroad," according to the Guayaquil daily *El Universo*. At year's end, the tussle continued, with Noboa and other government officials criticizing what they perceived as negative coverage of government affairs.

In August, a little-known group called Legión Blanca sent several lengthy e-mails to local human rights organizations and media outlets. In addition to issuing death threats against activists and claiming responsibility for harassing and intimidating them, the group threatened "alleged journalists who, hidden behind their computers, pens, microphones, or screens, promote communism, chaos, and destabilization of democracy."

The group also claimed to have murdered journalist Luis Fernando Maldonado, a news producer and host for the Quito-based television channel Telesistema who was killed on August 8 in an apparent robbery attempt. Local journalists dismissed the group's confession as unreliable and maintained that Maldonado was not killed for his journalistic work. One source suggested that the group was merely trying to engender fear among Ecuadoran journalists.

In some cases, politicians have used criminal defamation lawsuits to pressure journalists. In July, Ecuadoran Roldosista Party (PRE) parliamentary deputy Fernando Rosero filed a criminal defamation lawsuit against Jorge Vivanco Mendieta, deputy editor and columnist at the Guayaquil daily *Expreso*. The lawsuit stemmed from several articles by Vivanco, including a piece criticizing the army for not defending itself against allegations that Rosero had made accusing the army of purchasing defective weapons. Rosero also filed a civil lawsuit against Vivanco requesting damages for US$1 million. Both cases remained in the courts at press time.

Also in July, journalist Malena Cardona Batallas was fined and sentenced to a month in prison for defaming PRE parliamentary deputy Roberto Rodríguez in a May 2000 television interview in which Cardona questioned Rodríguez about the alleged misappropriation of a government vehicle. On December 14, Portoviejo's Superior Court of Justice upheld the sentence, which the journalist plans to appeal.

Ecuador's 1975 Law on the Professional Practice of Journalism requires all local journalists to have a university degree in journalism and to register with the Federación Nacional de Periodistas, a national press association. While the law is rarely applied, during 2001, journalists' unions, which argue that the restrictions hold the profession to a higher standard, called for increased enforcement. In a 1985 decision, however, the Costa Rica–based Inter-American Court of Human Rights found that such mandatory licensing laws violate the American Convention on Human Rights.

Article 81 of the 1998 constitution requires the state to guarantee freedom of information by releasing public documents on demand. But the government routinely ignores this obligation, which has not yet been codified. In August, a commission comprising members of several journalists' organizations met with the president's spokesman, Oscar Zuloaga, to call on the government to enforce Article 81. Authorities have not yet taken action.

EL SALVADOR

EL SALVADOR'S MEDIA CONTINUED TO BE POLARIZED, and journalists suffered from violent attacks and a lack of access to public information.

The tragic January and February earthquakes that left 1 million Salvadorans homeless revealed the vast rift that remained between leftist partisans and conservative groups 10 years after the end of a long and brutal civil war.

TV DOCE, a television station founded in 1984 and recognized as one of the few independent voices during the brutal conflict, was widely criticized for its coverage of the relief effort.

In a January 19 editorial, the conservative, pro-government daily *El Diario de Hoy* accused TV DOCE of fabricating "pathetic scenes" with victims that scared away foreign aid.

Only days before, TV DOCE had begun airing a daily program intended to give earthquake victims the opportunity to contact their relatives. Viewers began calling to denounce the government for handling the disaster poorly.

By all accounts, the government reacted by imposing an advertising boycott. Private advertisers apparently reduced their ad buys as well.

As a result, the station was forced to slash its operations. TV DOCE news director Mauricio Funes told CPJ that the station's news program, which used to air daily, is now only broadcast during the week. Jobs were cut and salaries were lowered. However, TV DOCE began to recover because the station gathered support from some organizations and local governments, according to Funes.

Official reticence toward releasing government information continued to impede journalists' work in 2001. Judges consistently used Article 272 of the Criminal Procedure Code, which allows them to bar reporters from courthouse proceedings to protect morality, public interest, or national security. According to the local press organization Asociación de Periodistas de El Salvador (APES), the judiciary restricted access to 11 proceedings in 2001.

APES, whose 1998 proposals for legal reform were not seriously considered, presented them again in 2001, along with another proposal. APES proposed that the Legislative Assembly repeal Article 324 of the Penal Code, which imposes six months' to three years' imprisonment for government officials who release information "that should remain secret." The law does not specify when the "secrecy" rule applies. Article 324 was thrust in the limelight on August 28, when Attorney General Belisario Artiga published a communiqué chastising an anonymous official who leaked the results of an investigation into several officials to *El Diario de Hoy*.

The attorney general called on the anonymous official to resign. After several protests, Artiga acknowledged that the government had an obligation to create guidelines for the release of official documents. But by year's end, no action had been taken.

APES and a nongovernmental organization called Probidad reported numerous incidents where judges, police officers, and others physically or verbally attacked reporters. Both organizations reported on the September 13 attack on a Canal 4 cameraman and a *La Prensa Gráfica* photographer. The journalists were covering a court hearing of a judge accused of practicing without a license when individuals said to be the judge's bodyguards assaulted them. In another case, police officers attacked two *El Diario de Hoy* reporters during a carnival celebration. One officer hit one of the journalists with a stick, and another tried to confiscate the other journalist's film, the organizations reported.

GUATEMALA

AMID HARASSMENT AND VIOLENCE AGAINST JOURNALISTS, human rights activists, and judges involved in high-profile cases, Guatemala's political stability deteriorated considerably in 2001, and press freedom along with it. The administration of President Alfonso Portillo Cabrera, a member of the right-wing Guatemalan Republican Front (FRG), showed little tolerance for criticism of any kind.

Several attacks set the tone for the year. On February 20, a group of protesters gathered in front of the offices of the Guatemala City daily *elPeriódico* and threatened the newspaper's staff. The protesters identified themselves as supporters of Luis Rabbé, then minister of communications, infrastructure, and housing. The threats apparently resulted from the newspaper's coverage of high-level government corruption, including *elPeriódico*'s strong criticism of Rabbé's official conduct. Rabbé later resigned.

In late March, four *elPeriódico* journalists were threatened and attacked after they uncovered mismanagement at a state-controlled bank. In another controversial story known as "Guategate," *Prensa Libre* revealed in 2000 that more than 20 FRG legislators had conspired to reduce a new tax on alcoholic beverages. Former military dictator and current president of Congress Gen. Efraín Ríos Montt was implicated in the scandal and stripped of immunity from prosecution in March 2001. In April, Ríos Montt complained that media coverage of "Guategate" was part of an orchestrated campaign to damage his prestige and ensure his "political lynching." In October 2001, the investigation of Ríos Montt and the other legislators was shelved after a highly controversial court ruling.

Early in the year, media tycoon Angel González, a Mexican national and brother-in-law of former minister Rabbé, used his broadcasting empire to wage a campaign to discredit *elPeriódico* and *Prensa Libre*. Through front companies, González owns all four of Guatemala's private television stations, which violates constitutional prohibitions against both monopolies and foreign ownership of the media. He has canceled two independent news programs and wields enormous influence over Guatemalan politics.

González has been a leading financial contributor to President Portillo's political campaigns, and Rabbé is a former executive in González's media empire. González has also been linked to shady business deals in Perú, where he allegedly attempted to gain control of TV channel Canal 13 in collusion with disgraced Peruvian intelligence adviser Vladimiro Montesinos, according to Peruvian sources.

Though President Portillo says he is concerned about González's TV monopoly, he has done little to dismantle it. While the president has pledged to open the remaining two broadcast TV channels to competitive bidding—they are state-owned and currently don't broadcast any programming—no concrete action has been taken.

On November 30, Guatemalan Journalists' Day, the single-chamber, FRG-controlled Congress passed a bill that requires all university graduates, including those with journalism degrees, to register with trade associations known as *colegios*. The bill was then sent to President Portillo, who was asked to veto it by the journalists' organization Asociación de Periodistas de Guatemala (APG) and other international press freedom organizations. Portillo promised a veto if he found that the bill was likely to damage the interests of journalists.

The Guatemalan press has recently made more of an effort to defend itself from government interference and harassment. In addition to APG activism, the press freedom organization Centro para la Defensa de la Libertad de Expresión organized its first seminar in June 2001.

Beyond Guatemala City, provincial journalists face harassment, threats, intimidation, and violence. On September 5, radio journalist Jorge Mynor Alegría Armendáriz was murdered outside his home in Puerto Barrios, a port city located on the Caribbean coast in Izabal Department. The journalist hosted an afternoon call-in show that often discussed corruption and official misconduct. Following Alegría's death, his colleague Enrique Aceituno resigned as host of a local news program, saying he had received threats for criticizing local authorities.

One journalist's murder was resolved in 2001. On February 19, a court sentenced former security guard Gustavo García to 15 years in prison for killing *Prensa Libre* photographer Roberto Martínez and two bystanders in April 2000, during a riot sparked by a bus-fare increase. García's security firm was ordered to pay Martínez's family 150,000 quetzales (US$20,000) in damages. The second defendant, also a security guard with the company, was acquitted.

HAITI

HAITI'S PRESS SUFFERED A CRACKDOWN THIS YEAR that coincided with the February inauguration of President Jean-Bertrand Aristide and continued after an apparent December coup attempt that sought to oust him. On December 17, about two dozen gunmen stormed the National Palace at dawn. At least 13 people were killed in the attack and ensuing mob violence in the streets of the capital, Port-au-Prince, and other cities.

Hours after the attack, hundreds of government supporters armed with machetes and guns accosted and threatened at least a dozen journalists working for private radio stations in the capital, prompting at least four media outlets to suspend broadcasts for the day. Other stations went off the air for several days. Several broadcasters also received anonymous phone threats, while Aristide partisans attacked radio stations and vehicles belonging to private news organizations.

Later that day, Aristide asked Haitians to respect the rights of political parties and journalists. Opposition parties maintained that the president was using the coup attempt as a pretext to crush dissent. As a result of the violent attacks, at least 15 journalists left the country to apply for asylum in the United States and France, and as many as 40 journalists went into hiding, according to international press reports.

Before the December violence, frequent setbacks plagued the investigation of the April 3, 2000, assassination of Jean Léopold Dominique, the country's most prominent journalist and a longtime pro-democracy activist whose station, Radio Haïti Inter, criticized Aristide's ruling Lavalas Family (FL) party. Dominique alone had dared to air investigative stories and name names in a country where a history of state repression has dictated that political coverage be elusive and evasive.

Though not officially accused, FL senator Dany Toussaint is widely suspected of masterminding Dominique's murder in reprisal for an October 1999 editorial that criticized him sharply. At least six people were arrested and more than 80 suspects were questioned, including Toussaint. But examining judge Claudy Gassant resigned in June, saying he had received inadequate protection from threats. Justice Minister Gary Lissade promised to ensure Gassant's security. The judge then returned to the case, but the threats continued.

Although former president René Préval asked Parliament in his final State of the Nation address to ensure that the Dominique case was quickly resolved, several senators were widely criticized for questioning why the probe deserved so much attention and whether the parliamentary immunity of their colleague and suspect Toussaint should be lifted. In protest, Radio Haïti Inter suspended its broadcasts for three days in February.

In June, Toussaint's supporters erected barricades of burning tires in Port-au-Prince suburbs and called for Gassant's arrest. In September, Gassant requested that Parliament lift the legislator's immunity, but by year's end no official decision had been made. Gassant left Haiti for the United States in January 2002 and is considering seeking asylum there. It is unclear whether the murder case will continue with an interim judge, or if a new judge will restart the entire investigation.

In Haiti, where as much as 55 percent of the population is illiterate and the price of a television can exceed the average yearly wage, radio remains the primary medium, with more than 40 stations on the air. Many are partisan— either government-backed or allegedly supported by conservative foreign organizations. Government officials tend to attack private radio stations when their coverage does not support the ruling party or the president.

The country has two major dailies, *Le Nouvelliste* and *Le Matin*, along with three partisan weeklies distributed in the United States and Haiti: *Haïti-Observateur*, *Haïti Progrès*, and *Haïti En Marche*. The 2-year-old *Haitian Times*, which is edited by former *New York Times* reporter Garry Pierre-Pierre and published in Brooklyn, New York, aims to inform English-speaking Haitians at home and abroad about current events in Haiti and among the Haitian diaspora.

Amid its charged politics and deteriorating economy, Haiti suffers from a dearth of independent journalism. Although private radio stations criticize the Aristide administration, they often fail to apply the same critical eye to civic organizations, opposition parties, and the private sector, whose paid advertisements help keep them afloat. Some journalists accept bribes and have been known to drop stories in exchange for money. There is virtually no investigative work because of the risks involved.

Press freedom abuses in 2001 coincided with a clampdown on government opposition. On January 9, FL militant Paul Raymond threatened media owners, former government officials, and opposition leaders with violence if they did not distance themselves from a minority party coalition's plan to launch a "shadow government." Journalists were targeted during March demonstrations, when pro-Aristide street militants erected flaming tire barricades nationwide and demanded the arrest of Gérard Gourgue, head of the opposition Democratic Convergence, who claimed to be the "shadow" president. Journalists said they were forced to conceal their press badges.

Jean Robert Delciné, a Radio Haïti Inter journalist, was assaulted, threatened, and had his radio equipment confiscated by police officers when he went to the Cité Soleil slum on October 13 to inquire about executions allegedly committed by police officers. Extrajudicial executions became an increasing problem after Aristide launched a "zero tolerance" anti-crime campaign in June, implying that street criminals caught red-handed could be summarily punished without trial. Opposition leaders and human rights groups denounced the policy, fearing that anybody deemed a criminal could become a target.

On December 3, Brignolle Lindor, news director of Radio Echo 2000, was hacked to death by a machete-wielding mob while en route to one of his other jobs as a customs official near the provincial town of Petit-Goâve. CPJ sources said that Lindor's name appeared on an FL deputy's list of opposition partisans who should be specifically targeted by the zero-tolerance policy.

In June, CPJ Americas program coordinator Marylene Smeets visited Haiti and met with media owners, government officials, foreign diplomats, local press associations, and journalists to discuss the Dominique case and other press freedom concerns.

HONDURAS

THE INDEPENDENT PRESS FACED PRESSURE FROM THE GOVERNMENT of President Carlos Roberto Flores Facussé. Powerful politicians dominated the media during the November 2001 presidential elections, while small political parties received little coverage and had very limited access to the press. Both the National Party (PN) and the ruling Liberal Party (PL) flooded radio and TV stations with advertisements, but PN candidate Ricardo Maduro emerged victorious, defeating PL candidate Rafael Pineda Ponce to become president.

In some cases, the media and politicians are indistinguishable. President Flores, member of the PL, owns the Tegucigalpa daily *La Tribuna*. Jaime Rosenthal, a businessman and unsuccessful candidate in the Liberal Party presidential primaries in 2000, owns the television channel Canal 11 and the San Pedro Sula–based daily *Tiempo*. Other politicians linked to the PL and the opposition National Party own national and regional radio and television stations.

The Tegucigalpa daily *El Heraldo*, known for its anti-government editorial line, fired Manuel Torres and Roger Argueta, opinion editor and investigative reporter, respectively, in May, reportedly under government pressure. In April,

El Heraldo editor Thelma Mejía resigned, also under government pressure. All three had criticized the government while working at the paper, and after they left, its coverage of the Flores administration became markedly less critical. Local sources have speculated that *El Heraldo*'s owner, Jorge Canahuati, who has lucrative government contracts through some of his other companies, may have acquiesced to the dismissals for business reasons.

Journalists often accuse media owners of interfering with work in the newsrooms. In late April, a group of intellectuals, including several journalists, sent an open letter to media owners urging them to allow their companies to report the news objectively and without interference. In an early May letter, the media owners' organization Asociación de Medios de Comunicación called the April letter a "slanderous document," and accused its senders of "discrediting the nation" and using "blackmail and psychological pressure."

Journalists are also vulnerable to bribery and other economic pressures because of their low salaries. Credible reports have revealed that politicians and businessmen have paid journalists in exchange for favorable coverage. Journalists have also been rewarded with loans, government advertising, or jobs with government agencies.

Defaming public officials is a criminal offense punishable by up to four years in prison, according to Article 345 of the Penal Code. The code also prescribes up to six years imprisonment for defaming the president.

JAMAICA

JAMAICA ENJOYS CONSIDERABLE PRESS FREEDOM. Despite gang warfare across the island nation, the media have not had problems covering controversial stories. "The media freely report on crime and violence in Jamaica, with these reports gaining prominence in the press and broadcast media," noted Donna Ortega, president of the Press Association of Jamaica.

However, journalists still have limited access to government information. "We in the media feel there's a culture of secrecy," said Ken Allen, opinion page editor of the daily newspaper *The Gleaner*. "The government keeps things close to their chest," he added.

Currently, access to information is governed by the 1911 Official Secrets Act. New legislation presented in the House of Representatives on December 4 would restrict access to government documents when disclosure could have an adverse effect on the ability of the government to manage the economy or would compromise national security. Parliament is currently examining the bill, according to Ortega.

Meanwhile, the Gleaner Company Limited continued to appeal a libel verdict stemming from a 1987 Associated Press story published in the company's daily, *The Gleaner*, and its afternoon tabloid, *The Star*, alleging that former tourism minister Eric Anthony Abrahams had accepted bribes. After the Court of Appeals reduced the judgment from 80.7 million Jamaican dollars (US$1.7

million) to 35 million Jamaican dollars (US$750,000) in 2000, the company appealed to the Privy Council in the United Kingdom, where the case was still pending at press time. (Jamaica is an independent country within the British Commonwealth, with the British monarch as titular head of state.)

MEXICO

PRESIDENT VICENTE FOX'S HISTORIC ELECTION IN 2000 MARKED THE END of the long-ruling Institutional Revolutionary Party's (PRI) domination of the country and its media. But the honeymoon between the president and the media ended in 2001 with increasingly critical coverage that reflected the public's frustration with the slow pace of reforms under the new government.

From the unresolved Chiapas conflict and rising unemployment to the lack of progress in addressing past human rights abuses, the media criticized the president for not delivering on his campaign promises. In November, Fox used his weekly radio program "Fox en vivo, Fox contigo" (Fox live, Fox with you) to complain about the criticism against his administration: "There is a lot of libel, a lot of deceit, a lot of lies recently in the media."

The Mexican government for the first time acknowledged responsibility for a rash of human rights abuses that took place during the counterinsurgency that the PRI-led government waged against leftist activists and guerrillas in Guerrero State during the 1970s. A November report issued by the National Human Rights Commission held the Mexican government accountable for detaining and torturing at least 275 men and women, but the commission did not disclose the names of some 74 officials who were implicated. While President Fox appointed a special prosecutor to investigate the disappearances, he did not establish a truth commission to probe state-sponsored repression, and little progress was made.

Emboldened by the government's reluctance to find and prosecute human rights violators, opponents of the investigations launched violent attacks against activists and journalists. On October 19, prominent human rights lawyer Digna Ochoa was murdered in her Mexico City office. Ochoa, a past victim of kidnapping and threats, had escaped an assassination attempt in 1999. A note found next to her threatened her colleagues as well.

On October 27, anonymous death threats were issued against human rights activists Miguel Sarre, Fernando Ruiz, Juan Antonio Vega, Sergio Aguayo, and Edgar Cortez. And on November 6, Germán Dehesa, a writer and columnist with the daily *Reforma*, received anonymous death threats via e-mail after he wrote a piece denouncing the harassment of human rights activists.

On December 4, robbers broke into the offices of the monthly magazine *Forum*, taking computer equipment worth about 65,000 Mexican pesos (US$7,000), along with CD-ROMs and zip discs containing archive materials. *Forum* is best known for publishing articles by jailed Gen. José Francisco Gallardo Rodríguez, who was arrested in 1993 after writing an article for

Forum calling for the armed forces to establish an independent, civilian ombudsman to monitor human rights abuses involving the military. While *Forum* director Eduardo Ibarra refrained from calling the robbery politically motivated, some journalists believed the break-in was connected to other attacks on human rights advocates. The investigation into the robbery had made no progress by year's end.

Mexican law does not currently guarantee public access to official information, but Congress is scheduled to consider two competing bills on the subject in the spring of 2002. One, drafted and supported by a coalition of journalists, academics, and nongovernmental organizations, would provide comprehensive measures that include sanctions for public officials who hide or destroy information. Critics charge that the other bill, sponsored by the government, offers unacceptably limited access and does not punish officials for failing to comply with the regulations.

The access to information bills have sparked a contentious debate. Ernesto Villanueva, an academic and frequent collaborator with the Mexico City weekly *Proceso*, told CPJ that he received threats after he criticized the government-sponsored version of the law.

The U.S.-Mexico border remained a dangerous place for journalists, who are often targeted by narco-traffickers and corrupt security personnel in the region. On February 19, José Luis Ortega Mata, the editor of the weekly *Semanario de Ojinaga*, in Chihuahua State, was shot to death. Friends and relatives linked the murder to his stories on drug trafficking in the region, including drug traffickers' ties to local politicians.

In August, a judge acquitted the two suspects in the 1998 murder of Philip True, a *San Antonio Express-News* (Texas) journalist who was killed while working on a story about the Huichols, an indigenous population that lives in a mountainous area stretching across Jalisco, Nayarit, and Durango states. The judge's ruling was under appeal at year's end. However, CPJ protested irregularities in the prosecution and the investigation that cast doubt on the validity of the proceedings.

NICARAGUA

DURING HIS LAST YEAR IN OFFICE, PRESIDENT ARNOLDO ALEMÁN continued to show intolerance and hostility toward the press. His administration supported a law requiring compulsory registration for journalists and doled out state advertising to punish or reward media outlets, depending on their coverage.

Most journalists agree that compared with the previous government, led by Violeta Chamorro, which repealed restrictive measures and allowed the media to flourish, press freedom has suffered under the Alemán administration.

Alemán's government has been plagued by corruption scandals, many of them uncovered by the press. The president himself has been accused of generously adding to his wealth while in office, and he has refused to make his tax returns public. Alemán has rejected corruption charges, calling them part of a media campaign designed to tarnish his achievements.

Nicaraguan journalists and media owners have challenged Law 372, which mandates that all journalists must register with the press organization Colegio de Periodistas de Nicaragua. After the National Assembly approved the bill in December 2000, President Alemán sent it back to the assembly for revisions, which included restrictive provisions such as penal sanctions for journalists not accredited with the Colegio. The assembly adopted the modified bill in March 2001.

In early June, Nicaraguan journalists and media owners challenged the legislation in the Supreme Court of Justice, which had yet to issue a decision at press time. In 1985, the Costa Rica–based Inter-American Court of Human Rights ruled that laws requiring the mandatory licensing of journalists violate the American Convention on Human Rights.

Despite having promised in 2000 that political considerations would no longer influence state advertising policy, the Alemán administration continued to face accusations that it manipulated the flow of state advertising to reward or punish the media. In late June, *El Nuevo Diario*, a leading daily close to the Sandinista National Liberation Front (FSLN), announced that the government had sharply curtailed the paper's share of state advertising, in addition to canceling the subscriptions of government ministries and agencies. The main beneficiary appeared to be the pro-government *La Noticia*, which, despite its low circulation, received a disproportionate share of state advertising.

The Managua daily *La Prensa*, meanwhile, is still awaiting a Supreme Court decision regarding government attempts to collect taxes based on a 1999 audit it conducted after the paper published a report on official corruption.

In presidential elections held on November 4, Constitutionalist Liberal Party candidate Enrique Bolaños beat the FSLN-led National Convergence candidate and former president Daniel Ortega. But during the campaign, according to prominent journalist Adolfo Pastrán Arancibia, unsubstantiated press allegations of corruption against both candidates seemed designed to advance political agendas rather than to present the news.

A bill that would allow increased access to public information remained stuck in the National Assembly at year's end, but President-elect Bolaños has promised to press for its passage. Local journalists say the law is sorely needed because of the government's instinctively secretive approach to information management.

PANAMA

DURING 2001, GOVERNMENT OFFICIALS PROPOSED LEGISLATION to toughen repressive press laws, castigated local journalists and media outlets, and prosecuted them for criminal defamation.

Panama's so-called gag laws include a range of articles, laws, and decrees—many promulgated under military governments—that criminalize criticism of public officials and permit prior censorship. In December 1999, following a pledge to repeal those regulations after she took office in September 1999, President Mireya Moscoso signed a bill that repealed some of the more onerous provisions. Under the law, the government was required to submit a bill before June 2000 that was expected to bring Panama's press laws in line with international standards.

But the bill was never submitted, neither in 2000 nor in 2001. In fact, the government considered presenting legislation that would have tightened press laws, though no new restrictions had been formally proposed by year's end.

In a positive development, the government passed a new access to information law based on a proposal from Transparency International, an international nongovernmental organization that aims to combat corruption. The bill establishes fines of up to 2,000 balboas (US$2,000) and even dismissal for government employees who do not release public information in a timely manner.

The government continues to use lawsuits to attack journalists, accusing the media of waging a campaign against public officials. Even President Moscoso, along with Winston Spadafora, the former minister of government and justice and a current Supreme Court justice, filed a criminal defamation suit. On September 17, the weekly *La Cáscara News* published a photomontage portraying Moscoso and Spadafora, both scantily dressed, in an intimate embrace. Several *La Cáscara News* employees were briefly detained, and on September 19, the Ministry of Government and Justice temporarily banned the weekly for violating parts of the press laws that had not been repealed in December 1999, including the requirement that publications provide the ministry with data such as the names of its editors and legal counsel.

Meanwhile, Attorney General José Antonio Sossa again proved to be a foe of the press. "There's a criminal aspect to Panamanian journalism that can only be eradicated with the application of penal laws," he was quoted as saying in the June 3 edition of the daily *La Prensa*. The chief prosecutor kept up a drum beat of criticism before and during a June visit to Panama by members from the Inter-American Commission on Human Rights (IACHR) and the IACHR's then-special rapporteur for freedom of expression Santiago A. Canton. The IACHR delegates used this visit, during which they also met with an indignant Sossa, to reiterate an earlier request to eliminate Panama's "disrespect" provisions.

Panamanian journalists have taken to the streets to protest their situation. On March 19, after two of their colleagues were handed suspended 18-month prison sentences, journalists picketed the Supreme Court. Nonetheless, in a country where, according to some estimates, one-third of journalists face criminal defamation prosecutions, self-censorship has become rampant, and even protests have become subdued.

On March 22, Panama's leading daily *La Prensa* was subjected to what has been dubbed a "boardroom coup" by Ricardo Alberto Arias, the foreign minister for former president Ernesto Pérez Balladares. The daily, which was created in 1980 to fight Panama's military dictatorship, later became a thorn in the side of Pérez Balladares because of its take-no-prisoners muckraking of his government's officials.

According to CPJ contacts, Arias persuaded a majority of the paper's shareholders to elect him as the new president of the paper. Previously, Arias had convinced a majority of executive board members to vote against renewing the contract of Peruvian journalist Gustavo Gorriti, who, as *La Prensa*'s associate editor, led the paper to break scandal after scandal about the Pérez Balladares administration during the late 1990s. A key member of *La Prensa*'s crack reporting team subsequently resigned, and others at the paper were demoted, leaving the once feisty paper a shadow of its former self.

PARAGUAY

JOURNALISTS IN PARAGUAY FACE ONE OF THE REGION'S most difficult working environments, in which threats, attacks, and criminal defamation lawsuits occur frequently. Throughout 2001, the Paraguayan press remained sharply divided between the ruling Colorado Party and the opposition Liberal Party. The press does cover official corruption, but media owners' allegiances to powerful politicians and businessmen, combined with a lack of balance and accuracy, damaged the credibility of much local journalism.

On July 16, President Luis González Macchi signed Law 1728 on Administrative Transparency and Free Access to Information. The law ostensibly codified Article 28 of the Paraguayan Constitution, which states that public sources of information "are free to all." In fact, Law 1728 made it extremely difficult for journalists to obtain any public records and left a dangerous amount of discretion in the hands of the president and other officials.

Journalists also argued that public officials could take advantage of the law to hinder or delay newspaper investigations into corruption, and that the complicated bureaucratic procedures required for obtaining official information hampered the media's ability to report news. After severe criticism from the media and civil society, the president repealed the law on September 24.

Parliament is currently considering new legislation to address the issue of access to information. One bill, drafted in collaboration with the local press union Sindicato de Periodistas del Paraguay (SPP) and other civil society groups, would shorten the waiting period to access official information and would require that all information be granted free of charge.

On September 20, the Chamber of Deputies passed a bill to amend Law 1682, which was originally intended to restrict the activities of credit reporting agencies. But journalists claimed that it did not distinguish between public figures and private citizens, making it almost impossible to monitor the finances of government officials. At year's end, the bill, which exempted the press from those restrictions, moved to the Senate. Senators then added modifications prohibiting the press from publishing "sensitive" personal data such as medical information, religious beliefs, race, and political affiliation. Paraguayan journalists sharply criticized the changes.

Criminal defamation laws were used throughout 2001 to stifle criticism. Several articles of the Penal Code establish penalties ranging from a fine to two years' imprisonment for libel, defamation, and slander. While journalists are rarely imprisoned for their work, they have been ordered to pay hefty monetary damages. In September, for instance, Telmo Tomás Ibáñez Jara, *ABC Color* correspondent in the city of Concepción, was ordered to pay a fine of 19 million guaraníes (approximately US$4,000) in connection with a criminal defamation lawsuit filed by three city officials. In November, the Concepción Appeals Court reversed the ruling.

In April, a judge ordered *ABC Color* editor Aldo Zuccolillo to pay a fine of 470 million guaraníes (around US$100,000) in a criminal complaint filed in 1998 by Colorado Party senator Juan Carlos Galaverna. The judgment was under appeal at press time. Another criminal defamation lawsuit, filed against Zuccolillo in May by former Colorado Party deputy Oscar González, was dismissed, according to *ABC Color*.

In December, community radio stations achieved a significant victory when the Comptroller General's Office ruled that they may now request permits from the National Telecommunications Commission without having to bid for frequencies in a public auction, according to the World Association of Community Radio Broadcasters (AMARC).

Paraguay remains a dangerous place for journalists. In January, an unidentified gunman murdered journalist Salvador Medina Velázquez. His family linked the attack to his reports on criminal gangs. Early in the year, police arrested four suspects. In September, a prosecutor charged one of them with Medina's murder and requested that charges against the others be dismissed. A court found the remaining suspect guilty and sentenced him to 25 years in prison. Medina's relatives, however, believe that the individuals who ordered the murder have not been brought to justice.

In May, journalist Séver del Puerto and his family were threatened with death, apparently because of del Puerto's free-lance investigation into the alleged involvement of a former interior minister and several judges in an August 2000 robbery at Asunción International Airport. Because of the threats, del Puerto and his family went into hiding. The journalist was later admitted to a hospital after an emotional breakdown.

Journalists outside major cities faced the most attacks and threats. In November, Vicenta Risso, correspondent for the Asunción daily *ABC Color* in Presidente Hayes Department, received several death threats after taking a picture of a local official who was using a public vehicle for election campaigns, according to the SPP. Also in November, *ABC Color* correspondent César Martínez reported that he had received death threats from Colorado Party politicians because of his critical coverage, the SPP reported.

PERU

PRESS FREEDOM CONDITIONS IMPROVED MARKEDLY in Peru during 2001. The victory of centrist Alejandro Toledo, who beat leftist candidate Alan García in the June 3 runoff presidential elections, brought democracy back to Peru, a country that suffered 10 years of authoritarian rule under former president Alberto K. Fujimori.

In June, Fujimori's sinister intelligence adviser, Vladimiro Montesinos, was captured in Venezuela and extradited to Peru. He is currently jailed in a maximum-security prison and faces scores of charges, including corruption, embezzlement, money laundering, and weapons trafficking. Fujimori, who remains in self-imposed exile in Japan, also faces numerous corruption charges in Peru.

Throughout 2001, the steady release of the "vladivideos," a collection of tapes that Montesinos had secretly recorded, most likely to extort money from those taped, continually shocked the country. The tapes first emerged in September 2000 when independent cable channel Canal N broadcast a video showing Montesinos bribing an opposition congressman. The recordings vindicated the independent press, which, led by the dailies *El Comercio*, *La República*, and *Liberación*, had endured defamation suits and harassment for covering corruption and human rights violations under Fujimori.

Each new installment of the "vladivideos" revealed the brazen measures that Montesinos and Fujimori had taken to corrupt the legislature, the judiciary, and the media. With the complicity of television channel owners, the pair orchestrated media coverage in order to secure Fujimori's third presidential term, widely considered unconstitutional, in April 2000. Their tactics included bribes, judicial persecution, manipulation of government advertising, threats, and tax incentives. In a video released in February, Montesinos bragged: "They [the broadcast channels] are all lined up. Every day I have a meeting with them and we plan what is going to come out in the nightly news shows."

Several media owners have been charged with crimes ranging from embezzlement and influence peddling to conspiring to commit crimes. In one set of "vladivideos," José Enrique Crousillat and his son José Francisco Crousillat, owners of América Televisión-Canal 4, can be seen taking thousands of dollars in cash from Montesinos. In February, José Francisco Crousillat admitted to having received US$9 million from Montesinos in exchange for a carte blanche to dictate Canal 4's programming content so as to favor Fujimori's candidacy. Both father and son are now fugitives. The brothers Samuel and Mendel Winter, minority owners of Frecuencia Latina-Canal 2, who conspired with Montesinos to wrest the channel from its owner, Israeli-born businessman Baruch Ivcher, are now in jail.

Another video, released in February, showed businessman Genaro Delgado Parker, former owner of Red Global de Televisión-Canal 13, negotiating the 1999 dismissal of outspoken Fujimori critic and TV journalist César Hildebrandt with Montesino in exchange for the latter's support in several legal disputes over the station's ownership. Delgado Parker now faces an investigation for conspiring to commit crimes.

The defamation campaign that the Fujimori government orchestrated against the independent press and the opposition from 1998 to 2000 was further exposed in 2001. The *prensa chicha*, a group of tabloids that reveled in publishing unsubstantiated allegations about independent journalists and opposition politicians, carried out the campaign. In March, a judge prohibited several tabloid owners from leaving the country after a public prosecutor's investigation revealed evidence that the government had directly bankrolled the tabloids.

The broadcast media's complicity with the Fujimori government prompted an intense national debate over what action to take against corrupt media owners and their TV stations. Some, like the reknowned Peruvian writer Mario Vargas Llosa, proposed empowering the judiciary to revoke the licenses of TV stations that had supported Fujimori.

In December, the Toledo administration proposed the Law of Modernization and Transparency of Telecommunications Services, which a congressional subcommittee was considering at press time. Designed to prevent manipulation and abuse of the broadcast media, the bill would create a radio and television commission, comprising government and civil society representatives, to oversee and review the TV licensing process.

Despite the marked improvement in press freedom conditions, attacks and threats against journalists continued in 2001. Journalists from the provinces were again the most endangered. Unidentified assailants attacked Luis Samuel Zevallos Hidalgo, a journalist with radio station Radio La Oroya in Yauli-La Oroya, Junín Department, apparently for broadcasting a recording of a local official bribing a business executive.

SURINAME

PRESIDENT RONALD VENETIAAN, LEADER OF A MODERATE COALITION of ethnic parties, proved as respectful of press freedom as journalists had hoped when he took office in August 2000. Since then, no major abuses have been reported in this former Dutch colony of less than half a million inhabitants.

Under the previous government, journalists were routinely harassed and subject to diatribes from strongman Dési Bouterse, leader of the then-ruling National Democratic Party (NDP). An August 12, 2000, meeting between Venetiaan and representatives of the media went a long way toward assuring local journalists that the press would have a good relationship with the new administration. Nita Ramcharan, editor-in-chief of Suriname's leading daily *De Ware Tijd*, reported that Venetiaan kept his promises throughout 2001. "Press freedom has been completely respected by this government," she said.

The NDP station Radio Kankantrie was taken off the air twice during the year for administrative reasons, but local sources said the actions might have come in reprisal for the station's anti-government broadcasts. However, Radio Kankantrie has been on the air without problems ever since.

Local journalists say that Bouterse, who remains a political force in Suriname as an opposition member of the National Assembly, and his followers kept fairly quiet in 2001. Bouterse is being investigated in Suriname for his role in the 1982 massacre of 15 political opponents. In a separate investigation, the Dutch Supreme Court ruled on September 18 that Bouterse cannot be tried in the Netherlands for the massacre. But on October 23, the same court upheld an 11-year sentence against him for cocaine smuggling.

Suriname's deep-seated culture of intolerance was revealed on the night of May 28, when three men attacked Dutch reporter Armand Snijders. The men blocked his car, beat and kicked him, and burned him with cigarettes. Snijders, who has lived in Suriname since 1993 and has worked for the Dutch news service Geassocieerde Pers Diensten for the last three years, told CPJ that the assault was probably related to his reporting about a former military officer whom he suspected of being involved in cocaine smuggling. The investigation into the attack has not yielded any results, Snijders said.

TRINIDAD AND TOBAGO

THIS OIL- AND GAS-RICH ISLAND NATION, whose population is equally divided between people of African and Indian descent, moved from crisis to crisis after elections in December 2000.

Former prime minister Basdeo Panday's United National Congress (UNC), supported mainly by Indo-Trinidadians, narrowly defeated the People's National Movement (PNM), generally supported by Afro-Trinidadians, in elections that the PNM charged were fraudulent. Both parties challenged some of the results, though the challenges became moot when the prime minister called for new elections in October after the UNC lost its legislative majority because three of its representatives defected.

The elections ended in a tie, with both the UNC and the PNM winning 18 seats, sparking yet another constitutional crisis. According to the constitution, the president may appoint a prime minister who he thinks will command a majority in Parliament. During the last week of December, PNM leader Patrick Manning was sworn in as prime minister after President Arthur N. R. Robinson chose him to break the tie.

In 2000, then-prime minister Panday refrained from his usual tirades against the press in advance of the elections. But in 2001 he lashed out at the media, which has actively covered several corruption scandals. According to John Babb, news editor of the popular paper *Newsday*, Panday called such reports "lies, half-truths, and innuendos." Babb told CPJ that when unfavorable stories appear, politicians often tell their supporters not to buy those papers and also to pull advertising from them.

Wesley Gibbings, a free-lance journalist and president of the recently launched Association of Caribbean Media Workers, said that in addition to government suppression, the business community has also tried to control the press. "While the principal, immediate threat appears to be the attitude of the government, a very real threat exists from among the ranks of the commercial sector," he pointed out. "It usually takes the form of withdrawal of advertising," he added. The fact that many media outlets are part of business conglomerates complicates the situation, Gibbings said.

In these tumultuous times, the country's 11 radio stations have played a very important role, according to Gibbings. Many feature shows where callers talk openly about controversial issues. "Most of the discussion," Gibbings noted, "has focused on claims of corruption."

UNITED STATES

Since its founding in 1981, CPJ has, as a matter of strategy and policy, concentrated on press freedom violations and attacks against journalists outside the United States. Within the country, a vital press freedom community marshals its resources and expertise to defend journalists' rights. CPJ aims to focus its efforts on those nations where journalists most need international support and protection.

However, CPJ did take up a number of U.S. cases in 2001, either because they were particularly serious, or because they had broad international implications. For the first time in its 20-year history, CPJ included an American on its annual list of imprisoned journalists. Two American journalists were killed in 2001: Free-lance photographer William Biggart died covering the attacks on the World Trade Center on September 11, and Robert Stevens, a photo editor for the tabloid *Sun* newspaper, died from inhalation anthrax in October.

On August 7, CPJ sent a letter to U.S. Attorney General John Ashcroft expressing concern about the detention of journalist Vanessa Leggett on contempt of court charges.

Leggett, a 33-year-old free-lance writer based in Houston, Texas, cited the confidentiality of her sources in refusing to turn over her research to a grand jury investigating the 1997 murder of a Houston socialite. CPJ's letter noted that the detention "sends exactly the wrong signal to authoritarian governments, who may now show even less restraint in using state power to restrict press freedom." Leggett, who was released on January 4, is believed to have been imprisoned longer than any journalist in U.S. history.

The Leggett case was not the only effort the Justice Department made to breach the journalist-source relationship. In August, Associated Press reporter John Solomon received notification that his home phone records had been subpoenaed in an effort to learn the source for a story on organized crime.

The September 11 attacks on the World Trade Center in New York City and the Pentagon in Washington, D.C., dramatically changed the media landscape in the United States and raised a number of troubling press freedom issues.

While the press earned widespread public support for its coverage of the attacks, some media observers questioned whether the U.S. media abandoned objectivity in covering the domestic response to terrorism as well as U.S. military operations in Afghanistan. Commentators in the U.S., but particularly in Europe and the Middle East, sharply criticized some of the U.S. media for its shallow coverage of Islam, for giving minimal coverage to civilian casualties in Afghanistan, and for timid reporting on such controversial U.S. policies as the detention without charge of hundreds of terrorism suspects.

The Bush administration also took several steps to influence both domestic and international coverage, particularly of Osama bin Laden and the Al Qaeda terrorist network.

Just a few days after September 11, the U.S. State Department contacted the Voice of America (VOA), a broadcast organization funded by the federal government, and expressed concern about the radio broadcast of an exclusive interview with Taliban leader Mullah Mohammed Omar. "We didn't think that the American taxpayer ... should be broadcasting the voice of the Taliban," explained State Department spokesman Richard Boucher. In December, Spozhmai W. Maiwandi, the VOA journalist who conducted the interview, was forced out of her job as head of the Pashto Service. Around the same time, VOA chief Robert Reilly distributed a memo barring interviews with officials from "nations that sponsor terrorism." VOA staffers criticized the policy as interfering with the station's newsgathering function.

On October 3, Secretary of State Colin Powell asked the Emir of Qatar to use his influence to rein in Al-Jazeera, a Qatar-based, Arabic-language satellite station bankrolled by the Qatari government. The request stemmed from concern about the station's alleged anti-American bias and its repeated airing of a 1998 exclusive interview with Osama bin Laden.

A week later, on October 10, National Security Adviser Condoleezza Rice asked a group of U.S. television executives to use caution when airing pre-recorded messages from Osama bin Laden and his associates. Rice argued that such statements were at best propaganda and could contain coded instructions to terrorist cells. Network executives agreed to consider editing future bin Laden videotapes to remove language that could incite violence against Americans.

While the appropriateness of Rice's conference call with the executives was debated in the United States, the actions taken by the Bush administration seemed to embolden repressive governments around the world to crack down on their own domestic media. In Russia, a presidential adviser said President Vladimir Putin planned to study U.S. limitations on reporting about terrorists in order to develop rules for Russian media.

A new section of CPJ's Web site (www.cpj.org), called "Covering the New War," tracked other war-related press freedom abuses in countries around the globe, including Benin, China, Indonesia, Israel, Liberia, Uganda, and Zimbabwe.

While journalists covering the war in Afghanistan risked detention by the Taliban as well as armed attack, many also complained about a lack of access to U.S. forces in the field. In December, several news organizations protested when reporters at a Marine base near Kandahar were confined to a warehouse to prevent them from photographing injured soldiers who were being transferred to the base for treatment after a friendly-fire incident.

Later that month, Afghan tribal forces detained three photojournalists at the behest of U.S. Special Forces operating in the Tora Bora region, according to *The New York Times.* Memory cards containing images of U.S. soldiers were seized from two digital cameras.

On January 31, 2002, CPJ also sent a letter to U.S. Secretary of Defense Donald Rumsfeld requesting clarification of the November 13, 2001, missile strike on the Kabul bureau of Al-Jazeera. The U.S. military described the building as a "known" Al Qaeda facility without providing any evidence. Despite the fact that the facility had housed the Al-Jazeera office for nearly two years and had several satellite dishes mounted on its roof, the U.S. military claimed it had no indications the building was used as Al-Jazeera's Kabul bureau.

A series of anthrax-laced letters sent to U.S. media figures and politicians in October created widespread anxiety among the press. Tainted letters were sent to NBC news anchor Tom Brokaw and to the *New York Post.* The child of an ABC news employee and several American Media Inc. employees in Florida were also infected, although the source of the anthrax could not be positively identified. American Media publishes supermarket tabloids, including *The National Enquirer*, which covers mostly celebrity gossip (although the paper did run stories attacking Osama bin Laden). *The Sun*, where Robert Stevens worked as photo editor, is filled with bizarre human-interest stories and astrological predictions. At the end of the year, authorities had not been able to link the letters to the September 11 attacks.

URUGUAY

ALTHOUGH URUGUAY BOASTS ONE OF LATIN AMERICA'S MOST VIBRANT and diverse media scenes, journalists say its quality has suffered during a three-year economic recession. Many journalists have lost their jobs, while increased competition with foreign publications, a decline in Uruguayans' buying power, and a decrease in advertising have exacerbated the crisis.

In a country where many publications depend almost entirely on state advertising, a sharp decrease in government advertising budgets has hurt many media outlets. Journalists also remain concerned that state agencies and enterprises continue to withhold advertising from critical media while rewarding media that provide favorable coverage.

The country's highly secretive banking and tax laws severely hinder coverage of corruption, journalists say. They also contend that media owners' ties to allegedly corrupt businessmen have suppressed coverage of links between Uruguayan companies and money-laundering schemes run by Argentine businessmen. Many Uruguayans only learned about the allegations by watching Argentine cable channels.

In another telling example, the journalists' union Asociación de la Prensa Uruguaya denounced local TV channel Canal 12 in early September for censoring parts of an Argentine show in which Argentine parliamentary deputy Elisa Carrió exposed alleged money-laundering involving Uruguayan companies.

Journalists also faced court battles for revealing government scandals. On May 30, an appeals court reversed a previous ruling that ordered the weekly *Búsqueda* to publish a letter by María Olmedo, an official of the General Tax Office (DGI) who took offense at a *Búsqueda* article denouncing alleged DGI corruption. The appeals court ruled that because the story did not mention any DGI officials by name, the paper was not required to print Olmedo's letter.

A right-to-information bill remains stalled in the Uruguayan Congress. Introduced in 1998, the law would guarantee the right to access public records kept in government archives and would give preferential treatment to media requests for such information.

Radio broadcasters have long been divided over the issue of community radio stations; currently, more than 20 of them operate without a permit in Uruguay. While commercial stations claim that community stations interfere with their frequencies, community stations argue that they cannot afford to buy frequencies, which are currently granted through auctions. In unprecedented October talks, representatives from both sides met with officials from the URSEC, the country's telecommunications regulatory agency, for preliminary negotiations on creating a legal framework in which community stations can operate.

VENEZUELA

DURING 2001, SUPPORTERS OF PRESIDENT HUGO CHÁVEZ FRÍAS clashed with the opposition over the government's political and economic policies, while in December the business sector called for street demonstrations to protest anti-business legislation. Venezuela's political situation—along with Chávez's popularity—appeared tenuous at the end of the year.

Amid such tension, the antagonistic relationship between the media and the president took a turn for the worse. While the local press can still report the news freely, Chávez's increasingly harsh rhetoric and a series of disturbing legal actions bode ill for freedom of expression in Venezuela.

Chávez has effectively used the media to solidify his popularity and marginalize the independent press. Through *cadenas*, his wildly popular impromptu radio and television shows, he has rallied support, recounted anecdotes from his daily life, and excoriated his opponents—including the press, which he has labeled the "anti-social communications media." In addition, Chávez routinely used public media to pursue his own agenda and that of his Fifth Republic Movement (MVR) party.

Last year, during a broadcast of Chávez's popular radio show, "Aló, Presidente," the president criticized Elías Santana, coordinator of the civic group

Queremos Elegir, host of the radio program "Santana Total," and a columnist for the Caracas-based daily *El Nacional*. Santana filed suit, demanding that he be given the right to reply on a subsequent broadcast of the show.

But the Supreme Court denied Santana's petition, ruling on June 12 that the right to reply was intended to benefit only individuals who do not have access to a public forum, not media professionals. The court then vastly exceeded the limits of the case and went on to create a set of criteria defining what constitutes "timely, truthful, and impartial information." The right to "truthful" information was incorporated into Venezuela's constitution in 1999 despite objections from media groups.

Under the Supreme Court ruling, journalists may now express opinions only if they do not contain insults that are "out of context, disconnected, or unnecessary for the topic; or offensive, insidious, or degrading." In addition, if a publication claims to be independent, but the majority of its columnists subscribe to the same ideological beliefs, the publication could be in violation of the new standards. The ruling also permits prior censorship in some cases.

On July 21, the newspaper association Bloque de Prensa Venezolano protested the Supreme Court ruling in a petition filed with the Inter-American Commission on Human Rights (IACHR). The commission was still evaluating the case at year's end.

On October 18, the Venezuelan National Telecommunications Commission (Conatel) began investigating the 24-hour news channel Globovisión to determine whether it had violated media broadcast regulations by reporting "false" news during an inaccurate September 29 report that the station corrected later the same day. Conatel could fine the station or suspend its license temporarily or permanently. On October 29, the office of the IACHR's special rapporteur for freedom of expression declared its concern about the investigation, and contended it was based on legislation contrary to the principle of press freedom. The case was ongoing at year's end.

In late October, the First National Conference of Popular Communicators, a group of community media representatives sponsored by President Chávez's party, issued worrisome recommendations, including "imposing censorship on sensationalist media and domestic media that distort truthful information" and asking Conatel to ban comic programs that "deteriorate the image of the President." ■

| CASES TABLE OF CONTENTS |

ARGENTINA

JANUARY 18

Análisis
ATTACKED

Unidentified individuals ransacked the offices of the weekly *Análisis*, based in the town of Paraná in Entre Ríos Province, north of Buenos Aires on the Uruguayan border.

The attack likely took place in the early morning hours, when the office was closed. The doors to the weekly's offices were not forced open, leading staffers to believe that the perpetrators had a key. The entire office was ransacked and drawer locks were tampered with, suggesting that the premises had been thoroughly searched.

The attackers took documents, audio recordings of interviews, a videotape, and two cellular phones. They also searched the desk of editor Daniel Enz, taking documents but leaving valuable items such as signed checks. Because they did not steal any expensive office equipment, robbery was not a likely motive.

In the January 25 issue of *Análisis*, Enz wrote that days before the break-in, individuals who appeared to be plainclothes intelligence agents kept the weekly's offices under surveillance.

Enz claimed the attack was intended to intimidate the paper's staff. He speculated that local officials ordered the attack in response to *Análisis*' critical coverage of the provincial government.

Later on January 18, local police visited the *Análisis* offices to gather evidence and dust for fingerprints. Examining magistrate Raúl Herzovich

was subsequently placed in charge of the investigation.

At press time, the inquiry into the assault was stalled, and Enz had not been called to testify.

MARCH 28

Marcelo Bonelli, *Clarín*
LEGAL ACTION
Julio Blanck, *Clarín*
LEGAL ACTION

Bonelli, a journalist with the national daily *Clarín*, and Blanck, *Clarín*'s national political editor, were charged with breaching tax confidentiality after an article by Bonelli in the June 5, 2000, edition of *Clarín* reported that Víctor Alderete, the former head of the Comprehensive Medical Attention Program, the national health service for retirees, was being investigated by the General Direction of Taxes (DGI) for tax evasion.

Bonelli reported that the DGI suspected Alderete, who claimed to have a negative income, of hiding income behind loans he obtained from a dummy corporation in order to purchase a farm for 4.5 million pesos (US$4.5 million). Bonelli also wrote that Alderete was suspected of bribery and channeling money from bribes to the dummy corporation.

In his article, Bonelli cited Alderete's 1997 and 1998 tax returns, the latest available.

On March 28, 2001, federal judge Claudio Bonadio did not deny the truthfulness of the article but ordered the prosecution of Bonelli under Law 11.683, which guarantees the confidentiality of tax information. In the same ruling, the judge dismissed the charges against Blanck, contending that he had fulfilled his responsibility to ensure that the information published was correct.

The charge against Bonelli carries a prison sentence of one month to two years, according to the local press freedom organization PERIODISTAS.

On July 17, the Federal Appeals Court overturned Judge Bonadio's decision and ruled that press freedom should prevail over individual privacy, especially when the news is of public interest or involves a public official. The judges further ruled that Law 11.683 did not apply to journalists.

On July 7, 2000, Alderete was prosecuted for tax evasion and held in preventive detention. He was released on September 18 of this year, but the investigation into his finances continued at press time.

SEPTEMBER 25

NOTICIAS
LEGAL ACTION
Jorge Fontevecchia, *NOTICIAS*
LEGAL ACTION
Héctor D'Amico, *NOTICIAS*
LEGAL ACTION

The Supreme Court upheld a lower court ruling against the weekly newsmagazine *NOTICIAS*, its director Fontevecchia, and its former editor D'Amico.

According to the judgment, *NOTICIAS* violated former president Carlos Saúl Menem's right to privacy by reporting on his extramarital relationship with Martha Meza, a former schoolteacher who is currently a parliamentary deputy.

In 1996, Menem sued *NOTICIAS*

for invasion of privacy over a series of 1995 articles about his relationship with Meza.

NOTICIAS reported that the relationship began in the early 1980s during Argentina's military dictatorship (the future president was detained in Formosa Province at the time), and that Menem was the father of Meza's illegitimate son, who was born in 1981. The weekly also reported that Menem gave various expensive gifts to Meza.

Meza, who by 1995 had become a provincial congressional deputy for Menem's Justicialist Party (PJ), currently serves as a PJ deputy in the federal parliament.

Menem lost the case, but an appeals court overturned the ruling in 1998. On September 25, five of nine Supreme Court justices voted to uphold the 1998 verdict against *NOTICIAS*, with four abstentions.

The Supreme Court's September 25 ruling also upheld an appellate court order requiring *NOTICIAS* to publish the judgment. However, the Supreme Court lowered Menem's damages award from 150,000 pesos (US$150,000) to 60,000 pesos (US$60,000).

Neither Menem nor the judges have ever questioned the accuracy of the magazine's reporting.

On November 15, Horacio Verbitsky and Eduardo Bertoni, secretary-general and legal adviser, respectively, of the Argentine press freedom organization PERIODISTAS, filed a petition on the *NOTICIAS* case with the Inter-American Commission on Human Rights (IACHR) in Washington, D.C.

Accompanied by CPJ board member and *Chicago Tribune* columnist Clarence Page and World Press

Freedom Committee executive director Marilyn Greene, Verbitsky and Bertoni presented a 68-page complaint to IACHR executive secretary Santiago A. Canton on behalf of PERIODISTAS and *NOTICIAS*. The complaint asked the IACHR to suspend the verdict while it examines the case, as well as to urge the Argentine government to amend its legal system in order to guarantee freedom of expression.

CPJ published an alert about the case that same day. At year's end, the IACHR was still reviewing the complaint.

BOLIVIA

JULY 29

Juan Carlos Encinas, free-lancer
KILLED

Encinas, 39, a free-lance reporter in the small town of Catavi in La Paz Department, died of wounds sustained while he was covering a fight between two mining cooperatives that were vying for control of a limestone quarry outside Catavi.

On July 29, about 50 armed members of the mining cooperative Marmolera Comunitaria Ltda surrounded and attacked members of Cooperativa Multiactiva Catavi Ltda, which controlled the quarry.

The attackers fired at least seven shots, wounding a worker and Encinas, who was shot in the groin. Encinas was initially treated at a local medical post but died on the way to a hospital in the city of El Alto.

Encinas was carrying a camera and a tape recorder, and his credentials identified him as a journalist. Three days before Encinas' death, a small

production company hired him to report on the story for La Paz-based TV channel Canal 21, according to the local press union Federación de Trabajadores de la Prensa de Bolivia.

Two days after Encinas' death, the El Alto police arrested eight men suspected of the killing. Though they were initially ordered released on bail, the Superior District Court of La Paz overturned that decision and the suspects remained in preventive detention.

SEPTEMBER 27

Tania Sandoval, ATB
ATTACKED
Alfredo Orellana, ATB
ATTACKED
Iván Canelas, *La Razón*
ATTACKED
Fernando Cartagena, *La Razón*
ATTACKED
Carlos Arévalo, UNITEL
ATTACKED
Dico Soliz, *Opinión*
ATTACKED

Six local journalists and three guides were attacked while covering clashes between coca growers and the military in Chapare, a tropical region in central Bolivia, according to local press reports. One of the guides was killed in the attack.

The journalists included Sandoval and Orellana, reporter and cameraman, respectively, with the television station ATB; Arévalo, a reporter for the television network UNITEL; Cartagena and Canelas, reporters with the national daily *La Razón*; and Soliz, a reporter for the Cochabamba-based daily *Opinión*.

The journalists were on their way to

interview an army commander. As they traveled down a road leading to the Loma Alta Military Camp, soldiers suddenly opened fire with live ammunition and tear gas canisters.

The gunfire lasted at least 15 minutes, forcing the journalists to hide in the bush and run uphill. The soldiers continued to shoot despite the fact that the journalists yelled, "We are from the press," and were wearing vests that identified them as members of the media.

On October 8, the journalists filed a written complaint with the Ombudsman's Office, supported with video evidence of the attack. At press time, the government had taken no action on the complaint.

NOVEMBER 29

Cecilia Saavedra, Canal 18 Megavisión
ATTACKED

Saavedra, a reporter with the television station Canal 18 Megavisión, was wounded by police fire while covering a protest by university students in the city of Santa Cruz.

The journalist and a cameraman were covering the second consecutive day of clashes between local police and students from the Universidad Autónoma Gabriel René Moreno who were demanding that the governor of Santa Cruz Department increase the university's budget.

At around 5 p.m., some students began pelting police with firecrackers. Police responded by throwing tear gas canisters and firing rubber bullets. The police then charged the protesters in an effort to break up the demonstration.

Choking on tear gas, Saavedra decided to leave the scene. As she was

walking past a university building, at least 11 rubber bullets struck her legs. A taxi took her to a private clinic where the bullets were surgically removed. Saavedra was released from the clinic two days later.

BRAZIL

MAY 4

Mário Quevedo Neto, *Folha de Vilhena*
LEGAL ACTION

Quevedo, a correspondent for the Vilhena-based daily *Folha do Sul* in the city of Porto Velho and a press adviser to Congressman Daniel Pereira of the Rondônia State Legislative Assembly, was convicted of criminal defamation and sentenced to community service.

The case stemmed from an article Quevedo wrote in March 1998, when he was the editor of *Folha de Vilhena*, reporting that inmates in Vilhena's prison were jailed under poor conditions, and that prison facilities were in a state of decay and abandonment. Quevedo held Judge Adolfo Theodoro Naujorks Neto (no relation to the journalist), who was in charge of inspecting state prisons, responsible.

Judge Naujorks filed a criminal defamation suit against the journalist and initially requested monetary damages, which he later withdrew.

According to the journalists' organization Federação Nacional dos Jornalistas, the Vilhena District Court ruled in 1998 that Quevedo had defamed Judge Naujorks, despite the fact that conditions at Vilhena's prison warranted judicial intervention.

The journalist was sentenced to four

months at a prison-shelter (which requires inmates to sleep at the prison but allows them to go to work during the day) and fined 1,300 reais (US$500).

After Quevedo appealed, the Rondônia State Court commuted his sentence to four months of community service at the State Ombudsman's Office in Porto Velho, the capital of Rondônia. In addition, Quevedo was ordered to pay the legal costs of the case and a 360 reais fine (US$145).

The journalist began serving his sentence on May 4, after missing a deadline to file an appeal at the federal level, and finished it on August 31.

JULY 21

Tribuna Popular
LEGAL ACTION

Officials confiscated the July 21 issue of *Tribuna Popular*, a weekly paper in the southern state of Rio Grande do Sul, after it reported on corruption charges against local authorities.

The confiscated issue contained a front-page story reporting that São Lourenço do Sul mayor Dari Pagel and five other former and current officials had recently been charged with embezzling about 20,000 reais (US$8,000) in 1997 and 1998 from a retirement fund created for municipal workers.

According to local newspapers, the same story was reported in the July 21 issue of the Pelotas-based daily *Diário Popular* and was subsequently picked up by the Pelotas daily *Diário da Manhã*, as well as the regional edition of the daily *Zero Hora*.

While Mayor Pagel took no legal action against these publications, he did file suit requesting the confiscation of the July 21 edition of *Tribuna Popular*, which he claimed had damaged his reputation.

On July 21, Judge Ana Paula Braga Alencastro ruled in favor of the mayor.

Tribuna Popular filed an appeal requesting that the impounded copies be released and planned to file a lawsuit requesting damages, according to the national daily *Folha de S.Paulo*. No further information on the case was available at press time.

AUGUST 16

Mário Coelho de Almeida Filho,
A Verdade
KILLED (MOTIVE UNCONFIRMED)

An unidentified gunman killed Coelho, administrative editor and publisher of the local thrice-monthly newspaper *A Verdade*, outside his house with a .45-caliber handgun.

The journalist was murdered just one day before he was scheduled to testify in a criminal defamation lawsuit.

Some local observers claimed that Coelho had persuaded local politicians to bankroll *A Verdade* in exchange for favorable coverage, according to the Brazilian media news Web site Comunique-se.com. Conversely, other sources claimed that Coelho had used the threat of negative coverage to extort money from politicians.

The suit against Coelho was brought by Magé mayor Narriman Zito and her husband, José Camilo Zito dos Santos, mayor of the local municipality of Duque de Caxias, after *A Verdade* printed the minutes of a state legislative assembly session during which a political rival of Zito accused her of having an affair with one of her security guards.

A Verdade often criticized local politicians for alleged corruption, and Coelho's father told the Brazilian daily *O Globo* that his son had received several phone threats five months before his death.

On September 14, acting on an anonymous tip, Magé police arrested retired Military Police sergeant Manoel Daniel de Abreu Filho as a suspect in the murder, according to *O Globo*. The person who tipped off the police also told them that de Abreu Filho had worked as a security guard for Rio de Janeiro state assemblywoman Andréia Zito, daughter of Duque de Caxias mayor Zito dos Santos.

At the time of his arrest, de Abreu Filho worked as a bodyguard for the wife of Waldir Zito, mayor of the city of Belford Roxo and brother of José Camilo Zito dos Santos.

After witnesses were shown a picture of de Abreu Filho and recognized him as the murderer, Judge Geraldo José Machado ordered that he be held in prison. The police seized two handguns from de Abreu Filho and said they would perform ballistic tests to determine if they were used in the crime. The police are also seeking to determine whether de Abreu Filho acted on his own or followed orders.

OCTOBER 4

Sérgio Fleury Moraes, *DEBATE*
`LEGAL ACTION`
DEBATE
`LEGAL ACTION`

In an ongoing civil defamation lawsuit, the Superior Court of Justice upheld a ruling ordering Fleury, publisher and owner of the Santa Cruz do Rio Pardo-based weekly *DEBATE*, to pay damages to Judge Antônio José Magdalena. As a result, his paper faced bankruptcy.

In a series of 1991 articles, *DEBATE* reported that the city government had given Judge Magdalena a home phone line for his private use, even though the local fire station had been denied telephone service. *DEBATE* also reported that Judge Magdalena's rent was paid with public funds, while the former residence for city judges remained vacant. *DEBATE* claimed that Judge Magdalena's living arrangements, although not illegal, constituted an "immoral perk."

In 1994, according to *DEBATE*, the National Audit Office ordered the city to stop paying the judge's rent.

In 1995, Judge Magdalena filed a civil action against Fleury and *DEBATE*. The judge argued that the paper had endangered him and his family, invaded their privacy, and damaged their reputation by publishing his phone number and a picture of his house. He requested monetary damages totaling US$140,000.

In 1996, a lower court in Santa Cruz do Rio Pardo ruled in Magdalena's favor. According to *DEBATE*, the sentencing judge was a close associate of Magdalena's.

A 1999 ruling from the São Paulo State Court of Justice upheld the sentence but lowered the award to US$67,000. Fleury maintained that Magdalena won the cases because judges tend to protect each other.

Fleury appealed the case to a five-judge panel of the Superior Court of

Justice. While two judges dismissed the appeal, one judge postponed the proceedings. On October 4, the appeal was rejected.

According to *DEBATE*, the award granted to Judge Magdalena, which may reach 400,000 reais (approximately US$150,000) including legal costs and interest, was excessive because the paper is a small-circulation publication.

In an October article, Fleury told the monthly *Imprensa* that his only property is the small offices that house the weekly, which are worth 100,000 reais (about US$37,000).

DEBATE appealed the case to a Superior Court of Justice panel comprising 10 judges, including the five who already rejected the appeal. If that appeal fails, Fleury can still appeal to the Supreme Federal Court, the highest court in the country. At year's end, the case was before the Superior Court of Justice.

CHILE

JANUARY 31

María Eugenia González, *El Mostrador.cl*
ATTACKED
Rocío Berrios, *El Mostrador.cl*
HARASSED
Fabio Díaz, Televisión Española
ATTACKED
Gonzalo Mazuela, *Primera Línea.cl*
ATTACKED

An angry crowd of supporters of Gen. Augusto Pinochet confronted González, Berrios, Mazuela, and Díaz while the journalists were covering the presentation of a warrant for house arrest to the former dictator.

The warrant charged Pinochet with masterminding the abduction and killing of 75 political prisoners in a 1973 military operation known as "the Caravan of Death."

At around 11 p.m., as the journalists were arriving outside the Pinochet family's country estate in the resort town of Bucalemu, southwest of Santiago, several dozen Pinochet supporters attacked them. According to the daily *El Mercurio de Valparaíso*, the supporters had been ferried from Santiago in three buses rented by the Pinochet Foundation in a show of support for the general.

The crowd spat on González, who works for the online daily *El Mostrador.cl*, and threw water, soil, and stones at her. Military police then came to González's rescue and escorted her into a police car.

The mob also damaged the car used by González and *El Mostrador.cl* reporter Berrios. González and Berrios subsequently filed a complaint with local police.

Díaz, a correspondent for Spanish TV channel Televisión Española, was kicked, insulted, and pelted with eggs. He was apparently targeted for his Spanish nationality as well as for being a journalist.

Spain became the object of the Pinochet sympathizers' wrath in October 1998, when Spanish judge Baltazar Garzón charged Pinochet with crimes against humanity and issued an international warrant for his arrest while the former dictator was visiting London. Pinochet returned to Chile in March 2000 after the British House of Lords ruled him medically unfit to stand trial.

Mazuela, who works for the online daily *Primera Línea.cl*, was reporting via cell phone on the attack against Díaz when the protesters approached and started kicking him. The three journalists suffered only minor injuries.

In addition to attacking journalists and accusing them of anti-Pinochet bias, the crowd chanted insults against members of the ruling coalition and against Chilean judge Juan Guzmán, who had issued the house arrest warrant.

FEBRUARY 5

Enrique Alvarado, *El Metropolitano*
`LEGAL ACTION`
Javier Urrutia, *El Metropolitano*
`LEGAL ACTION`
Mireya Muñoz, *El Metropolitano*
`LEGAL ACTION`
Patricio Ulloa, *El Metropolitano*
`LEGAL ACTION`
Pablo Valdés, *El Metropolitano*
`LEGAL ACTION`

Chilean senator and businessman Francisco Javier Errázuriz filed suit against Alvarado, editor of the daily *El Metropolitano*; Urrutia, editor of the paper's business section; and photographer Muñoz under Article 6b of Chile's State Security Law (LSE). Starting January 27, *El Metropolitano* had published a series of articles linking Errázuriz to a scandal involving forged documents. Muñoz photographed the office of a notary allegedly involved in the scandal.

On January 28, Errázuriz called Urrutia and asked that his version of the events be published in a front-page article of the same length as the paper's exposé, according to the Argentine press freedom organization PERIODISTAS.

The Peruvian press freedom organization Instituto Prensa Y Sociedad (IPYS) reported that Errázuriz sent three letters to *El Metropolitano* on Senate letterhead. One of the letters, dated February 19, noted, "All those in the public eye have the duty to make use of the LSE, precisely in order to protect the state and its spokespeople against those who commit an outrage against press freedom, such an important pillar of our society."

On March 19, the journalists testified before an Appeals Court judge, as required by the LSE. Meanwhile, however, the Chamber of Deputies was taking steps to abolish parts of the law that were formally repealed in late spring.

On March 22, Errázuriz filed a fresh complaint against the journalists with the Third Criminal Court, this time under criminal defamation provisions of the Penal Code, IPYS reported. In addition to Alvarado, Urrutia, and Muñoz, the new suit added *El Metropolitano*'s president, Patricio Ulloa, and editorial board member Pablo Valdés as defendants.

At the beginning of April, the parties tried unsuccessfully to settle their dispute. Apparently, Errázuriz would only agree to withdraw the new complaint if the paper published a front-page article denying everything it had written about him, according to IPYS.

CPJ was unable to determine the outcome of the case by press time.

AUGUST 23

Alejandra Matus, free-lancer
`LEGAL ACTION, CENSORED`

The Supreme Court of Justice refused to consider journalist and author

Alejandra Matus' appeal against the seizure of *The Black Book of Chilean Justice*, a muckraking exposé of the Chilean judiciary that was banned more than two years ago.

The Chilean judiciary seemed unwilling to lift the ban even though a new press law, signed in May, repealed the infamous articles of the State Security Law under which Matus was charged with criminal defamation and *The Black Book* was outlawed.

Matus' troubles began on April 14, 1999, when Santiago Appeals Court judge Rafael Huerta banned her book in response to a suit filed by Supreme Court justice Servando Jordán under Article 6(b) of the State Security Law, which made it a crime against public order to insult high officials.

After Judge Huerta ordered the seizure of the book's entire print run, Matus flew to Argentina to avoid imprisonment. Six months later, the United States granted Matus political asylum.

Matus filed a complaint with the Washington-based Inter-American Commission on Human Rights (IACHR), alleging that Chilean authorities had violated her basic human rights. On March 23, 2001, CPJ submitted an amicus curiae brief to the commission in support of Matus' complaint. The brief was prepared for CPJ by the New York law firm Debevoise & Plimpton, whose partners include CPJ board member and prominent First Amendment attorney James C. Goodale.

CPJ's brief argued that "public order" is threatened, not promoted, by the criminalization of defamation and that government officials should have no special protection from criticism.

The brief further argued that proof of actual malice should be required in all defamation cases, whether criminal or civil, and that the seizure of Matus' book violated international standards against censorship.

Based on these arguments, the brief urged the commission to recommend: the rejection of all efforts to criminalize defamation, and in particular the repeal of Article 6(b) of Chile's State Security Law and similar Chilean statutes; the dismissal of all charges against Matus; the adoption of an actual malice standard for all defamation cases involving public officials or public figures; the rejection of all prior censorship, and in particular the repeal of articles 16 and 30 of Chile's State Security Law; the distribution of *The Black Book* in Chile without legal penalty, and the return of all copies seized by the government.

In April, the Chamber of Deputies and the Senate passed a law on regulating "Freedoms of Opinion and Information and the Practice of Journalism." Among other provisions, the new law repealed articles 6(b) and 16 of the State Security Law. President Ricardo Lagos signed the bill into law on May 18.

On June 2, Matus' brother and lawyer, Jean Pierre Matus, requested that the Santiago Appeals Court close the case, drop the detention order against Matus, lift the ban on her book, and release the impounded copies.

The Matuses told CPJ that on June 29, Appeals Court judge Rubén Ballesteros dismissed the parts of the case stemming from the State Security Law. However, he did not overturn other charges, including those based on the Law on Publicity Abuses, even though the new press law repealed that statute entirely.

In the same June 29 decision, Judge Ballesteros upheld the detention order and book ban, pending possible challenges to his ruling dismissing charges stemming from the State Security Law.

The next day, Jean Pierre Matus filed a writ asking the Santiago Appeals Court to lift the detention order. On July 6, the court unanimously ruled in Matus' favor, enabling her to return to Chile.

When Matus arrived for a weeklong visit on July 14, she and her brother filed another writ requesting that the Appeals Court lift the ban on her book. On July 25, the court declared the writ inadmissible. Jean Pierre filed a complaint against that decision with the Supreme Court on July 31.

In an August 6 alert, CPJ executive director Ann Cooper said, "It seems as if some members of the Chilean judiciary are hanging on to any excuse to continue this unjustified case against Alejandra Matus. Clearly, the case should be dismissed in its entirety and the ban on *The Black Book of Chilean Justice* lifted."

On August 23, the Chilean Supreme Court also declared the writ inadmissible.

In an August 29 alert, Cooper said, "The Supreme Court's August 23 decision certainly casts a shadow over the recent repeal of some of Chile's most notorious and restrictive press provisions."

Meanwhile, Justice Jordán filed an appeal on June 30 against the partial dismissal of the case. Jean Pierre Matus then filed an appeal on July 25 urging the judge to dismiss the case entirely.

On September 17, the Appeals Court rejected both Jordán's and the Matus' appeal, Jean Pierre Matus said. On September 29, Jean Pierre Matus asked Ballesteros to end the book ban. On October 19, Ballesteros ruled on the request, allowing the book to be sold; dismissing State Security Law charges faced by Bartolo Ortiz and Carlos Orellana, CEO and chief editor of Editorial Planeta, respectively; and temporarily dismissing the charges under other laws faced by Matus, Ortiz, and Orellana.

Matus went back to live in Chile on November 15, she told CPJ. That day, the Appeals Court confirmed Ballesteros' decision, according to Jean Pierre Matus. From that day until December 12, he said, the file was "lost," but on December 13, Ballesteros authorized the return of Editorial Planeta's impounded books, which happened on December 17.

OCTOBER 29

Pablo Solís, *El Mostrador.cl*
ATTACKED
Luis Cáceres, *El Mostrador.cl*
ATTACKED

Solís and Cáceres, reporter and photographer, respectively, for the online newspaper *El Mostrador.cl* (www.elmostrador.cl), were attacked by a group of Mapuche Indians, apparently in retaliation for the site's articles on alleged financial irregularities involving Mapuche community leaders.

The journalists were covering an afternoon meeting between Mapuche leaders and Alejandra Krauss, minister of Cooperation and Planning, in downtown Santiago. *El Mostrador.cl* reported that when the meeting ended around 4:45 p.m., some 20 Mapuche Indians assaulted the journalists and destroyed Cáceres' digital camera.

The attackers expressed anger about *El Mostrador.cl*'s reports on alleged corruption within the National Corporation for Indigenous Development, the government agency for native Chilean affairs. The police then arrived and restored order.

The journalists chose not to file a police complaint about the incident.

DECEMBER 1

Eduardo Yáñez Morel
LEGAL ACTION

The Supreme Court filed a complaint against Yáñez, a regular panelist on Chilevisión's debate show "El Termó-Metro," for "disrespect," under Articles 263 and 264 of the Penal Code. Yáñez faces up to five years in prison if convicted.

The complaint stemmed from a November 27 episode of the show in which Yáñez described the judiciary as "immoral, cowardly, and corrupt" for not providing compensation to a woman who, it was revealed during the broadcast, had been imprisoned for a crime she did not commit. Yáñez, a businessman and environmental activist, also said the judiciary had shown "little manliness" in failing to apologize for the miscarriage of justice.

On November 30, the Supreme Court asked its then-president, Hernán Álvarez, to file a criminal complaint accusing Yáñez of "disrespect." Although Article 6b of the State Security Law, Chile's most infamous "disrespect" provision, was repealed in late spring

2001, government officials still have more legal protection against criticism than ordinary citizens.

In early January, the judge in charge of the case, Juan Manuel Muñoz Pardo, gave the parties 10 working days to reach a settlement. But the new Supreme Court president, Mario Garrido Montt, repeatedly refused to meet with Yáñez, who wanted to offer his apologies. According to a January 16 article in *El Mercurio*, Garrido contended that the judiciary deserved respect like any person. "If anyone refers to the judiciary with insults, we won't doubt to act in the same way," Garrido said.

On January 15, Judge Muñoz initiated proceedings against Yáñez and the panelist was detained overnight. The next day, the Santiago Appeals Court confirmed Judge Muñoz's decision to grant Yáñez a 100,000 peso (US$150) bail.

Yáñez's attorney announced that he would fight the case on constitutional grounds. The Inter-American Commission on Human Rights has interceded on Yáñez's behalf, asking the Chilean government to provide it with information on the case.

COLOMBIA

JANUARY 1

Jorge Enrique Botero, Caracol Televisión
THREATENED

Botero, head of current affairs programming for the Caracol Televisión network, received multiple death threats that forced him to send his family abroad and move out of his apartment in Bogotá.

The threats began in November

2000, a month after the journalist produced a documentary on government troops and police being held in jungle camps by the leftist Revolutionary Armed Forces of Colombia (FARC) guerrillas, Botero told CPJ.

Botero has had uneasy relations with the Colombian military since 1997, when FARC leader Alfonso Cano granted him a rare television interview. Since then, Botero says, senior army officers have publicly described him as a rebel sympathizer and "head of press for the FARC."

His film was due to open a new series of documentaries called "Grandes Reportajes" (Great Reports). But the series was scrapped and Botero was relieved of his duties, though not formally dismissed, after network directors told him "it was not convenient" to air the first show.

However, the network did air some of Botero's footage showing police and soldiers held captive behind barbed-wire fences. The complete documentary showed a variety of camp conditions, good and bad, and revealed that some 500 police and soldiers taken prisoner by rebels during the last four years had been virtually forgotten by their commanders and the government.

The guerrillas apparently believed that granting limited media access to the camps would pressure the government to swap captive troops for jailed guerrillas.

Botero told CPJ that he began receiving telephone threats at his home in downtown Bogotá a month after the program was scrapped. The caller said: "Shut your mouth motherfucker. We're coming to get you," and added that Botero had "five days to get lost." On other occasions, the caller phoned late at night, leaving the phone off the hook so Botero could hear background music from a bar or discotheque.

Sometimes, the caller played a recording of Botero's private phone conversations from a few minutes earlier, revealing that the reporter's phone was being tapped.

Botero reported the threats to Bogotá police and to the Human Rights Division of the Interior Ministry. He was not provided with personal security, but police asked the bodyguards of a number of senators living in the same apartment building to provide assistance to Botero if necessary.

In January 2001, two written death threats were delivered by hand to Botero's home. Both read, "We offer our condolences to the Botero family for the death of Jorge Enrique Botero."

Botero then sent his family to an undisclosed location abroad and moved out of his apartment. For about two months, he traveled on business in Europe. The threats resumed when he returned.

At year's end, Botero was working as a free-lance journalist in Colombia but was considering leaving the country again. He said that the Interior Ministry had offered to pay for his flight out of the country under its program to protect threatened journalists.

JANUARY 30

Claudia Gurisatti, RCN Televisión
THREATENED

Top Colombian TV anchor Gurisatti was forced to flee the country for Miami after government officials said they had uncovered evidence of a plot to kill her.

Gurisatti, 28, hosts the midday and evening news broadcasts on RCN Televisión and anchors the nightly news show "La Noche" (The Night), where she has interviewed leaders of both guerrilla and paramilitary groups, as well as a number of individuals and officials involved in alleged corruption.

Gurisatti spent nearly six months in Miami, where she continued to anchor "La Noche" via satellite. She returned to Colombia in June.

On February 23, then-attorney general Alfonso Gómez Méndez claimed that the country's largest guerrilla group, the Revolutionary Armed Forces of Colombia (FARC), was behind the failed plan to assassinate the journalist.

In a press conference, Gómez Méndez said that two men had confessed that the Teófilo Forero Column, a mobile combat unit of the FARC, had hired them to murder Gurisatti.

The attorney general's office identified the two men as Enod Romero Quiroz, alias "Flash," and Jailander Doncel Pedreros, alias "Panther." A third man, a Bogotá tailor, was allegedly in charge of the plan and conducted initial surveillance to determine Gurisatti's work and social routines, investigators said.

Doncel Pedreros was also accused of murdering Congressman Andrés Páez, who was killed in central Tolima Department on January 27. According to the confessions of Doncel Pedreros and Romero Quiroz, their next victim was to be Gurisatti, but they gave no motive for attacking her, Gómez Méndez said.

On the morning of July 16, Doncel Pedreros was found strangled to death in his cell at Bogotá's Modelo Prison, said Oscar Galvis, a spokesman for the nation's federal prison system. Romero Quiroz and the tailor were released in late 2001.

In comments to journalists on February 28, veteran FARC commander Manuel Marulanda rejected allegations that the FARC was behind the murder plot. "We have no people engaged in that type of work. This is not how we behave with the press," he said. "We have attempted no attack [on Gurisatti]."

Gurisatti said she doubts the FARC plotted to kill her. "If they really wanted to, they have people here in the capital who could have done it by now without much problem," she told CPJ.

APRIL 27

Flavio Bedoya, *Voz*
KILLED

Four unidentified gunmen on motorcycles shot and killed Bedoya, a regional correspondent for the Bogotá-based Communist Party newspaper *Voz*, as he stepped off a bus in the southwestern port city of Tumaco, police and colleagues said.

Bedoya, 52, had worked for *Voz* for about a year and a half, according to Álvaro Angarita, one of the weekly's senior correspondents.

Angarita linked the murder to a series of highly critical reports that Bedoya had published about collusion between security forces and right-wing paramilitary gangs in Nariño Department. Police confirmed the killing but gave no further details.

Southwestern Colombia, especially Nariño Department and neighboring

Cauca Department, experienced a number of paramilitary attacks in the two months before the killing.

Colombia's small Communist Party has political links to the left-wing guerrilla organization Revolutionary Armed Forces of Colombia (FARC), but has traditionally advocated social change through grassroots mobilization and the ballot box rather than armed revolution.

MAY 21

Voz
ATTACKED

Police bomb-disposal experts defused a cluster bomb found in a pickup truck parked outside the offices of the Communist Party newspaper, *Voz*, in downtown Bogotá.

The 550-pound bomb was concealed in a load of oranges and bananas. This particular cluster bomb is commercially manufactured in the United States to American military specifications and sold worldwide. Bogotá Metropolitan Police spokesperson Sgt. Alberto Cantillo said the bomb contained TNT and was designed to be dropped from a plane. Bogotá police chief Col. Luis Contento told reporters that the device "would have caused huge devastation" and would likely have destroyed buildings within a two-block radius.

Carlos Lozano, editor of *Voz*, said the truck was parked at 4 a.m. local time. When a secretary at the newspaper arrived at work some four hours later, she became suspicious and alerted the police.

Lozano was not at the office when the bomb was defused. After his secretary warned him of the problem, he and his bodyguards immediately left for

Communist Party headquarters elsewhere in the city.

"We have had a terrible shock. I believe the bombers were waiting for me to arrive before they detonated the device," Lozano told CPJ.

In April, Lozano was named to a four-person commission created to monitor official efforts to curb right-wing paramilitary attacks around the country. The commission, formed by government peace negotiators and the leftist Revolutionary Armed Forces of Colombia (FARC), is participating in talks aimed at ending the country's protracted civil war.

Voz has been a frequent target of censorship efforts and bomb attacks. On April 27, *Voz* correspondent Flavio Bedoya was murdered, in all likelihood because of a series of highly critical reports he had published about collusion between security forces and right-wing paramilitary gangs in Nariño Department (see April 27 case).

On May 21, CPJ circulated a news alert about the attempted bombing of *Voz*. A few days later, Carlos Castaño, leader of the paramilitary group United Self-Defense Forces of Colombia (AUC), took responsibility for the bomb attempt.

MAY 25

Carlos Lajud, Citytv
ATTACKED
Carlos Molina, Caracol Televisión
ATTACKED

Lajud and Molina were injured during the second of two back-to-back bomb attacks in Bogotá that left four dead and 25 injured. Both journalists were hospitalized but released after treatment.

Lajud, 27, a reporter for the news show "CityNoticias" at local Bogotá TV channel Citytv (owned by the El Tiempo Publishing House), suffered shrapnel wounds to the arm and leg. Molina, 36, a reporter for national TV network Caracol Televisión, was also injured by shrapnel, as was a press officer for the Bogotá Metropolitan Police.

The two blasts occurred 10 minutes apart at around 8 a.m. The first bomb exploded under a footbridge that crosses a main highway in northwest Bogotá, killing three people. Police, official investigators, anti-explosives teams, and journalists were already on the scene when the second bomb detonated.

Lajud and Molina told *El Tiempo* that they were reporting on the scene when the second explosion occurred. Their cameramen suffered shock but were not injured.

It was not clear whether the two bombs were directed at a specific target. Public buildings nearest to the site of the blasts include the National University, the Augustín Codazzi Geographic Institute, and the Industrial Standards Office, known as Icontec.

Interior Minister Armando Estrada speculated that the right-wing paramilitary United Self-Defense Forces of Colombia (AUC) may have planned the bomb attacks in retaliation for a wave of government-instigated searches the previous day of properties owned by suspected paramilitary financiers. Estrada, however, produced no specific evidence to back those suspicions, and the AUC did not claim responsibility.

JUNE 6

Citytv
ATTACKED
Javier Santoyo, Caracol Televisión
ATTACKED
Oscar Patiño, Caracol Televisión
ATTACKED
Wilfredo Pinto, RCN Televisión
ATTACKED

At least three journalists and a TV news studio were attacked during anti-government demonstrations across Colombia.

The demonstrators included teachers, health workers, other public-sector employees, and students. Thousands gathered to protest proposed legislation that would reduce the level of federal funding to regional and municipal authorities, a policy many feared would result in widespread cuts in provincial health care and education.

There were several attacks on the press during the demonstrations, at least one of them seemingly motivated by the perception that journalists covering the conflict were biased because they worked for media outlets owned by members of Colombia's political and economic elite.

The first attack took place on June 6 in the capital, Bogotá, when a small group of protesters threw homemade firecrackers at the downtown headquarters of the local TV station Citytv. Citytv is part of the El Tiempo Publishing House, owned by the wealthy Santos family.

Minutes before the attack, Finance Minister Juan Manuel Santos gave a televised speech in which he denounced the protests and pledged to push the federal funding legislation through Congress at all costs.

The Citytv building was targeted again during a protest on June 7. One firecracker broke the window of a TV studio on an upper floor during the live broadcast of a lunchtime chat show.

During protests held that same day in the northeastern city of Bucaramanga, Caracol Televisión regional correspondent Santoyo and his cameraman, Patiño, were beaten by a group of police officers who objected to their filming of the arrest of a student.

Santoyo told the newspaper *El Tiempo* that their camera was smashed in the incident and that RCN Televisión cameraman Pinto was also attacked. Santoyo added that he and his colleagues had lodged a formal complaint with the Bogotá police and had requested 15 million pesos (US$7,000) to cover damage to the camera. Bucaramanga police chief Gen. Fortunato Guañarita announced that he had launched an internal inquiry into the matter, but no further details were forthcoming.

JUNE 27

Pablo Emilio Parra Castañeda,
Planadas Cultural Estéreo
KILLED (MOTIVE UNCONFIRMED)
Leftist guerrillas shot Parra, 50, twice in the head after abducting him from his home in the Tolima Department township of Planadas. The body of Parra, who founded and directed the community radio station Planadas Cultural Estéreo, was found later that day along a rural road.

Col. Norberto Torres of the Planadas police said that after killing Parra, rebels from the Revolutionary Armed Forces of Colombia (FARC) attached a note to

his body that read: "For being a spy." FARC rebels control the area, according to local authorities.

The FARC, the nation's largest leftist rebel group, later claimed responsibility for the assassination in a communiqué that accused Parra of being an informant for the army, Torres said.

When contacted by CPJ, a spokesman for the army's 6th Brigade denied that Parra was an informant. The spokesman, who asked to remain unidentified, said no one at the brigade had heard of him. Parra's 30-year-old daughter, Liliana Parra, also denied that her father was an informant. She told CPJ that her father broadcast popular music and community news on his radio program but never discussed political subjects.

The radio station was based in Parra's house. The journalist also worked with the local office of the Red Cross and had never received death threats, Liliana Parra said.

The departmental prosecutor's office was investigating the murder but had made no arrests by year's end. Special Prosecutor Jairo Francisco Leal Alvarado said evidence found so far suggested that Parra was not killed because of his work as a journalist. He would not elaborate.

JULY 4

Arquímedes Arias Henao,
Fresno Estéreo
KILLED (MOTIVE UNCONFIRMED)
Arias, founder and director of the local radio station Fresno Estéreo, was killed during the evening when an assassin burst into his home in the Tolima Department township of Fresno

and shot him three times in the head.

After shooting Arias, the gunman fled on a motorcycle driven by a man waiting outside, said José Parra, an investigator at the Tolima Department prosecutor's office.

Parra said no arrests have been made, and that the reasons for Arias' assassination remain unclear. Parra reported that the region is crawling with fighters from Colombia's two main leftist guerrilla groups and a rival right-wing paramilitary army.

Before moving to Fresno earlier in the year, Arias founded and directed several other radio stations that, along with Fresno Estéreo, broadcast popular music and nonpolitical community programs, said his brother, Eduardo Arias.

Eduardo Arias told CPJ that his brother operated the radio station from his home and had never received death threats.

There had been no progress in the investigation by year's end, Parra said.

JULY 6

José Duviel Vásquez Arias, La Voz de la Selva
KILLED
Omar Orlando García Garzón, La Voz de la Selva
THREATENED

An unidentified gunman shot and killed Vásquez, director of the local radio station La Voz de la Selva (The Voice of the Jungle), and tried to kill his colleague García, news coordinator of the station.

The two journalists, who had just finished the first broadcast of their twice-daily news program, were driving home from work in Florencia, a city in southern Caquetá Department that is a former stronghold of the Revolutionary Armed Forces of Colombia (FARC), the country's largest leftist guerrilla group. More recently, the town has become a power base for an anti-Communist paramilitary group linked to the right-wing United Self-Defense Forces of Colombia (AUC).

García told CPJ that the gunman first shot Vásquez and then aimed at him. Vásquez's slumped body intercepted the second bullet, which merely brushed García, who was able to give the authorities a detailed description of the killer. The next day, García began receiving threatening phone calls. On July 9, an anonymous caller warned him to leave Florencia on pain of death.

In addition to witnessing the killing, García had assisted Vásquez in documenting corruption implicating local government officials and members of the FARC, the journalist told CPJ.

The journalists had investigated Caquetá governor Pablo Adriano Muñoz, who was reportedly elected with support from the FARC, for allegedly embezzling public funds. Muñoz accused Vásquez of "persecuting" him, whereupon Vásquez filed a defamation suit against the governor. Vásquez's lawyer, Carlos Alberto Beltrán, had to flee Florencia after a failed attempt on his life, according to García.

Vásquez stated during one of his broadcasts that if anything happened to him or his family, it would be the governor's fault.

García reported that Vásquez's last broadcasts dealt with an AUC communiqué in which the organization announced changes in its local leadership and promised to refrain from kidnapping and extortion.

The journalist's murder followed those of the station's former director, Alfredo Abad López, whom Vásquez had replaced, and another colleague, Guillermo Léon Agudelo. García, his wife, and their two young daughters have since left the country.

On July 11, CPJ issued an alert about Vásquez's murder.

JULY 8

Jorge Enrique Urbano Sánchez,
Mar Estéreo
`KILLED`

Two unidentified attackers shot Urbano four times at around 2 a.m. while he was celebrating his 55th birthday with friends in the coastal city of Buenaventura, family members and authorities said.

Urbano hosted a one-hour morning radio program broadcast on local station Mar Estéreo. He was also the administrator of the Néstor Urbano Tenorio Park.

Urbano apparently devoted his final radio broadcast to denouncing a local criminal gang called Tumba Puertas (Knock Down Doors). The gang was a frequent topic of discussion on Urbano's show; the broadcaster often blamed Tumba Puertas for rampant crime in the park and urged police to crack down on drug dealing there.

Urbano had also coordinated efforts to relocate street vendors and remove drug addicts from the park. Before his murder, he received death threats that he attributed to these public statements and actions.

JULY 16

Eduardo Estrada Gutiérrez,
radio journalist
`KILLED (MOTIVE UNCONFIRMED)`

Estrada, a community leader and local broadcaster, was killed in the early morning of July 16 in the municipality of San Pablo, located in Bolívar Department.

Unidentified attackers shot the journalist as he was returning home with his wife after attending a family reunion.

Estrada was the president of the Asociación para el Desarrollo de la Comunicación y la Cultura de San Pablo, a community organization affiliated to a network of community radio stations. At the time of his death, the journalist was working to launch a community station for San Pablo.

Investigations have not revealed the identity of the attackers or the possible motive.

SEPTEMBER 28

Víctor Tobar, Reuters
`HARASSED`
Hélver Viarraga, Reuters
`HARASSED`
Angel González, Caracol Televisión
`HARASSED`
Norvei Poloche, Caracol Televisión
`HARASSED`
César Velandia, RCN Televisión
`HARASSED`
Édinson Bautista, RCN Televisión
`HARASSED`
Érica Manchola, TV Hoy
`HARASSED`

Seven Colombian journalists were harassed by leftist guerrillas from the Revolutionary Armed Forces of

Colombia (FARC) while traveling to cover a protest march sponsored by Liberal Party presidential candidate Horacio Serpa.

The group included: Reuters cameraman Tobar; Tobar's assistant, Viarraga; Caracol Televisión correspondent González; González's cameraman, Poloche; RCN Televisión correspondent Velandia; Velandia's assistant, Bautista; and TV Hoy correspondent Manchola.

Eight FARC fighters erected a roadblock and stopped the journalists around noon outside the southern village of Balsillas, 125 miles south of the capital, Bogotá.

The rebels told the journalists that filming was forbidden in the area, and that FARC commanders had ordered them detained for their own safety. Fighting between rebel and government forces had killed at least two guerrillas in recent days. The fighters also told the journalists that the road ahead was mined.

When Tobar tried to drive away, a FARC fighter pointed a gun to his head while rebels deflated the tires of the journalists' cars, Tobar told CPJ.

The journalists had traveled to the region after hearing of demonstrations related to Serpa's peaceful march into rebel-controlled territory located less than a mile from Balsillas. Riding in more than 50 buses, Serpa and some 3,000 supporters left Bogotá on September 28 and were expected to pass through the area by the following day.

The caravan arrived in the area late in the morning of September 29 but was turned back by the rebels along the same mountainous, dirt road outside Balsillas where the journalists had been harassed. Serpa never reached San Vicente del Caguán, the main town inside the enclave, where he had planned to give a speech denouncing human rights abuses in rebel territory.

The journalists spent the night of September 28 near the checkpoint. They were allowed to film the Serpa caravan the next day. At around 4 p.m., after finding an air pump, the journalists headed back to nearby Neiva, the capital of Huila Department, where most of them live and work.

"[The FARC] never mistreated us, but it caught us by surprise," said Velandia, who has worked for RCN for three years. On October 5, CPJ issued an alert deploring the harassment of the journalists.

NOVEMBER 9

Cristina Castro, RCN Televisión
THREATENED
Oscar Torres, *Diario del Sur*
THREATENED
Alfonso Pardo, *Voz*
THREATENED
Germán Arcos, Caracol Televisión
THREATENED

Four Colombian journalists fled their homes in the southern Colombian department of Nariño after receiving death threats from a right-wing paramilitary faction that accused them of collaborating with leftist guerrillas.

The letter, signed by the Southern Liberators Front of the United Self-Defense Forces of Colombia (AUC), accused three reporters and a cameraman of giving government information to the National Liberation Army (ELN) and the Revolutionary

Armed Forces of Colombia (FARC).

Several news organizations in Pasto, Nariño's capital, received the one-page letter on November 9.

In the letter, a copy of which was obtained by CPJ, the paramilitaries wrote that they recognized the "important role" of journalists and said they would never attack the "real and honest press."

But the letter described the four journalists as "a danger to society" and declared that they would be executed if they did not quit their jobs and leave the area within 48 hours.

The journalists, who fled from Nariño to the capital, Bogotá, called the accusations lies.

The journalists said they met with Interior Minister Armando Estrada to discuss the threats. Even though the government offered them limited assistance to leave the country, Torres said the aid was not enough to support him and his family while he searched for work in exile. Torres said he would return to Pasto but feared for his life.

NOVEMBER 14

Julio César Romero, *El Caleño*
ATTACKED, HARASSED

Romero, a photographer for the Cali-based newspaper *El Caleño*, was assaulted by university students who were protesting the murders of two classmates who had been gunned down inside the public university the week before while playing chess.

Some 200 students marched from the university to the city center. Romero had taken several photos and was preparing to leave when about 20 protesters surrounded him and accused him of

taking pictures for the local police.

The attackers pummeled Romero with their fists, ripped off his shirt, and bashed his head with rocks as several journalists tried to fight them off, said Héctor Molina, a reporter who was covering the event for local TV station Noti 5. The attackers left after taking the film from Romero's camera.

Romero, a 20-year veteran photojournalist, was taken to a local hospital and treated for minor injuries.

Heriberto Cárdenas Escudero, retired radio and newspaper reporter
KILLED (MOTIVE UNCONFIRMED)

Four armed assailants wearing hoods burst into the home of Cárdenas, a retired journalist who lived in the western Colombian city of Buenaventura, killing him, his son, and his brother, police said.

Cárdenas was watching an evening soccer match on television when the attackers broke into the house and opened fire, said Col. Luis Alberto Ramírez of the Buenaventura Police.

Cárdenas, 51, died from gunshot wounds to his head and chest. His son and brother died two days later.

It was initially reported that Cárdenas' teenage nephew was killed in the attack. However, Colonel Ramírez said that the nephew was stabbed to death last year, and that the November 14 attack may have been related to his slaying.

Cárdenas had worked as a news announcer with radio Carcajal Stéreo in Buenaventura and as a local reporter for several newspapers, including *El Tiempo* and *El Espectador*, two of Colombia's most prominent national publications. In the past, journalists from both papers have been targeted by left-wing guerrillas and right-wing paramilitaries, as have provincial broadcast journalists all over the country.

During the last year, Cárdenas worked as a press officer at the local fire department.

At year's end, Colonel Ramírez said the investigation had turned up nothing new. Though no one had been captured, he still believed that Cárdenas was killed for personal reasons. The prosecutor handling the case in Buenaventura, Balmer Restrepo, refused to discuss the case over the phone.

DECEMBER 5

Héctor Mario Rodríguez,
primerapagina.com
HARASSED

Two National Police officers tried to detain Rodríguez, editor of the online and print publication *primerapagina.com*, the journalist told CPJ.

Rodríguez was covering an annual meeting of the troubled National Coffee Growers' Federation in the capital, Bogotá, when he was expelled from the press room and escorted out of the building by the federation's security chief and five private security guards.

Rodríguez said federation officials were angry with him because of several articles he had written about alleged corruption at the federation.

Immediately after Rodríguez left the building, two National Police officers stopped him and demanded that he turn over the printed copies of *primerapagina.com* that he was carrying.

The officers said they were responding to a complaint from the federation's security chief. When Rodríguez asked if he was being detained, the officers asked him to wait while they called a higher-ranking officer. Rodríguez then left in his car. The officers chased him on foot but quickly gave up.

Rodríguez said authorities had yet to respond to a complaint about the incident that his publication sent to National Police chief Gen. Luis Ernesto Gilibert Vargas.

Jenny Alvarado, a National Police press officer, said she did not know whether the complaint was being investigated. Gilibert did not return messages. Attempts to reach the National Coffee Growers' Federation for comment were unsuccessful.

DECEMBER 23

Álvaro Alonso Escobar, *La Región*
KILLED (MOTIVE UNCONFIRMED)

Escobar, the publisher of the monthly newspaper *La Región*, was shot and killed by a lone gunman after an argument, according to state police commander Luis Mesa. A visitor arrived at Escobar's home in the town of Fundación, Magdalena Department, at around 7 p.m. and shot the journalist three times in the head before fleeing on a motorcycle.

Magdalena Department is known as a violent area, with leftist guerillas and rightist paramilitary forces both active.

Mesa told CPJ that he believed Escobar had been murdered for personal reasons, but could provide no further details.

COSTA RICA

Mauricio Herrera Ulloa, *La Nación*
LEGAL ACTION

The Costa Rican Supreme Court rejected the appeal of journalist Herrera Ulloa and the San José daily *La Nación*, who were convicted of criminal defamation.

On November 12, 1999, the Penal Court of the First Judicial Circuit in San José convicted Herrera Ulloa and *La Nación* of criminal defamation based on 1995 articles by Herrera Ulloa that cited European press reports alleging corruption by former Costa Rican diplomat Félix Przedborski.

The court ordered Herrera Ulloa to pay a fine equivalent to 120 days' wages, the plaintiff's legal fees, and 60 million colones (US$190,000) in damages to Przedborski. It also ordered that the journalist's name be inscribed in an official list of convicted criminals. *La Nación* was instructed to remove all links to the offending articles from its Web site and to publish parts of the ruling.

In response, the newspaper and the journalist filed a petition with the Inter-American Commission on Human Rights, an entity of the Organization of American States (OAS).

According to Herrera Ulloa's lawyer, Fernando Guier, the petition recommended that the commission urge Costa Rica to bring its press laws into compliance with the American Convention on Human Rights, which the country ratified in 1970. On March 1, the commission's then-executive secretary, Jorge Taiana, asked the Costa Rican Penal Court to suspend its ruling while the commission studied the case.

When the Penal Court refused to comply, the commission asked the Inter-American Court of Human Rights, another OAS entity, to confirm the suspension. (The court's decisions are legally binding on Costa Rica and other countries that have accepted the court's jurisdiction.) On April 6, the Inter-American Court's president, Antônio Cançado Trindade, ordered the Costa Rican government to suspend the verdict. The Inter-American Court held a May 22 hearing on the matter.

On May 21, CPJ issued an alert about the hearing. Executive director Ann Cooper was quoted as saying, "It is shocking that journalists in Costa Rica can be branded as criminals simply for doing their professional duty."

On May 23, the Inter-American Court confirmed the ruling ordering the Costa Rican government to suspend the verdict.

Then on September 7, the court, which is based in San José, Costa Rica, issued "provisional measures" ordering Costa Rican authorities to keep Herrera Ulloa off the official list of convicted criminals until the Inter-American Court system resolves the case. The government was also instructed not to enforce the order requiring *La Nación* to publish the Penal Court's ruling.

That was the first time the court had taken such action in a freedom of expression case. Provisional measures are only issued in cases of "extreme gravity and urgency, and when necessary to avoid irreparable damage to persons," according to the American Convention on Human Rights.

On October 3, the Penal Court

confirmed that it would abide by the Inter-American Court's decision, Guier later told CPJ.

During its 113th regular session, held from November 12 to 16, the Inter-American Commission conducted a hearing to determine whether it would hear the case. At year's end, no decision had been made.

JULY 7

Parmenio Medina Pérez, "La Patada"
KILLED

Medina, producer and host of the weekly radio program "La Patada" (The Kick), was murdered by unknown assailants who shot him three times at close range with a .38-caliber weapon, once in the back and twice in the head.

Medina's 28-year-old program often denounced official corruption and earned him numerous threats. On-air accusations he had made since 1999 about alleged fiscal improprieties at a local Catholic radio station led to its closure and an investigation of its former director.

Two months before his murder, Medina received death threats in connection with the accusations, and unknown attackers fired bullets at his house. Although Medina had been under police protection, he asked that it be lifted just days before his death.

In a July 10 letter, CPJ praised President Miguel Ángel Rodríguez Echeverría for condemning the murder and encouraged the president to ensure that the perpetrators were caught. President Rodríguez responded with an e-mail message saying, "[M]y government is committed to cooperate as best as it can with the judicial

authorities to clarify these facts until their ultimate consequences and will do all it can to discover the material and intellectual authors."

No substantial progress in the investigation had been reported at year's end, however.

CUBA

MARCH 31

Jesús Hernández Hernández,
HavanaPress
HARASSED
Jadir Hernández Hernández,
HavanaPress
HARASSED

On the eve of an international conference of legislators, state security agents detained and threatened Jesús Hernández Hernández, a reporter for the independent news agency HavanaPress, in the western province of Habana.

The journalist was held for two hours and warned not to cover the activities of dissidents during the 105th Inter-Parliamentary Conference, held in Havana from April 1 to 7, according to HavanaPress. The agency also reported that Jesús Hernández Hernández had been ordered to quit working as a journalist.

The police lieutenant who questioned Jesús Hernández Hernández told him that he and his brother Jadir Hernández Hernández, who is also a reporter for HavanaPress, could be prosecuted at any time and given prison terms of up to 15 years for violating the Law for the Protection of Cuba's National Independence and Economy, which is also known as Law 88, or as the "gag law."

Law 88 mandates prison terms for "supporting, facilitating, or collaborating with the objectives of the Helms-Burton Law [U.S. legislation that imposes sanctions on foreign companies trading with Cuba], the embargo, and the economic war against our people, with the goal of ruining internal order, destabilizing the country, and liquidating the socialist state and Cuba's independence."

The lieutenant also threatened to reopen a six-month-old criminal case against the Hernández Hernández brothers. On September 15, 2000, agents from the government's Technical Department of Investigation (DTI), the criminal police, held the brothers for more than three days at the DTI offices in San José de las Lajas, near Havana. They accused the two journalists of smuggling Cuban immigrants to the United States.

APRIL 9

Ricardo González Alfonso, free-lancer
HARASSED

González Alfonso, 49, a free-lance journalist and the Cuba correspondent for the Paris-based press freedom organization Reporters sans frontières (RSF), was placed under house arrest by Cuban authorities.

National Revolutionary Police (PNR) detained the journalist after his former wife filed a complaint alleging that he had threatened her. (Like many divorced couples in Cuba, which suffers a severe housing shortage, González Alfonso and his ex-wife shared the same house.)

González Alfonso was released at around 5 p.m. Apparently, the police only discovered his profession when he was already in detention.

At 10 p.m., two police agents appeared at González Alfonso's home with a house arrest warrant, which lacked the required signature and stamp. Under Cuban law, house arrest can be imposed for up to 20 days, by which time the district attorney is required to rule on the matter.

It is highly unusual for Cuban police to impose house arrest in a domestic dispute, CPJ sources said. Given that González Alfonso still lived with his ex-wife, it is unclear why police would effectively lock them up together in response to her complaint.

In mid-May, González Alfonso told CPJ that "the police move was so sloppy that within days they had to lift the house arrest order for lack of evidence." He also told CPJ that he had been threatened with prosecution under the Law for the Protection of Cuba's National Independence and Economy (also known as Law 88). [See March 31 case.]

CPJ issued an alert about this case on April 12.

González Alfonso's affiliation with RSF has exposed him to repeated harassment from Cuban authorities. In February 2001, he was detained for four hours and interrogated about interviews he had given to a Miami radio station. Meanwhile, his house was placed under police surveillance.

AUGUST 1

Jesús Álvarez Castillo, CubaPress
THREATENED, HARASSED

Security officials threatened and harassed Álvarez Castillo, a journalist with the independent news agency CubaPress.

State Security Department (DSE) officers stopped the journalist in the streets of Morón, a city in the central province of Ciego de Ávila, and summoned him to the DSE's Morón headquarters, according to CubaPress. The officers interrogated Álvarez Castillo for two hours and threatened him with prosecution and prison if he continued working as a reporter in the area.

In mid-June, the journalist reported that he was unable to file stories over the phone to the Miami-based Web site Nueva Prensa Cubana because the DSE was disrupting his phone line.

Álvarez Castillo has covered Ciego de Ávila for CubaPress for the last three years. He also represents the independent journalists' organization Sociedad de Periodistas Manuel Márquez Sterling in Ciego de Ávila.

AUGUST 22

Dorka de Céspedes Vila, HavanaPress
THREATENED, HARASSED

Police and state security agents detained de Céspedes, a journalist with the independent news agency HavanaPress, while she was trying to cover a protest by a human rights group in Havana.

When the journalist arrived at the protest site around 8:30 p.m., National Revolutionary Police and State Security Department agents threatened her with jail and ordered her into a car. She was dropped about 6 miles (10 kilometers) from the point where she was detained.

OCTOBER 12

Sociedad de Periodistas Manuel Márquez Sterling
HARASSED

State security agents banned the independent press association Sociedad de Periodistas Manuel Márquez Sterling from giving training courses and harassed some of its members, according to local CPJ sources.

On the afternoon of October 12, two Department of State Security (DSE) officers came to the offices of the association and warned its president, journalist Ricardo González Alfonso, that they would not allow the group to offer courses during the 2001-2002 academic year.

The DSE officers also told González Alfonso that the courses were illegal because the journalists did not have a license to teach. The classes, including Spanish grammar, journalism, and English, were scheduled to open on October 15. They are free of charge for association members.

On October 14, the DSE officers visited the homes of independent journalists Jorge Olivera Castillo, Graciela Alfonso, Dorka de Céspedes Vila, and Aimeé Cabrera Álvarez, all of whom are very active in the organization, and warned them that attending the classes was illegal.

To avoid a confrontation with state security forces, the organization canceled the opening ceremony for the school year but confirmed that classes would open at a later date.

On October 16, the organization issued a statement condemning the prohibition. The following day, a lawyer from the Catholic Church's civic center Centro de Formación Cívica y Religiosa assured the group that the Cuban Penal Code does not bar their classes, and that teachers who give lessons for free do not need to obtain a license. Most teachers at the school do have licenses to teach in the Havana municipality of Playa, where the organization is based, González Alfonso informed CPJ.

The journalism classes, to be taught by respected independent journalist Raúl Rivero, are based on a Florida International University course.

On the morning of October 29, the day the courses were scheduled to start, about six DSE agents prevented journalists from attending classes, González Alfonso said. Rivero, who was already inside the association's office, was told to leave.

Journalist Carlos Castro was forced into a police car and driven to a neighborhood several miles away, where he was released. The association's offices were kept under police surveillance.

Although the organization has submitted all the required documentation to register as an association under Cuban law, the government had yet to approve the organization's application by year's end.

CPJ issued an alert about this case on October 24.

NOVEMBER 22

José Orlando González Bridón,
Cuba Free Press
IMPRISONED

González Bridón, a Cuban journalist and labor activist who was jailed for 11 months for distributing false information, was released on parole on November 22.

The journalist was first detained on December 15, 2000, and taken to the headquarters of the Technical Department of Investigations (DTI), the criminal police. On December 28, he was transferred to Combinado del Este Prison, where he was held several months without trial.

In early April 2001, a government prosecutor charged González Bridón with spreading false information about the death of a fellow labor activist and asked the court to sentence him to seven years in prison.

An article by the journalist posted to the Cuba Free Press site on August 5, 2000, reported that the Confederation of Cuban Democratic Workers national coordinator Joanna González Herrera had been attacked by her ex-husband, and that Cuban police had failed to prevent her death.

During González Bridón's trial, which was held behind closed doors on May 24, his lawyer argued that Joanna González Herrera had reported her ex-husband's threats to the police and was subsequently murdered by him. González Bridón reported these facts accurately, and therefore could not be accused of spreading false news.

González Bridón's attorney also argued that because ordinary Cubans lack access to the Internet, the journalist could not have caused alarm or discontent among the population through his work, which was published online. He then requested González Bridón's immediate and unconditional release.

In response, the state prosecutor changed the charges against González Bridón to "defamation of the institutions, heroes, and martyrs of the homeland" under Article 204 of the Penal Code, and requested a one-year prison sentence. The court announced that it would pass sentence within five days.

In early June, despite the new charge, the court found González Bridón guilty of distributing "false information for the purpose of disturbing the international peace, or to endanger the prestige or credibility of the Cuban State or its good relations with another State," a criminal offense under Article 115 of the Penal Code, and increased the sentence to two years imprisonment.

Under Cuban sentencing regulations, a one-year prison term would have led to González Bridón's release on June 15, since he would have been eligible for parole after serving half his sentence. In cases involving political dissidents, it is not uncommon for Cuban courts to pass longer sentences than those sought by prosecutors.

On June 8, a prison warden gave González Bridón a written copy of the sentence. On June 13, González Bridón's lawyer filed an appeal for annulment (*recurso de casación*) on procedural grounds.

DOMINICAN REPUBLIC

JUNE 28

Darío Medrano, Univisión, Color Visión-Canal 9
THREATENED
Ramón Carmona, Univisión
THREATENED

Medrano and Carmona, reporter and cameraman, respectively, for the U.S.-based Univisión television network, were threatened after they reported on street protests against a government-imposed economic adjustment package, which included higher taxes on gas and food and higher electricity rates, according to local press reports.

The journalists told the Santo Domingo daily *El Nacional* that they had received phone threats from people who identified themselves as government officials. The callers said they believed the reports damaged the Dominican Republic's image abroad. According to statements Carmona made to *El Nacional*, an unidentified caller told him that he had been blacklisted.

In addition to being Univisión's correspondent in the Dominican Republic, Medrano is a reporter for the Santo Domingo TV station Color Visión-Canal 9.

On June 30, the Santo Domingo daily *Última Hora* reported that the journalists' association Colegio Dominicano de Periodistas had issued a communiqué expressing its concern about the threats against Medrano and Carmona and requesting that they be investigated.

ECUADOR

JULY 20

Jorge Vivanco Mendieta, *Expreso*
LEGAL ACTION

Vivanco, 74, deputy editor and columnist at the Guayaquil daily *Expreso*, faced criminal and civil defamation charges filed by Fernando Rosero, a parliamentary deputy with the Ecuadoran Roldosista Party (PRE).

The lawsuits stemmed from several *Expreso* articles by Vivanco, including a July 15 piece criticizing Ecuadoran army generals for not defending themselves against Rosero's allegations that they had purchased defective weapons from Argentina in early 1995.

In the article, Vivanco referred to a political "offensive" by "Panamanian exiles" led by Rosero. This was an allusion to Rosero's relationship with former president and PRE leader Abdalá Bucaram, who was removed from his post in 1997 for corruption and has since lived in Panama with some of his closest supporters. Vivanco also wrote that Rosero was protected by his "parliamentary immunity-impunity."

Vivanco told CPJ that the 19th Criminal Court of Guayas would hear the criminal case. A judge scheduled settlement talks for December 21, but the journalist told CPJ that he had no intention of settling the case.

Rosero's civil suit requested US$1 million in damages. The 10th Civil Court of Guayas heard arguments in late December. On January 7, 2002, a judge dismissed the civil suit, ruling that Rosero had not proved any actual damage.

Rosero immediately appealed the ruling, taking the opportunity to issue veiled threats against Vivanco and to criticize the judge for alleged partiality. "In defense of honor, tomorrow those affected will have to take justice into their own hands," Rosero wrote in his request for an appeal, a copy of which was obtained by CPJ.

GUATEMALA

FEBRUARY 20

elPeriódico
ATTACKED

About 50 protesters gathered in front of the *elPeriódico* offices and threatened the newspaper's staff. According to CPJ sources, the protesters identified themselves as supporters of Luis Rabbé, then-minister of communications, infrastructure, and housing. Both *elPeriódico* and the daily *Prensa Libre* had strongly criticized Rabbé's official conduct.

Journalists at *elPeriódico* subsequently identified some of the protesters as employees of the Ministry of Communications, Infrastructure, and Housing. At least one car used to transport them was also traced to the ministry.

The mob attempted to force open doors and threw burning copies of the newspaper into the building, which also houses the Prensa Libre Group's daily *Nuestro Diario*.

The protesters also tried to attack three photographers, two from *elPeriódico* and one from *Nuestro Diario*, and damaged two vehicles belonging to *Nuestro Diario*. Local police took 40 minutes to respond to a call for help from *elPeriódico's* offices. When the police finally arrived, they did not make any arrests.

In various articles published since November 2000, *elPeriódico* exposed irregularities in the awarding of public works contracts by Rabbé's ministry. Early in January 2001, local press reports quoted Rabbé as saying he was the victim of a campaign of personal destruction by some journalists.

Radio and television stations owned by Ángel González, a Mexican national who is Rabbé's brother-in-law, also waged a campaign to discredit *elPeriódico*. Through front companies, González owns all four of Guatemala's private television stations, in violation of constitutional prohibitions against media monopolies and foreign ownership of media.

González has been a leading financial contributor to Guatemalan president Alfonso Portillo Cabrera's political campaigns, and Rabbé himself is a former executive in González's media empire. According to local sources, television crews from González's stations arrived outside *elPeriódico* 20 minutes before the attack.

In a February 22 letter to President Portillo Cabrera, CPJ urged him to ensure that all journalists in Guatemala are able to work without fear of threats or intimidation.

MARCH 27

Silvia Gereda, *elPeriódico*
`ATTACKED, THREATENED`
Luis Escobar, *elPeriódico*
`THREATENED`
Enrique Castañeda, *elPeriódico*
`THREATENED`
Walter Martín Juárez Ruiz, *elPeriódico*
`ATTACKED, THREATENED`

Escobar and Castañeda, reporters for the Guatemala City daily *elPeriódico*, were threatened after they broke a scandal involving the state-controlled bank Crédito Hipotecario Nacional (CHN).

Gereda and Juárez, respectively the investigative editor and a reporter with the paper, were also menaced over *elPeriódico*'s coverage of the scandal.

On March 26, *elPeriódico* broke a major story about irregular CHN loans totaling 47 million quetzales (US$6 million). *elPeriódico* reported that some of these loans were to companies and

individuals with close links to CHN stockholders and the bank's president, José Armando Llort.

On March 27, in direct response to *elPeriódico*'s reporting, the Banking Supervision Office ordered CHN to recover the total loan amount by the end of the month. On April 3, Llort and five other members of the CHN board of directors resigned. According to local press reports, President Alfonso Portillo Cabrera personally asked Llort to give up his post.

After the *elPeriódico* story broke, Llort placed several advertisements in local newspapers threatening legal action against media that covered the CHN story, according to CPJ sources in Guatemala.

On March 27, meanwhile, a man who identified himself as a CHN employee approached Gereda and said that Llort wanted to kill her as well as her colleagues Escobar and Castañeda. The man claimed that the *elPeriódico* journalists were being watched and filmed.

He then produced a folder containing personal information about Gereda and her family. He also gave her an oral account of Escobar and Castañeda's daily schedule.

That evening, Gereda told CPJ, another individual approached her and grabbed her by the neck as she left her literature class at the Universidad del Valle. After insulting Gereda, the man said they—an obvious reference to *elPeriódico* journalists— would be killed if they kept making trouble. Gereda was unable to identify the attacker.

On the morning of March 28, Gereda noticed a car with tinted windows parked outside her house. In the afternoon, Castañeda was trailed by an unregistered red vehicle.

Later that day, Gereda filed a complaint with the United Nations Verification Mission in Guatemala (MINUGUA), which monitors compliance with the peace agreements that ended Guatemala's long-running civil war. The next day, Gereda went to the Public Ministry and filed another complaint. Ministry officials provided her with several letters ordering police units based near the paper's offices to provide assistance in case of an emergency.

Also on March 28, following a phone conversation with Byron Barrera, President Portillo's secretary of social communication, CPJ issued a public statement expressing its concern about the threats against the *elPeriódico* journalists.

On March 30 at around 8 p.m., two masked gunmen in a car intercepted Juárez while he was driving in downtown Guatemala City. The attackers got out of their car and pointed their handguns at Juárez's head. Before fleeing the scene, the men told the journalist that they were going to kill him, Gereda, Escobar, and Castañeda because of *elPeriódico*'s work.

In a state of nervous collapse, Juárez sought refuge in a nearby fire station, where he was given a tranquilizer.

AUGUST 1

Eddy Castillo, *elPeriódico*
ATTACKED
Mynor de León, *Prensa Libre*
ATTACKED

Sandra Sebastián, *Siglo Veintiuno*
ATTACKED
Marvin del Cid, Emisoras Unidas
ATTACKED

Castillo, de León, Sebastián, and del Cid were attacked by police officers while covering public demonstrations against a two percent increase in the value-added tax.

As the protest ended on the afternoon of August 1 near Guatemala City's Plaza de la Constitución, a group of demonstrators engaged in a street battle with officers from the Civil National Police, who used tear gas and fired pistols into the air to disperse the crowds.

When police moved to make arrests, journalists attempted to interview and photograph the protesters who were being detained. The police tried to push the journalists away and beat up at least four of them. Police also shouted that they did not want to see any journalists around.

Members of the media who were assaulted by riot police included: Castillo, a reporter for the daily *elPeriódico*; de León, a photographer for the daily *Prensa Libre,* whose camera was destroyed; Sebastián, a photographer for the daily *Siglo Veintiuno*; and del Cid, a reporter for the radio station Emisoras Unidas.

Various sources reported that the assault occurred in front of police chief Santos Estrada Marroquín, who was in charge of riot control in the area. Apparently, he did not intervene.

On August 6, CPJ sent a letter of inquiry to Adolfo González Rodas, the attorney general of Guatemala, expressing its concerns about the attack and urging a prompt and thorough investigation.

Jorge Mynor Alegría Armendáriz,
Radio Amatique
`KILLED`
Enrique Aceituno, Radio Amatique
`THREATENED`

Alegría, host of the call-in show "Línea Directa," was shot at least five times outside his home in Puerto Barrios, a port city located on the Caribbean coast in Izabal Department.

Alegría, who also worked as a part-time correspondent for the national radio network Emisoras Unidas, had reportedly been threatened on three different occasions after broadcasting stories about corruption. In addition, one of his colleagues told the press that local officials had tried to bribe Alegría to keep him quiet about their activities.

Police detained two suspects in connection with Alegría's murder. One suspect had a 9 mm handgun whose bullets apparently matched those found at the crime scene. Preliminary investigations by the Puerto Barrios prosecutor's office revealed that the handgun had recently fired six shots.

On September 20, the Ombudsman's Office for Human Rights (PDH) released the results of its investigations. The report concluded that Alegría's murder was politically motivated and was probably masterminded by local officials in retaliation for the journalist's coverage of corruption in Puerto Barrios. The PDH added that the two suspects in police custody were scapegoats. A report with the PDH's findings was sent to the newly created Prosecutor's Office for Crimes against Journalists.

In early October, the two suspects were released after ballistics testing proved that the confiscated handgun was not the murder weapon.

At year's end, the Puerto Barrios prosecutor's office and police were investigating Alegría's murder as either a crime of passion, a politically motivated crime, or a common crime. However, they have not offered any evidence to support their theories. According to the news agency CERIGUA, a local prosecutor declared that a political motivation could neither be ruled out nor confirmed.

HAITI

Lilianne Pierre-Paul, Radio Kiskeya
`THREATENED`
Radio Kiskeya
`HARASSED`

Pierre-Paul, co-owner and program director of the independent Port-au-Prince station Radio Kiskeya, was threatened by Paul Raymond, leader of the religious organization Ti Kominote Legliz, during a press conference.

That same day, an unidentified individual tried to set Radio Kiskeya's offices on fire.

Raymond's organization supports the ruling Lavalas Family party. During his remarks at the press conference, Raymond read names from a list of people who he claimed were planning to form a shadow government.

The list included Pierre-Paul. Raymond gave those mentioned three days to distance themselves from the alleged plot, threatening violence should they not comply.

During his remarks, Raymond said

Pierre-Paul's name belonged on the list because she always referred to the lawmakers who won a seat in the controversial May 2000 parliamentary elections as "contested deputies."

Pierre-Paul told CPJ that at 7 p.m. that same evening, staff members found a gallon of gasoline in a plastic bag in the station's courtyard. Gasoline had also been poured on the ground.

A security guard and some neighbors later claimed to have seen someone running away from the offices just before the gasoline was discovered. The next day, a match was found stuck in the gate.

Local police declined to investigate the incident because there was no actual fire.

Pierre-Paul told CPJ that she received death threats on a weekly basis, mostly by mail. In insulting terms, the anonymous letters accused Pierre-Paul of corruption.

JUNE 9

Roosevelt Benjamin, Signal FM
THREATENED

Benjamin, news director at the private radio station Signal FM, based in the Port-au-Prince suburb of Pétion-Ville, received a series of telephone threats after a June 9 broadcast of his weekly political talk show "Moment Vérité" (Moment of Truth).

Benjamin told CPJ that one hour after his program, he received an anonymous call on his cell phone. "I see you are meddling in affairs that are none of your business," the caller said. "But we can force you to be silent."

Five minutes later, the same man called again, this time telling Benjamin

that he knew where the journalist lived and what car he drove. The next day at around 5 p.m., Benjamin received similar threats from a different caller. After the program was rebroadcast on the night of June 11, Benjamin received another, apparently threatening, call in which the caller remained silent.

All four calls were made with a prepaid phone card, Benjamin said, making it impossible for him to identify the callers.

Benjamin believes that he was threatened for stating, during his June 9 broadcast, that a recently launched political organization called the Mouvement de la Société Civile Majoritaire (Majority Civil Society Movement) was dominated by the relatives of senators from the ruling Lavalas Family party.

On June 13, CPJ wrote a letter to President Jean-Bertrand Aristide expressing its profound concern over the threats.

DECEMBER 3

Brignolle Lindor, Radio Echo 2000
KILLED

A machete-wielding mob hacked to death Lindor, news director of the private station Radio Echo 2000 that is based in the coastal town of Petit-Goâve, some 40 miles west of Port-au-Prince.

At 11 a.m., Lindor and a colleague were driving to one of Lindor's other jobs, as a customs official. Their car was ambushed by supporters of President Jean-Bertrand Aristide's Lavalas Family party. Lindor's colleague fled, but Lindor was attacked and killed after he tried to take refuge in the nearby home of a local town counselor.

Lindor hosted the political talk show "Dialogue." He had received numerous threats from local authorities for inviting members of the 15-party opposition coalition Democratic Convergence to appear on his show.

After Aristide launched a "zero tolerance" anti-crime campaign in June, implying that street criminals caught red-handed could be summarily punished without trial, Petit-Goâve deputy mayor Dumé Bony announced in public that the "zero tolerance" policy should be applied to Lindor. Opposition parties and human rights groups accused Aristide of issuing a carte blanche for extrajudicial executions.

Lindor's December 11 funeral turned violent when police used bludgeons and tear gas on mourners who were shouting anti-Aristide slogans, according to wire reports.

HONDURAS

MAY 1

Manuel Torres Calderón, *El Heraldo*
`CENSORED`
Roger Argueta, *El Heraldo*
`CENSORED`

Torres, op-ed editor for the Tegucigalpa daily *El Heraldo*, and Argueta, an investigative reporter for the paper, were fired under government pressure, according to the journalists and human rights organizations.

Torres told CPJ that prior to his dismissal, the government pressured the paper to tone down its editorials, which often criticized President Carlos Roberto Flores Facussé's government.

Management told Torres that the

decision to dismiss him had nothing to do with his work, but with "interests that come from above." After he left *El Heraldo*, the paper started extolling the Flores administration.

Argueta told the human rights organization COFADEH that he was gradually relieved of his daily assignments and then fired. According to COFADEH, *El Heraldo* deputy director Julio César Marín claimed that Argueta had given statements criticizing *El Heraldo* to other media outlets, and that he had requested information regarding business deals that *El Heraldo* owner Jorge Canahuati had made with the government.

Canahuati, who also owns the San Pedro Sula-based daily *La Prensa*, the country's largest paper, claimed that Torres' dismissal was a "normal work circumstance" and denied that he had acted under government pressure.

Torres worked as an editorial writer for *El Heraldo* for five years, and in September 1999 became an op-ed editor for the paper. Under Torres, *El Heraldo*'s op-ed section became one of the most respected in Honduras and one known for its openness to diverse opinions.

Argueta was hired by the former editor of *El Heraldo*, Thelma Mejía, who resigned in late April, allegedly under government pressure.

MEXICO

FEBRUARY 19

José Luis Ortega Mata, *Semanario de Ojinaga*
`KILLED`

Ortega Mata, 37, was the editor of

the weekly *Semanario de Ojinaga*, based in Ojinaga, Chihuahua State. He was shot twice in the head at close range with a .22-caliber firearm on the evening of February 19, according to local press reports.

Friends and relatives of the journalist linked his murder to a front-page story in the February 15 issue of *Semanario de Ojinaga* reporting that the federal Attorney General's Office (PGR) was investigating drug trafficking activities in the town of Aldama, near the state capital, Chihuahua. *Semanario de Ojinaga* also claimed that local traffickers were moving drugs from safe houses in Aldama through Ojinaga to the United States.

It has also been reported that the paper was about to publish a story alleging that drug traffickers were funding the electoral campaigns of local politicians, and that Ortega Mata had received threats in connection with the story. In the past, the weekly has run articles criticizing local politicians and police.

On April 29, a businessman named Jesús Manuel Herrera was arrested by state police and charged with Ortega Mata's murder based on eyewitness testimony. However, jail records show that the alleged eyewitness who identified Herrera as the assailant was in jail at the time of Ortega Mata's death. In addition, the Chihuahua Attorney General's Office was unable to provide a motive and offered no other evidence. Despite these revelations, Herrera remained imprisoned pending further investigations.

On July 13, after several hearings and more than 70 days in prison, an appeals court judge ruled that the evidence against Herrera was insufficient, and he was released.

APRIL 16

Carolina Pavón, *REFORMA*
LEGAL ACTION
Alejandro Junco de la Vega, *REFORMA*
LEGAL ACTION

Former Mexico City mayor Rosario Robles Berlanga brought criminal defamation charges against Pavón, a reporter with the Mexico City-based daily *REFORMA*, and Junco de la Vega, president and publisher of the paper. The charges stem from an April 12 cover story in which Pavón reported on official allegations that almost 10 percent of the mayor's administration's 2000 budget had gone missing.

The allegations appeared in a report from the Comptroller General's Office of Mexico City, which found that 6 billion Mexican pesos (US$650 million) were unaccounted for in last year's budget.

Robles, who was mayor of Mexico City until December 2000, did not dispute the allegations, but contended that she had no knowledge of the reported malfeasance and therefore could not be held responsible.

On April 16, Robles filed a criminal defamation complaint against Pavón and Junco de la Vega before federal district attorney general Bernardo Bátiz.

REFORMA's manager of legal affairs, Eugenio Herrera Terrazas, told CPJ that the suit was based on Article 350 of the Federal District's Penal Code. If convicted, Pavón and Junco de la Vega could be jailed for up to two years.

In a letter protesting the charges that

was sent to President Vicente Fox
Quesada on May 22, CPJ argued that it
was outrageous that Robles should
make a criminal matter of her
objections to a report on a matter of
obvious public interest.

OCTOBER 23

Ernesto Villanueva, *Proceso*
THREATENED, HARASSED

Villanueva, a university professor and
a frequent contributor to the Mexico
City weekly *Proceso*, was harassed and
threatened by unidentified individuals,
apparently in reprisal for criticizing a
government-sponsored access to
information bill.

At around 10:40 p.m., a car with its
high-beam lights on followed Villanueva
as he drove home. Upon his arrival, the
professor received an anonymous phone
call from an individual who said,
"Doctor, we want you to stop talking
crap about the [access to information]
law. Mexico City is a very dangerous
city and the family goes first. Take that
into account." The caller hung up when
Villanueva asked who was on the phone.

Villanueva, a professor at Mexico
City's Universidad Iberoamericana's
Communications Department, is also a
member of the Oaxaca Group, a
coalition of journalists, academics, and
nongovernmental organizations that in
late 2001 proposed a draft bill on
access to public information.

In his frequent articles for *Proceso*,
Villanueva had harshly criticized a
competing bill sponsored by
President Vicente Fox Quesada's
administration. Opposition deputies
in the Congress introduced the Oaxaca
Group version of the bill for debate in

early December 2001. It remained
under consideration at year's end.

The threats against Villanueva
came four days after the murder of
human rights lawyer Digna Ochoa and
threats against human rights activists
at the Miguel Agustín Pro Juárez
Human Rights Center, where Ochoa
used to work.

In a November 5 *Proceso* article,
Villanueva wrote that he had decided
against filing a complaint about the
incident because he did not want to
distract attention from the debate on
the bill.

NICARAGUA

AUGUST 25

Adolfo Pastrán Arancibia, Radio La
Primerísima
CENSORED

Pastrán, a prominent journalist
who hosted the radio show "Púlsar
Noticias" and was press director of
the Managua-based radio station
Radio La Primerísima, was forced to
cancel his show after the Sandinista
National Liberation Front (FSLN),
the country's main opposition party,
allegedly pressured the radio
station's management.

According to Pastrán, the radio
station had harshly criticized the
FSLN and its leader, Daniel Ortega.
In late July, Ortega met with the
station's management and resolved
his differences with them.

Shortly thereafter, Pastrán was given
a 20-day "vacation" while his show
was shortened from one hour to 45
minutes and moved to a new time slot.
The original slot was filled with a new

show hosted by FSLN parliamentary deputy Víctor Hugo Tinoco.

While on vacation, Pastrán performed consulting work for the civic organization Movimiento Viva Managua, whose leader, Pedro Solórzano, was a longtime friend. Solórzano's organization planned to mount a media campaign encouraging people to vote in the November 4, 2001, general elections.

When Pastrán returned from his vacation, he met with the station's general manager, William Grigsby, and told him about his consulting work, explaining that he had provided only technical assistance and did not see any conflict of interest. In addition, the journalist claimed that his contract with Radio La Primerísima allowed such work, and that he had performed media consulting work in the past for private and public institutions without problems.

Grigsby, however, told Pastrán that since Solórzano had just been chosen to run the electoral campaign in Managua for the ruling Constitutionalist Liberal Party (PLC) candidate Enrique Bolaños, Pastrán's work with him would damage the radio station's relationship with the FSLN.

Grigsby added that both Solórzano and Bolaños were political enemies of the FSLN and therefore of Radio La Primerísima. Although Pastrán offered to take an unpaid leave of absence and resign as press director, while keeping his show, on August 25 he was summoned to a meeting and told that his show would be canceled effective immediately.

"Púlsar Noticias," a highly rated daily show, first went on the air on

Radio La Primerísima in June 1999. Since mid-September, the show has been broadcast by the Managua-based station Radio Tiempo.

PANAMA

JANUARY 3

Julio Briceño, *La Prensa*
LEGAL ACTION
Stanley Muschett, *La Prensa*
LEGAL ACTION
La Prensa
LEGAL ACTION

Ricardo Arias Calderón, a former Panamanian vice president who later became president-for-life of the Christian Democratic Party (PDC), filed a criminal defamation case against Briceño, cartoonist with the Panama City daily *La Prensa*, and Muschett, then the paper's editor, over a cartoon that ran in the paper on December 30, 2000. He also filed a civil action against *La Prensa*.

Briceño's cartoon criticized a recent alliance between the PDC and the Democratic Revolutionary Party (PRD), which allowed the two opposition parties to take control of the Legislative Assembly. The cartoon depicted Arias Calderón holding hands with the Grim Reaper, a reference to PRD support for Panama's former military regimes.

The cartoon was published just after the remains of several political dissidents were found buried near military barracks outside of Panama City. On December 31, 2000, *La Prensa* published a letter by Arias Calderón responding to the cartoon.

In his civil suit, Arias Calderón asked for 1 million balboas (US$1,000,000) in damages. Briceño faced two years in jail. (Muschett was dropped from the suit, Briceño told CPJ.)

On June 29, Briceño testified before the Seventh Attorney General's Office. On July 4, the cartoonist was prohibited from leaving Panama and ordered to sign a government register every 15 days. Briceño told CPJ that he signed the register once before a higher court declared the measure void in mid-July.

Briceño was summoned for another hearing on December 28, but did not attend because a brief his lawyer wanted to present was not ready. They decided to wait for a second summons, which had not arrived at press time.

MARCH 12

Octavio Amat, El Panamá América
`LEGAL ACTION`
Jean Marcel Chéry, El Panamá América
`LEGAL ACTION`
Gustavo Aparicio, El Panamá América
`LEGAL ACTION`
John Watson Riley, El Panamá América
`LEGAL ACTION`

Then-minister of government and justice Winston Spadafora filed a criminal defamation case against Aparicio and Chéry, reporters with the Panama City daily El Panamá América; Watson, a photographer with the paper; and Amat, the paper's editor. In addition, Spadafora accused Chéry, Aparicio, and Watson of trespassing on private property.

The suit came after a March 8 article in El Panamá América reported that a remote road being built by the Social Investment Fund would pass by the country estates of Spadafora and comptroller Alvin Weeden. The article

was accompanied by aerial photos. The journalists claimed one of Spadafora's employees let them onto the property.

On March 20, agents of the Public Ministry visited El Panamá América's offices to notify the journalists of the suit. Public Ministry officials carried out an on-site inspection of the premises the next day. However, El Panamá América editor Rosa Guizado told CPJ that Panamanian law requires two days advance notice of such an inspection.

At year's end, Guizado said, the case was still in the hands of the Public Ministry.

MARCH 20

Marcelino Rodríguez, El Siglo
`LEGAL ACTION`

Rodríguez, a former reporter with the Panama City daily El Siglo, was convicted of defaming Panama's solicitor general, Alma Montenegro de Fletcher, and sentenced to serve 16 months in prison. The sentence was then reduced to a fine of 1,000 balboas (US$1,000), but Rodríguez was barred from holding public office for the 16-month period.

On August 4, 1998, Montenegro de Fletcher filed a criminal defamation case against Rodríguez after an El Siglo article published the previous day alleged that the prosecutor had used her influence to acquire government housing in the former Panama Canal Zone. Montenegro de Fletcher denied the allegations.

Shortly thereafter, Brittmarie Janson Pérez, a Panamanian anthropologist and columnist who resides in the United States, published a column in El Siglo saying that she was the source for

Rodríguez's story. Janson Pérez and Michelle Lescure, editor of *El Siglo* at the time, were later added as defendants in the defamation suit.

On March 4, 1999, CPJ sent a letter to then-president Ernesto Pérez Balladares urging him to fulfill his often stated promise to repeal the country's so-called gag laws. The letter mentioned the *El Siglo* case as an example of the many criminal defamation cases involving Panamanian journalists.

On January 10, 2000, Ninth Circuit district attorney Roberto Murgas Torraza asked that the case be dismissed, Lescure told CPJ. Montenegro de Fletcher subsequently filed a petition with the Attorney General's Office calling for an investigation into Murgas Torraza. The attorney resigned on January 20, 2000, claiming that he had been pressured and threatened, Lescure said.

Judge Ileana Turner Montenegro then dismissed the case against Lescure and Janson Pérez but ordered that Rodríguez be tried.

After the journalist was sentenced, Montenegro de Fletcher asked President Mireya Moscoso to pardon the journalist. Although the president promised to do so, she had apparently not kept her promise by year's end.

MAY 16

Miguel Antonio Bernal, *"Alternativa,"* *El Panamá América*
LEGAL ACTION

Radio journalist, columnist, and university professor Bernal was tried on criminal defamation charges filed originally in 1998 by then-National Police director José Luis Sosa.

During a February 1998 broadcast of the news program "TVN-Noticias," Bernal held the National Police responsible for the decapitation of four Coiba Island Prison inmates by fellow prisoners.

At the time, Sosa was quoted in the Panama City daily *La Prensa* as saying, "Apart from being false, Bernal's assertions are slanderous of the good name of the institution and help to debilitate the confidence and support that the community has given to the National Police."

Bernal faces an 18-month prison sentence if convicted.

Bernal hosts the daily radio program "Alternativa," which covers current affairs. He also writes a weekly column for the Panama City daily *El Panamá América* and contributes to the dailies *La Prensa* and *El Siglo*.

In a May 15 news alert about the upcoming trial, CPJ's executive director Ann Cooper said, "It is shocking that officials of a democratic country should abuse criminal defamation laws to stifle critical voices in the media."

On the day of the hearing, Bernal moved to have the charges dismissed, arguing that Sosa had no standing to file defamation charges because he was not directly affected by the remarks.

Bernal's petition was rejected in July. He appealed the rejection to the Second Superior Tribunal of Justice, which had not yet responded at press time.

PARAGUAY

JANUARY 5

Salvador Medina Velázquez
KILLED

Medina, 27, president of the board

of community radio station FM Ñemity in the town of Capiibary in the San Pedro Department, about 250 km (150 miles) from Asunción, was ambushed and shot by an unidentified gunman.

The journalist was driving a motorcycle with his brother Gaspar when a masked attacker came out from behind some bushes and shot him in the left side at point-blank range. The attacker then fled into the bush, according to local press reports. Medina lost control of his motorcycle, fell to the ground, and died immediately.

The journalist's family linked the attack to his reports on timber smuggling in state-owned forest reservations in Capiibary, local sources told CPJ. In particular, Medina had singled out a gang of alleged smugglers with ties to the National Republican Association (ARN), also known as the Colorado Party.

One of those whom Medina had accused was arrested in March for timber smuggling. In addition, Medina had covered incidents of livestock theft, along with organized crime in a nearby town.

In January and February, the Paraguayan police arrested four men suspected of killing Medina, but at least four other suspects were still at large.

In a hearing on September 6, Public Prosecutor Ramón Trinidad Zelaya charged Milcíades Maylin, one of the four suspects in police custody, with Medina's murder. Judge Silvio Flores granted Trinidad's request that the charges against the three other suspects be dismissed.

On October 16, a three-judge sentencing tribunal found Maylin guilty of murdering Medina and sentenced him to a 25-year prison term. Medina's

relatives, however, believe that the individuals who ordered the murder have not been brought to justice.

MAY 7

Séver del Puerto, Radio Cáritas-Universidad Católica
THREATENED, HARASSED

Radio journalist del Puerto and his family suffered death threats and other harassment related to his investigations linking a prominent government official to a high-profile robbery.

Del Puerto, a crime reporter for the Catholic radio station Radio Cáritas-Universidad Católica in Asunción, worked for the current-events radio programs "En el Cambio" and "El Pulso del País."

Beginning May 7, the journalist received numerous phone calls from anonymous individuals who threatened to kill him and his family. His car was also followed, according to local sources contacted by CPJ. Fearing for his life and his family, del Puerto took his family into hiding at several different locations. The threats intensified on May 14, prompting the journalist to seek refuge at the offices of the television station Canal 9.

The threats apparently came in retaliation for del Puerto's free-lance investigation into the alleged involvement of former interior minister Walter Bower and several judges in an August 2000 robbery at the Asunción International Airport.

Del Puerto spent five months investigating the robbery, in which heavily armed robbers stole 40 billion guaraníes (US$11 million) from armored trucks owned by

Prosegur del Paraguay S.A., a private security company. The journalist was planning to sell his story to leading media outlets in Paraguay, according to local sources.

After arriving at Canal 9 on May 14, del Puerto denounced the death threats and claimed to have evidence linking Bower, who is currently a parliamentary deputy for the Colorado Party, to the robbery. Later that evening, the journalist filed a complaint with the Attorney General's Office, backed up by video and audio recordings in which an eyewitness accused Bower of masterminding the robbery. The Paraguayan police then assigned six police agents to protect del Puerto and his immediate relatives, according to local news reports.

On May 20, del Puerto was admitted to the Hospital Universitario, where he received treatment for a nervous breakdown. He later received additional treatment at a private clinic.

On May 22, local and regional human rights activists filed a writ of habeas corpus with the Paraguayan Supreme Court, requesting security guarantees for del Puerto and his family. The signatories included the local press freedom organization Sindicato de Periodistas del Paraguay, the regional chapter of the U.S.-based Center for Justice and International Law, and the local human rights group Coordinadora de Derechos Humanos del Paraguay. CPJ was unable to confirm the status of this petition by press time.

On June 4, CPJ sent President Luis González Macchi a letter of protest expressing concern for the safety of del Puerto and his family.

JUNE 26

Telmo Tomás Ibáñez Jara, *ABC Color*
THREATENED, LEGAL ACTION

Ibáñez, correspondent for the Asunción daily *ABC Color* in the city of Concepción, faced a criminal defamation lawsuit filed by three city officials.

The case stemmed from a May 27 article in *ABC Color*, titled "The Mayor Has Accomplices and Accessories." Ibáñez's article cited official documents from the Comptroller General's Office, presenting evidence of financial misconduct in the administration of Concepción mayor Genaro Domínguez Bogado.

Ibáñez also wrote that city councilmen Andrés Villalba Barrios, Eulogio Echagüe Insfrán, and Blas Cáceres, who apparently ignored the audit's findings, were involved in the irregularities. On June 26, the three councilmen filed a criminal complaint against the journalist, accusing him of "aggravated libel."

A month later, on July 25, the Ministry of Interior took over Concepción's local government, temporarily removing Mayor Domínguez from office.

On September 21, Judge Juan Pablo Cardozo Notario found Ibáñez guilty of defamation and ordered him to pay a fine of 19 million guaraníes (approximately US$4,000) plus legal costs.

On September 24, the local press union Sindicato de Periodistas del Paraguay issued a statement condemning the sentence.

On September 25 and 26, the journalist received several anonymous phone threats, according to *ABC Color*. He was also trailed by an unidentified vehicle. The threats prompted Ibáñez to visit the local police headquarters.

On October 5, Ibáñez filed an appeal with the Concepción Appeals Court. On November 28, the court revoked Judge Cardozo's ruling and ordered the plaintiffs to assume the legal costs of the proceedings.

PERU

APRIL 19

Luis Samuel Zevallos Hidalgo, Radio La Oroya
ATTACKED

Unidentified individuals assaulted Zevallos, a journalist with radio station Radio La Oroya in the municipality of Yauli-La Oroya, Junín Department, after he broadcast an audio recording of a local official bribing a business executive.

The journalist, who worked for the news program "En las Noticias" (In the News), was attacked by four unidentified men as he was heading home at around 1 a.m. Cevallos told CPJ that the attackers covered him with a pillow and then beat him. They also took the audiotape, which Zevallos had broadcast two days earlier.

The tape was of a conversation between a local business executive who had been awarded a contract to supply milk for a community food program and Javier Izquierdo Yantas, head of supplies and logistics for the municipality of Yauli-La Oroya. In the conversation, Izquierdo asked the businessman for a bribe of 5,000 nuevos soles (about US$1,400).

Zevallos attributed the attack to Izquierdo and Yauli-La Oroya mayor

Georgina Ríos Quintanilla, who appointed Izquierdo. Ríos is a member of the Vamos Vecino political party, a junior member of former president Alberto K. Fujimori's ruling coalition.

As a result of the attack, Zevallos suffered multiple injuries and broke his collarbone. Afer surgery and a month of bed rest, he returned to Radio La Oroya on June 11.

MAY 8

Jesús Alfonso Castiglione Mendoza, free-lancer
LEGAL ACTION
Martín Gómez Arquiño, Radio Alpamayo
LEGAL ACTION
Hugo González Henostroza, Liberación
LEGAL ACTION

Castiglione, Gómez, and González faced criminal defamation charges filed by former governor Ildorfo Cueva Retuerto in Huaraz, a city in the central department of Ancash.

Cueva, a retired police colonel who headed the government anti-terrorism office in Huaraz in the early 1990s, was named governor of Ancash in late February 2001. After learning of his appointment, the three journalists accused him of committing numerous human rights violations under the authoritarian government of former president Alberto K. Fujimori.

On April 21, the Ministry of the Interior dismissed Cueva over these allegations.

On May 8, Cueva filed a criminal complaint against the journalists with the First Criminal Chamber of the Huaraz Superior Court. He requested civil damages of 1 million nuevos soles (US$280,000), in addition to criminal penalties.

González, president of the Huaraz chapter of the local journalists' organization Asociación Nacional de Periodistas (ANP) and local correspondent for the Lima-based daily *Liberación*, wrote an article quoting Gómez, a journalist with the local radio station Radio Alpamayo, who declared that Cueva was a human rights violator and that his appointment was an insult to the region's citizens. Speaking for the ANP, González also expressed the outrage of local journalists over Cueva's appointment.

Castiglione wrote a March 28 letter to the editor of the national weekly *Caretas* denouncing Cueva as a human rights violator and claiming he had been tortured while in Cueva's custody in 1993. Castiglione, the former owner of radio station Radio Amistad in the port city of Huacho, was arrested in April 1993 and accused of participating in a Shining Path terrorist attack in Huaraz. He was convicted in 1994 and pardoned in 1996.

Since his arrest in 1993, Castiglione has frequently condemned Cueva's record of human rights violations. The journalist told CPJ that he was concerned that Cuevas remained an influential person in the area and might use his clout to harass the journalists.

In the May 27 edition of the television news program "Reportajes" (Reports), broadcast by Panamericana TV-Canal 5, Cueva accused Castiglione of being a slanderer and a terrorist.

The journalists were formally notified of the lawsuit on June 7. On June 20, their lawyer requested that the criminal charges be dropped. On August

17, Judge Magdalena Sofía Salazar de Solís dismissed the charges, ruling that the journalists had done legitimate reporting on regional events.

Cueva appealed this ruling on August 27, Castiglione told CPJ. At press time, there were no new developments in the case, which was being heard in the Ancash Superior Court.

UNITED STATES

JULY 20

Vanessa Leggett, free-lancer
IMPRISONED

Leggett, a Houston-based free-lancer, was jailed without bail after refusing to hand over research for a book she was writing about the 1997 murder of Houston socialite Doris Angleton. Leggett, who is believed to have served in prison longer than any journalist in U.S. history, was released on January 4.

The journalist, 33, was asked to give her research materials to a federal grand jury. These materials include tapes of interviews she conducted with murder suspect Roger Angleton, the victim's brother-in-law, shortly before he committed suicide.

Since the Watergate era, federal prosecutors have needed permission from the U.S. attorney general before ordering a journalist to reveal his or her sources. The last federal jailing of journalists was in 1991, when four journalists were briefly detained for refusing to testify in a corruption trial.

Justice Department spokeswoman Mindy Tucker was quoted in the fall issue of *The News Media & The Law* as saying, "She was not handled as a member of the media, so [the department]

would not have followed the procedure that we have laid out for subpoenas of members of the media."

Leggett, who was clearly investigating a news story for public dissemination, refused to comply with the subpoena, citing confidentiality of her sources. In a closed hearing on July 19, District Judge Melinda Harmon found Leggett in contempt of court and gave her a one-day grace period to surrender to authorities. Leggett turned herself in on July 20.

Leggett's lawyer, Mike DeGeurin, filed an appeal with the U.S. Court of Appeals for the Fifth Circuit asking that bail be granted immediately and that the appeal be handled in an expedited manner. The court refused bail but granted the request for an expedited appeal hearing, which was held on August 15.

The Appeals Court denied requests by news organizations to argue on Leggett's behalf during the hearing. Initially, the court had closed the hearing to the public, but after the news organizations filed an emergency motion, the courtroom was opened on August 14.

During the August 15 hearing before a three-judge panel, Justice Department attorney Paula Offenhauser admitted that prosecutors were not sure what they were after.

But on August 17, the panel of the Appeals Court upheld Judge Harmon's ruling, saying, "The district court did not abuse its discretion in ordering Leggett incarcerated for contempt." DeGeurin told CPJ that the Appeals Court panel assumed Leggett to be a journalist but contended that reporter's privilege carries less weight in a federal grand jury investigation.

DeGeurin appealed to the full court,

but his request for a rehearing was denied in November. The Appeals Court also denied DeGeurin's motion to release Leggett during the appeals process.

DeGeurin then filed a petition for a writ of certiorari with the U.S. Supreme Court on December 31 asking for a review of the appeals court decision.

Leggett was released on January 4, 2002, the day the grand jury's term expired. "I'm very grateful to be free. I don't think anyone realizes how precious freedom is until it's threatened or taken away from them," Leggett told CPJ shortly after her release.

The appeal before the Supreme Court, however, remained important because Leggett could still be summoned as a witness in any future trial related to the Angleton murder. She could also face criminal contempt charges.

At press time, the Supreme Court was still reviewing the case.

SEPTEMBER 11

William Biggart, free-lancer
KILLED

Biggart, a free-lance news photographer, was killed in the terrorist attacks on the World Trade Center. The journalist's body was found on September 15 in the rubble at Ground Zero, near the bodies of several firefighters. Biggart had rushed to the scene with his camera shortly after hearing about the attacks.

SEPTEMBER 21

Voice of America
CENSORED

Under pressure from the U.S. Department of State, the Voice of America (VOA) delayed airing a story that contained parts of an exclusive interview with the leader of Afghanistan's Taliban movement, Mullah Mohammed Omar.

The federally funded broadcaster's decision came after Deputy Secretary of State Richard L. Armitage and senior National Security Council officials contacted members of VOA's board of governors to express their concern that broadcasting the interview would amount to providing a platform to terrorists, according to *The Washington Post*. The VOA board then relayed these concerns to staff members.

The news report, by VOA's Ed Warner, was scheduled to air on September 21. It contained excerpts from Warner's exclusive interview with Omar and also quoted U.S. president George W. Bush's September 20 address to Congress.

Warner's report also featured commentary by John Esposito, director of the Center of Muslim-Christian Understanding at Georgetown University, and by a spokesman for the Northern Alliance military coalition.

When asked in a September 24 press briefing to explain the State Department's opposition to VOA airing the Omar interview, department spokesperson Richard Boucher said, "We didn't think that the American taxpayer, the Voice of America, should be broadcasting the voice of the Taliban."

VOA ultimately aired the piece on September 25, despite State Department objections. The following day, Boucher expressed regret over VOA's decision to go ahead with the report and said that airing the interview was not in any way consistent with the traditions of the Voice of America.

VOA is an international multimedia broadcasting service funded by the U.S. government. Since 1998, when it was removed from direct State Department control, VOA has operated under the oversight of a government-appointed board of governors, although the secretary of state or his designee still sits on the board.

News of the controversy prompted more than 100 VOA employees to send a letter to newspapers protesting that their work was being censored, according to local news reports.

On September 27, CPJ issued an alert regarding the Department of State's attempt to dictate journalistic content at VOA.

A month later, Spozhmai W. Maiwandi, the journalist who conducted the interview with Mullah Omar, was involuntarily reassigned.

OCTOBER 5

Robert Stevens, *The Sun*
KILLED

Stevens, 63, a photo editor at the tabloid newspaper *The Sun*, died of inhalation anthrax in Boca Raton, Florida. Authorities opened a criminal investigation into the killing but have not determined where the anthrax came from. However, officials did confirm that the type of anthrax that killed Stevens is the same strain that was mailed to NBC Nightly News anchor Tom Brokaw.

VENEZUELA

JANUARY 8

Pablo Aure Sánchez, free-lancer
LEGAL ACTION

Military intelligence agents detained

lawyer and columnist Aure for allegedly insulting the military in a letter that was published in the Caracas daily *El Nacional* on January 3, 2001.

Aure's letter described the armed forces as weak and unworthy, dismissing Venezuelan soldiers as more "castrated" (*castradas*) than "military" (*castrenses*). In his letter, Aure claimed that public esteem for the military had sunk so low that "we imagine them parading...in multicolored panties"—a reference to an ongoing campaign in which colorful women's underwear was anonymously sent to military officers to insult their manhood.

Aure told CPJ that on January 4, then defense minister Gen. Ismael Eliécer Hurtado Soucre denounced him to the attorney general while asking that a military tribunal also try the case. On January 8, Aure was detained at his home and taken to the Board of Military Intelligence. There, Aure said, he was stripped and put in a small cell without a bathroom.

The next day, Aure was taken before a military judge, Lt. Col. César Rodríguez Urdaneta of the Third Military Tribunal, who ordered the columnist jailed in Ramo Verde Prison. Amid a national outcry, Aure was released the following day (January 10) on health grounds.

On February 2, Aure told CPJ, the Supreme Court of Justice ruled that military courts did not have jurisdiction in his case. Since then, the case has been pending with Judge César Sánchez Pimentel of the civil Eighth Tribunal of Control.

In June, the Attorney General's Office asked Sánchez to dismiss the case. At year's end, Aure told CPJ there had been no new developments in his case.

FEBRUARY 23

Pablo López Ulacio, *La Razón*
LEGAL ACTION

López Ulacio, exiled editor of the weekly *La Razón*, faces prison in connection with a criminal defamation case if he returns to his country. The Venezuelan government has refused to comply with recommendations from the Inter-American Commission on Human Rights (IACHR) of the Organization of American States (OAS) that Venezuelan authorities take steps to guarantee López Ulacio's basic rights.

In October 1999, Venezuelan businessman Tobías Carrero filed criminal defamation charges against *La Razón*. Carrero claimed that *La Razón* had damaged the honor and reputation of his insurance company, Multinacional de Seguros, in columns by Santiago Alcalá that were published in September 1999.

Carrero is known to have close ties to President Hugo Chávez Frías and other members of the government. Alcalá's columns alleged that Multinacional de Seguros had won government contracts due to favoritism. He claimed that favoritism had also influenced the auctioning of state-owned radio stations to a media company that Carrero controls.

The legal proceedings against *La Razón* have been marred by numerous due-process violations. Defense lawyers were barred from gathering evidence in the United States that might have confirmed *La Razón*'s allegations. The paper was prohibited from publishing any information relating to the case, a clear instance of prior censorship. And in August 2000, after López Ulacio boycotted several court hearings to protest what he saw as tainted proceedings, the court ordered him placed under house arrest.

López Ulacio's lawyer, Omar Estacio, argued that this order violated "basic rules of criminal procedure, which do not expressly prescribe house arrest for contempt." Fearing unjust detention, López Ulacio fled the country after the order was issued.

Estacio subsequently asked the IACHR to intervene with Venezuelan authorities on López Ulacio's behalf. On February 7, the commission granted his request, asking the authorities to respect due process in the case, to lift prior censorship of *La Razón*, and to refrain from arresting López Ulacio. The IACHR asked that these measures be taken within 15 days, Estacio told CPJ.

On February 22, Estacio filed a petition with the judge in the case, María Cristina Reverón, asking her to comply with the commission's recommendations. He renewed his petition on February 23 and 28, and on March 5 and 12.

On March 13, Judge Reverón ruled that Estacio could not act on behalf of López Ulacio until the journalist had actually been arrested. That same day, Estacio appealed the judge's ruling to the Caracas Penal Appeals Court. The court eventually overturned Judge Reverón's decision and ordered her to rule on Estacio's petition.

More than five months later, Judge Reverón was still defying the higher court's orders. On June 26, Estacio said, she confirmed the arrest order against López Ulacio, specifying that he should be detained in a Caracas police station.

Meanwhile, the Venezuelan

government, through the Ministry of Foreign Affairs, withheld official information concerning the IACHR decision from local judicial authorities until June 20.

On July 17, CPJ wrote a letter to IACHR's then-special rapporteur for freedom of expression Santiago A. Canton, urging him to do everything in his power to ensure that López Ulacio's case was heard by the Inter-American Court of Human Rights, the OAS body whose decisions are legally binding on Venezuela and other countries that have accepted its jurisdiction.

At press time, Venezuelan authorities had yet to comply with the commission's requests, and López Ulacio was still unable to return to his home country without running the risk of being unjustly detained.

OCTOBER 18

Globovisión
LEGAL ACTION

The Venezuelan National Telecommunications Commission (Conatel) opened an investigation into Globovisión, a 24-hour television news channel, to determine whether the station had violated media broadcast regulations by reporting false news. Conatel had the power to fine the station and suspend or cancel its license.

On September 29, Globovisión reported that nine taxi drivers had been attacked and killed the previous night. In fact, only one had been killed. Globovisión issued a correction that same day.

But during an October 4 public ceremony, President Hugo Chávez Frías railed against Globovisión for being against the "peaceful and democratic revolution" he had promised after taking office in 1999. Since then, Chávez has repeatedly assailed "the media of the oligarchy."

According to the Caracas-based daily *El Nacional*, the president stated that the government controls broadcasting frequencies and warned, "Don't be surprised if I, for reasons of national interest, revise these [broadcasting] concessions."

In an October 18 letter, a copy of which was obtained by CPJ, Conatel notified Globovisión that the commission was investigating the station's violation of 1941 broadcast media regulations, which forbid the transmission of false news and require information to come from trustworthy sources. The letter said Globovisión had 10 working days to present its defense.

On November 2, Conatel general director Jesse Chacón Escamillo told the Caracas daily *El Universal* that his agency was an independent, technical entity; that it had not received any request to investigate from any government agency; and that it had started looking into the Globovisión case before Chávez made his statements. However, most Venezuelan analysts believe that the investigation is a politically motivated act ordered by President Chávez.

CPJ issued an alert about the case on October 24. On November 8, *El Universal* reported that Conatel, at the request of Globovisión, had extended the station's deadline to respond to the charges until November 13. The case was ongoing at year's end. ■

239

OVERVIEW: ASIA

by Kavita Menon

Journalists across Asia faced extraordinary pressures in 2001. Risks included reporting on war and insurgency, covering crime and corruption, or simply expressing a dissenting view in an authoritarian state.

CPJ's two most striking indices of press freedom are the annual toll of journalists killed around the world and our list of journalists imprisoned at the end of the calendar year. Asian countries registered disproportionately high on both counts—with more journalists killed in Afghanistan than in any other country, and China once again the world's leading jailer of journalists. Nepal, shockingly, took second place on the imprisoned list, with 17 journalists detained as of December 31, 2001, due to a sweeping crackdown on the Maoist insurgency that had severe implications for the press.

Afghanistan was the biggest story in the region, if not the world. Soon after the September 11 terrorist attacks on the United States, hundreds of foreign correspondents made their way toward Afghanistan in anticipation of the eventual U.S.-led military campaign there. The U.S. justified its military action in Afghanistan as essential to destroy the al-Qaeda terrorist network headed by Osama bin Laden, the prime suspect behind the September 11 attacks, and to remove from power the ruling Taliban militia that had provided him refuge and a base of operations in Afghanistan.

Journalists faced myriad restrictions in reporting on the war. The Taliban barred virtually all foreign journalists from areas under its control. The U.S. military, citing the need for secrecy in its war on terror, did not allow the press access to its forces on the ground until late November, and even then imposed unusually tight restrictions on reporting.

Initially, most journalists entered Afghanistan from Tajikistan, with the help of Northern Alliance forces. As the battle lines shifted, journalists advanced with the Alliance troops. However, with greater access came sharply increased dangers. Reporting on the frontlines was extremely dangerous, with journalists vulnerable not only to the obvious threats posed by landmines, cross-fire, and hostile militias, but to the risks of simply living and working in a lawless land. Eight journalists were killed in Afghanistan during a particularly brutal two weeks in November. The dangers did not subside with the demise of the Taliban, and in some cases seemed more acute as rogue militias and bandits operated unchecked.

The risks to journalists covering civil war and ethnic insurgencies elsewhere in Asia received less attention, but were no less serious. The press in Nepal lost many of its legal protections at the end of November, when the government declared a state of emergency and suspended most civil and political rights in response to a growing Maoist insurgency. Anyone suspected of links to the Maoists could be branded a "terrorist" and detained for up to six months

Kavita Menon is CPJ's program coordinator for Asia. **A. Lin Neumann** is CPJ's Asia consultant. **Sophie Beach** is CPJ's Asia research associate.

without trial. Dozens of journalists were rounded up under these provisions in a matter of weeks. While most were detained briefly and then released, 17 journalists were in custody as of December 31, 2001.

Sri Lanka's long-running state of emergency, which had been in place since 1983, finally lapsed in 2001. But the administration of President Chandrika Kumaratunga used other existing legislation to retain its formidable powers. The Prevention of Terrorism Act (PTA), for instance, was invoked to allow authorities to detain anyone suspected of involvement with the rebel Liberation Tigers of Tamil Eelam for up to 18 months without charge. Activists from the Tamil Media Alliance registered concern that journalists could be detained under the PTA simply for "failing to provide information about the activities of terrorists."

In India, the loud protests of the national press succeeded in the elimination of a similar clause from proposed anti-terrorism legislation. Despite this important victory, journalists reporting on anti-government insurgencies in Kashmir and the Northeastern States continued to be vulnerable to harassment and even assault. In the most dramatic instance of abuse, Indian security forces in Kashmir attacked a group of 16 journalists who were documenting efforts by the Indian military to break up a funeral procession held for civilian victims of a suicide bomb attack.

In Nepal, Sri Lanka, India, and Indonesia, authorities tried to block the media's access to areas of civil conflict. Anti-government rebels also put pressure on journalists to get their side of the story out. Traveling to conflict areas without government authorization carried its own risks. In Sri Lanka, an American journalist who entered rebel-held territory was shot and seriously wounded by government soldiers who apparently mistook her party for members of the Liberation Tigers of Tamil Eelam. In the Indonesian province of Irian Jaya, also known as Papua, a faction of the rebel Free Papua Movement held two documentary filmmakers hostage to gain international attention to the independence movement there. And in the restive province of Aceh, threats from separatist guerrillas forced the only local independent daily to shut down for two weeks.

Fighting in the southern Philippines between government forces and Muslim separatist guerrillas was practically ignored by the international community prior to the United States-led anti-terrorism campaign, but longstanding tensions there have made journalism an extremely dangerous profession. A radio host was killed in May soon after receiving an on-air threat from a spokesman for the Abu Sayyaf, a guerrilla group that claims to be fighting for a separate Muslim state and is suspected of links to bin Laden's al-Qaeda network. His murder, along with that of another journalist killed in January for his reporting on the involvement of local officials in the drug trade, brought the total number of journalists killed since 1986, when democracy was restored in the Philippines, to 37. The death toll among the press in the Philippines is among the highest of any country in the world.

The alarmingly high incidence of violence against journalists in a democracy like the Philippines is far from exceptional. In fragile democracies with weak or politicized law enforcement agencies, including the Philippines, Indonesia, Sri Lanka, and Bangladesh, attacks against the press are common because they tend to go unpunished.

For the media in Bangladesh, 2001 was a particularly brutal year. Scores of journalists were subject to violent assault. At least two of them were left permanently crippled by their attackers. One journalist was assassinated for his reporting on local criminal syndicates. Another was killed for reasons that remain unknown. In volatile Indonesia, the Alliance of Independent Journalists documented 95 attacks and other incidents of harassment against journalists. The very real threat of violence in these countries encouraged self-censorship among journalists.

Ongoing political and social turbulence in Fiji, the Solomon Islands, and Papua New Guinea took its toll on local media. In Papua New Guinea, journalists were repeatedly targeted for attack during periods of unrest, while Fijian authorities exerted more subtle pressures to restrain political coverage.

The dangers faced by journalists in authoritarian Asian countries were of a different nature. Both China and Vietnam maintained a firm grip over all domestic media outlets and ruthlessly punished dissent. In these countries, the new possibilities for free expression that accompanied the advent of the Internet carried old risks of persecution. In 2001, China imprisoned eight people for publishing news and information online.

China held 35 journalists in prison at year's end, more than any other country in the world. One of them was Jiang Weiping, who received CPJ's International Press Freedom Award in 2001. Jiang landed in jail because of his reporting on local corruption. Though Communist Party officials have encouraged journalists to expose crime and corruption, reporters who overstepped government-mandated limits faced harsh reprisals.

In a backhanded compliment to growing independence and professionalism among elements of the country's press, the Chinese government undertook one of the most severe media crackdowns in recent years, shutting down publications, firing editors and reporters seen as too independent, and issuing new directives listing forbidden topics.

Despite its problems, the Chinese press remains far more vibrant than the press in countries such as Burma, North Korea, and Laos. Burma's military junta controls the local media through direct censorship and an elaborate regulatory system that prevent local journalists from reporting even the most mundane events. The regime also threatens dissident journalists with imprisonment—at least 12 Burmese journalists were jailed at the end of 2001. During a recent CPJ mission to Burma, one retired newspaper editor remarked that, "If you haven't been in jail you haven't been a reporter here." (See page 2 for CPJ's special report on press conditions in Burma.)

Pakistan's military dictatorship, headed by Gen. Pervez Musharraf, was not nearly as repressive as the Burmese junta. However, the unchecked power of the military government tended to encourage self-censorship among local journalists, who were vulnerable to illegal detention and frequent harassment by the country's intelligence agencies. After September 11, government scrutiny of the media became particularly intense.

The most serious problems facing the large numbers of foreign journalists who arrived in Pakistan in the fall, anticipating war in neighboring Afghanistan, were restrictions on access to the border areas and requirements that journalists reporting along the frontier region travel in the company of armed security officials. Local authorities argued that the restrictions were necessary to cope with the mounting threat of violence from groups angered by the U.S.-led attacks on Afghanistan.

Pressure on the government from religious extremists in Pakistan twice resulted in the closure of newspapers and the arrests of journalists on blasphemy charges.

Press freedom gains made across Southeast Asia in recent years seemed in danger of reversal in Thailand and Indonesia as new leaders took office with more restrictive attitudes toward the media. Many Thai journalists accused business tycoon Thaksin Shinawatra, the country's new prime minister, of trying to exercise undue influence over the media in violation of constitutional guarantees. Indonesian president Megawati Sukarnoputri worried journalists with her close links to the military and her decision to restore the post of information minister, an office that was used to control the media for decades under former dictator Suharto.

In Malaysia, the government further tightened its already firm grip on the mainstream media through political pressure, threats, and licensing restrictions. And in Singapore, where the local press is largely controlled by the ruling People's Action Party (PAP), the government restricted the foreign media from covering domestic politics and introduced new regulations to curb independent political commentary on the Internet. One political activist was arrested in November after posting an article on the Singaporeans for Democracy Web site that criticized alleged election law violations by PAP leaders in 1997. ■

AFGHANISTAN

IN RECENT YEARS, IT HAD BECOME COMMON FOR PEOPLE who care about Afghanistan to worry about its growing invisibility. The all-encompassing burqa gown, which the ruling Taliban forced women to wear, seemed a metaphor for the militia's efforts to hide Afghanistan's people and problems from the world. Visits by foreign correspondents were restricted; taking pictures was banned. In March, authorities expelled the only Western correspondent resident in Taliban-held territory, Kate Clark of the BBC, because of her reporting on the militia's destruction of ancient Buddhist statues in Bamiyan.

But the U.S.-led military campaign, which began on October 7, changed everything. Afghanistan—believed to harbor the man responsible for the September 11 attacks on the United States, Osama bin Laden—became the world's most important place, and the international media arrived in droves. With greater access, however, came sharply increased dangers: The threats posed by war and anarchy resulted in the deaths of eight journalists during a particularly brutal two weeks in November.

Within days after September 11, hundreds of foreign correspondents began massing along Afghanistan's borders with Pakistan and Tajikistan to try to make their way into the country, which was widely expected to be the first target of Washington's "war on terrorism." The Taliban, meanwhile, ordered all foreigners, including journalists, out of the country.

An unusually large number of foreign correspondents were already in Afghanistan to cover the high-profile trial of eight foreign aid workers accused of attempting to convert Muslims to Christianity, but most left after Taliban officials warned that foreigners would not be safe if the United States attacked.

Throughout September and October, most foreign journalists entered the country from Tajikistan with the help of the opposition Northern Alliance, which had been fighting the Taliban for years for control of Afghanistan. The Northern Alliance, eager for the world's attention and support, had developed a reputation for being media-friendly.

Some feared that Northern Alliance forces might view reporters with suspicion after two men posing as journalists killed their revered military commander, Ahmed Shah Massood, in a September 9 suicide bomb attack. (An Afghan journalist in the room to cover the supposed "interview" was injured in this explosion.) Alliance leaders identified the killers as Arabs whom they suspected were linked to al-Qaeda. While most foreign journalists said Alliance soldiers treated them well, Arab journalists were viewed with suspicion. In November, the Northern Alliance expelled a reporter for the Qatar-based, Arabic-language satellite channel Al-Jazeera.

The Taliban were largely hostile toward foreign reporters, suspecting that any Westerner in their territory was spying for the Americans or the British. Though some journalists managed to slip briefly into the country from Pakistan undetected, this proved dangerous. Between the end of September and the end of

November, the Taliban arrested four journalists and their guides on suspicion of espionage. Reluctantly, the Taliban did allow a few visits for groups of foreign reporters to show off damage from U.S. air strikes, but these trips were brief and closely minded. A handful of foreign journalists were finally allowed to enter Kabul toward the end of the Taliban's hold over the city, beginning with Kathy Gannon, Afghanistan and Pakistan bureau chief of The Associated Press (AP), who arrived on October 25 along with AP photographer Dimitri Messinis. Before their arrival, the most consistent source of reliable information about what was happening in Taliban territory came from local agency reporters Amir Shah of the AP, Sayed Salahuddin of Reuters, and Said Mohammad Azam of Agence France-Presse—all Afghan nationals working under tremendous pressures.

Another crucial source of information about the consequences of the U.S. bombing campaign was Al-Jazeera, the only television broadcaster in Taliban-held Afghanistan present throughout the first phase of the war. However, U.S. officials viewed the channel as antagonistic and in October asked Qatari authorities to rein in the station's coverage. Al-Jazeera further angered the U.S. government when it became the conduit for Osama bin Laden's occasional video statements, which were delivered to the station's Kabul office and then broadcast internationally.

U.S. bombs destroyed Al-Jazeera's Kabul headquarters during the early morning hours of November 13 while Taliban soldiers retreated from Kabul and Northern Alliance forces were poised to take control of the city. Though U.S. missile strikes damaged other news bureaus in the hours before Kabul fell, including those of The Associated Press and the BBC, no evidence surfaced that they were targeted. In a terse letter to Al-Jazeera dated December 6, U.S. assistant secretary of defense Victoria Clarke said that "the building we struck was a known al-Qaeda facility in central Kabul," adding that "there were no indications that this or any nearby facility was used by Al-Jazeera."

Generally, there was very limited media coverage of U.S. military operations in Afghanistan. This was especially true during the first phase of the war, when U.S. Special Forces carried out most of the missions. Even when the Pentagon began allowing the press access to some of its ground troops at the end of November, military officials tightly circumscribed journalists' ability to report on much of anything. Journalists based at Camp Rhino, near Kandahar, complained that their colleagues in Washington, D.C., who relied largely on official briefings for information, tended to break significant stories about U.S. action in Afghanistan.

CPJ documented several incidents in which U.S. military officials in Afghanistan violated the stated Pentagon policy of providing "maximum media coverage, and minimum hassle." On December 5, officials at Camp Rhino prevented journalists from reporting on a "friendly fire" incident in which a misdirected American B-52 bomb killed three U.S. Special Forces soldiers and five anti-Taliban Afghan fighters. News organizations loudly protested this effort to censor coverage of the casualties and received an apology from the U.S. Defense Department.

However, on December 20, Afghan tribal fighters harassed and detained three photojournalists, apparently at the behest of U.S. Special Forces soldiers who did not want to be photographed. And on December 31, officials at the U.S. Marine base in Kandahar barred Associated Press photographer John Moore from the base after he took photographs of U.S. troops in combat gear boarding helicopters for a mission to Baghran, where Taliban leader Mullah Omar was believed to be hiding. Several major news organizations had reported on this mission, basing their stories on eyewitness accounts, statements from Afghanistan's interim prime minister Hamid Karzai and other local authorities, and interviews with Pentagon officials. Officials did not offer an immediate justification for lifting Moore's credentials.

Journalists reporting from U.S. military bases agreed to adhere to guidelines requiring that they refrain from coverage that could endanger service members' lives or jeopardize the security of an operation. However, journalists said access to information about American military operations was even tighter than during the tightly scripted Persian Gulf War. U.S. defense secretary Donald Rumsfeld agreed in principle to honor the terms of a 1992 agreement between the Pentagon and major news organizations promising that "open and independent reporting will be the principal means of coverage of U.S. military operations," but he and other top officials routinely invoked the special nature of the war on terrorism to justify curbs on information.

Reporting outside the ambit of the U.S. military was limited only by safety considerations. On November 11, three journalists were killed when the Northern Alliance convoy they were traveling with came under Taliban fire. On November 19, a group of gunmen waylaid four journalists en route from Jalalabad and Kabul and executed them not far from the road. One week later, in the northern city of Mazar-e-Sharif, a journalist was roused from his sleep and killed in the middle of the night by a group of robbers. Foreign journalists, with their large amounts of cash and expensive equipment, were particularly vulnerable to banditry.

At the end of November, a rumor circulated that Mullah Omar had announced a bounty of US$50,000 on the heads of Western journalists, but this was never substantiated. Stories that the Kabul Intercontinental Hotel, where many journalists were staying, had recently been targeted for a bomb attack heightened the sense of danger.

The local press, which was decimated by more than two decades of war, along with much else in the country, showed signs of reviving by year's end. Within days of the Taliban's retreat from Kabul, Radio Afghanistan had replaced the militia's stern Voice of Shariah, which was used mainly to broadcast official edicts and religious pronouncements. Kabul Television also celebrated its rebirth, five years after the Taliban banned it.

Most Afghans, however, do not have access to television and have relied for years on short-wave radio broadcasts by the BBC and the Voice of America for information. A handful of print publications also resumed publication in Kabul by the end of the year, but were desperately short of resources. Few printing presses survived the decades of war, newsprint was scarce, and the electricity supply remained spotty, even in the capital.

Press freedom advocates advised donor countries and international agencies that nurturing a strong, independent local media would be far more helpful to building a sustainable peace than would foreign initiatives such as the U.S. plan to launch a Radio Free Afghanistan.

BANGLADESH

IN 2001, THE ANTI-CORRUPTION WATCHDOG GROUP Transparency International ranked Bangladesh the most corrupt country in the world. The almost complete collapse of law and order in the country was seen as one of the prime reasons behind the fall from power of the Awami League.

The year began with a brutal attack on a young reporter that shocked a press corps already hardened by death threats, harassment, and assaults. On January 25, the private army of a local politician in the southeastern Feni District, Joynal Hazari, beat Tipu Sultan, a correspondent for the United News of Bangladesh, with iron rods and wooden bats, crushing the bones in his hands, arms, and legs so that he would never be able to work as a reporter again. The reporter was attacked for his writing on Hazari's abuse of power.

Outraged local journalists organized a campaign on Tipu's behalf to raise money for his medical treatment abroad. They also aggressively pursued his story, covering the circumstances of his attack, naming those responsible, and consistently holding the government accountable for its failure to prosecute the assailants.

The government of Prime Minister Sheikh Hasina did little or nothing to investigate the attack because Hazari was a member of parliament from the ruling Awami League in a constituency that the party decided it could not afford to lose. But when Hasina's term ended in mid-July, Parliament was dissolved, and a politically neutral caretaker government was established to supervise the forthcoming general elections.

Once the Awami League no longer held the reins of government, Joynal Hazari's once formidable powers in Feni seemed to evaporate. On July 31, the caretaker government charged Hazari—along with dozens of his associates—in connection with the murders of three villagers in an attack that seemed politically motivated. That same week, according to the Bangladesh Centre for Development, Journalism, and Communication, the government replaced Feni's police chief and deputy commissioner and ordered the new officials to investigate the attack on Tipu Sultan thoroughly.

Hazari went into hiding. He ultimately lost his parliamentary seat in October elections that brought to power an alliance led by the Bangladesh Nationalist Party (BNP).

Tipu's story revealed the dangers facing Bangladeshi journalists who expose corruption, the active involvement and tacit complicity of political leaders in violence against journalists, and the politicization of law enforcement agencies. "It seems that we, the people in the press, have become the most vulnerable group of professionals in the country right now," wrote *The Daily Star*, Bangladesh's leading English-language daily, a few days after the attack on Tipu.

Even after the cries for help and pledges from the government to uphold press freedom, local journalists continued to come under attack. Nahar Ali, a reporter for the Khulna newspaper *Anirban*, was killed in April because "he knew too much" about the workings of local criminal syndicates and the complicity of some local authorities in their activities.

Another local reporter, Ahsan Ali (not related to Nahar Ali), was tortured and killed in July. As is often the case in Bangladesh, the motive for his murder remained unclear. Because of the extent of local corruption, police investigations are themselves often suspect, making it difficult to determine the reasons behind a journalist's murder, let alone secure justice in a case.

Pressure from local journalists did help in efforts to prosecute the assassins of Shamsur Rahman, a senior correspondent for the daily *Janakantha* who frequently contributed to the BBC's Bengali service and had reported on smuggling gangs and illegal arms trafficking along Bangladesh's western border with India. Rahman was gunned down on July 16, 2000, as he was working alone at night at his office in downtown Jessore. His case, like Tipu's, galvanized the media and forced police to launch a high-profile investigation.

Though the investigation moved slowly, and some journalists remain skeptical of the results, police filed charges against 16 people in May 2001. In a bizarre twist, five of those accused were journalists, including the Jessore bureau chief of the daily *Inqilab*. By August, at least 10 of the suspects had been arrested, but no trial date was set, according to local journalists.

During the last five years, six Bangladeshi journalists have been killed for their reporting. None of those cases has yet been successfully prosecuted. Equally disturbing were the increasingly vicious attacks. Tipu Sultan was not the only one left crippled by an assault. Reporter Prabir Shikder had his bullet-ridden right leg amputated following an attack that also left him with multiple stab injuries and bullet wounds in his right hand and arm. Shikder was attacked for his reporting on alleged war crimes committed by a prominent businessman during Bangladesh's 1971 war for independence from Pakistan, according to police.

Bulu Sharif, a reporter for the daily *Jugantor*, was stabbed in his face, neck, and left eye one day after he wrote an article explaining why a local BNP leader seemed unlikely to win a seat in the October parliamentary elections. Death threats, which for years have been common in Bangladesh, were taken much more seriously, and small groups of journalists sometimes evacuated their towns, going underground for periods when they felt particularly insecure.

Unfortunately, there was no particular reason to believe that conditions for the press would improve under the leadership of Prime Minister Khaleda Zia, the archrival of Sheikh Hasina. Zia heads the Bangladesh Nationalist Party, the leading partner in a four-party coalition government that includes two religious parties not known for their tolerance of press freedom, the Jamaat-e-Islami and Islami Oikya Jote. Though the new home minister promised to launch fresh investigations into the murders of all journalists killed during the Awami League's rule, no action had been taken by year's end. CPJ sources said the announcement might have been nothing more than a partisan jab at the previous government.

The most direct threat to press freedom from the central government actually occurred under Zia, when authorities arrested Shahriar Kabir, a documentary filmmaker and newspaper columnist, for reporting on a wave of attacks against Bangladesh's Hindu minority community following the parliamentary elections. Supporters of Zia's Bangladesh Nationalist Party were allegedly responsible for these attacks, targeting Hindus in part for their tendency to favor the Awami League.

Kabir was arrested on November 22 under Bangladesh's notorious Special Powers Act, a law that Zia, while out of power, had pledged to abolish since authorities have often abused it to punish the political opposition. He was later charged with treason, a crime punishable by death. Kabir was released on bail on January 20, 2002.

BRUNEI

AN ABSOLUTE MONARCHY WHOSE LEADER, Sultan Hassanal Bolkiah, rules by decree, tiny Brunei has enormous oil and gas reserves and is one of the richest countries in the world on a per capita basis. This wealth has not made for a free press, however. The government controls the electronic media through Radio Television Brunei, and newspapers must exercise caution when covering religious and political issues to survive in the conservative, Muslim-dominated country.

Sultan Bolkiah, reputed to be one of the richest people in the world, rules under an ideology he calls "Malay Muslim Monarchy," according to which the monarchy is the defender of the Islamic faith. The ideology, introduced in 1991, appeared aimed at stalling calls for democratization and further isolating the country's wealthy Chinese minority.

In October, harsh amendments to the Press Law went into effect. The revised law gives the home affairs minister power to suspend local newspapers and withdraw permits for imported publications, an authority that is not subject to appeal or judicial review. The legislation also imposes stiff fines and jail sentences on journalists who publish "false news."

Foreign journalists must now secure government permits to work for local publications, and media outlets must have government approval to receive foreign financing. Because many foreigners in Brunei work for the English-language media, these journalists are almost certain to come under increased pressure to mute their coverage or risk losing their jobs.

It appeared that the Press Law was aimed largely at the country's sole independent newspaper, the *News Express*. The paper, which employs many ethnic Chinese from neighboring Malaysia and Singapore, exists outside the country's traditional power structure and has often provided critical coverage. The other English-language daily, the *Borneo Bulletin*, has close links to the sultan's family and is seen as a semiofficial government voice. Local sources report that censorious articles in the *News Express* about a financial scandal involving members of the royal family may have helped trigger the new media restrictions.

In September, CPJ protested the law as an attack on press freedom in a country that had previously been known for its relatively liberal media climate. The legislation seemed to be modeled on similar tough statutes in Malaysia.

BURMA

CONTROLLED BY A HARSH MILITARY JUNTA and operating under a regime of severe censorship and threat, Burma's media are barred from reporting even the most mundane local events. Debate about government policies or the dire state of the economy is unheard of, and most political news consists of glowing stories recounting the presumed achievements of the ruling State Peace and Development Council. There is virtually no coverage of opposition leader and Nobel laureate Daw Aung San Suu Kyi's political party, the National League for Democracy (NLD). An ongoing dialogue of sorts between the NLD and the junta is similarly off-limits to the press.

The only recent development that has encouraged some observers is the 1999 opening of the privately owned—but junta-controlled—English-language *Myanmar Times*. A project encouraged by the Office of Strategic Studies (OSS), headed by military intelligence chief Lt. Gen. Khin Nyunt, the weekly paper is nominally owned by Australian publisher Ross Dunkley and targets foreign investors. It is allowed more latitude in its reporting and presentation than staid mouthpieces such as the official daily *New Light of Myanmar*.

The *Times* might indicate a subtle split in the ruling junta, with the OSS and Khin Nyunt seeking to present a more polished, if no less dictatorial, image of Burma. In February, the respected Thailand-based Burmese exile publication, *The Irrawaddy*, reported that OSS officials have privately cited *The Myanmar Times* as the best source of information for the intelligence agency's views.

Some 50 private weekly and monthly journals are allowed to publish in the capital, Rangoon, but they must negotiate a gauntlet of state censors and pay regular, hefty bribes. Journalists from some of these publications told CPJ during a visit that they are prevented from covering floods, natural disasters, or fires. They must frequently scrap entire print runs of their magazines if an article violates official sensibilities. Even coverage of many international events, such as the September 11 terrorist attacks on the United States, is banned.

Virtually no foreign journalists are allowed to live in Rangoon. (The sole exception is the representative of China's official Xinhua News Agency.) Local stringers for international wire services say the military closely monitors their activities. Although the junta allowed certain visiting reporters greater access in 2001, foreigners still require special visas and are monitored while in the country.

Communications in general are restricted in Burma. Government permits are needed to own a fax machine, mobile phones are extremely difficult to obtain, and there is no public Internet access. A few thousand e-mail accounts are available, but they are run through a government server and subject to long delays while censors screen messages.

Exile publications that operate along the border with Thailand say they try to distribute their materials inside the country, but since their couriers often risk capture, they can send only a few hundred copies at a time into border areas. Almost no underground press exists because students, the mainstay of such activities in the past, have been brutally repressed by the government.

At the end of 2001, 12 journalists were imprisoned in Burma, many of them for having had contact with the NLD. In July, free-lance journalist San San Nwe was released from prison after serving seven years of a 10-year sentence for allegedly conveying information that showed the regime in a bad light to foreign journalists and diplomats. Journalists in Rangoon told CPJ that San San Nwe suffered from ill health while in detention.

In 2001, the World Association of Newspapers gave her the Golden Pen of Freedom Award. The co-winner of the award, another veteran Burmese journalist, U Win Tin, remains in detention. San San Nwe's release appeared to be linked to the ongoing dialogue between the junta and Aung San Suu Kyi, which has resulted in the release of some 200 political prisoners and the reopening of several NLD offices. Aung San Suu Kyi, however, remains under house arrest and is prohibited from talking to the press.

Chinese premier Jiang Zemin's December trip to Burma—the first visit to the country by a Chinese leader since 1988—reinforced ties between the junta and one of its few international allies. Chinese investment has grown in Burma since the junta crushed the 1988 pro-democracy uprising, slaughtering thousands of people in the process. China is one of the few countries in the world that did not break ties with Rangoon over the incident, instead using the country's isolation to increase Chinese influence. (Another taboo subject for the Burmese press is growing domestic resentment of China's presence, especially in central Burma.) The government-controlled media, predictably, hailed Jiang's visit as a major event.

(See special report on page 2.)

CAMBODIA

WITH THE GOVERNMENT OF STRONGMAN HUN SEN and his Cambodian People's Party firmly entrenched in power, the press was largely spared from the harsh political battles that once divided the country into armed camps.

The major political event looming for Cambodia in 2002 will be the long-delayed trial of remaining leaders of the Khmer Rouge, the radical communist movement that laid waste to the country from 1975 to 1979. With some current political leaders tainted by association with the Khmer Rouge, passions are certain to run high over the trials.

In January, Foreign Minister Hor Namhong sued three staff members of the English-language *Cambodia Daily* for US$1 million dollars for printing two stories alleging that he had once run a Khmer Rouge prison camp. In September, a judge ordered the paper to print a retraction of the story and fined the journalists nearly US$8,000. The case was currently under appeal at press time.

In May, some 200 local journalists representing three different press associations gathered under the umbrella of the Southeast Asian Press Alliance and UNESCO to celebrate World Press Freedom Day. The event marked the first time that the often politically divided Khmer-language press joined together for such a celebration. Speakers at the event noted that while Cambodian newspapers operate with relative freedom, the broadcast media in the country remain strictly controlled, with few opposition voices given access to radio and television.

The ruling party runs Cambodia's six television stations. Of the country's 11 radio stations, all but two are essentially pro-government. FM102, run by the Women's Media Center in the capital, Phnom Penh, provides the most balanced news and commentary.

Government spokesman Khieu Kanharith, a longtime Hun Sen associate, defended the government's record in March by saying that Cambodian airwaves are more open than those in neighboring countries such as Vietnam, Burma, and Laos, all of which are one-party states. "We have many political debates on the radio and television, some organized by non-governmental organizations," he told The Associated Press. "Compared to the region, you can say Cambodia has among the freest media." He did not mention neighboring Thailand, which actually does have the region's freest press.

Meanwhile, in the print media, years of turmoil have impoverished the countryside and drastically reduced literacy, so much so that even the largest Khmer-language daily, *Rasmei Kampuchea*, prints just 15,000 copies a day for a country of 12 million people.

Lack of professionalism in the media is also an ongoing problem. Journalists are paid a pittance and frequently use extortion to supplement their incomes. Cambodian journalists told CPJ that reporters commonly threaten businessmen with negative publicity unless they pay a bribe.

The government has repeatedly pledged to amend the country's already restrictive press laws with a subdecree that could drastically reduce the number of newspapers allowed to publish by mandating that publishers obtain licenses and meet stringent capital requirements. The subdecree, which local journalist associations universally oppose, was withheld from Parliament in 2001.

The political battles that once turned virtually all Khmer newspapers into partisan attack vehicles have subsided since Hun Sen consolidated his power following a 1997 coup against his main political rival. Now some of the larger newspapers, despite their ties to Hun Sen, publish more balanced coverage. The most independent papers remain the *Cambodia Daily* and the excellent biweekly *Phnom Penh Post*, both foreign-owned, English-language newspapers launched during the United Nations peacekeeping mission in the early 1990s.

CHINA

IN 2001, THE CHINESE GOVERNMENT FINALLY ACHIEVED two long-standing goals that brought the country closer to full integration in the international community. In July, Beijing won a bid to host the 2008 Olympic Games, and in November, the World Trade Organization officially accepted China as a member. These developments helped secure the legacy of President Jiang Zemin, Premier Zhu Rongji, and National People's Congress Chairman Li Peng, who are slated to retire after the 16th Party Congress. Nevertheless, in the waning days of the current administration, the country's rulers took full advantage of entrenched media control to stifle critical reporting about their leadership and plans for their succession.

Chinese media outlets experienced one of the most severe crackdowns in recent years. Publications were closed, outspoken reporters were arrested, and hundreds of journalists were sent to Beijing for so-called political training sessions. CPJ documented eight arrests in 2001, and only one release (that of journalist Guo Xinmin). New research revealed the cases of six more journalists jailed in previous years, bringing the total number of journalists imprisoned at year's end to 35. China's record as the world's leading jailer of journalists helped ensure that, for the fifth straight year, Jiang appeared on CPJ's list of the Ten Worst Enemies of the Press. (See page 597.)

In August, China Central Television announced the "Seven No's," topics that the government can ban a publication for covering. Among the prohibited topics are "state secrets," a loosely defined term that can encompass information in publicly available official documents. The arrests and subsequent expulsions of several foreign-based scholars conducting research in China this year highlighted the government's arbitrary use of the charge.

The year opened on an ominous note with the murder of journalist Feng Zhaoxia, the first case CPJ has documented of a reporter killed for his work in China. In January, Feng, an investigative reporter for the Xi'an newspaper *Gejie Daobao*, was found in a ditch outside the city with his throat cut. CPJ believes he was killed for reporting on local officials' alliances with criminal gangs.

While the government officially encourages reporters to uncover local corruption, in practice, those who do face harassment, threats, or arrest. Veteran journalist and economist He Qinglian, who has written extensively about corruption, fled to the United States in June after escalating surveillance on her home made her fear imminent arrest.

One of CPJ's 2001 International Press Freedom awardees, Jiang Weiping, was sentenced to eight years in prison after writing a series of articles for the Hong Kong magazine *Qianshao* (Frontline) about high-level corruption in northeastern Chinese cities. A veteran journalist for the Xinhua News Agency and the newspaper *Wen Hui Bao*, Jiang knew the risks he faced by covering local elites' misconduct, so he wrote the stories under various pen names and published them in Hong Kong. Nevertheless, Jiang was tracked down and detained in December 2000, then held for nine months before being tried.

The Chinese media suffered a huge blow in the spring when several editors at the newspaper *Nanfang Zhoumo* (Southern Weekend) were either demoted or fired after they published a report examining how poverty and other forms of inequality might have led members of a local gang to a life of crime. *Nanfang Zhoumo* had long pushed the boundaries of media control by reporting frankly on social problems such as AIDS, crime, and the trafficking of women. After the crackdown, the pioneering newspaper became a bland publication, indistinguishable from hundreds of other official papers in China.

While the central government finally acknowledged the rapid spread of AIDS in the country, journalists who tried to report on the subject were harassed, threatened, or detained by local officials unwilling to expose the severity of the problem in their territory. AIDS patients have been routinely warned not to talk to the media, and a group of Beijing-based journalists who traveled to Suixian, Henan Province, in November to investigate the epidemic there were detained for two days in a government guest house, according to *The New York Times*.

With more than 26 million people online, Internet chat rooms have become an important forum for political debate. Chinese authorities view this phenomenon with alarm and throughout 2001 used various methods to restrict or monitor online communications. Internet cafés became a prime target in 2001, with 17,000 closed beginning in April. Those remaining were forced to install software to block Web sites that the government considers politically or morally objectionable.

During the year, eight people were arrested for publishing or distributing information online. At year's end, five of those tried were still awaiting a verdict, including Huang Qi, who was jailed in 2000 for publishing a Web site that included articles about the democracy movement and the banned spiritual movement Falun Gong. The four others were tried for organizing an informal group that discussed current political and social issues and distributed essays online.

In what could be perceived as an opening in the Internet industry, the government said it will allow foreign companies to provide Internet access on the mainland. AOL–Time Warner was the first company to win such a contract when it signed a joint venture deal with Legend Holdings, China's largest personal computer manufacturer. Under the deal, the details of which have not been made public, AOL software will be pre-installed on all Legend computers. Privacy and free speech advocates raised concerns about how AOL might deal with Chinese laws requiring all Internet service providers to make detailed records of their customers' online activities available to the government.

Foreign television companies also won the right to broadcast inside the mainland. In October, AOL–Time Warner signed a deal to broadcast its Mandarin-language China Entertainment Television (CETV) via cable providers in southern Guangdong Province. In return, AOL will broadcast the official China Central Television on channels in the United States, beginning with 24-hour broadcasts on its affiliates in Houston, New York City, and Los Angeles. Rupert Murdoch's News Corporation signed a similar deal for its Star TV channel in December.

However, these deals seem unlikely to expand television viewers' choices significantly, since the government will require foreign broadcasters to use a state-owned satellite system controlled by censors. The companies that have already signed deals said they will restrict programming to entertainment shows only. A China-based spokesman for News Corporation defended the decision, telling Agence France-Presse that, "There are certain programs we wouldn't air in the Middle East because they would be considered offensive for religious reasons. If you call this self-censorship, then of course we're doing a kind of self-censorship."

HONG KONG

HONG KONG CHIEF EXECUTIVE TUNG CHEE-HWA, hand-picked by Beijing to run the territory, told the World Association of Newspapers at its annual congress that, "The current leadership in China is one of the most enlightened and progressive in our history." However, after four years of Chinese rule, many of Hong Kong's civil liberties, including press freedom, continued to erode as Beijing took steps to consolidate its power over local politics.

In January, Anson Chan, head of the civil service and one of Hong Kong's staunchest defenders of a free press, resigned. Chan's departure, which came a year and a half before her term expired, surprised most in Hong Kong, although Beijing officials had warned her repeatedly to tone down her independent views. Chinese vice premier Qian Qichen told Chan in September 2000 that if she could not give "better support" to Tung, she should retire, according to a report in the *Far Eastern Economic Review*. Without Chan as a defense, the Hong Kong government will be far more susceptible to pressure from the mainland to crack down on civil liberties, including press freedom.

Pro-Beijing officials renewed pressure this year on the public broadcaster, Radio Television Hong Kong (RTHK), which they believe should serve as a conduit for Chinese government views. In October, Chief Executive Tung reprimanded Lam Chiu-wing, host of RTHK's satirical talk show "Headliner," after he made a joke comparing Tung's administration to the Taliban. After the incident, senior producers at the station were required to vet his program's script, a change from earlier practice.

The Hong Kong Press Council, an industry organization founded in 2000 and designed to encourage the media to regulate itself, expanded its powers this year when it began accepting complaints against media sensationalism. However, only member newspapers are required to abide by council rulings. The council also introduced a draft bill to change its current status as a company into a "statutory body with qualified privilege," making it immune from libel lawsuits when it publicly criticizes publications. Many local journalists opposed the move.

EAST TIMOR

EAST TIMOR'S MEDIA FACED THEIR FIRST REAL TEST under a democratic environment when they covered September's United Nations–supervised poll electing a constituent assembly and a transitional government. The press performed admirably, with few cases of political harassment and most Timorese journalists attempting to be fair and balanced in their reporting.

Two daily newspapers, about a half-dozen weekly and monthly magazines, and a handful of community radio stations now operate freely, in stark contrast to the 24 years of Indonesian occupation, which ended in 1999 following a popular referendum and a maelstrom of violence directed by the Indonesian military and its local militia allies. The election of the assembly paves the way for full independence, expected in mid-2002.

The electoral victory of the Revolutionary Front for an Independent East Timor (Fretilin), the formerly Marxist political party that led the independence movement, caused some anxiety among journalists, who accused the party of interfering with media efforts to cover opposition parties. On the eve of the vote, a senior Fretilin official called an editor of the largest daily newspaper, *Suara Timor Loros'ae*, and warned him that the paper would face reprisals for allegedly backing a rival political party during the campaign.

The new transitional government is charged with drafting a constitution, and while press freedom seems likely to be guaranteed in any charter, there is concern over the shape that broadcast regulations will take. A halting effort by the United Nations Transitional Administration for East Timor to push through legislation creating an independent public broadcasting authority failed prior to the elections. Instead, the transitional government signed a "cooperative protocol" with the territory's former colonial ruler, Portugal, to establish an authority to broadcast radio and television in Portuguese. The Timor Loros'ae Journalists' Association criticized the agreement, which was made without public discussion. It also ignores the vital role of the Tetum and Indonesian languages, both far more widely spoken in the territory than the official language, Portuguese.

In December, CPJ commended a U.N.-administered court for convicting members of an anti-independence militia of crimes against humanity, including the murder of Agus Muliawan, an Indonesian journalist slain in the violent aftermath of the 1999 referendum. The murderers of Dutch journalist Sander Thoenes, whom investigators believe was killed by Indonesian infantry soldiers after the referendum, have yet to be brought to justice.

FIJI

ONGOING POLITICAL TURBULENCE CONTINUED TO PLAGUE FIJI'S MEDIA. Tensions between indigenous Fijians and those of Indian descent are often played out in the media, which is divided along ethnic and linguistic lines.

The year began with Court of Appeal hearings to determine the legality of prime minister Laisenia Qarase's interim government, which was installed with military backing in July 2000 after a failed coup by businessman George Speight tipped Fiji into chaos. The court was also charged with deciding whether Fiji's 1997 constitution, which the military suspended last year, remained in force.

During the legal proceedings, some journalists warned that media outlets were practicing self-censorship or giving in to official requests to tone down their political coverage. An editorial in the privately owned daily *Fiji Sun* complained of a "more sinister type of media control," in which the interim government "may have gained tacit agreement from private broadcasters who believed they were helping the nation by avoiding some content, perhaps deemed 'inflammatory.'"

In February, police stopped the filming of a political affairs television program on partially government-owned Fiji TV by forcibly preventing participants from entering the venue and threatening to arrest them if the program proceeded. The show, which was to discuss Fiji's future, was scheduled to coincide with the Court of Appeal proceedings. Police told producers that they needed a license because the filming was considered a public gathering, even though the participants were all issued private invitations. Many guests backed out after the incident, and Fiji TV was forced to reschedule the program until after the court hearings.

In March, the court upheld the constitution and declared the interim government illegal. Elections were called for August.

During the campaign, local journalists, government information officials, minority groups, and the Fiji Media Council held a conference on the role of the press in the election process. The five-day workshop, "Steering Fiji Back to Democracy: A Challenge for the Journalists Working in Fiji," focused on teaching journalists how to cover post-conflict and reconciliation issues. The government also issued a statement calling on the media to "use its code of checks and balances and ensure that published or broadcast material is indeed fair and balanced."

Qarase, an indigenous Fijian, won the elections but did nothing to ease racial tensions beyond urging the media to exercise restraint when reporting on racial issues. He refused to form a multiethnic coalition government with the Indo-Fijian Labour Party, the country's second largest party, even though his party had failed to win enough seats to govern alone—virtually guaranteeing continued political instability.

INDIA

INDIA'S FREE PRESS IS PERHAPS THE STRONGEST PILLAR of its democracy, but Indian journalists continued to face numerous challenges in 2001, including physical threats, legal harassment, and more subtle pressures applied by the central government.

In the disputed territory of Kashmir, where fighting between local separatists, foreign fighters, and Indian security forces has long forced journalists to tread carefully in their reporting, the press continued to suffer violent assault. Most of the attacks against journalists documented by CPJ in 2001 were committed by security forces. In January, police beat up Surinder Singh Oberoi, a correspondent for the Agence France-Press news agency, as he was attempting to cover an attack on a security bunker in Srinagar by suspected militant separatists. Soldiers beat up several staff members of the Urdu-language weekly *Chattan*, one of Kashmir's most well-respected and widely circulated publications, after unknown assailants threw a grenade at a group of soldiers in Srinagar.

The most spectacular press freedom abuse in Kashmir occurred in May, when Border Security Forces (BSF) attacked at least 16 journalists who were covering the BSF's attempts to break up a funeral procession held for civilian victims of a suicide bomb attack. BSF troops first assaulted several of the mourners in apparent anger over the previous day's attack, and then turned on journalists who were covering the action.

The incident was widely publicized, leading Indian authorities to order an inquiry into the assault on the journalists. The formal investigation only got underway at the end of 2001.

Journalistic coverage of Islam can spark fierce protests in Kashmir, which is mostly Muslim. In April, for example, some 5,000 angry demonstrators threw stones at police in Srinagar and set cars ablaze to protest the April 16 edition of *Time* magazine, which contained an illustration portraying the Prophet Mohammed. (In Islam, it is considered blasphemous to create images of Mohammed.)

Secessionist rebellions in the Northeastern States—Assam, Manipur, Meghalaya, Mizoram, and Nagaland—took their toll on the media. Competing groups of separatist militants are active throughout the region, home to numerous ethnic minorities, and have often resorted to violence and intimidation against the press to get their point across.

On September 26, journalists in Manipur went on strike to protest increasingly aggressive attempts by militant groups to influence editorial content. The strike lasted for two weeks, resulting in a total news blackout in Manipur during the aftermath of the September 11 terrorist attacks in New York and Washington, D.C.

Indian security forces also targeted the press in the Northeastern States though local journalists were often reluctant to publicize these abuses for fear of reprisal. Early in the year, a local journalist in Assam was held incommunicado for two weeks after he interviewed members of the rebel United Liberation Front of Assam (ULFA). "We want to know who you met, and we want all your notes," security forces told the reporter, who did not wish to be identified. According to one of the reporter's colleagues, he was forced in the end to comply with the demand. "He had to buy his freedom with his notes," the colleague said.

Foreign correspondents were not immune from such harassment. In June,

Karin Steinberger, a German editor for the newspaper *Sueddeutsche Zeitung,* and Steve McCurry, an American photographer associated with Magnum, were detained by police in Assam while on assignment for the magazine *GEO.* Local authorities detained the journalists for two days at various locations, accused them of contacting ULFA rebels in neighboring Bhutan, and ultimately ordered them to leave India.

Across India, local politicians used law enforcement agencies to suppress dissent. In June, for example, police in the southern state of Tamil Nadu arrested and assaulted dozens of journalists at the behest of Chief Minister Jayaram Jayalalitha, who was engaged in a broad political crackdown on the main local opposition party.

Party activists also targeted journalists covering political demonstrations. During a strike in Maharashtra State called by labor unions with the support of the Shiv Sena, a militant Hindu organization, about 30 demonstrators in Mumbai beat up Vaibhav Purandare, a reporter for the national daily *The Asian Age.*

Criminal violence against journalists seemed to decrease last year, although one journalist was killed for his reporting on local corruption in the northern state of Uttar Pradesh. Moolchand Yadav, a free-lance reporter who regularly contributed to Hindi-language dailies, including *Jansatta* and *Punjab Kesari*, was shot dead on the street in Jhansi, Uttar Pradesh, after writing a series of exposés on land deals in the area.

In general, journalists working for the vernacular press and living outside major urban centers tend to be far more vulnerable to attack. A rare news report about the dangers facing journalists working in regions such as the Bundelkhand, where Yadav was based, noted that reporters "most often receive threats from politicians, the mafia, the police, and the district administration." The article, written by Ajay Uprety of the English-language magazine *The Week,* reported that of the 250 journalists in the Bundelkhand region, more than half had guns or bodyguards.

Unfortunately, the difficulties facing provincial reporters are compounded by the fact that most elite journalists, especially those who work for the English-language press in media hubs such as Bombay and Bangalore, tend to disregard them as colleagues. Yadav's assassination, for instance, received far less attention from the national press than did the accidental deaths of four young journalists who were killed in a plane crash along with Congress Party politician Madhav Rao Scindia. Anju Sharma, of *The Hindustan Times*; Sanjiv Sinha, of *The Indian Express*; Ranjan Jha and Gopal Bisht, both of the television channel Aaj Tak, died in a tragic accident on September 30 when their chartered plane crashed en route to Kanpur, Uttar Pradesh, where they had planned to attend a Congress Party rally.

Cameraman Vikram Singh Bisht narrowly escaped death during the December 13 terrorist attack on the Indian Parliament by a suicide squad armed with AK-47s, grenades, and other explosive devices. Bisht was struck by a bullet that became embedded in his spinal cord, resulting in partial paralysis. It seemed unlikely he would ever work as a cameraman again.

With the Parliament attack, the Indian government's efforts to link its fight against militants in Kashmir with the United States' so-called war on terror began to garner some international support. But India's threat to go to war with Pakistan, which it blamed for sponsoring the militants suspected of carrying out the attack, was greeted mostly with alarm. India's often-nationalistic press contributed to the jingoistic atmosphere: the BBC reported that the Indian media were on balance far more hawkish than the average Indian on the street.

India's own anti-terror war had not had any negative impact on the local press by year's end. The first draft of a proposed anti-terrorism ordinance included a controversial clause that would have made it a criminal offense *not* to provide the government with "information about offenses." After loud protests by the country's leading journalists, who complained that the legislation would force journalists to become police informants, the government dropped the egregious provision.

Authorities continued to use existing laws against journalists. One penal code clause sets criminal penalties for promoting "disharmony" or "feelings of enmity" between different communities. The charge tends to be invoked at the whim of local officials, as in the case of Rajesh Bhattarai, a West Bengal editor who was arrested by police from neighboring Sikkim in August. Bhattarai, who ran a small Nepali-language daily, was accused of stirring unrest by publishing an article that embarrassed Sikkim's chief minister. He was released following protests by CPJ.

Indian judges also have abused contempt of court provisions to punish journalists for criticizing the judiciary in print. The biggest contempt case of the year involved Booker Prize–winning novelist Arundhati Roy, who was charged with contempt, along with two other activists, for protesting the Supreme Court's authorization of continued construction on a controversial dam project.

The protests in question were made verbally during public demonstrations and not through the media. But as Roy pointed out in her affidavit, the Supreme Court's actions indicate a "disquieting inclination on the part of the court to silence criticism and muzzle dissent, to harass and intimidate those who disagree with it."

On August 28, the Supreme Court dismissed the contempt petition against Roy's colleagues, but issued a second contempt notice against Roy for the remarks made in her affidavit. This trial—from which journalists were barred—was ongoing at year's end.

Similarly disturbing issues were raised by a lesser-known contempt case filed against Vineet Narain, founding editor of the muckraking newspaper *Kalchakra*. The Jammu and Kashmir High Court served Narain with a contempt notice after he published an article that questioned the role of Justice T.S. Doabia in resolving a land dispute. Narain's case, too, was pending at year's end.

The government used other administrative tools to stifle the press. At the end of May, tax inspectors raided the leading news magazine *Outlook* and spent 26 hours ransacking its offices. Though the target of the raid was ostensibly the Raheja Group, which owns *Outlook,* the raid followed the magazine's publication of a series of articles examining corporate influence in the prime minister's office. Agents also confiscated property from the editorial department, including reporters' notebooks and computer discs.

The investigation was ongoing at year's end, according to sources at *Outlook,* who added that the magazine's editorial content had been toned down in response to the government pressure.

In March, a corruption scandal exposed by the news Web site Tehelka.com at first threatened to bring down the government. Tehelka caught senior officials on camera accepting bribes from journalists posing as arms dealers. The government appointed a special commission that seemed more interested in investigating the news outlet's questionable reporting methods than in following up on its dramatic revelations of government corruption. Although Defense Minister George Fernandes was among the senior officials who resigned in the wake of the exposé, the prime minister reinstated him in October, even as the commission of inquiry continued its probe.

INDONESIA

ANOTHER YEAR OF POLITICAL TURMOIL saw the Indonesian press clinging to its hard-won freedoms. But President Megawati Sukarnoputri, who took over from the quixotic Abdurrahman Wahid in July, is showing worrying signs of being less friendly toward the press than her predecessor.

One of Megawati's first acts in office was to appoint a state minister for communications and information, leading to fears that her government would eventually re-establish the notorious Information Ministry, which Wahid disbanded in 1999. For decades, former dictator President Suharto used the ministry to license and sanction the media, controls that were lifted after he was forced from office in 1998.

The ministry itself had not been formally reintroduced at press time. But in December, Communication and Information Minister Syamsul Muarif complained that the press was "out of control." Testifying before a parliamentary committee, Muarif, a member of Suharto's Golkar Party, announced plans to strengthen criminal sanctions against the media in a new law to be introduced at a later date.

With regional rebellions, economic trouble, and the strain of a difficult transition toward democracy, Indonesia's press often faces threats and assaults. In the restive northern Sumatra province of Aceh, the largest daily newspaper, *Serambi Indonesia,* was forced to suspend publication for two weeks in August following a series of threats from the Free Aceh Movement (GAM), an Islamic separatist movement battling the army for control of the region. The rebels claimed the newspaper published too many reports reflecting the government position, a charge that the paper's editor denied. *Serambi*'s journalists have frequently been accused of bias by both sides in the bloody conflict, but press groups have defended them, praising the paper's courage and balance in a time of virtual civil war.

In August, GAM rebels abducted three technicians from the state broadcaster TVRI after accusing the station of airing pro-government reports. The men were finally released unharmed nearly two months later. In late December, Zahrial, a reporter for *Serambi* in Aceh, was pulled off a public bus and beaten severely by Indonesian army officers after they saw the journalist's press card, according to the Southeast Asian Press Alliance in Jakarta. The soldiers threatened to kill Zahrial if he reported the assault.

Journalists covering street demonstrations in Jakarta and elsewhere were attacked on several occasions, sometimes by police and other times by demonstrators or political groups. The Alliance of Independent Journalists reported that at least 95 instances had been recorded in which journalists were attacked or harassed because of their work.

In addition, journalists say that self-censorship is common, especially when reporting on religious conflict. "There are still pressures," said Aristides Katoppo, veteran publisher of the newspaper *Sinar Harapan*. "The pressures may not be from the government side as they were in the past, but there is a lot from society."

Advocacy groups and journalists also readily admit that ethical and professional lapses continue to plague the Indonesian media and undermine credibility. So-called envelope journalism, when journalists receive bribes and payments from their sources, occurs frequently, and "fake" journalists often use bogus press cards to extract favors from public officials and money from businessmen.

In the aftermath of the September 11 attacks on the United States, some mainstream media in Indonesia, the world's largest Muslim country, also seemed to allow sectarian passions to color their reporting. It was widely reported that Israel, or simply, "the Jews," were responsible for the attacks on the Pentagon and the World Trade Center, inflaming anti-U.S. demonstrations. Fortunately, moderate leaders helped calm the situation and urge restraint.

The foreign press remained free from harassment through the year, for the most part, although all journalists face the same risks when covering street demonstrations and other turmoil. In January, it was reported that foreign journalists visiting Indonesia would be banned from conflict areas such as Aceh, Irian Jaya, and the Maluku islands. Officials, however, have not enforced the ban, and no coordinated government policy emerged on the issue. Indonesia continues to require visiting foreign correspondents to secure special visas prior to entering the country, a practice that CPJ has repeatedly urged the government to abandon since it was used in the past to blacklist some reporters.

In the legal arena, no progress was made toward drafting constitutional protections for the press. Political and business interests have similarly stalled long-promised broadcast reform legislation, which most journalists' groups hope will eventually open up a traditionally opaque licensing process to greater competition and public accountability. Also in doubt are efforts to create a BBC-style, independently chartered public broadcast authority to replace the current state-controlled television and radio services.

CPJ remains concerned over Indonesia's apparent unwillingness to cooperate with United Nations investigators seeking to bring the murderers of Dutch journalist Sander Thoenes to justice. Thoenes, a correspondent for the *Christian Science Monitor* and the *Financial Times*, was killed in 1999 during East Timor's fight for independence from Indonesia. Witnesses and investigators have identified his assailants as members of the Indonesian army's notorious Battalion 745. Thus far, the government has shown little indication that it will prosecute anyone for the murder. In September, *Tempo* magazine reported that the Attorney General's Office had quietly declared the case closed. Indonesian officials denied the claim and say they are cooperating with U.N. authorities, but no arrests have been made.

LAOS

WITH A GROWING REPUTATION AS A HAVEN for Western travelers looking for a less-developed, more "authentic" Asian experience, tiny landlocked Laos is slowly emerging from the cocoon of isolation in which it has dwelt since the communist victory in 1975. Unfortunately, openness to visitors has not translated into tolerance of free expression, and the country's press remains among the most restricted in Asia.

The government owns all media outlets and strictly monitors the activities of local journalists. The degree of control here is striking—even by the harsh standards of communist regimes—with none of the dissenting voices that have emerged in China or Vietnam. Major activities of the state-sanctioned Lao Journalists Association include explaining government restrictions to visitors and running a popular tourist restaurant in the capital, Vientiane.

The law prohibits criticism of the ruling party and requires journalists to write "constructive" articles. Failure to do so can result in up to 15 years' imprisonment. It is nearly impossible for international media outlets to gather information from Laos. No foreign reporters are allowed to be based in the country, and it is notoriously difficult to obtain comment even from official government sources. Moreover, foreign news reports appearing in Lao publications are subject to censorship.

In June, Information and Culture Minister Phandouangchit Vongsa announced that the government intended to strengthen the Penal Code to include free-lance journalists who report "false news" about the country. The minister said he would soon publish guidelines listing which "truths" benefit the state. He told Reuters "there will certainly be penalties for those free-lancers who have caused misunderstandings about Laos to the rest of the world."

The new law seemed to be a response to a spate of anonymous bomb attacks in 2000 that disturbed the country's placid image. If enacted, the regulations could make life even more difficult for international news agencies that rely on local stringers for information. But the president of the Lao Journalist Association, Khamkong Kongvongsa, defended the new regulations as necessary to give the media "better direction."

Those living near the porous border with Thailand have access to more information since that country's television and radio signals are freely available. For news about Laos itself, however, most people must rely on the shortwave broadcasts of the Lao Service of Radio Free Asia. Commercial Internet access is available relatively cheaply through a government-managed service provider. The government seems to make little effort to block access to external news and information sites, despite regulations allowing it to do so and prohibiting the use of the Internet to protest against the Lao government.

MALAYSIA

In 2001, Malaysia's ruling National Front coalition, led by aging strongman Prime Minister Mahathir Mohamad, sought to broaden already tight controls on the press through coercion, ownership changes, verbal bullying, and backroom personnel moves.

Currently, all publications must obtain an annual press license to operate, and the permit can be withdrawn without judicial review. Radio and television are even more tightly controlled, with almost no independent news allowed. In addition, the government owns virtually all major media, either through the ruling National Front parties or Mahathir's allies.

In January, Mahathir became irate when Hong Kong's *Asiaweek* magazine printed an unflattering photo of him on its cover. A special office in the Home Affairs Ministry that screens foreign publications then delayed distribution of *Asiaweek* in Malaysia by a week or longer. Joining the queue was an issue of another regional magazine, the *Far Eastern Economic Review*. While *Asiaweek* ceased publication late in the year, the *Review* continues to be censored with no formal explanation from Malaysian authorities, although the delayed issue did contain an article about opposition to Mahathir within the ruling party.

In late December, the normally cautious English-language daily *The Sun*, which is owned by one of the prime minister's closest associates, drew Mahathir's ire with a Christmas Day report that police had uncovered a plot to assassinate Mahathir. The prime minister denied any knowledge of the alleged plot and sharply criticized the newspaper. On December 27, *The Sun* ran an apology, and the paper's editor-in-chief and another editor resigned. The paper also suspended the two senior editors, the reporter, and the photographer credited with reporting the story. But the ousted news editor stood by the article, telling reporters that the prime minister's office was aware of the report but had not issued any instruction to pull the piece.

On December 31, some 40 *Sun* journalists, including representatives of the usually staid National Union of Journalists, staged a demonstration outside the newspaper's office in protest against both the apology and the suspensions.

In May, the Malaysian Chinese Association (MCA), a senior partner in the ruling National Front coalition, dealt a paralyzing blow to the Chinese-language press—traditionally the country's most independent—by acquiring two major Chinese-language dailies, *Nanyang Press* and *Nanyang Siang Pau*. The move effectively brought the papers under government control, and journalists protested what they saw as pre-emptive censorship of the Chinese-language media. Even some MCA members opposed the takeover because it might erode support from Chinese constituents who feared that Mahathir was using the party to further his political interests.

Concerns that the newspapers would lose their independence seemed justified when the senior editorial staff of both papers were dismissed after ownership changed hands. A subsequent consumer boycott of both publications led to a steep drop in newsstand sales, according to the independent online newspaper *Malaysiakini*. MCA's takeover left only one major Chinese daily out of government control, *Sin Chew Jit Po*.

The sole bright spot in this bleak landscape is the Internet, which has thus far escaped government control or censorship, largely because Mahathir wishes to attract foreign investment to his high-tech "Multimedia Super Corridor" project.

Since 1999, the news Web site *Malaysiakini* has provided daily online news for a growing base of consumers while attracting international attention. However, the government stepped up pressure on the publication during 2001. In February, the *Far Eastern Economic Review* reported that *Malaysiakini* had received start-up funding from a foundation controlled by currency trader George Soros, whom Mahathir has branded an enemy of his country's financial system.

The site denied the report, but Mahathir told the nation that "loyal Malaysians" should stop reading *Malaysiakini*. Around the same time, *Malaysiakini* reporters were barred from attending government press conferences on the grounds that they did not carry government-issued press cards. Throughout the year, other government officials warned that the site would be prosecuted if its reporting endangered "national security."

In May, the prime minister's office announced that laws were being prepared to require online journalists to observe the same draconian restrictions that impede the rest of the media. By year's end, however, no formal action had been taken. Fortunately, another Internet site seeking to expand Malaysia's journalistic horizons was launched in 2001. Radiqradio.com, a Malay-language Internet radio site, began broadcasting online in August to bypass government controls regulating radio licenses for independent operators.

Also in May, CPJ named Mahathir one of the Top Ten Enemies of the Press. (See page 597.)

MONGOLIA

THE YEAR BEGAN WITH A TRAGIC ACCIDENT that claimed the lives of three journalists, who died on January 14 when their United Nations–chartered plane crashed in northwestern Mongolia. Tsevegmid Batzorig, a photographer associated with the private Mongolian photo agency Gamma; Takahiro Kato, a reporter for the Japanese broadcaster NHK; and Minoru Masaki, a cameraman for NHK, were traveling to cover U.N.-sponsored relief efforts in the region, which had been devastated by extraordinarily cold weather and heavy snows. Six other people died in the crash, which was apparently caused by pilot error.

The May 2001 re-election of President Natsagiin Bagabandi further cemented the power of his Mongolian People's Revolutionary Party (MPRP), the formerly communist party that ruled the country for decades as a satellite of the Soviet Union. The party also swept parliamentary elections in 2000, winning 72 of 76 seats in the legislative body, known as the Great Hural.

Upon his re-election, Bagabandi pledged to defend press freedom and human rights, saying that the MPRP, which held exclusive power from 1924 until 1990, would not use its political dominance to suppress opposition views. Prime Minister Nambar Enkhbayar, chairman of the MPRP, has also stated his commitment to upholding press freedom.

A 1998 Law on Freedom of the Media contains many important provisions, including a requirement that "the state shall not impose control (censoring) over the contents of public information." However, in practice, politicians in Mongolia remain uncomfortable with media scrutiny, and officials tend to limit journalists' access to information about the government. Old habits of self-censorship remain common, and in-depth political reporting is rare.

The press law also requires the state to relinquish control over all print and broadcast media. Yet Mongolian National Television and Radio (MNTR) remained in the government's hands at the end of 2001, despite repeated promises to turn it into an independent public broadcaster. The head of MNTR is a political appointee, and its news coverage is heavily tilted toward the ruling party.

While there are private broadcast outlets in Mongolia, none have the range of MNTR, which reaches across Mongolia's vast and often inhospitable landscape. Radio is a particularly powerful medium in a country where roughly half the population are nomadic herders, and many journalists and political observers note that no government has yet been willing to relinquish control over such a useful tool.

In recent years, the government has lifted restrictions on publishing licenses, leading to the growth of a tabloid press that devotes most of its attention to crime, celebrity gossip, and sex scandals. Journalists worry that these publications may fuel a perception that the press has abused its freedom, thereby giving politicians an excuse to impose censorship. This year, the Ministry of Justice prepared a draft revision of Mongolia's criminal code that included tougher punishments for libel. Though the legislation had not been finalized at press time, criminal penalties for libel and defamation appear likely to remain on the books.

NEPAL

A YEAR OF EXTRAORDINARY VIOLENCE AND POLITICAL UPHEAVAL severely strained Nepal's young democracy and posed profound challenges for the country's media. Scores of journalists were detained after the declaration of emergency regulations in November, and 17 remained in prison at year's end.

The first major crisis for the press in 2001 began on June 1, when Crown Prince Dipendra shot and killed his parents, King Birendra and Queen Aishwarya, and seven other relatives before turning the gun on himself. The government's initial reluctance to discuss the details of the tragedy publicly, followed by shifting official accounts of the murders, helped feed a welter of conspiracy theories.

In the days following the massacre, the English-language daily *Kathmandu Post* reported that "the public mood is changing from spontaneous outburst of grief to anxiety and frustration over not being able to get the 'real facts' of the unfortunate incident." Journalists said that angry demonstrators in the capital city of Katmandu were protesting not only against the government for withholding information but also against the foreign media for reporting that their crown prince was a murderer.

An official report eventually concluded that Dipendra had committed the shooting spree while under the influence of drugs and alcohol, but many Nepalese have refused to accept that explanation. Eyewitnesses and sources close to the royal family have said that Dipendra was enraged by his mother's refusal to allow him to marry the woman he loved.

During the uncertain days following the palace massacre, government attempts to squelch the rumors included arresting three journalists from Nepal's leading daily, *Kantipur*, on charges of treason. Authorities arrested them on June 6, after the paper published a column by Baburam Bhattarai, a senior leader of Nepal's Maoist rebels, suggesting that the royal murders were the result of an international conspiracy. Yubaraj Ghimire, *Kantipur*'s editor-in-chief, told *The New York Times* that the decision to publish Bhattarai's column was consistent with his newspaper's policy of airing the uncensored views of "every person whose opinion is important to the nation."

Ghimire and two of his colleagues were detained for nine days before a Special Court panel ordered their release pending trial. After strenuous protests from local and international groups, including CPJ, the government dropped the case.

Since 1990, when King Birendra transformed Nepal from an absolute monarchy in response to pro-democracy demonstrations, the press has stoutly defended its freedoms against occasional government interference. However, nothing in the country's relatively brief history of democracy could have prepared journalists for the struggle they faced after November 26, when King Gyanendra—Birendra's brother, crowned following the royal massacre—declared a state of emergency in response to a spate of killings by Maoist rebels.

Maoist insurgents, who model their movement after Peru's Shining Path, have been fighting since 1996 to topple Nepal's constitutional monarchy. By the end of 2001, the conflict had claimed more than 2,000 lives. While many Nepalese abhor the rebels' violent tactics, much of the public sympathizes with the Maoists' stated plans to redistribute land and reform a political system that has done little to alleviate widespread poverty. Journalists who report on rebel activities, or who work for publications seen as sympathetic to the Maoist cause, have long faced government persecution, but these dangers increased sharply after November.

Under the emergency order, the king suspended articles of the constitution guaranteeing some of Nepal's most cherished civil liberties, including press freedom. The king also issued an ordinance permitting authorities to detain suspected terrorists without trial for six months, and the Interior Ministry declared the Maoist Communist Party of Nepal a "terrorist organization." On the very day these orders were issued, police raided the offices of three publications believed to be associated with the Maoist movement and arrested nine media workers.

On November 27, the Nepalese army issued a notice informing media outlets that they should seek permission from the army's Information Department before publishing any news about military affairs.

On November 28, authorities seized all copies of the *Kathmandu Post* after the newspaper ran a photo of several Maoist militants. Government officials warned the paper's editors not to publish articles or photos that "glorify" the Maoist movement. The same day, the Ministry of Information and Communication issued a statement listing several proscribed topics, including reports that "create hatred and disrespect against His Majesty the King and the Royal Family" or "harm national dignity, create social disintegration and instigate terror." The statement also encouraged the media to publish official news and reports "regarding bravery and achievements of [the] Royal Nepal Army, police and civil servants."

Journalists told CPJ that they were alarmed to see how swiftly and easily their rights could be curtailed. Many were disappointed that the international community failed to challenge the government's sweeping restrictions. A U.S. government spokesman said on November 30 that Washington was not worried about Nepal because "we hear from most mainstream journalists in Nepal that they're confident that they and their work will not be affected by the restrictions." That statement was met with surprise and frustration by some of the country's leading reporters and editors.

The Federation of Nepalese Journalists reported that more than 50 media workers were detained in the weeks following the declaration of emergency regulations. CPJ confirmed that 17 remained in jail as of December 31. Journalists also complained that they were banned from covering military operations against the rebels, and that government efforts to keep the media informed about casualty figures and other details of the civil war were at best inadequate and at worst, not credible.

NORTH KOREA

UNDER THE TOTALITARIAN RULE OF NORTH KOREAN LEADER KIM JONG IL, the press is nothing but a government propaganda instrument. One political observer noted that the only variation in the country's media is the relative degree of vitriol directed against South Korea, Japan, and the United States, calibrated to suit the foreign policy priorities of the regime.

Overtures from South Korea's president Kim Dae Jung, who won a Nobel Peace Prize in 2000 for his "Sunshine Policy" of improving relations between North and South Korea, were scorned for most of the year as part of Pyongyang's angry response to being snubbed by the United States. After the White House suggested that North Korea could not be trusted as a negotiating partner, Kim Jong Il targeted his diplomatic efforts toward China and Russia.

Foreign journalists have had more access to North Korea during the last two years, but their movements within the country are still highly restricted and monitored. In May, a record 75 foreign journalists—including journalists from South Korea—were permitted to spend two days in North Korea to cover the visit of a European Union delegation, led by Swedish prime minister Goeran Persson.

However, when the notoriously reclusive Kim Jong Il embarked on his epic train journey across Russia at the end of July, no journalists were invited. Though it was a historic trip—the first time Kim had traveled to a foreign country apart from China—the leader apparently preferred to keep a profile so low as to be almost invisible.

The North Korean press was not permitted to mention his absence for days, and the foreign media were kept at a distance throughout the trip. *The Times* of London noted that Kim's trip "will make the Guinness record for the longest train journey taken by a visiting head of state, [but] it has also been one of the most secretive since the Germans shipped Lenin in a sealed train to the Finland Station."

The North Korean government's efforts to control the media have helped ensure that its chronic food shortage is one of the most underreported disasters in the world. This year, a book by Andrew Natsios, head of the United States Agency for International Development, presented shocking evidence that at least 2.5 million people—one-tenth of North Korea's population—have died in the famine, which began in 1994.

Domestic media are forbidden to report on either the famine or the roots of the crisis. While it is true that, in the words of one activist, people do not need the media to tell them when they are starving, the lack of access to accurate information within North Korea is a tragedy. Meanwhile, the country's harsh Penal Code cites listening to foreign broadcasts and possessing dissident publications as "crimes against the state," which are punishable by death.

PAKISTAN

WORKING AS A JOURNALIST IN PAKISTAN has long been a tricky business, and the threats only intensified after September 11, when the military government repudiated the Taliban regime in Afghanistan and then Islamist militant groups at home in order to align itself with the United States in a global "war on terror."

With the resulting external and internal pressures on the Pakistani government, officials were acutely sensitive about how their actions were being portrayed by the media. Some local journalists said the huge influx of foreign journalists afforded them some protection, because the intense international media scrutiny restrained the government from overt attempts to control the local press. However, other journalists told CPJ that they actually came under closer observation when working with foreign correspondents.

In June, less than two years after he seized power in a military coup, Gen. Pervez Musharraf promoted himself from "chief executive" to president, and hinted that he would remain the country's head of state even after national elections scheduled for October 2002.

The unchecked power of the military government tended to encourage self-censorship in the Pakistani press. Even under democratic rule, journalists had complained of routine surveillance and harassment by state intelligence agencies, especially the feared Inter-Services Intelligence (ISI), which is controlled by the Pakistani army. The ISI operates with considerable independence, giving rise to speculation that its domestic and foreign policy agenda might not be entirely aligned with that of the Musharraf government.

In this environment, local journalists who were targeted tended to keep a low profile rather than risk further reprisals by calling attention to themselves. In March, Shakil Shaikh, chief reporter for the English-language daily *The News*, was abducted around midday by a group of five unidentified men riding in a jeep. His captors bound and blindfolded him, and then beat him for several hours, saying, "You write too much. Now you will not write anymore."

Sources at *The News* said the precise motive for the attack was unclear, since Shaikh reported on a range of political and military issues. Afterward, Shaikh refused to discuss the incident, and never identified his assailants. Similarly, toward the end of September, a local reporter based in Peshawar, a city located along the border with Afghanistan, was abducted and detained incommunicado for nearly a month by military intelligence, according to CPJ sources. However, following his release, he asked colleagues not to publicize his case.

Local journalists were far more vulnerable to harassment than the foreign correspondents who came to Pakistan in droves following the September 11 attacks on the United States. The country's location alongside Afghanistan, the first target of Washington's "new war," made Pakistan a natural destination for journalists. (Afghanistan itself was declared off-limits by the then-ruling Taliban militia, though large numbers of journalists did enter the country from Tajikistan with the help of opposition Northern Alliance forces.)

An initially lax visa policy that allowed citizens of most Western countries and other "friendly" nations to obtain 30-day tourist visas upon arrival was tightened by September 24. "After the incidents of September 11, we felt the need for a more stringent visa policy," foreign office spokesman Riaz Ahmed Khan said, as reported by Pakistan's daily *Dawn*. The article said that the visa policy "was being tightened primarily because an army of journalists had landed in Pakistan and more were expected."

Though Western journalists did not experience significant processing delays, journalists from neighboring India complained that their visa applications languished indefinitely. *The News* reported that the government was "not issuing visas to Indian journalists, saying that they have nothing to report...except anti-Pakistan stories." The unofficial ban on virtually all journalists of Indian origin remained in place despite international protests.

Even the handful of ethnic Indians who did manage to get visas to Pakistan were subject to intense scrutiny and arbitrary treatment. Rajiv Chandrasekaran, a U.S. citizen who works for *The Washington Post*, reported from Pakistan for a couple of months without serious incident. But when his visa came up for renewal toward the end of November, authorities simply delayed processing it. When the visa expired, officials ordered him out of the country, citing unspecified "security implications." Philip Bennett, the *Post*'s assistant managing editor for foreign news, protested the government's action, calling it "unexplained and unjustified."

Two British journalists were even more unceremoniously expelled, apparently because of their reporting on the activities of the ISI. Christina Lamb and Justin Sutcliffe, a reporter and photographer, respectively, for *The Sunday Telegraph*, were arrested at their hotel in the middle of the night, detained, and ultimately bundled off on the next flight to London without ever being told the reason for their deportation.

Foreign correspondents reporting along Pakistan's border with Afghanistan complained of restrictions on access to Afghan refugee camps and requirements that armed government security officers accompany them at all times. In Quetta, a Pakistani city close to a major border crossing en route to Taliban headquarters in Kandahar, Afghanistan, authorities so closely circumscribed the movements of foreign journalists that some reporters said they felt like "prisoners" in their luxury hotel. Local officials argued that the restrictions were necessary to cope with the mounting threat of violence from groups angered by the U.S.-led attacks on Afghanistan. On a few occasions, anti-American protesters threatened and harassed foreign correspondents in their midst.

Access to the border itself was severely limited. One newspaper reported that this was in response to Taliban demands that foreign journalists be kept away from the border, in case they were really working as spies. On October 13, after the Taliban arrested two foreign journalists and their local assistants for crossing from Pakistan into Afghanistan without permission, Pakistan's foreign office warned foreign journalists that the government would hold news organizations accountable for any employee who entered Afghanistan illegally.

"If someone goes inside Afghanistan without proper identification...we will also take action against the particular agency or network sponsoring that person," said Pakistani foreign ministry spokesman Riaz Mohammad Khan, as reported by Agence France-Presse. "Advise your own colleagues not to be adventurous."

Before the announcement, Pakistani authorities had already arrested two French television journalists and the three local reporters working with them, as well as a French magazine reporter in a separate incident, all for reporting in the tribal areas without permission.

Local journalists working in the tribal areas faced a different sort of threat from local administrators who wield absolute power over their domains under the Frontier Crimes Regulation (FCR), a legacy of British colonial rule. Officials often invoke the FCR to punish journalists for their reporting. Persons accused under the FCR are denied due process of law, including the right to counsel. FCR trials are held by a tribal council, known as a jirga, whose members are appointed by the political agent.

The jirga's decisions cannot be appealed to the provincial High Court or the Supreme Court of Pakistan. In July, a reporter in North Waziristan Agency was threatened with arrest under the FCR after writing about clashes between two tribal groups.

Pakistani journalists are extremely vulnerable to pressure from religious parties. This became starkly apparent early in the year, when the Peshawar-based newspaper *The Frontier Post* came under fire for its inadvertent publication of a letter to the editor that included derogatory references to the Prophet Mohammed. Although senior management at the newspaper claimed the letter appeared by mistake and apologized for failing to stop its publication, district officials responded to complaints from local religious leaders by shutting down the paper and ordering the immediate arrest of seven staff members on charges of blasphemy.

On January 30, hundreds of demonstrators gathered outside *The Frontier Post*'s offices and set fire to the building housing the paper's printing press. Despite the paper's unequivocal public apology, religious groups continued to stage violent demonstrations, with some protesters calling for the journalists to be executed. Authorities did nothing to protect the staff of the newspaper.

In June, local authorities in the town of Abbotabad used the blasphemy law to shut down a newspaper that had published an article contesting the view of certain Muslim clerics that a beardless man cannot be a good Muslim.

Criticism of the blasphemy law itself was barely tolerated. In September, government Press Department officials censored an issue of *Newsweek* magazine that contained an article entitled "Talking is Dangerous." The piece reported on the prosecution of Shaikh Mohammed Younus, a professor who had recently been sentenced to death for allegedly making blasphemous remarks about the Prophet Mohammed during his lectures.

By the end of the year, the military government was taking steps to curb the activities of religious militants, in response to the threat of war from India and under pressure from the United States. The crackdown seemed bound to provoke dangerous passions, as some of these groups had previously enjoyed close ties with the military establishment. Journalists feared that any serious instability would further threaten their already precarious freedoms.

PAPUA NEW GUINEA

ALTHOUGH THE PAPUA NEW GUINEAN PRESS REMAINS ONE OF THE FREEST in the Pacific, political unrest in 2001 led to several violent episodes in which journalists were attacked.

With the exception of Papua New Guinea's largest radio broadcaster, the state-run National Broadcasting Corporation (NBC), all media outlets are privately owned. Of the three major newspapers, foreign companies own two. There is only one television channel, EM-TV.

In mid-March, soldiers staged an armed protest against government proposals to reduce the army's size amid rumors that Australia would deploy troops on the island. When Prime Minister Mekere Morauta failed to attend a meeting with the protesters, they rioted and attacked journalists reporting on the conflict. Kevin Ricketts, a reporter for the Australian Associated Press; Richard Dinnen, a reporter for the Australian Broadcasting Corporation (ABC); and Peter Dip, a cameraman for ABC, were beaten by soldiers before police escorted them away. Soldiers stole ABC equipment, including Dinnen's two-way radio.

NBC managing director Bosky Tonny was fired in March, soon after Prime Minister Morauta issued a statement accusing NBC of acting "totally irresponsibly" in airing "incorrect and inflammatory statements" about the military standoff. Despite his termination, Tonny told the Malaysian-owned daily *National* that, "The government does not control [NBC's] program and editorial output despite its 100 percent ownership. It is the people's radio and it must remain that way."

In June, students at the University of Papua New Guinea in Port Moresby conducted a sit-in outside of government offices to protest the privatization of public utilities and foreign influence over the country's economic policies. After five days, police broke up the peaceful demonstrations by opening fire and killing four protesters. An EM-TV film crew was threatened during the violence, and their car was set on fire. Two reporters for the *Papua New Guinea Post-Courier*, the nation's largest daily, were also punched and kicked by protesters while reporting at a hospital. As ABC reporter Richard Dinnen wrote, "Clearly, journalists working in PNG can expect retaliation or retribution if people disagree with their reporting of the events."

In August, NBC suspended news director Joe Ealadona over his coverage of the military and student protests. Ealadona's suspension notice said the broadcasts "threatened national security."

On August 30, the government granted autonomy to the island of Bougainville, ending the province's 10-year struggle for independence, which killed up to 20,000 people and has been called the bloodiest conflict in the Pacific since World War II. As part of the peace deal, Bougainville will receive financial assistance to establish a government infrastructure. Under these plans, the island's local media, currently limited to one radio station that broadcasts from Radio Australia, are expected to expand and develop.

PHILIPPINES

DESPITE A TUMULTUOUS POLITICAL CULTURE PLAGUED BY CORRUPTION, social unrest, poverty, and ethnic conflict, the Philippines steadfastly adheres to a tradition of free expression that makes it one of the most open societies in Asia. The constitution guarantees press freedom, and few government regulations control the print or broadcast media. The Philippine press proved stronger than ever in 2001.

In early January, President Joseph Estrada was forcibly ousted through a combination of popular protest and military intervention amid charges of corruption and abuse of power, many of which originated with reports prepared by the respected Philippine Center for Investigative Journalism. President Gloria Macapagal Arroyo succeeded Estrada.

In October, retired newspaper publisher Eugenia Apostol received the Knight International Press Fellowship Lifetime Achievement Award from the International Center for Journalists in Washington, D.C., for her role in using the press to help oust dictator Ferdinand Marcos in 1986 and Estrada in 2001.

The next month, prominent businessman Raul Concepcion called on the government to consider "whether the (country's) free-wheeling democracy and press are a deterrent to economic growth." As a longtime supporter of democratic reform and the chairman of the largest trade and industry group in the country, Concepcion's question made headlines. Journalists and government officials answered him forcefully: President Arroyo, herself frequently criticized by the press, countered that, "In the context of press freedom, I'd rather say that [some] reports are wrong and that I am irritated than clamp down on the freedom of the press."

However, in the strife-torn island of Mindanao, where separatist Muslim guerrillas are battling the Philippine army for control of several areas, journalists are frequently attacked. Both the military and the guerrillas, principally the Abu Sayyaf, a radical group that engages in hostage-taking and has been linked to the al-Qaeda terrorist network, also use local radio commentators to score propaganda points against one another.

Outspoken commentators may find themselves in lethal danger. In May, unidentified gunmen murdered radio announcer Candelario Cayona in Zamboanga City. He had recently received an on-air death threat from an Abu Sayyaf spokesman. Including the January murder of radio reporter Roland Ureta in the province of Aklan, 37 journalists have been killed since democracy was restored to the country in 1986, making the Philippines one of the most dangerous places in the world to practice journalism. No one in the Philippines has ever been convicted of murdering a journalist.

SINGAPORE

In the run-up to November's general elections, entrenched government control of the media and new regulations governing the Internet and the foreign press virtually silenced public dissent. The ruling People's Action Party's (PAP) overwhelming dominance in the media sector helped guarantee the party's supremacy: It won more than 75 percent of the vote, its biggest victory since 1980.

Singapore Press Holdings (SPH), a company closely linked to the PAP, owns all but one of the country's newspapers. In 2000, SPH secured licenses to operate television and radio stations, which were launched in May 2001. The only alternative to SPH is the government-owned Media Corp, which publishes a free daily newspaper, runs several television channels, and operates 12 of the country's 18 FM radio stations.

The government also tightened control over the foreign media, one of the country's only sources of independent coverage. In April, Parliament passed a bill granting the government broad power to prevent foreign broadcasters from "engaging in domestic politics."

Kevin Liew, youth leader of the opposition Singapore Democratic Party, told the *International Herald Tribune* that, "With the local media in the hands of the ruling party and the continued restrictions on the foreign media, the Internet is the only other avenue for the opposition to conduct its campaign activities."

But authorities promulgated new regulations in 2001 limiting online speech as well. In April, the government ordered nonprofit organizations that promote press freedom and other political reforms to register as political organizations, thus prohibiting them from receiving foreign funding. These regulations affected free expression advocacy groups, such as Think Centre, Open Singapore Center, and Sintercom.

Additional rules banned non-party-affiliated political Web sites from publishing campaign materials or running election advertisements. In effect, only PAP or PAP-affiliated content was officially allowed online during the campaign. Soon after the regulations were announced, Sintercom closed, and Think Centre shut its online Speakers Corner forum in protest.

Free-lancer Robert Ho was the first person charged for violating the new regulations. On November 16, Ho was arrested after posting an article on the Singaporeans for Democracy Web site that criticized four PAP leaders for violating election laws in 1997. Ho was forced to undergo a psychiatric evaluation. If convicted, he faces three years in jail.

In 2000, the government opened Speakers Corner, a Hyde Park Corner–style experiment in free expression. But by 2001, the experiment had clearly failed. Participants are required to register before speaking, the government has banned certain topics, and security officials monitor what is said. In September, local civil society activists commemorated Speakers Corner's first year in a ceremony designed to highlight the initiative's failings. At the ceremony, activist James Gomez said, "The only thing which has grown at Speaker's Corner is the grass."

SOLOMON ISLANDS

THROUGHOUT THE YEAR, A VOLATILE POLITICAL SITUATION and a destitute economy made survival the media's primary goal. Although a peace agreement ended the country's 2-year-old civil war in October 2000, tension pervaded the country, with two ethnic militia groups—the Isatabu Freedom Movement and the Malaita Eagle Force (MEF)—remaining heavily armed.

Militants angered by coverage of the conflict frequently target journalists for attack. At least two reporters fled the country in 2001 to escape intimidation, while other journalists routinely censored themselves for fear of retribution.

Meanwhile, the economic devastation resulting from the civil war had a predictable impact on the country's press. The islands boast three weekly papers, two monthly publications, and a few radio broadcasters. The Solomon Islands Broadcasting Corporation (SIBC), the country's main radio broadcaster, operates primarily on a Parliament-approved budget but did not receive any of its government funding in 2001.

In mid-December, parliamentary elections were held for the first time since the MEF's failed coup attempt in June 2000. International election monitors helped stabilize what was widely expected to be a violent period, and the media was able to report on the campaign and the poll with relative freedom.

In a step forward for local journalists, SIBC launched the country's first media Web site in time for the election. The site, www.sibconline.com.sb, posted daily news updates and analyses of the campaign. While Internet access is limited on the islands with only a handful of Internet cafés available, the site was widely read overseas.

Sir Allen Kemakeza, who had been fired as deputy prime minister in August amid accusations of financial malfeasance, was chosen prime minister. But because no party won a majority at the polls, Kemakeza was elected without a popular mandate. It remained uncertain at year's end whether his administration would improve conditions for the country's journalists.

Nevertheless, during 2001, local journalists reported that rural residents and other disfranchised groups increasingly rely on the media to publicize their complaints. Even some members of militia groups are learning that the media can act as a forum for their views.

SOUTH KOREA

DURING 2001, A STATE CRACKDOWN ON ALLEGED FINANCIAL MISCONDUCT by the country's major media companies further embittered already contentious relations between President Kim Dae Jung and the South Korean press.

In January, the president stated that "it is incumbent upon the news media to practice fair and balanced reporting with responsible criticism." Only weeks later, on February 8, the National Tax Service launched a major audit of 23 media conglomerates in what authorities conceded was the most extensive investigation of any single industry in South Korean history. On February 12, the Fair Trade Commission began investigating 13 newspapers and three major broadcasting outlets. And then, in April, the Regulatory Reform Committee announced the need to revive guidelines regulating newspaper marketing and distribution to curb unfair business dealings.

The so-called Big Three newspapers, *Chosun Ilbo*, *JoongAng Ilbo*, and *Dong-A Ilbo*, together account for about 70 percent of the country's newspaper market. These dailies, all of which have featured articles skeptical of President Kim and his "Sunshine Policy" of engaging North Korea, maintain that, "The motivation behind this [tax] investigation is to muzzle the Big Three papers, because they are critical of the president and his policies," Kim Young Hie, vice president of *JoongAng Ilbo*, told *The New York Times*.

In June, the National Tax Service fined 23 media companies a total of 505.6 billion won (US$393 million). While state broadcasters and the liberal newspaper *Hankyoreh*, an old supporter of President Kim, were also fined, some of the stiffest penalties fell on the Big Three, whose size made them liable for larger amounts.

On August 16, government prosecutors asked the Seoul District Court to issue arrest warrants for five media executives accused of large-scale tax evasion and embezzlement. The next day, the court approved arrest warrants for three of them: Bang Sang Hoon, president and owner of *Chosun Ilbo*, South Korea's largest-circulation newspaper; Kim Byung Kwan, principal owner and honorary chairman of *Dong-A Ilbo*; and Cho Hee Joon, controlling shareholder of *Kookmin Ilbo*, a smaller newspaper owned by the Full Gospel Church. The other two were denied warrants for lack of evidence.

Though the court initially rejected defense lawyers' pleas for their clients' release, it abruptly reversed itself months later. On October 25, the court ordered the immediate release on bail of Kim Byung Kwan on medical grounds. On November 6, the court ordered the release of Bang, and on November 8, of Cho. All three had been jailed since August 17. Their trials were still in progress at year's end, as were those of several other media executives, who were also indicted for tax evasion but were not jailed.

While some argued that the government's heavy-handed tactics were reminiscent of the country's authoritarian past, many journalists, civil society groups, and political observers agreed that the South Korean media business is rife with corruption, and that no business should be exempt from paying taxes. At a June rally held by the Korean Federation of Press Unions and the nongovernmental group People's Action for Press Reform, activists released a declaration stating that they would "strongly resist any government bid to control the media" but supported the audits.

Large segments of the public have been frustrated by the bullying tactics some newspapers use to boost circulation figures. In South Korea, the big newspaper groups often use high-pressure sales techniques to lure customers—offering expensive gifts and delivering free copies for months on end. There is a saying that "quitting papers is harder than quitting cigarettes," wrote the English-language daily *Korea Herald*.

In October, the Korean Newspaper Association (KNA) drafted its own set of newspaper regulations, including a ban on newspapers giving presents and free copies exceeding 20 percent of paid circulation. Though newspaper publishers considered industry-sponsored regulations preferable to guidelines designed by the Regulatory Reform Committee, many of them still complained that the KNA had bowed to government pressure and was effectively opening the door for future state interference.

While the administration's long battle with the major media companies grabbed most of the headlines in 2001, scant attention was paid to the arrests of three journalists from the left-leaning monthly *Jajuminbo*, which backs the reunification of North and South Korea. On October 23, National Intelligence Service agents arrested chief editor Lee Chang Gi and reporters Park Joon Young and Baek Oon Jong. They were charged with violating South Korea's National Security Law, which has been used to punish those who disseminate allegedly anti-state views, especially those seen as supportive of North Korea or of communism generally. The journalists' trial was still in progress at year's end.

It remained unclear why authorities targeted *Jajuminbo*, but some human rights activists contended the arrests were a sign that hard-liners opposed to any engagement with communist North Korea were gaining strength. Kim's influence had certainly diminished, with his approval rating hitting a low of 25 percent in 2001. Clashes with the political opposition forced him to reshuffle his cabinet in September, and he resigned as head of the ruling Millennium Democratic Party in November.

With Kim Dae Jung barred by law from running for re-election and his Millennium Democratic Party in disarray, the opposition Grand National Party (GNP) began gearing up for the December 2002 presidential election. A loud champion of the embattled newspaper owners, the GNP is likely to win the support of the mainstream press.

SRI LANKA

SRI LANKA'S METTLESOME MEDIA ENDURED ANOTHER YEAR of extraordinary political volatility. Although the administration of President Chandrika Kumaratunga finally lifted onerous censorship regulations and eased restrictions preventing journalists from reporting fully on the country's long-running civil war, journalists were still routinely threatened and harassed for their reporting. Impunity for crimes against journalists continued to be the norm, contributing to a culture in which political violence occurs frequently because it goes unpunished.

On May 30, Kumaratunga ordered the Media Ministry to revoke a June 1998 order imposing censorship on the press. The administration had enforced the restrictions, which were tightened further in 2000, as part of an effort to curb reporting on politically sensitive issues, including the government's handling of the war against the Liberation Tigers of Tamil Eelam (LTTE), who are fighting for an independent homeland for the country's ethnic Tamil minority. The civil war has dragged on for nearly 20 years, costing more than 60,000 lives and shattering Sri Lanka's economy.

Local journalists had hoped that lifting censorship regulations would be followed by a broader effort to grant reporters freer access to the conflict areas. Currently, journalists require permission from the defense ministry to travel to war zones in the north and east of the country, though their requests are seldom granted. The occasional media visits were typically limited to military guided tours.

A July announcement by the government's Special Media Information Center that access restrictions had been lifted on areas in the north and east was followed within weeks by a Defense Ministry clarification stating that areas held by the LTTE remained off-limits. Journalists did say they were able to obtain permits to visit government-controlled conflict areas more quickly and easily than in previous years and acknowledged government efforts to improve communication between the military and the media. However, an initiative sponsored by the Sri Lankan Editors' Guild to work with government officials to formulate a set of rational guidelines on war coverage foundered as the administration was consumed with various political crises.

In April, Marie Colvin, a veteran war correspondent for London's *Sunday Times* newspaper, did manage to cross the front lines and report from the LTTE-controlled Wanni region, only to be shot by Sri Lankan soldiers on her way out of rebel territory. Colvin was hit by shrapnel from a grenade fired by the Sri Lankan army, receiving wounds in her head, chest, and arms. Her left eye was permanently blinded by the attack. Though Colvin was traveling with a group of unarmed civilians, soldiers apparently mistook the group for LTTE members. Colvin shouted out that she was a journalist, but the soldiers fired anyway.

Colvin was beaten, threatened, and interrogated by soldiers before being taken to a military hospital in a nearby army garrison town. The next day, the government Department of Information issued an ominous statement noting that Colvin had overstayed her visa and appeared to have "her own secret agenda with the LTTE." Sri Lanka's overseas missions were "asked to be cautious when recommending journalists for visas."

Though authorities decided not to press charges against Colvin, they did arrest six men for allegedly helping to arrange her visit to rebel territory.

In early July, Kumaratunga allowed the country's harsh emergency laws to lapse rather than face certain defeat in parliament, where her ruling People's Alliance no longer held a majority of seats. The emergency regulations were first imposed in March 1983 and required monthly approval by parliament in order to be extended. The regulations gave the executive branch broad authority to take whatever measures it deemed necessary to preserve law and order—including the authority to restrict the press.

However, the government immediately invoked the Prevention of Terrorism Act (PTA) to preserve the administration's sweeping powers, including the authority to detain anyone suspected of involvement with the LTTE for up to 18 months without charge. Activists from the Tamil Media Alliance protested that journalists could be detained under the PTA simply for "failing to provide information about the activities of terrorists."

Tamil journalists are already particularly vulnerable to official harassment. In March, A.S.M. Fasmi, a reporter for the Tamil-language newspaper *Thinakkural* who is based in the town of Mannar, was detained, interrogated, and threatened repeatedly with death after he reported on the alleged rape of two Tamil women while in the custody of local security forces.

In July, the acting army brigadier in Batticaloa summoned three Tamil journalists for interrogation and warned them that they could be charged under the PTA if they continued to criticize the government and security forces in print.

On July 10, President Kumaratunga abruptly suspended parliament, in order to avoid a no-confidence motion scheduled for the following week, and called for a nationwide referendum on whether the constitution should be amended to allow greater regional autonomy, a key demand of the country's Tamil minority. Independent media fiercely criticized the move, which many considered anti-democratic. On July 22, after days of vocal protests led by the opposition United National Party (UNP), the chief elections commissioner invoked the long-dormant Referendum Act No. 7 of 1981 to threaten the press that publishing "false statements" regarding the referendum was illegal. The vaguely worded order encouraged self-censorship because it did not specify a punishment.

Parliament reconvened on September 6. By October 11, Kumaratunga faced another round of crippling defections and a looming no-confidence vote. Instead of holding a referendum, the president eventually decided to dissolve parliament altogether and call new elections, which were scheduled for December 5.

During the run-up to the parliamentary elections, Kumaratunga used state media to spread the accusation that one of the defecting lawmakers, S.B. Dissanayake, had suggested murdering two editors to silence criticism of the government. Dissanayake, who had been a senior minister in Kumaratunga's cabinet, responded that the president herself had been complicit in a series of attacks against journalists and opposition figures. Journalists said the exchange lent credence to their suspicions that the most high-level government officials had plotted attacks on the press.

Particularly during the election campaign, state media often fed dangerous passions by irresponsibly accusing Kumaratunga's political opponents of maintaining links with the Tamil Tigers. Earlier in the year, in June, state media outlets accused the veteran journalist and TamilNet Web site editor Dharmeratnam Sivaram of being an LTTE spy, a charge that seriously endangered Sivaram and his family.

In Sri Lanka, where the civil war has exacerbated interethnic tensions and political violence is frequent, branding someone an LTTE spy can be tantamount to issuing a death warrant. The government almost never prosecutes attacks against journalists, fostering a climate of impunity that heightens the dangers for all members of the press.

Perhaps the most shocking example of this impunity was the government's failure to prosecute the October 2000 murder of Mylvaganam Nimalarajan, a Jaffna-based journalist who covered the civil war for various news organizations, including the BBC's Tamil and Sinhala-language services, the Tamil-language daily *Virakesari*, and the Sinhala-language weekly *Ravaya*. Police ignored evidence suggesting that militias backed by a pro-government party may have murdered Nimalarajan in retaliation for his reporting on vote rigging and intimidation during the 2000 parliamentary elections in Jaffna. CPJ's repeated queries to government officials requesting information about the status of the investigation into Nimalarajan's assassination went unanswered.

CPJ's advocacy did seem to stimulate prosecution efforts in a case involving Iqbal Athas, defense columnist for the Colombo-based, English-language weekly *The Sunday Times*, who was harassed and threatened by military officers after writing a series of exposés on corruption in the armed forces. In February 1998, Athas and his family were subject to an attack on their home during which five armed men forcibly entered the residence and threatened him, his wife, and young daughter at gunpoint.

Athas and his wife identified Air Force squadron leaders H.M. Rukman Herath and D.S. Prasanna Kannangara as two of the assailants. After CPJ sent letters to the Sri Lankan attorney general and justice minister in February and April, respectively, trial proceedings finally began in May. Hearings were still in progress at year's end.

Criminal defamation laws remain on the books and continue to be used to harass journalists. In 2001, Victor Ivan, editor of the Sinhala-language newspaper *Ravaya*, faced four separate criminal defamation suits, most of them filed by government officials whom the paper had accused of wrongdoing.

After the opposition United National Party won the December parliamentary elections, media activists hoped to secure a slew of media reforms, including the elimination of criminal penalties for libel and defamation. Prime Minister Ranil Wickremasinghe of the UNP campaigned on a pro-media platform, as did his archrival Kumaratunga years ago.

One local journalist told CPJ that any reforms would need to be passed within the first six months of 2002, before power clouded the judgment of the new victors.

TAIWAN

AN INDEPENDENT AND LIVELY PRESS REMAINS A BEDROCK of Taiwan's democratic society, though debates over the limits of free expression persist. The media's penchant for covering scandals was checked by a high-profile lawsuit lodged by the vice president and by an attack on the racy tabloid *Taiwan Next*. Meanwhile, Taiwan's acute concern about safeguarding national security led a court to imprison a military officer for allegedly leaking information to the press.

In January, proceedings began in a libel suit that Vice President Annette Lu filed against the popular weekly news magazine *The Journalist*. In what was dubbed "the soap opera trial of the century," the magazine's editors claimed that Lu had telephoned the editor with information about President Chen Shui-bian's romantic affair with an aide. Lu, who denied the story, said the magazine had damaged her name and reputation and asked editors to issue an apology. Though criminal penalties for libel, defamation, and insult remain on the books in Taiwan, Lu decided to pursue the case as a civil matter. The case had not been resolved by year's end.

In August, a group of baseball bat-wielding thugs attacked the offices of the tabloid weekly *Taiwan Next*, smashing windows and damaging equipment. The paper, owned by Hong Kong media tycoon Jimmy Lai, had been threatened before over its risqué coverage of scandals involving celebrities and politicians.

The ongoing war of words with mainland China, which regards Taiwan as a renegade province, had negative repercussions on the media. In August, a military court sentenced Maj. Liu Chih-chung to nine years in jail for charges that included leaking so-called military secrets to the press. The charges stemmed from a story that appeared on the eve of President Chen's May 20, 2000, inauguration alleging that three warships from mainland China were entering the Taiwan Straits. Observers noted that while the information did not endanger the Taiwanese military, it did embarrass the army. A legislator publicly declared the ruling unfair and "a blow to freedom of speech."

Soon after the sentencing, President Chen told a gathering of journalists that they should not sacrifice national security in their quest for press freedom but instead should "remain alert to disasters, risks and Beijing's hostility."

Recent media exchanges between Taiwan and mainland China were a positive development, although not free of tension. In November 2000, a new policy allowed mainland journalists to be based on the island; the first two correspondents arrived on February 8. However, Chinese officials complained that Taiwan only allowed month-long visits and refused to renew permits for reporters from the official Xinhua News Agency. Meanwhile, Taiwanese officials accused Xinhua of publishing "incorrect reports" about Taiwanese politics.

The contentious Taiwan-mainland relationship worsened in December when President Chen's Democratic Progressive Party, which supports independence from China, consolidated its power by winning the majority of seats in legislative elections.

After the elections, the government announced the formation of a task force to oversee the reform of Taiwan's three major television stations. Various political talk shows on the stations, which are all partially owned by different political parties, were accused of slanting election coverage. The task force will work to eradicate political, military, and partisan influence from the broadcast media and support editorial independence, according to government officials.

THAILAND

WHEN POPULIST TELECOMMUNICATIONS BILLIONAIRE Thaksin Shinawatra and his Thai Rak Thai (Thai Love Thai) party came to power with a solid majority in January, the stage was set for an ongoing confrontation between the new prime minister, eager to contrive a positive public image, and the freewheeling Thai press.

In February, 23 news employees of iTV, Thailand's only non-government-owned television station, were summarily fired after they claimed that they had been pressured to provide pro-Thaksin news coverage during the election campaign. The firings led to protests from local and international press advocacy groups, largely because Shin Corporation, which Thaksin founded and his family holds, had recently acquired a controlling interest in iTV.

In June, the government's Labor Relations Commission sided with the sacked iTV employees, who had filed a petition with the commission, and ordered the company to reinstate them with full compensation. Management of iTV appealed the decision in court, but by year's end the case had not been resolved. In October, iTV employees released a book about the drama, *Testimony of the Rebels.*

Also in June, the army ordered its radio and television stations to air "constructive news" about the prime minister and cabinet ministers, as well as to publicize government policies and measures, an action that the Thai Journalists Association complained violated the Thai constitution.

In August, Thaksin was narrowly acquitted in the Constitutional Court of falsely concealing assets when he served in a previous government, charges that would have barred him from office if upheld. Thaksin was indicted in December 2000 after a series of aggressive, award-winning investigative reports in the Thai business newspaper *Prachachart Thurakij.* Many Thai newspapers argued that the verdict was politically motivated.

Shortly after the acquittal, police warned two local dailies, *Thai Rath* and *Krungthep Thurakij,* that they could face closure for carrying a critical foreign news agency report about the case. In addition, the prime minister's office tightened restrictions on journalists interviewing cabinet ministers. Thai journalists complained privately to CPJ that Thaksin aides were pressuring editors to cover the administration more favorably in the verdict's aftermath. There were also reports that companies close to Thaksin were pulling advertisements from critical media outlets.

While the print press is overwhelmingly privately owned, most radio and television stations remain in the hands of the army and government agencies, a legacy of past military rule. The 1997 constitution includes a provision calling for the privatization of broadcast outlets, but the process has been slow and fraught with political infighting.

In August, popular television personality and opposition senator Chirmsak Pinthong was ousted as host of a talk show on state-owned Channel 11, which is operated by the prime minister's office. In addition, the Mass Communications Organization of Thailand told Chirmsak's production firm, Watchdog Company, that its contract to produce two shows on state-run Channel 9 was being revoked. A number of journalist groups and opposition politicians complained that the actions against Chirmsak violated the 1997 reform constitution, which guarantees press freedom and ensures the rights of journalists to work without interference. "There is a climate of fear," Chirmsak said, " People are censoring themselves and that is dangerous."

Beyond the capital, provincial journalists were again targeted for violent attack in 2001. Commentator Withayut Sangsopit, a radio host in the town of Surat Thani, was murdered after reporting on corruption allegations involving the local municipal council. Prominent editor Amnat Jongyotying of the *Northern Daily* newspaper in Chiang Mai continued without success to pursue a court case against four men accused of shooting him in April 2000. Amnat told CPJ that he and his family received numerous death threats during the year, allegedly from local officials he criticized in print.

Thailand's revered monarch, King Bhumibol Adulyadej, seemed to address the media controversies in his December speech to the nation on his 74th birthday. Looking toward Thaksin, who was in the audience, the king warned that the country was on a course to "catastrophe" and that "everybody needs to lower his ego." Widely perceived to be a backer of political reform, the king added, "People get angry at others who express a different opinion while in fact they should be angry at themselves."

VIETNAM

DURING 2001, VIETNAM FORGED CLOSER TIES with the international community. In July, the country hosted the Association of Southeast Asian Nations conference, and in November, the national assembly signed a long-awaited trade agreement with the United States. Spurred by China's admission, the Vietnamese government moved ahead with efforts to enter the World Trade Organization. Yet Vietnam made no progress in improving press freedom.

The state owns all of the country's nearly 500 media outlets and gives journalists strict guidelines that specify what they can and cannot publish. At a national conference on the press and publishing industry in October, Nguyen Khoa Diem, secretary of the Party Central Committee, said the media should focus on "promoting patriotism and national pride."

Journalists who publish restricted information can be prosecuted for revealing state secrets, a broadly defined term that covers even basic economic data, such as money supply and inflation. Individuals who dare to write about the country's leaders or the political situation face especially harsh reprisals, including dismissal, imprisonment, or house arrest.

On June 12, authorities confiscated the memoirs of Lt. Gen. Tran Do, one of the country's most prominent political dissidents. The writings contained a critical analysis of the 9th Party Congress held in April, as well as Tran's thoughts on the future of the nation. Tran was held under strict surveillance, first at a hospital and then at his home in Hanoi.

In early September, just as the U.S. House of Representatives was preparing to vote on the trade bill and the accompanying Vietnam Human Rights Act, the Vietnamese government detained about a dozen dissidents for questioning— including journalist Nguyen Vu Binh and writer Nguyen Thanh Giang—in connection with an anti-corruption organization that several of the activists had founded. They were released soon after.

While dissidents do use the Internet to circulate independent news and opinion, government controls and limited access impede such efforts. High service charges and the fact that Vietnam only has 3.2 telephone lines per 100 people prevent many citizens from going online.

For the first time since 1997, the government this year issued new regulations governing Internet use. The statutes, which took effect on September 7, liberalized the sector by allowing private companies to become Internet Service Providers (ISPs) as long as they have two years experience in the industry. Previously, only state-owned businesses were allowed to provide Internet services.

However, the decree states that Internet Access Providers (IAPs), which control the physical connection between Vietnamese ISPs and the rest of the world, must lease telephone lines from the state-run Vietnam Post and Telecommunications Corporation. IAPs are also responsible for installing firewalls and other censorship mechanisms.

The new regulations impose fines of up to 20 million dong (US$1,330) for illegal Internet activity, including distributing restricted information and pornographic material and stealing personal information from private citizens.

Government firewalls already block sites containing information on dissident movements or pornography. Nevertheless, a government official acknowledged that firewalls are "no longer effective," and that those who wanted to evade government controls could do so, according to a report in the *San Jose Mercury News*, an American newspaper.

While the government cracks down on domestic Internet opposition, foreign correspondents have also faced censorship and criticism. In October, the People's Army daily *Quan Doi Nhan Dan* published an article condemning foreign reporters for "supporting, coordinating, and praising [the dissidents] in a concerted effort by Western media in a choir against Vietnam."

On October 11, the government issued new regulations requiring all news video transmitted via satellite by foreign journalists to be inspected by the government first. Officials have up to three days to approve videos, a prohibitively long time in the television news world. ■

| CASES TABLE OF CONTENTS |

AFGHANISTAN

MARCH 14

Kate Clark, BBC
EXPELLED

Taliban authorities ordered Clark, a Kabul-based correspondent for the BBC, to leave the country within 36 hours. The expulsion came in response to BBC reports about the militia's destruction of ancient Buddhist statues in Bamiyan, some 100 miles northwest of Kabul.

The Pakistan-based Afghan Islamic Press agency published the Taliban's statement defending Clark's expulsion, in which the BBC is accused of "broadcasting false news about Afghanistan and vicious propaganda against the Islamic Emirate of Afghanistan (IEA) by its enemies." The statement took issue with a BBC report in which an American professor criticized the Taliban's order to destroy the statues.

On March 14, CPJ circulated a news alert regarding the case.

On March 15, Clark arrived in Pakistan, where she continued to cover Afghanistan for the BBC.

SEPTEMBER 9

Faheem Dasty, Ariana Afghan
ATTACKED

Dasty, director of the Ariana Afghan news agency and stringer for the French television station France 2, was critically injured in the suicide bomb attack that killed Ahmed Shah Massood, the revered military commander of the Afghan Northern Alliance.

The two suicide bombers posed as journalists, and Dasty was in the room with them to cover their "interview" with Massood at his base in Khoja Bahauddin, in northern Afghanistan's Takhar Province. One of the attackers detonated the bomb, which had apparently been strapped to their video camera, soon after beginning the interview at around 4 p.m.

The explosion fatally wounded Massood, killed a close aide, and injured Afghanistan's ambassador to India. (At that time, most of the world still recognized the Northern Alliance leaders who ruled Afghanistan from 1992 to 1996 as the country's legitimate government.)

One of the bombers was killed in the blast, and the other was shot by Massood's security guards, according to Dasty.

Dasty, who spent several days in a coma, suffered severe burns, according to the Paris-based press freedom organization Reporters Sans Frontières (RSF). Dasty had worked for RSF as the group's correspondent in the Panjshir Valley, where the Ariana Afghan news agency was based.

After receiving medical treatment in Paris, Dasty returned to Afghanistan. At the end of 2001, he was in Kabul trying to relaunch the *Kabul Weekly* newspaper, an RSF-sponsored project.

SEPTEMBER 9

Foreign journalists
HARASSED, CENSORED

Taliban regime officials barred journalists covering the trial of eight foreign aid workers from leaving Kabul's Intercontinental Hotel. Authorities also searched some of the journalists' rooms for cameras, pictures, and videotapes.

Taliban officials said they took action against the journalists for illegally photographing and videotaping the detainees. The Taliban officially banned all forms of photography on religious grounds but had relaxed these rules during major news events.

The trial of the foreign aid workers on the criminal charge of preaching Christianity began on September 4. The foreigners (two Americans, two Australians, and four Germans) were arrested in early August along with 16 Afghan colleagues from the German-based charity Shelter Now International.

In July, the Taliban announced that the penalty for a foreigner suspected of proselytizing was jail and expulsion. (Under the Taliban, Afghans who preached or converted to a religion other than Islam faced the death penalty.)

Though Taliban foreign minister Wakil Ahmed Muttawakil had initially promised that the trial would take place in an open court, he later clarified that journalists, diplomats, and other outside observers would be admitted only during the "second phase" of the proceedings. As it turned out, journalists were allowed to cover the trial on September 8, when the aid workers appeared for the first time since their arrest, but were prevented from returning the next day.

On September 9, authorities briefly detained the government interpreters who were accompanying the journalists, apparently because the interpreters had not prevented the journalists from taking pictures, according to wire service reports. A Foreign Ministry spokesman denied that the interpreters had been detained,

claiming they were attending a seminar, according to Agence France-Presse.

Foreign correspondents and photographers covering the aid workers' trial were required to stay at the Intercontinental Hotel and travel in the company of an official interpreter.

Journalists had no access to the detained Afghan employees of Shelter Now, and little was known about their condition.

In a September 10 statement, CPJ condemned the Taliban's harassment of journalists covering the trial.

SEPTEMBER 28

Yvonne Ridley, *Sunday Express*
IMPRISONED

Soldiers from the ruling Taliban militia arrested Ridley, a reporter for London's *Sunday Express* newspaper, along with two male Pakistani guides in a village near the eastern city of Jalalabad.

Taliban authorities initially detained Ridley in Jalalabad. On October 6, they moved her to a prison in Kabul, where she was jailed along with six of eight foreign aid workers on trial at the time for preaching Christianity, a violation of Taliban law.

Taliban officials said they arrested Ridley, who carried no travel documents and was disguised under an all-encompassing burqa gown, on suspicions that she was in the country as a spy.

Ridley said she repeatedly apologized to the Taliban for entering the country without a passport or visa. She had applied for a visa to Afghanistan several times without success, according to her newspaper, but the Taliban banned foreign correspondents from the country following the September 11 terrorist attacks on the United States.

On October 3, the Taliban's information minister, Qudratullah Jamal, said in an interview with Reuters news agency that Ridley "must have had ill intentions" in coming to Afghanistan. "America and Britain talk of having their special forces in Afghanistan. She could be one of those special forces," Jamal said.

On October 4, the Afghan Islamic Press (AIP), a Pakistan-based news agency closely linked to the Taliban, quoted the Taliban's deputy foreign minister Mullah Abdur Rahman Zahid as saying, "She will be tried because she broke the laws of our land and entered the country without permission."

Zahid went on to remark that officials would "determine if she is really a journalist or [if] she had some other intentions."

Under the Taliban, anyone found guilty of spying faced a possible death sentence.

However, on October 6, hours after British Prime Minister Tony Blair visited Pakistan, the AIP quoted a Taliban official as saying Ridley would be released. "Taliban leader [Mullah Mohammad Omar] issued the order following the British government's request for her release," said Abdul Salam Zaeef, the Taliban's ambassador to Pakistan. Zaeef had been involved in negotiations for days with consular officials at the British High Commission, as well as with a delegation sent by Northern and Shell, publishers of the *Express* newspapers.

Late on the evening of October 8, Taliban escorts drove Ridley to the Pakistani border crossing at Torkham,

near Peshawar, and handed her over to Pakistani officials. In an account of her ordeal published on October 9 in the daily *Express*, Ridley said that pressure from Pakistani and British officials helped win her freedom.

In her *Express* article, Ridley wrote that she began a hunger strike the day of her arrest after she was denied access to a telephone.

Ridley reported that from her prison cell in Kabul she could clearly see bombs dropping on the evening of October 7, the first night of U.S.-led air strikes against Afghanistan.

Commenting on her decision to go to Afghanistan, Ridley wrote, "It was not a silly stunt, I was trying to find out what Afghans thought about the situation."

After her release, Ridley was taken first to Peshawar and then to Islamabad, where she was in the care of the British High Commission. She left Islamabad for London on October 9.

CPJ issued several statements calling on the Taliban to release Ridley and her two Pakistani guides, Gul Muhmand and Jan Ali. After the Taliban retreated from Kabul in late November, Muhmand and Ali were released and returned to Pakistan.

OCTOBER 9

Michel Peyrard, *Paris Match*
IMPRISONED
Mukkaram Khan, *Nawa-i-Waqt*
IMPRISONED
Peyrard, a reporter for the French weekly *Paris Match*, was arrested with Khan and Mohammad Irfan, both Pakistani nationals, about 20 miles outside the eastern city of Jalalabad.

Khan, a correspondent for the national Urdu-language daily *Nawa-i-Waqt*, and Irfan, an administrator at an Islamic school in Peshawar, were working as Peyrard's guides when he entered Afghanistan under the cover of a head-to-toe burqa gown.

Soon after the three were arrested, Taliban intelligence chief Mullah Taj Meer told the Afghan Islamic Press, a Pakistan-based news agency with close links to the Taliban, that the three men had been caught with "spying equipment," including a satellite phone, and would be tried for espionage.

A Pakistani journalist who visited the detainees in Jalalabad in mid-October said all three were being held in a large house and were in good health, according to *Paris Match* managing editor Olivier Royant, who was in Islamabad working for their release.

Peyrard has worked at *Paris Match* since 1983 and has reported from Kosovo and Chechnya, as well as from Kuwait during the Gulf War.

On November 3, Taliban officials escorted Peyrard to the Torkham border crossing in northwest Pakistan, where he was met by Pakistani officials and the French ambassador to Pakistan. Though the reasons for his release were unclear, it came after lengthy negotiations between French government officials, *Paris Match* representatives, and the Taliban.

On November 10, the Taliban released Irfan and escorted him to the Torkham border crossing. He was briefly detained by Pakistani officials before being released. Khan was released on November 12 and returned to Pakistan.

CPJ issued several statements calling for the release of the three men.

OCTOBER 22

Daigen Yanagida, free-lancer
IMPRISONED

Yanagida was arrested in the Afghan town of Asadabad, near the border with Pakistan, and was brought to Jalalabad for questioning, according to Japanese and international news sources.

The free-lance journalist was arrested on suspicion of illegal entry into Afghanistan. On October 29, he spoke by telephone with a Japanese colleague in Pakistan and said he was detained but well treated.

Yanagida was based in Nairobi, Kenya, but traveled extensively around the world. According to his family, he left Japan on October 15 after notifying a Tokyo publishing company that he intended to write a book about Afghanistan.

On October 27, the Taliban Foreign Ministry warned that all foreigners entering the country without proper papers would face "serious measures," including spying charges, according to the Afghan Islamic Press (AIP), a Pakistan-based news agency with close ties to the Taliban. Under Taliban law, espionage was punishable by death.

Yanagida was released on November 16, after Taliban forces abandoned Jalalabad. On his way to the Pakistani border, he was detained at a checkpoint by local anti-Taliban Pashtun forces because he was not carrying a passport (it had been confiscated by Taliban authorities).

Yanagida was sent back to Jalalabad, where he stayed in the residence of a local leader sympathetic to former Afghan king Zahir Shah, according to international news reports. On

November 17, Yanagida again left Jalalabad for Pakistan. He returned to Japan on November 19.

NOVEMBER 7

Ali Al-Arab, Al-Jazeera
EXPELLED

Northern Alliance soldiers expelled Al-Arab, a reporter for the influential Arabic-language news channel Al-Jazeera, from Afghanistan. An Al-Jazeera source told CPJ that soldiers escorted Al-Arab to the Tajik border and advised the reporter to return "in a time of peace."

Al-Arab said later on Al-Jazeera that he was not given any official expulsion order but "was told from the moment I arrived that Arabs are not welcome in Northern Alliance areas," according to a translation of the report broadcast by the BBC.

On September 9, two men posing as Arab journalists detonated a bomb that killed the Northern Alliance's revered military commander, Ahmed Shah Massood. An Al-Jazeera source said the station had not had a reporter in alliance-held territory since Massood's assassination.

Soldiers expelled Al-Arab despite the fact that he had obtained a valid visa from the Afghan embassy in Dushanbe, which was controlled by the opposition government led by Northern Alliance president Burhanuddin Rabbani.

NOVEMBER 11

Gary Skurka, free-lancer
ATTACKED

Skurka, a free-lance television producer on assignment for the documentary program "National Geographic Explorer," was wounded by shrapnel while he, *USA Today* reporter Tim Friend, and aid worker Greg Long were watching an exchange of fire between Taliban and Northern Alliance troops on the front line near Kalakata.

Skurka suffered shrapnel wounds to his legs from a Taliban shell that hit just below where the three men were sitting, according to an account by Friend published in *USA Today*. Skurka was immediately rushed to a field hospital in Khoja Bahauddin and then transferred to Dushanbe, Tajikistan, according to sources at National Geographic Television. After treatment, he was released from the hospital and was expected to make a full recovery.

Friend was not injured in the incident, but Long suffered a concussion. Skurka had been in Afghanistan for about two weeks to film a documentary about relief workers.

Johanne Sutton, Radio France Internationale
KILLED
Pierre Billaud, Radio Télévision Luxembourg
KILLED
Volker Handloik, free-lancer
KILLED

Sutton, a reporter for Radio France Internationale; Billaud, a reporter for Radio Télévision Luxembourg; and Handloik, a free-lance reporter on assignment for the German news magazine *Stern*, were killed on the evening of November 11 when Taliban forces fired on a Northern Alliance military convoy.

The reporters were among a group of six journalists who were riding with

Northern Alliance soldiers in an armored personnel carrier (APC). The soldiers were advancing toward Taliban positions near the city of Taloqan, the capital of Takhar Province and the Alliance's former headquarters.

Taliban forces opened fire on the convoy and hit the APC carrying the journalists with a rocket-propelled grenade. The jolt from the grenade's impact caused some people to fall off the tank while others may have jumped off. It was unclear whether the journalists who died were killed in the cross fire, or whether Taliban soldiers later executed at least two of them.

Three journalists survived the attack: Paul McGeough, a reporter for the Australian newspaper *The Sydney Morning Herald*; Véronique Rebeyrotte, a reporter for France Culture radio; and Levon Sevunts, a reporter for the *Montreal Gazette*.

NOVEMBER 13

Al-Jazeera
ATTACKED

During the early morning hours of November 13, U.S. aircraft dropped two 500-pound bombs on the building housing the Arabic-language television station Al-Jazeera, according to a U.S. Central Command spokesperson.

No Al-Jazeera staff were in the building at the time of the bombing, which destroyed the facilities.

In a letter to Al-Jazeera dated December 6, U.S. Assistant Secretary of Defense Victoria Clarke made no apology for the bombing and stated that "the building we struck was a known al-Qaeda facility in central Kabul." (Al-Qaeda is the terrorist network led by Osama bin Laden, the prime suspect behind the September 11 attacks against the United States.)

"There were no indications this or any nearby facility was used by Al-Jazeera," Clarke added.

Al-Jazeera's Kabul bureau was located in a residential neighborhood and was used solely by Al-Jazeera staff, according to sources at the station. Al-Jazeera had occupied the same building in Kabul for nearly two years, and the location of its office was well known to local residents, including members of the diplomatic community. The building, which housed three satellite dishes on its roof, was clearly identifiable as a broadcast facility.

On January 31, 2002, CPJ sent a letter to U.S. secretary of defense Donald H. Rumsfeld requesting information about the circumstances behind the bombing.

NOVEMBER 19

Azizullah Haidari, Reuters
KILLED
Harry Burton, Reuters Television
KILLED
Julio Fuentes, *El Mundo*
KILLED
Maria Grazia Cutuli, *Corriere della Sera*
KILLED

Haidari, an Afghan-born photographer for the Reuters news agency; Burton, an Australian cameraman for Reuters; Fuentes, a Spanish correspondent for the Madrid-based newspaper *El Mundo*; and Cutuli, an Italian correspondent for the Milan-based daily *Corriere della Sera*, were killed by a group of gunmen who ambushed their convoy.

The journalists were traveling through eastern Nangarhar Province at the head of a convoy of about eight vehicles when they were stopped by a group of armed men near the town of Sarobi, some 55 miles (90 kilometers) east of Kabul. Gunmen dragged the four journalists out of two of the front cars and executed them using Kalashnikov rifles, according to a driver and translator who were allowed to flee and later spoke to reporters.

On the morning of November 20, the bodies were brought to Jalalabad, where colleagues identified them.

Although an anti-Taliban coalition in Jalalabad had chosen a new governor for Nangarhar that weekend, local authorities had not secured full control over the province.

NOVEMBER 22

Foreign journalists
EXPELLED

About 100 foreign journalists were expelled from Afghanistan by Taliban officials after being invited to visit areas of the country still under Taliban control.

On November 20, the journalists entered Spin Boldak, a town near the Pakistani border, after obtaining 10-day visas from the Taliban. The reporters were allowed to visit a refugee camp and were invited to Kandahar, the Taliban's southern stronghold.

However, on November 22, before bringing the journalists to Kandahar, Taliban officials suddenly notified them that they had 90 minutes to pack their belongings and leave. The journalists were then escorted to the Pakistani border town of Chaman.

The reason for the expulsion was unclear. A *New York Times* journalist present reported that the order followed a debate between moderate and hard-line Taliban officials over whether the journalists should be allowed to stay. Other reporters suggested that Taliban officials no longer felt they could protect Western journalists from Afghan crowds angered by the intensified U.S. bombing campaign.

NOVEMBER 24

Andrea Catherwood, ITN
ATTACKED

Catherwood, a reporter for the British television news network ITN, was injured by shrapnel from a grenade that a Taliban soldier set off outside the Qalai Jhangi fort near Mazar-e-Sharif, according to the ITN press office in London.

The explosion occurred while Northern Alliance soldiers were searching Taliban troops who had recently surrendered.

Catherwood was standing about 10 yards (9 meters) away from the Taliban soldier when he detonated a hand grenade, killing himself, two other Taliban fighters, and a Northern Alliance official standing nearby. Catherwood received shrapnel wounds in the leg; her translator was also injured.

NOVEMBER 25

Ken Hechtman, free-lancer
IMPRISONED

Hechtman, a free-lancer who contributed articles to the weekly *Montreal Mirror* and the Web site straightgoods.com, was detained by

Taliban authorities just after arriving in the border town of Spin Boldak.

Hechtman later described the initial round of interrogations as "friendly" but said the mood changed when U.S. air strikes hit the area, because Taliban officials suspected that the Americans had dispatched him to guide the attacks.

The Taliban had largely barred foreign journalists from areas under their control during this phase of the war, and Hechtman did not have a visa for travel to Afghanistan.

Hechtman, who had been shuttled between the office of a local commander and the Taliban Foreign Office for most of the day, was then taken to the home of someone he identified as the "city commander, who doubled as the city judge." The judge questioned him for two hours and then sent him to the city jail pending an investigation.

Hechtman was kept shackled in a cell with other prisoners and was threatened at gunpoint. After the second day, Hechtman managed to convince the jailer to send a relative to Pakistan with news about the journalist's detention. On November 27, Mohammedzai, the jailer's cousin, approached two Western journalists in the Pakistani border town of Chaman and told them that Taliban soldiers were holding Hechtman and had threatened to kill him if they did not receive a ransom.

Hechtman later said the Taliban had never demanded a ransom. The journalists alerted Canadian authorities immediately, and international news media carried the story widely. Taliban officials were eventually persuaded to release Hechtman on December 1, after meetings with Canadian diplomats and Pakistani government representatives.

NOVEMBER 26

Ulf Strömberg, TV4
KILLED

Strömberg, a cameraman for the Swedish channel TV4, was murdered in the early morning during a robbery at the house in Taloqan where he and several other journalists were staying.

At around 2 a.m., armed gunmen broke into the house and entered the room where two journalists from the Swedish newspaper *Aftonbladet* were sleeping. The intruders demanded money, which they were given, and also stole equipment including cameras, computers, and a satellite phone, according to *Aftonbladet*.

The robbers threatened to kill the two journalists—Martin Adler, a photographer, and Bo Liden, a correspondent—but left the room after an Afghan translator intervened on their behalf, according to a Reuters report. The gunmen then proceeded to the room Strömberg was sharing with his TV4 colleague Rolf Porseryd, a correspondent. Porseryd told reporters that Strömberg went to the door and slammed it shut when he saw the gunmen, who fired several shots before fleeing.

Strömberg, 42, was apparently hit in the chest by a bullet fired through the door. Though colleagues rushed him to a local hospital, his wounds were fatal.

DECEMBER 5

The Associated Press
CENSORED
Associated Press Television News
CENSORED
The Baltimore Sun
CENSORED

CBS News
CENSORED
CNN
CENSORED
Gannett
CENSORED
Newsweek
CENSORED
The New York Times
CENSORED
Reuters
CENSORED
The Wall Street Journal
CENSORED
The Washington Post
CENSORED

U.S. military officials at Camp Rhino, a Marine base in southern Afghanistan, prevented journalists from reporting on a "friendly fire" incident in which a misdirected American B-52 bomb killed three U.S. Special Forces soldiers and five anti-Taliban Afghan fighters.

Journalists from 11 U.S. news organizations were confined to a warehouse while injured soldiers were transferred to the base for treatment. That night, the journalists were pulled out of Afghanistan altogether.

The reporters, who entered the Marine base on November 25, were the first journalists permitted to accompany U.S. ground troops in Afghanistan. Under terms agreed upon with the Pentagon, the journalists were required to pool their reports with other news media.

Jonathan Wolman, executive editor of The Associated Press (AP), told the AP that Defense Department policy "allows for coverage of casualties, but it was subverted in this case."

Jill Abramson, the Washington bureau chief of *The New York Times*, said: "This was a gross abuse of the ground rules for the press pool. It is very difficult to understand what operational security issues would have been violated by allowing the reporters access to the efforts to recover and evacuate the wounded."

On December 6, Victoria Clarke, U.S. assistant secretary of defense for public affairs, sent a letter to Washington bureau chiefs of major news organizations saying "we owe you an apology" for the "severe shortcomings" in the way the Pentagon treated the news media. She pledged that the Defense Department was committed to providing "maximum media coverage with minimal delay and hassle."

DECEMBER 20

David Guttenfelder,
The Associated Press
THREATENED, HARASSED, CENSORED
Joao Silva, *The New York Times*
THREATENED, HARASSED, CENSORED
Tyler Hicks, *The New York Times*
THREATENED, HARASSED, CENSORED

Guttenfelder, chief Asia photographer for The Associated Press (AP), and Silva and Hicks, both photographers for *The New York Times*, were taking pictures of American Special Operations forces in the Tora Bora region of eastern Afghanistan when an Afghan interpreter working for the U.S. soldiers asked them to stop.

The photographers complied with the request and were driving toward a nearby village when a group of Afghan tribal fighters intercepted them.

"They pointed their guns at us, took off the safeties, pulled out the bayonets and pointed them in our faces in the car," Guttenfelder told the AP. "We didn't know what was going on. We thought they were bandits."

The Afghan fighters forced the journalists to accompany them to a base camp, where they seized their cameras, computers, and other belongings. The photographers noticed two American soldiers in the area and called out for help.

The soldiers came over but refused to assist the journalists. According to Guttenfelder's account, one soldier said, "We know what journalists are trying to do, but we had to do this because taking our pictures puts us in danger."

Guttenfelder told the soldiers that any pictures that compromised the American forces' security could simply be deleted from their digital cameras and asked them to intervene with the Afghan fighters. "We have no more control over them than you do," one of the soldiers said. As they walked away, one soldier added, "Don't worry, they won't kill you," according to Guttenfelder.

The Afghan fighters detained the journalists for more than an hour before releasing them and returning their money and equipment. However, the fighters confiscated memory discs containing pictures of the American soldiers.

The Pentagon, which had openly discussed the presence of American Special Forces in Tora Bora, pledged to cooperate with the media "as long as operational security is not hindered, people's lives are not put at risk, and we are not revealing classified information," according to Pentagon spokesperson Victoria Clarke.

"We strongly protest this action and have asked the Pentagon to immediately investigate the matter," said AP vice president and executive photo editor Vin Alabiso.

DECEMBER 31

John Moore, The Associated Press
`CENSORED`

United States military officials in Kandahar banned Moore, an AP photographer, from the military base there after he took photographs of American troops in combat gear boarding helicopters in preparation for a mission.

On December 31, the AP reported that, "Combat-ready U.S. Marines launched a mission Monday to capture Taliban leader Mullah Mohammed Omar, thought to be hiding in the remote mountains of central Afghanistan." The first story carried Moore's byline, along with that of reporter Matt Kelley.

Several major news organizations carried similar versions of the story based on eyewitness accounts, statements from Afghan interim prime minister Hamid Karzai and other local authorities, and interviews with Pentagon officials.

However, officials from the U.S. Central Command dismissed reports of the deployment as "completely wrong." Rear Adm. Craig Quigley, a top spokesman for the U.S. Central Command in Tampa, Florida, was quoted by *The Washington Post* as saying, "No one has gone anywhere.

They're flat wrong." He reportedly added, "There've been no helos flying from Kandahar," and "There are no Marines who have left Kandahar." Another Central Command spokesperson, Air Force Maj. Bill Harrison, said, "We know there is no such operation going on."

At a press conference on January 2, 2002, Rear Adm. John Stufflebeem, deputy director of operations for the Joint Chiefs of Staff, confirmed that U.S. Marines had been deployed from Kandahar but said that the units were seeking information, not specific individuals. At the same briefing, Pentagon spokeswoman Victoria Clarke admitted that official responses to the reports had been confusing.

When asked whether a photographer had been banned from the U.S. military base in Kandahar, Clarke said, "Not that I know of."

The Associated Press requested that the U.S. military restore Moore's press credentials for the base.

BANGLADESH

JANUARY 25

Tipu Sultan, United News of Bangladesh
ATTACKED

Tipu, a correspondent for the independent wire service United News of Bangladesh (UNB), was crippled in a brutal attack in the southeastern district of Feni.

On the night of January 25, Tipu was stopped along a road by a group of armed men working for Joynal Hazari, a member of parliament from Feni for the ruling Awami League. Tipu later told CPJ that he heard one of the attackers call Hazari on a cell phone and receive instructions to "cut off my hands and legs." The gang first took Tipu to a community center, where they beat him severely and told him, "This is the order of Hazari." They then moved him to another building, where he was beaten unconscious with bats, hockey sticks, and iron rods.

Tipu was hospitalized with gaping wounds and multiple broken bones and fractures in his hands, arms, and legs. Doctors feared he would suffer permanent disabilities.

Tipu says the attack came in reprisal for his reporting on Hazari, who had an infamous reputation as the "Godfather of Feni." In 2000, the journalist won UNB's award for best correspondent in recognition of his courageous and enterprising reporting.

On January 28, Tipu failed in his initial attempt to file a police report accusing Hazari and 14 others of assaulting him. Police refused to register the case because one of Hazari's followers had already filed a report accusing local opposition party activists of involvement in the attack. Local journalists said the false case was registered to frustrate Tipu's efforts to secure legal redress.

However, Tipu successfuly filed a police report against Hazari on September 17, during the rule of the non-partisan caretaker government that presided over Bangladesh in the run-up to parliamentary elections. Hazari had, by that time, gone underground in order to avoid prosecution on murder charges in an unrelated case.

The attack on Tipu Sultan became symbolic of the rising tide of violence directed against the press in Bangladesh.

Leading journalists championed Tipu's cause, and two of the leading national dailies, the Bengali-language *Prothom Alo* and English-language *Daily Star*, launched a fund drive to help pay for his medical treatment abroad. That money, together with funds raised by international organizations (including CPJ), allowed Tipu to seek treatment at the world-class Bumrungrad Hospital in Bangkok.

By the end of 2001, after multiple operations and extensive physical therapy, Tipu had regained the use of his right hand, which attackers had taken special pains to destroy. "Now I am going to start my previous profession within the shortest possible period," he wrote in an e-mail to CPJ in December. "Though I am still not fully cured, now I can write with my right hand."

APRIL 19

Purbokone
ATTACKED
Iskander Ali Chowdhury, *Purbokone*
ATTACKED
Jalaluddin Ahmed Chowdhury,
Purbokone
ATTACKED

At around 1:30 a.m., a group of men led by Mamunur Rashid Mamun, a ward commissioner in the Chittagong City Corporation, forced their way into the offices of the local Bengali-language daily *Purbokone*.

The intruders assaulted chief subeditor Iskander Ali Chowdhury and journalist Jalaluddin Ahmed Chowdhury and forced them out of the building. The journalists were threatened and then shoved into a nearby roadside ditch.

In an April 24, front-page interview in the Bengali-language daily *Sangbad*, Mamun admitted going to the *Purbokone* offices but denied attacking the journalists. Mamun maintained that he visited the newspaper to ask why *Purbokone*, an independent publication, did not give favorable coverage to the ruling Awami League.

In the *Sangbad* interview, the commissioner also stated that he had the blessings of senior party officials and expressed confidence that he would not face legal reprisals over the incident. However, police in Panchlaish Thana charged him under the Public Safety Act.

In an April 24 letter to Prime Minister Sheikh Hasina, CPJ noted an alarming spate of violence directed against journalists in Bangladesh and urging her government to take immediate action to ensure that these crimes were prosecuted vigorously. Among the cases raised in the letter was the attack on the *Purbokone* journalists.

On April 28, police seized Mamun's property, under court orders, in an effort to force the politician to face the charges against him. Meanwhile, Mamun had gone into hiding to avoid arrest. The Associated Press reported that the seizure was "the first step by the government after a string of attacks by politicians and criminal gangs against Bangladesh's beleaguered journalists."

On May 5, in another unprecedented move, the government offered a 100,000 takas (US$5,400) reward for information that would help find Mamun. On May 6, two brothers of the politician were arrested for allegedly violating wildlife preservation laws. "Our main aim is to draw him out of hiding," a police officer told the AP. On May 7, Mamun surrendered before the Chief Metropolitan Magistrate's Court in Chittagong.

Mamun's case was referred to the Public Safety Act Tribunal in Chittagong, with hearing dates set for June 24, 25, and 26, according to the Dhaka-based newspaper *The Independent*. CPJ was unable to determine the outcome of these proceedings.

APRIL 20

Prabir Shikder, *Janakantha*
ATTACKED

Shikder, Faridpur correspondent for the national Bengali-language daily *Janakantha*, was on a reporting assignment when a group of armed men ambushed him on the outskirts of town.

The attackers, who had been waiting by the roadside in a van, threw several Molotov cocktails at Shikder as he approached on his motorcycle, according to eyewitness accounts from the local press. Several of the men then shot the journalist and stabbed him repeatedly before fleeing the scene.

The reporter was rushed to Faridpur Medical College Hospital and later transferred to the National Institute of Cardiovascular Diseases in Dhaka. Doctors amputated Shikder's right leg, which was shattered by bullets. The journalist also sustained multiple stab injuries and bullet wounds in his right hand and arm.

Local journalists say Shikder was most likely attacked for reporting on the alleged collaboration of prominent local figures with Pakistani forces during the country's 1971 war for independence from Pakistan. Shikder had also covered organized crime and its links to local police.

APRIL 21

Nahar Ali, *Anirban*
KILLED

Ali, a correspondent for the Khulna-based, Bengali-language daily *Anirban*, died shortly before midnight on April 21, while undergoing treatment at Khulna Medical College Hospital for injuries sustained in an attack days earlier. Late on the night of April 17, masked men kidnapped Ali from his home in the village of Shovna, according to local press reports. The assailants stabbed him, beat him severely, and broke his hands and legs before abandoning him on the outskirts of his village, according to police.

Ali was found unconscious and taken to the hospital in Khulna, a major city in southwestern Bangladesh. Doctors said he died due to major brain damage and profuse bleeding.

Police suggested that members of the outlawed Biplobi Communist Party may have killed Ali because of a dispute over ownership of a shrimp farm. However, journalists in Khulna said that the investigation lacked credibility because Ali's reporting had uncovered links between police and smuggling rings in the region. CPJ sources said that Ali, who worked as the Dumuria subdistrict correspondent for *Anirban*, was killed because "he knew too much" about the workings of local criminal syndicates and the complicity of some local authorities in their activities.

JULY 20

Ahsan Ali, free-lancer
KILLED (MOTIVE UNCONFIRMED)

Ali, a stringer for the daily

newspaper *Jugantor*, was reported missing on July 20 and found dead on July 22 in an irrigation canal in Rupganj Village, where he lived. Assailants had bound the journalist's hands and legs, burned his face and chest with nitric acid, and stabbed him to death, according to police.

Ali had received death threats that same week from a local leader of the ruling Awami League's youth wing, according to his wife, Shahida Akhter. Akhter told journalists that the threats followed Ali's reporting months earlier that party activists were linked to incidents of highway robbery on the road from Dhaka to Chittagong. However, she also suggested that Ali might have been killed over a land dispute with some relatives.

NOVEMBER 22

Shahriar Kabir, free-lancer
IMPRISONED

On November 22, police at Dhaka's Zia International Airport arrested Kabir when he returned to Bangladesh from India, where he had interviewed minority Bangladeshi Hindus who fled there following attacks against their community after Bangladesh's October 1 parliamentary elections. Kabir—a documentary filmmaker, regular contributor to the national Bengali-language daily *Janakantha*, and author of several books about Bangladesh's war for independence— was arrested for "anti-state activities on the basis of intelligence reports and at the instruction of higher authorities," according to a police report. Police seized his passport, five videotapes, 13 audiotapes, several rolls of unprocessed film, and his camera, according to news reports.

A November 25 statement issued by the Home Ministry alleged that Kabir was "involved in a heinous bid to tarnish the image of Bangladesh and its government," according to a report published by *The Daily Star*, a leading national paper. "Kabir had made a whirlwind tour across India with ulterior motives to shoot video films," it said, noting that the video footage and other materials seized from Kabir upon his arrest were "objectionable, misleading, instigating and provocative to destroy communal harmony." That same day, a district magistrate's court authorized the government to detain Kabir for up to 30 days under the provisions of Bangladesh's Special Powers Act. Authorities in Bangladesh frequently abuse this act, which allows for the arbitrary arrest and detention of any citizen suspected of engaging in activities that threaten national security.

On December 8, the government charged Kabir with treason. His detention was later extended by another three months.

On January 12, 2002, in response to a habeas corpus petition, a High Court bench declared the extension of Kabir's term of detention to be illegal and ordered the journalist's release. However, Kabir continued to be held on the treason charge. On January 19, a separate High Court bench ordered Kabir to be released on interim bail for six months, pending his treason trial. The High Court also issued a "show cause" notice to the government asking prosecutors to demonstrate why Kabir should not be granted permanent bail.

On January 20, authorities released

Kabir from Dhaka Central Jail, where he was greeted by hundreds of colleagues, relatives, and other supporters. At press time, the government had not dropped the treason charge against Kabir, a charge that carries a maximum penalty of death.

BRUNEI

OCTOBER 1

All journalists
LEGAL ACTION

Sweeping amendments to an existing press law were expected to severely curtail freedom of information in Brunei by imposing strict licensing requirements on newspapers and imposing jail terms on journalists who published "false news."

The law, the Local Newspapers (Amendment) Order 2001, went into effect on October 1. It requires newspapers to apply to the minister of home affairs for annual publishing permits. The minister has sole discretionary power to grant permits, which are not subject to appeal or judicial review. In addition, the new law grants the government absolute power to bar the distribution of foreign periodicals in Brunei.

The law requires newspapers applying for permits to deposit 100,000 Bruneian dollars (US$57,700) in cash with the government. Anyone who publishes without a license is liable to a fine of up to 40,000 dollars (US$23,100) or three years in jail. Other provisions allow the minister of home affairs to charge journalists with publishing malicious reports or false news, a crime punishable by a fine of 40,000

dollars, three months in jail, or both.

The law also requires individuals who are not Bruneian citizens or permanent residents to obtain prior approval from the Office of the Prime Minister before working in the press. The majority of the staff at Brunei's two English-language dailies, the *Borneo Bulletin* and the *News Express*, are foreigners. If enacted, the law could threaten the survival of these newspapers.

On September 25, CPJ wrote a letter to His Majesty Sultan Haji Hassanal Bolkiah Mu'izzaddin Waddaulah, warning him that if the new law was allowed to stand, it would severely limit the free flow of information in Brunei and would provide a negative example to the rest of Southeast Asia.

CHINA

JANUARY 15

Feng Zhaoxia, *Gejie Daobao*
KILLED

Feng, a reporter for the Xi'an-based daily *Gejie Daobao*, was found in a ditch outside Xi'an with his throat cut, according to Chinese and international press reports.

Feng was an investigative reporter who wrote about criminal gangs and their links to corrupt local politicians. He had received repeated death threats, and his rented room had been broken into many times. In the days before his death, he told colleagues he was being followed and that he feared for his life, according to Reuters. On January 14, he moved to new lodgings as a safety precaution.

Soon after Feng's body was found,

police ruled his death a suicide and banned the local press from writing about it. According to relatives who identified his body, there was a four-inch gash in his throat and no blood on his clothes, making it unlikely he could have killed himself. One relative told Reuters, "He had no reason to commit suicide. He had a happy, healthy family, a good job, and no psychological problems."

Feng's relatives and colleagues believe he was killed for his journalistic work. They have petitioned local authorities to reopen the case but have received no response.

Feng, a former farmer, began writing articles and sending them to local publications in the hope of becoming a journalist. After his first article was published in 1980, he won several awards for his writing before being hired by *Gejie Daobao* in 1996.

MARCH 13

Yang Zili, free-lancer
IMPRISONED
Xu Wei, *Xiaofei Ribao*
IMPRISONED
Zhang Honghai, free-lancer
IMPRISONED
Jin Haike, free-lancer
IMPRISONED

Yang, Xu, Jin, and Zhang were detained on March 13 and charged with subversion on April 20, according to the Hong Kong–based Information Center for Human Rights and Democracy. The four were active participants in the "Xin Qingnian Xuehui" (New Youth Study Group), an informal gathering of individuals who explored topics related to political

and social reform and used the Internet to circulate relevant articles.

Yang and Xu were detained separately on March 13. Less is known about the circumstances under which Zhang and Jin were detained, but they were also taken into custody around mid-March, according to the Information Center.

Yang, the group's most prominent member, is well known in liberal academic circles for his technological expertise in evading government firewalls and creating e-mail accounts that cannot be monitored, according to a report in *The New York Times*. His Web site, "Yangzi de Sixiang Jiayuan" (Yangzi's Garden of Ideas), featured poems, essays, and reports by various authors on subjects ranging from the shortcomings of rural elections to broad discussions of political theory.

Authorities shut down the site after Yang's arrest, according to a well-informed U.S.-based source who did not wish to be identified. The source created a mirror site (www.bringmenews.com/China/freeyzl/mirror/).

When Xu, a reporter with *Xiaofei Ribao* (Consumer Daily), was detained on March 13, authorities confiscated his computer, other professional equipment, and books, according to an account published online by his girlfriend, Wang Ying. Wang reported that public security officials also ordered the *Xiaofei Ribao* to fire Xu. The newspaper has refused to discuss Xu's case with reporters, according to The Associated Press.

All four were tried on September 28 by the Beijing Number One Intermediate People's Court, but no verdict had been announced by year's end.

MARCH 15

Liu Haofeng, free-lancer
IMPRISONED

Liu was secretly arrested in Shanghai in mid-March while conducting research on social conditions in rural China for the dissident China Democracy Party (CDP). On May 16, Liu was sentenced to "reeducation through labor," a form of administrative detention that allows officials to send individuals to such camps for up to three years without trial or formal charges.

After Liu's arrest, friends and family members were not informed of his whereabouts, and CDP members say they only found out what had happened to him when they received news of his sentence in August.

Sentencing papers issued by the Shanghai Reeducation through Labor Committee cited several alleged offenses, including a policy paper and an essay written by Liu that were published under various pen names on the CDP's Web site. The essay focused on the current situation of China's peasants. The committee also accused Liu of trying to form an illegal organization, the "China Democracy Party Joint Headquarters, Second Front."

The journalist previously worked as an editor and reporter for various publications, including the magazine *Jishu Jingji Yu Guanli* (Technology Economy and Management), run by the Fujian Province Economic and Trade Committee, and *Zhongguo Shichang Jingji Bao* (China Market Economy News), run by the Central Party School in Beijing.

Beginning in 1999, he worked for Univillage, a research organization focusing on rural democratization, and managed their Web site. He was working as a free-lance journalist at the time of his arrest.

Lu Xinhua, free-lancer
IMPRISONED

Lu was arrested in mid-March in Wuhan, Hubei Province, after articles he had written about rural unrest and official corruption appeared on various Internet news sites based overseas. On April 20, he was charged with "inciting to subvert state power," a charge frequently used against journalists who write about politically sensitive subjects. Lu's trial began on September 18. On December 30, Lu was sentenced to four years in prison.

APRIL 3

Guo Qinghai, free-lancer
IMPRISONED, LEGAL ACTION

Guo was arrested in September 2000 after posting several essays on overseas online bulletin boards calling for political reforms in China. In almost 40 essays posted under the pen name Qing Song, Guo covered a variety of topics, including political prisoners, environmental problems, and corruption. In one essay, Guo discussed the importance of a free press, saying, "Those who oppose lifting media censorship argue that it will negatively influence social stability. But according to what I have seen...countries that control speech may be able to maintain stability in the short term, but the end result is often violent upheaval, coup d'etats, or war."

Guo, who worked in a bank, also

wrote articles for Taiwanese newspapers. He was a friend and classmate of writer Qi Yanchen, who was sentenced to four years in prison on subversion charges just four days after Guo's arrest. One of Guo's last online essays appealed for Qi's release.

On April 3, 2001, Guo was tried on subversion charges by a court in Cangzhou, Hebei Province. On April 26, he was sentenced to four years in prison.

APRIL 8

Wu Jianming, free-lancer
IMPRISONED

Wu was detained in the southern city of Shenzhen and investigated on suspicion of spying for Taiwan, according to numerous sources. He was formally charged on May 26.

Until 1986, Wu taught at the Communist Party's Central Party School in Beijing. From 1986 to 1988, he was a reporter at the newspaper *Shenzhen Qingnian Bao* (Shenzhen Youth Daily). He became a U.S. citizen after moving to the United States in 1988 and has since divided his time between Queens, New York, and Hong Kong.

Wu's writing covered a number of politically sensitive topics. In 1990, for example, he published a book on the Tiananmen Square massacre of June 4, 1989. Printed by a Taiwanese publisher under the title *Wangpai Chujin de Zhongnanhai Qiaoju* (Zhongnanhai Has Played Its Trump Cards), the book analyzed decisions of senior Communist Party officials during the crisis.

From January 1995 until mid-1999, Wu wrote a column under the pen name Jiang Shan for the Hong Kong–based newspaper *Apple Daily*. The column discussed Chinese political, economic, and foreign-policy issues, including mainland China-Taiwan relations and the 1989 protest movement. From 1996 to 1997, Wu also served as an editor at the now defunct Hong Kong paper *Kuai Bao* (Express).

In an August 2 letter to President Jiang Zemin, CPJ urged him to ensure that Wu is given a fair and open trial under international legal standards of due process.

On September 28, before being tried, Wu was suddenly released and deported to the United States. The circumstances behind his release were unknown, but it came just before U.S. president George W. Bush's October 21 visit to China.

MAY 1

Jiang Weiping, free-lancer
IMPRISONED, LEGAL ACTION

Jiang, a free-lance reporter, was arrested on December 5, 2000, after publishing a number of articles in the Hong Kong magazine *Qianshao* (Frontline) that revealed corruption scandals in northeastern China. Jiang wrote the *Qianshao* articles, which were published between June and September 1999, under various pen names. His coverage exposed several major corruption scandals involving high-level officials. Notably, Jiang reported that Shenyang vice mayor Ma Xiangdong had lost nearly 30 million yuan (US$3.6 million) in public funds gambling in Macau casinos. Jiang also revealed that Daqing mayor Qian Dihua had used public funds to buy apartments for each of his 29 mistresses.

Soon after these cases were publicized in *Qianshao* and other Hong

Kong media, central authorities detained Ma. He was accused of taking bribes, embezzling public funds, and gambling overseas. Ma was executed for these crimes in December 2001. After his arrest, Ma's case was widely reported in the domestic press and used as an example in the government's ongoing fight against corruption.

However, in May 2001, Jiang was indicted on the charge of "revealing state secrets."

An experienced journalist, Jiang had worked until May 2000 as the northeastern China bureau chief for the Hong Kong paper *Wen Hui Bao*. In the 1980s, he worked as a Dalian-based correspondent for Xinhua News Agency. He contributed free-lance articles to *Qianshao*, a monthly Chinese-language magazine focusing on mainland affairs.

The Dalian Intermediate Court sentenced Jiang to eight years in prison following a secret trial held on September 5, 2001. On November 20, 2001, CPJ honored Jiang with an International Press Freedom Award.

Wang Jinbo, free-lancer
IMPRISONED

Wang, a free-lance journalist, was arrested in early May 2001 for e-mailing essays to overseas organizations arguing that the government should change its official line that the 1989 protests in Tiananmen Square were "counterrevolutionary." In October, Wang was formally charged with "inciting to subvert state power." On November 14, the Junan County Court in Shandong Province conducted his closed trial; only the journalists' relatives were allowed to attend. On

December 13, Wang was sentenced to four years in prison.

Wang, a member of the banned China Democracy Party, had been detained several times in the past for his political activities. In February, days before the International Olympic Committee (IOC) visited Beijing, he was briefly taken into custody after signing an open letter calling on the IOC to pressure China to release political prisoners. A number of Wang's essays have been posted on various Internet sites. One, titled "My Account of Police Violations of Civil Rights," describes his January 2001 detention, when police interrogated him and held him for 20 hours with no food or heat after he signed an open letter calling for the release of political prisoners.

MAY 9

Zhu Ruixiang, free-lancer
IMPRISONED

Zhu was arrested and charged with subversion after distributing articles via the Internet. Prosecutors accused him of distributing "hostile" materials, including copies of *Dacankao* (VIP Reference), a Chinese-language, pro-democracy electronic newsletter that Zhu had allegedly e-mailed to several friends, according to U.S.-based sources close to the case.

Dacankao, which is compiled in the United States and e-mailed to more than 1 million addresses in China every day, contains articles from various sources about social and political topics banned from China's tightly controlled domestic media.

Following his September 10 trial, the Shaoyang Municipal Intermediate

People's Court signaled its intention to sentence Zhu to a nine-month jail term. However, the Political and Legal Committee of Shaoyang Municipality reviewed the case and insisted that the court impose a more severe sentence. On September 11, Zhu was sentenced to three years in prison.

Zhu, a respected lawyer in Shaoyang City, had previously worked as an editor at a local radio station. He was also the founder and editor-in-chief of the *Shaoyang City Radio and Television Journal*.

MAY 18

Hu Dalin, free-lancer
IMPRISONED

Hu was arrested four days after posting an essay by his father, Lu Jiaping, on the Internet. The essay, titled "Finally the Official Media Has a Different Voice," praised a newspaper article that criticized China's leaders for being too soft on the United States.

Hu, who runs an art supply business, had created a Web site that featured the political essays of his father, Lu Jiaping. Lu is a 60-year-old, left-leaning intellectual based in Beijing.

According to an account written by his father, nine public security officers arrived at Hu's house on May 18; three of them took Hu to the local precinct while the others searched his house and confiscated his computer, copies of his father's essays, and other materials, including books and letters.

At first, the officers told Hu's fiancée that, according to law, he would be released or his family would be notified within 48 hours. However, when she inquired 48 hours later, officials told her

that Hu could not be released because his case concerned state secrets.

Police later told her that Hu was a political criminal who would be held for at least 15 days while they conducted an investigation. The Public Security Bureau did not allow Hu's family to visit him in detention, and they charged his fiancée 320 yuan (about US$40) for his incarceration.

During Hu's interrogation, police officers questioned him about Lu Jiaping's essays, and told him that while his father was allowed to write such essays, he could not post them on the Internet, according to his father's account.

On June 4, Hu Dalin was released after his fiancée paid the detention center a 500 yuan (US$62) fee.

JUNE 1

Qian Gang, *Nanfang Zhoumo*
HARASSED
Chang Ping, *Nanfang Zhoumo*
HARASSED

In early June, Qian and Chang, respectively the deputy editor and front page news editor of the Guangdong-based newspaper *Nanfang Zhoumo* (Southern Weekend), were demoted from their posts under pressure from the local propaganda bureau, according to a journalist close to the case.

Another editor and a reporter were fired and banned from ever working in journalism again.

The personnel changes came after the newspaper published a report about a criminal gang, led by Hunan Province native Zhang Jun, that killed 28 people in a spree of murder and theft. The piece featured interviews with gang members and their families. The author also analyzed problems such as poverty and other forms of inequality that may have led the gang members to a life of crime.

One of China's most progressive and adventurous newspapers, *Nanfang Zhoumo* has pushed the boundaries of media control by publishing explicit reports on social problems such as AIDS, crime, and the trafficking of women.

The paper's daring reporting has made it a longtime target of authorities. In January 2000, editor Jiang Yiping was demoted after publishing reports that angered government censors. Qian Gang was hired to replace her.

After the recent personnel crackdown, one employee told the *South China Morning Post*, "This is a death sentence.... They cannot shut it down but the paper as we know it will no longer exist."

JUNE 14

He Qinglian, *Shenzhen Fazhi Bao*
HARASSED

Chinese journalist He Qinglian fled to the United States after security agents broke into her house in the southern city of Shenzhen.

During a 2000 crackdown on liberal intellectuals, He was demoted from her position as editor of *Shenzhen Fazhi Bao* (Shenzhen Legal Daily). Afterward, police regularly followed her and tapped her phone. The government also banned He's writing.

He was planning to leave China in late June 2001 to start a sabbatical at the University of Chicago. In April, after she received the official invitation from the university and a U.S. visa, a security agent was assigned to shadow

her as she rode the bus to work each day.

In early June, security agents broke into He's apartment in Shenzhen and confiscated her belongings, including invitations to conferences abroad and other personal documents. Because this action followed the arrests of several scholars on charges of spying, she feared that police were planning a case against her and decided to flee the country immediately.

In 1998, He made a name for herself with her book *Zhongguo de Xianjing* (China's Pitfalls), in which she argued that corruption is endemic to China's political and economic system. Her recent book, *Women Rengran Zai Yangwang Xingkong* (We Are All Still Gazing at the Stars), criticizes President Jiang Zemin's theory of "Sange Daibiao" (generally translated as "The Three Represents"), which says the Communist Party should represent the advanced forces of production, advanced culture, and grassroots interests.

The book was based on an essay He wrote for *Shuwu* (Reading Room) magazine in March 2000. After the essay was published, the book was banned and several editors were demoted.

JUNE 15

Liu Weifang, free-lancer
IMPRISONED, LEGAL ACTION

Liu was arrested sometime after September 26, 2000, when security officials from the Ninth Agricultural Brigade District, in the Xinjiang Uighur Autonomous Region came to his house, confiscated his computer, and announced that he was being officially investigated, according to an account that Liu posted on the

Internet. Liu's most recent online essay was dated October 20, 2000.

Liu had recently posted a number of essays criticizing China's leaders and political system in Internet chat rooms. The essays, which the author signed either with his real name or with the initials "lgwf," covered topics such as official corruption, development policies in China's western regions, and environmental issues. At press time, the articles were available online at: http://liuweifang.ipfox.com.

"The reasons for my actions are all above-board," Liu wrote in one essay. "They are not aimed at any one person or any organization; rather, they are directed at any behavior in society that harms humanity. The goal is to speed up humanity's progress and development." The official *Xinjiang Daily* characterized Liu's work as "a major threat to national security."

According to a June 15, 2001, report in the *Xinjiang Daily*, Liu was sentenced to three years in prison by the Ninth Agricultural Brigade District's Intermediate People's Court. Liu's sentencing was announced amid government attempts to tighten control over the Internet.

JUNE 18

Nanfang Zhoumo Internet forum
CENSORED
"Minzhu he Renquan" Internet forum
CENSORED
Remen Huati
CENSORED

A number of popular online chat rooms were closed for posting comments critical of the government, according to the Hong Kong-based Information Center

for Human Rights and Democracy.

A chat room organized by the Guangzhou newspaper *Nanfang Zhoumo* (Southern Weekend) was closed on June 18 after several users criticized the recent firing of two of the paper's editors for their coverage of organized crime and other sensitive topics.

Another popular Internet forum, "Minzhu he Renquan" (Democracy and Human Rights), operated by a Web site called Xici Hutong, was also closed after users posted more than 100 essays attacking the government's press crackdown. And on June 18, the Internet magazine *Remen Huati* (Hot Topic), which frequently ran politically controversial articles, ceased publication under severe government pressure, according to the center.

On June 25, an anonymous posting on the Xici Hutong site called on users to respect relevant Internet regulations and refrain from posting "subversive" material.

JULY 13

Tuomo Pesonen, YLE
HARASSED
Janne Niskala, free-lancer
HARASSED

Authorities detained Pesonen, the Beijing-based Asia correspondent for YLE, Finland's national public broadcasting company; Niskala, a free-lance cameraman; and their Chinese colleagues while the crew was reporting in an area of northwest Beijing slated to be demolished in preparation for the 2008 Olympic Games. (The Chinese nationals did not want to disclose their identities.)

Pesonen told CPJ that he and his

crew were ordered not to film in the area or talk to residents and were brought to a police station for questioning. While they were detained, Pesonen called his station on his cell phone and gave a live report. The crew was released after about an hour and told to leave the area.

The journalists were detained just hours before the International Olympic Committee officially announced it had selected Beijing as host for the 2008 Games. In making their Olympic bid, Beijing officials pledged to give the media complete freedom to report when they come to China.

JULY 19

William Foreman, The Associated Press
HARASSED

Foreman, Taipei bureau chief for The Associated Press, was detained and questioned for a day when he traveled to the town of Mafang, in mainland China's Shaanxi Province, to investigate a bomb explosion that killed at least 69 people.

While interviewing farmers in a neighboring village, Foreman was detained by police in a noodle restaurant. After about four hours, he was taken to a hotel in the nearby city of Yulin, where police confiscated the photos he had taken in Mafang. He was held until about 7 p.m. The next morning, police escorted him to the airport.

Upon his release, Foreman was forced to sign a statement acknowledging that he had violated Chinese law by traveling to Mafang without official permission. Chinese law requires foreign correspondents to register with provincial foreign affairs offices before reporting outside of Beijing, but permission is rarely granted to visit the scenes of violent or otherwise sensitive incidents.

AUGUST 8

All journalists
CENSORED

The Chinese government announced on national television that publications could be summarily closed down for reporting on any one of seven proscribed topics, known as the "Seven No's."

The policy banned all press reports that:

1. Negate the guiding role of Marxism, Mao Zedong Thought, or Deng Xiaoping Theory;

2. Oppose the guiding principles, official line, or policies of the Communist Party;

3. Reveal state secrets, damage national security, or harm national interests;

4. Oppose official policies regarding minority nationalities and religion, or harm national unity and affect social stability;

5. Advocate murder, violence, obscenity, superstition, or pseudo-science;

6. Spread rumors or falsified news, or interfere in the work of the party and government;

7. Violate party propaganda discipline, or national publishing and advertising regulations.

Government authorities first communicated the seven banned topics to Chinese editors in January, but the August 8 announcement marked the first public acknowledgment of the policy.

Authorities also progressively stiffened penalties for violating the bans. In January, editors were told that offending publications would receive a warning. After the first warning, editors could be dismissed. After repeated warnings, the publication could be closed down.

In June, media outlets received copies of an internal government document announcing that publications could be closed immediately for violating the ban.

In the August 8 announcement, the central government upped the ante yet again by warning that any province, autonomous region, or municipality in which two or more newspapers are closed down for violating one of these stipulations will not be allowed to launch any new publications in the following year.

AUGUST 14

Huang Qi, Tianwang Web site
IMPRISONED, LEGAL ACTION

Huang Qi published the Tianwang Web site (www.6-4tianwang.com), which featured articles about pro-democracy activism in China, the independence movement in the Xinjiang Uighur Autonomous Region, and the banned spiritual group Falun Gong. He was arrested on June 3, 2000, and later charged with subversion.

The Chengdu Intermediate Court in Sichuan Province held a secret trial on August 14, 2001. Family members were not allowed to attend, and no verdict or sentencing date was released. However, in China, criminal cases brought to trial usually result in a guilty verdict. The charges against Huang Qi carry a punishment of up to 10 years in prison. Huang's trial was postponed several times throughout 2001 in an apparent effort to deflect international attention from China's human rights practices during the country's campaign to host the 2008 Olympic Games. Two of the trial delays—on February 23 and June 27—coincided with important dates in Beijing's Olympics bid.

SEPTEMBER 12

All journalists
CENSORED

The day after the terrorist attacks on New York City and Washington, D.C., the Chinese government directed all media, including Internet portals, to refrain from publishing anti-American statements, according to international news reports.

A few days later, on September 16, the Central Propaganda Department issued another directive ordering all domestic news organizations to refrain from publishing commentaries expressing support for either the United States or the terrorists.

"We are supposed to report the facts only," a journalist told the *South China Morning Post*. "Anything with value judgment such as condemning the terrorists or supporting the Americans to retaliate is prohibited."

Detailed background on terrorist activities, including how the September 11 attacks were prepared, was also banned.

Commentators speculated that the measures were intended to give the Chinese government room to formulate its own foreign policy in the wake of the September 11 attacks.

Lam Chiu-wing, Radio Television Hong Kong
HARASSED

Hong Kong chief executive Tung Chee-hwa reprimanded Lam, host of the satirical television talk show "Headliner" on the public Radio Television Hong Kong, after he jokingly compared Tung's administration to the Taliban. After the incident, senior producers of the show were required to vet all scripts, a change from earlier practice.

The Broadcasting Authority, a government body responsible for complaints against broadcast media, issued a statement that "Headliner," which is considered a "current affairs program and not classified as a Personal View Program, should observe the provisions governing impartiality."

The Hong Kong Journalists Association replied that as a satirical program, "Headliner" was not subject to journalistic standards of impartiality.

Pro-Beijing officials had recently renewed pressure on RTHK, which they believe should present only official Chinese views. Following Tung's comments, Ma Lik, a deputy to mainland China's National People's Congress, said: "Enough is enough. It's time for the Government to spell out the role of RTHK to the public. The Government should disband it if it no longer has a role to explain government policies."

FIJI

FEBRUARY 22

Fiji Television
CENSORED

Filming of "Leader's Forum," a political affairs program on Fiji Television, was postponed after police forcibly prevented participants from entering the venue and threatened to arrest them if the program proceeded.

The program was scheduled to coincide with court hearings into the legality of Prime Minister Laisenia Qarase's interim government, which was installed with military backing in July 2000 after a failed coup by businessman George Speight.

Police told producers at Fiji Television that they needed a license to film the program because the filming was considered a public gathering, even though the participants had all been issued private invitations. Many participants backed out after the police threat, and Fiji TV was forced to reschedule the program until after the court proceedings had concluded.

INDIA

JANUARY 19

Surinder Singh Oberoi, Agence France-Presse
ATTACKED

Oberoi, a correspondent for Agence France-Presse, was beaten by police officer G.M. Dar while covering an attack on a security bunker in Srinagar, Kashmir, by suspected militant Muslims. After the attackers threw a grenade at the bunker, killing one person and injuring nine others, security forces cordoned off the area and ordered journalists to leave the scene.

Dar struck Oberoi repeatedly with his rifle. The officer only stopped the assault after other journalists at the scene intervened. Minutes later, however, when Oberoi approached another officer to complain, Dar started hitting him again.

Local journalists say they often bear the brunt of the security forces' anger and frustration when they arrive on the scene of an attack. In this particular grenade attack, two officers were among the nine injured.

Oberoi said he did not know why he had been targeted. Dar later apologized for the attack.

MAY 10

Aijaz Rahi, The Associated Press
ATTACKED
Sanam Aijaz, Eenadu Television
ATTACKED
Merajuddin, Associated Press Television
ATTACKED
Syed Shujaat Bukhari, *The Hindu*
ATTACKED
Nissar Ahmed Bhat, *The Hindu*
ATTACKED
Sheikh Mushtaq, Reuters
ATTACKED
Fayaz Kabli, Reuters
ATTACKED
S. Irfan, Press Trust of India
ATTACKED
Fayaz Ahmad, United News of India
ATTACKED
Naseer Ahmad, Zee TV
ATTACKED
Bilal Ahmad Bhat, Asian News International
ATTACKED
S. Tariq, New Delhi Television
ATTACKED
Tauseef, Agence France-Presse
ATTACKED
Javid Ahmad Shah, *Indian Express*
ATTACKED

Sayed Muzaffar Hussain, *Srinagar Times*
ATTACKED
B. Kumar, Eenadu Television
ATTACKED

At least 16 Indian journalists were attacked by Indian Border Security Force (BSF) troops in the Kashmir town of Magam. The journalists were covering the aftermath of the previous day's suicide bombing against a BSF camp. The explosion killed 11 people, eight of them civilians, according to local press sources.

The journalists included Rahi, a photographer for The Associated Press; Aijaz, of Hyderabad-based Eenadu Television (ETV); Merajuddin (who, like many Indians, uses only one name), a cameraman for Associated Press Television News; Bukhari, a correspondent for *The Hindu* newspaper; Nissar Ahmed Bhat, photographer for *The Hindu*; Mushtaq, a Reuters correspondent; Kabli, a Reuters photographer; Irfan, of the Press Trust of India; Fayaz Ahmad, of the United News of India; Naseer Ahmad, of Zee TV; Bilal Ahmad Bhat, of Asian News International; Tariq, of New Delhi Television; Tauseef, of Agence France-Presse; Shah, of the *Indian Express* newspaper; Hussain, of the daily *Srinagar Times*; and Kumar, a cameraman for ETV.

The journalists were covering a funeral procession for three of the civilian victims when a BSF convoy approached the crowd. Members of BSF's Battalion 194 got out of their vehicles and began firing in the air and attacking members of the funeral procession, according to journalists at the scene.

As the crowd scattered, BSF soldiers turned on journalists documenting the assault, beating them with rifle butts and batons and destroying their camera equipment.

Some journalists took shelter in the homes of local residents. Others fled to the Magam police station, where they managed to contact colleagues in the capital, Srinagar, about 30 kilometers (17 miles) to the south. After these colleagues alerted the BSF headquarters in Srinagar, BSF deputy inspector general R.P. Singh left immediately for Magam.

When Singh arrived at the police station, he asked the journalists there to take him to the scene of the attack and explain what had happened. Four journalists escorted him to the site and also began searching for any camera equipment that could be recovered.

Local BSF commander Deputy Inspector General A.K. Mallick then approached the journalists and told them they had no right to enter the area without his permission. Mallick quickly became enraged when this was disputed. Mallick threatened twice to shoot the journalists before ordering his forces to attack them, according to CPJ sources. Some 20 BSF soldiers then descended on the four journalists and bludgeoned them with rifle butts.

Singh called a halt to the attack, but Mallick challenged Singh's authority, saying, "Who are you? This is my operational area." Mallick then threatened once again to shoot all four journalists, accusing them of being "anti-national" Pakistan sympathizers.

The journalists returned to the safety of the Magam police station, by which time other officials had arrived from Srinagar.

Among the most seriously injured of the journalists was Kumar, who was severely beaten and thrown into a stream. Kumar suffered head injuries requiring 15 stitches, according to sources at ETV. Rahi received a hairline fracture to his knee when he was hit with a wooden board.

On May 17, CPJ sent a letter to Home Minister Lal Krishna Advani asking him to ensure that the official inquiry into the matter was thorough and impartial, and that the findings were made public. However, the government never released the results of the preliminary inquiry. Local journalists told CPJ that the Indian Border Security Force began a formal investigation into the incident only at the end of 2001. This investigation was ongoing at the end of the year.

JUNE 1

Vineet Narain, *Kalchakra*
HARASSED, LEGAL ACTION

A division bench of the Jammu and Kashmir High Court ordered the arrest of Narain, founding editor of the investigative journal *Kalchakra*, for his failure to appear in court to face a contempt-of-court charge.

The court declared Narain an "absconder" and directed a New Delhi district magistrate to attach the property of *Kalchakra*, as well as a printing press where the journal was produced. The High Court scheduled the next hearing for July 13 in Jammu.

Narain said he never received official notice of the order, which was published in local newspapers in Jammu, and also argued that his life would be in serious danger if he traveled to Jammu and Kashmir State.

The contempt case arose from a paragraph in an article published in the December 16, 2000, edition of *Kalchakra*. It questioned the role of Jammu and Kashmir High Court justice T.S. Doabia in resolving a land dispute and suggested that Doabia had been unduly influenced by his friendship with Indian Supreme Court chief justice A.S. Anand, who formerly served as chief justice of the Jammu and Kashmir High Court.

The court said that the paragraph "appears to be per se contempt of the court as it has the tendency of bringing the administration of justice to disrepute by attributing disparaging motives and bias to a sitting judge of this court."

In addition, the February 16, December 1, and December 16, 2000, editions of *Kalchakra* contained allegations that Chief Justice Anand had helped secure legal victories for close family members and associates in various property disputes.

Narain believes that his contempt case was brought at the behest of Chief Justice Anand.

In response to the High Court summons, Narain filed two petitions with the Supreme Court of India. The first petition asked that the contempt case be dropped altogether. In the event that the case was pursued, Narain also petitioned that the venue be transferred to New Delhi in light of security concerns in Srinagar.

The Supreme Court ordered Narain to petition the Jammu and Kashmir High Court directly for a change of venue. The High Court eventually agreed to transfer the case not to New Delhi but to Jammu, the winter capital of Indian-controlled Kashmir.

Narain said he had been threatened by militant groups in Kashmir who were angered by his investigations into their underground funding networks. Narain is well known in India for exposing the so-called *hawala* scam, a US$18 million bribery scandal that implicated some of the country's leading politicians. He reported that some of those allegedly involved in channeling payoffs to politicians were also transferring money to militant groups in Kashmir.

The Indian government acknowledged the potential threat to Narain's safety by providing him with special security protection between 1996 and 1998, at the height of efforts to prosecute those involved in the *hawala* scandal.

Narain said that in the current case, local officials largely ignored his repeated requests for protection in Kashmir. He also informed the High Court that security concerns prevented him from traveling to Kashmir to face the contempt charge.

On July 6, CPJ and Human Rights Watch issued a joint letter addressed to Prime Minister Atal Behari Vajpayee, noting that the prosecution of Vineet Narain represented an abuse of the contempt of court law, which should never be used to shield members of the judiciary from scrutiny by the press.

CPJ urged the prime minister to order an inquiry into possible political motivations behind Narain's prosecution and to ensure that police did not arrest Narain for having missed previous court dates in Jammu, given that he had clearly conveyed his security concerns to the various courts.

On August 4, twelve Jammu police officers came to Narain's office to arrest him (the journalist was not in Delhi at the time). The court also placed advertisements in Delhi newspapers declaring Narain a "proclaimed offender." CPJ sent another letter to Prime Minister Vajpayee on August 8, describing the ongoing harassment.

In December, the Jammu High Court canceled all orders of arrest, but scheduled the next hearing date for February 5, 2002, in Jammu.

JUNE 27

G. Suresh, Sun TV
HARASSED
Chennai Journalists
ATTACKED, HARASSED

Police arrested G. Suresh, reporter and cameraman for Sun TV in Villupuram District, Tamil Nadu. Suresh was one of nearly 20 journalists who went to a government-owned rice storage facility to report on a grain scandal. After the broadcast of Suresh's report, which embarrassed the Tamil Nadu state government, police went to Suresh's home and arrested him on assorted charges ranging from trespassing to physical intimidation.

Sun TV is owned by relatives of Muthuvel Karunanidhi, Tamil Nadu's former chief minister and the main rival to current chief minister Jayaram Jayalalitha.

Senior journalists in the state capital, Chennai, immediately organized a petition to secure Suresh's release. On June 28, a group of about 50 journalists assembled outside the office of Chief Minister Jayalalitha to present the petition, but she refused to accept it. Police then ordered the journalists to disperse and beat several with batons in

an effort to break up the demonstration.

On the morning of June 29, a group of 150 journalists gathered to march toward the State Secretariat to protest Suresh's arrest, as well as their rough treatment the previous day. Police dressed in riot gear and armed with tear gas and water pistols halted the demonstration and arrested all the journalists. They were detained at Vepery Police Station for about seven hours. They agreed to be released only after receiving confirmation that Suresh had been released on bail.

On July 3, CPJ issued a statement condemning a whole series of attacks against the press that accompanied a political crackdown in Tamil Nadu. Suresh's arrest was the first of several state government attempts to intimidate local journalists. (See June 30 and July 2 cases.)

JUNE 30

Sun TV
HARASSED

At around 9 a.m., police dressed in riot gear surrounded the offices of Sun TV in Chennai, the capital of Tamil Nadu. The station, which is owned by relatives of former chief minister Muthuvel Karunanidhi, had been repeatedly broadcasting video of the opposition politician's recent arrest, which was part of a broad state government crackdown on his Dravida Munnetra Kazhagam (DMK) party.

Police had arrested Karunanidhi, the main rival to Tamil Nadu chief minister Jayaram Jayalalitha, and several DMK activists in pre-dawn raids on June 30.

Sun TV staff did not allow the police to enter, and they made no attempt to enter by force. However, police did prevent Sun TV reporters from entering the premises. One Sun TV editor described the incident as a "siege."

That same day, Police Commissioner K. Muthukaruppan issued an order preventing Sun TV from broadcasting video of Karunanidhi's arrest. "If the Sun TV continued the telecast, action would be taken against it in accordance with the law," the order read, according to the *Times of India* newspaper.

Sun TV responded with a letter stating that the police commissioner did not have the authority to censor programming and continued with its regular broadcasts.

On July 3, CPJ issued a statement condemning a series of attacks against the press in Tamil Nadu, including the state government's attempts to censor Sun TV. No further action was taken against the station. (See June 27, June 30, and July 2 cases.)

V. Ganesan, *The Hindu*
`ATTACKED`
Sam Daniel, New Delhi Television
`ATTACKED`
R. Chandran, New Delhi Television
`ATTACKED`
N. Swaminathan, Sun TV
`ATTACKED`
K. Jayakoti, Raj TV
`ATTACKED`

Five Indian journalists were attacked by police while covering the arrest of M.K. Stalin, mayor of Chennai and son of opposition leader Muthuvel Karunanidhi.

The journalists were: Ganesan, a photographer for *The Hindu* newspaper; Daniel, a reporter for New Delhi

Television (NDTV); Chandran, a cameraman for NDTV; Swaminathan, a reporter for Sun TV; and Jayakoti, a cameraman for Raj TV.

Opposition supporters had gathered outside Madurai Central Jail to protest Stalin's arrest, and police began beating the demonstrators. Journalists covering the violence were also targeted.

On July 3, CPJ issued a statement condemning attacks against the press that accompanied the political crackdown in Tamil Nadu. (See June 27, June 30, and July 2 cases.)

JULY 2

R. Sendhil Kumar, Jaya TV
`ATTACKED`
S. Kumar, Jaya TV
`ATTACKED`

R. Sendhil Kumar, a cameraman for Jaya TV, and S. Kumar, his assistant, were assaulted in the Tamil Nadu state capital, Chennai, by activists from the opposition Dravida Munnetra Kazhagham (DMK) party.

Jaya TV is owned and operated by allies of Tamil Nadu chief minister Jayaram Jayalalitha. The two Jaya TV journalists were singled out of a group of journalists in front of the home of DMK leader Muthuvel Karunanidhi.

The incident followed a spate of attacks against the press in Tamil Nadu that accompanied a political crackdown orchestrated by Jayalalitha. (See June 27 and June 30 cases.)

JULY 30

Moolchand Yadav, free-lancer
`KILLED`

Yadav, a free-lance reporter who regularly contributed to Hindi-language dailies, including *Jansatta* and *Punjab Kesari*, was shot dead on the street in Jhansi, Uttar Pradesh. Colleagues said that Yadav had been murdered at the behest of two powerful landowners angered by his exposés about local corruption.

AUGUST 11

Tahir Mohiudin, *Chattan*
ATTACKED

A group of soldiers stormed into the office of the Urdu-language weekly *Chattan*, one of Kashmir's most well-respected and widely circulated publications. The soldiers beat up several staffers, including Mohiudin, the weekly's owner and editor.

The attack on the paper came after unknown assailants threw a grenade at soldiers patrolling a busy street in the commercial district of Srinagar, Kashmir. Security forces retaliated by beating up civilians in the area, near *Chattan*'s office. Four members of India's Border Security Forces and five civilians were injured in the blast.

AUGUST 20

Rajesh Bhattarai, *Aajo Bholi*
LEGAL ACTION

At around 1 p.m., an officer from the crime branch of the Sikkim police arrived at the *Aajo Bholi* office in Siliguri, in the neighboring state of West Bengal, and arrested Bhattarai under the provisions of Section 153(a) of the Indian Penal Code, which states that anyone whose words, "whether spoken or written," promote "disharmony" or "feelings of enmity" between different communities faces up to three years in prison.

Sources at the Nepali-language daily told CPJ that the charge related to an article that had appeared in the paper more than a year ago. On May 3, 2000, *Aajo Bholi* reported that Sikkim's chief minister Pawan Kumar Chamling, had described the flag of the Gorkha National Liberation Front (GNLF) as a symbol of murder during a May Day speech two days earlier.

Chamling denied ever making this statement. Sources at *Aajo Bholi* told CPJ that in response to complaints from Chamling and other political leaders in Sikkim, they published three separate apologies for the article.

During the 1980s, the GNLF led an armed movement to create an independent ethnic Gorkha state called Gorkhaland. In 1988, the group signed a peace accord with national and state government officials that resulted in the formation of the Darjeeling Gorkha Hill Council, currently headed by GNLF leader Subhash Ghisingh. The council was intended to give greater autonomy to the Gorkha people, who originally come from Nepal but represent a significant percentage of the population in West Bengal and Sikkim.

Although Bhattarai was granted interim bail on medical grounds, he was required to appear by August 31 before a judge in Sikkim's capital, Gangtok, to face a criminal charge.

On August 29, CPJ sent a letter to Chief Minister Chamling, calling on Sikkimese authorities to cease their unjust persecution of Rajesh Bhattarai. Bhattarai later arranged a private meeting with Chamling in New Delhi and apologized again for publishing the article, after which the government dropped the charge against him.

DECEMBER 13

Vikram Singh Bisht, Asian News International
`ATTACKED`

Bisht, a cameraman for the New Delhi-based news agency Asian News International (ANI), was critically injured in an attack by a suicide squad on the Indian Parliament. Thirteen people were killed in the raid, including the five attackers.

The assailants, armed with AK-47s, grenades, and other explosive devices, drove into the heavily guarded Parliament compound in what looked like an official car. Shortly thereafter, a gun battle broke out between the attackers and Indian security forces.

Bisht was standing by one of the main compound gates along with several other cameramen, waiting to film arriving and departing politicians. Early in the attack, one of the gunmen turned and fired in the direction of the journalists, according to a cameraman who was there.

Bisht, 28, was hit by a bullet that became embedded in his spinal cord, resulting in partial paralysis. Doctors said that an operation to remove the bullet would be too risky and suggested that with further treatment and physical therapy, Bisht may recover some movement.

At the end of 2001, Bisht was still hospitalized at the All India Institute of Medical Sciences, where he remained largely immobile. "I have been here for nearly a month," Bisht told *The Asian*

Age newspaper in January. "For days I could not move my hands. Now my left hand has shown some life. But my legs seem to have no life."

INDONESIA

MAY 24

Agus Wijanarko, *Republika*
`ATTACKED`
Yon Daryon, Rajawali Citra Televisi Indonesia
`ATTACKED`
Thomas, Televisi Pendidikan Indonesia
`ATTACKED`
Marsis, *Pikiran Rakyat*
`ATTACKED`
Bambang Mudjono, *Radar Tegal*
`ATTACKED`
Sarjono, *Sinar Pagi*
`ATTACKED`

Six journalists were attacked by supporters of President Abdurrahman Wahid during a rally in Tegal, Central Java.

The attack was perpetrated by members of a group calling itself Laskar Diponegoro, which was composed of Wahid supporters from both the ruling National Awakening Party and the Nahdlatul Ulama, a grassroots Islamic organization.

On May 24, Laskar Diponegoro held a violent rally against Wahid's political rival, the National Mandate Party (PAN), during which the house of a PAN official was torched.

After noticing the presence of journalists, several protesters abused them verbally and then assaulted them with metal poles and sticks, according to local and international news sources.

Six reporters were injured in the

attack, including Wijanarko of the Jakarta-based daily newspaper *Republika*, who was beaten so severely that he suffered a concussion and spent five days in the hospital. The other injured journalists were Daryon, of the private television station Rajawali Citra Televisi Indonesia; Thomas, of the private television station Televisi Pendidikan Indonesia (like many Indonesians, he is known by only one name); Marsis, of the daily newspaper *Pikiran Rakyat*; Mudjono, of the local newspaper *Radar Tegal*; and Sarjono, of the national newspaper *Sinar Pagi*.

On May 31, CPJ sent a letter to President Wahid urging him to ensure that those responsible for these attacks are prosecuted. On June 13, CPJ received a personal e-mail message from the president's daughter Yenny Zannuba Wahid, a former journalist who was then working as an adviser to her father. She wrote that President Wahid had ordered a special investigation into this incident and pledged that "we'll try as hard as we can to prevent [such attacks] from happening in the future."

On July 23, Wahid was impeached by the Indonesian Peoples' Consultative Assembly, and Megawati Sukarnoputri was appointed president. At year's end, the status of the investigation ordered by Wahid was unclear.

MAY 25

Torgeir Norling, free-lancer
HARASSED

Norling, a Norwegian free-lance journalist based in Bangkok, was stopped by Indonesian security forces as he was traveling by bus from Banda Aceh to Lhokseumawe, in Aceh Province, along with two Acehnese human rights activists.

At a checkpoint about 50 kilometers (31 miles) outside of Lhokseumawe, three police officers boarded the bus and headed straight for Norling, according to his own account. One of the officers pointed to him and said, "You are a journalist," and ordered Norling and his two colleagues off the bus. Police took the group to the Jeumpa police headquarters in Bireuen City, Agence France-Presse (AFP) reported.

Norling told CPJ that police and army officers interrogated the group for five hours, quizzing them about the purpose of their trip to Lhokseumawe. Police detained them overnight and early the next morning ordered them to take a bus to Lhokseumawe and report to the main police station there on arrival.

At the Lhokseumawe Police Station, Norling and his Acehnese associates were interrogated for about two hours. They were released abruptly after one of the officers received a phone call that Norling believes may have come from a senior official in the provincial capital, Banda Aceh. By that time, AFP had already reported the group's arrest.

Norling said that while he was not officially expelled from the province, an officer told him he would be in danger if he stayed in Aceh. He interpreted this warning as a veiled threat.

Aceh police operations spokesman Commissioner Sudharsono told AFP that the group was detained and interrogated because Norling did not have official authorization to report in the restive province. "We expect all foreign journalists to get letters of permission from the government if they want to come to Aceh, because the armed forces are responsible [for their safety]," Sudharsono said.

Philippe Simon, documentary filmmaker
IMPRISONED
Johan van Den Eynde, documentary filmmaker
IMPRISONED

Simon and van Den Eynde, two Belgian documentary filmmakers, were taken hostage on June 7 by a faction of the separatist Free Papua Movement (Organisasi Papua Merdeka, or OPM). The two had been working in a remote area in Irian Jaya, also known as Papua. They were last seen when they left for the jungle east of Nabire, a coastal city about 500 kilometers (310 miles) southwest of the provincial capital, Jayapura.

The OPM is fighting for independence from Indonesian rule, and the faction responsible for the kidnapping apparently believed that taking the two filmmakers hostage would attract international attention to their cause.

After weeks of difficult and often confusing negotiations involving church mediators, Belgian and Indonesian officials, Papuan activists, and the Jakarta office of the Southeast Asian Press Alliance (SEAPA), Simon and van Den Eynde were released on August 16.

Titus Murib, leader of the OPM faction responsible for the kidnapping, told a representative from the Jakarta office of SEAPA who witnessed the release that OPM would guarantee the safety of journalists reporting in the restive territory.

CPJ issued two statements expressing concern about the filmmakers' safety. In

an August 16 press release welcoming their release, CPJ said, "We hope the OPM pledge means the group will never again seek to achieve its propaganda goals by kidnapping journalists."

CPJ also called on rebel groups and state security forces in Indonesia to respect the right of all journalists to work without fear of harassment, abduction, or other reprisals.

Serambi Indonesia
THREATENED, CENSORED

Serambi Indonesia, the largest daily newspaper in Aceh Province, suspended publication under pressure from the separatist Free Aceh Movement (Gerakan Aceh Merdeka, or GAM).

GAM leaders were angered by an article about the massacre of 31 villagers in eastern Aceh that appeared in the August 10 edition of *Serambi*. The police held GAM responsible for the killings, while GAM blamed Indonesian security forces.

A GAM spokesman called the newspaper's offices after the article was published and accused *Serambi* of siding with the government in its coverage of the massacre.

"I have forbidden [the newspaper] to publish lies," a GAM spokesman told The Associated Press. "People here say they will burn down the building and kill workers."

Representatives of GAM told *Serambi* management that they could not guarantee the safety of newspaper employees if they continued publishing, according to the Jakarta office of the Bangkok-based Southeast Asian Press Alliance.

Aceh is the scene of a 26-year-old struggle between armed separatist rebels and Indonesian security forces. Journalists who report on the conflict routinely face pressure from all sides, including GAM, the police, and the Indonesian military.

In June, *Serambi Indonesia* was also forced to suspend operations temporarily, due in part to threats from GAM.

On August 24, *Serambi* resumed publication.

OCTOBER 15

Medo Malianza, Metro TV
`ATTACKED`
Agung Nugroho, Indosiar TV
`ATTACKED`
Dadang, Reuters
`ATTACKED`
Lamhot Aritonang, *Pantur Daily*
`ATTACKED`

Police assaulted four local journalists covering an anti-American demonstration in front of the House of Representatives in Jakarta, according to Indonesian and international news sources.

The victims were: Malianza, a cameraman for Metro TV; Nugroho, a cameraman from Indosiar TV; Dadang, a Reuters photographer who, like many Indonesians, uses only one name; and Aritonang, a photographer from the newspaper *Pantur Daily*.

The police were trying to disperse a rally of some 1,500 people organized by several Islamic groups to protest U.S. military action in Afghanistan and demand that the Indonesian government sever diplomatic relations with the United States. After firing warning shots, police attacked the crowd using tear gas, water cannons, and clubs.

As Malianza filmed police officers vandalizing a car, police beat him and forced him to hand over the tape. During the melée, officers damaged several cars, including one owned by Reuters, according to the *Jakarta Post*. Police also seized a videotape from Nugroho.

After several local press organizations protested the actions, Jakarta police chief Sofjan Jacoeb formally apologized and returned the confiscated videotapes to Metro TV and Indosiar.

NEPAL

MARCH 10

Krishna Sen, *Janadesh*
`IMPRISONED, HARASSED, MISSING`

Sen, editor of the weekly *Janadesh*, contacted journalists and asked them to appear at Rajbiraj Jail the next morning, when he expected to be released, following a March 8 Supreme Court ruling that his long detention violated Nepal's habeus corpus protections. But when the press arrived at the jail on March 11, Hom Nath Khatri, a prison official, told them that Sen had been released the previous night. Local journalists and human rights advocates promptly reported him missing.

Police first arrested Sen in Kathmandu on April 19, 1999, and detained him under provisions of the Public Security Act, which allows preventive detention of those considered to be a threat to domestic security and tranquility. CPJ believes the arrest was prompted by that week's edition of *Janadesh*, which featured an interview with Baburam Bhattarai, one of the leaders of the Maoist insurgency in Nepal. On the day Sen was arrested, police reportedly confiscated 20,000 copies of the weekly in order to prevent the interview from being widely read.

The Supreme Court first ordered Sen's release on August 10, 1999. But according to his attorney, Yekraj Bhandari, police and district officials conspired to keep the journalist in detention by forging release papers and then rearresting him days later on false charges.

Prison authorities forced Sen to sign papers certifying his release from Bhadragol Jail in Kathmandu on February 9, 2000, according to Bhandari. Sen was not released, however. Instead, he was secretly transferred to the southeastern district of Siraha, where police said he was detained on February 13. Authorities then charged him with carrying illegal weapons under the provisions of the Arms and Ammunitions Act. Around August 2000, Sen was transferred yet again, this time to Rajbiraj Jail.

Legal proceedings in Sen's case were postponed repeatedly throughout 2000. On March 8, 2001, the Supreme Court of Nepal ruled his detention illegal and ordered his release.

On March 12, CPJ sent a letter to Prime Minister Girija Prasad Koirala asking him to ensure that the Supreme Court's order was enforced, and to confirm publicly that Sen had been released. Under mounting national and international pressure, the government ordered Sen's release from Jaleswor Jail, in Mahottari District, where he had been transferred after his purported March 10 "release" from Rajbiraj Jail.

On the afternoon of March 15, Sen was turned over to a delegation from the Federation of Nepalese Journalists.

JUNE 6

Yubaraj Ghimire, *Kantipur*
IMPRISONED
Kailash Shirohiya, Kantipur Publications
IMPRISONED
Binod Raj Gyawali, Kantipur Publications
IMPRISONED

Ghimire, editor of the Nepali-language daily *Kantipur*; Shirohiya, managing director of Kantipur Publications; and Gyawali, director of the publishing house, were arrested at around 6 p.m. and told they were being charged with treason, according to sources in Kathmandu.

The charges stemmed from that day's edition of *Kantipur*, which contained an article by Maoist rebel leader Baburam Bhattarai that called on Nepalese citizens to reject the newly crowned King Gyanendra as a "puppet of Indian expansionist forces."

Bhattarai's article also challenged official and media accounts of the June 1 palace massacre, in which King Birendra and nine other members of the royal family were killed. Bhattarai criticized the new king and called on Nepal's army to take action to "safeguard the nation, although they could not save their king."

All three journalists were released on June 15, though Ghimire was required to post bail of 2,000 rupees (US$27). They were ordered to appear in court on July 16 to face sedition charges.

The July 16 trial was postponed, and on August 17, the government withdrew the charges against the three journalists.

CPJ issued a June 6 statement condemning the journalists' arrest, a June 12 letter to Prime Minister Girija Prasad Koirala protesting their prolonged detention, and a June 18 press release urging that the sedition charges be withdrawn.

NOVEMBER 26

All journalists
THREATENED, LEGAL ACTION

On Monday, November 26, King Gyanendra declared a state of emergency and suspended civil liberties, including press freedom, in response to an upsurge of violence between Maoist rebels and government security forces that killed at least 100 people over the previous weekend.

Articles of the constitution that were suspended included those guaranteeing freedom of expression and opinion (Article 12.2a), press and publication rights (Article 13), and the right to information (Article 16). Under Nepalese law, a state of emergency can last for up to six months.

The palace also announced on November 26 that the government could detain suspected terrorists for up to six months without trial. That same day, the Interior Ministry publicly declared the Communist Party of Nepal-Maoist (CPN-M) to be a terrorist organization. The ministry added that any organizations or individuals supporting the CPN-M and its activities would also be considered terrorists, according to local news reports.

On November 29, CPJ sent a letter to Prime Minister Sher Bahadur Deuba protesting the government's use of the emergency measures to harass and persecute journalists who report on rebel activities or who work for publications seen as sympathetic to the Maoist cause.

Om Sharma, *Janadisha*
IMPRISONED
Dipendra Rokaya, *Janadisha*
IMPRISONED
Govinda Acharya, *Janadesh*
IMPRISONED
Khil Bahadur Bhandari, *Janadesh*
IMPRISONED
Deepak Sapkota, *Janadesh*
IMPRISONED
Manarishi Dhital, *Dishabodh*
IMPRISONED
Ishwarchandra Gyawali, *Dishabodh*
IMPRISONED

On November 26, police raided the offices of three publications closely associated with Nepal's Maoist movement: the daily *Janadisha*, the weekly *Janadesh*, and the monthly *Dishabodh*. The police arrested nine staff members, including seven journalists, and also confiscated equipment and written materials. The arrested journalists included Sharma, an editor for *Janadisha*; Rokaya, whose position at *Janadisha* was not known; Archarya, an editor of *Janadesh*; Bhandari, executive editor of *Janadesh*; Sapkota, a reporter for *Janadesh*; Dhital, a reporter for *Dishabodh*; and Gyawali, executive editor of *Dishabodh*.

All were arrested about two hours before the government declared a state of emergency and enacted the Terrorist and Destructive Activities (Control and Punishment) ordinance, which named the Communist Party of Nepal-Maoist (CPN-M) a terrorist organization and therefore illegal. The government announcement also stipulated that any organizations or individuals supporting the CPN-M and its activities would be considered terrorists, according to local news reports. Under the new regulations, terrorism carries a life sentence.

On January 9, 2002, lawyers for the journalists filed a habeas corpus petition to the Supreme Court, which then issued a show cause notice to the government. The government responded that six of the journalists were charged under the terrorism ordinance for engaging in activities supporting the Maoist movement, according to a lawyer for the journalists. At press time, the government had not yet issued a response for Om Sharma's case, and the hearing date for all the cases would not be set until it did. The defense lawyers argue that the journalists' detention is illegal because they were arrested before the terrorist ordinance was officially declared.

NOVEMBER 28

All journalists
`CENSORED`

The Ministry of Information and Communication issued a directive prohibiting press coverage of numerous topics related to the country's civil war. The directive came after King Gyanendra declared a state of emergency on November 26, when the government suspended civil liberties, including press freedom. The statement also encouraged the media to publish official news and reports "regarding bravery and achievements of [the] Royal Nepal Army, police, and civil servants."

The ministry did not specify the penalties for violating the November 28 order.

"Matters not to be published [or] broadcast" included:

a. "Anything that aims to create hatred and disrespect against His Majesty the King and the Royal Family."

b. "Anything that is likely to harm [the] sovereignty and territorial integrity of the Kingdom of Nepal."

c. "Anything that disturbs security, peace and order in the Kingdom of Nepal."

d. "Anything that is likely to create misunderstanding and communal hatred among the people of different castes, communities, religions, classes and regions."

e. "Anything that is likely to hurt the decent behavior, morale, and social dignity of people."

f. "News that [is] against the spirit of the Constitution of the Kingdom of Nepal, 1990."

g. "News that hurts the fundamental values of multi-party democracy."

h. "Anything that is likely to harm national dignity, create social disintegration and instigate terror."

i. "Anything that is likely to create hatred against [the] Royal Nepal Army, police and civil servants and lower their moral[s] and dignity."

j. "News that support[s] Maoist terrorist[s] including individual[s] or groups."

k. "Any matters that aim at overthrowing elected government."

l. "Matters that are likely to create unusual fear and terror among people."

m. "Matters that misinterpret and disrespect and underestimate any caste, language, religion and culture."

Kathmandu Post
`CENSORED`

The government seized all copies of the *Kathmandu Post*, the country's largest English-language daily, after the newspaper ran a photo of several Maoist militants, according to sources in Nepal.

Government officials then warned the paper's editors not to publish articles or photos that "glorify" the Maoist movement.

In a statement issued the same day, the Ministry of Information and Communication listed several proscribed topics, including reports that "create hatred and disrespect against His Majesty the King and the Royal Family" or "harm national dignity, create social disintegration and instigate terror."

On Monday, November 26, King Gyanendra declared a state of emergency throughout the country in response to increasing violence between Maoist rebels and government forces that killed at least 100 people over the previous weekend.

The decree suspended several articles of the constitution, including those guaranteeing freedom of the press.

CPJ protested these abrogations in a November 29 letter to Prime Minister Sher Bahadur Deuba.

Dev Kumar Yadav, *Janadesh*
IMPRISONED

Yadav, a reporter for the weekly *Janadesh*, was arrested in Siraha. Although the circumstances surrounding his detention were unclear, at year's end he was being held in Siraha, according to the Informal Sector Service Center (INSEC), a Kathmandu-based human rights organization.

DECEMBER 2

Ganga Bista, Nepal Television,
Chautari Times

Shankar Khanal, Radio Nepal,
Spacetime Daily
IMPRISONED

Bista, a reporter for Nepal Television and *Chautari Times*, and Khanal, a reporter for Radio Nepal and *Spacetime Daily*, were arrested by the army along with *Nepal Samacharpatra* reporter Indira Giri, according to INSEC. Giri was released on December 6.

DECEMBER 6

Sama Thapa, *Yugayan*
IMPRISONED

After his arrest in Kailali District, Thapa, publisher of *Yugayan*, was brought to the local police station in Tikapur, according to the Federation of Nepalese Journalists (FNJ) and INSEC. He was then shifted to the Regional Police Unit Office in Dhangadhi, where he was being held at year's end.

Chitra Choudhary, *Nawa Paricharcha*
IMPRISONED

Choudhary is an adviser-editor of *Nawa Paricharcha* weekly in Tikapur and the former editor-in-chief of *Yugayan*. He was also the principal of the National Lower Secondary School in Patharaiya. School personnel arrested him on the morning of December 6. He was brought with Sama Thapa to police stations in Tikapur and Dhangadhi. At year's end, he was being held in Army Barracks, Dhangadhi, according to INSEC.

DECEMBER 21

Komal Nath Baral, *Swaviman*
IMPRISONED

Baral, an editor at *Swaviman*

weekly, was arrested at his home in Kaski district, Pokhara, according to FNJ and INSEC.

Prem Bahadur Diyali, *Blast Daily*
IMPRISONED

Diyali, a reporter at *Blast Daily*, was arrested by police at his residence in Sunsari District, according to FNJ and INSEC. He was put under preventive detention on December 23. Local journalists have said *Blast*, based in Dharan, was targeted because it had published reports criticizing local leaders.

DECEMBER 25

Badri Prasad Sharma, *Baglung Weekly*
IMPRISONED

Sharma, editor and publisher of *Baglung Weekly*, was arrested by security personnel from his house in Baglung, according to INSEC and FNJ.

DECEMBER 27

Chandra Man Shrestha, *Janadisha*
IMPRISONED

Shrestha, a managing director at the daily *Janadisha*, was arrested from Maharajgunj, Kathmandu. His whereabouts were unknown at year's end.

DECEMBER 31

Janardan Biyogi, *Swaviman*
IMPRISONED

Biyogi, a subeditor of *Swaviman* weekly, was arrested by the army in Kaski District, Pokhara, according to FNJ.

Pushkar Lal Shrestha, *Nepal Samacharpatra*

HARASSED
Kapil Kafle, *Nepal Samacharpatra*
HARASSED

Shrestha, publisher and editor-in-chief of *Nepal Samacharpatra*, and Kafle, an editor at the paper, were summoned for interrogation by Chief District Officer Kirti Bahadur Chand, the country's top law enforcement official.

Chand telephoned Shrestha and ordered him and Kafle to visit his office immediately to discuss an article in that day's paper that quoted the leader of Nepal's Maoist rebels. Chand told the journalists to refrain from publishing any statements from the Communist Party of Nepal's Maoist faction, which the government declared a "terrorist organization" on November 26.

On November 26, King Gyanendra declared a state of emergency in Nepal and suspended civil liberties, including press freedom. On November 28, the Ministry of Information and Communication issued a list of proscribed topics for the media, among them any expression of support for the Maoists and news likely to "lower the morale and dignity" of the security forces.

Shrestha and Kafle argued that the article in question could not have violated the ministry's decree because the story described the decline of the Maoists' influence in urban areas and praised the efforts of the army and police. They were released after about an hour of questioning.

PAKISTAN

JANUARY 29

The Frontier Post
CENSORED, ATTACKED

Munawwar Mohsin, *The Frontier Post*
IMPRISONED
Imtiaz Hussain, *The Frontier Post*
IMPRISONED
Qazi Ghulam Sarwar, *The Frontier Post*
IMPRISONED
Aftab Ahmed, *The Frontier Post*
IMPRISONED
Mehmood Afridi, *The Frontier Post*
LEGAL ACTION
Javed Nazir, *The Frontier Post*
LEGAL ACTION
Kifayatullah, *Maidan*
HARASSED

On January 29, *The Frontier Post* published a letter to the editor entitled "Why Muslims Hate Jews," which included derogatory references to the Prophet Muhammad.

Although senior management at the newspaper claimed the letter was inserted into the copy by mistake and apologized for failing to stop its publication, district officials responded to complaints from local religious leaders by shutting down the paper and ordering the immediate arrest of seven staff members on charges of blasphemy. In Pakistan, anyone accused of blasphemy is subject to immediate arrest without due process safeguards; those found guilty may be sentenced to death.

That evening, police sealed the offices and the printing press of *The Frontier Post*, and arrested Mohsin, sub-editor; Hussain, chief reporter; Sarwar, feature writer; and Ahmed, news editor, along with computer operator Wajihul Hassan. Police did not arrest the two others charged—Afridi, the paper's managing editor, and Nazir, joint editor—since both went into hiding.

On January 30, *The Frontier Post* placed prominent advertisements on the front pages of the country's major Urdu- and English-language dailies, noting that it "profoundly regrets the publication...of highly blasphemous material masquerading as a letter to the editor, and identifies with the injured feelings of the nation over the issue." Afridi, the paper's managing editor, urged the government to launch an immediate judicial inquiry into the circumstances of the letter's publication.

Despite the paper's unequivocal public apology, religious groups continued to stage violent demonstrations, with some protesters calling for the journalists to be executed. On January 30, hundreds of demonstrators gathered outside *The Frontier Post*'s offices and set fire to the building housing the paper's printing press. The fire caused extensive property damage. Local journalists told CPJ that police stationed outside the building did not act swiftly to stop the destruction, and charged that some officers even aided the arsonists.

On January 31, at approximately 6:30 p.m., police raided the offices of the Urdu-language daily *Maidan*, the sister publication of *The Frontier Post*. Police detained about six people from the newspaper, including the news editor, Kifayatullah (who, like some Pakistanis, uses only one name). Local journalists told CPJ that the group was briefly taken in for interrogation, as police were trying to determine the whereabouts of Afridi.

At the direction of the federal government, authorities in Northwest Frontier Province established a one-man tribunal to investigate the circumstances in which the offending letter had been published. On February 15, as this inquiry was ongoing, Hussain, Sarwar, and Hassan were released on bail.

On March 9, Justice Qaim Jan Khan submitted a report to the provincial government summarizing his findings. Though the judge found that the letter was published due to "negligence" and not to any malicious intent, the government ultimately decided to proceed with its prosecution of the journalists on blasphemy charges.

On March 13, Ahmed was released on bail.

The Frontier Post was forced to suspend publication until June 26, when it was relaunched from the eastern city of Lahore.

At the end of 2001, the blasphemy case was ongoing, although Munawwar Mohsin was the only *Frontier Post* journalist still in prison. Mohsin admitted responsibility for publishing the letter, which he said he had not read carefully. He told *The New York Times* that he "could never think of abusing our Holy Prophet," but confessed that, having only recently completed a drug rehabilitation program, his mind may have been slightly addled.

CPJ sent a letter to Chief Executive Pervez Musharraf on January 31, noting that in light of the prompt public apology offered by *The Frontier Post*, punitive action against the journalists was unwarranted and would only contribute to a hostile atmosphere for the press.

MARCH 28

Shakil Shaikh, *The News*
ATTACKED

Shaikh, chief reporter for the national English-language daily *The News*, was abducted around midday by a group of five unidentified men riding in a jeep. After cutting off Shaikh's car on the Kashmir Highway, less than a mile from the main commercial center of Islamabad, the men forced Shaikh into their jeep and drove him to a deserted area on the outskirts of the city.

Shaikh, blindfolded and with his hands bound by rope, was then beaten for more than three hours. The assailants kicked Shaikh, stomped on his body, and struck him on the head with the butt of an AK-47.

"You write too much. Now you will not write anymore," Shaikh's assailants said repeatedly as they beat him. They also threatened to harm his parents, wife, and children.

After several hours, the men abandoned Shaikh and drove off. He eventually managed to untie himself and found that his car had been left for him nearby. Shaikh drove back to his home in Islamabad and was then taken by ambulance to the Pakistan Institute of Medical Sciences for treatment.

Colleagues who saw him that evening said that he suffered from severe emotional trauma in addition to his physical injuries.

Sources at *The News* said the precise motive for the attack was unclear, since Shaikh reported on a wide range of political and military issues. The journalist told colleagues he could not identify his captors.

On March 29, CPJ wrote a letter to Chief Executive Pervez Musharraf urging him to ensure that the men who brutalized Shaikh were brought to justice. There was no progress in the case by year's end.

JUNE 3

Jamil Yousaf, *free-lancer*
`LEGAL ACTION`
Mohammed Shahid Chaudhry,
Mohasib
`IMPRISONED`
Raja Mohammed Haroon, *Mohasib*
`IMPRISONED`
Shakil Ahmed Tahirkheli, *Mohasib*
`IMPRISONED`
Mohammed Zaman Khan, *Mohasib*
`IMPRISONED`
Mohasib
`CENSORED`

On June 3, police in Abbottabad registered a case against Yousaf and two editors at the Urdu-language daily *Mohasib*, charging them with blasphemy under sections 295-A and 295-C of the Penal Code. Section 295-C carries a mandatory death penalty, according to a Federal Shariat Court decision of October 1990.

The charges arose from a May 29 *Mohasib* article titled "The Beard and Islam," by Yousaf, a well-known poet and author. The article contested the view of certain Muslim clerics that a beardless man cannot be a good Muslim. The piece also criticized the exploitation of religious faith for personal gain.

After local religious leaders protested against Yousaf's article, police went to the office of *Mohasib* on the afternoon of June 3 and began questioning Chaudhry, the newspaper's managing editor, and Haroon, a sub-editor. The two men were taken into custody on the pretext that they needed protection from religious extremists, according to a CPJ source.

When Chaudhry and Haroon said they would prefer to meet with religious leaders to explain their position, police said such a meeting could be held at the police station.

At around 8 p.m., a group of religious leaders arrived at the Cantonment Police Station, where the journalists were being held. However, instead of resolving the dispute, one of the men filed a First Information Report with police, accusing Yousaf and the *Mohasib* journalists of committing blasphemy. That night, police sealed the offices of *Mohasib*.

Chaudhry and Haroon were detained overnight at the station. The next morning, June 4, police arrested *Mohasib* news editor Tahirkheli at his home. All three journalists were remanded to police custody for two days and then transferred to Abbottabad District Jail.

Mohasib editor Zaman Khan was arrested on the night of June 8, despite having obtained pre-emptive bail from a judge in the neighboring district of Haripur.

Police also issued an arrest warrant for Yousaf, who went into hiding.

On June 14, CPJ sent a letter to Chief Executive Gen. Pervez Musharraf (who declared himself president on June 20), calling for the immediate and unconditional release of all four journalists.

As international pressure mounted to free the journalists, federal and provincial authorities took action. The Federal Ministry of Religious Affairs and the Northwest Frontier Province Law Department each issued statements arguing that the *Mohasib* article contained nothing that could be considered blasphemous.

In early July, following the provincial law department's review of the case, the inspector general of police in Northwest Frontier Province sent a notice to the senior superintendent of police in Abbottabad, urging local authorities to drop the case registered against *Mohasib* and to release the jailed editors.

However, Abbottabad officials refused, citing pressure from religious groups.

On July 18, a Sessions Court judge in Abbottabad ordered the release of the journalists on bail. The government later withdrew the case.

JULY 24

Hayat Ullah, *Ausaf*
THREATENED, LEGAL ACTION

Hayat Ullah, a correspondent for the Urdu-language daily *Ausaf* in Mirali, North Waziristan Agency, went into hiding after North Waziristan authorities ordered his arrest for reporting on clashes between local tribal groups.

According to Hayat Ullah, officials began attempting to curb his reporting in December 2000, after he published an article about an attack on the office of the North Waziristan political agent. (In Federally Administered Tribal Areas such as North Waziristan Agency, the political agent is the chief federal administrator in the territory.)

At that time, Political Agent Mohammad Mushtaq Jadoon summoned Hayat Ullah to his office and complained that the report had exposed the weakness of the local administration. Jadoon warned the journalist never to publish such stories. He also ordered him to apologize and to submit all future articles for

approval by the local administration before sending them on to *Ausaf*.

In June 2001, without consulting Jadoon, Hayat Ullah began reporting on persistent clashes between two tribal groups in the area. He told CPJ that Jadoon's assistant threatened him with arrest on July 5. On July 24, after he reported on Jadoon's criticisms of local tribal elders, he received a telephone call from another official notifying him that his arrest was imminent. On July 26, Hayat Ullah fled his home in Mirali.

Hayat Ullah told CPJ that local authorities issued an arrest warrant under the Frontier Crimes Regulation (FCR), a legacy of British colonial rule that grants virtually unchecked powers to government administrators in tribal areas. Parties accused under the FCR are denied due process of law, including the right to counsel and the right to an appeal.

The journalist told CPJ that his family members and colleagues were under extreme pressure to reveal his whereabouts. On July 26, police detained Hayat Ullah's relative Abbas Khan and told him he would be released only after Hayat Ullah turned himself in to authorities. Khan, a tribal elder and schoolteacher, was released on August 2 after a public protest led by local teachers' unions. Police also sealed the *Ausaf* office in Mirali and a newspaper distribution center in Speenwam that Hayat Ullah runs.

On August 7, CPJ wrote a letter to President Pervez Musharraf expressing outrage at the persecution of Hayat Ullah. Local sources said that local authorities then backed down in the face of international attention to Hayat Ullah's case. The journalist was able to resume his work without further harassment.

SEPTEMBER 1

Newsweek
CENSORED

Pakistani censors ruled that the current issue of *Newsweek* magazine could only circulate in the country if the local distributor agreed to cut out an article by Zahid Hussain, a *Newsweek* correspondent in Islamabad.

The censored article, titled "Talking Is Dangerous," was about the prosecution of Shaikh Mohammed Younus, a professor who had recently been sentenced to death under Pakistan's controversial blasphemy laws. The prosecution claimed that Younus had insulted the Prophet Mohammad.

Customs officials blocked distribution of the magazine and then referred the matter to the government's Press Information Department. On September 1, press department officials ordered *Newsweek*'s local distributor, Liberty Books, to remove the article before circulating copies of the magazine, according to international wire reports.

Local journalists said that *Newsweek*, which normally begins circulating on Tuesdays, did not appear until Sunday, September 2, after the article had been ripped out.

On September 4, CPJ issued a statement condemning Pakistani authorities' decision to censor the article.

SEPTEMBER 1

Asadullah, free-lancer
KILLED (MOTIVE UNCONFIRMED)

Asadullah, an occasional contributor to the news agency Kashmir Press International (KPI), was shot dead on the streets of Karachi by unidentified gunmen. KPI is run by the Jamaat-i-Islami, a conservative religious party. Local journalists said Asadullah was also an active member of the party, and that members of a rival political party may have killed him. The motive behind the shooting was unclear at year's end.

OCTOBER 5

Olivier Ravanello, LCI
IMPRISONED
Jérôme Marcantetti, LCI
IMPRISONED
Rifatullah Orakzai, *Khyber Mail*
IMPRISONED
Muhammad Iqbal Afridi, *Al-Akhbar*
IMPRISONED
Syed Karim, free-lancer
IMPRISONED

Authorities in Khyber Agency arrested Ravanello, a reporter for the French television channel LCI; Marcantetti, a cameraman and producer for LCI; Orakzai, a reporter for the Peshawar-based English-language newspaper *Khyber Mail*; Afridi, a district correspondent based in Bara, Khyber Agency, who contributes to the national Urdu-language daily *Al-Akhbar*; and Karim, a local free-lance journalist.

The French journalists were released without charge on October 8 after officials from the French embassy intervened. The other journalists remained in jail on the authority of the political agent of Khyber Agency, Dr. Fida Wazir.

Political agents exercise virtually unchecked power in the Federally Administered Tribal Areas, which include Khyber Agency, and have routinely used their authority to punish journalists for their reporting.

On October 10, CPJ sent a letter to the governor of Northwest Frontier Province, Syed Iftikhar Hussain Shah, asking him to intervene with local authorities to secure the journalists' immediate and unconditional release.

Orakzai, Afridi, and Karim were released on October 18, according to local journalists.

OCTOBER 8

Susan Taylor Martin, *St. Petersburg Times*
THREATENED, HARASSED
Jamie Francis, *St. Petersburg Times*
THREATENED, HARASSED

Martin, a reporter for the *St. Petersburg Times*, and Francis, a photographer for the paper, were threatened and harassed by Pakistanis angered by the recent U.S.-led bombing campaign against neighboring Afghanistan. The two were reporting in Sakot, a town in Pakistan's Northwest Frontier Province.

At around 11 a.m., Martin and Francis arrived in Sakot by car, along with a Pakistani guide and driver. When they encountered a large crowd of anti-American demonstrators, Francis got out of the car to take photographs. Several police officers rushed toward the journalists and advised them to leave the area immediately.

Their guide led the journalists to a nearby building, which turned out to be a mosque housing a *madrassa*, or Islamic school. Francis started taking pictures through a window of the demonstrators outside, and Martin began interviewing the men gathering around them.

In an account of the incident that she wrote for the *St. Petersburg Times*, Martin said the group began getting larger and angrier, with masses of demonstrators coming up from the street and blocking the stairs to the exit.

One man she interviewed said, "I request you to leave this place. People are emotional and may do you some harm." Another shouted "Get out!" repeatedly in Martin's face. Someone else started ominously quizzing the pair about where they were from and for what media outlets they worked.

Several armed police officers eventually pushed their way into the crowd and ushered Martin, Francis, and their guide out of the mosque, advising them to run to safety. The police took them to the office of the chief constable of Malakand Agency, in Northwest Frontier Province, who said, half-joking, "For you, the situation was dangerous because any person with white skin we think is Bush."

Martin credited police with "rescuing us from the mob and perhaps saving our lives."

CPJ published an alert about the incident on October 10.

OCTOBER 8

Aziz Zemouri, *Figaro Magazine*
IMPRISONED

Zemouri, a reporter for the French weekly *Figaro Magazine*, was detained by Pakistani authorities in North Waziristan Agency when Afghan officials turned him over at the border.

Zemouri told CPJ that he had entered Afghanistan on October 8 but was turned back by the Taliban at the first checkpoint over the border.

After one night at a military camp in North Waziristan Agency, local authorities sent Zemouri to Peshawar. Traveling without an escort, Zemouri tried again to cross the Afghan border. He was caught by Pakistani police as he boarded a bus.

Zemouri was held under police guard for two nights in Miranshah, North Waziristan Agency, before being escorted to Peshawar, where he was jailed. When he refused to be handcuffed to his jail cell bars, guards hit him. He was not allowed access to a lawyer or translator while members of Pakistan's Inter-Services Intelligence agency interrogated him.

Zemouri believes he was detained for crossing into a tribal area near the Afghan border without a permit.

Zemouri was not charged with any crime and was released on October 16. He returned to France on October 20.

OCTOBER 25

Aditya Sinha, *Hindustan Times*
EXPELLED
Indian journalists
HARASSED

Pakistani security officials ordered Sinha, a reporter for the Indian daily *Hindustan Times*, to leave Pakistan immediately.

Sinha had been reporting from Peshawar for more than a month and had obtained a 15-day visa extension from the Interior Ministry the previous week.

Before putting him on the first available flight out of the country, a security official told Sinha, who holds a U.S. passport, "You are a U.S. national, but on the inside you are an Indian," according to Sinha's account

published in the October 27 edition of the *Hindustan Times*.

Pakistani officials admitted privately that Indian journalists would generally not be allowed into the country, according to CPJ sources. As early as September 25, the Pakistani daily *The News* reported that the "Pakistan government is not issuing visas to Indian journalists, saying that they have nothing to report from here except anti-Pakistan stories."

This restrictive policy seriously impeded the Indian press, as well as international media companies including the BBC, which has a large South Asia bureau based in New Delhi.

Indian journalists, as well as journalists of Indian origin holding citizenship from Western countries, told CPJ that visa applications submitted in mid-September seemed to languish indefinitely in the Pakistani bureaucracy. Meanwhile, non-Indian journalists typically received visas within days, if not hours, of submitting their applications.

On October 29, CPJ sent a letter to President Pervez Musharraf, urging him to ensure that journalists would not be barred from Pakistan on the basis of their nationality or ethnic background.

NOVEMBER 9

Christina Lamb, *The Sunday Telegraph*
HARASSED, EXPELLED
Justin Sutcliffe, *The Sunday Telegraph*
HARASSED, EXPELLED

At around 2:30 a.m., five male police officers in plain clothes and two policewomen forced their way into Lamb's hotel room in Quetta and ordered *The Sunday Telegraph* correspondent to accompany them. The officers refused to say which agency they were from, though Lamb suspected they were members of Pakistan's Inter-Services Intelligence agency (ISI).

When Lamb refused to leave, an officer finally showed her a faxed copy of a letter from the Interior Ministry ordering her expulsion and that of *Sunday Telegraph* photographer Sutcliffe on the grounds that the pair had been "acting in a manner prejudicial to the external affairs and national security of Pakistan."

After arresting Sutcliffe, the officers led him and Lamb outside the Serena Hotel and ordered the journalists into separate vehicles. Sutcliffe and Lamb refused to split up and were eventually taken together to a building adjacent to the Quetta railway station, where they were detained overnight. In an account of the incident published later in *The Sunday Telegraph*, Lamb wrote that she "wondered if anyone would ever hear of us again."

The next day, armed guards took the two journalists to the Quetta airport and put them on a flight to Islamabad. Fortunately, they were met at the airport by a member of the British Parliament, Paul Marsden, who was at the end of a fact-finding mission to Afghan refugee camps. Marsden had learned that morning of the pair's arrest and spent hours trying to find them. Lamb later wrote that their treatment improved markedly after Marsden came on the scene.

In Islamabad, the journalists were taken to the immigration director's office and allowed to meet a British consular official. The assistant director of immigration denied any knowledge

of the reasons behind the deportation order. Despite repeated requests, the journalists were never permitted to speak to a government official who could explain their treatment. That night, officers took Lamb and Sutcliffe to the international airport, where they were to board an early morning flight to London.

At the airport, "our 19 guards were reduced to six," Lamb wrote, but she described being treated roughly nonetheless.

Lamb claimed that she and Sutcliffe were expelled for investigating alleged ISI involvement in supplying arms to the Taliban militia in Afghanistan.

British foreign secretary Jack Straw raised the issue of the journalists' expulsion with his Pakistani counterpart, Abdul Sattar. Straw conveyed the British government's "concern" that the journalists were never informed of the charges against them and never given the opportunity to defend themselves.

Lamb was expelled from Pakistan once before, in September 1989, after writing about an alleged army plot to overthrow the government of Prime Minister Benazir Bhutto.

DECEMBER 8

Robert Fisk, *The Independent*
ATTACKED
Justin Huggler, *The Independent*
ATTACKED

Fisk, Middle East correspondent for the London daily *Independent*, was severely beaten by Afghan refugees in the village of Kila Abdullah in western Pakistan.

Fisk, his *Independent* colleague

Huggler, driver Amanullah, and translator Fayyaz Ahmed were driving past Kila Abdullah, near the Afghan border, when their car broke down. A large crowd gathered around the car and started throwing stones and hitting Huggler and Fisk. As the two reporters tried to board a bus, Fisk was dragged off, beaten, and kicked by about 60 men. The assailants were mostly Afghan refugees, according to Fisk.

In a December 10 report in *The Independent*, Fisk wrote that, "Pebbles and small stones began to bounce off my head and shoulders.... My head was suddenly struck by stones on both sides at the same time....Then a fist punched me in the face, splintering my glasses on my nose, another hand grabbed at the spare pair of spectacles round my neck and ripped the leather container from the cord."

Fisk was rescued when a man escorted him away from the skirmish and into a police van. The police brought him to a Red Cross and Red Crescent convoy, where he received medical treatment. Huggler was not harmed.

PAPUA NEW GUINEA

MARCH 20

Kevin Ricketts, Australian Associated Press
`ATTACKED`
Richard Dinnen, Australian Broadcasting Corporation
`ATTACKED`
Peter Dip, Australian Broadcasting Corporation
`ATTACKED`

Three Australian journalists were attacked by soldiers during a military riot in the capital, Port Moresby.

In mid-March, armed soldiers staged a violent protest against government proposals to reduce the size of the armed forces. The soldiers were also angered by rumors that Australian troops would be deployed on the island.

About 100 soldiers stole weapons from the barracks armory. When Prime Minister Mekere Morauta failed to show for a meeting with the protesters, the soldiers rioted and attacked journalists reporting on the conflict. Ricketts, Dinnen, and Dip were beaten by soldiers before being escorted away by police.

Australian Broadcasting Corporation reporter Dinnen said he was struck by a length of pipe. A soldier then told him, that he "knew where I lived and that he would deal with 'you *** Australians' in a most violent manner," according to Dinnen. During the scuffle, soldiers stole ABC equipment, including Dinnen's two-way radio.

PHILIPPINES

JANUARY 3

Roland Ureta, DYKR Radio
`KILLED`

Radio journalist Ureta was gunned down on the night of January 3 when two motorcycle-riding men waylaid him en route from Kalibo, the capital of Aklan Province, to the town of Lezo.

Ureta was program director of the radio station DYKR, an affiliate of the Radio Mindanao Network. Police estimated that he was killed within an hour of leaving the radio station, where he had just hosted "Agong Nightwatch," his evening radio program.

Ureta was apparently murdered as a result of his radio commentaries, which included pieces about local government corruption and police involvement in the drug trade.

Mohammad Yusop, DXID Radio
KILLED (MOTIVE UNCONFIRMED)

Yusop, a commentator for the radio station DXID in Pagadian City, was shot in the back of the head by two men on a motorcycle while he was riding in a three-wheel pedicab. He died on the spot.

Yusop hosted a religious program and was not known to have broadcast any controversial reports. The station manager at DXID, owned by the Islamic Radio Broadcasting Company, said that he was not aware of any threats against Yusop, and no group claimed responsibility for his murder.

Candelario Cayona, DXLL Radio
KILLED

At about 6 a.m. on May 30, three unidentified men ambushed Cayona, a radio commentator for the local station DXLL, as he left home on his motorcycle to host a morning broadcast. Cayona died on the spot from four gunshot wounds, including two to the face. The assailants, all identified as young males, fled the scene.

Cayona was an outspoken commentator who often criticized local politicians, the military, and Muslim separatist guerrillas. The journalist had recently received several death threats, including an on-air threat that was

phoned in by Abu Sabaya, spokesman for the guerrilla group Abu Sayyaf. Although Cayona reported the threats to station officials, he was not escorted by a bodyguard on the morning of the attack.

Cayona is the second DXLL staffer to be murdered in recent years. In 1998, Rey Bancayrin, another outspoken commentator for the station, was actually killed on the air when two unidentified gunmen burst into the studio and shot him dead.

Joy Mortel, *Mindoro Guardian*
KILLED (MOTIVE UNCONFIRMED)

Mortel, a reporter for the *Mindoro Guardian*, was killed in her home in Barangay Talabanhan, Occidental Mindoro Province, according to local press reports. Two unidentified armed men reportedly shot Mortel after a heated argument. She died from multiple gunshot wounds.

The motive for Mortel's murder remained unclear at year's end. Local police told the *Manila Times* that communist rebels had targeted Mortel because of her allegedly questionable financial dealings relating to local cooperatives she had organized in the region. However, police did not exclude the possibility that the murder was related to her journalism.

DYHB Radio
ATTACKED

A bomb exploded in the early morning hours of June 6 outside DYHB Radio Station in Bacolod City, Negros Occidental Province, injuring two bystanders and a security guard and tearing a three-meter hole in a wall.

DYHB is known for its hard-hitting reports on local crime and drug syndicates, according to the Manila-based Center for Media Freedom and Responsibility (CMFR). The station had also broadcast reports on the military's battle against Abu Sayyaf, a separatist guerrilla group that at the time was holding 13 Filipino and American hostages. DYHB is part of the Radio Mindanao Network (RMN), which aired interviews with Abu Sabaya, spokesperson for the separatists.

The station manager at DYHB linked the bombing to the station's coverage of the Abu Sayyaf hostage crisis, although local journalists argued that DYHB's coverage of crime and corruption could also be a factor, according to CMFR. Local police said the ingredients of the bomb would be available only to bomb experts or the military.

SINGAPORE

APRIL 19

Foreign broadcast media
CENSORED

The Singaporean Parliament passed a bill designed to curb foreign broadcast coverage of local issues. The new law gives the government broad power to restrict or suspend broadcasters for "engaging in domestic politics."

With Singapore's local media overwhelmingly controlled by the ruling People's Action Party, foreign media have been a crucial source of independent news in the country. The legislation, an amendment to the Singapore Broadcasting Authority Act,

would affect the operations of the BBC, CNN, CNBC, Bloomberg, and the Hong Kong-based Chinese Television Network.

The legislation "makes it clear to foreign broadcasters that whilst they can sell their services to Singaporeans, they should not interfere with our domestic politics," said Information Minister Lee Yock Suan, according to Agence France-Presse. "Foreign broadcasters are outsiders and not participants on our political scene."

Foreign print media are already subject to similar legislation.

CPJ protested the legislation in a statement issued on April 19.

NOVEMBER 16

Robert Ho, free-lancer
IMPRISONED, LEGAL ACTION

Ho, a free-lance journalist, was arrested after posting an online essay that accused government officials of breaking the law during the 1997 elections.

After being charged with posting online content that was "likely to lead to a breach of peace," Ho was forced to undergo a psychiatric evaluation. On November 30, he posted bail of Singapore $5,000 (US$2,778).

Ho is the first person to be charged under legislation regulating Internet content that was passed in the run-up to the November 3 general elections. The regulations stipulate that Web sites not administered by a political party may not publish political material during the election. On October 19, Ho's essay was posted on Singaporeans for Democracy, a nongovernmental, pro-democracy Web site.

Ho's essay accused Prime Minister

Goh Chok Tong and other People's Action Party officials of violating the law by entering polling stations without a permit on election day in 1997. He called on all Singaporeans to protest by breaking the same law during the upcoming election.

If convicted, Ho could be sentenced to three years in prison. No trial date had been set by year's end.

SOUTH KOREA

OCTOBER 23

Lee Chang Gi, *Jajuminbo*
`IMPRISONED`
Park Joon Young, *Jajuminbo*
`IMPRISONED`
Baek Oon Jong, *Jajuminbo*
`IMPRISONED`

Agents from South Korea's National Intelligence Service arrested Lee, chief editor of the monthly *Jajuminbo*, and Park and Baek, both reporters for the magazine. The journalists were charged with violating South Korea's National Security Law, which has been used to punish those who publish or broadcast views deemed anti-state, especially material seen as supportive of North Korea or of communism generally.

Jajuminbo, which also publishes an online edition at www.jajuminbo.com, is a small-circulation, private magazine that promotes the reunification of North and South Korea.

During the trial, prosecutors accused *Jajuminbo* of publishing articles that promoted North Korea's vision of reunification. The three journalists were also accused of maintaining contact with "pro-North Korean" activists in Japan.

The district attorney asked that each of the journalists be sentenced to four years in prison. The court was scheduled to announce its verdict on February 9, 2002. As this book went to press, all three journalists were being held at the Seoul Detention Center.

SRI LANKA

MARCH 21

A.S.M. Fasmi, *Thinakkural*
`THREATENED`

Fasmi, a reporter for the Tamil-language newspaper *Thinakkural*, said he was detained, interrogated, and threatened repeatedly with death after reporting on the alleged rape of two Tamil women detained by local security forces in February.

On the morning of March 21, the day Fasmi's report on the rape charges appeared in *Thinakkural*, intelligence officers from the 21-5 Army Brigade on the northern island of Mannar summoned the journalist for interrogation, according to his own account. Fasmi, who is based in Mannar, said the officers accused him of plotting to bribe members of the armed forces and thereby tarnish their image. An army officer told him he was under arrest and transferred him to the crime branch of the Mannar Police.

Fasmi was released at around 4 p.m. after signing a sworn statement. The journalist later reported receiving numerous phone calls threatening his life.

On April 16, CPJ wrote a letter to President Chandrika Kumaratunga asking her to guarantee Fasmi's safety.

APRIL 16

Marie Colvin, *The Sunday Times*
ATTACKED

Colvin, an award-winning American journalist who works for the British newspaper *The Sunday Times*, was hit by shrapnel from a grenade fired by the Sri Lankan army, receiving wounds in her head, chest, and arms. Colvin's left eye was permanently blinded by the attack.

Though she was traveling with a group of unarmed civilians, soldiers apparently mistook the group for members of the rebel Liberation Tigers of Tamil Eelam (LTTE). Colvin shouted out that she was a journalist, but the soldiers fired anyway.

Even after she was hit, Colvin continued shouting that she was a journalist, an American, and that she needed a doctor. Eventually, soldiers told her to approach them with her hands in the air. According to her account, later published in *The Sunday Times*, soldiers then pushed her down on the ground, flat on her back, and began kicking her. After searching her for weapons, they led her away at gunpoint.

At the next location, an officer interrogated her and tried to force her to admit that her party had fired first, which she denied. Finally, soldiers took her to a military hospital in the garrison town of Vavuniya. She was later flown to Colombo.

An April 17 statement issued by Sri Lanka's Department of Information noted that Colvin did not have official clearance to travel to the rebel-held Wanni region, where she had spent two weeks with LTTE guerrilla forces.

Colvin is one of the few foreign correspondents who have managed to reach rebel-held territory in Sri Lanka in recent years.

In addition, the statement contended that Colvin had overstayed her visa and suggested she "had her own secret agenda with the LTTE." Sri Lanka's overseas missions were "asked to be cautious when recommending journalists for visas."

CPJ issued an alert on April 17, expressing concern for Colvin's safety and cautioning the Sri Lankan government against imposing additional bureaucratic restrictions on journalists.

MAY 23

Ravaya
ATTACKED

Unidentified assailants threw a smoke bomb into the office compound of *Ravaya*, a Sinhala-language weekly paper published from Maharagama, a southern suburb of the capital, Colombo. There was no serious damage.

The nonlethal smoke bomb was of a type commonly used by Sri Lankan security forces and is not available to the general public, police told the BBC.

Ravaya editor Victor Ivan, who has been an outspoken critic of the government, told CPJ that he thought the bomb attack was intended as a warning. "My feeling is that this is only a signal," he said. "This is a small thing, but journalists have also been killed in Sri Lanka—and nothing happens."

CPJ issued a press release on May 25, noting the alarming frequency of attacks against journalists in Sri Lanka and urging the administration to issue a prompt and full report on the status of the police investigation into the *Ravaya* attack.

JUNE 8

Dharmeratnam Sivaram, TamilNet
`THREATENED`

In early June, several state-owned newspapers accused Sivaram, a veteran journalist and the editor of the TamilNet Web site, of being a spy for the rebel Liberation Tigers of Tamil Eelam (LTTE). The charges seriously endangered Sivaram and his family.

TamilNet (www.tamilnet.com) is an online news service that covers Sri Lankan affairs, with special emphasis on news of interest to the Tamil community. The service is widely acknowledged as an indispensable source of information about the long-running civil war between government forces and the LTTE.

On June 8, the English-language government newspaper *The Daily News* included Sivaram on a list of alleged LTTE spies. On June 17, the state-run Tamil-language daily *Thinakaran* ran similar accusations in a front-page story that included a color photograph of Sivaram. That same day, the independent Sinhala-language newspaper *Divaina* followed the lead of the state media by accusing Sivaram of acting as an LTTE agent.

None of the newspapers provided any substantive evidence to prove the allegations against Sivaram.

In Sri Lanka, where the civil war has exacerbated ethnic tensions and political violence is common, branding someone as an LTTE spy can be tantamount to issuing a death warrant.

On June 21, CPJ sent a letter to President Chandrika Kumaratunga asking her to guarantee personally that no harm came to Dharmeratnam Sivaram or his family as a result of the state media's irresponsible and vicious campaign.

JULY 17

Aiyathurai Nadesan, *Virakesari*
`THREATENED`
S. M. Gopalaratnam, *Thinakathir*
`THREATENED`
K. Rushangan, *Thinakathir*
`THREATENED`

Nadesan, Batticaloa correspondent for the Tamil-language daily *Virakesari*, was summoned for interrogation by the coordinating officer of the Sri Lankan army's 23-3 brigade. Nadesan identified the officer as Colonel Manawaduge.

The officer warned Nadesan that he would be arrested under the Prevention of Terrorism Act (PTA) if he continued writing against the government and the security forces, according to the journalist's account.

The officer also delivered an oblique threat, reminding Nadesan that political activists have been killed in Sri Lanka for putting up posters critical of the government. Nadesan said he was then photographed from different angles, which he feared would make it easier for security forces to target him in the future.

Nadesan, who uses the pen name Nellai G. Nadesan, is an award-winning journalist with a reputation for independent reporting.

Manawaduge had summoned two other journalists for a similar interrogation just days earlier, according to the East Lanka Journalists

Association: S. M. Gopalaratnam, editor of *Thinakathir*, Batticaloa's only Tamil-language daily, and K. Rushangan, the paper's deputy editor.

JULY 22

All journalists
THREATENED

Following opposition protests against President Chandrika Kumaratunga's July 10 decision to suspend parliament and call a nationwide referendum, Chief Elections Commissioner Dayananda Dissanayake warned the press that publishing any "false statements" regarding the referendum was illegal and would be punished under the long-dormant 1981 Referendum Act No. 7.

Section 58 (1) of the act criminalizes the publication of "any false statement concerning or relating to (a) the utterances or activities at a Referendum of any recognised political party or any person; or (b) the conduct or management of such Referendum by any such recognised political party or person, and such statement [as] is capable of influencing the result of such Referendum," according to the government-run *Daily News*.

The act places the burden of proof on journalists, who are considered "guilty of an illegal practice unless such person proves that such publication was made without his consent or connivance, and that he exercised all such diligence to prevent such publication as he ought to have exercised having regard to the nature of his function in such capacity and in all the circumstances."

TAIWAN

AUGUST 22

Taiwan Yi Zhoukan
ATTACKED

Around midday, a group of men wielding baseball bats charged into the downtown Taipei offices of *Taiwan Yi Zhoukan* (Taiwan Next), a popular tabloid-style newsmagazine, and smashed windows, computers, and office furniture. No one was injured in the attack.

"The violence was apparently a warning to Next Media Ltd.," said a police officer quoted by Agence France-Presse. Next Media, the company that publishes *Taiwan Yi Zhoukan*, is owned by Hong Kong media tycoon Jimmy Lai.

Though it had only been publishing for about three months at the time of the attack, *Taiwan Yi Zhoukan* had already developed a reputation for exposing scandals involving politicians, celebrities, and criminals. Pei Wei, the magazine's editor-in-chief, told reporters that while staffers had received many threatening phone calls in the past as a result of such coverage, "We have no idea who did this."

On August 23, CPJ wrote to President Chen Shui-bian, urging him to ensure that the police investigation was thorough and professional and that the perpetrators were prosecuted to the fullest extent of the law. On September 3, three young men were arrested by Taipei police and charged with perpetrating the attack, according to Taiwan government sources. One suspect, Tzi-wen He, confessed to the crime and said he was angered over *Taiwan Yi Zhoukan*'s reports that an assemblyman had links to the pornography industry in Chiayi City. By year's end the suspects had not been brought to trial and the investigation was ongoing.

THAILAND

APRIL 10

Withayut Sangsopit
KILLED

Withayut, a radio journalist and commentator, was gunned down on April 10 in the southern city of Surat Thani.

According to police, Withayut was approached by several gunmen and shot five times as he was about to enter his radio studio to begin his popular morning program, "Catch Up With the World." Withayut's program was carried on Fourth Army Radio, the regional affiliate of the Royal Thai Army Radio and Television network.

Surat Thani police believe Withayut, 56, was killed as a result of his reporting on irregularities involving a 50 million baht (US$1.1 million) real estate deal for a municipal garbage dump. The reports began in 1999 and eventually led the Interior Ministry to investigate and to order a portion of the money returned to the government.

Police arrested two men in connection with the shooting, one of them a municipal official implicated in the garbage dump scandal.

A well-known radio commentator in southern Thailand, Withayut was for many years a correspondent for the Bangkok-based, Thai-language *Daily News* before starting his radio program. Police said the journalist had received

numerous death threats and was under police protection prior to the murder. However, Withayut's protection was lifted shortly before the killing, according to several Thai newspapers.

MAY 2

Kaset Puengpak, *Thai Rath*
KILLED

Kaset, a stringer for the Thai-language newspaper *Thai Rath*, was shot dead in Viset Chaichan District, Ang Thong Province. Kaset was known for his reporting on local drug gangs linked to powerful politicians and police officers, according to *Thai Rath* and several Thai journalists. The Thai Journalists Association issued a statement saying that Kaset was likely murdered for his journalistic work. After the killing, authorities interrogated a police corporal who had quarreled with Kaset over law enforcement issues in the area. No arrests have been reported in the case.

NOVEMBER 18

Suchart Charnchanavivat, *Chao Mukdahan, Siam Rath*
KILLED (MOTIVE UNCONFIRMED)
Settha Sririwat, *Naew Na*, Channel 3
KILLED (MOTIVE UNCONFIRMED)
Chuvit Chueharn, iTV, *The Nation, Krungthep Thurakij*
KILLED (MOTIVE UNCONFIRMED)
Somboon Saenviset, *Daily News*
ATTACKED

Paiboon Bunthos, a stringer for the daily *Thai Rath* in the provincial town of Mukdahan, near the Laotian border, opened fire on four of his colleagues during dinner on a floating restaurant, killing three, before committing suicide by turning his weapon on himself, according to police reports.

The reporters killed were Suchart, 62, editor of the newspaper *Chao Mukdahan* and a stringer for the daily *Siam Rath*; Settha, 38, a stringer for the daily *Naew Na* and Channel 3 television; and Chuvit, 38, a stringer for iTV, *The Nation* newspaper, and the daily *Krungthep Thurakij*. Also injured in the attack were Somboon, a stringer for the *Daily News*, and Vichian Susonna, a lawyer.

The motive behind the attack was unclear. At the time of the shooting, police reported that one of the victims, Suchart, had recently published articles in his local newspaper, *Chao Mukdahan*, accusing unidentified local journalists of bribe taking and extortion. According to Thai journalists, there were other long-standing differences among the men, including allegations of theft lodged by the gunman against others in the group.

The dinner at the floating restaurant was supposedly organized so that the men could settle their differences.

Officials of the Thai Journalists Association say that the incident in Mukdahan might have been related to the journalists' illegal business activities. It is not uncommon in Thailand for provincial newspaper stringers, who are notoriously underpaid, to use their positions to solicit bribes or favors from local officials.

Mukdahan is a center for a thriving border trade with neighboring Laos, which may also have played a role in the killing, according to Thai journalists. In the aftermath of the incident, the Press Council of Thailand

issued a December 10 letter calling on national newspapers to exercise more care in training and recruiting their provincial stringers in order to minimize corruption and unethical behavior.

The Thai Journalists Association did not consider the attack to be related directly to journalism, but the bizarre nature of the tragedy made it difficult to sort out the gunman's motive.

VIETNAM

JUNE 12

Tran Do, free-lancer
HARASSED, CENSORED

Police in Ho Chi Minh City confiscated a manuscript section of the memoirs of Lt. Gen. Tran Do, Vietnam's most prominent political dissident.

Tran, a former general in the Vietnam People's Army, had previously served as head of the Culture, Literature, and Art Department of the Party Central Committee and as deputy chairman of the National Assembly. He was expelled from the Communist Party in 1999 after writing essays calling for political reform.

Tran's memoirs, written in three separate sections, contain his thoughts on the future of the country, as well as his analysis of the 9th Party Congress held in April, according to international media reports. The second section was published overseas last year.

On June 12, the Hanoi-based Tran was in Ho Chi Minh City visiting his son. He brought the 83-page third section of his memoirs. On arrival in Ho Chi Minh City, Tran took the manuscript to a copier, where he printed 15 copies to distribute to his family and friends, according to a U.S.-based journalist familiar with the case.

On his way back from the copy shop, state security officers stopped Tran's car and confiscated all the copies of his manuscript. He was then brought to the local precinct and questioned before being released.

Authorities brought Tran in for questioning again on June 22. Soon after the interrogation session, the 77-year-old Tran fell ill and was taken to a local emergency room. He was later transferred to the Friendship Hospital in Hanoi, where he was put under tight surveillance. He was later released from the hospital, and is recovering at home, where he remained under surveillance at year's end.

Tran repeatedly asked authorities to return his manuscript. He also wrote to the Vietnam Writers' Union, of which he is a member, asking for their support.

On August 23, CPJ wrote to President Tran Duc Luong urging him to ensure that all copies of Tran's manuscript are returned, and that he be allowed to write and publish without fear of reprisals.

OCTOBER 11

All foreign journalists
CENSORED

The Foreign Ministry and the Department of Post and Communications issued new regulations requiring the government to inspect and approve all video footage transmitted via satellite by foreign journalists working in Vietnam.

Under the regulations, foreign journalists must apply for a permit and describe in detail the contents of each video to be transmitted. The government can take up to three days to approve the video.

Previously, foreign journalists had to describe the contents of a video in general terms to get a "letter of introduction" from the Foreign Ministry to the satellite feeding company, according to a Hanoi-based foreign correspondent.

The new regulations state, "Organizations and individuals must not abuse international satellite feeds to oppose the Vietnamese state, create national animosity, instigate violence or undermine traditional Vietnamese customs and values."

Such broadly worded charges are commonly used to crack down on critics of the government, which has repeatedly accused the foreign media of supporting political dissidents.

On October 22, the People's Army daily newspaper, *Quan Doi Nhan Dan*, published an article accusing foreign media of using "these dissidents to propagate the capitalist political and economic model, the bourgeois concepts of democratic values, freedom and human rights." ■

OVERVIEW: EUROPE AND CENTRAL ASIA

by Alex Lupis

THE EXHILARATING PROSPECT OF BROAD PRESS FREEDOMS that followed the collapse of the Soviet Union a decade ago has faded dramatically in much of the post-communist world. A considerable decline in press freedom conditions in Russia during the last year, along with the stranglehold authoritarian leaders have imposed on media in Central Asia, the Caucasus, Ukraine, Belarus, and Moldova, has put journalists on the defensive across the region.

Even in the Balkans, press freedom gains have remained modest despite the election of reformist governments in Croatia, Serbia, and parts of Bosnia. Interethnic tension, political extremism, official corruption, organized crime, and weak government institutions ensure that journalists remain highly vulnerable. In Central Europe, journalists work in a relatively safe environment yet must still contend with politicized state broadcasters, as well as with threats and legal intimidation from politicians. Criminal libel laws and monopolies over media ownership afflict most of Eastern Europe and Central Asia.

In May 2001, CPJ placed Russian president Vladimir Putin on its annual Ten Worst Enemies of the Press list. Throughout 2001, his government imposed censorship on journalists covering the conflict in Chechnya, legally harassed private media outlets, and granted sweeping powers of surveillance to security services. Despite Putin's professed goal of imposing the rule of law, numerous journalists across Russia have been violently attacked with impunity. Russia has one jailed journalist, Grigory Pasko, who was sentenced in December 2001 to four years in prison on spurious treason charges.

In an ominous and dramatic move in April 2001, the state-run Gazprom corporation took over NTV, Russia's most prominent independent national television network. At the same time, Gazprom took over the Sem Dnei Publishing House, which owned a prominent Moscow daily and a prestigious newsweekly. Within days, the new Gazprom management had shut down the newspaper and ousted top journalists at the weekly.

Despite Gazprom's insistence that the changes were strictly business, the main beneficiary was Putin himself, whose primary critics were silenced. The government wrested even more control from media when a January 2002 court ruling ordered the liquidation of the parent company of TV-6, an independent national television network that has criticized the Kremlin.

Alex Lupis is the program coordinator for Europe and Central Asia and wrote the analyses of Albania, Bosnia, Bulgaria, Croatia, Cyprus, Czech Republic, Hungary, Macedonia, Romania, Slovakia, Slovenia, and Yugoslavia. **Olga Tarasov** is the research associate for Europe and Central Asia and wrote the analyses of Armenia, Azerbaijan, Belarus, Georgia, Kyrgyzstan, Moldova, Poland, and Ukraine. **Emma Gray** is the consultant for Europe and Central Asia and wrote the analyses of Italy, Kazakhstan, Latvia, Russia, Tajikistan, Turkmenistan, United Kingdom, and Uzbekistan. **Joel Simon** is deputy director of CPJ and wrote the analysis of Spain. The CPJ fact-finding and advocacy mission to Serbia and Bosnia in May was funded by a grant from the **Freedom Forum**.

While many former Soviet republics have used naked repression to muzzle their journalists, the takeover of NTV and the liquidation of TV-6 marked the debut of a more refined technique of political action disguised as capitalism. These developments provoked anxiety among journalists in neighboring former Soviet republics. Many fear that their own governments will follow Russia's precedent by orchestrating the state takeover of independent media and then calling it a business dispute.

Press freedom conditions along Russia's southern periphery in Central Asia, where journalists continue to struggle under the harshest of conditions, were even grimmer. Authoritarian leaders either strengthened their hold on the few remaining independent media outlets or reinforced their complete control over media.

In both Kazakhstan and Kyrgyzstan, the government aggressively kept local independent and opposition media from publishing. The Kazakh government used pliant judges, the tax police, and other economic levers to convict or impose fines on prominent opposition journalists. Press freedom in Kyrgyzstan, meanwhile, suffered major setbacks as politically motivated civil libel suits filed by government officials resulted in heavy damage awards, forcing newspapers such as the independent weekly *Res Publica* and *Asaba*, the country's oldest and most popular Kyrgyz-language publication, to either shut down or operate on the brink of bankruptcy.

Tajikistan continues to suffer from the aftermath of its civil war, which ended in 1997. Local journalists work in dire conditions of instability and poverty, exacerbated by stifling restrictions from President Imomali Rakhmonov. Turkmenistan, meanwhile, remained completely isolated under President Saparmurat Niyazov's totalitarian cult of personality, and the state retained control over all publishing and broadcast licenses.

President Islam Karimov's brutal repression of all domestic dissent continued in Uzbekistan. The July dismissal of Alo Khodzhayev, the increasingly outspoken editor-in-chief of the Russian-language daily *Tashkentskaya Pravda*, and the decision of Shukhrat Babadjanov, director of the independent TV station ALC in Urgench, to flee the country for fear of his life, ensured that the government's control of the media, including the Internet, remained all but absolute. Uzbekistan also remains the region's most active jailer of journalists. Despite the release of radio journalist Shodi Mardiev in January 2002 under an amnesty, three other journalists continued to serve long sentences.

Following the September 11 attacks on the United States, some Central Asian leaders were eager to utilize the "war on terrorism" as an excuse to stifle domestic dissent further. Even in Russia, there was anxiety that political leaders might harness the crisis for their own advantage. Aleksei Pankin, a media analyst with *The Moscow Times*, wrote that "here in Russia the authorities are always most eager to borrow from the worst elements of Western experience."

Most state-run or pro-government independent media outlets in Central Asia downplayed the war in Afghanistan and the presence of U.S. troops in the region in an effort to quell potential anti-Western and anti-government sentiment.

Wherever possible, local residents turned to Russian television channels and Western radio broadcasts in Russian and other Central Asian languages for news.

In the Caucasus, press freedom conditions continued to stagnate under the weight of widespread poverty, polarized politics, corruption, and political instability. Dire economic conditions proved to be the greatest obstacle for independent media outlets in Armenia, where self-censorship and reporting in exchange for financial support from wealthy patrons undermined journalists' independence.

In Azerbaijan, the government of President Heydar Aliyev continued to crack down on independent and opposition media through state-sponsored harassment, defamation lawsuits, financial pressure, imprisonment, and physical assault. Courts forcibly closed the independent weeklies *Milletin Sesi* and *Bakinsky Bulvar*, for example, after high-level government officials sued the papers. A government-mandated switch from the Cyrillic to the Latin alphabet and licensing problems placed additional financial burdens on the Azeri media.

Rampant corruption, organized crime, and political instability in Georgia ensured that journalists who dared to cover the country's volatile politics and influential criminal gangs faced reprisals, often from President Eduard Shevardnadze's strong-armed government. In late October, agents from the National Security Ministry raided the headquarters of the independent television station Rustavi-2, sparking large anti-government demonstrations and a political crisis that only subsided after Shevardnadze dismissed his entire cabinet.

Along Russia's western periphery, press freedom in Moldova, Ukraine, and Belarus remained under fire and showed no significant signs of improvement. Government pressure on Moldovan media outlets increased following Communist Party victories in parliamentary and presidential elections.

In Ukraine, President Leonid Kuchma's government stepped up its habitual censorship of opposition newspapers and increased attacks and threats against independent journalists, earning Kuchma a spot on CPJ's annual list of the Ten Worst Enemies of the Press. The disappearance and presumed murder of Internet editor Georgy Gongadze in late 2000 brought the plight of Ukrainian journalists into sharp focus. Allegations that Kuchma himself may have ordered Gongadze's murder sparked a political crisis that threatened to bring down his government.

The July murder of Igor Aleksandrov, director of the independent television company Tor, and the unsolved Gongadze case highlight a pattern of Ukrainian police stalling criminal investigations and claiming attacks are unrelated to journalists' work. As a result, violence against journalists continues with impunity.

President Aleksandr Lukashenko continued his assault on the independent and opposition press in Belarus. Lukashenko managed to cling to power in September 9 presidential elections amid charges of human rights violations and electoral fraud. The government made little progress in the case of Dmitry Zavadsky, a cameraman who disappeared in July 2000, while independent publications faced harassment, censorship, seizure, and closure for criticizing the regime.

Following the demise of the Milosevic and Tudjman regimes, press freedom in the Balkans showed only modest improvement under reformist governments in Serbia, Croatia, and parts of Bosnia, where fragile ruling coalitions often sought to co-opt state-run and independent media outlets.

Unresponsive police forces, particularly in Serbia and Bosnia, ensured that journalists reporting on organized crime, official corruption, and war crimes continue to be intimidated, beaten, and murdered with impunity. Simmering interethnic tensions in Bosnia, Kosovo, and Macedonia also inhibited the ability of journalists to move freely and securely within their own countries

In Macedonia, journalists faced harassment and assault as the conflict between state security forces and ethnic Albanian rebels escalated throughout the year. Widespread poverty, weak government institutions, and faltering political and economic reforms inhibited free expression throughout much of the Balkans, particularly in Romania and Albania.

Central European countries pressed ahead with political reforms in their efforts to join the European Union (EU). But in the Czech Republic, Hungary, and elsewhere, powerful officials wielded criminal libel charges and other aggressive tactics to intimidate critical journalists in both state and public media.

On the Mediterranean island of Cyprus, which is also in line for EU membership, opposition media outlets in the northern Turkish-occupied sector, such as the daily *Avrupa*, faced harassment, intimidation, and violence in retaliation for criticizing Rauf Denktash, leader of the breakaway northern Cypriot regime.

In Western Europe, sectarian violence and political protests posed significant risks for both journalists and media executives. The Basque separatist group ETA continued to target media outlets in Spain in retaliation for their news coverage. In 2001, ETA maimed Basque journalist Gorka Landaburu with a letter bomb on May 15 and killed newspaper executive Santiago Oleaga Elejebarrieta on May 24.

Two months later, in late July, journalists covering the Group of Eight summit of the world's industrialized nations in Genoa, Italy, suffered brutal attacks from police officers and demonstrators. A parliamentary commission created to investigate allegations of police misconduct released a report on September 14 that praised the police for keeping order and blamed the violence on the protesters.

In 2001, seven journalists in Europe and Central Asia were killed in retaliation for their reporting. This was an increase from the five killed in 2000, but an average figure for the region during the mid-to-late 1990s, by which time civil wars in Tajikistan, Georgia, and the former Yugoslavia had, for the most part, subsided.

Four of the journalists were killed for investigating official corruption or organized crime in provincial areas of Russia, Ukraine, Latvia, and Serbia. In the summer of 2001, a popular television journalist with the embattled Rustavi-2 station in Tbilisi, Georgia, was also murdered.

Two other journalists were killed while covering conflicts. An Associated Press Television News correspondent was killed just inside Kosovo while reporting on NATO operations related to fighting in neighboring Macedonia. Investigative journalist Martin O'Hagan, shot dead outside his home in the Northern Irish town of Lurgan, was the first reported fatality of a journalist covering the conflict in Northern Ireland. ∎

ALBANIA

INDEPENDENT JOURNALISTS IN ALBANIA CONTINUE TO STRUGGLE with economic underdevelopment, highly partisan politics, and security risks. Low professional standards and stalled government reforms of media laws further compounded journalists' problems in 2001.

High taxes and printing costs, poor distribution networks, low advertising revenues, limited business skills, and endemic corruption keep editors and publishers dependent on financial subsidies from political parties. Because most media owners are affiliated with one of two dominant political parties—either Prime Minister Ilir Meta's ruling Socialist Party (SP), or Sali Berisha's opposition Democratic Party (DP)—news coverage tends to be highly partisan.

While a sluggish economy has led to a decline in the print media's advertising revenue and thus decreased circulation, some broadcast media outlets have begun to gain a degree of financial stability from their rising advertising revenues.

Politicians often bribe or otherwise induce journalists to write negative articles about their rivals. University training for journalists is poor, and the media training provided by Western nongovernmental organizations usually has little influence on journalistic ethics. As a result, the public remains generally mistrustful of journalists.

Parliamentary elections in the summer of 2001 were highly partisan, and the press coverage mirrored the bitter political feud between the SP and the DP's Union for Victory coalition. Albanian Television (TVSH), the influential public broadcaster, helped contribute to an SP victory via positive coverage of the party.

Nonetheless, media coverage of the elections improved somewhat over previous years, with private broadcast media providing a broader variety of information, according to political analyst Fatos Lubonja. Two new private television stations—TV Arberia and TV Klan—gave rural viewers an alternative to TVSH. While TV Klan favored the SP in its electoral coverage, two local channels based in Tirana—TV Shijak and ATN-1—openly supported the DP.

A number of journalists working for pro-DP media outlets were reportedly harassed during the campaign. On June 15, police officers detained Enis Fani, a free-lance cameraman working for ATN-1, for several hours in the city of Durres while he was filming an argument between police officers and DP political candidate Hajdar Kovaci, the Tirana-based Free Media Albanian Forum reported.

Journalists investigating politically sensitive issues, such as organized crime or corruption, also continue to face security risks. On November 8, an unknown assailant assaulted and threatened Nikolle Lesi, publisher of the independent Tirana daily *Koha Jone*, after the paper published allegations that a hotel in the city of Durres was built illegally, according to the Tirana-based Albanian Human Rights Group. Meanwhile, police officers continued to threaten and detain journalists.

A new press law drafted at the end of 2000 remained stalled in 2001. The draft law protects the confidentiality of sources and limits the state's ability to confiscate printed material. However, the legislation also establishes a "right to reply" statute—which requires publications to print letters to the editor from individuals mentioned in articles—as well as a press council to regulate the media.

The government failed to decriminalize libel in 2001. Even compliance with previously passed laws—such as the Freedom of Information on Official Documents Law, which codifies how journalists can obtain government information—remains poor since journalists must often bribe government clerks to obtain official documents.

The ability of journalists to influence media reforms or to protest attacks on their colleagues was limited by their disunity. The country boasts several press associations, but they are fragmented and unable to speak with one voice.

ARMENIA

WIDESPREAD POVERTY, POLARIZED POLITICS, AND FLAWED LEGISLATION kept the media at the mercy of government officials and wealthy sponsors during 2001. Libel remained a criminal offense punishable by imprisonment, though it was not used against journalists during the year.

Dire economic conditions proved to be the greatest obstacle for the independent media in Armenia, where most people cannot afford to buy newspapers. Readership and print runs remained miniscule, particularly outside the capital, Yerevan. Advertising also remained an insignificant source of revenue. As a result, journalists censored themselves and slanted their reporting in exchange for the financial support of wealthy patrons.

In this politically polarized country, President Robert Kocharian and his supporters retained control of leading media outlets, including state television—the only nationally broadcast channel. The president's political opponents control only a few publications. In addition, journalists continue to face significant security risks in covering the government's investigation into the October 1999 armed attack on the Parliament, which left eight high-level politicians, including the prime minister, dead.

Relations between Armenia and neighboring Azerbaijan remained strained in 2001 due to tensions over the status of the unrecognized Republic of Nagorno-Karabakh, a formerly autonomous region within Azerbaijan currently controlled by ethnic Armenian separatists. In November, the Yerevan Press Club temporarily halted journalist exchanges between the two countries due to growing anti-Armenian sentiment in leading Azerbaijani publications, local and international sources reported. However, both sides stated that cooperation would resume when the inflammatory statements subsided. By year's end, the Azeri media had toned down their coverage of the disputed region, mostly because they had problems of their own working under the authoritarian regime of President Heydar Aliyev.

A controversial Law on Television and Radio adopted in October 2000 drew a barrage of domestic and international criticism in 2001 for granting the president excessive powers over the broadcast industry, including the State Broadcast Council (SBC) and the National Commission on Television and Radio

(NCTR). Experts claimed the law would impede the development of independent broadcast media in Armenia by giving the president wide latitude to favor media outlets loyal to him. With presidential and parliamentary elections set for 2003, these broad new presidential powers seemed even more troubling.

In January 2001, the Constitutional Court ruled that several provisions of the law were unconstitutional. Later that month, in an unprecedented protest designed to push legislators to amend the law, all of Armenia's television and radio stations stopped broadcasting for 45 minutes. On January 30, the Yerevan Press Club, Internews Armenia, and the Journalist Union of Armenia submitted proposed amendments to Parliament.

Lawmakers adopted amendments that simplified licensing procedures for producing television and radio programs and granted currently functioning TV and radio stations priority in frequency auctions. The parliament also passed measures designed to decrease the president's control over the SBC and the NCTR.

AZERBAIJAN

ALTHOUGH PRESIDENT HEYDAR ALIYEV CLAIMED to be the "guarantor of freedom of speech and the press in Azerbaijan," his government continued to crack down on independent and opposition media while suppressing public criticism. Journalists who dared to criticize officials suffered harassment, defamation lawsuits, imprisonment, and physical assaults. Publications faced financial pressure and closures, as well as more indirect forms of censorship.

Meanwhile, the pan-European intergovernmental human rights organization Council of Europe, which admitted Azerbaijan last year, vocally criticized the country's sluggish democratization and restrictive media policies.

In June, President Aliyev issued a decree requiring the press to print exclusively in the Latin script by August 1, a move intended to reduce the dominance of the Russian language in Azerbaijan. (Josef Stalin imposed the Russian-derived Cyrillic script on Azerbaijan in 1939. Since then, most Azeri-language newspapers in the country have been printed in Cyrillic.)

The circulation of some newspapers and magazines dropped after the decree because many older readers are not accustomed to the Latin script. That reduction hurt independent publications, which rely heavily on newsstand sales.

In August, when the independent weekly *Impuls* defied the decree and continued to publish in Cyrillic, the government pressured the paper's printer to block the issue, and the Baku prosecutor's office issued a warning to *Impuls'* owner. The newspaper has since ceased publication.

In August, Baku's Narimanov District Court closed two independent weeklies for allegedly defaming government officials. The court then found several editors and reporters guilty of defamation, and jailed two of them. CPJ protested the imprisonment of *Milletin Sesi* editor-in-chief Shahbaz Khuduoglu and *Bakinsky Bulvar* founder Elmar Huseynov in an October 16 letter to President Aliyev. On October 17, Aliyev signed a pardon releasing the two in honor of the 10th anniversary of Azerbaijan's independence. The pardon did not reverse the guilty verdicts against the journalists, however, and both *Bakinsky Bulvar* and *Milletin Sesi* remain closed.

In November, officials accused the opposition dailies *Azadliq*, *Yeni Musavat*, and *Hurriyyet* of "undermining Azerbaijan's statehood." Subsequently, a number of printing houses refused to print those publications.

On December 12, picketers gathered in the center of Baku to protest state harassment of the three newspapers, according to Azer Hasret, chairman of the Journalists' Trade Union. More than 20 journalists were injured when police violently dispersed the rally.

A domestic and internatinal uproar ensued. A few days later, President Aliyev met with journalists and pledged government support for independent and opposition media outlets. Aliyev subsequently ordered the state publishing house to institute a one-year moratorium on collecting debts owed by independent publications.

On December 27, Aliyev instructed the Cabinet of Ministers and his executive staff to implement assistance measures for independent and opposition media outlets. The measures include financial subsidies, support for the development of private publishing companies, and assurances that the state publishing house will print non-state publications. The president also asked the prosecutor general to investigate cases of journalists allegedly persecuted because of their work and to punish the offenders. However, the order did not specify implementation deadlines.

Throughout the year, officials tried to close the independent distribution company Gaya. Authorities claimed that Gaya lacked proper documentation and that its kiosks did not meet the government's aesthetic standards. In reality, authorities were trying to monopolize printed press distribution. At the end of the year, the company's representatives appealed to Baku officials to allow Gaya to distribute without further harassment.

In January and February, authorities closed the regional television stations DMR TV, Mingechevir TV, Khayal TV, and Gutb TV, which had been operating unlicensed for years because the government had repeatedly denied their applications for no reason. On February 6, officials announced that the stations would be allowed to reopen, and they resumed broadcasting by the end of February.

Extensive international pressure finally prompted President Aliyev to order that broadcast licenses be awarded to regional television stations. On December 21, accordingly, the Cabinet of Ministers Frequencies Committee finally awarded licenses to five regional stations: Khayal TV, Gutb TV, Aygun TV, Mingechevir TV, and Dunya TV.

In December, parliament considered a draft Law on Mass Media that drew fierce international and domestic criticism. Articles 19, 27, and 50 would have allowed officials to close media outlets if the courts order publications to retract stories three times in one year. The articles also empowered authorities to ban media outlets that "undermine Azerbaijan's statehood" and to annul the accreditation of journalists who distribute "inaccurate information."

After strong objections from the Council of Europe, the contentious sections of the law were removed, according to local press reports. At the end of December, parliament adopted amendments to the Law on Mass Media that excluded articles 19, 27, and 50. In part, the amended law lifted restrictions on the sources of a media outlet's funding and abolished current registration procedures. In addition, journalists can only be forced to disclose their sources to protect public health, prevent grave crimes, or exonerate persons charged with grave crimes.

Despite this small legislative victory, the government demonstrates a visceral hatred of the press. In a December speech, President Aliyev's brother, Jalal Aliyev, railed that the media "are enemies. Nowhere can you find such enemies to a nation as in this nation…"

BELARUS

PRESIDENT ALEKSANDR LUKASHENKO CONTINUED HIS ASSAULT on the independent and opposition press in 2001, and he managed to cling to power in September 9 presidential elections amid charges of human rights violations and extensive electoral fraud. Throughout the year, independent publications faced harassment, censorship, seizures, and closures for criticizing the regime. Little progress was made in the infamous case of disappeared cameraman Dmitry Zavadsky, and troubling legal "reforms" were proposed at end of the year.

Press freedom abuses intensified in the month prior to the September poll. On August 17, police from the State Committee for Financial Investigation seized 400,000 copies the special election issue of the independent triweekly *Nasha Svaboda*, which endorsed opposition candidate Vladimir Goncharik and predicted Lukashenko's defeat.

While the government launched spurious tax audits against several opposition newspapers in advance of the poll, the most significant crackdown occurred on August 22, when the State Committee for Financial Investigation seized equipment and froze bank accounts of the Magic publishing house, which prints most Minsk-based independent papers. Authorities sealed Magic's printing presses, blocking the publication of dozens of independent newspapers, Stepan Zhirnostyok, Magic's executive director, told CPJ.

Magic's owner, Yuri Budko, told Radio Free Europe/Radio Liberty that the committee officials justified their actions by referring to an earlier court order that Budko had successfully challenged in 2000.

The publishing house resumed work five days later, after Budko agreed to appoint the deputy head of the State Press Committee, Vladimir Glushakov, as the acting director of Magic during the ongoing investigation, local and international sources reported. While at Magic, Glushakov censored the independent publications *Rabochy*, *Predprinimatelskaya Gazeta*, and *Narodnaya Volya* for allegedly defaming President Lukashenko. Glushakov stopped working at the Magic publishing house three days after the election, local sources told CPJ.

During the election period, Belarusian authorities denied a number of international monitors entry into the country, including a CPJ consultant who intended to monitor press conditions in Belarus prior to the September 9 poll.

Meanwhile, little progress was made in the investigation into the case of Dmitry Zavadsky, a cameraman with the Russian public television station ORT who vanished on July 7, 2000. Zavadsky's disappearance shocked Belarusian society and also served as a grim reminder of the security risks journalists face in Belarus.

Credible leads have implicated high-level Belarusian government officials in the disappearance. In June, Dmitry Petrushkevich, a member of the investigative team on the Zavadsky case, and Oleg Sluchek, a former Prosecutor's Office employee, went into exile in the United States and alleged that a "death squad" created by high-level government officials to eliminate Lukashenko's political opponents killed Zavadsky.

Throughout the year, CPJ issued numerous statements calling for an independent, international investigation and urging the government to bring the perpetrators to justice. However, a year and a half after the journalist's disappearance, Zavadsky's fate remains unknown.

The investigation has focused on four suspects—Valery Ignatovich, Maksim Malik, Aleksei Guz and Sergei Saushkin—known as the Ignatovich Group. Officials claim that Ignatovich, a former officer of the elite special forces unit, Almaz, and a member of the ultranationalist organization Russian National Unity, led the gang that abducted the journalist.

Although Belarusian authorities have neither found Zavadsky's body nor established a plausible motive, in May, they charged members of the Ignatovich Group with kidnapping the journalist. According to the official theory, he was abducted in revenge for filming Belarusian military servicemen, including Ignatovich, as they fought alongside rebel forces in Chechnya.

On October 24, the Minsk Regional Court began the trial of the Ignatovich Group, according to local and international sources. Despite the fact that Zavadsky's wife, along with local civic organizations and opposition activists, demanded an open trial, it remains closed to the public. Proceedings continued into 2002, and in January, Interior Minister Naumov announced that regardless of the trial's outcome, the investigation into Zavadsky's disappearance would continue.

Legislation amending the 1995 Media Law, slated for review by the National Assembly in spring 2002, will further restrict the independent press in Belarus. Although the draft law simplifies registration procedures and increases the number of warnings the government must give publications before closing them for violating regulations, the legislation contains many vague provisions that can be used to curb independent media.

The amended law prohibits the mere mention of unregistered political parties or civic organizations; enjoins media outlets from receiving money from foreign or anonymous donors; and introduces new regulations for publications with a print run of less than 500 copies that could be used to censor them.

The law allows the Information Ministry to annul a media outlet's registration without judicial authorization. If it passes, the draft law will only add to the sizable arsenal of tactics used by the Lukashenko regime to stifle the independent press.

BOSNIA AND HERZEGOVINA

WHILE BOSNIA'S ETHNICALLY FRAGMENTED MEDIA showed modest signs of integration in 2001, independent journalists endured threats, harassment, and violence from political parties and government officials.

Nationalist and reformist parties battled in the November 2000 elections, with mixed results. The Bosnian Serb nationalist SDS party, formerly led by indicted war criminal Radovan Karadzic, handily won in the Serb entity of Republika Srpska (RS). The Croat nationalist HDZ party gained an absolute majority from ethnic Croat voters in the western and southwestern regions of the Muslim-Croat Federation, the other political entity within Bosnia.

The reformist SDP party, meanwhile, narrowly beat the Bosnian Muslim nationalist SDA party in central Bosnia and other areas of the federation.

After taking power in Republika Srpska, the SDS reinstated numerous party loyalists to senior police and security posts in early 2001. The return of SDS officials who had orchestrated the wartime ethnic cleansing campaigns made journalists cautious about reporting on war crimes, official corruption, and organized crime.

The RS police investigation into the October 1999 assassination attempt against Zeljko Kopanja, editor of the Banja Luka-based daily *Nezavisne Novine*, who lost both legs to a car bomb after publishing articles about Serbian war crimes, faltered after SDS officials took over the Interior Ministry.

The HDZ continued to resist international efforts to integrate Croat-dominated western Herzegovina within the federation. During the first several months of 2001, the HDZ boycotted the Parliament, threatened to establish its own ethnic Croat mini-state, and orchestrated a mutiny by ethnic Croat soldiers in the federation army. In March, the international officials who still effectively run Bosnia responded by sacking HDZ leader Ante Jelavic from the country's tripartite presidency.

Most media outlets in western Herzegovina remain under the control of the HDZ and backed the party's rebellion, while the HDZ pressures the few independent media outlets in the region. The intimidation became so intense in early 2001 that independent journalists asked press freedom organizations not to publicize their cases, for fear of worsening the situation.

In May, a CPJ delegation traveled to Bosnia to press RS authorities to move forward with the the Kopanja investigation and to address security threats to journalists. Zivko Radisic, the Serb chairman of the Bosnian Presidency, promised to discuss the case with RS prime minister Mladen Ivanic and Interior Minister Perica Bundalo, but no progress in the investigation had been reported by the end of 2001.

Meanwhile, press freedom conditions continued to deteriorate in Republika Srpska. In July, the director and news editor of Banja Luka's independent Alternativna Televizija (ATV) station and the editor of the Banja Luka youth magazine *BUKA* all received death threats for their coverage of war crimes and former Yugoslav president Slobodan Milosevic. The sluggish police response reinforced the impression that journalists can be intimidated with impunity.

There was also a sudden change in the management of the official Republika

Srpska news agency, SRNA, which was established during the war as an SDS mouthpiece. SRNA had recently gained some professional credibility and financial stability under director and editor Dragan Davidovic. But the RS government abruptly dismissed Davidovic in August in an apparently political move.

War crimes remained a dangerous topic for journalists to investigate, even in the relative safety of urban centers such as Sarajevo, where a reformist government was in power. On the evening of January 22, unknown assailants attacked Kristijan Ivelic, a reporter for the Sarajevo weekly magazine *Start BiH*, after he published a series of articles on the execution of 12 Yugoslav People's Army soldiers in the central park of Sarajevo in 1992.

Foreign journalists also remained vulnerable. In early June, a Belgian state television crew working on a documentary film about Karadzic was briefly detained at gunpoint after leaving Pale, a town where Karadzic lived during the Bosnian war. Masked gunmen blocked the road and confiscated their videotape.

One of the most significant developments in 2001 was the emergence of *Nezavisne Novine* as Bosnia's first truly national newspaper. It expanded coverage of local events throughout the country by opening bureaus in Muslim-dominated Sarajevo and in the Croat-Muslim city of Mostar. *Nezavisne Novine* also gained a truly national readership that crossed ethnic boundaries when it started using the Roman script, which is favored by Croats and Muslims. Moreover, the newspaper's moderate editorial policy and balanced coverage of Bosnia's appalling wartime history have earned it credibility.

Certain media reforms progressed due to pressure from the lead international agency in Bosnia, the Office of the High Representatives (OHR), as well as the Bosnia mission of the Vienna-based Organization for Security and Cooperation in Europe (OSCE).

In February, the OHR and the OSCE jointly proposed a draft defamation law for parliamentary approval in Republika Srpska and the federation. The proposed legislation would eliminate criminal defamation and restrict liability for civil defamation. The RS Parliament adopted the law in July, but the federation Parliament had failed to pass it by year's end.

International authorities also reformed Bosnia's internationally supervised broadcast regulatory agencies. In March, the OHR merged the International Media Commission and the Telecommunications Regulatory Agency to form a single Communications Regulatory Agency to regulate programming standards, election coverage, and frequency distribution.

BULGARIA

DURING 2001, MEDIA OUTLETS THAT CRITICIZED RULING AUTHORITIES faced harassment, while journalists investigating politically sensitive issues, such as official corruption and organized crime, continued to suffer threats and intimidation for their work.

A crisis erupted at Bulgarian National Radio (BNR), the country's largest and most influential media outlet, after the director's term expired on January 18. On

February 6, the National Council for Radio and Television (NCRT), a quasi-governmental media oversight board, appointed Ivan Borislavov, a supporter of the ruling Union of Democratic Forces (UDF) party, as the new BNR director. Staff members worried that the station would lose its editorial independence, particularly in the face of upcoming parliamentary elections, because of Borislavov's ties to the UDF. The following day, 200 BNR staff threatened to strike if he did not resign.

During the following weeks, demonstrations escalated and management dismissed a dozen popular news anchors for participating in the protests. On April 5, the Supreme Administrative Court annulled the appointment, concluding that it had violated administrative procedures, BTA news agency reported. While the decision was being appealed, BNR management dismissed an additional six protesters on April 10 and brought in journalists from the pro-UDF, Sofia-based daily *Demokratsia* to replace them. Finally, on May 15, the Supreme Court reaffirmed the April 5 ruling.

On May 28, the NCRT appointed a compromise candidate, journalist Polya Stancheva, as BNR director in order to defuse the conflict. Though also considered a UDF loyalist, Stanchev rehired the journalists who had been dismissed for participating in the protests.

The episode at BNR highlighted the problems with the NCRT. While it was originally established to limit excessive political influence over the media, "all nine members of the board were known to be supporters of the ruling [UDF] party," said Ognian Zlatev of the Sofia-based Media Development Center.

Independent media outlets continued to face indirect government harassment, especially when politicians used their influence to divert advertising revenue to loyal media outlets and away from more independent and critical outlets.

On March 5, Ivo Prokopiev and Filip Harmandjiev, editors-in-chief of the Sofia-based weekly *Kapital* and the Sofia-based daily *Dnevnik*, respectively, both accused Prosecutor General Nikola Filchev of launching multiple tax audits against them in retaliation for an article published in *Dnevnik* in early February. (The article detailed alleged criminal activities of the prosecutor general's brother.) The two editors also charged the audits were in reprisal for numerous *Kapital* articles criticizing the Prosecutor's Office.

On April 23, the Union of Bulgarian Newspaper Publishers, which represents the independent publishers of Bulgaria's 13 leading dailies, issued a statement expressing its "grave concern and categorically denounce [sic] increasing instances, in which the levers of power are used to exert pressure on daily newspapers and interfere in the editorial policy of many publications," Reuters reported.

The harassment of *Dnevnik* and *Kapital* occurred just as Bulgaria was preparing for crucial parliamentary elections on June 17. The state-run media—both BNR and Bulgarian National Television (BNT)—continued their tradition of providing preferential coverage of the ruling UDF party government.

But broad public frustration with political corruption and declining standards of living led angry voters to dump the ruling UDF coalition. The National Movement of Simeon II, a front representing the former Bulgarian king, who had recently returned from exile in Spain, won the election with nearly 43 percent of the vote. Later in the year, in two presidential election rounds held on November 11 and 18, Georgi Parvanov, leader of the opposition Socialist Party, defeated incumbent president Petar Stoyanov.

CROATIA

THE SHAKY COALITION OF REFORMIST PARTIES ELECTED IN 2000 after the death of the nationalist President Franjo Tudjman pressed ahead with political and economic reforms in 2001 and pushed to join the European Union. As a result, press freedom conditions in Croatia continued to improve. The government and the Parliament made some tentative efforts to revise media laws and reform state media institutions, though narrow political interests within the ruling coalition and efforts to retain influence over the press led to mixed results.

Tudjman's nationalist HDZ party fared surprisingly well in local elections held throughout Croatia on May 20, highlighting public frustration with poverty, painful economic reforms, and cooperation with the United Nations war crimes tribunal, which is investigating and prosecuting Balkans war crimes suspects. When it was in power during the 1990s, the HDZ used the police, judiciary, and domestic intelligence services to threaten, harass, and prosecute independent journalists. Out of power in 2001, the HDZ and its right-wing supporters became opportunistic defenders of press freedom.

On May 6, some 20,000 nationalists, war veterans, and HDZ supporters gathered in the Dalmatian city of Split to protest the demotion of Josip Jovic, editor of the state-owned Split daily *Slobodna Dalmacija*. (Jovic was made a columnist.) The newspaper was known for its aggressive use of ethnic hate speech under Jovic's editorial leadership, according to local media analyst Sasa Milosevic. Through the management change, the government hoped to discourage the promotion of interethnic hatred in the media.

While physical attacks on journalists decreased overall in 2001, right-wing political activists behaved aggressively toward journalists who reported on war crimes, according to the Croatian Helsinki Committee. On March 1, a group of ax-wielding men surrounded and beat photographer Rino Belan and journalist Damir Pilic, both from the Split weekly *Feral Tribune*, while they were visiting the southern town of Pakostane to investigate an indicted war criminal.

In many other cases, the HDZ sought to censure individuals who had questioned its policies while the party was in power. On October 1, for example, state-run Croatian Television (HTV) broadcast *Storm Over Krajina*, a groundbreaking documentary about war crimes committed by the Croatian Army against ethnic Serbs in Croatia in 1995. HTV journalist Denis Latin hosted a televised discussion after the film with both right- and left-wing commentators, but the HDZ was outraged and called for the dismissal of Latin and Croatian Radio Television (HRT) director Mirko Galic.

In late October, Parliament amended the Information Law to require media outlets to disclose their ownership to the government. However, according to the Croatian Helsinki Committee, the amendment does not require public disclosure.

Another piece of legislation passed in October seeks to reform and depoliticize the state-run HINA news agency, which served as an HDZ mouthpiece during the 1990s. Parliament did not, however, revise the Law on Telecommunication, leaving many of the country's radio stations in the hands of HDZ supporters who received licenses during Tudjman's reign. Some local media analysts support this conservative approach, arguing that because most licenses will expire in 2002 or 2003, waiting until then to reassess the distribution of broadcast licenses will be the least politicized way to reform the process.

Hundreds of outstanding libel cases filed against independent journalists who criticized the HDZ during the Tudjman regime are still making their way through the overburdened judicial system. A local media analyst noted that judges are no longer under constant government pressure as they were during the 1990s, making it more likely that they will dismiss the cases.

While the number of libel cases has decreased significantly, in late July, Montenegrin president Milo Djukanovic sued Ivo Pukanic, owner of the sensationalistic Zagreb weekly *Nacional*, along with editor-in-chief Sina Karli and reporters Jasna Babic and Berislav Jelinic. The suit was based on *Nacional* articles implicating Djukanovic in a multimillion-dollar illegal cigarette smuggling operation run by Balkan organized crime groups. The journalists could face up to three years in prison if convicted, The Associated Press reported. In November, Djukanovic sought US$100,000 in damages for the articles, but no progress was reported in the case at the end of the year.

In November, the Interior Ministry finally released some 120 surveillance files on "disloyal" journalists that the notorious Service for the Protection of the Constitutional Order (SZUP) had compiled in the 1990s. The ministry only allowed journalists to examine their own files, under highly restricted conditions. Both the Split weekly *Feral Tribune*—a frequent target of harassment during the Tudjman regime—and the Croatian Journalists Association called for the former SZUP officials, many of whom still occupy senior positions in the state intelligence service, to be held accountable for their actions, the HINA news agency reported. The current government has resisted pressure to prosecute these individuals.

CYPRUS

SOME **35,000** TURKISH TROOPS ARE STATIONED in the self-styled Turkish Republic of Northern Cyprus, which only Turkey recognizes as legitimate. The island remains divided into a more prosperous ethnic Greek sector in the south and an isolated and impoverished ethnic Turkish sector in the north. Cyprus' capital, Nicosia, sits in the middle of the island and is divided into two halves, one controlled by the internationally recognized Greek Cypriot authorities and the other by the Turkish government in Ankara.

During 2001, journalists in northern Cyprus frequently criticized the Turkish

Cypriot breakaway regime, founded after Turkey invaded the northern half of this Mediterranean island in 1974. In response, they were harassed and intimidated by Turkish Cypriot authorities and their supporters.

The daily *Avrupa*, based in northern Cyprus, is known for its aggressive reporting on Rauf Denktash, leader of the northern Cypriot regime, senior politicians in Ankara, and Turkish military officials based on the island. During 2001, the newspaper received regular threats and was also the victim of several violent attacks.

On May 24, a bomb blast caused significant damage to *Avrupa*'s printing offices. Agence France-Presse, citing eyewitnesses, said unidentified assailants placed the bomb at the printing house gate and fled the scene in a waiting car. CPJ protested the bombing, for which no one claimed responsibility.

The harassment of *Avrupa* intensified during the run-up to Denktash's December 4 meeting with Glafcos Clerides, the Greek Cypriot president of the Republic of Cyprus. The two leaders, who had not met in four years, planned to begin negotiating a settlement in hopes that all of Cyprus—not just the southern sector—could join the European Union in the near future.

On November 9, northern Cypriot authorities confiscated *Avrupa*'s computers over an unpaid 1997 tax debt, Agence France-Presse reported. The paper's editor, Sener Levent, charged that the seizure was related to articles critical of Turkish prime minister Bulent Ecevit and Foreign Minister Ismail Cem, who threatened to annex the island if the Greek Cypriot government joined the European Union on its own. In the end, Denktash backed away from this harsh rhetoric during his meeting with President Clerides and agreed to additional talks in January.

On December 9, a high school teacher in northern Cyprus was dismissed for criticizing the Turkish military presence in articles published in *Avrupa*. Some 350 students protested the dismissal in the Turkish-held sector of Nicosia.

On December 12, northern Cypriot authorities confiscated money and property from *Avrupa*. Authorities seized office furniture, equipment, and about 5 billion lira (US$3,500) in cash. The confiscations stemmed from a court-imposed fine of some 200 billion Turkish lira (US$138,000) resulting from a libel case that Denktash filed against the newspaper in 1999.

On December 15, the newspaper reappeared after a brief absence and announced that it had changed its name to *Afrika* to illustrate its contention that "the law of the jungle" ruled in northern Cyprus. The following day, *Afrika* reported that both Levent and *Afrika* reporter Ali Osman were preparing to sue the Turkish government in the European Court of Human Rights for arresting and detaining them on spurious espionage charges in July 2000. The journalists also planned to challenge the continued use of military courts in northern Cyprus.

Other cases of harassment and intimidation were reported as well. Sevgul Uludag, a journalist with the progressive, Turkish-language online magazine *Hamamboculeri* (www.hamamboculeri.org), told CPJ that in August, Turkish Cypriot militants threatened her and the publication in retaliation for articles that criticized the northern Cypriot regime.

In November, northern Cypriot authorities prevented a group of cartoonists from crossing the buffer zone dividing the island on their way to a joint exhibition of Greek and Turkish Cypriot cartoonists in the Greek sector of Nicosia, according to Huseyin Cakmak, president of the Turkish Cypriot Cartoonists' Association.

CZECH REPUBLIC

DESPITE THE CZECH REPUBLIC'S STATUS AS A LEADING CANDIDATE to join the European Union, local journalists continue to face significant risks for criticizing politicians and government policies, while political interference in the media inhibits the expansion of press freedom.

The country's entire political establishment was shaken at the beginning of the year by a crisis at Czech Television (CT). On December 20, 2000, CT's supervisors—all of them politically appointed—abruptly dismissed the general director and named journalist Jiri Hodac, a loyalist of Parliament speaker Vaclav Klaus' Civic Democratic Party (ODS), as the station's new head.

According to international reports, Hodac was appointed in a backroom deal between the ruling coalition and the powerful, conservative ODS. Klaus, a former prime minister, was suspected of trying to consolidate control over CT in advance of parliamentary elections, scheduled for sometime in 2002. CT staffers were so outraged that they occupied the station's offices and began broadcasting their protests during prime time.

The dispute also divided the country's political leaders, with President Vaclav Havel publicly supporting the journalists and criticizing Klaus, his main rival. On January 3, 2001, about 100,000 people gathered in Prague's Wenceslaus Square to demand Hodac's resignation. As popular support for the journalists grew, senior politicians backed away from Hodac. On January 11, 2001, with 50,000 protesters in Wenceslaus Square calling for him to step down, Hodac resigned.

On January 23, the lower house of Parliament—the House of Chambers—overrode Senate opposition and amended the country's Media Law in an effort to depoliticize the station. The nine-member Czech Television Council (CTC), which oversees the network, was dismissed and expanded to 15 members. The new legislation gave professional and civic organizations the right to nominate new CTC members, subject to Parliament's approval.

On February 9, Jiri Balvin, an experienced and respected journalist, was appointed as the interim CT director. CT staffers ended their strike on February 10 after receiving assurances from Balvin that he would maintain editorial independence. Parliament finally approved new CTC members in late May. On October 31, the CTC selected Balvin for a six-year term as CT general director.

Even as the CT crisis ebbed, independent journalists who criticized government policies continued to face considerable risk. On October 22, Prime Minister Milos Zeman threatened legal action against the independent, Prague-based weekly *Respekt* because of its sharp attacks on government corruption.

Zemen characterized the weekly as "the garbage pail of Czech journalism." After protests from CPJ and other press freedom organizations, Zemen abandoned his threatened lawsuit.

On February 28, a court ordered Zeman to offer a public apology for suggesting that Ivan Brezina of the Prague weekly *Reflex* had accepted bribes to write articles about a nuclear power plant. Zemen was also ordered to pay 300,000 koruny (US$8,000) in damages, the CTK news agency reported. On December 6, the ruling was overturned on appeal.

On October 23, Frantisek Zamecnik, former editor of the controversial, pro-communist regional weekly *Nove Bruntalsko*, was convicted of libeling three local officials and sentenced to 16 months in prison. The case was under appeal at year's end.

In a positive development, Tomas Smrcek, a former television reporter, was acquitted in June of "endangering classified information." Smrcek faced eight years in prison for displaying a confidential government document during a 1994 television interview that aired on the Nova channel. He had used the document to support allegations of corruption against the chief of the State Security Service.

The U.S. government–run news service Radio Free Europe/Radio Liberty (RFE/RL) has offices in Prague, and Czech authorities took steps throughout the year to protect the station from a number of threats. On April 22, for example, Czech authorities expelled Iraqi diplomat Ahmed Khalil Ibrahim Samir al-Ani for conducting surveillance of the RFE/RL headquarters. There were unconfirmed international press reports that al-Ani was planning a terrorist attack on the RFE/RL building, which also houses the U.S.-funded Radio Free Iraq.

After September 11, Czech authorities deployed troops and armored personnel carriers outside the RFE/RL building as a security precaution. Because of the physical vulnerability of the building, Prime Minister Zeman called on the United States to relocate RFE/RL headquarters from downtown Prague to a more secure location, The Associated Press reported.

GEORGIA

RIFE WITH CORRUPTION, ORGANIZED CRIME, AND POLITICAL INSTABILITY, Georgia is full of stories that are dangerous to tell. Journalists who dare to report on them risk reprisals, often from President Eduard Shevardnadze's strong-armed government.

Most chilling for journalists was the July murder of Georgy Sanaya, a popular, 26-year-old reporter for the Tbilisi-based independent television station Rustavi-2. Sanaya, who anchored "Night Courier," a nightly political talk show featuring interviews with Georgia's leading politicians, was found dead in his apartment on July 26. He had been shot once in the head at close range. His murder shocked the country and shook public confidence in its political leaders. A sluggish, secretive investigation only fed public discontent.

While Sanaya's work was not generally controversial, he had recently hosted a segment on Georgia's Pankisi Gorge, near Chechnya, an area that had been the scene of kidnappings and conflict between Georgians and Chechens. A former parliamentary deputy who appeared on "Night Courier" speculated that criminals from the Pankisi Gorge region may have been responsible for Sanaya's murder.

On December 6, they arrested former police officer Grigol Khurtsilava after a ballistic analysis traced the murder weapon to him, according to the Georgian news agency *Black Sea Press*. However, law enforcement officials continued to insist that Sanaya's murder was not politically motivated. Local journalists and the Georgian public generally dismissed the official theory, expressing a common view that Sanaya was murdered for his work.

Feeding this belief was the government's continued harassment of Rustavi-2, which has been punished repeatedly for its hard-hitting investigative reports on corruption and abuse of power. In October, Interior Minister Kakha Targamadze publicly threatened that he would take revenge on the station for its reports on allegations of corruption in the Interior and National Security ministries.

On October 31, National Security Ministry agents raided the station's headquarters, claiming they were searching for financial records in connection with charges that the station had not paid some 1 million laris (US$480,000) in taxes. But according to station manager Nika Tabatadze, tax authorities had audited and cleared the station a week before the raid. Station officials believe the move came in reprisal for Rustavi-2's coverage of unrest in the Pankisi Gorge region, its reporting on allegations that Georgia was harboring Chechen rebels, and its reports on ministerial corruption.

Once news of the raid spread, thousands of protestors gathered in central Tbilisi demanding the resignations of Shevardnadze, his entire government, and the Georgian Parliament. Tensions subsided in the following days only after Shevardnadze dismissed his cabinet. The speaker of the parliament, Zurab Zhvaniya, and Prosecutor General Georgy Meparishvili also resigned. Shevardnadze remained in power, but the political crisis weakened him even further, leaving Georgia on the verge of civil unrest.

Reporting on conflict in the Caucasus proved risky for Japanese free-lance journalist Kosuke Tsuneoka, who was kidnapped in the Pankisi Gorge in midyear and held for several months. Tsuneoka was reportedly captured while en route from Georgia to Chechnya to interview Chechen rebels. His captors were not identified, and Tsuneoka was finally freed on December 7 during a Georgian military operation.

HUNGARY

EVEN AS HUNGARY MOVED CLOSER TO JOINING THE EUROPEAN UNION, Prime Minister Viktor Orban and his right-wing Fidesz-Hungarian Civic Party (Fidesz-MPP) continued to bully Hungary's public service broadcasters and retaliate against unfavorable coverage in the independent media.

Hungary's ruling coalition—which includes Fidesz and two other parties—

used its control over the National Radio and Television Board (ORTT) and three other broadcast boards to promote its own political agenda.

Meanwhile, the ORTT took punitive measures against independent broadcasters. After the independent television station RTL aired an interview in April in which a guest identified as a hit man was asked how much he would charge to kill the prime minister, the ORTT fined the station US$17,600 and ordered it off the air for 10 minutes during prime time. On October 2, the ORTT criticized certain domestic television stations for overdramatizing their coverage of the terrorism crisis in the United States, rather than seeking to calm their audience.

In late March, Fidesz parliamentary deputies proposed a new privacy bill that would have amended the criminal code to allow media outlets to be prosecuted for invasion of privacy. The bill also contained a "right to reply" provision that would have forced media outlets to publish responses to editorial comments.

Despite protests from local press groups, Parliament adopted the law on May 30. But on June 12, President Ferenc Madl refused to sign the law and instead referred it to the Constitutional Court for an opinion. On December 4, the court ruled the law unconstitutional. Nevertheless, the Fidesz parliamentarian who proposed the bill said he planned to modify and reintroduce it.

In a positive development, Hungary's first Roma-language radio station, Radio C, which reaches Budapest's 100,000-strong Romany community, was granted a permanent license. In addition, a new press freedom group was established in 2001. The Budapest-based Hungarian Press Freedom Center seeks to protect and enhance press freedom in Hungary through advocacy, research, training, and legal assistance for journalists.

ITALY

BECAUSE PRESS FREEDOM IS GENERALLY RESPECTED IN ITALY, CPJ does not routinely monitor conditions in the country. However, CPJ did protest brutal attacks by police officers and demonstrators on journalists during the July 20-22 Group of Eight (G-8) summit of the world's industrialized nations in Genoa.

International reports and CPJ's own research concluded that the Italian police were responsible for most of the attacks. Officers beat several journalists during demonstrations on July 20, as well as during the night of July 21-22 when police raided a school that housed the Genoa Social Forum, an umbrella group of some 1,000 anti-globalization groups. The Independent Media Center (IMC), which helped many independent journalists file stories about the demonstrations, was housed in one of the buildings.

According to an Italian government report, some 13 police commanders and 70 police officers participated in the raid, in which about 90 people were arrested, the IMC was ransacked, and several independent journalists were beaten.

An internal government inquiry published on August 1 pointed to "errors and omissions" in the policing of the summit. On August 2, the Interior Ministry announced that three senior police officers responsible for security would be transferred from their posts. The police denied having used excessive force and claimed to have found numerous weapons and other evidence that protestors were planning violent attacks.

Demonstrators were also responsible for a number of assaults on journalists during the summit. On July 21, a group of militant anarchists attacked journalists and television crews from Germany and Japan, according to the London-based *Independent*.

On August 2, CPJ sent a letter to Italian prime minister Silvio Berlusconi protesting the attacks and urging an official inquiry. CPJ also expressed concern over reports that some police officers had disguised themselves as journalists in order to infiltrate the demonstrations. The letter noted that this tactic endangers all journalists. CPJ called for a thorough investigation.

CPJ also condemned calls by Italian judicial authorities that media outlets turn over photographs, audiotapes, and videotapes of the Genoa street violence. Reuters, The Associated Press, Agence France-Presse, and Italy's RAI state television network all received such orders in the two weeks following the raids, Reuters reported. Under Italian law, stiff penalties can be imposed on journalists or organizations that do not comply with such requests, and there is no possibility of appeal to the judiciary.

The Italian journalists' association advised its members not to give unpublished material to the authorities, and CPJ found no instances where material that had not already been made public was handed over. In its letter to Berlusconi, CPJ expressed concern that forcing journalists to act as police informants could severely jeopardize their safety and credibility.

On September 14, a parliamentary commission created to investigate allegations of police misconduct released its findings. The report praised the police for keeping order and blamed the violence on the protesters, who were accused of using criminal tactics.

The report stated that the police behavior during the Genoa Social Forum raid was lawful and justified by the officers' fear that some protestors had weapons. Criticism of the police was mild; tactical errors, such as "shortcomings and confusion" in coordination of police units were cited, as was some evidence that individual police officers used excessive force in carrying out their duties. The findings did not specifically address police brutality against journalists.

KAZAKHSTAN

ON MAY 3—WORLD PRESS FREEDOM DAY—President Nursultan Nazarbayev approved restrictive amendments to Kazakhstan's already burdensome Mass Media Law. Under the law, organizations designated as members of the "mass media" are subject to a host of harsh provisions. But Nazarbayev's amendment widened the legal net by designating Web sites as "mass media" as well. This change mainly affected independent journalists and politicians, who tend to publish on the Internet. Most of the country's newspapers and televisions stations are owned, directly or indirectly, by the president's family or business associates.

The amendments also limited the amount of foreign programming Kazakh media outlets are allowed to air. Local independent broadcasters complained that because foreign programming is so popular, any reduction would decrease advertising revenues. In addition, small independent stations cannot afford to produce original material to replace foreign broadcasts.

Finally, a tightening of criminal libel laws made it even easier to prosecute editors and media owners in a country where any government criticism brings harsh legal reprisals.

On April 17, CPJ wrote to President Nazarbayev to protest the one-year prison term handed to Yermurat Bapi, editor of the opposition weekly *SolDat*, who was convicted of "publicly insulting the dignity and honor of the president" in a published article. Though Bapi was pardoned, he remained a convicted criminal and was barred from traveling abroad.

On April 20, unknown individuals broke into *SolDat*'s editorial offices. Software and files were destroyed, and expensive electronic equipment was damaged. Local sources told CPJ that the robbers were trying to prevent the paper from being published. Meanwhile, Bapi's colleagues told local reporters that at least five printers in the city of Almaty had refused to produce the paper.

Bapi was kept from leaving Kazakhstan to attend a U.S. congressional hearing on repression in Central Asia, which was held on July 18. CPJ testified at the hearing and condemned the Kazakh regime's abysmal press freedom record.

CPJ also protested the politically motivated charges against Bigeldi Gabdullin, editor of the opposition weekly *XXI Vek*. Gabdullin was accused of criminal defamation after publishing two articles in October 2000 alleging that the president was involved in corruption. The case was dismissed in April 2001. On January 9, meanwhile, Gabdullin was fined 5 million tenge (nearly US$34,500) when a court found him guilty of slandering a company owned by the president's son-in-law, Rakhat Aliyev.

Aliyev also sued the privately owned biweekly *Vremya Po* for insulting his personal dignity and honor in its coverage of an argument between him and a political rival. On December 14, 2001, the paper was ordered to pay Aliyev 3 million tenges (about US$20,000) in damages.

The state controls all of Kazakhstan's printing houses, as well as the country's two main Internet service providers. Officials often block access to politically sensitive material, including the Web site of the Moscow-based Information Analytical Center Eurasia (www.eurasia.org.ru), which is funded by exiled members of Kazakhstan's opposition party, the Republican People's Party of Kazakhstan.

KYRGYZSTAN

PRESS FREEDOM IN KYRGYZSTAN SUFFERED MAJOR SETBACKS in 2001 as President Askar Akayev continued his increasingly repressive curtailment of dissent.

Politically motivated civil libel suits resulted in exorbitant damage awards, driving some newsapers to the brink of bankruptcy.

In March, a Bishkek court ordered the Uchkun Publishing House to stop printing *Asaba*, the oldest and most popular Kyrgyz-language publication in the country, until the paper had paid fines and damages totaling 8 million soms (about US$160,000).

For two weeks in March, the Bishkek-based opposition weekly *Res Publica* published articles by *Asaba*. But when officials began confiscating *Asaba*'s property on March 15, they also impounded 6,600 pounds (3,000 kilograms) of newsprint stored at Uchkun. That effectively blocked the publication of both newspapers, since *Res Publica* has no paper reserves of its own. On March 19, *Asaba*'s owner announced that the newspaper was suspending publication indefinitely. *Asaba* remains closed, but in October government loyalists opened a new, pro-government newspaper under the same name.

In a separate case, the Pervomaisky District Court found *Res Publica* guilty on October 17 of defaming Aleksandr Yeliseyev, a former member of the Kyrgyz Committee for Human Rights (KCHR). The newspaper was ordered to pay 300,000 soms (more than US$6,300) in damages for publishing several articles earlier in the year about the circumstances surrounding Eliseev's 1997 dismissal from the KCHR.

Sardarbek Botaliyev, another former KCHR member, also sued *Res Publica*, accusing the paper of defaming him in a series of articles about his 1996 dismissal from the KCHR.

These cases followed a February ruling that forced *Res Publica* to pay an overdue fine stemming from two 1999 libel cases. Though the paper has been publishing somewhat regularly online, it has had difficulty producing hard copies.

The government also used convoluted registration regulations to curb the opposition press. In April and May, the Justice Ministry granted registration to 16 new media outlets, including the independent newspapers *Moya Stolitsa*, *Agym*, *Techeniye*, and *Joltiken*, only to rescind all 16 registrations in June. The ministry explained that the 16 new outlets were registered before all existing media outlets had renewed their registration, which violated a decision that the ministry had secretly adopted on April 5.

In separate lawsuits, *Moya Stolitsa* editor-in-chief Aleskandr Kim and Bakyt Jamalidinov, the publisher of *Agym*, *Techeniye* and *Joltiken*, challenged the ministry's actions. Jamalidinov dropped his case after the Justice Ministry registered his papers in early November. They began publishing later that month, according to Radio Free Europe/Radio Liberty. *Moya Stolitsa*'s lawsuit was still pending in early 2002, although the newspaper's staff was working at another newly registered publication, *Moya Stolitsa-Novosti*.

Despite lengthy debates and high expectations, parliament failed to repeal criminal libel statutes. Parliamentary committee member Azimbek Beknazarov told local reporters that the Justice Ministry, the Prosecutor General's Office, and the Supreme Court felt it was "too early" to repeal the laws.

Meanwhile, the government proposed other legislation that critics said could be used to jail journalists who criticize the government. The broad and vague Decree 358, unveiled in July, would have revised Article 297 of Kyrgyzstan's Criminal Code to establish prison terms for activities aimed at overthrowing or undermining constitutional order. After loud domestic and international protests, the decree was withdrawn. The government said it would revise the proposal, but had not done so by year's end.

LATVIA

MOST OF LATVIA'S NEWSPAPERS, TELEVISION STATIONS, AND RADIO OUTLETS are privately owned, and press freedom is generally respected in this Baltic nation. But the murder of a Latvian investigative reporter in 2001 highlighted the dangers that face local journalists who cover organized crime.

Gundars Matiss, a 35-year-old crime reporter with the Liepaja-based daily *Kurzemes Vards*, was attacked on November 15 in the stairwell of his apartment. He was struck several times on the head, arms, and legs with a truncheon or club. After three operations, he fell into a coma. Matiss died of a brain hemorrhage on November 28.

Matiss had not been robbed and does not seem to have been involved in any serious personal dispute. His editor, Andzilss Remess, told CPJ: "Matiss knew a lot about the criminal world. He was one of those reporters who went deep." His latest project was an investigation of the contraband alcohol trade in Liepaja, according to Remess. At press time, the police investigation was still ongoing.

The Matiss case notwithstanding, most Latvian journalists work largely without interference. However, local journalists say they sometimes practice self-censorship because of laws that impose stiff penalties for libel and "propagating racial, ethnic, or religious superiority."

When Latvia became an independent country in 1991 after several decades of Soviet rule, about half the population spoke Russian. The issue of language and other rights for ethnic Russians remains perennially contentious for the country's politicians. In 1995, Latvia adopted the Law on Radio and Television, which stipulates that no more than 25 percent of all broadcasting can be in languages other than Latvian. Although President Vaira Vike-Freiberga said in April that the requirement "may change in a couple of years," it had already been used in March to impose a one-week broadcasting suspension on a radio station owned by the media group Bizess & Baltija. The company challenged the suspension, but the case remained unresolved at year's end.

MACEDONIA

FIGHTING BETWEEN THE MACEDONIAN GOVERNMENT and ethnic Albanian rebels seeking increased civil liberties escalated throughout the year, pushing the country to the edge of civil war. Unprofessional reporting and outright hate speech by both ethnic Macedonian and ethnic Albanian journalists played a central role in radicalizing their respective communities and polarizing the political atmosphere.

Several weeks before the initial outbreak of fighting in February, a scandal branded the "Macedonian Watergate" shook the country's political establishment. Branko Crvenkovski, leader of the country's largest opposition party, accused Prime Minister Ljubco Georgievski of illegally wiretapping the conversations of top government officials and other prominent figures, including some 25 journalists. Crvenkovski produced 140 pages of transcripts in which several journalists recognized their telephone conversations with politicians.

Journalists began avoiding using their phones, particularly mobile phones, for work-related conversations, according to local media analyst Vesna Sopar.

Also in February, Macedonian authorities withdrew a proposed Law on Public Information after local journalists and international press freedom groups criticized it. The draft legislation would have required all media outlets to seek government accreditation, provided inadequate access to official information, and codified standards for ethical journalism.

Later that month, ethnic Albanian rebels calling themselves the National Liberation Army (NLA) began occupying swathes of territory in northern and western Macedonia. On February 16, NLA rebels detained and questioned a television crew from the independent station A1. The rebels also confiscated the journalists' equipment. Interior Ministry forces, meanwhile, harassed journalists and limited their ability to travel to NLA-controlled territory.

On March 14, protesters beat up Sitel Television cameraman Dusan Kardalevski and A1 reporter Atanas Sokolovski, who were covering an ethnic Albanian rally in the western city of Tetevo, Sitel Television reported.

Government officials took steps to censor certain Western news organizations whose coverage of the conflict displeased them. On March 11, the director of state-run Macedonian Radio, Antoan Sereci, announced that the station would no longer air BBC news bulletins in the Macedonian and Albanian languages, The Associated Press reported.

Macedonian authorities also targeted ethnic Albanian publications. On March 22, Interior Ministry officials at Skopje's Petrovec International Airport confiscated the international edition of *Fakti*, a nationalistic, Albanian-language daily newspaper, as it was about to be shipped to Switzerland, according to local news reports. An Interior Ministry spokesman said the edition was confiscated because it contained an article calling on ethnic Albanians émigrés to join the rebels. Later, in an effort to downplay the incident, ministry officials described the confiscation as unlawful and mistaken.

As the conflict intensified, Macedonian government officials struggled to retain editorial and political control over increasingly pro-NLA Albanian-language news programs on state-run Macedonian Television. On April 30, Macedonian Television suspended its late-night Albanian-language news program because of its "ethnic intolerance" and anti-state broadcasts,

Deutsche Press Agentur reported. Daytime news programs in Albanian were suspended for three weeks in August when NATO troops were entering Macedonia to disarm the NLA, according to one CPJ source.

As Western officials became more involved in mediating the conflict and pressuring the government to grant ethnic Albanians broader civil rights, foreign correspondents became convenient targets for angry Macedonian Slavs. On the evening of June 25, after the European Union brokered a cease-fire that allowed rebels to leave a town just outside the capital, Skopje, without disarming, a massive riot erupted in protest. Some 5,000 Macedonian Slavs marched through Skopje firing guns. The protesters occupied the parliament building for a few hours and beat up several foreigners, including two BBC journalists.

In some cases, police were barely able to protect journalists. On August 12, an angry mob in a northern village surrounded and assaulted three Danish journalists and their ethnic Albanian driver. When the police pulled them to safety, the crowd pulled the journalists out and continued beating them. Police officers were eventually able to return the journalists to Skopje, but the fate of the driver was not known.

The conflict also resulted in the death of one foreign correspondent. On March 29, the Macedonian Army launched a mini-offensive against the NLA in northern Macedonia. Just across the border in Kosovo, meanwhile, NATO-led peacekeepers tried to prevent Albanian guerrillas from crossing into Macedonia.

Kerem Lawton, 30, a British national and producer for Associated Press Television News, was killed when a mortar shell struck his vehicle in the Kosovo village of Krivenik as he was arriving to cover the NATO operation. Both Macedonian military officials and ethnic Albanian insurgents denied responsibility. CPJ protested Lawton's death, but at the end of the year it still remained unclear where the shell came from and whether the attack was deliberate.

In the later stages of the conflict, there were also reports that the government harassed Macedonian-language media outlets in retaliation for their reporting. On June 2, the state-run Nova Makedonija publishing company dismissed the editor-in-chief of the pro-government Skopje daily *Nova Makedonija* after one of his articles proposed resolving the conflict by exchanging territory and populations with neighboring countries, the SAFAX news agency reported.

While fighting between the NLA and government forces subsided after a peace accord was signed on August 13, one of the conflict's gravest casualties remained journalistic professionalism and impartiality. A1 Television director Aco Kabranov said, "What is difficult is the polarization of the media space—the Albanian propaganda on one side and the regime's on the other pushed by Macedonian national television," Agence France-Presse reported.

By the end of the summer, even the popular, independent A1 Television gave in to pressure and started supporting the government. "The media, like everything else in Macedonia, is divided into two camps, broken along ethnic lines," Dejar Georgievski, a Skopje-based media analyst, told *The Christian Science Monitor*.

MOLDOVA

GOVERNMENT PRESSURE ON THE MOLDOVAN MEDIA increased in 2001 after the Communist Party won a majority in the February parliamentary elections. The Communist candidate, Vladimir Voronin, was elected president in April.

Soon after the presidential elections, the Chisinau-based Independent Journalism Center reported that journalists from the opposition publications *Flux*, *Tara*, *Jurnal de Chisinau*, and *Trud-Moldova* were denied accreditation for President Voronin's April 7 inauguration. The stated reason was lack of space, but the journalists were told unofficially that access was denied because they worked for "bourgeois" newspapers.

In mid-July, the Moldovan Parliament approved an amendment to the Press Law banning domestic news media from receiving foreign funding. The government claimed the amendment would reduce foreign interference in Moldova's internal affairs, but with the country sliding deeper into poverty, the legislation is more likely to put a financial strain on opposition and independent publications, which are not state subsidized.

National and local officials frequently keep public information from reporters, especially those affiliated with independent media outlets. The European Institute for the Media, a nonprofit research organization, reported that Moldova's Administrative Code was amended in 2001 to impose a fine of up to 2,700 lei (US$210) for violating the Access to Information Law.

The Criminal Code was also amended and now punishes deliberate failure to grant access to information of public interest with up to three years in prison. It is unclear if these new regulations will be enforced.

Growing tensions between the official government in the capital, Chisinau, and authorities in the breakaway region of Trans-Dniester, which is dominated by ethnic Russians and Ukrainians, added to the hardships of journalists on both sides of the conflict. In early October, Moldova's Prosecutor General asked a Chisinau district court to close the Russian-language weekly *Kommersant Moldovy* for backing the Trans-Dniester separatists.

The court banned *Kommersant Moldovy*. However, in mid-December, the paper resumed publication under the name *Kommersant Plus*.

In later October, Chisinau police detained a television crew from Trans-Dniester's official news agency, Olvia Press, and questioned them about their work and their stance on Moldova's territorial integrity. They were held for several hours and their videotapes were confiscated.

In retaliation, Trans-Dniester authorities rescinded the accreditation of 17 Moldovan journalists and ordered them to leave the territory by November 1. Trans-Dniester officials said they would not reconsider their decision until they received an official apology and the confiscated videotape. Two weeks later, Moldovan authorities apologized, and the Trans-Dniester authorities reinstated the journalists' accreditations.

POLAND

SCANDAL MONGERING AND MUDSLINGING BLACKENED THE IMAGES of both politicians and the press in 2001, particularly during the run-up to September's parliamentary elections.

The first scandal erupted in January after *Rzeczpospolita*, a leading Warsaw daily, published a series of investigative pieces on official corruption. Justice Minister Lech Kaczynski accused the paper of conspiring with the Polish Special Services to uncover compromising evidence designed to ruin officials' reputations and force them to resign; the paper denied the charge. Kaczynski implied that the paper's evidence was invalid and opened an investigation to find out who had leaked the compromising information.

Kaczynski subsequently retracted these claims in a January 13 letter of apology to *Rzeczpospolita* and promised to investigate the newspaper's allegations. But the paper, along with politicians and media and civic groups, accused Kaczynski of assaulting press freedom. The controversy finally died down in August, when Kaczynki's initial investigation into the paper's alleged collusion with the Special Services was dropped.

Kaczynski was at the center of a second scandal that shook Poland in June, when the public television network TVP accused the minister and his brother, Jaroslaw, of embezzling US$600,000 during the 1990s that had been earmarked to repay part of Poland's foreign debt. The network, whose management has close ties to Poland's former communist SLD movement, charged that the Kaczynski brothers used the money to finance their right-wing Law and Justice party, an SLD rival.

A group of parliamentarians from several parties charged that TVP's report was a biased and politically motivated effort to discredit the SLD's rival candidates during the parliamentary election campaign. The Association of Polish Journalists also accused the network of allowing political bosses to exploit it for political ends. "Freedom of speech was supposed to exist in a free Poland, and public television was supposed to be reliable and unbiased," the association said, according to the Polish news agency Polska Agencja Prasowa. "Never have we departed so far from these values and standards." The association called for amendments to the national broadcasting law to prevent media exploitation for political purposes.

On July 2, the Kaczynski brothers sued TVP and sought an apology for the network's allegations. The case was still pending at the end of the year.

Meanwhile, Poland's goal of joining the European Union, which has called for legal and constitutional reforms, boosted legislation that promotes greater press freedom in 2001. After long delays, parliament approved a new Access to Public Information Law. In October, a month after its final approval, the law was tested in a Lublin District Court case when Miroslaw Sznajder, editor-in-chief of the Krasnik-based newspaper *Nowiny Krasnicke*, filed a complaint against local mayor Piotr Czubinski. The court found Czubinski guilty of witholding public information and ordered him to pay a 2200 zloty (US$540) fine to the Press Freedom Monitoring Center. The mayor also promised never to obstruct press investigations again.

ROMANIA

WIDESPREAD POVERTY, FALTERING POLITICAL AND ECONOMIC REFORMS, and slowing progress toward European Union membership continue to inhibit the expansion of press freedom in Romania, where Ion Iliescu and his leftist coalition won presidential and parliamentary elections held in late 2000.

On January 10, 2001, Prime Minister Adrian Nastase's government placed the official Rompres news agency—generally know for its objectivity—under the direct control of the Ministry of Public Information. Two weeks later, the government appointed journalist and party loyalist Ioan Mihai Rosca as the agency's new director. Though no significant changes in Rompres' editorial policy were reported, local press freedom groups were concerned that the new government moved so quickly to consolidate power over a respected public media outlet.

Soon after, Parliament took several initiatives that frightened press freedom advocates. On February 7, parliamentary deputy Ristea Priboi, a close adviser of Prime Minister Nastase, was elected chairman of the Foreign Intelligence Service Oversight Committee. Evidence then emerged that Priboi had worked for communist dictator Nicolae Ceausescu's notorious Securitate, or secret police, during the Cold War. Priboi was also involved in intimidating journalists from the Romanian service of the Radio Free Europe/Radio Liberty (RFE/RL), a U.S. government–funded radio network, when it was based in Munich. He was forced to resign in April.

On March 7, Parliament approved a vaguely defined and highly restrictive Law on State Secrets. The law would punish individuals who obtain or publish state secrets with up to seven or 10 years in prison, respectively. After Prime Minister Nastase, the Romanian Press Club, and the U.S. Department of State criticized the law, Romanian Radio reported that President Iliescu would return it to the Parliament for revisions. A new version was drafted, according to the Media Monitoring Agency, but there were no reports that Parliament had considered it by the end of the year.

Parliament also managed to pass a Freedom of Access to Information Law (FOIA), Rompres reported. Several local nongovernmental organizations, including the Media Monitoring Agency and the Center for Independent Journalism, participated in analyzing and revising the draft law, which was passed on April 18. Rompres reported that the legislation guarantees citizens and journalists access to information "of public interest," but limits access to national security information and information on judicial proceedings. There are also sanctions for civil servants who violate the law.

Romanian libel laws favor plaintiffs, and politicians and government officials often use them to intimidate media outlets and discourage critical reporting. Estimates suggest that hundreds of libel cases are currently pending against journalists, and that the lawsuits themselves force media outlets to divert significant amounts of time and resources away from reporting. Cartoonist Marius Nitov, for example, was convicted and fined 8 million lei (US$400), a large sum by Romanian standards, for drawing a cartoon depicting his communist village mayor as a pig, the Cartoonists Rights Network reported.

Even senior politicians felt free to lash out at journalists in response to negative press coverage. On September 17, Romanian Radio news director Paul Grigoriu broadcast an interview with far-right parliamentarian Corneliu Vadim Tudor, who accused President Iliescu of having allegedly authorized government officials to provide military training for members of the militant Palestinian group Hamas in 1995. That same day, President Iliescu denounced the radio host for not defending his president, Romanian Radio reported. Grogoriu was suspended the following day.

In one positive case, a Bucharest court reversed a ruling against Alison Mutler, a reporter for the The Associated Press in Bucharest. She was sued for libel by Bishop Laszlo Toekes over a June 1998 story that cited a statement Toekes had made about his forced collaboration with Romania's communist-era secret police. Though Mutler was acquitted of libel, she was convicted of having caused "moral damages" and was ordered to pay Toekes 700 million lei (US$22,000). On November 5, the fine was overturned.

On November 18, two men wearing ski masks and wielding iron bars attacked Lucian Valeriu of the Arad daily *Observator* after he published a series of articles about links between criminals and local police, The Associated Press reported. Valeriu's editor said a police officer had recently threatened to kill the journalist if he continued writing articles on the police.

RUSSIA

A DECADE AFTER THE DEMISE OF THE SOVIET UNION, Russia still struggled to define the limits of free expression. Nowhere was the struggle more intense than in the media. President Vladimir Putin's administration was either directly involved in or held responsible for a broad range of abuses, including the selective use of tax audits, prosecutions, and police raids to stifle independent media outlets, as well as the stealthy amassing of control over information. In addition, widespread violence against journalists continued, with official investigations stagnant and perpetrators rarely punished.

In May, CPJ named Putin to its annual list of the Ten Worst Enemies of the Press, the first time since the collapse of the Soviet Union that a Russian leader was included. (See page 597.) And while Putin did improve relations with the United States and other Western democracies during 2001, he still faced strong international protests over his media policies.

The year's biggest story was the battle waged for control over NTV—one of the only independent television networks in Russia with national reach. The fight pitted Media-Most, a holding company owned by the exiled media magnate Vladimir Gusinsky, against its main creditor, the state gas monopoly Gazprom. The saga began when armed police and tax officials raided Media-Most's Moscow headquarters in May 2000, and it ended 11 months later after a boardroom coup handed the government-dominated corporation formal control of NTV.

Independent NTV was the jewel in the crown of Media-Most. The network's news and current affairs programs regularly criticized government policies, particularly the war in Chechnya. Gazprom pursued Gusinsky and Media-Most through the courts, charging fraud, tax evasion, and financial mismanagement. The gas company backed up its boardroom takeover with direct action: A new management team forcibly occupied NTV on April 14, 2001.

Gazprom swiftly closed two more Media-Most outlets, targeting publications also known for criticizing the government. On April 16, the staff of the daily *Segodnya* was ousted and its editor fired. The next day, security guards barred the employees of the weekly newsmagazine *Itogi* from entering their offices and dismissed the editor. The management of Media-Most's Ekho Moskvy, the country's largest privately held news radio station, remained in place, though the station suffered a spate of police raids and tax inspections.

Officials—including Gazprom-Media's then-general director Alfred Kokh, who visited CPJ's New York City offices on March 6—insisted that the dispute between Media-Most and Gazprom was purely financial. CPJ argued that Gazprom's heavy-handed tactics revealed political motives behind the takeover. In an April 30 letter to President Putin, CPJ emphasized that financial concerns could not account for the dismissal of the editor of *Itogi*, a magazine that was both profitable and highly respected.

Though media analysts said that NTV retained some of its independent voice under the new management, the station's anti-Kremlin tone softened significantly. After their ouster, many NTV journalists moved to TV-6, the remaining private network with national reach.

Boris Berezovksy, a Yeltsin-era media and oil tycoon and a bitter opponent of Putin, controlled TV-6 until Press Minister Mikhail Lesin ordered the channel off the air at midnight on January 22, 2002. The move came after a legal battle between the network and a minority shareholder, LUKOIL-Garant, resulted in the liquidation of TV-6's parent company. The oil giant LUKOIL has strong links with the Kremlin, and TV-6's fate was seen by many Russian politicians and journalists as part of a state-orchestrated campaign to control Russian citizens' access to information. At press time, TV6 was off the air but planned to bid in March 2002 to regain its old frequency.

Not content with solidifying Kremlin control over national television, Putin signed an August 13 decree re-establishing federal control over the entire national network of broadcasting and relay stations for television and radio signals. The state-owned Russian Television and Radio Broadcasting Network (RTRS) now controls the stations and reports to the Ministry of Press and Information, whose chief, Mikhail Lesin, is seen by many as an opponent of independent media. The decree created state subsidies for channels serving areas with a population of less than 200,000. Since state-run channels broadcast nationwide to rural communities, state television will benefit from the subsidies. The new rules also gave Lesin and the Kremlin vital new leverage over all private radio and television stations.

State surveillance of the Internet continued through regulations requiring Russian Internet Service Providers to install a monitoring device that routes all their traffic through servers controlled by local law enforcement agencies. The creation of the Kremlin-backed Media Union to rival the existing Russian Union of Journalists (RUJ) also alarmed press freedom advocates. The RUJ reportedly irritated the government with its active support of press freedom. In September, the head of the RUJ said the trade union was fighting an eviction order from the Ministry of State Property.

Moscow also imposed increasingly tight restrictions on journalists reporting on the Chechen war, who already face the risk of violence and kidnapping in the region. One kidnapping victim, French free-lance photographer Brice Fleutiaux, who was held hostage in Chechnya for eight months in 1999 and 2000, committed suicide in France on April 24.

On February 20, Russian security forces in Chechnya detained *Novaya Gazeta* war correspondent Anna Politkovskaya, who was investigating Russian military abuses against Chechen civilians. Politkovskaya was accused of entering Chechnya without correct accreditation and of not registering her whereabouts with the Russian military. She told CPJ that Russian soldiers threatened to shoot her during her three-day ordeal. In September, Politkovskaya received several death threats in connection with her Chechnya reports, and in early October she fled temporarily to Vienna, Austria. CPJ met her in Vienna to discuss and publicize her plight.

In March, the Media Ministry warned the Moscow daily *Nezavisimaya Gazeta* that it had violated the law by publishing an interview with Chechen leader Aslan Maskhadov. Officials also complained about several other interviews with Maskhadov published on the Web site Grani.ru, in the business daily *Kommersant*, and in the twice-weekly *Novaya Gazeta*. Presidential aide Sergei Yasterzhembsky said on August 30 that he was seeking to ban news reporting on the views of Chechen fighters. At the end of the year, the Duma passed a measure forbidding the media from broadcasting "propaganda" from terrorists.

On February 8, Radio Free Europe/Radio Liberty announced plans to start broadcasts in Chechen and two other languages of the Northern Caucasus. But Russian lawmakers and Media Ministry officials labeled the plans "very inappropriate," and by year's end the broadcasts had not begun.

In a final, year-end blow, a Russian military court sentenced military journalist Grigory Pasko to four years in prison on December 25. Pasko was convicted of "treason in the form of espionage" for the crime of "intending" to give classified documents to Japanese news outlets. He had been reporting on environmental damage caused by the Russian navy for his newspaper, *Boyevaya Vakhta* (Battle Watch).

In early June, a CPJ delegation traveled to Vladivostok before Pasko's trial to publicize concerns over the charges. The trial was conducted in a secret military court, calling into question the impartiality and independence of the proceedings. The case, which had dragged on for years, was emblematic of the persecution that environmental whistle-blowers have come to expect in Russia.

Officials also used economic pressure to harass the media, including tax raids, police confiscations of print runs or videotapes, and official pressure on businesses to withhold advertising from publications deemed troublesome. During a CPJ visit to Moscow in March, *Novaya Gazeta* editor Dmitry Muratov told CPJ staff that his paper, a harsh critic of the government, had endured dozens of lawsuits and several major tax inspections. In addition, said Muratov, advertisers had come under intense pressure to pull their ads from the paper.

Such harassment was even more commonplace in Russia's provinces, where media outlets are more vulnerable to the whims of local leaders. In the Primorsky Region, for example, defamation suits were frequent, and the courts imposed large fines on journalists and media outlets, sometimes pushing them into bankruptcy.

Low advertising revenues and high distribution costs sent other media companies, particularly newspapers, begging to federal or local officials for government subsidies and tax breaks. Meanwhile, broadcasters unable to pay their electricity bills were shut down in the regions of Khabarovsk, Primorye, Kamchatka, and Altai.

During 2001, only one journalist was killed for his work in Russia, compared with three in 2000. Eduard Markevich, editor and publisher of the local newspaper *Novy Reft* in Sverdlovsk Region, was found dead on September 18. Markevich's paper often criticized local officials, and he had suffered at least one violent attack and many death threats during the last several years.

Journalists were assaulted throughout Russia in 2001, with dozens of cases recorded by CPJ and Moscow watchdog groups such as the Center for Journalism in Extreme Situations and the Glasnost Defense Foundation. On February 7, two armed men stormed the offices of the opposition newspaper *Vozrozhdeniye Respubliki* in Cherkessk, the capital of the southern Karachai-Cherkessia Republic, and severely beat two editors. Editor Rashid Khatuyev linked the attack to critical articles that the newspaper had published about the republic's president.

In the southern city of Belgorod, local authorities used violence against investigative reporter Olga Kitova after she published a series of articles in *Belgorodskaya Pravda* in May 2000 that questioned the credibility of a local prosecutor's case. Even though police assaulted the journalist, Kitova was charged with using force against officers, as well as with slander. On December 20, she received a two-and-a-half year suspended sentence, a large fine, and was banned from elected office for three years.

SLOVAKIA

As Slovakia adopts political reforms aimed at European Union membership, the government remains slow to change press laws and revamp the state-run media. Criminal libel cases against journalists and political influence over media outlets also hindered the Slovak press in 2001.

Politicians continue to influence the editorial policies of Slovak Television (STV) and Slovak Radio (SRO) through the governing STV and SRO councils, whose members they appoint. Officials also control membership on the Broadcasting and Retransmission Council, which regulates the broadcast media. Political manipulation tends to be most blatant during election campaigns, when lawmakers pressure STV to broadcast their speeches, according to local media expert Andrej Skolkay. Other, more subtle forms of pressure, such as phone calls to editors, are also common.

Strong disagreements between the current government and the Parliament over state media reform and, particularly, the degree of autonomy that government-run media outlets should have, stalled crucial reforms this year. Lawmakers failed to strengthen financial oversight of STV and SRO, which both suffered from significant mismanagement and accumulated a massive debt of 927 million korunas (US$19 million) in 2001. Slovakia's state privatization agency, the National Property Fund, was forced to bail out both stations in July.

Reflecting a broader pattern of discrimination against the country's Roma minority, few Romany journalists served on state media editorial boards. On November 13, some 50 Romany associations called for Romany journalists to be appointed to the boards, in part, to ensure that state media present more objective information about issues affecting the Romany community, the CTK news agency reported.

In June, President Rudolf Schuster filed a defamation suit against Ales Kratky, a reporter for the Bratislava daily *Novy Cas*, after Kratky wrote that the president's state of the union address indicated that Schuster showed a "mental incapacity to lead the country." Kratky faces up to two years in prison if convicted. His case was still pending at press time.

Meanwhile, some politicians use their financial resources to influence the editorial policies of independent media outlets. In some cases, media executives become actively involved in politics. Media tycoon Pavol Rusko, chairman of Markiza TV, the country's most popular private television station, has used his station to promote the New Citizens' Alliance, a political party he created in May 2001.

SLOVENIA

While press freedom is generally respected in Slovenia, a brutal attack against one journalist and the potential prosecution of another have raised some concerns about the government's commitment to protecting the press.

Miro Petek, a journalist for the Maribor daily *Vecer*, Slovenia's second-largest newspaper, was attacked outside his home in the small town of Mezica on the evening of February 28 by two unknown men. Petek sustained severe skull fractures and spent five months recovering from the nearly fatal attack.

Local sources and press reports linked the attack to an investigation into financial irregularities in the business partnership between a local company and a bank that Petek had been pursuing for more than a year. President Milan Kucan denounced the attack, and an inquiry was launched under the supervision of the National Police. However, police investigators chose to focus their attention on the personal lives of Petek and his associates.

Grega Repovz, President of the Slovenian Journalistic Society, told CPJ that local investigators had identified two suspects, but that the National Police had not detained them. Repovz did not know why the investigation was moving so slowly, but he said, "The lack of progress...has definitely caused self-censorship [among journalists] in the Koroska region where Petek lives and works."

The second case involved Blaz Zgaga, an investigative journalist who also works for *Vecer*. On June 10, 2000, *Vecer* published an article by Zgaga questioning the legality of a joint intelligence operation conducted by the Slovenian Ministry of Defense's Intelligence and Security Service (OVS) and the U.S. Defense Intelligence Agency (DIA). Zgaga had obtained a secret document revealing that the DIA had used OVS agents in Yugoslavia to gather intelligence for the U.S. military during the NATO air war against Yugoslavia in 1999.

Following the article's publication, Zgaga was immediately placed under surveillance and his apartment was searched. On October 9, 2000, a formal criminal investigation was launched against Zgaga for revealing military secrets. The investigation was launched at the request of Defense Minister Janez Jansa. Zgaga told CPJ that the court justified the investigation by accusing him of identifying intelligence agents, revealing intelligence methods, and publishing material that could harm the Slovenian armed forces. He faced up to five years in prison.

At a hearing on January 22, 2002, a district court dismissed the case for lack of evidence and ruled that the information in Zgaga's article was true. The prosecutor has the option to retry the case, though local sources thought that unlikely.

SPAIN

WHILE PRESS FREEDOM IS GENERALLY RESPECTED IN SPAIN, CPJ has been extremely concerned about a series of violent attacks against journalists and media professionals carried out by the Basque separatist group ETA during the last several years. In 2001, ETA continued its terrorist campaign against the press, maiming Basque journalist Gorka Landaburu with a letter bomb on May 15 and gunning down newspaper executive Santiago Oleaga Elejebarrieta on May 24.

Oleaga, who was the chief financial officer of the regional daily *El Diario Vasco*, was shot seven times in the head, neck, and back by a lone gunman as he exited his car in a parking lot outside Matia Hospital, in the Basque port city of San Sebastian. Oleaga had driven to the hospital to undergo physical therapy for an injured shoulder. One hour after Oleaga's murder, a car exploded within a mile of the murder scene. Police theorize that his attackers destroyed the car after using it to flee.

In July, ETA issued a public communiqué claiming responsibility for the letter bomb sent to Landaburu, which severed several of his fingers. Landaburu, who covers the Basque region for the Madrid weekly *Cambio 16*, was protected by armed guards at the time because of repeated threats against him. In its statement, ETA described Landaburu, whom it accused of collaborating with the Spanish government, as a "journalist-policeman."

Oleaga, on the other hand, had not received any threats. It was unclear why ETA targeted a news executive rather than a journalist. Some analysts suggested that the very randomness of the attack was intended to maximize terror. Both attacks came immediately after regional Basque country elections in May in which the political party closest to ETA fared poorly. The results were widely interpreted as a rejection of ETA's violent tactics. A CPJ report on the Basque conflict published just after the Oleaga murder noted that, "the [ETA] guerillas regard the Spanish media...as adjuncts of the state, and therefore, legitimate targets in its 'liberation war.'"

While ETA attacks against the press have long fueled widespread outrage in Spain, the situation began to receive considerable international attention in 2001. The Paris-based World Association of Newspapers (WAN) visited Spain in March to express its concern directly to Spanish officials, including Prime Minister José María Aznar. In September, WAN, along with several Spanish press organizations, hosted an international conference on terrorism against the media in the Basque city of Bilbao. The conference was co-hosted by Grupo Correo, a Basque media conglomerate whose offices were bombarded with Molotov cocktails by ETA sympathizers in March.

In October, the Washington, D.C.–based International Women's Media Foundation honored Carmen Gurruchaga Basurto, a political reporter for the Madrid daily *El Mundo*, with a 2001 Courage in Journalism Award for her coverage of ETA. Gurruchaga has endured a campaign of violence and intimidation in retaliation for her reporting, yet she continues to cover the terrorist group for *El Mundo*.

TAJIKISTAN

ALTHOUGH TAJIKISTAN'S CIVIL WAR ENDED IN 1997, its devastating effects endure. Journalists work in dire, impoverished conditions, exacerbated by the stifling restrictions imposed under President Imomali Rakhmonov. Investigative reporting is rare, especially on sensitive issues such as trafficking in weapons and drugs, border tensions, and power struggles among the political and military elite.

Tajikistan's sole publishing house is controlled by the state, which freely blocks publication of critical stories. Journalists who persist in speaking their minds are threatened with police intimidation, tax harassment, and legal challenges under insult laws that carry prison sentences of up to two years.

On June 14, according to local and international sources, officials from the State Security Ministry questioned reporter Khrushed Atovulloyev of the newspaper *Dzhavononi Tojikiston* about a June 8 article that described abysmal living conditions endured by university students and bribe-taking by teaching staff. Atovulloyev was released with a warning to stop covering such topics.

A reporter for *Badakhshon* in the Gorno-Badakhshansky region was fired on June 10 after he wrote an article criticizing local officials. Saidnazar Aliyev was apparently dismissed after the editor received phone calls from local authorities complaining about the story.

On July 5, Russian officials in Moscow arrested Dododjon Atovullo, the exiled publisher and editor of the Tajik opposition newspaper *Charogi Ruz* (Daylight). Atovullo, who was traveling through Moscow on his way to Tashkent, Uzbekistan, when he was detained, is an outspoken critic of the Tajik government, which asked Russia to arrest and extradite him. His paper has frequently accused Tajik government officials of corruption, nepotism, and drug trafficking. Atovullo faced charges of sedition and insulting the president, and would have faced the death penalty if extradited, according to his lawyer. Russian authorities denied the extradition request, and on July 11, Atovullo returned to Germany, where he now lives in exile.

Under the country's media laws, the state Committee for Television and Radio has legal authority to invoke prior censorship of broadcast programming. Applications for broadcasting licenses can take years to be processed; the news agency Asia-Plus, for example, has waited in vain for three years to obtain a radio broadcasting license.

Tajik officials are notoriously secretive and unaccountable to the public for their actions. Journalists are often arbitrarily denied access to press conferences, and Russian journalists accredited in Tajikistan complain that officials harass them in response to criticism.

In this bleak picture, one relatively bright spot is the northern province of Sugd, near Tajikistan's Uzbek border. A July report by the United Nations Integrated Regional Information Network reported that 16 independent television and radio stations operate in the region without undue pressure from local authorities. International organizations such as the Organization for Security and Co-operation in Europe, the Eurasia Foundation, the U.S. Agency for International Development, and Internews support the new ventures. Local observers attribute the relative freedom in Sugd to the government's desire to foster nationalism in an area where people tend to have close ties with Tajikistan's neighbor, Uzbekistan. Sugd, which avoided much of the civil war's economic and political turmoil, is also more stable than the rest of the country.

Tajikistan has an 800-mile (1,300-kilometer) border with Afghanistan and was the main point of entry for foreign journalists covering the U.S. military operations against Afghanistan after the September 11 terrorist attacks on the

United States. The Tajik Foreign Ministry reported in October that in the previous month, 1,300 foreign journalists had arrived in the capital, Dushanbe, compared with a total of 1,600 over the previous eight years. Dushanbe was unprepared for the influx, and there were reportedly high prices charged for scarce resources and transportation over the border into northern Afghanistan.

TURKMENISTAN

IN A REGION WHERE FREEDOM OF THE PRESS AND FREE EXPRESSION are endangered concepts, the authoritarian regime of President Saparmurat Niyazov still manages to set a horrible example. Niyazov often takes his repression to absurd extremes. In April, for example, he banned opera and ballet from his country on the grounds that they are "alien" to Turkmen culture.

Niyazov also works hard to maintain a Soviet-style cult of personality. On October 19, the government adopted *Rukhnama*, his 400-page book of moral commandments based on Turkmen customs and traditions, as a national code of spiritual conduct. Delegates to a May conference of the Humanitarian Association of Turkmen in the capital, Ashgabat, bestowed on Niyazov the title Turkmenbashi the Great, though they stopped short of elevating him to the status of "prophet" after Niyazov professed to be weary of overly lavish praise.

The state controls all publishing and broadcast licenses, and Internet access is only available through the state provider, Turkmentelecom. In late March, Niyazov berated Turkmenistan's media outlets, saying that television in particular failed to reflect the nation's traditions and culture. On April 4, he restructured the state's media monopoly by abolishing the national broadcasting corporation and establishing three new television channels and three new radio stations. The channels are controlled by the Coordination Council for Broadcasting, which was created at the same time and answers to the Turkmenistan Cabinet of Ministers.

Turkmenistan has 10 Turkmen-language publications and one in Russian. A few Russian newspapers are also available, and the government carefully selects five hours of material for the country's one Russian-language television channel. In late April, a supplement to the Russian-language newspaper *Neutral Turkmenistan* titled *Serdar Yeli* (The Way of the Leader) was immediately withdrawn because it had been published without official permission.

Radio Free Europe/Radio Liberty (RFE/RL) Turkmen service correspondent Saparmurat Ovesberdiyev was searched at Moscow's Domodedovo Airport on February 27. Customs officials found US$4,000 in false notes in the journalist's luggage, which Ovesberdiyev believes one of the officers planted. After five hours of questioning, he was released without charges.

Few dare to speak out against a regime that routinely persecutes political and religious dissidents. A handful of Turkmen journalists write for foreign publications, but only under pseudonyms. Government security forces regularly refuse reporters entry to events sponsored by other countries, such as embassy parties or corporate press conferences, and journalists often face reprisals if they travel abroad. The Council for the Supervision of Foreigners also controls outside influences by strictly monitoring the activities of all international visitors.

UKRAINE

LEGAL HARASSMENT, VIOLENCE, AND DEATH continued to stalk Ukrainian journalists in 2001. Two murders underscored the continuing dangers, as did the stalled investigation into the murder of Internet journalist Georgy Gongadze. More than a year after Gongadze's headless corpse was discovered in November 2000, and after months of allegations about possible presidential involvement in his death, the case remained unsolved.

The high-profile Gongadze scandal, branded "Kuchmagate" after audiotapes implicating President Kuchma in the murder were released in November 2000, sparked a domestic political crisis and compromised Ukraine's reputation abroad. In July, U.S. national security adviser Condoleezza Rice stressed that U.S.-Ukrainian relations largely depended on the outcome of the case and other democratic reforms. Despite tremendous international and local pressure on Kuchma throughout 2001, Ukrainian authorities seemed determined to obstruct the investigation.

Adding insult to injustice was Kuchma's June speech marking the country's Day of the Journalist. "It is hard to remember some significant event, pluses or minuses in the life of our society," he said, "that have not been freely written about, including by those who call themselves the opposition media."

Kuchma's claim angered a press corps chilled by two years of press freedom assaults. Though the Gongadze murder occurred in 2000, it dominated Ukrainian news throughout 2001, with almost monthly developments that often bordered on the bizarre.

In February 2001, Kuchma announced that Russian forensic analysts had confirmed that the headless corpse found in 2000 was Gongadze's. In early March, after the Prosecutor General's Office ordered another forensic examination of the body, DNA analysis conducted in Germany concluded that the body was not Gongadze's. Soon after, Kuchma invited the U.S. FBI to help in the investigation. The FBI found that the corpse was Gongadze's after all.

Another bombshell came in May, when Internal Affairs Minister Yuri Smyrnov announced that the murder had been solved. He claimed the crime was an act of hooliganism linked to an elusive mafia boss named Cyclops. Smyrnov also announced that the two perpetrators were dead. In a statement, CPJ expressed severe doubts about Smyrnov's statements, but the prosecutor and law enforcement officials clung to their theory.

On the first anniversary of Gongadze's disappearance, his widow, Myroslava Gongadze, called for the creation of a special international commission to investigate the case. CPJ supported the request, as did the Council of Europe, but the Ukrainian government did not respond.

In an attempt to close the case, the pro-Kuchma Labor Ukraine political party hired the private American investigative agency Kroll Associates to investigate Gongadze's murder. While Kroll concluded that no convincing evidence implicated Kuchma in the murder, critics charged that the scope of Kroll's investigation was very limited. Nor did Kroll determine a motive for the crime or name its perpetrators. No significant developments have been reported since then.

In 2001, two journalists were murdered in Ukraine, and both cases remained unsolved at year's end. On June 24, Oleh Breus, publisher of the regional weekly *XXI Vek* in the provincial city of Luhansk, was shot dead outside his home. Although the ongoing investigation had produced no results at press time, a confidential source told CPJ that evidence links Breus' murder both to his business interests and to material published in *XXI Vek*. CPJ continues to follow the case.

Igor Aleksandrov, director of Tor, an independent television company based in Slavyansk in eastern Ukraine, was brutally attacked by club-wielding thugs on the morning of July 3, as he entered Tor's offices. He was rushed to the local city hospital, but he never regained consciousness and died from head injuries four days later.

Aleksandrov's colleagues believe the murder was connected to his television program, "Bez Retushi" (Without Retouching), which often addressed government corruption and organized crime. In late August, law enforcement officials arrested a suspect and claimed that Aleksandrov's murder was a case of mistaken identity, unconnected to his journalism.

In December, a parliamentary commission examining the case voiced its doubts about the "mistaken identity" theory and accused the Ukrainian Security Service (SBU) of falsifying evidence. Despite these concerns, the Prosecutor General's Office charged the suspect, and the Donetsk Regional Court scheduled his trial for September 11, 2002. Due to domestic outrage over this long delay, the court first rescheduled the trial of the alleged murderer for late January 2002 but then postponed it until early March, the local news agency Interfax-Ukraina reported. Aleksandrov's colleagues and family still believe that he was killed because of his work, and CPJ's research on the case also indicates the murder came in reprisal for his hard-hitting television program.

These murders led to a strange government decision. In December, the Internal Affairs Ministry authorized journalists covering sensitive topics, such as corruption, to carry guns with rubber bullets. Authorities appeared to be either acknowledging their powerlessness to maintain law and order or abdicating their responsibility for doing so. Either way, the move drew widespread criticism from the media and press freedom organizations.

In April, citing declining press freedom and human rights conditions in Ukraine, the Parliamentary Assembly of the Council of Europe Monitoring Committee recommended suspending Ukraine's membership in the Council of Europe. While Ukraine retained membership at year's end, the

Monitoring Committee's highly unusual step demonstrated the gravity of human rights and press freedom abuses in the country.

Ukraine's new Criminal Code, which took effect in September, repealed criminal penalties in libel cases. It also introduced severe punishments, including fines and prison terms, for obstructing journalistic work and for persecuting journalists who criticize the government. Whether officials will enforce the new law remains to be seen. In May, CPJ named Kuchma one of the Top Ten Enemies of the Press. (See page 597.)

UNITED KINGDOM

PRESS FREEDOM IS GENERALLY RESPECTED IN THE UNITED KINGDOM, and CPJ does not routinely monitor conditions in the country. However, CPJ was extremely alarmed by the September 28 murder of investigative reporter Martin O'Hagan, the first working journalist to be killed in Northern Ireland since the outbreak of violence more than three decades ago. O'Hagan was shot dead outside his home in the town of Lurgan on September 28.

O'Hagan worked in the Belfast office of the Dublin-based *Sunday World*, Ireland's best-selling tabloid weekly. He regularly covered the paramilitary underworld, and had received death threats from both sides of the Protestant-Catholic divide.

A Protestant paramilitary group called the Red Hand Defenders claimed responsibility for O'Hagan's murder in a telephone call to the BBC. Police consider the group a cover name for armed militants of the Loyalist Volunteer Force (LVF) and of the larger Ulster Defense Association (UDA). Colleagues believe the LVF targeted O'Hagan because he exposed their narcotics trafficking network and their involvement in extortion and murder. At press time, the police investigation was continuing, but no one had been charged.

Though physical attacks on journalists are rare in Northern Ireland, death threats are common.

On July 2, Barry George was convicted of the April 1999 murder of Jill Dando, a prominent television presenter on the BBC's "Crimewatch" program. Dando was shot once in the head at point-blank range just outside her West London home. George, 41, who also lived in West London, was fascinated by the military, collected guns, and was said to be obsessed with celebrities.

Following the trial, however, several British newspapers questioned the conviction, pointing out that the murder weapon was never recovered, there were no witnesses to the crime, and no motive was ever established. On December 13, George was granted leave to appeal his sentence. Three appeals court judges were scheduled to hear the case in the summer of 2002.

Citing concerns that video footage from Al-Qaeda and Osama bin Laden, who is suspected of masterminding the September 11 terrorist attacks on the United States, might contain coded messages to terrorists, the British government's communications chief met with executives from the networks BBC1, ITN, and Sky

News on October 15. The head of the BBC said later that "there had been talk of censorship and suggestions that the BBC would be squeezed by the government. That hasn't happened, and it isn't likely to." The executives also affirmed their "right to exercise our own independent, impartial editorial judgement."

UZBEKISTAN

TORTURE OF POLITICAL AND RELIGIOUS DISSIDENTS REMAINS COMMONPLACE under the brutal regime of President Islam Karimov. In February, writer Emin Usman died in detention, and the July death of imprisoned human rights activist Shovriq Rusimorodov confirmed the deteriorating political situation. Karimov has also cracked down on civil liberties by jailing thousands of Muslims under the pretext of fighting Islamic terrorism and fundamentalism.

The state of press freedom in Uzbekistan is no less bleak. CPJ detailed the systematic repression that journalists suffer in its report, "Silencing Central Asia: The Voice of Dissidents," which was presented to the U.S. House subcommittees on International Operations and Human Rights and Middle East and South Asia on July 18, 2001.

Control of the media, including the Internet, is pervasive in Uzbekistan: The government monopolizes printing presses and newspaper distribution, finances the main newspapers, and has the power to grant or deny licenses to media outlets. Uzbekistan is also one of the few countries in the world that practices prior censorship. The State Press Committee can order any material to be withdrawn, and it is not unusual for newspaper editors or radio producers to receive phone calls from officials demanding revisions.

Fighting the censor is a risky business, as Alo Khodzhayev, editor-in-chief of the Russian-language daily *Tashkentskaya Pravda*, learned when he was dismissed on July 7. Authorities said Khodzhayev's position had been eliminated, but the editor told CPJ that the move came in reprisal for an exhibition, titled "Without Censorship," that his paper opened in mid-June. The exhibition included a wall covered with newspaper articles that Uzbek authorities had banned.

In the summer edition of *Dangerous Assignments*, CPJ's biannual magazine, an Uzbek journalist writing under a pseudonym gave a detailed report of the local censorship regime in the country.

In 2001, Muhammad Bekjanov and Iusuf Ruzimuradov, of the banned opposition newspaper *Erk*, continued to serve 14- and 15-year sentences, respectively, for their involvement with the publication. According to a human rights activist incarcerated with Bekjanov, prison authorities have treated him with particular harshness, including torture.

In a positive development, Shodi Mardiev, a reporter with the state-run Samarkand radio station, was released on January 5, 2002, under a presidential amnesty. In June 1998, Mardiev was sentenced to 11 years in prison for defamation and extortion after he produced a broadcast that satirized the alleged corruption of a local government official. The journalist's health was greatly damaged by the ordeal. Shortly after his arrest in November 1997, he suffered two brain hemorrhages while in a pretrial detention center. He was hospitalized twice in 1999 for a heart condition and experienced pain and difficulty in walking.

In April, local journalists formed the Union of Independent Journalists of Uzbekistan. The need for such an organization was dramatically underscored weeks later, when Security Ministry police tried unsuccessfully to beat up union president Ruslan Sharipov. On August 31, Sharipov was briefly detained and questioned by the police after publishing a series of articles on human rights violations in Uzbekistan. In July, Interior Ministry officials interrogated another member of the new union, Asadullo Ortikov, and ordered him to stop criticizing the government in print.

Serious threats led one journalist, Shukhrat Babadjanov, to flee into exile. Babadjanov, director of the independent TV station ALC in Urgench, had been fighting authorities for nearly two years after the politically motivated closure of his station. On June 28, he was again refused a broadcasting license. On July 24, he was ordered to vacate the station's premises. Authorities then ordered him to appear at the prosecutor's office in the capital, Tashkent, on August 6, to face charges of criminal forgery. Instead, he fled and later told CPJ he feared that authorities intended to silence him by putting him in prison on spurious charges.

UPI's Tashkent correspondent, Marina Kozlova, was followed and harassed by police on three separate occasions during the summer of 2001. Kozlova told CPJ that the police targeted her for criticizing Uzbek security organizations.

In March, several Uzbek human rights groups and opposition politicians charged that the head of the Tashkent bureau of Radio Free Europe/Radio Liberty (RFE/RL) was not airing the criticisms of opposition members. While RFE/RL's head office in Washington, D.C., denied the charges, some local RFE/RL staffers agreed, accusing bureau chief Aziz Dzhurayev of being too close to Uzbek authorities, of censoring reports, and of wrongfully dismissing several of the service's journalists.

Uzbekistan shares a 115-mile (190-kilometer) border with Afghanistan and saw an influx of foreign journalists during the U.S. military campaign in Afghanistan after the September 11 terrorist attacks on the United States. The Uzbek government gave U.S. troops permission to use the Khanabad airfield in the south of the country for operations in Afghanistan. There has been no official information about any security guarantees or economic benefits that Uzbekistan hopes to gain from backing the United States. Independent Uzbek journalists and human rights activists, however, told CPJ they are concerned that the new rapprochement may lead the U.S. government to soften its criticism of Karimov's repressive regime.

YUGOSLAVIA

THE REVOLUTIONARY POLITICAL CHANGES OF LATE 2000 AND EARLY 2001 that ousted former Yugoslav President Slobodan Milosevic ended a decade of repression for

Yugoslavia's independent journalists. But after a year in power, the Democratic Opposition of Serbia (DOS), which replaced Milosevic, failed to enact needed reforms in media-related laws. And while the DOS proved far less heavy-handed than Milosevic, its leaders have not hesitated to apply more subtle pressures on independent media that do not embrace DOS policies.

The 18-party DOS coalition represented a broad array of political and ideological loyalties: Serbian nationalists, former Milosevic allies, and pro-Western reformists. The coalition took power in two stages. Stage one came in the aftermath of federal presidential elections, held in September 2000, which Milosevic tried to steal. A popular uprising in early October drove Milosevic from power, clearing the way for DOS presidential candidate Vojislav Kostunica to take office. Then, in December 2000, the DOS won a majority in the Serbian parliamentary elections, and appointed coalition member Zoran Djindjic prime minister the following month.

Kostunica's presidency brought a dramatic, and almost immediate, end to the intense state-sponsored persecution of journalists that marked Milosevic's reign. Within four months, the Yugoslav courts and parliament had dismantled the notorious Public Information Law, used under Milosevic to impose huge fines and equipment confiscations on media outlets that criticized the government.

The new rulers promised further media reform, sending a wave of optimism through the independent press corps. Veran Matic, chairman of the Association of Independent Electronic Media (ANEM) in Belgrade, said local media groups enthusiastically submitted ideas for new laws on broadcasting and information. But, said Matic, with the exception of the new telecommunications minister, Kostunica's government "did not wholeheartedly engage in" the reform process. In fact, although the independent reporting of ANEM and other media had played a key role in Milosevic's fall, the coalition that replaced him soon came to see truly independent journalism as a threat to the cohesion of its 18-party alliance.

Within that alliance, informal political factions began to form, most significantly around Kostunica, who enjoyed strong public support, and Djindjic, who was less popular but more committed to the reform process. The growing competition between Kostunica and Djindjic heightened each politician's efforts to harness media support for his own political benefit.

Independent and wealthy television stations such as TV Pink and BK TV were particularly attractive to DOS politicians because of their large national audiences. Because they were loyal to the Milosevic regime, these stations benefited from subsidies and regulatory favor throughout the 1990s. When the DOS took power, they quickly switched their allegiance to the new government.

Meanwhile, a decade of physical abuse, legal harassment, heavy fines, and periodic confiscation of property under Milosevic left other media outlets financially weak but determined to preserve their independence under the new government. But without government patronage, ANEM's broadcasters and other independent media lacked both the financial support and political protection to compete in the new market.

This vulnerability was noticeable in early May, when CPJ conducted a fact-finding mission to Serbia. In meetings with senior Yugoslav and Serbian government officials, CPJ urged greater accountability for individuals who target journalists, with particular emphasis on the April 1999 assassination of *Dnevni Telegraf* editor-in-chief Slavko Curuvija. CPJ also called for a timely reallocation of broadcast frequencies to ensure that a broad range of views is available on television and radio. And CPJ urged a thorough government audit of private, pro-Milosevic media that had profited from illegal financial support during the 1990s.

Several weeks after the CPJ mission, two attackers killed Milan Pantic, a 47-year-old crime reporter for the Belgrade daily *Vecernje Novosti*, as he was entering his apartment building. Pantic had received numerous telephone threats in response to his articles, which covered corruption and organized crime. Local authorities launched an investigation into the case, but no progress was reported at the end of the year.

The media reform effort stalled in July, when the government abolished the Federal Telecommunications Ministry, the only government office that had aggressively supported new media laws. The ruling coalition took no further action to push reform. As a result, smaller, independent media outlets remained financially vulnerable. Long denied national broadcast licenses by the Milosevic regime, they were still unable to obtain them under the new government—and thus could not compete for national advertising revenues that went instead to state television and the two pro-government broadcasters, BK TV and TV Pink.

Government inaction on several other crucial issues exacerbated the economic bias in favor of pro-government broadcasters. Despite calls from international press freedom groups and independent media outlets, the ruling coalition never audited the financial gains that pro-Milosevic stations made during the 1990s. Furthermore, only some of the equipment confiscated from independent media outlets under Milosevic's Public Information Act was actually returned, despite promises to the contrary. And though the government pledged to return the 31 million dinars (US$450,000) that the independent media paid in Public Information Law fines during the last years of the Milosevic regime, only about a third of that amount had been repaid as of August, according to ANEM.

Government efforts to reform the bloated state broadcasting service, Radio Television Serbia (RTS), also lagged significantly. RTS broadcasts, which had been a crucial element of Milosevic's efforts to control public opinion, now enthusiastically supported the coalition that replaced him. RTS journalists apparently feared losing their jobs if they criticized the coalition, and the network's financial dependence on the state seemed to guarantee its docility.

Security conditions in the southern Serbian province of Kosovo remained difficult, with journalists reporting physical threats and intimidation from political parties and organized crime figures.

On October 19, an ethnic Albanian journalist for the Albanian-language daily *Bota Sot*, Bekim Kastrati, was killed in a drive-by shooting. United Nations police were still investigating Kastrati's murder at the end of the year. Local sources told CPJ that another passenger wounded in the attack, a former commander of the Kosovo Liberation Army, was the likely target of the shooting.

Kerem Lawton, a British national and producer for Associated Press Television News, died on March 29 when a mortar shell struck his vehicle in the village of Krivenik, in Kosovo. Lawton had arrived to cover NATO operations along the border with Macedonia.

Political debate in Montenegro, meanwhile, continued to focus on whether the republic should remain in the Yugoslav federation. With Milosevic's dictatorship gone, international and domestic support for Montenegrin independence weakened considerably. As a result, President Milo Djukanovic and his pro-independence allies barely held on to power in April parliamentary elections, with former Milosevic supporters and pro-Yugoslav politicians gaining new seats.

Podgorica's political establishment was shaken in the spring by the "tobacco affair." In neighboring Croatia, the sensationalist Zagreb weekly *Nacional* published a series of articles alleging that Djukanovic was skimming money from an illegal cigarette smuggling operation. The Podgorica daily *Dan* reprinted the articles, whereupon Djukanovic filed libel charges against *Dan* editor-in-chief Vladislav Asanin. On December 6, Asanin was convicted and given a three-month prison sentence. The judgment was under appeal at press time. ■

| CASES TABLE OF CONTENTS |

ARMENIA

Haikakan Zhamanak
`LEGAL ACTION`

The National Scout Movement (NSM) requested that criminal libel charges be filed against the Yerevan daily *Haikakan Zhamanak*, the Nayan Tapan news agency reported.

The NSM claimed that a February 21 article in the paper libeled the group by accusing it of supporting the October 27, 1999, attack on the Armenian parliament that left eight politicians dead, including Prime Minister Vazgen Sarkissian.

In March, the Prosecutor General's Office rejected NSM's request.

MARCH 28

Chorrord Ishkhanutyun
`HARASSED`

Interior Ministry officers seized unspecified equipment used by the opposition weekly *Chorrord Ishkhanutyun* since 1996, claiming it belonged to the ministry. An eyewitness told the newspaper Aravot that some of the equipment was a gift from former interior minister Vano Siradegian.

Siradegian also founded the Shamiram Party, of which Shoger Matevosian, the newspaper's editor, is the president, according to CPJ sources. *Chorrord Ishkhanutyun* is well known for its sharp criticisms of President Robert Kocharian and his government.

MAY 16

Chorrord Ishkhanutyun
`HARASSED`

Armenian tax police conducted an audit of the Ogostos Agency, publisher of the Yerevan-based opposition weekly *Chorrord Ishkhanutyun*, without the required written order from the Ministry of State Revenues, local sources reported. A large number of documents were seized.

The Ministry of State Revenues issued the official audit order two days later. The tax police then conducted another audit of the Ogostos Agency, which began on May 23.

This was illegal: according to the Law on Audits, tax authorities cannot inspect the same organization more than once each year. Officials claimed that the May 16 audit was merely a "visit."

MAY 18

Shoger Matevosian, *Chorrord Ishkhanutyun*
`HARASSED`

Matevosian, editor of the opposition weekly *Chorrord Ishkhanutyun* and leader of the Shamiram Party, was summoned to the military prosecutor's office for questioning, according to local sources.

She was interrogated about several recent articles that criticized the official investigation into the October 27, 1999, attack on the Armenian Parliament, which left the prime minister and seven other officials dead.

JUNE 26

Vahagn Gukasian, free-lancer
`ATTACKED`

A bus owned by opposition free-lance journalist Gukasian, which he used as a workshop where he manufactured leather accessories in order to support his journalism, was destroyed by fire.

Gukasian maintains that the fire came in deliberate retaliation for his work, specifically his investigative reports on the October 1999 attack on the Armenian parliament, which left the prime minister and seven other officials dead.

Gukasian's most recent articles on the attack, published in the newspaper *Haikakan Zhamanak*, alleged that in addition to the five assailants who were on trial for the crime, a sixth remained at large. He also accused the Ministry of National Security of being involved in the attack, the Russia-based Prima Human Rights News Agency reported.

According to local and international reports, Gukasian received telephone threats following the publication of the stories.

In early September, law enforcement authorities closed the investigation into the fire without further explanation.

SEPTEMBER 10

Ashtarak TV
CENSORED

Law enforcement agents and tax police disrupted Ashtarak TV's live interview with Ashot Manucharian, leader of the opposition political movement Front of National Accord and the political secretary of the Socialist Armenia Association, according to the Yerevan Press Club.

Prior to the broadcast, police surrounded the television station's building and demanded that it close immediately. The police claimed that the station was unlicensed and had not paid its electricity bills.

Ashtarak TV broadcast the Manucharian interview anyway. Fifteen minutes into the interview, however, electricity to the station was cut off.

Two days later, the Republican Telecommunications Center and the National Security Ministry shut down Ashtarak TV and sealed its technical equipment over the licencing issue.

Vagram Botsinian, head of Ashtarak TV, maintains that the station was unable to obtain a license from the National Commission on Television and Radio due to bureaucratic stonewalling. The station remained closed at year's end.

AZERBAIJAN

JANUARY 5

ABA TV
HARASSED, LEGAL ACTION

Acting on the orders of a Baku court, tax police conducted a 12-hour search of the independent station ABA TV's offices to gather evidence for a criminal case that could result in a five-year ban on the station and a three-year jail term for its director.

The raid was the latest chapter in a financial dispute between ABA TV and the government. In October 2000, the station was shut down for two weeks after the Ministry of Communications claimed the station owed money to the state.

ABA president Fariq Zulfuqarov denied charges that his company owed billions of manats and claimed the police found no evidence of wrongdoing in ABA TV's account books. He said that by revealing information about an ongoing investigation to the media, the authorities had violated the Criminal Procedural Code and slandered his company.

The investigation was ongoing at year's end. Meanwhile, ABA TV remained closed.

JANUARY 8

DMR TV
CENSORED

Authorities closed DMR TV, the only independent source of local news in the town of Balakan, northwest Azerbaijan, for nearly six weeks under the pretext that the station was not properly licensed.

On the morning of January 8, police and a tax official detained DMR TV president Mustafa Dibirov and took him to a police station. Dibirov was forced to write a letter promising to keep his station off the air until he received an official government license. The letter also specified that failure to keep his promise would lead to criminal charges.

Like most regional stations in Azerbaijan, DMR TV's license applications have been repeatedly denied. As a result, the station has been operating without a license for 10 years.

On February 6, Azeri officials announced that DMR TV and three other regional television stations closed in the previous month would be allowed to reopen immediately. DMR TV resumed broadcasting on February 18.

JANUARY 25

Mingechevir TV
CENSORED

Vahid Mamedov, president of Mingechevir TV, an independent station based in the town of Mingechevir, shut down the station after the local police chief threatened to prosecute him for broadcasting without a license.

Major Tahir Badalov allegedly acted on orders from the State Radio Frequencies Commission and the Ministry of Internal Affairs.

Like many other regional independent broadcasters, Mingechevir TV had repeatedly applied for a broadcast license but was refused by authorities.

On February 6, Azeri officials announced that Mingechevir TV and three other regional stations that had been closed in the previous month would be allowed to reopen immediately. The station resumed broadcasting on February 15.

FEBRUARY 6

Gutb TV
CENSORED
Khayal TV
CENSORED

The provincial stations Gutb TV and Khayal TV were closed for about two weeks by a local governor, who said he was acting on orders from officials in the capital, Baku.

Governor Mehman Ibrahimov later justified his action by claiming that neither station was properly licensed, Internews Azerbaijan reported.

Gutb TV president Mahir Orujiev later announced that Governor Ibrahimov had told him on February 14 that the station was being shut down because authorities in Baku did not want more than one television station broadcasting per region.

Like many other regional independent stations in Azerbaijan, Gutb TV and Khayal TV had applied repeatedly for broadcast licenses. In each case, local authorities cited a lack of available frequencies as an excuse to reject the application, even though all the stations operate in rural areas where they compete only with state television.

Khayal TV resumed broadcasting on February 19. Gubt TV was back on the air by February 21.

Namik Ibrahimov, *Ekho*
`ATTACKED`

Ibrahimov, a reporter for the independent daily *Ekho*, was attacked by a half-dozen police officers while covering a police raid on an unauthorized street market in Baku.

When Ibrahimov started taking pictures of the raid, the officers kicked him and beat him with their police batons, damaging his camera in the process. Ibrahimov was taken to a police car and then released soon afterwards on the orders of a senior police officer.

MARCH 3

Idrak Abbasov, *Impuls*
`ATTACKED`

Police attacked and beat Abbasov, a reporter with the newspaper *Impuls*, when he attempted to photograph them closing down a newspaper kiosk owned by Gaya, the company that distributes the publication. He was detained at a police station for several hours, and then released.

The police also assaulted Gaya's deputy director, who, along with other employees, was trying to stop them from closing the kiosk.

APRIL 21

Heydar Oguz, *Hurriyyet*
`IMPRISONED, ATTACKED`
Jasur Mammedov, *Hurriyyet*
`IMPRISONED, ATTACKED`
Suleyman Mammedli, *Hurriyyet*
`ATTACKED`

Police attacked and arrested Oguz and Mammedov, reporters with the thrice-weekly Baku newspaper *Hurriyyet*, while the journalists were covering an illegal protest rally by the opposition Democratic Party of Azerbaijan.

Meanwhile, the deputy chief of the Baku Senior Police Department assaulted Mammedli, the newspaper's editor-in-chief, according to local sources.

A group of police officers attacked and beat Oguz and Mammedov before they had a chance to show their press credentials. The reporters were then taken to a police station, where Oguz was sentenced to seven days in prison and Mammedov was sentenced to 12 days. Both were released on April 28.

MAY 12

Idrak Abbasov, *Impuls*
`ATTACKED`
Suleyman Mammedli, *Hurriyyet*
`ATTACKED`
Seymur Verdizade, *Bu Gun*
`ATTACKED`
Aybeniz Velikhanli, *Milletin Sesi*
`ATTACKED`

Parvin Sadai, *Milletin Sesi*
`ATTACKED`
Rahim Qadimov, *525-ci Qezet*
`ATTACKED`
Rasim Mustafaoglu, *Hurriyyet*
`ATTACKED`

Seven journalists were beaten by uniformed police and individuals in civilian clothing while covering an opposition Democratic Party of Azerbaijan (DPA) rally in the capital, Baku.

A DPA report on the incident alleged that the plainclothes attackers were members of the police, the national security service, and a private security firm called Amay.

Abbasov, a reporter with the newspaper *Impuls*, was assaulted when he tried to photograph the police beating women DPA members. His camera was confiscated and broken. Later that day, the journalist was hospitalized with head injuries.

Mammedli, editor-in-chief of the newspaper *Hurriyyet*; Verdizade, a reporter with the newspaper *Bu Gun*; Velikhanli and Sadai, reporters with the newspaper *Milletin Sesi*; Qadimov, a reporter with the newspaper *525-ci Qezet*; and Mustafaoglu, editor of the newspaper *Hurriyyet*, were also assaulted during the demonstration.

According to CPJ sources in Baku, police detained Mammedli after attacking him. Verdizade and Sadai's tape recorders were confiscated, as was Mustafaoglus' press card.

JULY 15

Yaqub Abbasov, *Ulus*
`IMPRISONED, LEGAL ACTION`

Surkhay Qojayev, *Ulus*
`IMPRISONED, LEGAL ACTION`

Abbasov and Qojayev, founder and deputy editor, respectively, of the independent newspaper *Ulus*, were detained and charged with hooliganism, according to local reports.

The charges came after former *Ulus* contributor Aybeniz Ilqar filed a complaint claiming that Abbasov, Qojayev, and and a member of the opposition Democratic Party, with which the paper is allied, physically assaulted her when she came to the *Ulus* offices on July 5 to have Abbasov stamp her work documents, local sources reported.

The journalists claim they were framed in order to suppress their independent publication, which often criticized the government, and because of their affiliation with the Democratic Party.

On July 15, the Sabayil District Court ordered the two journalists jailed for three months pending trial. However, they were detained until December 6, when the Sabayil District Court in Baku found them guilty but ordered them released. Abbasov was given a suspended prison term of 14 months, while Qojayev was given a suspended sentence of one year.

JULY 17

ABA Television
`HARASSED, CENSORED`

The independent Baku station ABA Television closed its doors, apparently under government pressure. Tax Ministry officials then confiscated some of the station's equipment.

For several months, ABA had been the subject of intense scrutiny by tax officials. Shamil Safiyev, the head of the station's finance department, has been in jail since his May 22 arrest on charges of tax evasion and the intentional use of false documents.

ABA president Fariq Zulfuqarov announced the station's closure in a videotaped message sent to his employees on July 16 from the United States, where he had been living for more than two months.

In a July 18 interview published in the Baku newspaper *Ekho*, Zulfuqarov said he closed the station to protest the Tax Ministry's investigation, which he viewed as a government-orchestrated attempt to take control of ABA.

At approximately 1:00 a.m. on the night of July 16-17, Tax Ministry officials seized two trucks containing ABA Television equipment. The equipment, which ABA staff members were apparently moving out of the station in an attempt to save it from confiscation, was said to be worth 1.5 billion manats (US$320,000).

Sources in Baku told CPJ that the Tax Ministry will hold the equipment until officials finish investigating alleged financial improprieties at the station. At year's end, the station remained closed, and the investigation was ongoing.

CPJ send a letter of inquiry about this case to President Heydar Aliyev on August 27.

AUGUST 7

Milletin Sesi
LEGAL ACTION, CENSORED

The Narimanov District Court in Baku ordered the independent weekly *Milletin Sesi* to cease publication after finding the paper guilty of defaming Nadir Nasibov, the former chairman of the State Property Committee, and his deputy, Barat Nuriyev.

The defamation charge came in reprisal for an article in the July 22-28 edition of *Milletin Sesi* titled, "Who Testified Against Heydar Aliyev?" The article accused Nasibov and Nuriyev of financial misconduct in a privatization deal, the Turan news agency reported.

These allegations had already appeared in numerous international publications, including *Forbes*, *The New York Times*, and the Russian magazine *Kommersant-Dengi*, the Moscow-based Center for Journalism in Extreme Situations (CJES) reported. According to Azerbaijan's Law on Mass Media, media outlets are not responsible for information republished from other media sources.

The court ignored 126 pages of articles that were submitted to support *Milletin Sesi*'s allegations against Nasibov and Nuriyev. *Milletin Sesi* editor Shahbaz Khuduoglu told CJES that he planned to appeal the ruling, to the Supreme Court if necessary. He added that *Milletin Sesi* would continue publishing until all legal recourses have been exhausted.

The paper ceased publication soon after September 17, when the District Court ruled for the plaintiff in a separate case of alleged defamation against President Heydar Aliyev's chief of staff (see September 17 case).

On October 22, the former editors of *Milletin Sesi* released a statement noting that the Court of Appeals had upheld the earlier conviction.

AUGUST 9

Impuls
CENSORED

Azerbaijani authorities blocked distribution of the August 9 edition of the newspaper *Impuls* because it was printed in Cyrillic script.

A June presidential decree required local publications to print exclusively in the Latin script (by August 1, 2001).

The government ordered the paper's printing house to block the issue, and officials summoned *Impuls'* owner, Khan Husseyn Aliyev, to the Baku prosecutor's office and gave him an official warning for violating the regulation. The newspaper subsequently ceased publication.

The decree was intended to reduce the dominance of the Russian language in Azerbaijan. Josef Stalin imposed the Russian Cyrillic script, which is derived from Russian, on Azerbaijan in 1939. Since then, most Azeri-language newspapers in the country have been printed in Cyrillic.

AUGUST 15

Etimad
LEGAL ACTION, CENSORED

The Yasamalsky District Court in the capital, Baku, shut down the newspaper *Etimad* for allegedly insulting Azerbaijan's senior Muslim cleric, Sheikh-ul-Islam Allakhshukur Pashazade.

The charge came in response to an article titled, "Isa Gambar and the Two Armenians," which appeared in the July 28-August 3 edition of *Etimad*. The article contained critical comments about Pashazade, according to local and international press sources.

In an August 13 television address, President Heydar Aliyev condemned the article and called for sanctions against the newspaper.

"In connection with this article, we have received hundreds of letters.... In all these letters, people express their outrage at such an incident and ask me, the president of Azerbaijan, to punish the newspaper that insulted Azerbaijan's religious leader, Sheikh ul-Islam. I agree with all these thoughts," the president declared. *Etimad* subsequently ceased publishing.

SEPTEMBER 4

Elmar Huseynov, *Bakinsky Bulvar*
IMPRISONED
Irada Huseynova, *Bakinsky Bulvar*
LEGAL ACTION
Bella Zakirova, *Bakinsky Bulvar*
LEGAL ACTION

Huseynov, founder of the independent Russian-language weekly *Bakinsky Bulvar*; Huseynova, a reporter for the paper; and Zakirova, the editor-in-chief, were found guilty of defamation and fined 80 million manats (US$17,400) by Baku's Nizaminsky District Court.

Baku mayor Hajibala Abutalibov sued *Bakinsky Bulvar* for defamation and sought to close the paper after it published an article by Irada Huseynova criticizing the mayor for demolishing commercial kiosks, a move that left many unemployed.

According to CPJ sources, the court ordered *Bakinsky Bulvar* to issue a written apology to the mayor, but shut it down before it could publish such a statement. On September 6, the court forbade publishing houses and distributors from printing and circulating copies of *Bakinsky Bulvar*.

Following the paper's closure, the court launched criminal prosecutions against Huseynov, Huseynova, and Zakirova. All three were charged with defaming the mayor, an offense punishable by one to three years in prison

On September 20, Huseynova requested political asylum in Germany after attending a conference in Warsaw, according to local press reports. She was still abroad at year's end.

On September 21, both Huseynov and Zakirova were found guilty of criminal defamation. The court sentenced Huseynov to six months in prison and gave Zakirova a six-month suspended sentence. CPJ protested these actions in an October 16 letter to President Heydar Aliyev.

On October 17, Aliyev signed a pardon authorizing Huseynov's release in honor of the 10th anniversary of Azerbaijan's independence. The pardon came in response to numerous appeals received by his office, according to Leyla Yunus, chairperson of an Azerbaijani organization called the Committee to Protect Imprisoned Journalists and Freedom of Expression.

The pardon did not reverse the guilty verdict against Huseynov, and *Bakinsky Bulvar* remained closed at year's end, according to local CPJ sources.

The Azerbaijani news agency Turan reported that on November 13, the Court of Appeals upheld the convictions of Huseynov and Zakirova.

SEPTEMBER 17

Shahbaz Khuduoglu, *Milletin Sesi*
IMPRISONED, LEGAL ACTION

Gulnaz Qamberli, *Milletin Sesi*
LEGAL ACTION
Eynulla Fetullayev, *Milletin Sesi*
LEGAL ACTION
Milletin Sesi
LEGAL ACTION

Ramiz Mehdiyev, President Heydar Aliyev's chief of staff, filed defamation charges against three journalists from the independent weekly *Milletin Sesi*.

The group included editor-in-chief Khuduoglu, correspondent Qamberli, and deputy editor Fetullayev.

The charges arose from an article in the paper that criticized Mehdiyev and other officials for restricting public access to a popular resort area where they were vacationing with unidentified women.

Local and international sources reported that during the trial, the court denied Khuduoglu access to a defense attorney. On September 17, Khuduoglu was sentenced to six months in prison, while Qamberli received a three-month suspended sentence.

Fetullayev's trial began on January 8, 2002, the Azerbaijani news agency Turan reported. On January 11, Fetullayev was summoned to the Narimanov Court, where Judge Babayev informed him that Ramiz Mehdiyev had officially withdrawn his lawsuit against the deputy editor, Turan news agency reported.

At another September 17 hearing, the Narimanov Court ordered *Milletin Sesi* to cease publication, according to local reports. Soon after, the paper ceased publication.

CPJ protested these actions in an October 16 letter to President Aliyev.

On October 17, Aliyev signed a pardon authorizing Khuduoglu's release in honor of the 10th anniversary of

Azerbaijan's independence. The pardon came in response to numerous appeals received by his office, according to Leyla Yunus, chairperson of a local organization called the Committee to Protect Imprisoned Journalists and Freedom of Expression.

The pardon did not reverse the guilty verdict against Khuduoglu. On October 22, the former editors of *Milletin Sesi* released a statement noting that the Court of Appeals had upheld the earlier conviction.

NOVEMBER 15

Shahbaz Khuduoglu, *Milletin Sesi*
ATTACKED, HARASSED
Elmar Huseynov, *Bakinsky Bulvar*
ATTACKED, HARASSED

Khuduoglu, editor-in-chief of the banned independent weekly *Milletin Sesi*, and Huseynov, founder of the banned independent weekly *Bakinsky Bulvar*, were arrested and detained when they and their staff attempted to stage a protest in front of the monument to the founder of the first Azerbaijani newspaper, according to local press reports. The two journalists were released later that day with a warning, CPJ sources said.

DECEMBER 6

Shahnaz Metlebqizi, *Yeni Musavat*
ATTACKED

Metlebqizi, a correspondent with the Baku-based independent daily *Yeni Musavat*, was attacked outside her home by an unknown assailant, according to local press reports.

As the journalist approached her house, the attacker grabbed a fresh edition of *Yeni Musavat* out of Metlebqizi's hand and cut it into small bits with a knife. He then hit the journalist repeatedly over the head and threatened to harm other journalists at the newspaper.

The police launched a criminal investigation into the attack, but no progress had been made by year's end, the chairman of the local Journalists' Trade Union told CPJ.

DECEMBER 12

Rauf Arifoglu, *Yeni Musavat*
ATTACKED, HARASSED
Azer Hasret, Chairman of the Journalists' Trade Union
ATTACKED, HARASSED
Elman Maliyev, *Express*
ATTACKED, HARASSED
Ramiz Najafli, *Azadliq*
ATTACKED, HARASSED
Ali Rza, *Azadliq*
ATTACKED
Idrak Abbasov, *Impuls*
ATTACKED
Khatire Askerova, *Hurriyyet*
ATTACKED
Jesaret Aliyev, *Hurriyyet*
ATTACKED
Elchin Yusifoglu, *Hurriyyet*
ATTACKED
Vasif Mammedoglu, *Hurriyyet*
ATTACKED
Salim Mammedov, *Ulus*
ATTACKED
Namiq Mayilov, Turan Information Agency
ATTACKED
Salim Azizoglu, *Yeni Musavat*
ATTACKED
Konul Shamilqizi, *Yeni Musavat*
ATTACKED

Tale Seyfeddinoglu, *Yeni Musavat*
ATTACKED
Shahin Jeferli, *Yeni Musavat*
ATTACKED
Elshad Pashasoy, *Yeni Musavat*
ATTACKED
Shahnaz Metlebqizi, *Yeni Musavat*
ATTACKED
Suheyle Yasharqizi, *Yeni Musavat*
ATTACKED
Mubariz Jeferli, *Yeni Musavat*
ATTACKED
Mahir Rufatoglu, *Yeni Musavat*
ATTACKED
Ilhame Namiqqizi, *Yeni Musavat*
ATTACKED
Javid Jabbaroglu, *Yeni Musavat*
ATTACKED
Rena Jamaqizi, *Yeni Musavat*
ATTACKED
Anar Natiqoglu, *Yeni Musavat*
ATTACKED
Sebine Avazqizi, *Yeni Musavat*
ATTACKED

More than 20 journalists were injured when police violently dispersed a rally in front of President Heydar Aliyev's ruling New Azerbaijan Party (NAP) headquarters.

Fifty picketers and 100 supporters had gathered to protest recent NAP calls to destroy the independent, opposition dailies *Yeni Musavat*, *Azadliq*, and *Hurriyyet*, according to Azer Hasret, chairman of the Journalists' Trade Union. Police also took protesters' signs and ripped them apart.

The Baku mayor's office had refused the organizers' petition to hold a demonstration.

Following the NAP statements, several printing houses refused to print the three publications, according to local sources. Hasret told CPJ that all three newspapers filed lawsuits against the New Azerbaijan Party in response.

Najafli, a correspondent with the independent daily *Azadliq*, was badly injured by the police and taken to the hospital, where he was diagnosed with a severe concussion. At year's end he was recovering at home but remained unable to work, according to CPJ sources.

Meanwhile, Arifoglu, editor of the independent daily *Yeni Musavat*; Maliyev, correspondent with the daily *Express*; and Hasret were arrested. Baku's chief of police Nagiyev personally beat up Hasret and Maliyev in the back seat of a police vehicle while two police officers restrained them, the newspaper *525ci Qezet* reported.

The arrested journalists were released half an hour later after parliamentarian Aqbal Agazade, a member of the Civic Unity Party, intervened on their behalf, Hasret told CPJ.

Following the violent events of December 12, the entire staff of *Azadliq* asked U.S. Ambassador Ross Wilson to grant them political asylum in the United States, according to the Azerbaijani news agency Turan. Their application was pending at year's end.

BELARUS

JANUARY 16

Svobodnaya Zona
CENSORED

On the orders of the regional Press Department, the Brest Regional Printing Press refused to publish the first issue of the independent newspaper *Svobodnaya Zona*, which was intended as a business supplement to the weekly *Brestsky Kuryer*.

The paper was banned on the pretext that its publisher did not have a contract with the printer.

Svobodnaya Zona was registered with the State Press Committee on January 21, 2000. Under the Press Law, all new publications must print their first issue within a year to keep their registration certificates valid.

The day after the print run was blocked, *Svobodnaya Zona's* publisher arranged to have the paper printed in Minsk.

De-Fakto
CENSORED

The state-run Sverdlov Printing Press, the only printing house in Mogilyov Region, refused to publish an issue of the independent weekly *De-fakto* unless the newspaper agreed to cut an article about President Aleksandr Lukashenko's mental health.

The story discussed a January 12 article by psychiatrist Dmitry Shchigelsky that ran in the independent newspaper *Nasha Svaboda*. Shchigelsky suggested that Lukashenko suffers from a serious psychiatric disorder and is unfit for office.

According to the *De-fakto* staff member who delivered the issue to the printer, a foreman noticed the article on Lukashenko and demanded that it be removed. After the staff member protested, the foreman referred him to the printer's director and to the state security services. Ultimately, *De-fakto* agreed to replace the article with a collection of jokes.

The next week, the newspaper published a front-page story about the episode, denouncing it as an incident of illegal censorship.

JANUARY 17

Valery Shchukin, *Narodnaya Volya*
IMPRISONED, ATTACKED, LEGAL ACTION

Shchukin, a correspondent with the Minsk-based independent daily *Narodnaya Volya*, was charged with hooliganism after trying to enter a restricted press conference held by Internal Affairs Minister Naumov the day before, local sources reported.

Only journalists on a previously approved list were allowed to attend the press conference. Although Shchukin had called ahead, he was refused access because the list had already been compiled, said local sources. When the journalist attempted to enter the press conference, the guards stopped him and physically removed him.

Shchukin was sentenced to three months in prison, according to local and international sources. He unsuccessfully appealed the verdict and began serving his prison term on June 12, local sources reported. Shchukin was released on September 12, 2001.

Nasha Svaboda
LEGAL ACTION

At the request of the State Press Committee, the General Prosecutor's Office filed criminal libel charges against the twice-weekly independent newspaper *Nasha Svaboda* over an article that questioned the mental health of President Aleksandr Lukashenko.

The article, published on January 12 under the headline "Doctor's Verdict," was written by a psychiatrist who claimed Lukashenko suffers from a serious psychiatric disorder that makes him unfit for office.

The paper's editor argued that to determine whether the article was libelous, a court would have to order an independent psychiatric evaluation of Lukashenko.

Under Belarus's new Criminal Code, which took effect on January 1, persons convicted of libeling the president face fines, up to two years of community service, or up to four years in prison.

In mid-June, the online information agency Yu. S. News (www.yusnews.com) reported that the charges against *Nasha Svaboda* had been dropped.

JANUARY 26

Brestsky Kuryer
LEGAL ACTION

The State Press Committee issued a warning to the independent Brest weekly *Brestsky Kuryer* for reporting on a meeting of the Regional Belarus Civil Movement, a local non-governmental organization.

The press committee ruled that the story made a statement on behalf of an organization not registered with the Justice Ministry, a violation of Article 5 of the Media Law.

According to Belarusian law, a media outlet can be closed if it receives two such warnings in one year. The newspaper filed an appeal in mid-February.

On April 13, the High Economic Court of Belarus revoked the warning, ruling that the article in question was a news report and could therefore not be classified as a statement on behalf of the Regional Belarus Civil Movement.

FEBRUARY 6

Belorusskaya Delovaya Gazeta
LEGAL ACTION

After publishing a story on abuses by state security police, the independent Minsk daily *Belorusskaya Delovaya Gazeta* was warned for allegedly breaching Article 5.2 of the Press Law by reporting on a continuing investigation.

Under Belarusian law, a media outlet can be shut down after two official warnings.

Deputy Prosecutor Gen. Mikhail Snegir's warning to editor Pyotr Martsev came in response to a December 19, 2000, article entitled "The Blood of Almaz." It described crimes allegedly committed by former members of a special police unit called Almaz.

The focus of the article was former Almaz member Valery Ignatovich, the main suspect in the July 2000 kidnapping of Dmitry Zavadsky, a cameraman for Russian Public Television (ORT). The article asserted that Belarusian officials were deliberately covering up the crime.

Gen. Snegir claimed the newspaper had violated the press law by disclosing details of an ongoing investigation. *Belorusskaya Delovaya Gazeta's* management argued that they had not violated the law because the information was obtained independently.

FEBRUARY 14

Narodnaya Volya
LEGAL ACTION
Komsomolskaya Pravda v Belarusi
LEGAL ACTION

The State Press Committee issued warnings to the independent daily

Narodnaya Volya and to the local edition of the Moscow-based *Komsomolskaya Pravda v Belarusi* for breaching Article 32 of the Media Law, which stipulates that media outlets are responsible for the accuracy of the information they publish.

Under Belarusian law, a news organization can be shut down after two warnings from the Press Committee.

The committee argued that both newspapers had violated the law by describing the prominent Belarusian writer Vasil Bykov as an exile. The committee claimed that Bykov was not forced out of the country but had left of his own free will.

FEBRUARY 20

Sergei Nerovny, *Volny Horad*
HARASSED, LEGAL ACTION
Nikolai Motorenko,
Nash Volny Horad
HARASSED, LEGAL ACTION
Vadim Stefanenko, *Malady Front*
HARASSED, LEGAL ACTION

Nerovny, editor-in-chief of the daily newspaper *Volny Horad* in the city of Krichev; Stefanenko, Krichev leader of the opposition organization Malady Front; and Motorenko, editor of the newspaper *Nash Volny Horad*, were convicted of illegal production and distribution of printed materials.

Each was fined the equivalent of 50 monthly minimum-wage salaries (3,600 rubles, or approximately US$150).

On February 2, 2001, police searched a night train delivering *Volny Horad* from Smolensk, Russia, just across the border from Krichev, and confiscated 507 copies of the newspaper.

On February 7, police detained Stefanenko at the Krichev railroad station. He had just arrived from Smolensk with 296 copies of *Volny Horad* and 302 copies of *Nash Volny Horad*. The police later destroyed the newspapers.

Five days later, the Krichev City Council sent a letter to Smolensk city authorities asking them to do everything in their power to prevent *Volny Horad* from being printed in Smolensk. Krichev authorities justified the request by claiming that the newspaper had criticized the prospective political union between Russia and Belarus.

On February 13, 2001, police attempted to seize copies of the two newspapers at the Krichev railroad station. But when officers arrived, they found a group of journalists with video cameras waiting. A search of Stefanenko revealed a single copy of the government newspaper *Sovetskaya Belarus*.

Nerovny and Stefanenko were each fined 50 minimum wages at a February 20 hearing. In a separate hearing on March 2, the Krichev City Court convicted Nerovny of illegal entrepreneurial activities and fined him another 50 minimum wages, which by March had risen to 5,700 rubles (approximately US$250).

Motorenko was fined 50 minimum wages at a March 6 hearing.

MAY 8

ORT
HARASSED
RTR
HARASSED
NTV
HARASSED

Government officials interrupted the

broadcasts of ORT, RTR, and NTV, three leading Russian television channels operating in Belarus, and replaced their programming with Belarusian president Aleksandr Lukashenko's Victory Day speech.

Victory Day is a national holiday that celebrates the Soviet Union's World War II victory over Nazi Germany. Authorities did not restore the Russian channel's regular broadcasts until late Wednesday morning.

Lukashenko explained that a technical error caused the channels to be shut off and his speech broadcast all over the country. He dismissed the delay in restoring regular programming as simple clumsiness.

MAY 14

Yuri Svirko, *Diena*
HARASSED

At the request of the Belarusian Presidential Protection Service (BPPS), the Belarusian Foreign Ministry's Commission for Accrediting Foreign Media Correspondents issued a warning to Svirko, a reporter for the Latvian newspaper *Diena*.

The warning came after an April 10 confrontation in which Svirko, who had a valid pass to the Belarusian National Assembly's House of Representatives, was denied entry into the session hall to hear President Aleksandr Lukashenko give a speech. An officer stopped the journalist at the building's third security checkpoint. When Svirko tried to enter the hall, the officer twisted the reporter's arms behind his back and hauled him to the press center.

On April 17, 2001, Svirko filed a

complaint with the Prosecutor General of the Republic of Belarus, but no action was taken.

JULY 12

Vadim Stefanenko, *Volny Horad*
LEGAL ACTION
Sergei Nerovny, *Volny Horad*
LEGAL ACTION
Nikolai Motorenko, *Volny Horad*
LEGAL ACTION

Krichev authorities launched a criminal case against journalists Stefanenko, Nerovny, and Motorenko of the Krichev-based weekly *Volny Horad*, according to local reports.

The journalists were accused of holding police officer Rybchinsky (first name unavailable) hostage on July 12, when police raided the newspaper's offices and seized technical equipment. The offices were also serving as the local headquarters of opposition presidential candidate Semyon Domash.

The journalists maintained that Rybchinsky burst into the offices and failed to identify himself as a police officer; the journalists simply closed the door behind him, according to the Belarusian news agency BelaPan.

Three months later, the prosecutor dropped the criminal case against the journalists for lack of evidence, Belarusian sources reported. At the end of October, the Krichev Prosecutor's Office reopened the case and then promptly closed it once again.

On November 12, BelaPan reported that local authorities again filed criminal charges against the three journalists but less than a month later closed the case again. No charges were pending at year's end.

Volny Horad
HARASSED

Police raided the offices of the Krichev-based weekly *Volny Horad* and seized three computers, a scanner, a television set, and a VCR, according to local and international press reports.

On July 18, a court in Krichev found the newspaper guilty of violating Decree No. 8, which bars the use of foreign grants for activities that encourage agitation. The court rubber-stamped the confiscation of the newspaper's computer equipment.

On August 3, the U.S. State Department condemned the seizure, noting that two of the three computers belonged to the U.S. embassy in Minsk. Under the 1996 U.S.-Belarus Bilateral Assistance Agreement, U.S. government assistance is exempt from Decree No. 8.

CPJ circulated an alert about this incident on August 23, 2001.

JULY 17

Den
ATTACKED

The offices of the independent, thrice-weekly newspaper *Den* were burglarized twice within a one-week period, according to local and international sources.

On July 17, unknown individuals broke into *Den*'s offices and stole computer equipment. The robbery took place after *Den*'s published reports criticizing high-level government officials.

The paper was about publish a special issue implicating the government in the disappearances of several well-known people, according to Belarusian and international reports. All materials related to the special edition disappeared after the robbery, according to the non-governmental organization Charter 97.

On July 24, the newspaper's offices were again burglarized and critical computer equipment was stolen, local and international sources reported.

Prior to the robberies, the editorial team completed work on the special issue. CPJ could not confirm if *Den* published the issue, but the paper was still publishing at year's end.

The newspaper's editor-in-chief, Aleksandr Tomkovich, linked the two robberies, pointing out that in both cases there were no signs of forced entry and that the thieves only stole equipment needed for publication, Radio Free Europe/Radio Liberty reported.

JULY 20

Belaruski Uskhod
HARASSED

Officials from the Markovka village Prosecutor's Office, accompanied by police, seized a computer, a printer, and a fax modem from the weekly *Belaruski Uskhod*, according to local press reports.

The equipment had been provided by the international nonprofit organization IREX, which successfully contested the seizure in the Khotimks Regional Court on August 15. The equipment was returned to the newspaper's headquarters five days later, on August 20.

CPJ circulated an alert about this incident on August 23, 2001.

AUGUST 17

Nasha Svaboda
CENSORED

Police from the State Committee for Financial Investigation seized 400,000 copies of the independent, thrice-weekly newspaper *Nasha Svaboda* in advance of the September 9 presidential elections.

The special election issue, which endorsed Vladimir Goncharik, the only opposition candidate running against incumbent president Aleksandr Lukashenko, predicted the president's defeat in the upcoming poll. (Lukashenko ultimately won what most observers dismissed as a fraudulent election.)

Officials did not file actual charges against *Nasha Svaboda*, but claimed that they confiscated the paper's print run at the Magic publishing house in Minsk because Magic had not adequately prepared certain financial documents.

However, *Nasha Svaboda* editor-in-chief Pavel Zhuk maintains that because the newspapers were the property of *Nasha Svaboda* and not of Magic, police had no right to seize them.

Though officials took nearly the entire 480,000 print run, Nasha Svaboda staff managed to retain 80,000 copies and distribute them by hand in Minsk.

CPJ published an alert about the seizure on August 20.

AUGUST 21

Narodnaya Volya
HARASSED

Officials from the State Committee for Financial Investigation seized several computers and other technical equipment from the independent daily *Narodnaya Volya*.

Officials claimed they confiscated the computers in order to determine whether the paper had a legal right to use them, given that they were borrowed from private individuals. Radio Free Europe/Radio Liberty reported that the investigation was slated to continue until September 19, but no charges were ever filed.

Despite these difficulties, Vyachaslau Orhish, a correspondent with the newspaper, maintained that *Narodnaya Volya* would continue to publish.

Around the same time, the State Committee for Financial Investigation also launched audits of two other independent newspapers, *Belarusskaya Delovaya Gazeta* and *Nasha Svaboda*. Neither publication was charged.

CPJ issued an alert about this case on August 23, 2001.

AUGUST 22

Magic publishing house
HARASSED

The State Committee for Financial Investigation seized equipment and froze bank accounts of the Magic publishing house, which prints most Minsk-based independent publications.

Magic's owner, Yuri Budko, told Radio Free Europe/Radio Liberty that the committee officials justified their actions by referring to an earlier court order that Budko successfully challenged last year.

Authorities sealed Magic's printing presses, preventing the publishing house from printing *Narodnaya Volya*, *Rabochy*, and more than a dozen other independent newspapers, Stepan Zhirnostyok, Magic's executive director, told CPJ.

On August 27, the publishing house resumed work after Budko reached an agreement with the State Press Committee to appoint the deputy head of the committee, Vladimir Glushakov, as the acting director of Magic during the ongoing investigation.

Local sources told CPJ that Glushakov stopped working at Magic three days after the election. CPJ issued an alert about the case on August 23, followed by a protest letter to President Aleksandr Lukashenko on September 5.

AUGUST 27

Rabochy
CENSORED

Deputy head of the State Press Committee Vladimir Glushakov, who was appointed acting director of the Magic publishing house in advance of September 9 presidential elections, suspended printing of a special issue of the independent newspaper *Rabochy* after about 40,000 copies had already been printed.

Glushakov claimed that printing could not proceed without a preliminary payment from *Rabochy*, according to CPJ sources.

Although *Rabochy* delivered a payment the next day, printing did not resume. Instead, a Minsk district prosecutor's office seized the copies already printed and submitted them as evidence in a criminal defamation case stemming from an article in the special issue that accused president Lukashenko and his administration of corruption.

CPJ protested this incident in a September 5 letter to Belarusian president Aleksandr Lukashenko.

Nasha Svaboda
HARASSED
Den
HARASSED

Rabochy
HARASSED
Belaruskaya Maladzyozhnaya
HARASSED

The Central Election Committee warned an opposition candidate for the presidency against distributing four independent newspapers to voters free of charge.

The committee issued an official warning to Vladimir Goncharik, electoral opponent of Belarusian president Aleksandr Lukashenko, for allegedly "bribing" voters by distributing free copies of the independent newspapers *Nasha Svaboda*, *Den*, *Rabochy*, and *Belaruskaya Maladzyozhnaya*.

Another warning from the committee could have resulted in Goncharik's being disqualified. CPJ protested the incident in a September 5 letter to President Lukashenko.

AUGUST 31

Predrinimatelskaya Gazeta
CENSORED

Deputy head of the State Press Committee Vladimir Glushakov, who was appointed acting director of the Magic publishing house in advance of September 9 presidential elections, censored two articles from an issue of the independent newspaper *Predrinimatelskaya Gazeta*.

One of the censored articles pointed out that Lukashenko was violating the Belarusian Constitution by seeking a third term in office. Another piece reminded readers that it is a criminal offense for government officials to falsify election results. In place of the articles, the paper ran blank spaces.

CPJ protested the incident in a September 5 letter to Belarusian president Aleksandr Lukashenko.

SEPTEMBER 5

Narodnaya Volya
`CENSORED`

Deputy head of the State Press Committee Vladimir Glushakov, who was appointed acting director of the Magic publishing house in advance of September 9 presidential elections, censored the independent *Narodnaya Volya*.

The September 5 print run was allowed to proceed only after editors removed a collage that expressed support for President Aleksandr Lukashenko's electoral opponent, Vladimir Goncharik.

Narodnaya Volya was also forced to remove allegedly defamatory phrases from an upcoming special issue.

CPJ protested the incident in a September 5 letter to President Aleksandr Lukashenko.

SEPTEMBER 9

Belarusskaya Delovaya Gazeta
`HARASSED`
Nasha Svaboda
`HARASSED`
Belarusskaya Gazeta
`HARASSED`
BelaPan news agency
`HARASSED`
Radio Racyja
`HARASSED`
Radio Free Europe/Radio Liberty Belarusian Service
`HARASSED`
Charter 97
`HARASSED`

Independent Monitoring
`HARASSED`
TV-6
`HARASSED`
Narodnaya Volya
`HARASSED`
Diena
`HARASSED`

During the September 9 presidential election, authorities blocked access to online versions of several major opposition newspapers, including *Belarusskaya Delovaya Gazeta*, *Nasha Svaboda*, and *Belarusskaya Gazeta*.

The Web sites of the independent BelaPan news agency, Radio Racyja, and the Belarusian Service of the U.S. government-funded Radio Free Europe/Radio Liberty also experienced unexplained service interruptions on election day.

Until they were blocked, the independent media outlets were posting up-to-the-minute reports of violations at polling stations, local press and election monitors reported.

The Internet campaign site of Vladimir Goncharik, President Aleksandr Lukashenko's main opponent, was also jammed, as were the sites of the civic organizations Charter 97 and Independent Monitoring.

Prior to the elections, Charter 97 had criticized Lukashenko for a range of alleged offenses. In particular, Charter 97 publicized credible allegations by former government officials implicating the president in the murder of Dmitry Zavadsky, a cameraman with the Russian public television network ORT who has been missing since July 7, 2000.

Several hours after the polls closed on September 9, according to Charter 97, President Lukashenko announced plans to ban the Russian channel TV-6 from operating in Belarus, though he never followed through on the threats.

Unlike the propaganda-filled Belarusian state television, Russian television stations have not shied away from criticizing Lukashenko. In return, the president has periodically threatened to expel Russian journalists.

On September 10, correspondents from the independent newspaper *Narodnaya Volya*, the BelaPan news agency, and the Latvian newspaper *Diena* were denied access to a presidential news conference, according to Charter 97. At the press conference, President Lukashenko promised to "support journalists the way I supported them before."

CPJ documented all these abuses in a September 21 news alert.

SEPTEMBER 24

Brestsky Kuryer
LEGAL ACTION, CENSORED

The State Press Committee warned the independent Brest-based weekly *Brestsky Kuryer* for publishing the statement of an unregistered political organization, a violation of the Press Law.

The statement, titled "Stop the persecution of democratic candidates for president of the Republic of Belarus!," was signed by leaders of local opposition parties, civic organizations, and labor unions, some of which were not registered with the government.

The High Economic Court of Belarus rejected the newspaper's appeal, according to Radio Racyja.

On November 5, the Brest regional printing house refused to print *Brestsky Kuryer* because of the

September warning. Printing house officials maintained that printing could resume only if they received written permission from the Regional Executive Committee.

The newspaper requested permission from the committee, without success. In mid-November, *Brestsky Kuryer* was forced to print its upcoming edition in Smolensk, Russia, local sources reported.

Soon after, the Brest regional printing house resumed publishing *Brestsky Kuryer*.

NOVEMBER 12

Pahonya
LEGAL ACTION

The Hrodno-based independent weekly *Pahonya* was shut down after the Belarusian High Economic Court found the publication guilty of insulting President Aleksandr Lukashenko and publishing the statements of an unregistered civic organization, according to local and international press reports.

The newspaper had received two prior warnings in relation to these charges.

Pahonya received the first warning on November 17, 2000, and the second warning in early September 2001. Prior to the second warning, the regional prosecutor's office confiscated *Pahonya*'s entire print run and opened a criminal case against the newspaper.

Pahonya's editor-in-chief, Mikola Markevich, filed a complaint in December with the High Economic Court of Belarus regarding its decision. At year's end, the newspaper continued to publish online.

NOVEMBER 19

Andzhei Pisalnik, *Pahonya*
LEGAL ACTION
Paval Mazheika, *Pahonya*
LEGAL ACTION
Mikola Markevich, *Pahonya*
LEGAL ACTION

Markevich, editor of the Hrodno-based independent weekly *Pahonya*, was charged with participating in an unsanctioned rally to protest the recent banning of the paper. *Pahonya* reporters Pisalnik and Mazheika were charged with the same offense.

Pahonya was shut down on November 12, after the Belarusian High Economic Court found the publication guilty of insulting President Aleksandr Lukashenko and publishing the statements of an unregistered civic organization (see November 12 case).

The rally was held on November 19. That same day, the three journalists were asked to come to the Leninsky District Police Department, where they were charged with violating the Belarusian Administrative Code.

On November 26, the Leninsky District Court found Mazheika and Pisalnik guilty of participating in an unsanctioned rally and issued them a warning, local and international sources reported.

Markevich's hearing was scheduled for December 5, but was postponed because the court misplaced his file, Radio Free Europe/Radio Liberty reported. On December 13, the Leninsky District Court found Markevich guilty of organizing and participating in an unsanctioned rally and fined him the equivalent of 50 minimum wages.

CYPRUS

MAY 24

Avrupa
ATTACKED

A bomb blast ripped through the printing facility of the daily *Avrupa* in northern Cyprus, causing significant damage.

No one claimed responsibility for the blast, according to international press reports. Quoting eyewitnesses, Agence France-Presse said unidentified assailants placed the bomb at the printing house gate and fled the scene in a waiting car.

Avrupa is known for criticizing the government of Rauf Denktash, leader of the self-styled Turkish Federated State of Cyprus, which Turkey alone recognizes.

Some 35,000 Turkish troops are stationed in the north Cypriot state, founded after Turkey invaded the northern half of the island in 1974.

Avrupa has faced numerous lawsuits over the years in response to its reporting. In July 2000, three staffers were arrested and accused of espionage. In November, *Avrupa*'s printing plant was the target of another bomb attack.

In a May 31 press release, CPJ condemned the bombing and called on northern Cypriot authorities to launch an investigation and bring the perpetrators to justice.

CZECH REPUBLIC

OCTOBER 22

Respekt
THREATENED

Prime Minister Milos Zeman

threatened to bankrupt the independent, Prague-based weekly *Respekt* with a series of debilitating lawsuits in retaliation for its criticism of his government.

Zeman announced that his government was planning to file suit against *Respekt* and its editor-in-chief, Pyotr Holub, after Holub wrote an article calling the ruling Social Democrat (CSSD) government corrupt, the CTK news agency reported.

The prime minister later told a group of journalists that members of his cabinet would file separate complaints against Holub, all demanding financial compensation, "so that *Respekt* finally ceases to exist."

Zeman valued the reputations of his 17 cabinet ministers at 10 million crowns (US$270,000) each, implying that his government would seek 170 million crowns (US$4.5 million) in damages.

He went on to say that he wanted an "equality-based partnership to reign between the government and the press" but added that journalists should not be surprised by his cabinet's "allergic" reaction to lies.

Respekt has often reported on scandals and conflicts of interest within the CSSD.

After strong protests from CPJ and other press freedom organizations, Zeman and the members of his cabinet dropped the threatened lawsuits.

FRANCE

JUNE 17

Nicolas Giudici, *Nice-Matin* and *Corse-Matin*
KILLED (MOTIVE UNCONFIRMED)
Giudici's body was found in some bushes on the edge of a dirt track near the village of Piedriggio in northern Corsica on the morning of June 17. Giudici, 52, had been shot three times, in the left arm, chest and right hip, according to local reports. His torched car was found 50 kilometers (30 miles) away at the bottom of a ravine near the town of Cervione.

Guidici frequently covered the separatist movement on the French island of Corsica as a reporter for the regional weekly *Nice-Matin* and the daily *Corse-Matin*. He was also the author of *Le Crépuscule des Corses* (Twilight of the Corsicans), a critical assessment of Corsican society that was published in 1997.

Local police launched an investigation into Giudici's murder, according to The Associated Press, but by year's end the inquiry was virtually at a standstill. Several possible motives, related both to Guidici's private life and his profession, were listed in local newspapers—including a possible connection to a local theft of rare paintings that concerned Guidici, who was a collector.

Political and criminal violence are part of life in Corsica. But Guidici's colleagues were unaware of any politically sensitive work that might have led to his murder.

GEORGIA

FEBRUARY 24

Tamaz Tsertsvadze, *Meridiani*
ATTACKED
Tsertsvadze, editor of the Tbilisi-based weekly *Meridiani*, was attacked near his home by a group of unknown

individuals. The journalist, who lost consciousness after he was beaten with steel bars, was later taken to hospital in critical condition and treated for a concussion, a broken nose, and broken ribs.

Tsertsvadze told the nonprofit International Center for Journalists that he was not robbed in the attack.

The assault may have been related to Tsertsvadze's journalism. Prior to the attack, *Meridiani* staff received a number of telephone threats demanding that the newspaper stop criticizing government authorities.

Police launched an investigation into the attack but had not identified any suspects by year's end.

APRIL 1

Meridiani
HARASSED

The editorial offices of the Tblisi-based weekly *Meridiani* were burglarized. The burglars stole computers containing the latest edition of the newspaper, along with layout templates and other critical files and technical equipment, according to international press reports.

The burglars also rummaged through the desk of *Meridiani* editor Tamaz Tsertsvadze. Computer cables were slashed, while other valuables, including money, remained untouched.

Tsertsvadze claimed that the robbery was connected to the newspaper's criticism of the Citizen's Union of Georgia, President Shevardnadze's political party, which controls the parliament.

The theft forced *Meridiani* to halt publication. The police launched an

investigation, but no progress had been reported by year's end.

MAY 21

Rustavi-2
LEGAL ACTION

Former minister of culture Valery Asatiani filed a defamation lawsuit against Rustavi-2, a Tbilisi-based independent television station.

The case stemmed from an April 1 exposé on the news program "60 Minutes" alleging Asatiani's involvement in a murder and subsequent cover-up. Asatiani sought 20,700,000 laris (US$10,000,000) in damages.

According to "60 Minutes" producer and anchor Akaki Gogichaishvili, the program presented an interview with Asatiani's former assistant Irakli Kereselidze, who is serving a life sentence for murdering a man named Bichi Bakhtadze.

The program also included a hidden camera interview with assistant of Asatiani's, Roman Bendeliani, which implicated the minister in the murder, Gogichaishvili told CPJ.

Prosecutor General Georgy Meparishvili later released a statement accusing "60 Minutes" of violating the law by using a hidden camera during the second interview, Rustavi-2 told CPJ. Meparshvili also claimed that "60 Minutes" acted illegally by convincing the victim's relatives to exhume the body.

Rustavi-2 maintains that its staff obeyed the law. Meparishvili resigned later in the year after a failed raid on Rustavi-2 caused mass protests. Asatiani's lawsuit was still pending at year's end.

JULY 1

Kosuke Tsuneoka, free-lancer
MISSING

Tsuneoka, a Japanese free-lance journalist, was kidnapped in Georgia's notorious Pankisi Gorge and held for several months.

Tsuneoka was reportedly travelling from Georgia to Chechnya to interview Chechen rebels when he was abducted by unidentified individuals. Prior to this trip, Tsuneoka had worked in Moscow as a free-lance journalist.

Tsuneoka, 32, last communicated with his family via e-mail at the end of July after arriving in Tbilisi, Georgia's capital, the Japan Economic Newswire reported. He wrote that he planned to visit Chechnya.

Tsuneoka also e-mailed his friend Kendziro Kato, a Tokyo-based military journalist, telling him that he would return from Chechnya to Georgia by August 15. Tsuneoka was traveling on a one-month Georgian visa, ITAR-TASS reported.

Tsuneoka was first thought to have gone missing in Chechnya. The Kremlin claimed he was not accredited to work in the Northern Caucasus Region and denied any knowledge of the journalist's whereabouts. But Russian officials pledged they would try to find him.

The Georgian Interior Ministry stated that it had no information on Tsuneoka's location, while the Georgian Foreign Ministry's press center said the journalist had not requested accreditation, according to ITAR-TASS.

Tsuneoka was freed on December 7 during a Georgian military operation, according to international reports.

JULY 26

Georgy Sanaya, Rustavi-2
KILLED

Sanaya, a popular 26-year-old Georgian journalist, was found dead in his Tbilisi apartment. He had been shot once in the head at close range with a 9 mm weapon. Sanaya anchored "Night Courier," a nightly political talk show in which he interviewed Georgia's leading politicians on the independent television station Rustavi-2.

Nika Tabatadze, news director of Rustavi-2, told CPJ that Sanaya's colleagues became concerned when he failed to report for work at the usual time on the afternoon of July 26 and did not answer his home or cellular telephones. That evening, a group of co-workers went to his apartment and knocked repeatedly on the door. When no one answered, they called the police, who entered the apartment and discovered Sanaya's body.

In a special television address, President Eduard Shevardnadze directed the minister of internal affairs, the prosecutor general, and the minister of state security to oversee the investigation personally. On July 27, President Shevardnadze met with U.S. chargé d'affaires Philip Remler and asked for the FBI's help in the investigation, according to Georgian and Russian press sources.

Although the police, assisted by a group of FBI agents, immediately launched an investigation, it failed to produce significant results. A suspect was detained in August but was later released due to lack of evidence, CPJ sources reported.

Sanaya's Rustavi-2 colleagues firmly believe that the murder resulted from his professional work, although they were not aware of any specific threats against the journalist. Erosi Kitsmarishvili, executive director of Rustavi-2, told CPJ that the murder could have been intended to intimidate the station, which is known for its investigative reporting on state corruption and misuse of power in Georgia. The station has frequently been the target of government harassment in recent years.

While Sanaya's work was not generally controversial, he had recently hosted a segment on Georgia's Pankisi Gorge, a lawless area near the Chechen border that is known for drug smuggling and kidnapping. A former parliamentary deputy who appeared on the program speculated publicly that criminals from the Pankisi Gorge region may have been responsible for Sanaya's murder.

On December 6, police arrested former police officer Grigol Khurtsilava after a ballistic analysis traced the murder weapon to him, the Georgian news agency Black Sea Press reported. Acting on his confession, police found the murder weapon and keys to Sanaya's apartment. Khurtsilava was then officially charged with Sanaya's murder. In early February 2002, the Prosecutor General's Office announced that it will forward Khurtsilava's case to the courts and insisted that Sanaya's murder was not politically motivated, the Moscow-based Center for Journalism in Extreme situations reported. Sanaya's colleagues maintain he was killed because of his work.

OCTOBER 31

Rustavi-2
HARASSED

Some 30 agents from Georgia's National Security Ministry raided the independent television station Rustavi-2's headquarters in the capital, Tbilisi, in an effort to obtain the station's financial records.

Rustavi-2, Georgia's most influential and respected broadcast outlet, is known for its exposés of government corruption and other abuses of authority.

National Security Ministry officials claimed the station was suspected of not paying some one million laris (US$480,000) in taxes, Radio Free Europe/Radio Liberty (RFE/RL) reported. But according to the station manager, Nika Tabatadze, tax authorities had audited and cleared the station a week earlier.

Several days before the raid, Interior Minister Kakha Targamadze publicly threatened Rustavi-2, according to local sources. Targamadze accused Rustavi-2 of "conspiring" against the Interior Ministry and threatened to "knock them on their backs," the Moscow-based Center for Journalism in Extreme Situations reported.

Targamadze's threat came in response to recent allegations about corruption in the Interior and National Security ministries that were made on the Rustavi-2 program "Night Courier."

Akaki Gogichaishvili, head of Rustavi-2's popular "60 Minutes" news program, attributed the raid to Rustavi-2's coverage of the restive Pankisi Gorge Region, near the Chechen border, where kidnapping and drug smuggling flourish.

In the weeks prior to the raid, Rustavi-2 had also reported extensively on allegations that Georgia was harboring Chechen rebels.

Rustavi-2 responded to the raid by broadcasting live the standoff between security agents and station officials outside its office in the center of Tbilisi, local sources reported.

Once news of the raid spread throughout Tbilisi, members of Parliament and local nongovernmental organizations immediately denounced the government crackdown. Hundreds of Rustavi-2 supporters gathered outside the station in an effort to prevent further government actions, according to news reports.

On October 31, thousands of protesters gathered in central Tbilisi to protest the raid, RFE/RL reported. President Shevardnadze, meanwhile, accepted the resignation of National Security Minister Vakhtang Kutateladze over the affair.

Shevardnadze also instructed Prosecutor General Georgy Meparishvili to investigate the legality of the raid, local sources reported. Meparishvili ruled that the raid was legal but later resigned.

NOVEMBER 12

Rustavi-2
ATTACKED, HARASSED

Police detained and assaulted a television crew from the popular investigative program "60 Minutes," which airs on the independent station Rustavi-2. The crew was working on a story about the narcotics trade in the Pankisi region at the time.

The crewmembers were stopped at a police checkpoint as they entered the region. When they identified themselves as journalists, they were taken to the local police station and beaten up.

A few hours later, the crew was released. When questioned by Rustavi-2 officials, the police denied any impropriety.

NOVEMBER 14

Izida Chaniya, *Nuzhnaya Gazeta*
HARASSED

Chaniya, editor of the independent weekly *Nuzhnaya Gazeta*, received a threatening telephone call giving her 72 hours to leave the Abkhazia region, local and international sources reported.

One week earlier, the newspaper had published a front-page article arguing that Georgia needed a new president.

Abkhazia is a volatile region with a strong separatist movement and a conflict-ridden history. Over the past few years, *Nuzhnaya Gazeta* has published numerous articles about high-level corruption and abuse of power in Abkhazia, according to the Georgian news agency Black Sea Press. As a result, the paper has often faced official harassment.

HUNGARY

MAY 7

Magyar Hirlap
HARASSED

Prime minister Viktor Orban's ruling Young Democrats-Civic Party (FIDESZ) banned employees of the newspaper *Magyar Hirlap* from attending party functions, The Associated Press reported.

The ban came after *Magyar Hirlap*

published a March article saying that "no one wants the liquidation of Viktor Orban and [FIDESZ party chairman] Laszlo Koever from public life." FIDESZ officials were outraged at the implication that Orban and Koever might be murdered.

Magyar Hirlap editor-in-chief Ilona Kocsi wrote an editorial apologizing for the article. On May 11, a FIDESZ official stated publicly that he considered the matter closed after Kocsi's apology, Hungarian Radio reported.

Magyar Hirlap journalists were unable to cover a FIDESZ congress in the southern Hungarian city of Szeged while the ban was in effect.

MAY 17

RTL Klub
LEGAL ACTION

The National Radio and Television Board ordered RTL Klub television to pay a US$17,600 fine and go off the air for 10 minutes during prime time, Agence France-Presse reported.

The ruling came in retaliation for an April interview on RTL Klub during which the presenter asked a man posing as a contract killer how much he would charge to kill Prime Minister Viktor Orban.

ITALY

JULY 20

Sam Cole, Associated Press Television News
ATTACKED
Timothy Fadek, GAMMA
ATTACKED

AP Biscom
ATTACKED
Jerome Delay, The Associated Press
ATTACKED

Police assaulted a number of journalists covering the Group of Eight (G-8) summit of the world's industrialized nations in Genoa from July 20 to July 22.

Cole, a Rome-based producer for Associated Press Television News, was clubbed and suffered a head injury. Fadek, of the GAMMA Press photo agency, was flung to the ground and beaten extensively, according to The Associated Press. An AP Biscom news agency reporter, whose name was not disclosed, was beaten even after he showed officers his press credentials and identified himself as a member of the press.

Violent demonstrators were also responsible for a number of assaults on journalists during the summit, according to international press reports. Delay, a Paris-based photographer for The Associated Press, sustained a fractured rib when a demonstrator struck him with a metal bar. In addition, CPJ received troubling reports that police officers masqueraded as journalists during the summit.

CPJ protested these attacks in an August 2 letter to Prime Minister Silvio Berlusconi.

JULY 21

The Independent Media Center
ATTACKED
Michael Geiser, free-lancer
ATTACKED
Philipp Stein, Independent Media Center
ATTACKED
Mark Covell, Indymedia
ATTACKED

At around midnight, police raided two buildings occupied by the Genoa Social Forum, an umbrella group of anti-globalization organizations. The Independent Media Center (IMC, www.indymedia.org), which helped many independent journalists file stories about the demonstrations, was based in one of the buildings.

The police, who claimed to be seeking violent demonstrators, ransacked the IMC and searched the premises for film and photographs, Agence France-Press reported.

Along with numerous activists, Italian police assaulted several independent journalists and IMC members who were in the building during the raid. Gieser, a Belgian journalist, suffered facial cuts when he was beaten as he lay on the ground. Stein, a German journalist and IMC member, was struck when he implored officers to stop the violence, according to Agence France-Press.

Covell, a British reporter who worked for Indymedia, was seriously injured by the police in the attack, during which he sustained a broken rib, internal bleeding, and an injury to his left arm.

In addition to the police brutality, a group of militant anarchists attacked journalists and television crews from Germany and Japan on July 21, the London-based *Independent* reported.

CPJ protested the attacks in an August 2 letter to Italian prime minister Silvio Berlusconi.

JULY 22

The Associated Press
LEGAL ACTION

Reuters
LEGAL ACTION
Agence France-Presse
LEGAL ACTION
RAI
LEGAL ACTION

Italian prosecutors ordered media outlets to turn over photographs, audiotapes, and videotapes of the violence that occurred in Genoa during the Group of Eight (G-8) summit of the world's industrialized nations from July 20 to 22.

Reuters, The Associated Press, Agence France-Presse, and the Italian state television network RAI all received the orders between July 22 and August 2.

Italian law imposes stiff penalties on journalists who do not comply with such orders. There is no right of appeal.

CPJ protested the orders in an August 22 letter to Italian prime minister Silvio Berlusconi.

KAZAKHSTAN

JANUARY 9

Bigeldy Gabdullin, *XXI Vek*
LEGAL ACTION

After a four-month trial, an Almaty court imposed a fine of 5 million tenge (about US$34,500) on Gabdullin, editor of the opposition weekly *XXI Vek*, for slandering a company controlled by Rakhat Aliyev, the son-in-law of President Nursultan Nazarbayev.

Aliyev's firm, Sakharny Tsentr Company, claimed that Gabdullin hurt its business reputation in an interview he gave to the independent television station Channel 31.

Gabdullin argued that his remarks had been taken out of context. On

February 16, his lawyer filed an appeal with a higher court.

XXI Vek was an opposition newspaper allied with exiled former prime minister Akezhan Kazhegelden, Nazarbayev's main rival. The paper has suffered frequent harassment in recent years and was effectively banned when no local printer would agree to produce it.

The paper was subsequently brought out by its own staff, who used a broken-down printing press and distributed copies by hand.

The last issue of *XXI Vek* appeared on January 25, 2001. In February, Gabdullin fled to the United States, where he now lives in exile.

JANUARY 25

Bigeldy Gabdullin, *XXI Vek*
LEGAL ACTION, CENSORED

The Almaty prosecutor's office opened a criminal case against Bigeldy Gabdullin, editor of the opposition weekly *XXI Vek*, for alleged defamation of President Nursultan Nazarbayev.

The charges were based on two *XXI Vek* articles, both published October 20, 2000, about Nazarbayev's alleged personal corruption. The prosecutor claimed that the articles had "negative connotations and [were] aimed at harming the honor and dignity of the President," local sources reported.

On April 6, the prosecutor's office issued a press release saying that it had dropped the case due to the "absence of [a] crime," although the newspaper had yet to receive formal notification to this effect. Additionally, *XXI Vek* had been ordered by the prosecutor's office to suspend its publication indefinitely on March 14.

APRIL 3

SolDat
HARASSED

Unknown individuals broke into SolDat's offices 17 days after Yermurat Bapi, the paper's editor-in-chief, was sentenced for "publicly insulting the dignity and honor of the president" (see April 3 case).

Computer files with a fully prepared edition of the newspaper, as well as a book ready for print, were destroyed. Expensive electronic equipment was damaged. The paper was forced to delay the printing of its next issue.

Bapi suspects that computer specialists carried out the break-in, since the targeted software and files were damaged irreparably and infected with a computer virus.

No criminal case was filed because, according to the police team on arrival, the doors and windows did not show evidence of forced entry.

Yermurat Bapi, *SolDat*
IMPRISONED, LEGAL ACTION

Bapi, editor of the opposition weekly *SolDat*, was convicted of "publicly insulting the dignity and honor of the president," an offense under Article 318.2 of the Criminal Code.

The journalist was sentenced to one year in jail and ordered to pay about US$280 in court expenses. The court also ordered that the July 6 print run of *SolDat* be burned.

Although he was immediately given a presidential amnesty, Bapi was banned from traveling abroad and subjected to other restrictions as a result of his conviction, which he appealed.

The case stemmed from two articles

that appeared in the May 30 and July 6 issues of *SolDat*. The first argued that President Nursultan Nazarbayev was responsible for violent ethnic clashes in the former Kazakh capital, Almaty, in December 1986.

The prosecution claimed that the second article, written by prominent Kazakh historian and dissident Karishal Asanov, had insulted Nazarbayev by describing him as illiterate, incompetent, and corrupt. Asanov was a co-defendant in the case but was acquitted for lack of evidence.

KYRGYZSTAN

FEBRUARY 13

Res Publica
CENSORED

A local court in Bishkek ordered the Uchkun Publishing House not to print the independent weekly *Res Publica* until the paper settled overdue fines from two libel cases.

Zamira Sydykova, the weekly's editor, said that because the newspaper had no money to pay the fines, it was unable to print its February 27 and March 6 issues. The fines were then paid and the newspaper released its March 13 issue.

Res Publica's March 30 and April 6 editions were also censored when Uchkun refused to print them after the Justice Ministry warned *Res Publica* not to publish work by reporters from *Asaba*, an opposition weekly that had been forced to close.

On April 5, *Res Publica* hired all of *Asaba*'s former journalists in order to overcome legal issues with publishing their materials. Four days later, Justice

Ministry officials said that the printer could resume printing *Res Publica*.

Res Publica owed one-quarter of a 200,000 soms (about US$4,200) fine imposed in March 1999 for allegedly violating the "honor and dignity" of Amanbek Karypkulov, president of the National Radio and Television Corporation.

The paper incurred Karypkulov's wrath by publishing an open letter from the company's employees calling for his dismissal.

Res Publica had been paying the fine in installments. The paper also owed 20,000 soms (about US$420) under a March 2000 judgment that it had defamed local politician Sadyrbek Botaliyev. *Res Publica* had reported that Botaliyev was attempting to undermine the Kyrgyz Human Rights Committee by launching a rival organization.

MARCH 6

Asaba
LEGAL ACTION, CENSORED

A Bishkek court ordered the Uchkun Publishing House to stop printing issues of *Asaba*, the oldest and most popular Kyrgyz-language publication in the country, until it had paid fines and damages totaling 8 million soms (about US$160,000), including an unprecedented US$100,000 damage award to parliamentary deputy Turdakun Usubaliyev. The court also ruled that any money coming into the newspaper's bank accounts would be garnished to pay the fines.

For two weeks in March, articles by *Asaba* journalists appeared in another paper, *Res Publica*. But when officials began confiscating *Asaba*'s property on

March 15, they also impounded 3,000 kilograms of newsprint stored at Uchkun. That action effectively blocked the publication of both newspapers, since *Res Publica* had no paper reserves of its own.

On March 19, *Asaba*'s owner announced that the newspaper was suspending publication indefinitely. Because the joint project with *Res Publica* was unprofitable, he said, *Asaba* would have to seek other solutions for its financial problems.

Asaba's effective closure followed several years of harassment from Kyrgyz tax authorities. In 1998, authorities demanded some US$42,000 in allegedly overdue taxes. The charges were dropped last year. But on February 27, chief tax official Aziz Momunkulov again charged the newspaper with tax evasion.

The newspaper's financial troubles were exacerbated by a financial dispute with the Kumtor Operating Company (a subsidiary of Canada's Cameco Corporation), which reportedly has close links to the Kyrgyz government. Kumtor claimed that the newspaper owed it more than one million soms (about US$22,000). Asaba disputed the claim in the Court of Appeals, which on February 20 ruled in favor of Kumtor.

On March 20, CPJ protested the harassment of *Asaba* in a letter to Kyrgyz president Askar Akayev. The paper remained closed at year's end, but in October, government loyalists opened a new, pro-government newspaper under the same name.

MARCH 13

Moldosaly Ibraimov, *Akyykat*
LEGAL ACTION

The Jalal-Abad District Court reversed its decision to free Ibraimov, a reporter with the newspaper *Akyykat*, who was cleared of criminal libel charges in June 2000.

A local judge, Toktosun Kasymbekov, brought libel charges against Ibraimov after the journalist reported that Kasymbekov had accepted a 730,000 som (US$15,000) bribe in connection with a legal dispute between two local politicians.

On June 19, 2000, Ibraimov was convicted and sentenced to two years in prison and a 107,000 som (US$2,200) fine. After winning an appeal, the journalist was freed on July 20, 2000.

Kasymbekov appealed that ruling to the Supreme Court, which instructed the district court to review its decision. On March 13, the original conviction was reinstated. The court then suspended the jail sentence.

Ibraimov's defense lawyer, Akmat Alagushev, filed a complaint with the Supreme Court. In April, Kasymbekov withdrew his charges against Ibraimov after the journalist printed a retraction of his original allegations, Alagushev told CPJ.

APRIL 24

Viktor Zapolsky, *Delo N*
LEGAL ACTION

The Pervomaisky District Court of Bishkek ordered Zapolsky, editor-in-chief of the independent weekly *Delo N*, to pay 50,000 soms (US$1,000) in damages for allegedly defaming Security Council secretary Misir Ashyrkulov.

Ashyrkulov had filed a lawsuit against Zapolsky seeking 1 million soms (more than US$21,000) in damages.

Originally, Secretary Ashyrkulov

lodged a 3 million som (more than US$60,000) suit against the newspaper *Komsomolskaya Pravda v Kyrgyzstane* and its editor-in-chief, Arkady Gladilov, for publishing an interview with Zapolsky in which he criticized the National Security Service. Ashyrkolov claimed that Zapolsky's statements damaged his professional reputation, Radio Free Europe/Radio Liberty reported.

In February, Ashyrkulov dropped his suit against *Komsomolskaya Pravda v Kyrgyzstane*. The next month he dropped the suit against Gladilov but elected to pursue his case against Zapolsky.

JUNE 20

Moya Stolitsa
LEGAL ACTION
Agym
LEGAL ACTION
Techeniye
LEGAL ACTION
Joltiken
LEGAL ACTION
Radio Dream Land
LEGAL ACTION
Pozitsiya
LEGAL ACTION
Zhilishchnye Vesti
LEGAL ACTION
Obrazovaniye v Kyrgyzstane
LEGAL ACTION
Pravo i Obrazovaniye
LEGAL ACTION
TV Almaz
LEGAL ACTION
Fergana
LEGAL ACTION
MK-krossvord
LEGAL ACTION

Minzhyldyk
LEGAL ACTION
Zdravstvuy
LEGAL ACTION
Studencheskaya Televizionnaya Set-STS Television and Radio Company
LEGAL ACTION
Ala TV Times Television
LEGAL ACTION

The Kyrgyz Justice Ministry rescinded certificates of registration for 16 new media outlets.

Throughout April and May, the Justice Ministry granted media certificates and then rescinded them, citing a previously unknown decision halting the registration of new media outlets until established media outlets had completed the registration process. The ministry claimed to have issued that decision on April 5, 2001.

On June 26, *Moya Stolitsa* editor-in-chief Aleskandr Kim filed a lawsuit against the Justice Ministry challenging the validity of both the April 5 decision and the ministry's subsequent cancellation of the 16 certificates.

Six days later, Bakyt Jamalidinov, the publisher of *Agym*, *Techeniye*, and *Joltiken*, filed a separate lawsuit against the ministry on the same grounds. During the following weeks, the Bishkek Arbitration Court postponed hearings for both cases several times.

On July 30, the court declined to review the *Moya Stolitsa* case and transferred the suit to a civil court. While the newspapers were preparing their cases, the ministry extended the reregistration deadline for registered media outlets to October 1.

After that, new publications were able to register. While the *Moya Stolitsa* case continues to be disputed in court, the newspaper's staff registered a new publication, *Moya Stolitsa-Novosti*, and published it in early November, RFE/RL reported.

Also in early November, the Justice Ministry finally registered *Agym*, which began publishing later that month, according to RFE/RL.

CPJ protested the extreme delays in registering media outlets in an August 22 letter to President Askar Akayev.

JULY 18

All media
LEGAL ACTION

The Presidential Administration of the Kyrgyz Republic adopted a decree to amend Article 297 of the Criminal code, making it easier to jail journalists who criticize the government.

The revised Article 297 states that activities intended to change or weaken the established constitutional order by force are punishable by up to three years' imprisonment. If such activities are funded by foreign organizations, they are punishable by three to five years in prison.

Meanwhile, the new Article 297-1 prescribes up to three years in prison and allows for confiscation of any property owned by persons who produce or distribute information intended to overthrow or undermine the constitutional order of the Kyrgyz Republic.

Parliament was scheduled to review the proposed legislation in September, according to the London-based Institute for War and Peace Reporting. However, due to domestic and international pressure, the Presidential Administration retracted the amendment decree.

CPJ protested the decree in an August 22 letter to President Askar Akayev.

OCTOBER 3

Res Publica
LEGAL ACTION

Bishkek's Pervomaisky District Court began its trial of the opposition weekly *Res Publica*, which was charged with slander by former Kyrgyz Committee for Human Rights (KCHR) member Sardarbek Botaliyev, according to Kyrgyz and international sources. Botaliyev sought 1,000,000 soms (about US $21,000).

The case stemmed from a series of articles published earlier in the year. According to former KCHR head Ramazan Dyryldayev, who lives in exile in Vienna, Botaliyev was dismissed from the organization in 1996 for theft and was prosecuted on those charges. However, the authorities later dismissed the charges against Botaliyev in exchange for his testimony against Dyryldayev in relation to other criminal charges.

Res Publica editor Zamira Sydykova did not attend all court proceedings, maintaining that the lawsuit's outcome was predetermined, according to Radio Free Europe/Radio Liberty. The case was still before the court at year's end.

OCTOBER 17

Res Publica
LEGAL ACTION

The Pervomaisky District Court found the Bishkek opposition weekly *Res Publica* guilty of defaming Aleksandr Yeliseyev, a former member of the Kyrgyz Committee for Human

Rights (KCHR), according to local and international reports. The newspaper was ordered to pay damages of 300,000 soms (about US $6,300).

Yeliseyev filed a lawsuit against the weekly after it published several articles by the current and former KCHR leadership about his 1997 dismissal from the committee. According to *Res Publica* editor-in-chief Zamira Sydykova, the articles' authors came to *Res Publica* after Yeliseyev published a story in another publication that allegedly insulted them.

At the trial, which began in September, Yeliseyev sought 1,500,000 (about US $31,600) in damages. Sydykova planned to appeal the verdict, reported Radio Free Europe/Radio Liberty.

LATVIA

November 28

Gundars Matiss, *Kurzemes Vards*
KILLED

Matiss, a crime reporter with the Liepaja-based daily *Kurzeme Vards*, was attacked on November 15 in the stairwell of his apartment building after he returned home from a shopping expedition. In a phone conversation from the hospital two hours after the attack, Matiss told the paper's editor-in-chief, Andzilss Remess, that someone followed him home and hit him from behind with a truncheon or club. He was struck several times on the head, arms, and legs. The assailant fled when neighbors interrupted the attack.

Matiss underwent three operations and fell into a coma. He died on November 28 from a brain hemorrhage.

The reporter had most recently investigated the contraband alcohol trade in Liepaja, according to Remess.

Though the police cited robbery, personal revenge, and retaliation for his journalism as possible motives, Matiss had not been robbed, and does not seem to have been involved in any serious personal dispute. His editor told CPJ: "Matiss knew a lot about the criminal world. He was one of those reporters who went deep." At press time, the police investigation was still ongoing.

MOLDOVA

January 10

Vremya
LEGAL ACTION
Yuliya Korolkova, *Vremya*
LEGAL ACTION

The Prosecutor General's Office filed criminal charges against the Russian-language newspaper *Vremya* and against *Vremya* correspondent Korolkova.

The charges were filed after the Association of Graduates of Romanian and Western Universities (CAIRO) complained that an article in the newspaper had insulted Moldova's national honor and instigated interethnic strife.

The story addressed the problems of Russian-speaking Moldovans, claiming that they have limited access to positions of power and that ethnic Moldovan officials take bribes.

According to local and international sources, *Vremya*'s editor-in-chief believes that the lawsuit is aimed to discredit the Russian-language press in Moldova.

The lawsuit was still pending at year's end.

MAY 12

Valentina Ushakova, *Argumenty i Fakty*
HARASSED

Ushakova, editor of the Moldovan edition of the Russian weekly *Argumenty i Fakty*, was dismissed after the paper's owner, Ion Musuc, eliminated her position.

According to Ushakova, she was fired for refusing to publish pro-communist political propaganda during the parliamentary election campaign.

Several journalists at the paper subsequently resigned in protest.

OCTOBER 5

Kommersant Moldovy
HARASSED, LEGAL ACTION

Moldova's prosecutor general asked a Chisinau district court to shut down the Russian-language weekly *Kommersant Moldovy*.

The Prosecutor General's Office accused the newspaper of publishing material that threatened Moldova's territorial integrity. *Kommersant Moldovy*, known for its sympathetic reports on Trans-Dnienster, a breakaway republic in eastern Modova that borders Ukraine, received a similar warning in January 2000 for its coverage of the region.

In the October 12 issue, the newspaper stated that it had not received the Prosecutor General's official notification and continued to publish.

In the beginning of November, the Moldovan Economic Court denied the publication's appeal to dismiss the lawsuit. On November 30, the court found *Kommersant Moldovy* guilty of threatening Moldova's territorial integrity

and national security and ordered the paper to cease publication, the Moscow-based Center for Journalism in Extreme Situations reported.

The newspaper plans to appeal the decision to a higher court. Meanwhile, in mid-December, the paper resumed publication under the name *Kommersant Plus*.

OCTOBER 30

Oleg Yeltsov, Olvia Press
HARASSED
Ivan Azmanov, Olvia Press
HARASSED

Several members of a television news crew from the news agency Olvia Press were detained by police in the Moldovan capital, Chisinau, according to local and international sources.

Correspondent Yelkov, cameraman Azmanov, and their driver were with the secretary of the Socialist Party of the Republic of Moldova, Valentin Krylov, whom they intended to interview, when they were taken into custody.

Olvia Press is the official news agency of the breakaway republic of Trans-Dniester, which is dominated by ethnic Slavs. All three crew members were questioned about the nature of their work in the country and their stance on Moldova's territorial integrity. The three men remained in custody for several hours, and their footage was confiscated.

In retaliation, Trans-Dniester authorities rescinded the accreditation of 17 Moldovan journalists, who were ordered to leave the territory by November 1. Trans-Dniester officials said they would not reconsider their decision until the Moldovan government issued an official apology and returned the videotape to the Olvia Press crew. Moldova denied detaining the journalists.

Two weeks later, however, Moldovan authorities apologized, and the Trans-Dniester authorities reinstated the journalists' accreditation.

NOVEMBER 25

RTR
LEGAL ACTION, CENSORED

Authorities in the breakaway Trans-Dniester region of Moldova blocked the broadcast of a report about the region by the Russian state television network RTR.

The report, part of RTR's regular program "Vesti Nedeli" (News of the Week), reported on allegedly widespread corruption, smuggling, and arms trafficking in Trans-Dniester and implicated the son of the current president, Igor Smirnov, in illegal activities.

The Trans-Dniester information minister, Boris Akulov, claimed the program was interrupted for technical reasons. "Vesti Nedeli" was then rebroadcast on the Trans-Dniester television station TV PMR with official commentary, Moldovan sources reported.

In response to RTR's report, Trans-Dniester authorities sued RTR for slander. The case remained in court at year's end.

In addition, RTR was banned from working in Trans-Dniester. Akulov announced that the regional Ministry of Information would not accredit RTR journalists until the network's management apologized for the program.

RUSSIA

FEBRUARY 6

Rashid Khatuyev, *Vozrozhdeniye*
ATTACKED
Vladimir Panov, *Vozrozhdeniye*
ATTACKED

Two men armed with guns and rubber truncheons stormed into the offices of the opposition newspaper *Vozrozhdeniye* in Cherkessk, the capital of the southern republic of Karachayevo-Cherkessiya.

The men beat up the paper's editor, Khatuyev, and his deputy, Panov. The attackers, who wore black balaclavas and special police force uniforms, also destroyed several computers before leaving the premises.

Khatuyev was taken to a local hospital, where he was diagnosed with concussion and a broken rib. Panov refused hospitalization for his injuries.

Vozrozhdeniye, which began publishing in January, is closely linked to the Vozrozhdeniye Respubliki political movement, which opposes the republic's president, Vladimir Semyonov.

Panov later told Moscow's *Kommersant-Daily* that the attack was prompted by a series of articles criticizing Semyonov 's regime. Panov claimed that the government had sanctioned the raid. Local officials dismissed the allegations, blaming the incident on mysterious "destabilizing" forces within the political elite, according to a report by the Institute for War and Peace Reporting.

FEBRUARY 20

Anna Politkovskaya, *Novaya Gazeta*
IMPRISONED, HARASSED

Novaya Gazeta correspondent Politkovskaya was detained by Russian security forces in the village of Khatuni in the Vedeno Region of Chechnya, where she was investigating a so-called filtration camp for Chechen civilians.

Russian military forces had allegedly committed numerous atrocities at the camp, including beatings, rapes, and murders.

Politkovskaya was arrested and accused of entering Chechnya without correct accreditation and of not having registered her whereabouts with the military. She was released on February 23.

Politkovskaya told CPJ that Russian soldiers threatened to shoot her during her ordeal.

APRIL 14

NTV
HARASSED, CENSORED
Itogi
CENSORED
Segodnya
CENSORED

After a tense 11-day standoff, the state-dominated Gazprom corporation succeeded in occupying the headquarters of NTV, formerly Russia's only independent national television station.

At 3:30 a.m. on Saturday, April 14, Boris Jordan, a controversial American financier appointed by Gazprom to head NTV, arrived at the station's headquarters with a court order. Security officers hired by Gazprom then took control of the station's offices and control room, which had been occupied by dissident NTV journalists.

The crisis began on April 3, when NTV creditor Gazprom staged a boardroom coup that wrested control of the network from media tycoon Vladimir Gusinsky, who was then in Spain fighting a Russian government effort to extradite him on corruption charges. NTV journalists refused to recognize the new Gazprom management team's authority, and a standoff ensued.

Early Saturday morning, Jordan and other Gazprom-appointed officials met with NTV staff and accepted resignations from more than 40 employees, including 10 journalists and five news presenters. By 10 a.m., the Gazprom-controlled NTV was back on the air with a skeleton newscasting crew.

Meanwhile, a group of some 15 former NTV journalists, led by ousted general director Yevgeny Kiselyov, moved swiftly to revive some of their former news programs at the cable station TNT, which was also controlled by Gusinsky. Later, many high-profile NTV journalists joined TV-6, a private nationwide television network. (See TV-6 case on page 452.)

On Monday, April 16, a group of dissident shareholders in Gusinsky's Media-Most holding company, including Gazprom, shut down the influential daily *Segodnya*, which was considered to be one of Moscow's most liberal newspapers.

That same day, Russian tax police filed tax-evasion charges against TNT's chief accountant. And on Tuesday, April 17, a Media-Most official acting on behalf of the dissident shareholders fired the editor of Media-Most's weekly newsmagazine *Itogi*, a joint venture with the U.S. magazine *Newsweek*. *Itogi* staffers were locked out of their offices and told that they could either resign or be fired.

CPJ published an alert about the case on April 17 and sent a formal protest letter to President Vladimir Putin on April 30.

MAY 18

RTR
HARASSED

Police arrested a film crew from the RTR network program "Vesti" in the city of Ivanovo while they were on their way to interview Deputy Mayor Sergei Brazer about interruptions in the municipal power supply.

Despite receiving preliminary permission to conduct the interview, the journalists were not allowed to enter the building where the deputy mayor's office is located. The police rudely demanded that the video camera be turned off and arrested the reporters when they did not comply. The crew was released only after the personal intervention of Gennady Panin, head of the Interior Affairs Department for the Ivanovo Region.

MAY 22

Olga Kitova, *Belgorodskaya Pravda*
IMPRISONED, ATTACKED,
LEGAL ACTION

Police in the southern city of Belgorod assaulted and jailed Kitova, a reporter with the newspaper *Belgorodskaya Pravda* who also contributes to the Moscow daily *Obshchaya Gazeta*.

On May 22, police officers arrested Kitova at her apartment in Belgorod and took her to a temporary holding cell, according to local news reports. Although Kitova was suffering from high blood pressure and heart complications as a result of the arrest, the police initially refused to provide her with medical treatment, according to Yuliya Ignatyeva of the *Obshchaya Gazeta* legal department. Later that day, Kitova was treated at Belgorod Hospital No. 1.

During the first week of her detention, Kitova was not allowed to meet privately with legal counsel. In addition, she was forbidden to receive phone calls or visitors apart from hospital staff and her attorney.

The arrest stemmed from a series of *Belgorodskaya Pravda* articles by Kitova, published in May 2000, that questioned the credibility of the Belgorod prosecutor's case against four local university students charged with sexually assaulting a male fellow student.

Kitova reported that the charges were largely based on forced confessions and testimony from the victim's mother, a politically well-connected health inspector who had been diagnosed as a paranoid schizophrenic.

In January 2001, the prosecutor's office began investigating Kitova for allegedly slandering the victim and his mother.

On March 21, ten police officers surrounded Kitova outside her home. One officer twisted her arm behind her back and shoved her into a police car, where she was beaten unconscious. Kitova was later treated for bruises and hypertension at Belgorod Hospital No. 1, her attorney told CPJ.

Local prosecutor Dimitriy Khlebnikov then launched an investigation against Kitova for allegedly insulting and using force against the police officers who had abducted and beaten her.

On May 28, Khlebnikov charged Kitova with five criminal offenses: slander, insulting an individual's honor, obstruction of justice, using force against state officials, and insulting state officials.

On the same day, local sources reported that Kitova had been released from police custody after she signed an agreement not to leave the city of Belgorod.

On June 1, CPJ sent a letter to Russian president Vladimir Putin protesting Kitova's prosecution and imprisonment.

On December 20, the court handed Kitova a 30-month suspended sentence, fined her 20,000 rubles (US$656), and banned her from elected office for three years, the Moscow-based Center for Journalism in Extreme Situations reported.

JUNE 7

NTV
THREATENED, CENSORED

A news crew from the national television network NTV was threatened by Vladivostok mayor Yuri Kopylov, local sources reported. The crew was filming Vladivostok officials greeting former governor Yevgeny Nazdratenko at the airport.

Kopylov became irate when he realized that he was being filmed. "Take the tape away from the bearded one!" he yelled. "Did I give you permission to tape me? Get away from here! Tolya,

take him away or punch him in the snout!" Kopylov's bodyguard then forced the crew to stop filming.

CPJ protested the threat in a June 11 letter to President Vladimir Putin.

Dalyokaya Okraina
HARASSED, CENSORED

Vladivostok police officers seized the June 7 edition of the newspaper *Dalyokaya Okraina*. According to local sources, some 20 police officers raided the Vladivostok post office, preventing the newly printed edition from being loaded into delivery trucks for several hours.

Police then confiscated the entire print run of 380,000 copies, local sources said, and took them to a district police station.

Vladimir Gilgenberg, editor-in-chief of *Dalyokaya Okraina*, said the police did not present a court order authorizing the confiscation and only referred to supposed verbal orders from Col. Vladimir Krivoshvili, the Vladivostok chief of police. Colonel Krivoshvili apparently acted on a complaint from Sergei Knyazev, chairman of the Regional Election Commission, who alleged that the edition contained material that violated election campaign law.

It appears that *Dalyokaya Okraina* was targeted for reporting on gubernatorial candidate Sergei Darkin's alleged links with criminal elements in Vladivostok. The newspaper's information came from the regional Internal Affairs Administration. Darkin, who is backed by prominent local politicians, won the first round of elections on May 27.

On June 12, officials again targeted

Dalyokaya Okraina, seizing 150,000 out of 600,000 copies of that day's edition. The raid came in advance of the second round of elections, scheduled for June 17. According to Gilgenberg, the police said they were acting on verbal orders from their superiors.

Darkin won the June poll and currently serves as the region's governor.

CPJ protested the harassment of *Dalyokaya Okraina* in a June 12 letter to President Vladimir Putin.

JULY 26

All journalists in Chechnya
HARASSED

The commandant of the Russian military base of Khankala in Chechnya imposed new restrictions requiring journalists covering the ongoing conflict there to be accompanied at all times by an official from the press service of the Interior Ministry.

The new rules were announced after a television crew traveling with Chechen security forces tried to enter the Chechen capital, Grozny, without permission from Russian authorities.

The media's access to the war-ravaged region is already severely restricted by cumbersome accreditation procedures and rules that make travel within Chechnya dependent on the whims of local officials. Reporters say the new regulations represent another Russian military attempt to control press coverage of the Chechen conflict.

The new escort requirement gives the military significant leverage, since officials can now discriminate between journalists based on their coverage.

Journalists based in Khankala say their reporting will also be limited by

the military's lack of resources. The government press centers have only three cars at their disposal, according to the local press, and journalists questioned whether officers would be willing to travel to areas that lack a military presence, or to places where authorities do not want the media covering military activities.

AUGUST 29

TVK Lipetsk
HARASSED, LEGAL ACTION

Authorities illegally took over TVK, the first private television station in the Lipetsk Region. The station was both a popular source of news and a harsh critic of Governor Oleg Korolyov, who is running for re-election in April 2002. TVK management had openly backed the governor's main electoral rival.

For several years, minority and majority shareholders of the station were locked in a deeply politicized conflict over management of the station. According to local press reports, TVK's ownership dispute began in 1998, when Leonid Trufanov, the founder and former owner of the station, sold a controlling stake to the Moscow-based Zenit Bank.

In 2000, a pro-Korolyov group of TVK shareholders sold their shares to the Moscow-based Energiya Corporation. Energiya's general director, a deputy in the Lipetsk Legislative Assembly, is closely allied with the Korolyov administration.

Energiya then challenged Zenit's 1998 share purchase in court, seeking to gain a controlling stake of TVK and replace its management.

Energiya lost its case. Earlier in

2001, Moscow's Kuntsevsky Court prohibited Energiya from conducting a TVK shareholders' meeting. The Sovetskiy District Court in Lipetsk later upheld that decision. Despite these rulings, Energiya had a shareholders' meeting on August 24 where delegates named pro-Korolyov business executive Dmitry Kolbasko as TVK's new general director.

In the early hours of August 29, police officers from the security service of the local Internal Affairs Administration took control of TVK's offices, according to local and international press reports. Claiming to act on Kolbasko's behalf, the police prevented station staff from entering the building.

In an interview with the Moscow daily *Kommersant*, TVK's ousted general director, Aleksandr Lykov, claimed that the Energiya-led shareholders' meeting took place in the office of Lieutenant Governor Sergei Dorovsky. Lykov and a local source told CPJ they believe the Korolyov administration backed the takeover in an effort to influence TVK's news programming ahead of the gubernatorial election.

Soon after, TVK's deposed management filed a legal complaint with the local prosecutor's office and also asked the Media Ministry in Moscow to suspend the station's broadcasting license until the courts resolved the dispute. On September 1, Deputy Media Minister Andrei Romanchenko suspended TVK's license for 10 days. When the suspension expired on September 11, Romanchenko extended it until October 11.

On September 17, the Sovetsky District Court reversed all previous rulings and upheld the results of Energiya's August 24 shareholders' meeting. The ruling also affirmed Kolbasko's appointment as the station's new general director and required Lykov to give TVK's seal, keys, and documentation to the new management.

On October 10, however, the Lipetsk Arbitration Court reinstated Aleksandr Lykov as TVK's general director. Though this ruling remains in effect and the station is still broadcasting, the case remained before the courts at year's end.

SEPTEMBER 18

Eduard Markevich, *Novy Reft*
KILLED

Markevich, 29, editor and publisher of *Novy Reft*, the local newspaper in the town of Reftinsky, Sverdlovsk Region, was found dead on September 18. He had been shot in the back.

Novy Reft often criticized local officials, and Markevich's colleagues told the Itar-Tass news service that he had received threatening telephone phone calls prior to the attack.

This was not the first attack on Markevich, the Region-Inform news agency reported. In 1998, two unknown assailants broke into his apartment and severely beat him in front of his pregnant wife. They were never caught.

In 2000, Markevich was illegally detained for 10 days after the local prosecutor's office charged him with defamation over a *Novy Reft* article questioning the propriety of a lucrative government contract that gave a former deputy prosecutor the exclusive right to represent the Reftinsky administration in court.

In May 2001, federal prosecutor general Vladimir Ustinov reprimanded the local prosecutor for violating Markevich's constitutional rights.

Police have launched an investigation into Markevich's murder. Almost four months after the journalist's death, authorities have made no progress, the Moscow-based Center for Journalism in Extreme Situations has reported. Markevich's wife continues to publish *Novy Reft.*

SEPTEMBER 27

TV-6
LEGAL ACTION

The independent national television network TV-6 was sued by a minority shareholder that sought to have the network liquidated on grounds of insolvency.

The suit was filed by the pension fund of LUKoil-Garant, a subsidiary of the giant LUKoil Corporation, which owns 15 percent of TV-6. The Russian industrial magnate Boris Berezovsky, who is a bitter opponent of President Vladimir Putin, owns 75 percent of the network, either outright or through other companies that he controls.

Originally, the Moscow Arbitration Court ruled to close MNVK on the basis of an obscure Russian law that prohibits companies from running a deficit for more than two years. TV-6 appealed, and though a Moscow appellate court upheld the liquidation in November, another appeal from TV-6 led to a ruling in the network's favor on December 29.

As of January 1, 2002, however, the Russian parliament repealed a law that allowed shareholders to liquidate their own companies, thus eliminating the legal basis for proceedings against TV-6.

But on January 4, 2002, the deputy chairman of the Highest Arbitration Court, Eduard Remov, disputed the December decision and filed a protest with the Presidium of the Highest Arbitration Court.

In its January 11 ruling, the Arbitration Court rejected TV-6's argument against liquidation. Instead, Judge Remov argued that since the original ruling came while the shareholder liquidation law was still in force, LUKoil's claim was valid and should be upheld.

Although TV-6 exhausted all appeals with the Russian arbitration court system, the network planned to appeal the case to the Russian Constitutional Court and the European Court of Human Rights.

U.S. State Department spokesman Richard Boucher said after the ruling, "We continue to urge Russian officials to ensure that TV-6 gets a full and fair hearing and ensure that press freedom and the rule of law can be best served by keeping TV-6 on the air," according to The Associated Press.

Although TV-6 was given up to six months to complete the liquidation, the Ministry of Information and Press had the authority to take away the network's broadcasting license at any moment. A shareholder meeting to set a time frame for liquidating TV-6's assets was scheduled for January 14. Press Minister Mikhail Lesin ordered TV-6 off the air at mighnight on January 22, 2002. TV-6 remains off the air but plans to bid in March to regain its old frequency.

OCTOBER 10

Anna Politkovskaya, *Novaya Gazeta*
THREATENED

Politkovskaya, a correspondent with the Moscow-based newspaper *Novaya Gazeta*, fled to Vienna, Austria after receiving threats stemming from her work in Chechnya.

Politkovskaya is known for her investigative reports on human rights abuses committed by the Russian military in Chechnya.

Novaya Gazeta's deputy editor-in-chief, Sergei Sokolov, told CPJ that the threats stemmed from a September 10 article in which Politkovskaya accused a Russian military officer named Sergei Lapin (whose nickname is "Kadet") of committing atrocities against civilians in Chechnya.

In mid-September, *Novaya Gazeta* received a threat via e-mail saying that Lapin was coming to Moscow to take revenge for the article, Sokolov reported.

Vyacheslav Izmailov, a military correspondent for *Novaya Gazeta*, told the English-language daily *The Moscow Times* that the most recent threat, received by *Novaya Gazeta* on October 10, was signed "Kadet."

Initially, security guards were assigned to protect Politkovskaya, and she was instructed by *Novaya Gazeta* not to leave her home.

However, *Novaya Gazeta*'s senior staff decided that these safety precautions were insufficient and sent her temporarily to Vienna.

Novaya Gazeta then petitioned local prosecutors to launch an investigation into Politkovskaya's case, Sokolov told CPJ.

Although the e-mails allegedly came from Lapin, Politkovskaya said the threats could also be linked to her coverage of a Russian military helicopter shot down in Chechnya in September. Though the Russian government has claimed that a lone Chechen rebel shot down the helicopter, Politkovskaya suggested in an article and in newspaper interviews that the Russian military was responsible for the accident.

Ten high-ranking military officials, including Lt. Gen. Anatoly Pozdnyakov, were killed when the aircraft was shot down. Pozdnyakov was on his way to Moscow to report to President Putin on the conduct of Russian military forces in Chechnya.

Politkovskaya came to the United States in November on a tour to promote her new book on Chechnya, *A Dirty War*. In early December, she returned to Moscow.

OCTOBER 16

TV-6
ATTACKED
Ren-TV
ATTACKED

Camera crews from the Moscow-based independent stations TV-6 and Ren-TV were attacked while filming a hostile takeover of the Moscow Soap-Making Plant, according to local news reports.

During an unscheduled shareholders' meeting, a group of unknown individuals attacked security guards in an attempt to physically occupy of the plant. During the raid, the attackers also assaulted TV-6 and Ren-TV journalists, breaking a video camera and other technical equipment, and tried to confiscate recorded videotapes.

According to local sources, the attackers fled when police arrived at the scene.

NOVEMBER 30

Ildar Zhandaryov, TV-6
ATTACKED

In the early hours of November 30, three unknown individuals assaulted and robbed Zhandaryov, a well-known Russian television journalist.

Zhandaryov co-hosted "Bez Protokola" (Without Protocol), a widely watched talk show, and the movie review program "Interesnoye Kino" (Interesting Movie). Both appeared on TV-6, a national network that was liquidated and taken off the air as CPJ went to press (see September 27 case).

Zhandaryov was attacked at approximately 3 a.m. as he returned from his late-night program and entered his apartment building. The masked attackers struck the journalist with a blunt object, taped his mouth and eyes shut, and then handcuffed him, according to local press reports. The attackers stole Zhandaryov's money and apartment keys, as well as valuables from his apartment.

Zhandaryov's assailants said that someone had "ordered" the attack and that he and his program "got on people's nerves," Zhandaryov told the Moscow-based radio station Ekho Moskvy.

He was taken to the Sklifosovsky Institute, where he was treated for head injuries and later released. The police launched an investigation into the attack, but by year's end no suspects had been detained.

DECEMBER 25

Grigory Pasko, *Boyevaya Vakhta*
IMPRISONED, LEGAL ACTION

Pasko, an investigative reporter with *Boyevaya Vakhta* (Battle Watch), a newspaper published by the Pacific Fleet, was convicted of treason and sentenced to four years in prison by the Military Court of the Pacific Fleet in Vladivostok. Russian prosecutors had demanded a nine-year sentence.

The ruling also stripped Pasko of his military rank and state decorations, Russian news agency Interfax reported. The journalist was taken into custody in the courtroom and subsequently jailed, Sergei Ivashchenko, a member of the Vladivostok Committee for the Defense of Pasko, told CPJ.

Pasko's attorney, Anatoly Pyshkin, filed an appeal with the Military Collegium of the Russian Supreme Court seeking full acquittal, Ivashchenko told CPJ.

Pasko was first arrested in November 1997 and charged with passing classified documents to Japanese news outlets. The journalist maintains that he revealed no classified material, and that he was prosecuted for publicizing environmental hazards at the Pacific Fleet's facilities. He spent 20 months in prison while awaiting trial.

In July 1999, Pasko was acquitted of treason but found guilty of abusing his authority as an officer. He was immediately amnestied, but four months later the Military Collegium of the Russian Supreme Court canceled the Vladivostok court's verdict and ordered a new trial.

Pasko's second trial began on July 11, after three postponements since March.

During the trial, Pasko's defense demonstrated that the proceedings lacked a basis in Russian law. Article 7 of the Federal Law on State Secrets, which stipulates that information about environmental dangers cannot be classified, protects Pasko's work on issues such as radioactive pollution.

In addition, the prosecution relied on a secret Ministry of Defense decree (No. 055) even though the Russian constitution bars the use of secret legislation in criminal cases.

The defense also challenged the veracity of many witnesses, several of whom acknowledged that the Federal Security Service (FSB) falsified their statements or tried to persuade them to give false testimony.

An FSB investigator was reprimanded for falsifying evidence in the first trial, for example. Also, the signatures of two people who witnessed a search of the reporter's apartment were shown to have been forged.

Throughout the year, CPJ issued numerous statements calling attention to Pasko's ordeal, and in early June, a CPJ delegation traveled to Vladivostok before Pasko's trial to publicize concerns over the charges.

SPAIN

MAY 15

Gorka Landaburu, *Cambio 16*
ATTACKED

Landaburu was severely injured after opening a letter bomb sent to his home in Zarauz, a town in the Basque region of northern Spain, near San Sebastian. While no one claimed responsibility for the attack, most observers link it to the Basque separatist group ETA.

Landaburu, a reporter for the national magazine *Cambio 16* and several national television stations, was injured at 10:20 a.m., according to local and international press reports. Landaburu lost at least one finger and suffered significant wounds to his hands, face and abdomen. The bomb was reportedly packed inside a book

Landaburu's brother directs the Basque edition of the national daily *El País*, and another brother is a senior official at the European Commission. In 1998, Molotov cocktails were thrown into Landaburu's residence. Three years earlier, masked men painted pro-ETA graffiti on the house.

TAJIKISTAN

JULY 5

Dodojon Atovullo, *Charogi Ruz*
IMPRISONED

Atovullo, a Tajik journalist and opposition activist who had been detained in Moscow since July 5 while Russian authorities considered extraditing him to Tajikistan, was released and returned to Germany, where he lives in exile with his family.

Russian authorities apprehended Atovullo at the Sheremetevo Airport outside Moscow on the evening of Thursday, July 5, while he was en route from Germany to Uzbekistan, local and international media reported.

The arrest allegedly came in response to a request from Tajik officials, who in April charged the journalist with insulting Tajik president Imomali Rakhmonov; supporting the violent removal of the constitutional order; and inciting ethnic, racial, and religious hatred.

If Russia had granted the extradition request, Atovullo would have faced prosecution under Tajikistan's harsh criminal libel and defamation laws. He would also have risked violence in a country where local law enforcement agencies are responsible for frequent harassment, beatings, and threats against journalists, according to CPJ research.

A Russian prosecutor told Atovullo that President Putin had personally ordered his release. But the prosecutor urged Atovullo to leave the country at once, claiming that the Russian government could not provide him with protection.

According to Atovullo's lawyer, Andrei Rakhmilovich, the charges against Atovullo resulted from articles about Tajik government corruption that he published in his own newspaper and in the Russian press.

Atovullo, 46, is the publisher of the influential Tajik opposition newspaper *Charogi Ruz* as well as a prominent opposition activist. Tajik authorities banned *Charogi Ruz* in 1992, and Atovullo moved the paper to Moscow a year later. The paper, which is distributed throughout Central Asia, has been a vocal critic of Tajikistan's notoriously corrupt and autocratic ruling elite.

On July 12, CPJ published a news alert about Atovullo's release.

UKRAINE

JANUARY 30

Yanina Sokolovskaya, *Izvestia*
ATTACKED
At around 8:20 p.m. on January 30,

an unidentified, knife-wielding assailant assaulted Sokolovskaya, Kyiv correspondent for the Moscow daily *Izvestia*, in the entranceway of her apartment building.

The journalist managed to escape and hide in an apartment on the ground floor, and the assailant fled after threatening to return to finish her off, Sokolovskaya told local media. She suffered knife cuts on her hands and face.

Izvestia editor Mikhail Kozhokin told Russian television that Sokolovskaya had been under surveillance for a week prior to the attack, presumably by the Ukrainian police or security services.

Kozhokin claimed that the attack was provoked by Sokolovskaya's recent interview with Yuliya Tymoshenko, a former deputy prime minister who had recently been ousted from the government amid charges of corruption. The interview was published January 26 in *Izvestia*'s Moscow edition and on the paper's Web site, but it did not appear in the Ukrainian edition.

Sokolovskaya agreed with her boss, arguing that the assault was related either to the Tymoshenko interview or to a series of articles she wrote on the alleged involvement of President Leonid Kuchma and other high-ranking officials in the September 2000 abduction and murder of Internet journalist Georgy Gongadze.

Two days after the attack on Sokolovskaya, Ukrainian deputy prosecutor general Sergei Vinokurov told reporters he had no evidence linking the assault to her reporting.

On February 5, police announced they had arrested a suspect who confessed to attacking the journalist in order to rob her. Neither the journalist nor her alleged assailant recognized each other in police lineups, however.

Sokolovskaya accused police of trying to present the attack as an attempted robbery in order to close the investigation as soon as possible.

FEBRUARY 5

Lyudmila Kokhanets, *Golos Ukrainy*
ATTACKED

Kokhanets, a reporter for the Kyiv daily *Golos Ukrainy*, was attacked in the entryway of her apartment building.

She said that the unknown assailant choked her and demanded that she stop reporting on President Leonid Kuchma's alleged involvement in the September 2000 abduction and murder of Internet journalist Georgy Gongadze.

The attacker let Kokhanets go, saying he would return if she continued to cover that story. Kokhanets told local reporters that she had received several telephone threats before the attack.

MARCH 9

Dmytro Shurkhalo, *Postup*
IMPRISONED, ATTACKED, HARASSED

Shurkhalo, a reporter with the independent daily *Postup*, in the city of Lviv, was detained by police at the railway station in the capital, Kyiv, where he was covering an opposition protest rally.

At around 7 p.m., Shurkhalo began interviewing students who were arriving from Lviv to participate in the rally. While he was conducting the interviews, a police officer approached him and asked for his identification papers.

Shurkhalo complied and presented his press ID to the officer, who passed it on to a man dressed in civilian clothing, and that man in turn passed it on to someone else. The journalist was immediately approached by another police officer and asked to show his identification papers again.

When Shurkhalo explained that another police officer had already taken his identification papers a few moments earlier, he was arrested and his tape recorder was confiscated. While being fingerprinted, he was questioned about his newspaper's ownership and editorial policies.

The next day, the Kyiv Municipal Court sentenced Shurkhalo to 15 days in prison for hooliganism and using obscenities.

On Wednesday, March 14, the court reversed its sentence and ordered Shurkhalo's release.

JUNE 7

Oleg Lyashko, *Svoboda*
LEGAL ACTION

The Minsk District Court in Kyiv found Lyashko, editor of the independent Kyiv weekly *Svoboda*, guilty of defaming former prime minister Vasyl Durdynets and Gen. Ivan Hryhorenko, the head of the Interior Affairs Administration for the Odessa Region.

The Prosecutor General's office began investigating Lyashko for alleged criminal defamation in July 1997, according to the local news agency UNIAN. The charges stemmed from several articles by Lyashko that appeared in the independent weekly *Polityka* in July 1997. Lyashko accused Durdynets and Hryhorenko of arbitrary and heavy-handed rule. Lyashko also alleged that both officials had engaged in illegal activities.

The verdict came almost four years after charges were first filed against Lyashko and after an earlier trial ended in acquittal. Lyashko was given a two-year suspended sentence and barred from all journalistic activities during that time, according to CPJ sources in Kyiv.

Almost a year later, in June 1998, Lyashko was formally charged with defamation under Section 2 of Article 125 of the Ukrainian Penal Code. In November of that year, the case was submitted to Kyiv's Pechersky District Court. On December 23, 1998, Judge Mykola Zamkovenko acquitted Lyashko of the defamation charges, ruling that the articles did not violate Ukraine's mass-media laws.

In November 2000, the Kyiv Municipal Court nullified Judge Zamkovenko's acquittal and sent the case to the Minsk District Court in Kyiv for a retrial, which resulted in the June 7 verdict against Lyashko.

June 24

Oleh Breus, *XXI Vek*
KILLED (MOTIVE UNCONFIRMED)

Breus, publisher of the regional weekly *XXI Vek* in the provincial city of Luhansk, was shot dead at approximately 11 p.m. while driving up to his house accompanied by his wife and a friend.

As Breus exited his car, he was shot four or five times in the head and back at point-blank range. Neither passenger was harmed.

Eyewitnesses heard the shots and saw two men fleeing, one of them holding a pistol. The Luhansk weekly *Kuryer* reported that both perpetrators left in a car that was parked nearby.

The motive for the murder remains unclear. As publisher of *XXI Vek*, Breus was mainly responsible for financial matters. He had other business interests apart from the newspaper and also held a senior position in the regional Communist Party of Workers and Peasants.

XXI Vek editor Yuri Yurov told CPJ that the newspaper generally reflected Breus' political positions and business interests.

Local police have launched an investigation into Breus' murder. At year's end, a confidential source told CPJ that there is some evidence linking Breus' murder to both his business interests and to material published in *XXI Vek*.

July 7

Igor Aleksandrov, Tor
KILLED

Aleksandrov, 44 and director of Tor, an independent television company based in Slavyansk, Donetsk Region, in eastern Ukraine, was attacked on the morning of July 3.

Unknown attackers assaulted Aleksandrov with baseball bats as he entered Tor's offices, according to local news reports. Tor deputy director Sergei Cherneta described the attack to the regional newspaper *Donbass*: "All of a sudden we heard...blows and screams, after that we heard a moan. I ran downstairs.... Our manager was lying in the lobby in a pool of blood with his head cracked open. Two large baseball bats were left nearby."

Aleksandrov was rushed to the local city hospital, where he underwent surgery. The journalist never regained consciousness and died from the head injuries on the morning of July 7.

Aleksandrov's colleagues believe the murder was connected to his television program, "Bez Retushi" (Without Retouching), which featured investigative coverage of government corruption and organized crime. The program often criticized Slavyansk municipal authorities.

Soon after the attack, Donetsk regional prosecutor Viktor Pshonka launched an official investigation. The chief of the Donetsk Administration of Internal Affairs, Gen. Vladimir Malyshev, stated that revenge was the leading motive in the murder but did not elaborate.

Aleksandrov became well known in 1998, when prosecutors brought a criminal case against him for insulting the honor and dignity of a parliamentary deputy. The Slavyansk City Court initially found the journalist guilty but later reviewed its decision after criticism from Ukrainian journalists and international human rights organizations.

The deputy withdrew his defamation complaint against the journalist last year. That removed the immediate legal threat but did not clear Aleksandrov's name, since his conviction was still technically under review. Claiming damage to his professional reputation, Aleksandrov appealed to the European Court of Human Rights, where the case was pending at the time of his murder.

In late August, law enforcement officials arrested a suspect, according to local press reports. The officials claimed that Aleksandrov's murder was a case of mistaken identity and was not connected with his journalism.

A parliamentary investigative commission was established in September to examine Aleksandrov's murder. In December, the commission voiced its doubts about the validity of the "mistaken identity" theory and stated that it knew who had really killed Aleksandrov, according to local reports.

While the commission refused to forward this information to law enforcement officials, it accused the Ukrainian Security Service of falsifying evidence in the case.

In mid-December, the General Prosecutor's Office officially charged the suspect detained in August, Yuri Verdyuk, with Aleksandrov's murder, local and international sources reported. On December 27, the Donetsk Regional Court scheduled Verdyuk's trial for September 11, 2002. After public calls for an immediate trial, the court re-scheduled proceedings for January 2002; they were then postponed until March.

The journalist's colleagues and family maintain that he was killed for his work, local sources told CPJ.

JULY 11

Oleh Velichko, Avers
ATTACKED

Oleh Velichko, head of the Avers media corporation in western Ukraine, was brutally beaten by two unknown assailants.

The assault took place outside Velichko's home between 11 p.m. and midnight. His attackers repeatedly said, "We are sick of you!" while they beat him, the Ukraina Sohodni news Web site reported.

Approximately US$250 was taken from Velichko during the attack, according to some local press accounts. He was taken to a local hospital where he was diagnosed with a concussion, broken ribs, and a bruised arm.

Velichko's Avers Corporation owns the television station Avers and the local newspapers *Avers Press* and *Lutskaya Yarmarka* in the provincial city of Lutsk. Velichko's colleagues believe he could have been attacked in retaliation for his television station's news reporting.

Avers TV director Volodimir Sinkevich told CPJ that the station frequently criticized the misdeeds of local police officials, politicians, business executives, and gangsters. In recent weeks, Sinkevich said, the station had investigated the illegal construction of a private garage in a nearby national park.

The local police launched an official investigation into the assault, which they treated as a robbery. No progress was reported by year's end.

AUGUST 26

Aleksei Movsesian, Efir-1 Television
ATTACKED

Movsesian, a 23-year-old cameraman with the independent TV station Efir-1, in the eastern Ukrainian city of Luhansk, was assaulted by an unknown individual.

The attacker struck Movsesian with a hard object between 11 p.m. and midnight while the journalist and a friend were walking in a park near Movsesian's home.

Movsesian lost consciousness and fell to the ground; the attacker then trampled him. The journalist's friend was not harmed in the incident, Efir-1 director Tatyana Kozhanovskaya told CPJ.

According to CPJ sources, Movsesian was taken to a local hospital, where he was treated for critical head injuries. In October, Movsesian regained consciousness and was released, the Ukrainian News Agency UNIAN reported.

Although local police have detained a suspect, they told the station director that their case hinges on Movsesian's positive identification of that suspect, even though several other people witnessed the attack.

Police have not released the suspect's name, and Movsesian was unable to identify him.

According to Kozhanovskaya, the police are treating the assault as a drunken brawl. However, a doctor at the hospital told Efir-1 that the cameraman's alcohol level was below the legal limit.

Movsesian's colleagues suspect the attack was linked to Movsesian's work. "It is difficult not to connect [the attack] with local political developments," Kozhanovskaya told CPJ. "Aleksei covered all the political clashes."

One such clash occurred in April, when a faction of Luhansk City Council deputies forced Mayor Anatoly Yagofyorov out of office. During a City Council meeting, council deputy Vladimir Ladnyk allegedly assaulted Movsesian and tried to take away his camera. The police opened a criminal case against Ladnyk in connection with this attack.

UNITED KINGDOM

SEPTEMBER 28

Martin O'Hagan, *Sunday World*
KILLED

O'Hagan, a 51-year-old investigative journalist with the Dublin newspaper *Sunday World*, was shot dead outside his home in the Northern Ireland town of Lurgan.

O'Hagan was shot several times from a passing car while walking home from a pub with his wife, who was not hurt in the attack. The vehicle used in the attack was found on fire not far from the crime scene. O'Hagan, who worked in the Belfast office of the *Sunday World*, was an Irish Catholic journalist who had become well known for his coverage of both Catholic and Protestant paramilitary groups.

More than 20 years ago, before he became a journalist, O'Hagan was convicted of running guns for the Irish Republican Army and served five years in prison. But he later turned away from radical politics, studying sociology at the Open University and the University of Ulster and then entering journalism as a free-lancer for local newspapers. His connections in both Catholic Republican and Protestant Loyalist circles, as well as in the British security forces, gave him unusual insight into the conflict but also made him a target for paramilitary reprisals.

In 1989, he was kidnapped and interrogated by the Irish Republican Army, which tried unsuccessfully to force him to divulge his sources, and in the early 1990s he was forced to flee to Dublin after receiving death threats from a top loyalist gunman. O'Hagan returned to Belfast in 1995 after most paramilitary groups had declared cease-fires.

While O'Hagan had received threats from Protestant militants in the past, it is not clear if he had been threatened prior to the shooting. The Red Hand Defenders, which police consider a cover name for Protestant militants from the Loyalist Volunteer Force (LVF) and the Ulster Defense Association, claimed responsibility for his murder.

Police initially identified the LVF as a primary suspect. Prior to his murder, O'Hagan had been working on several stories about the LVF, the BBC reported. Colleagues believe the LVF targeted O'Hagan for exposing the narcotics network they controlled, as well as assassinations and intimidation rackets they orchestrated.

The police investigation continues, and at press time no one had been charged for the killing.

UZBEKISTAN

MAY 7

Marina Kozlova, United Press International
HARASSED

The Ministry of Internal Affairs denied Kozlova press accreditation on the grounds that she dressed inappropriately and had the wrong hairstyle for a journalist.

Kozlova, a reporter for United Press International (UPI) who is known for asking senior government officials hard-hitting questions, was also accused of "defiant behaviour."

After protests from UPI and the U.S. embassy in Tashkent, Kozlova's accreditation was issued on May 17.

In a July 19 incident, Kozlova was followed by two men, one in police uniform, while traveling to a shopping center with her mother. Kozlova believes the intimidation resulted from her published criticims of Uzbek security authorities.

JULY 7

Alo Khodzhayev,
Tashkentskaya Pravda
HARASSED

Khodzhayev, editor of the state-owned daily *Tashkentskaya Pravda*, was fired after Tashkent regional authorities eliminated his job.

The groundwork for Khodzhayev's dismissal was laid by a July 5 edict that announced changes in the paper's organizational and financial structure.

The Russian-language *Tashkenskaya Pravda* was merged with its Uzbek-language partner, *Toshkent Khakikati*, under a single editor. Many analysts, and Khodzhayev himself, say the action came in response to the paper's frequent criticisms of censorship and the ruling regime.

The final straw for the authorities, according to Khodzhayev, came on June 18, when the newspaper organized a public exhibition called "Without Censorship." Part of the exibition was a wall covered with newspaper articles that Uzbek authorities had banned.

JULY 24

Shukhrat Babadjanov, TV ALC
HARASSED, LEGAL ACTION

Babadjanov, director of TV ALC, an independent station based in the town of Urgench, was charged with forgery.

The charges relate to a 10-year-old letter of recommendation for Babadjanov that was evidently written by Babadjanov himself but signed by Ruzi Chariyev, a prominent Uzbek painter. The journalist, who is also a well-known artist, was applying to join the Uzbekistan Union of Artists. He claims that Chariyev asked him to draft the letter because Chariyev does not write well in Uzbek.

According to information received by CPJ, Babadjanov was forced to flee Uzbekistan after the Tashkent prosecutor's office summoned him for questioning on August 6 in connection with the case.

These charges came after prolonged government harassment of Babadjanov and TV ALC, which was forced off the air in November 1999 despite protests from thousands of Urgench residents and appeals from the international community.

Since the closure, the Uzbek government has repeatedly denied Babadjanov's applications for a new broadcasting license. On July 24, 2001, Babadjanov was ordered to vacate his station's premises within a week because he had been refused a license again.

CPJ protested this case in an August 14 letter to Uzbek president Islam Karimov.

AUGUST 1

Madzhid Abduraimov, *Yangi Asr*
IMPRISONED

Abduraimov, a correspondent with the national weekly *Yangi Asr*, was convicted of extortion and sentenced to 13 years in prison.

In a January 15 article in *Yangi Asr*, Abduraimov charged that Nusrat Radzhabov, head of the Boisunsky District grain production company Zagotzerno, had misappropriated state funds and falsified documents.

Abduraimov also accused the businessman of killing a 12-year-old in a car accident and alleged that Radzhabov's teenage son was part of a group that had beaten and raped a 13-year-old boy.

Radzhabov claims that Abduraimov asked him for money and threatened to publish more accusations unless he was paid. According to the Institute for War and Peace Reporting (IWPR), Radzhabov tried to sue Abduraimov for slander, but dropped the suit after a local prosecutor's investigation confirmed the facts in the article.

Authorities arrested Abduraimov and accused him of receiving a US$6,000 bribe. He and a witness quoted by the IWPR claimed that a man threw the money into the back seat of his car immediately before police stopped his vehicle, searched it, and arrested him.

Abduraimov was held in Termez Regional Police Department jail until his trial began in Termez City Court on July 4.

According to Abduraimov, the court proceedings were influenced by local officials who objected to his reporting on corruption in the oil business. His request for a change of venue was not granted. He refused to attend the hearings and was sentenced in absentia.

Abduraimov is known for his investigative reporting and critical stance toward local law enforcement bodies and authorities. The journalist and his family have been persecuted for several years with threatening phone calls, and his son was reportedly beaten by police and sentenced to four months in jail for disorderly conduct.

Supporters say Abduraimov was most likely framed, and it is not known where he is being held. His family plans to appeal the sentence to the Supreme Court.

YUGOSLAVIA

MARCH 29

Kerem Lawton, Associated Press Television News
KILLED

Lawton, 30, a British national and producer for Associated Press Television News, died from shrapnel wounds sustained when a shell struck his car. At least two other civilians were feared dead in the attack, and at least 10 others were injured.

On March 28, the Macedonian Army launched a mini-offensive against Albanian insurgents in the village of Gracani in northern Macedonia. Just across the border in Kosovo, NATO-led peacekeepers stepped up patrols to intercept Albanian guerrillas crossing into Macedonia.

At the time of his death, Lawton had just arrived in the village of Krivenik to cover the deployment of additional NATO-led peacekeeping forces. Both Macedonian military officials and ethnic Albanian insurgents denied responsibility for Lawton's death and the other civilian casualties.

JUNE 11

Milan Pantic, Vecernje Novosti
KILLED

Pantic, a reporter for the Belgrade daily *Vecernje Novosti*, was killed shortly before 8 a.m. as he was entering his apartment building in the central Serbian town of Jagodina.

Pantic had gone to fetch a loaf of bread. As he entered the front door of his building, attackers grabbed him from behind, broke his neck, and then struck him several times on the head with a sharp object as he lay face down on the ground, according to *Vecernje Novosti*.

An eyewitness saw two attackers—both aged 20 to 30 and wearing masks and black shirts—running from the scene, sources at *Vecernje Novosti* said. Local authorities launched an investigation, but no progress was reported at year's end.

The 47-year-old journalist worked as the *Vecernje Novosti* correspondent for the Pomoravlje region of central Serbia. He reported extensively on criminal affairs, including corruption in local companies. His wife, Zivka Pantic, told *Vecernje Novosti* that Pantic had received numerous telephone threats in response to articles he had written.

JUNE 28

Milos Petrovic, Studio B Television
ATTACKED
Suzana Rafailovic, Beta
ATTACKED
Petar Pavlovic, Fonet
ATTACKED

Petrovic, of Studio B Television; Rafailovic, a reporter for the Beta news service; and Pavlovic, a photographer with the news agency Fonet, were attacked by enraged supporters of former Yugoslav president Slobodan Milosevic at a rally in central Belgrade.

The attacks against the journalists occurred in Belgrade's Republic Square, where several thousand supporters of

Milosevic's Socialist Party of Serbia (SPS) and the allied Serbian Radical Party (SRS) were protesting Milosevic's sudden extradition to the International War Crimes Tribunal in The Hague earlier that day. The demonstrators were also angry at the local media's coverage of the story.

The first attack occurred just before 7 p.m., when reporters from Studio B Television were walking toward the rally. Several men approached the journalists and punched cameraman Petrovic, knocking him to the ground.

At approximately 10 p.m., Rafailovic was interviewing an SPS activist when several people approached to inquire which media outlet she worked for, Beta editor-in-chief Dragan Janjic told CPJ. When the SPS activist responded that the journalist worked for Beta, the men started threatening and manhandling her.

About 30 minutes later, a group of SPS supporters assaulted Pavlovic when he approached the rally to take pictures, Fonet editor-in-chief Zoran Sekulic told CPJ.

Several SRS supporters then surrounded Pavlovic, tried to take his camera, and began punching and kicking him. Pavlovic was knocked to the ground several times but eventually escaped to the safety of a nearby park.

On June 29, CPJ issued an alert about the attacks.

Jelena Bozovic, Reuters
ATTACKED
Zoran Culafic, Fonet
ATTACKED

Reuters reporter Bozovic and Culafic, a journalist with the Fonet news agency, were attacked by Serbian Radical Party (SRS) supporters at a pro-Milosevic rally in front of the Federal Parliament building in Belgrade, Fonet reported.

Two SRS supporters approached Bozovic and asked for her affiliation. When she identified herself, they accused her of being a traitor on the payroll of foreigners. One of the men grabbed Bozovic's arm and took her notepad.

When Culafic attempted to intervene, he was thrown to the ground and roughed up by several SRS supporters.

Fonet reported that a cordon of police officers standing nearby made no effort to intervene.

CPJ issued an alert about the attacks on June 29.

OCTOBER 19

Bekim Kastrati, *Bota Sot*
KILLED (MOTIVE UNCONFIRMED)

Kastrati, an ethnic Albanian journalist for the Albanian-language daily *Bota Sot*, was shot on October 19 at around 8 p.m. in the village of Lausa, west of the provincial capital, Pristina, along with two other men who were riding in his car at the time. One of the passengers was killed, and the other was wounded.

Kastrati's employer, the Geneva-based *Bota Sot*, supports politician Ibrahim Rugova and his leading ethnic Albanian party, the Democratic Alliance of Kosovo.

A second man killed in the attack, Besim Dajaku, was reported to have been a current or former bodyguard of Rugova. The third man injured in the attack, Gani Geci, was a former member of the now-disbanded Kosovo Liberation Army. According to local sources, Geci was believed to be the true target of the shooting, but the murder investigation is still open.

NOVEMBER 22

Reporter
LEGAL ACTION
Blic
LEGAL ACTION

The Third Municipal Prosecutor's Office began investigating the independent Belgrade weekly *Reporter* the day after its November 21 edition went on sale, local sources reported.

The investigation was apparently triggered by an article listing the names of Yugoslav police officials that the United Nations International Criminal Tribunal for the Former Yugoslavia suspected of complicity in war crimes in Kosovo.

On Friday, November 23, two police investigators made an unannounced visit to *Reporter*'s office to question editor-in-chief Vladimir Radomirovic and reporter Jovica Krtinic, author of the article in question.

Later that day, investigators also questioned Veselin Simonovic, editor of the independent Belgrade daily *Blic*, which reprinted *Reporter*'s list in its November 22 edition.

The two police investigators who questioned Radomirovic and Krtinic invoked two Milosevic-era laws in an attempt to pressure the journalists into divulging their sources for the list. Article 218 of the Serbian Criminal Code proscribes "spreading false information" and was used to imprison several Serbian journalists in the late 1990s. The journalists were also threatened with prosecution under Serbia's notorious Public Information Law, which had in fact been repealed in February.

"We stand behind the story that the list is accurate," Radomirovic, according to the Belgrade daily *Danas*. "We expect further steps from the government and are ready for anything."

On the evening of November 25, Serbian prime minister Zoran Djindjic claimed that *Reporter* had published the war crimes list in order to "...upset the police, and turn them against the government," Belgrade's Radio B92 reported. That same day, Djindjic's Democratic Party issued a statement encouraging police officers named in Reporter's list to sue the publication for damages.

On December 4, police spokesman Milorad Simic confirmed that Serbia's Interior Ministry had notified all police departments that the ministry would cover legal expenses for any officer interested in suing *Reporter* or *Blic* for libel, according to local news reports.

Three days later, 12 police officers from the town of Valjevo whose names appeared on the list announced that they were filing a libel suit against the two publications.

A week later, 13 police officers from the city of Nis filed libel lawsuits against Simonovic. ■

OVERVIEW: THE MIDDLE EAST AND NORTH AFRICA

by Joel Campagna

BUCKING A WORLDWIDE TREND TOWARD DEMOCRACY in the post–Cold War era, the political landscape of the Middle East and North Africa remained dominated by an assortment of military-backed regimes, police states, autocracies, and oligarchies.

A new, younger generation of leaders has emerged in some countries in recent years, inheriting power and bringing hope for political and social liberalization. The 1999 royal successions in Morocco and Jordan, followed by the ascension of Bashar al-Assad to Syria's presidency in 2000, resulted in some positive developments for press freedom, including the end of the state's print media monopoly in Syria, the abolishment of some restrictive press law provisions in Jordan in 1999, and more open media discourse in Morocco.

But even in these countries, press freedom was undermined by censorship, harassment, and new, onerous legislation. Meanwhile, in the rest of the region, governments have failed to loosen shackles on the media. Abdel Rahman al-Rashed, chief editor of the influential London-based daily *Al-Sharq al-Awsat*, commented that despite the optimistic predictions of some analysts in recent years, the state of press freedom in the region has remained largely static. "We…know that what we are allowed to publish is not what the readers want," al-Rashed wrote. "The margin that has improved in most Arab countries is just cosmetic and far from the alleged claim of the freedom of the media and political democracy."

In the more repressive and centralized states of the region, such as Iraq and Libya, the state owns and controls all media and allows no dissent. But such total control has become less prevalent. In Syria, the state relinquished its media monopoly in 2001 by permitting the first nonstate papers in nearly 40 years. While governments still largely controlled local broadcast media and maintained their hold over influential print media, private publications have proliferated.

Countries such as Algeria, Egypt, Iran, Jordan, Lebanon, Kuwait, Morocco, Turkey, and Yemen, where journalists enjoy varying degrees of press freedom, boasted numerous independent papers. However, reporters had to contend with a familiar battery of official tactics used to hinder their work: censorship, criminal prosecution, arrest, detention, and intimidation by security forces.

Tough press laws and criminal statutes remained on the books and were used to prosecute journalists or to close or confiscate newspapers in Algeria, Egypt, Iran, Lebanon, Morocco, Sudan, Tunisia, and Turkey.

Perhaps nowhere in the region were the courts and media laws used more aggressively than in Iran and Turkey. In Iran, the conservative-dominated

Joel Campagna is program coordinator for the Middle East and North Africa at CPJ.
Hani Sabra is research associate for the Middle East and North Africa. **Nilay Karaelmas**, a consultant to CPJ, provided important research on Turkey for this report.

judiciary continued its relentless assault on the country's pro-reform media, banning at least 20 papers and publications during the year. Since April 2000, at least 47 publications have been closed. Meanwhile, journalists continued to be detained and prosecuted for a variety of ill-defined infractions.

Turkish journalists remained vulnerable to a long-standing collection of harsh criminal laws, especially when they tackled controversial political topics such as the Kurdish question, political Islam, or the military's controversial role in national politics. During the year, several journalists were indicted, tried, or imprisoned, and the authorities continued to use the laws to suspend alternative publications.

Some governments tried to enact even harsher legislation. Algeria and Jordan introduced legal amendments to their respective penal codes that defined new press-related "crimes" and increased prison penalties and fines. In Syria, a new press law provided a detailed guide to what cannot be published, and imposed tough penalties for offenders.

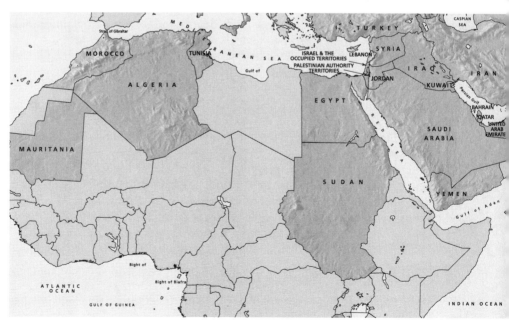

Foreign publications were not spared from state censorship. Many countries continued to ban distribution of foreign newspapers and magazines when they contained news that cast the government in a negative light. Confiscations again took place in Tunisia and Morocco, to name a few.

Security forces in several countries frequently harassed and intimidated journalists, often with impunity. Arbitrary arrests, interrogations, phone calls, and surveillance were used to intimidate reporters in Algeria, Jordan, the Palestinian Authority territories, Tunisia, and Yemen, among others. In Lebanon, security authorities confiscated the passport of Samir Qassir, a journalist with the daily *Al-Nahar*, apparently because an article the journalist wrote had offended the army and security forces. In Tunisia, the government cut telephone lines and monitored the activities of journalists and rights activists. In Syria, the government reportedly harassed the family of exiled journalist Nizar Nayyouf in retribution for his criticisms of the Syrian regime.

Many serious attacks against journalists remained unresolved. The Algerian government again failed to conduct transparent investigations into the murders of 58 journalists killed in the 1990s, mostly by Islamist extremists. The fate of two "disappeared" Algerian journalists—Djamel Eddine Fahassi and Aziz Bouabdallah, who were detained by men believed to be state agents—also remained unknown, and the government did not appear anxious to solve the cases.

One year after the drive-by shooting attack on former editor Riad Ben Fadhel, Tunisian President Zine al-Abidine Ben Ali's promise to bring the perpetrators to justice rang hollow; there was no indication that the government had launched a serious investigation or apprehended the perpetrators. Despite local and international pressure, the Israeli army and security forces absolved themselves of wrongdoing in several high-profile incidents in which Israeli fire wounded journalists while they were working.

Impunity, coupled with repressive laws and prosecution, often had a stultifying effect on press coverage and contributed to self-censorship across the region. In many countries, coverage of regional and international affairs is often of good quality, but journalists tend to avoid criticizing heads of state, government performance, official corruption, grave human rights abuses, and other official misdeeds.

Yet, many local journalists displayed great courage and continued to push the limits of freedom. Reformist papers in Iran continued to publish, while their supporters defiantly protested the press crackdown. Amid increasing government harassment, Morocco's feisty publications *Le Journal Hebdomadaire* and *Demain Magazine* persevered in broaching controversial topics, such as official corruption and dark aspects of the country's political past. In Lebanon, the top-notch weekly cultural supplement of *Al-Nahar*, edited by novelist Elias Khoury, continued to set high standards for journalism in the Arab world by tackling topics often avoided by other newspapers, including human rights and press freedom.

Some journalists were particularly savvy at navigating around state censorship. Journalists who were censored in places such as Syria and Tunisia used the international media to express themselves. The rise of several respected Europe-based, pan-Arab newspapers, regional satellite channels, and the Internet demonstrated that government control over information is weakening.

A number of Europe-based newspapers have become some of the most influential in the Arab world. Spurred on by new technologies, people across the region increasingly have access to satellite dishes and regional satellite channels. Networks such as Al-Jazeera, LBCI (Lebanese Broadcasting Corporation International), and the Middle East Broadcasting Centre were among the networks most widely watched for news and entertainment.

Qatar's influential Al-Jazeera took center stage after the September 11 attacks on the United States when, for several weeks, it was the only foreign broadcaster in Taliban-controlled Afghanistan. It was also the station Osama bin Laden used to convey his taped messages to the world. In doing so, Al-Jazeera angered the U.S. administration, which urged Qatar to censor the network for its allegedly "inflammatory" and anti-American coverage. U.S. pundits accused the network of being anti-American, a mouthpiece for Osama bin Laden, and a purveyor of anti-Semitism. U.S. media also intensified their scrutiny of other Arab media, analyzing them in a similar light.

Defenders of Al-Jazeera called it a vital and reliable news source that covers news professionally from an Arab perspective. They pointed out that the channel often draws the ire of many Arab governments for its hard-hitting coverage of Middle East affairs. At the same time, Arab commentators and other critics accused U.S. media of hypocrisy, drawing attention to their alleged pro-Israel bias, and racist or anti-Arab news coverage.

One thing was clear: Al-Jazeera was the most influential news channel in the region. In the more than five years since its founding, the channel has revolutionized television news in the Arab world and has set the tone for regional television news coverage, especially for the conflict in Afghanistan.

Spurred by Al-Jazeera's popularity, governments across the region sought to harness the power of radio and television for their advantage. At a meeting of Arab ministers of information, delegates discussed the need to develop Hebrew- and English-language satellite broadcasts in an effort to sway Israeli and U.S. opinion on certain issues. In January 2002, the Egyptian satellite channel Nile TV began airing 30 minutes of Hebrew-language news programming a day. Israel and the United States, meanwhile, floated the idea of an Arabic-language satellite channel to rival Al-Jazeera, while Hezbollah's Al-Manar TV in Lebanon, which already broadcasts Hebrew and English segments, was planning a full-time Hebrew channel.

It remained difficult for foreign journalists to enter many countries. In countries such as Algeria and Iraq, security forces monitored them closely. Journalists were also provided with government "minders" who restricted their movements.

In Israel and the Occupied Territories, where the Palestinian intifada entered its second year, journalists faced the threat of gunfire from the Israel Defense Forces and security forces. Such attacks again occured with disturbing regularity during 2001. In some cases, evidence suggested that soldiers might have targeted the journalists. Journalists also suffered physical attacks and harassment from the Israeli army and militant Jewish settlers. Authorities barred journalists from covering street clashes and military operations in certain areas under their control.

The Palestinian Authority also employed crude methods of censorship. In one highly publicized case, security forces prevented journalists from covering the reactions of Palestinians who celebrated the September 11 attacks on the United States. Similar measures were taken at subsequent political rallies and other news events.

There were an estimated 4 million Internet users in the Arab world, a figure expected to double by the end of 2002. Though much less widespread than television and beyond the financial reach of many, the Internet allowed access to a wealth of news and information that was otherwise unavailable. The Gulf States continued to boast one of the highest per capita rates of Internet use. Countries such as the United Arab Emirate of Dubai have fashioned themselves as regional hubs for the Internet. In 2001, the emirate launched an Internet City and one of the region's first online e-governments.

Activists and journalists in many countries used the Internet to disseminate news and opinions on political topics. During the intifada, Palestinians used the Internet to report breaking news and to organize dissent. Palestinian and Israeli activists mobilized support online for their respective views, as did other activists across the region.

Governments across the region have employed various techniques to control information online. The most common has been the use of proxy servers to ban controversial sites. But these efforts seem increasingly futile when savvy surfers evade them by using sophisticated hacking techniques, dialing in to outside servers, or using encrypted sites. ■

ALGERIA

ALGERIA'S BOISTEROUS PRESS HAS BEEN AT ODDS with president Abdel Aziz Bouteflika since he took office in 1999. In 2001, the animosity took a more serious turn when the government promulgated harsh new press legislation.

In June, despite intense local and international protest, the Algerian Parliament approved a series of new amendments to the Penal Code that prescribe prison terms of up to one year and fines up to 250,000 dinars (US$3,200) for defaming the president. A separate amendment imposes similar punishments for defaming Parliament, the courts, the military, or other state institutions. Writers, publishers, and responsible editors are held accountable for offending articles, along with publications themselves, which can be fined up to 2.5 million dinars (US$32,000).

In an interview with the London-based daily *Al-Sharq al-Awsat*, Bouteflika explained that the amendments were a response to "aggressive journalism," echoing the complaints of other officials who claimed that the press persistently libeled them and government bodies.

Although authorities had not enforced the amendment's harsher penalties by year's end, journalists were prosecuted for criminal libel. In one case, journalist Faouzia Ababsa, managing editor of the French-language daily *L'Authentique*, was convicted of defaming the head of a private trade association and given a suspended six-month prison sentence and a 1,500 dinar (US$20) fine.

Journalists must also contend with the controversial Information Code of 1990, which imposes jail sentences of five to 10 years for offenses such as publishing "false or misleading information" that harms "state security."

For the first time since Bouteflika took office, authorities banned a publication: the Arabic weekly *Al-Mouad* was suspended for six months after police seized copies of the paper from kiosks in late November without explanation. The action appeared to stem from an article about the 1999 assassination of Islamic Salvation Front leader Abdelkader Hachani, as well as another piece about an Islamist militant.

Ever since civil strife erupted between Islamist extremists and government forces a decade ago, Algeria's press has maintained its energy and vibrancy. However, it has yet to regain the diversity it enjoyed before the regime closed newspapers that were affiliated with or sympathetic to the Islamic opposition.

Between 1993 and 1996, 58 reporters and editors were murdered in Algeria, along with numerous other media workers. While Islamist militants were blamed for most of the killings, many local journalists suspect state involvement in some of the assassinations. The government's failure to conduct open investigations of the killings, or to allow independent international inquiries, leaves many questions unanswered. In 2000, Algerian Ministry of Justice officials reported that they had identified 20 of the journalists' killers and had sentenced 15 to death in absentia. These reports were impossible to verify, along with the government's contention that it had launched investigations into other murders.

The fate of "disappeared" journalists Djamel Eddine Fahassi and Aziz Bouabdallah remains unknown. Compelling evidence suggests that state security agents abducted the two in 1995 and 1997, respectively. Neither man has been seen since, and Algerian authorities have denied any knowledge of their arrests.

Fear of government reprisal, ideological prejudices, and limited information lead the media to avoid covering sensitive topics, such as human rights, military involvement in disappearances and other abuses, military courruption, and the military's controversial role in national politics.

At the same time, papers regularly attack human rights critics and other whistle-blowers, such as former army officer Habib Souaidia, whose highly publicized book *The Dirty War*, published in February, alleged that the Algerian army had executed suspected militants and committed other grave rights abuses.

In mid-February, the Arabic daily *Al-Youm* published an interview with Omar Chikhi, a former emir of the militant Armed Islamic Group (GIA). In the interview, Chikhi expressed no regret for killing journalists during the GIA's bloody campaign against the media between 1993 and 1996, and he agreed with Islamists' strategy of killing journalists and intellectuals.

The interview caused an uproar among local journalists, who were angered that Chikhi had benefited from the government's political amnesty of 1999. It was later revealed, however, that the interview with Chikhi had actually been conducted nearly two years earlier, leading some to suspect that the military had pressured the paper to publish the interview to deflect attention away from revelations in *The Dirty War*.

Security forces keep a close watch over the press, according to some Algerian journalists. During the year, agents monitored and questioned some journalists, while military security forces forged or maintained relationships with others in an attempt to influence their work.

Authorities also continued to restrict the work of foreign journalists, requiring them to be accompanied by bodyguards, supposedly for safety reasons. But many say that the government escorts are there to control rather than protect media workers. Foreign reporters often had difficulty in obtaining visas to work in the country. Some foreign journalists allege they have been blacklisted in retaliation for their unfavorable coverage of the regime.

BAHRAIN

MAJOR POLITICAL REFORMS AUGURED WELL FOR PRESS FREEDOM in the tiny Persian Gulf country of Bahrain, which was plagued by social tension and political unrest for part of the 1990s. In a mid-February referendum, voters overwhelmingly approved Emir Sheikh Hamed Bin Issa al-Khalifa's national charter, which seeks to transform the country into a constitutional monarchy with an elected Parliament and other reforms.

Many hope that these changes, expected to be implemented in 2004, will lead to greater press freedom. In November, the Ministry of Information said it had received several applications for new publications. Plans to unveil a new Press Law are under review.

Despite the spirit of reform, authorities still targeted journalists. On November 11, Bahraini journalist Hafedh al-Shaikh Saleh was charged with "harming national unity" in a suit brought by the Ministry of Information in response to unspecified articles that Saleh had published in the Bahraini daily *Akhbar al-Khaleej*. However, the journalist believed that the prosecution was actually triggered by an article he wrote for a Lebanese paper criticizing Bahrain's foreign policy toward the United States. The ministry also banned Saleh from writing for *Akhbar al-Khaleej*. Saleh later sued the ministry over the ban, and in January 2002 he won the case.

EGYPT

EGYPT'S PRESS REMAINS ONE OF THE MOST INFLUENTIAL in the Arab world. The editorial and opinion pages of the leading daily papers are widely read in many Arab countries for their coverage of regional affairs. On a local level, newspapers deal with a wide range of issues. Opposition papers, in particular, often criticize government officials and policies.

However, Egypt's press operates under numerous formal restrictions, and self-censorship prevails on several sensitive topics. Journalists avoid criticizing the president, the army, high-level officials, the security forces, and generally steer clear of reporting on serious government human rights abuses. The state owns the broadcast media, as well as shares in the major daily newspapers, whose editors are appointed by President Hosni Mubarak. Authorities maintain a strict licensing regime for the press, making it difficult for new independent titles to emerge without government consent.

Egypt has officially been in a state of emergency since the assassination of president Anwar Sadat in 1981. This allows authorities to try journalists and others in state security courts and military-style tribunals whose decisions cannot be appealed. Harsh libel laws and other statutes have been used to prosecute and jail several journalists in recent years.

Between 1998 and 2000, six Egyptian journalists were jailed for libel and other criminal offenses related to their work. Three of them have been imprisoned more than once. Tough provisions in Egypt's Press Code, approved in 1996, stipulate prison sentences of up to one year for journalists convicted of defamation, or up to two years if a public official files the suit. Fines can reach £E20,000 (US$4,400) for each offense. Other crimes—such as "inciting hatred," "violating public morality," "harming the national economy," and offending a foreign head of state—carry prison sentences of one to two years.

In the most notorious case of 2001, Mamdouh Mahran, editor of the weekly sister tabloids *Al-Nabaa* and *Akher Khabar*, was sentenced to three years in prison after he published an article, accompanied by graphic photos, alleging that a Coptic monk was having sexual relations with women in a monastery and then blackmailing them with videotapes of the interludes.

The story provoked riots by Coptic Christians in Egypt, who contended that the articles insulted their religion. Mahran failed to clarify that the monk had been defrocked in 1996. He claimed not to have known this, but few Copts believed him. Although Egypt's minority Coptic Christian polulation generallly lives at peace with the majority of Muslims, Muslim-Christian relations are a sensitive topic because Copts complain of official discrimination.

The Journalists' Syndicate in Cairo quickly distanced itself from Mahran and moved to revoke his membership. Mahran sued the syndicate and won, asserting that his expulsion violated the group's rules. In July, an administrative court revoked the publishing licenses of both papers.

Mahran's trial received a great deal of press coverage. Several editorials in the mainstream press decried Egyptian "yellow journalism," but other pundits argued that the decision to suspend the publication was rash. Though the State Security Court ruling took effect immediately, Mahran reportedly suffered a heart attack the day before he was to begin his prison term. At year's end, he had not gone to jail but remained in hospital under guard.

During the year, government officials tried to tighten the country's already harsh press laws. In March, journalists and human rights advocates protested after Minister of Culture Farouk Hosni sent amendments to the Public Records Law to Parliament for consideration. Had the proposal been incorporated into the law, it would have imposed a five-year prison sentence and a £E10,000 fine (about US$2,200) for publishing or photocopying a government document without prior written consent from the Cabinet. The amendment had not been passed or even debated at press time. Yet the threat remains. Such a vague, wide-ranging law could cut off debate on any issue and could potentially give the state wide latitude to define what constitutes a government document. Opposition papers in Egypt, notably *Al-Wafd*, battled the law in the lines of their columns.

The Political Parties Committee banned several parties this year, along with their party newspapers. The Egypt Party and its newspaper *Egypt*, as well as the National Conciliation Party and its newspaper *Al-Qarar*, were banned in October and August, respectively. It is unclear whether or not the parties will be able to resume activities. These closures follow the May 2000 closure of the Socialist Labor Party and its mouthpiece, *Al-Sha'b*. The editors of *Al-Sha'b* have launched an online version of the paper, which reaches a limited audience due to low rates of Internet access in Egypt.

To circumvent the convoluted licensing regime, some journalists register their papers as foreign publications in countries such as Cyprus and then print them inside Egypt, in the Free Investment Zone in Nasser City, or abroad. However, such newspapers are subject to review by the foreign publications censor, who reports directly to the minister of information and can ban publications deemed to contain objectionable material. To avoid censorship and financial loss from suspensions, some papers have informal arrangements with the censors to get their copy approved before printing.

IRAN

THE IRANIAN JUDICIARY PUSHED AHEAD WITH ITS YEAR-OLD CRACKDOWN on media dissent, further exacerbating an ongoing power struggle between conservative and reformist factions in the Islamic Republic.

The crackdown began in April 2000, when Supreme Leader Ayatollah Ali Khamenei delivered a fiery speech accusing the country's reformist press, which generally backs President Muhammed Khatami's agenda of social and political liberalization, of being foreign agents. Conservative judicial authorities took the speech as their cue to close dozens of newspapers and jail several journalists.

The repression continued throughout 2001. At least 20 newspapers and other publications were suspended by the courts on an array of vague charges such as "publishing lies" and "defamation." By year's end, at least five journalists were in jail on charges related to their journalistic work, while dozens more had been summoned to court, were appealing pending prison sentences, or had been fined and barred from practicing their profession.

On May 3, World Press Freedom Day, CPJ placed Khamenei at the head of its annual Ten Worst Enemies of the Press list. Khatami was re-elected in June, at a difficult time for the reformist movement that he inspired. (See page 597.)

In 1997, Khatami came to office promising Iranians more freedom of expression, democracy, and respect for the rule of law. His first term saw the emergence of a new liberal press that quickly began to debate sensitive topics such as official corruption, the undemocratic behavior of the ruling clerical establishment, and even Iran's theocratic form of government.

While the press helped mobilize Iran's burgeoning reform movement, conservative forces within the regime quickly used their control over key institutions, such as the courts, to target the media.

The Tehran Press Court prosecuted reformist publications throughout 2001, despite vocal protests from journalists and members of the reform-dominated Majles, or Parliament. In December, three Iranian parliamentarians were convicted of libel and other offenses in connection with their scathing criticisms of the judiciary. Among them was Hossein Loghmanian, who was jailed for libeling the courts after he denounced the press crackdown.

The Press Court closed newspapers and prosecuted journalists for vague offenses such as "insulting the leadership" and publishing lies, falsehoods, slander, or "propaganda against the State." Other courts, such as the Special Court for Clergy and the revolutionary court system, were employed to similar effect against newspapers and journalists.

Since April 2000, the courts have closed at least 47 publications, the vast majority of which were reformist in their editorial orientation. Only a handful of banned newspapers have been allowed to resume publishing. Several previously suspended newspapers were banned for good in 2001.

In December, the head of the judicial administration in Tehran, Abbas Ali

Alizadeh, said that the mass closures of newspapers and publications were undertaken for "the sake of God."

"One of our greatest glories is [the] closure of offending newspapers," Alizadeh boasted. "Based on our assessments, by doing this, we have done the greatest service to the people."

In spite of the crackdown, a handful of reformist papers were still publishing in Tehran at year's end, along with a number of smaller provincial and student publications. The surviving newspapers have generally toned down their reporting and analysis.

Many journalists were forced to take jobs at conservative papers or abandon journalism altogether. In addition to the five journalists behind bars for press offenses, several other writers and journalists, many of them active in the reform movement, were jailed without charge or for reasons related to the peaceful expression of opinions and ideas. Many were denied access to their families or lawyers.

In January, the prominent investigative reporter Akbar Ganji, whose articles on the murders of Iranian intellectuals and dissidents in 1998 implicated several top government officials, was sentenced to 10 years in prison followed by five years of internal exile. Ganji was convicted based on his participation in a 2000 conference in Berlin on the future of the Iranian reform movement.

In May, an appellate court reduced Ganji's sentence to six months, half the time he had already served. A higher court struck then struck down that verdict. In July, Ganji was sentenced to six years in jail by another appellate court. At press time, he still faced additional charges in the Press Court.

In a positive development, Iranian editor Mashallah Shamsolvaezin was released from prison on September 12, after spending 17 months behind bars. Shamsolvaezin, who edited the groundbreaking dailies *Jameah*, *Tous*, *Neshat*, and *Asr-e-Azadegan* before each was closed, had been serving a 30-month sentence for publishing an article that criticized capital punishment in Iran. In 2000, Shamsolvaezin received CPJ's International Press Freedom Award for courage and independence in news reporting. Another jailed editor, Latif Safari, director of the banned daily *Neshat*, was also released during the year.

Although local journalists bore the brunt of state harassment, foreign reporters were also targeted at times. In early February, Reuters bureau chief Jonathan Lyons and his wife, *Guardian* and *International Herald Tribune* reporter Geneive Abdo, fled the country, fearing official reprisals over an interview that they had conducted with the jailed Ganji.

In the interview, Ganji criticized conservatives and warned of a social explosion in Iran. Iranian authorities later barred Lyons from returning to the country and apparently warned the couple that they might face unspecified criminal charges.

The Internet remained a small but important source of alternative information for many Iranians. According to one estimate, there are some 380,000 Internet users in Iran, out of a population of 73 million. The country had about 100

Internet Service Providers (ISPs) and about 1,500 Internet cafés in the capital, Tehran. Some ISPs do take it upon themselves to filter objectionable political and moral content.

In May, the authorities closed down some 450 Internet cafés in an apparent attempt to protect the state telecommunications monopoly against competition from low-cost Internet telephone service. The cafés were allowed to reopen in June after they obtained new licenses.

That month, however, state telecom ordered Iranian ISPs to block material deemed immoral or threatening to state security, including dissident Web sites. It was unclear whether the order was practical or enforceable. And in November, the Supreme Cultural Revolution Council, a government body, issued a decree requiring all private ISPs to dismantle their operations and hand over their assets to the state. The controversial decree had not yet been implemented at press time.

Likewise, it remained unclear whether the directive was enforceable and whether the council had the constitutional authority to pass it in the first place. Parliament was expected to debate the issue in 2002.

Television and radio remained in the hands of the conservative establishment and largely reflected its views. Satellite dishes remained popular, despite a 1995 ban on their use, allowing Iranians access to international programming. In late October, however, authorities confiscated some 1,000 dishes and arrested several dish owners.

The dish crackdown was an apparent state response to provocative broadcasts by satellite channels affiliated with secular Iranian opposition groups based in the United States. Satellite broadcasts of Iranian soccer matches were introduced by commentators who condemned the Islamic regime and called on Iranian citizens to hold street demonstrations. They also broadcast footage showing soccer fans vandalizing property after the matches. The authorities later threatened to confiscate thousands more dishes.

IRAQ

SADDAM HUSSEIN'S REPRESSIVE REGIME MAINTAINED its stranglehold over all of Iraq's institutions, including the press. Print and broadcast media are closely controlled by the government or by Hussein's infamous son Uday, who owns or runs a number of influential media outlets.

Criticism of the Hussein family or top officials is not tolerated in any form. Insulting the president or other government authorities is punishable by death. Hagiographic coverage of the country's political leaders and vilifications of their enemies fill the press.

The Iraqi government, which is the country's sole Internet service provider, began offering limited online access to the public for the first time in 2000. Internet content is heavily censored, and only a few locations allow users to surf the Web. Private Internet access is forbidden, modems and cellular telephones are said to be banned, and fax machines can be used only with government permission.

It is also a criminal offense to possess a satellite dish. In late 1999, the government announced that it would allow restricted access to satellite television on a subscription basis. In May 2001, Iraqi newspapers reported that implementation was imminent. It is unclear, however, whether the service actually became available or not.

Foreign correspondents who are permitted to enter Iraq face numerous obstacles. Foreign journalists are required to travel with government minders from the Ministry of Information. Travel outside Baghdad requires written approval, and traveling to a location not specified in the request is forbidden. During the last year, authorities banned foreign correspondents from traveling to Kurdish-controlled areas in the north of the country, citing security concerns.

In the U.N.-mandated northern enclaves, which are not controlled by the government, rival Kurdish factions operate their own television stations and newspapers beyond the reach of official Iraqi repression.

ISRAEL AND THE OCCUPIED TERRITORIES

ISRAEL'S HEBREW-, ARABIC-, AND ENGLISH-LANGUAGE MEDIA are extremely lively and, despite some military censorship, mostly free. Yet, journalists covering the second intifada, which began in September 2000 in Gaza and the West Bank, faced a variety of restrictions and hazards from the Israeli army and militant Jewish settlers, including bullets, tear gas, shrapnel, and physical assault.

Gunfire from Israel Defense Forces (IDF) was the most dangerous and immediate threat to journalists in Israel. In February, French journalist Laurent van der Stock was shot in the leg, apparently by an Israeli bullet, while covering Palestinian demonstrators who were throwing rocks at Israeli soldiers near the West Bank city of Ramallah. A few weeks later, an IDF soldier in an armored personnel carrier opened fire without provocation in the direction of three Reuters journalists at the Netzarim Junction in Gaza.

An Israeli soldier struck Abu Dhabi TV correspondent Layla Odeh in the leg with a live round while she was filming in the Gaza Strip in April when no clashes were taking place in the area. And in mid-May, French correspondent of TF1 Bertrand Aguirre was wounded in the chest by another live round, apparently fired by an Israeli border policeman, in Ramallah. Video footage appeared to show the border policeman aiming in the direction of Aguirre and a group of journalists, even though the officer was not in a life-threatening situation.

In all, CPJ documented 16 cases in which journalists were wounded by live rounds or rubber-coated steel bullets between September 2000 and June 2001. The actual number of casualties appeared to be far greater; the Paris-based press freedom organization Reporters Sans Frontières reported more than 40 such cases.

Circumstantial evidence suggests that, in some cases, Israeli forces may have deliberately targeted journalists. Sometimes, journalists were shot in the legs, head, or even hands as they held cameras. In one case, a bullet hit a journalist's camera lens. In many cases, reporters hit by gunfire were far removed from clashes and easily recognizable as journalists because of their conspicuous camera equipment.

At the very least, the IDF or security forces behaved recklessly in firing live rounds or rubber-coated steel bullets that injured journalists. A six-person CPJ delegation met with Israeli ambassador David Ivry in June at the Israeli Embassy in Washington, D.C. Ivry promised to relay CPJ's concerns to the Israeli Foreign Ministry but vehemently denied that the IDF had intentionally targeted journalists.

On July 26, IDF chief of staff Lt. Gen. Shaul Mofaz "reiterated the standing orders concerning the safeguarding of journalists and called upon the army's commanders to strengthen the awareness of those orders throughout the ranks." On November 18, following months of pressure from the Jerusalem-based Foreign Press Association (FPA), CPJ, and other international press freedom groups, the IDF presented its findings on several cases in which journalists were wounded by gunfire.

Unfortunately, the IDF report failed to shed any light on the cases it reviewed. In fact, the findings rejected accusations of IDF responsibility in several of the shootings, despite strong evidence of deliberate targeting or recklessness. The FPA noted that, "the absence of concrete results in practically all of the cases does not suggest that the investigations were thorough and comprehensive."

In addition to gunfire, journalists reporting on the intifada risked physical attack and beatings from the Israeli army, security forces, and militant Jewish settlers, all of whom acted with seeming impunity. Jewish settlers often attacked journalists in the presence of soldiers who showed little interest in stopping the assaults or apprehending the assailants.

Perhaps nowhere was the dual daily threat of the IDF and Jewish settlers to journalists more pronounced than in the West Bank city of Hebron. In November 2001, CPJ gave an International Press Freedom Award to Palestinian journalist Mazen Dana, a Reuters cameraman from Hebron who for years has braved bullets and beatings to cover political unrest in the city.

By year's end, reported gunfire injuries to journalists had dropped sharply. The decline was probably due to a decrease in the number of street demonstrations, the use of armored press cars and other security precautions by journalists, and greater caution on the part of the IDF.

Palestinian journalists in the West Bank and Gaza (many of whom work for international media, including all the major wire services) continued to face significant bureaucratic obstacles. In order to enter Israel or East Jerusalem, Palestinians have for many years been required to obtain special permits, which are awarded sparingly and often for limited time periods. As a result, it remained nearly impossible for Palestinian journalists to travel between the West Bank and Gaza. Many Palestinian journalists also complained that Israel's Government Press Office (GPO) denied them press accreditation, which facilitates passage through Israeli checkpoints and grants them entry to official government events and press conferences.

When Israeli authorities proclaim a heightened threat of Palestinian violence, they seal off the Occupied Territories. No Palestinians, even those with permits, can enter Israel or East Jerusalem.

Within the Occupied Territories, Israeli checkpoints have been fortified with concrete roadblocks, dirt barriers, and ditches since the intifada began to keep Palestinians from leaving their towns and villages. Only Israeli bypass roads, which connect Israeli settlements, are consistently open, and Palestinians are banned from them. Authorities also divided the 360 square kilometer (about 144 square mile) Gaza Strip into three sections and cut off travel between them intermittently, sometimes for weeks at a time.

Even when the internal travel restrictions eased, cars were still delayed at checkpoints for hours. Not even foreigners and Israelis were exempt from such inconveniences. A normally one-hour drive from certain parts of the West Bank to Jerusalem could take hours.

On December 13, 2001, following a number of suicide bombings and armed attacks in Israel, Israel used missiles and bulldozers to destroy the Voice of Palestine (VOP) radio station's broadcasting headquarters in the West Bank city of Ramallah. Israel has long charged the VOP, the Palestinian National Authority's official radio station, with inciting violence. In October 2000, after a mob killed two Israeli reservists in the West Bank town of Ramallah, Israeli forces destroyed the station's transmission towers. CPJ condemned the attacks, describing them as a violation of international humanitarian law.

An analysis of Voice of Palestine broadcasting by CPJ found that while the station reflected the political perspective of the Palestinian Authority, there was no evidence that the station was used for military purposes.

In March, Israeli authorities officially barred Israeli citizens from traveling to areas of the West Bank and Gaza Strip under Palestinian control. Israeli journalists were exempted provided they signed a waiver that the government was not responsible for their safety. However, some Israeli journalists who traveled to Palestinian-controlled territory refused to sign such a document.

In Israel and East Jerusalem, the local and international press remain subject to Israeli military censorship when officials feel that a particular report will harm the country's defense interests. Journalists, however, have the option of appealing to the High Court of Justice. Most Hebrew-, Arabic-, and English-language media are able to circumvent the restrictions by attributing sensitive stories to foreign news outlets. Foreign journalists generally find enforcement erratic.

In May, the Israeli daily *Haaretz* reported that the Shin Bet, the Israeli security service, had called in Arab-Israeli authors, journalists, and publishers for "clarification and explanatory conversations" about their writing. The paper reported that some were asked not to write anything, including poetry, that could be considered "incitement" to violence.

The London-based, Arabic-language newspaper *Al-Sharq al-Awsat* reported that in July, Israeli forces impersonated a journalist in order to attack a Hamas office in Nablus. According to the paper, a man identifying himself as a BBC reporter called the office and asked to speak with Hamas leader Jamal Mansour. Mansour and a Palestinian journalist who was in the office to interview the Hamas leader were killed in the missile attack, which the paper said began just after the callers confirmed that Mansour was in the building. (See also "Palestinian Authority Territories," page 489.)

JORDAN

KING ABDULLAH II, WHO PROMISED POLITIAL REFORM when he began his reign in February 1999, has repeatedly affirmed that "the sky is the limit" for press freedom in Jordan. The reality is very different. Harsh new legal restrictions, along with familiar hardships such as threats and detentions, led to a deterioration in press freedom conditions during 2001.

On October 8, the government of Prime Minister Ali Abu al-Ragheb introduced "temporary" amendments to an already harsh Penal Code in response to the U.S.-led international "war on terror." However, the legislation went beyond anti-terrorism provisions to impose tough general restrictions on freedom of expression.

Approved by King Abdullah, the new amendments stipulate that publications can be temporarily or permanently banned by the courts for publishing "false information or rumors," harming "national unity," "aggravat[ing] basic social norms," "sow[ing] the seeds of hatred," or harming "the honor or reputation of individuals." Offending editors and owners face prison sentences of between three and six months, fines of 5,000 Jordanian dinars (about US$7,000), or both.

The new amendments also expanded a Penal Code article that criminalizes "insulting the dignity of the king" by making it an offense to publish any rumors or falsehoods regarding the king, whether in print, in cartoons, or online. The law also criminalizes those who "incite" others to commit similar offenses. Violators face between one and three years in prison. Charges brought under the new amendments are to be tried primarily in state security courts, rather than civil courts.

The amendments came after Jordanian officials warned they would not tolerate any efforts to destabilize the country in the aftermath of the U.S. military strikes on Afghanistan. Government officials blamed the new law on weekly newspapers that practice "irresponsible journalism." But government efforts to rein in dissent also appeared to reflect the depth of political uncertainty in Jordan, where the economy continued to stagnate and fears persisted of domestic spillover from Palestinian-Israeli violence next door.

Parliament is expected to review the amendments when it reconvenes in September 2002, though by year's end the government had not prosecuted any journalists under the law. Nevertheless, its potential chilling effect was difficult to dispute.

Jordanian officials also continued to employ a number of indirect methods to hinder journalists and foster self-censorship. The country's formidable security forces admonished journalists behind the scenes. Sometimes, the mere presence of security agents was enough to stifle independent reporting. Reverting to a practice that seemed on the decline in 2000, security forces detained a number of journalists during the year, including a reporter for the Qatar-based Al-Jazeera satellite station, who was interrogated after filming clashes between Jordanian police and demonstrators.

In March, six Israeli journalists were prevented from covering the Arab Summit in Amman. Jordanian security authorities requested that they leave the country, citing threats to their safety. A senior Jordanian official, however, said later that the action was taken because the participants did "not wish to see Israelis."

Some writers, including powerful and influential political figures, suffered severe professional consequences when they attempted to tackle politically sensitive issues. Former chief of the Royal Cabinet and former deputy prime minister Jawad Anani was asked to resign from his appointed Senate seat for criticizing the government in an article for the United Arab Emirates daily *Al-Bayan*.

The government amended the Jordan Radio and Television Corporation Law in 2000, technically ending the state monopoly on broadcast media. However, the new guidelines have not been formalized, and no initiatives to establish private broadcast stations are planned.

In late October 2001, King Abdullah called for the abolition of the Ministry of Information, which for years has enforced a host of restrictions on the press. The government replaced the ministry with the Higher Media Council, an 11-member supervisory body responsible for recommending and overseeing media policy. The council is expected to include both government officials and private citizens, though all will be appointed by the king. However, because of the council's ambiguous mandate, it is uncertain whether the media will fare better under it than they did under the Ministry of Information.

In 2001, the government sold its shares in the Jordan Press Foundation (JPF), publisher of the influential daily *Al-Rai* and the English-language weekly *Jordan Times*. But the foundation's majority shareholder is now the Social Security Corporation (SSC), run by the Minister of Labor. The SSC also holds shares in the daily *Al-Dustour* and in the once feisty *Al-Arab Al-Youm*, whose chairman resigned in 2000 after selling his shares, apparently due to government pressure. Other pro-government private interests also held stakes in *Al-Arab Al-Youm*.

The generally pro-government Jordan Press Association (JPA), which sometimes pushes for journalists' rights, also worked to restrict press freedoms in 2001. Under the Press and Publications Law and the JPA's bylaws, all journalists must belong to the organization in order to practice their profession. The JPA pressured the Ministry of Information to take action against foreign and Jordanian correspondents who were not JPA members but continued to work as journalists—a long-tolerated practice. Although King Abdullah promised that he would work to eliminate such restrictions, the requirement remained.

In February, the High Court of Justice upheld the JPA's lifetime ban on editor Nidal Mansour. In September 2000, the JPA expelled Mansour, who at the time was the group's secretary-general and editor of the weekly *Al-Hadath*, for launching a press freedom organization called the Center for Defending the Freedom of Journalists (CDFJ). The JPA claimed that Mansour violated the organization's bylaws by accepting foreign funding for the CDFJ and by not working full-time as a journalist. Mansour was eventually forced to step down as the editor of *Al-Hadath*.

KUWAIT

KUWAIT'S PRESS REMAINS ONE OF THE MORE OPEN in the Arab world. Newspapers often cover local political affairs aggressively and are not shy about criticizing senior officials. Nevertheless, journalists still practice self-censorship and avoid taking on the emir and other members of the ruling family.

The Press and Publications Law (PPL) has been used in recent years to prosecute journalists and suspend newspapers. Under the PPL, newspapers can be suspended and journalists jailed for sullying public morals, "disparaging God [and] the prophets," or "violating the national interest."

In the year's most shocking incident, veteran journalist Hidaya Sultan al-Salem, the owner and editor of the weekly magazine *Al-Majales*, was murdered on her way to work when an armed assailant opened fire on her chauffer-driven car in Kuwait City in late March. The motive for the murder remained unclear.

The main suspect, a police officer named Khaled al-Azmi, admitted to the killing. However, he later recanted, saying police had forced him to confess. Early in the investigation, Kuwaiti authorities said that al-Azmi killed al-Salem in revenge for an *Al-Majales* article that allegedly insulted the women of his tribe. The article was written some eight months earlier, however, leading some to doubt that the officer would have waited that long to take his revenge.

Some observers speculated that alleged financial disputes within al-Salem's family, or other alleged disputes with some of her employees, motivated the murder. In the last edition of *Al-Majales* before she was killed, according to press reports, al-Salem published an open letter claiming police had harassed her. In November, a source in Kuwait said that al-Azmi may have killed al-Salem because of a personal dispute between the two involving al-Azmi's sister.

Authorities monitored foreign papers for objectionable material, and censored at least one paper during the year, the Lebanon-based *Al-Tadamun al-Arabi wal Dawli*.

Two journalists were jailed in Kuwait at year's end: Fawwaz Muhammad al-Awadi Bessisso and Ibtisam Berto Sulaiman al-Dakhil. Both were imprisoned in June 1991 and later sentenced to life in prison because of their work with the collaborationist newspaper *Al-Nida*, which was published under the Iraqi occupation. Both remained imprisoned despite the release of some 15 former *Al-Nida* journalists since 1996, many by royal decree.

LEBANON

LEBANON BOASTS NUMEROUS PRIVATELY OWNED NEWSPAPERS and magazines, as well as television and radio stations that feature lively criticism of officials and government policies. Throughout 2001, however, Lebanese authorities used both the legal system and informal bullying to rein in outspoken journalists.

During 2001, Lebanese security forces harassed several journalists in retaliation for their professional work. In one widely publicized case, in June, a military court prosecuted Raghida Dergham, the New York bureau chief for the London-based *Al-Hayat* newspaper, for "dealing with the enemy" because of her participation in a 2000 panel discussion in Washington, D.C., that also featured an Israeli official.

The real motivation for the action was thought to be official anger at Dergham's critical coverage of a Lebanese dispute with the United Nations over the demarcation of the Lebanese-Israeli border. In 2000, authorities cancelled Dergham's passport while she was visiting Beirut. On November 30, 2001, the court dismissed the charges. In late March, security agents confiscated the Lebanese passport of Samir Qassir, a journalist with the daily *Al-Nahar*. That action appeared to come in response to Qassir's March 16 editorial criticizing the Lebanese army and security services. The passport was eventually returned, but authorities said they were investigating the legality of his Lebanese citizenship. The issue had not been resolved at press time.

Lebanese journalists tend to avoid criticizing the president, the army and state security services, official corruption, or Syria's controversial military and political role in the country. But in August, the armed forces filed criminal charges in a military court against the Paris-based weekly *Al-Watan Al-Arabi*. The magazine had published an article alleging that Syrian soldiers, some 20,000 of whom are stationed in Lebanon, were disguising themselves in Lebanese army uniforms. The case was still pending at years' end.

One week later, amid a government crackdown on opposition Christian groups, the army sued an editor and writer for *Al-Nahar* for defamation after the paper ran an article criticizing the country's compulsory military service.

Leaders of Lebanon's various political and religious factions tend to see media outlets as little more than political tools. Prime Minister Rafiq Hariri, for example, owns the station Future TV, which strongly backed Hariri during the 2000 elections. Politicians and others have also been known to pay journalists in exchange for positive press coverage, according to local sources.

One positive development has been the top-notch weekly cultural supplement of *Al-Nahar*, edited by novelist Elias Khoury. The paper continued to tackle topics often avoided by other newspapers, such as human rights, press freedom, and the Syrian military presence.

Broadcasters are also subject to restrictive laws, such as Decree 7997 of 1996, which bans stations broadcast news that seeks to "inflame or incite sectarian or religious chauvinism" or results in "slander, disparagement, disgrace, [or] defamation."

The Audiovisual Law of 1994 empowers the Ministry of Information to close television and radio stations that break the rules. State security agents continued to screen foreign publications entering the country and occasionally censored publications containing objectionable material.

As in other Middle East countries, many in Lebanon are able to bypass the local media entirely if they so chose. Many Lebanese have satellite dishes and can tune in to a wide variety of regional and international news programming.

MAURITANIA

THE RULING REPUBLICAN DEMOCRATIC PARTY SWEPT GENERAL AND LOCAL elections in October, and President Maaouya Ould Sid Ahmed Taya remained firmly in control of the country.

Authorities have for years used prior censorship and Article 11 of the 1991 Press Ordinance to harass journalists who cover sensitive issues. Under the harsh statutes, the minister of the interior can ban any publication that undermines Islam, the state's authority, or public order, or that defames foreign heads of state. Any person who sells or disseminates a banned publication can be imprisoned and fined.

In April, Mohammed Lemine Ould Bah, a correspondent for two French radio stations, was temporarily banned from practicing journalism after the minister of communications objected to his reports on the state of relations between Senegal and Mauritania.

MOROCCO

WHEN HE ASSUMED THE THRONE IN 1999, 38-year-old King Muhammad VI kindled hopes that he would usher in a period of greater political freedom in Morocco. The independent press continued to push the limits of free expression—and just as quickly found them. In 2001, as in previous years, Moroccan authorities used criminal prosecutions, censorship, and harassment to restrict the media.

The current Press Code imposes tough penalties on journalists who defame public officials or offend members of the royal family. Authorities also have the legal power to confiscate, suspend, or revoke the licenses of publications deemed to threaten public order.

In December 2000, the Moroccan government permanently closed the country's three most audacious independent publications—the weeklies *Le Journal*, *Al-Sahiffa*, and *Demain*—for printing a letter alleging that Prime Minister Abderrahamane Youssefi was involved in a 1972 leftist plot to assassinate the late King Hassan II.

The publications, which earned their reputations by publishing daring stories about corruption, the disputed Western Sahara region, and unsavory aspects of Morocco's political history, resumed publishing in 2001 under new, but similar sounding, titles. However, the authorities continued to pressure them in various ways, including through defamation suits.

In March, a Casablanca court convicted Abou Bakr Jamai and Ali Ammar, directors of the weekly *Le Journal Hebdomadaire* (formerly *Le Journal*) of defaming Foreign Minister Muhammad Ben Aissa after an article in *Le Journal* alleged that Ben Aissa had profited from the purchase of an official residence during his tenure as Morocco's ambassador to the United States. The two journalists were sentenced to jail terms of three and two months, respectively, and ordered to pay fines and damages totaling 2,020,000 dirhams (about US$200,000). Jamai and Ammar appealed the decision; their case was still pending at year's end.

Reporters and photographers also reported threats and harassment from state security agents, and some were briefly detained. In July, security agents followed and threatened France 3 Public Television editor Alain Chabod and *Demain Magazine*'s Ali Lmrabet while they were investigating explosive revelations that top Moroccan officials had tortured and killed prominent leftist dissident Mehdi Ben Barka in 1965. Agents also visited *Demain Magazine*'s printer and ordered the presses stopped so that they could read the current edition.

In July, King Muhammad issued a veiled threat against the Moroccan press during an interview with the London-based daily *Al-Sharq Al-Awsat*. Press freedom should be used in a "responsible" way, and journalists should respect state institutions, the king said. While professing respect for the press, Muhammad warned that he had "judicial means that I have not yet used, but if need be I will be forced to use in accordance with the law."

Meanwhile, Moroccan officials were not shy about using censorship. Authorities confiscated editions of *Al-Risala wal Futawwa* published by the local Islamist group Justice and Charity. By year's end, the authorities had also seized copies of *Demain Magazine* and suspended the magazine indefinitely, maintaining that the paper had failed to pay a fine from a November defamation conviction. The magazine claimed that the fine had been paid in full.

Officials also continued to ban issues of foreign publications that contained politically sensitive material, including several European newspapers that criticized the king, exposed human rights abuses, documented the country's social problems, or referred to the dispute over Western Sahara.

Morocco had one imprisoned journalist at year's end, Noureddine Darif, a journalist for the leftist weekly *Al-Amal al Democrati* who was arrested in Western Sahara in November for attempting to interview individuals injured during anti-government demonstrations. He was taken to a police station and reportedly beaten. Darif is accused of "collusion with a foreign party" and of stirring up violent disturbances. He is currently being held in Ayoun Prison.

PALESTINIAN AUTHORITY TERRITORIES

As the Palestinian uprising, or intifada, entered its second year, Palestinian National Authority (PNA) chairman Yasser Arafat appeared to be fighting for his own survival amidst escalating Israeli military attacks and intense diplomatic pressure from the United States. Despite the PNA's precarious situation and increasing alienation from the population at large, the PNA showed that it was still capable of cracking down on press freedom in 2001.

In March, PNA security forces closed the Ramallah office of the popular, Qatar-based satellite news channel Al-Jazeera for three days because it had broadcast an unflattering image of Arafat. Al-Jazeera has become popular among Palestinians for its coverage of the intifada, and the shutdown triggered widespread local and international protest. The station was allowed to reopen three days later.

In the aftermath of September 11, Palestinian security forces prevented several journalists from covering celebrations among Palestinians in the West Bank city of Nablus of the attacks on the United States. In one well-publicized incident, a PNA official told an Associated Press (AP) cameraman that his safety could not be guaranteed if footage of the rallies was aired. Fearing for the cameraman's safety, AP elected not to broadcast the images.

In October, security forces barred foreign journalists from entering the Gaza Strip in an apparent effort to prevent them from covering the aftermath of bloody clashes between Palestinian security forces and Palestinian demonstrators in Gaza City. The demonstrators were protesting U.S. military strikes against Afghanistan, and some expressed support for Osama bin Laden. A few days later, a number of journalists were prevented from covering another protest in a Gaza refugee camp.

Security forces continued to operate outside the law by censoring, intimidating, physically abusing, and arbitrarily arresting journalists from local print and broadcast media outlets.

The PNA's heavy-handed and arbitrary treatment of journalists has fostered an oppressive climate of self-censorship in the Palestinian press. In 2001, local newspapers continued to avoid coverage of issues such as PNA corruption and mismanagement, human rights abuses by security forces, or any issue that might reflect negatively on Arafat. Palestinian journalists continued to complain in private about their inability to print dissenting viewpoints in the mainstream press and about the lack of investigative reporting on Palestinian affairs.

The three major Palestinian dailies maintain close ties with the PNA. Arafat aide Akram Haniyya edits the daily *Al-Ayyam*, while Nabil Amr, another Arafat confidant, founded the daily *Al-Hayat al-Jadida*. In addition, the PNA covers the payroll of the latter. The privately owned *Al-Quds* is nominally independent but remains staunchly pro-PNA. The continuation of the intifada seemed to make journalists even more reluctant to criticize the PNA or its leadership.

Under intense U.S. and Israeli pressure to crack down on extremists who carried out a number of deadly suicide bombings against Israelis during the year, the PNA in December closed a number of offices of the radical groups Hamas and Islamic Jihad. The Islamist weeklies *Al-Risala* and *Al-Istiqlal*, Gaza-based publications affiliated with the Khalas Party (comprising former Hamas members) and the Islamic Jihad, were shut down in the process.

The PNA controls the official Palestine TV and the Voice of Palestine radio, both of which are PNA mouthpieces. However, a range of private radio and television stations sprang up across the West Bank in the 1990s, providing local news, debates, at times during the current intifada, important information about services, such as economic aid and counseling, that are available to beleaguered Palestinians.

But broadcast outlets remain vulnerable to PNA reprisals. On September 20, PNA security forces temporarily closed Al Roa TV, a private television station in the West Bank town of Bethlehem that had broadcast a statement from a militant group affiliated with Arafat's Fatah organization claiming responsibility for an attack on two Jewish settlers. The news apparently embarrassed the PNA since it suggested that a group technically under Arafat's control might have violated a recently announced Palestinian cease fire.

Citing safety concerns, fewer Israeli journalists ventured into the Palestinian-controlled territories during the intifada. In February, a Fatah leaflet, published in the Palestinian daily *Al-Quds,* warned that Israelis entering Bethlehem, including journalists, could be killed. The threat followed an Israel Radio report on the allegedly corrupt activities of a Fatah official. Palestinian West Bank security chief Col. Jibril Rajoub told the *Jerusalem Post* that the threats were irresponsible and did not reflect the PNA's position. Nevertheless, Fatah activists once again threatened Israeli journalists a month later, according to reports on Israel radio.

In late May, Palestinian militants detained two Western journalists working with *Newsweek* magazine in the Gaza Strip. The militants claimed to be members of the Fatah Hawks, an organization that was thought to be defunct. They announced that the journalists were being detained "to protest unfair American and British press coverage of the Israeli-Palestinian conflict."

The journalists, who were allowed to leave unharmed after four-and-a-half hours, said they never felt seriously threatened. (See also "Israel and the Occupied Territories," page 480.)

QATAR

FOR MANY OUTSIDE THE ARAB WORLD, the small Gulf state of Qatar is synonymous with the Al-Jazeera satellite channel, which for more than five years has provided bold news coverage on regional affairs. The feisty channel, which subsists on government funding but has earned a reputation for its editorial independence, has incurred the wrath of regimes throughout the Middle East for its provocative news reporting and energetic political debate programs. In 2001, Tunisia protested a talk show featuring Tunisian dissidents; Israel mulled the idea of barring local subscriptions to the channel; and other countries issued formal complaints or took reprisals against local Al-Jazeera reporters.

After the September 11 attacks on the United States, Al-Jazeera angered the Bush administration and was harshly criticized by both officials and pundits for its allegedly "inflammatory" anti-U.S. coverage and its broadcasts of Osama bin Laden's taped messages. CPJ expressed concern when U.S. secretary of state Colin Powell urged Qatar's Emir Sheikh Hamed bin Khalifa al-Thani to rein in the channel.

Although Al-Jazeera was a bright spot in Qatar's media landscape, the press does not operate entirely freely. While the government abolished the Ministry of Information and ended formal censorship of newspapers in the 1990s, self-censorship remains pervasive. Even at the normally lively Al-Jazeera, there is little aggressive reporting on Qatari affairs. According to critics, the station never directly criticizes the emir or the ruling family and avoids criticizing powerful neighbor Saudi Arabia.

During the year, Qatari authorities jailed a U.S. national who worked in the Qatari Foreign Ministry for allegedly defaming the emir on a Web site he was accused of operating. The site had featured a poll asking whether the emir's wife or a Qatari professor was the more attractive woman.

In June, Ahmed Ali, editor of the Qatari daily *Al-Watan*, was attacked and beaten by three relatives of Minister of Energy and Electricity Abdullah Hamad Al-Attia, who were angered by an article Ali had written that criticized one of the minister's proposals.

Qatari officials also censor the Internet for morally objectionable material.

SAUDI ARABIA

SAUDI ARABIA IS ONE OF THE MOST CLOSED SOCIETIES IN THE WORLD. The ruling al-Saud family tolerates no political dissent of any kind, especially in the press. Newspapers are deferential toward the ruling family and government policies. Although papers now report more openly on topics such as crime and unemployment, there is no open criticism of the government.

Since the Ministry of Information appoints newspaper editors, the government can exert pressure or dismiss them at will if they publish any objectionable material. Writers are also subject to the same pressures. During the year, CPJ received credible reports that the Ministry of Interior barred several columnists from writing for the daily *Al-Watan* and other Saudi publications because the ministry objected to their views on religion and other social issues.

The Saudi-owned daily *Arab News* reported that in July the Council of Ministers, a government body over which the king presides, approved a new press law that for the first time allows journalists to form a professional union. There seemed to be little hope, however, that such an organization would actually increase press freedom.

Saudi authorities exert tight control over all outside sources of information. Foreign publications are closely monitored and censored if they contain any news that offends Islam or casts the kingdom in a negative light.

Foreign journalists continued to have trouble entering the country. When they were allowed access, it was difficult to conduct serious investigations. In October, several foreign correspondents were reportedly barred from conducting interviews in the Abha region, where four of the hijackers involved in the September 11 terrorist attacks on the United States were thought to hail from.

The Internet has been available to the public since 1999. Although several private Internet Service Providers (ISP) and Internet cafés operate in the kingdom, a government proxy server filters out objectionable moral and political content. But savvy Web surfers can easily elude the crude controls. According to press reports, many Internet cafés boast in-house hackers who, for a fee, connect users to banned sites. Alternatively, those who can afford it evade the censors by making an international phone call to an ISP outside the country. During the year, there was talk that the authorities were preparing a new law to govern Internet use and specify punishments for such "illegal" online activities.

Satellite television is a more common source of alternative news for many Saudis. Though legally banned in Saudi Arabia, satellite dishes are widely available.

SUDAN

SUDAN'S INDEPENDENT AND OPPOSITION NEWSPAPERS occasionally feature lively coverage of local political affairs, but the government quickly stifles discussion when the press becomes too bold. Coverage of topics such as the 18-year civil war, government corruption or mismanagement, or other official misdeeds has triggered arrests, prosecutions, and censorship, and has led to a rise in self-censorship.

In September, the Press and Publications Council (PPC) imposed a three-day ban on the *Khartoum Monitor*, an independent, English-language daily, for publishing stories about the Nuba people in southern Sudan. The PPC claimed that the articles caused friction between the country's peoples. Several staff members were also detained. The PPC, which reports directly to the president, is responsible for enforcing Sudan's restrictive Press Law.

The PPC also suspended several newspapers. In early October, the council issued one-day suspensions to the dailies *Al-Usbu* and *Alwan* because some of their articles allegedly offended other journalists, according to press reports.

Sudanese authorities also used criminal and civil statutes to prosecute journalists who criticized officials or the government. A Khartoum court jailed Amal Abbas, editor-in-chief of the daily *Al-Rai al-Akher*, and Ibrahim Hassan, a reporter for the paper, for three months for failing to pay fines in a libel suit. The two were found guilty of libeling Khartoum governor Majzoub Khalifa in a 2000 article that accused him of corruption and nepotism. They were ordered to pay fines of 15 million pounds (US$5,900) each. *Al-Rai al-Akher* was also hit with a 1 billion pound fine (US$390,000), reportedly the largest fine ever imposed in a libel suit in Sudan.

In April, at least two journalists were detained in Khartoum while covering a banned Easter gathering at the All Saint's Church. In late October, Alfred Taaban and another reporter from the *Khartoum Monitor* were detained and held for several days after the paper published an article about the difficulties of covering the conflict in southern Sudan. Tabaan, who was accused of "inciting religious and ethnic hatred," was to be officially charged on December 27.

The Ministry of Information, meanwhile, continued to monitor and censor publications. In November, 22 Sudanese journalists from the *Al-Watan* newspaper were detained after they marched on the ministry. The journalists were protesting an order not to publish an article alleging that the government had distributed expired medicines in the countryside. The editors of the paper decided to hold the entire issue in protest. The detained journalists were transported to prison in three trucks and were released the following day. At press time, it was unclear whether they would still face charges.

SYRIA

A YEAR AND A HALF AFTER THE YOUTHFUL BASHAR AL-ASSAD came to power following the death of his father, Hafez al-Assad, in 2000, hopes that the new president would usher in an era of greater press freedom gave way to cynicism and disillusionment. President al-Assad's regime has made it abundantly clear that while it will tolerate the existence of a few independent media outlets, the margins of acceptable discourse are strictly limited.

The Syrian government allowed CPJ to conduct an investigative mission to Syria in April—the first officially sanctioned visit by an international human rights organization since 1995. During the two-week trip, Middle East program coordinator Joel Campagna met with Syrian journalists and intellectuals and sampled Syria's new press freedom climate firsthand.

When he took office, al-Assad replaced the heads of the state-controlled media, and officials began promoting greater transparency in government. The normally rigid state papers began to publish cautious discussions about political reform and democracy, and the ruling Baath Party eventually allowed the publication of the first nonstate newspapers in nearly four decades—including the pro-regime Syrian Communist Party newspaper *Sawt al-Shaab* and the Socialist Unionist Party mouthpiece *Al-Wahdawi*. More significantly, the privately owned satirical weekly *Al-Domari* was launched in late February.

The press liberalization took place against the backdrop of a more general opening in Syrian civil society. Syrian intellectuals and activists began to issue statements urging political and social liberalization. Many began to convene discussion groups, or salons, in their homes to discuss social and political issues—actions that could have easily landed them in jail under the iron-fisted rule of Hafez al-Assad.

But the changes quickly generated a backlash from Baath Party hard-liners, and the effect was soon felt in the state press. Essays about reform and democracy disappeared, and state newspapers reverted to their old leaden style, heaping praise on the regime and launching attacks against dissidents and activists.

In June, the Ministry of Information excised two pages of *Al-Domari* that contained unflattering items about Prime Minister Muhammad Mustafa Miro.

Several other private and party newspapers were eventually allowed to publish—among them *Al-Nour*, a paper affiliated with an offshoot of the Syrian Communist Party, and the weekly economics magazine *Al-Iqtisadiya*. But they too avoided controversial political topics and any substantive criticism of the regime.

On September 22, Bashar al-Assad announced tough restrictions on the print media. While his decree took the important step of legalizing private newspapers for the first time in nearly 40 years, it also severely limited what they can print.

The decree codified strict content bans on several topics, including "national security" and "national unity." Publications can be suspended for up to six months for violating the content bans, and the prime minister can revoke the licenses of repeat offenders. The new legislation criminalized a host of vague offenses, such as publishing "falsehoods" and "fabricated reports," which carry prison terms of one to three years and fines of between 500,000 and 1 million lira (US$9,456-$18,913). Publications that violate these restrictions face suspensions of up to six months. Libel and defamation are punishable by fines and up to a year in jail.

All periodicals must obtain a license from the prime minister, who can reject any application for the sake of the "public interest." Individuals who publish without a license can be jailed for up to three months. The law also allows censorship of foreign publications—copies of which must be submitted to the Ministry of Information—and requires that journalists divulge their sources when authorities ask them to do so.

To avoid the restrictions on the local media, Syrian writers continued to express dissenting views in regional Arabic newspapers, such as Lebanon's *Al-Nahar* and London's *Al-Hayat*, or on satellite channels such as Qatar's popular Al-Jazeera.

In August, Syrian authorities appeared to close this loophole by harassing or arresting a number of Syrian writers and intellectuals who had expressed critical views about Syria in pan-Arab media.

Despite the May release of jailed journalist and human rights activist Nizar Nayyouf, who had served nine years of a 10-year sentence for allegedly disseminating false information and belonging to an unauthorized organization, authorities continued to pressure him. Shortly after his release, Nayyouf was kidnapped and held for two days, presumedly by security agents. In early September, while he was in France receiving medical treatment, Nayyouf was charged with "trying to change the constitution by illegal means and issuing false reports from a foreign country"—an offense punishable by five years in prison, according to his lawyer. The charges apparently stemmed from critical remarks Nayyouf made about the regime after his release. Authorities were also said to have harassed Nayyouf's relatives because they refused to condemn his statements.

Under Bashar al-Assad, whose government is the country's sole Internet Service Provider (ISP), public Web access continued its gradual spread. According to some estimates, there were more than 10,000 Internet users in Syria last year. Several thousand more were thought to have connected via Jordanian and Lebanese ISPs to avoid government censorship. Internet cafés also have sprung up across the country.

Web sites with content about Israel, sexual matters, or criticism of Syria's poor human rights record are frequently blocked, as are sites that allow access to free e-mail accounts, which are difficult for the government to monitor. Some newspapers' sites were also banned, but enforcement is erratic and Web surfers can easily navigate around the restrictions.

Authorities are believed to monitor e-mail traffic. In December 2000, security forces detained and held a woman for several months without charge after she forwarded an e-mail that contained an off-color cartoon of Bashar al-Assad and Lebanese president Emile Lahoud. She was released late in the year.

(See special report on page 25.)

TUNISIA

THROUGHOUT HIS 15 YEARS IN POWER, President Zine al-Abidine Ben Ali has sought to stifle all dissent while portraying Tunisia as a progressive and democratic nation. Sadly, he has had considerable success. Members of the U.S. Congress, for example, continued to heap praise on Ben Ali while ignoring his dismal human rights and press freedom record. Meanwhile, CPJ named Ben Ali to its Ten Worst Enemies of the Press list for the fourth consecutive year. (See page 597.)

Though mostly privately owned, Tunisia's press is one of the meekest in the Arab world. And for good reason: Over the years, authorities have banned some newspapers and used economic pressure to intimidate others. Journalists who criticize the regime have been assaulted, dismissed from their jobs, denied accreditation, and put under police surveillance. They have had their phone lines cut and have been prevented from leaving the country.

Other journalists, including members of the state-controlled Tunisian Journalists Association (AJT), enthusiastically perform Ben Ali's dirty work by attacking human rights activists and other critics of the regime.

Ben Ali and other officials continued to blame the press for its own submissiveness and encouraged papers to be more critical. "I will say to you once more loud and clear: Do write on any subject you choose," Ben Ali trumpeted in a May interview with the dailies *As-Sabah* and *Ech-Chourouq*. "There are no taboos except what is prohibited by law and press ethics."

While the press deserved some of the blame for its poor coverage, it was difficult to take Ben Ali's words seriously given the state's ongoing crackdown on dissent. Authorities often confiscated the few papers that were critical, such as the small, poorly funded opposition paper *Al-Mawkif*, on the rare occasions that they were printed.

In late April, parliament passed a series of cosmetic amendments to the Press Code, eliminating an ambiguously worded article prohibiting "defaming public order," eliminating prison penalties for violating advertising regulations and other restrictions, and decreasing the period of time the government can suspend newspapers.

However, Tunisian journalists continued to work in a highly restrictive environment. They faced threats, monitoring, disconnected phone service, and arrest. In January, authorities barred human rights activist Jalel Zoghlami from publishing a new newspaper, *Kaws al-Karama*, and then assaulted him and several of his supporters when they tried to distribute unlicensed copies in Tunis. Zoghlami is the brother of exiled journalist Taoufik Ben Brik, who captured international attention in 2000 when he launched a 43-day hunger strike to protest government harassment of himself and his family.

Tunisian journalists and activists have used foreign newspapers, the Internet, and satellite television to express their views. Exiled dissidents and domestic critics appear frequently on the Qatar-based satellite channel Al-Jazeera or on Al-Mustaqila, a London-based satellite channel run by a Tunisian opposition figure. Hungry for uncensored political news, many Tunisians devour the lively debates in these media.

In June, Sihem Bensedrine, a human rights activist who edits the weekly online magazine *Kalima*, was arrested upon her return to Tunisia from Europe, where she had criticized Tunisia's judiciary and human rights record on an Al-Mustaqila talk show that was broadcast in Tunisia. Bensedrine was held for six weeks and denied visits from her family and lawyers. In August, plainclothes security forces attacked a group of supporters and family members who had gathered to celebrate her August 12 release. Charges against Bensendrine were still pending at year's end.

In 2001, Tunisia protested an Al-Jazeera program featuring Bensedrine and other dissident Tunisian intellectuals.

In August, a Tunisian judge filed a complaint against Al-Mustaqila with the British Independent Television Commission (ITC), a regulatory body that oversees standards in private television. Alleging that the station had misrepresented Tunisia's political situation and personally libeled him, the judge sought sanctions against the station that could have included fines or closure. The ITC rejected that complaint, whereupon Tunisian authorities filed another in late December.

The government bans foreign publications that criticize Tunisia and also blocks access to Web sites that highlight human rights abuses in the country, including the Amnesty International site and CPJ's own site (www.cpj.org).

More than one year after an assassination attempt against former editor Riad Ben Fadhel, Ben Ali has failed to deliver on promises to bring the perpetrators to justice. Ben Fahel was wounded in a drive-by shooting outside his home in Tunis on May 23, 2000, just days after publishing a negative article about Ben Ali. The attack took place a few hundred meters from the presidential palace, one of the most secure areas in Tunisia.

Now that the ruling Constitutional Democratic Rally party appears poised to push through a constitutional amendment allowing Ben Ali to stand for an unprecedented fourth term in 2003, the prospects for press freedom appear bleak. And despite Ben Ali's abysmal record, the president has largely escaped international criticism so far. On March 19, U.S. Senator Joseph Lieberman (D-Ct.) and other Senators paid tribute to Tunisia on the 45th anniversary of its independence. Lieberman stated that "the United States and Tunisia have shared a mutual commitment to freedom, democracy, and a peaceful resolution of conflict."

TURKEY

IN AN EFFORT TO IMPROVE ITS CHANCES TO JOIN the European Union, the Turkish Parliament in October approved more than 30 amendments to the country's restrictive constitution, which was passed in 1982 after a military coup two years before.

Lawmakers are currently considering a proposal that would bring some of the nation's repressive laws used to punish expression in line with the new constitution, but it was unclear at year's end what these new laws would look like. However, critics warned that, despite the October changes, the state still has the constitutional power to censor, prosecute, and jail journalists and others for covering such controversial topics as the country's Kurdish minority, political Islam, and the military's role in national politics.

Kurdish-language broadcast media—thought permitted under the new amendments—can still be censored if it threatens "national security" or "unity." And even with the modified language of other amendments, the government will still be able to prosecute journalists or suspend newspapers thought to conduct anti-state "activity."

But there could be some short-term benefits. Some observers think that many journalists and critics currently jailed could be released if certain laws are revised or dropped. These legal changes could result in the suspension of dozens— possibly hundreds—of court cases against journalists or activists prosecuted for their statements or writing. It is also possible that some of the 13 Turkish journalists who continue to languish in jail could be freed.

Even as Parliament tried to make Turkey's laws more palatable to the democracies of the EU, authorities continued to prosecute journalists and censor publications. While alternative pro-Kurdish, leftist, and Islamist media were primarily targeted, several prominent, mainstream journalists also faced legal harassment.

In February, free-lance journalist Metin Munir was charged with "insulting" the Turkish judiciary and faced a six-year prison sentence for an article he wrote criticizing the appointment of a state prosecutor with alleged links to organized crime. Two months later, Fehmi Koru, a columnist for the Islamist-leaning daily *Yeni Safak* and a well-known political commentator, was tried for allegedly inciting "enmity and hatred" after criticizing secular Turks for being intolerant of Islamist views during a 1999 television appearance. He faces up to four years in prison if convicted.

In another prominent prosecution, Nese Deuzel, a respected journalist with the daily *Radikal*, was indicted in three separate cases for articles and interviews she published about the Alevi religious minority and drug trafficking. Popular liberal columnist Ahmet Altan, meanwhile, endured at least three criminal cases during the year because he criticized the military's involvement in politics.

One Turkish journalist was jailed in 2001: Fikret Baksaya was sentenced to 16 months in prison for a column he wrote in 1999 criticizing state policies toward the country's Kurdish minority. Baksaya joined 12 other Turkish journalists who were in prison, mainly because of their affiliation with leftist or pro-Kurdish publications. While this number represents a dramatic decline from several years ago, dozens of Turkish journalists and writers are believed to be facing prosecution and the prospect of jail.

Authorities continued to ban or confiscate newspapers and books, especially leftist, pro-Kurdish, and pro-Islamist publications. In August 2001, a Turkish court banned the book *Temple of Fear* by journalist Celal Baslangic because it allegedly insulted the army by implicating Turkish security forces in human rights abuses. However, authorities took no action to censor the same articles when they were originally published in the daily *Radikal*.

Even prevailing in court does not always end journalists' travails. Free-lancer Nadire Mater, the author of a previously banned book, was acquitted in 2000 on charges of insulting the military. Then, in the summer of 2001, *Hurriyet* columnist Emin Colaslan and *Cumhuriyet* columnist Deniz Som published a series of spurious columns attacking Mater and the fact that she had received a grant from the liberal John D. and Catherine T. MacArthur Foundation, which they accused of being a CIA-backed organization. Some Turkish journalists privately speculated that the military was behind the smear campaign, although no conclusive evidence was found.

Journalists did not escape Turkey's severe economic crisis, which erupted after a public feud between President Ahmet Nedcet Sezer and Prime Minister Bulent

Ecevit over government efforts to combat official corruption triggered a run on the national currency in February. Between 3,000 and 5,000 media workers were laid off in two months, and media companies complained of lower advertising, circulation, and revenue. While the economic situation was indeed dire, many journalists charged that management exploited the crisis to fire enterprising journalists who frequently covered controversial topics.

The layoffs also highlighted Turkish journalists' perennial complaint: the concentration of media ownership and the negative effect it has on the diversity of opinions and the coverage of sensitive issues. For years, two private holding companies, Dogan Medya and Sabah, have controlled much of the print and broadcast media. The Sabah group plunged into crisis in 2001 when its head, Dinc Bilgin, was jailed on embezzlement and corruption charges; the turmoil left the Dogan group in control of more than 60 percent of Turkey's media.

The corporate-controlled, mainstream media continued to suffer from its usual vices, including self-censorship, editorial censorship, and ideological prejudice. The major papers often avoided criticizing the military and high-level corruption.

While private radio and television stations have proliferated in Turkey since the mid-1990s when the government began permitting private broadcasting, authorities applied tough laws and regulations to close or censor certain channels. In several cases, the Supreme Radio and Television Board (RTUK), a regulatory body established in 1994 with broad powers to sanction broadcast outlets, suspended television and radio stations for airing violent, sensational, or politically controversial programming. During 2001, Turkish-language broadcasts of the BBC and the German national station Deutsche Welle were banned because they harmed "national security."

In June, President Sezer vetoed a worrisome RTUK law that would have increased fines for violating RTUK regulations, relaxed restrictions on media ownership, and subjected Internet publications to harsh restrictions and punishments, much like traditional media. Even though no specific legislation exists regulating the Internet, authorities did punish Web users whose content they deemed inappropriate. In March, Coskun Ak, who administered an online discussion forum for the Internet company Superonline, was sentenced to 40 months in prison for insulting the state in a harsh critique of government human rights abuses that was posted on the discussion forum by an unknown participant. Ak was held liable because he failed to remove the posting.

UNITED ARAB EMIRATES

THE UNITED ARAB EMIRATES, IN PARTICULAR THE EMIRATE OF DUBAI, has transformed itself into a center for media and new information technology. In 2001, the emirate launched Dubai Media City to serve as a regional news hub for international media organizations, along with a separate Internet City. Dubai also began providing government services online. Citizens can now use the Web to pay traffic fines or get driver's licenses, for example. Despite these innovations, authorities use filtering technology to block sexually explicit and politically sensitive Internet content.

As far as print media are concerned, the government tolerates little criticism, and self-censorship is endemic when it comes to government affairs, the ruling family, and religion. Journalists who have dared to broach these topics frankly have been detained and threatened.

Authorities also prescreen foreign publications that enter the country.

YEMEN

WHILE YEMEN IS KNOWN FOR ITS VOCAL INDEPENDENT and opposition press, the practice of journalism carries considerable risk. In 2001, the government continued to use criminal prosecutions, censorship, arrests, and intimidation against the press.

For years, officials have prosecuted journalists under Yemen's vaguely worded Press and Publications Law and Penal Code, which prohibits criticizing the president and bars any news that "jeopardizes the supreme interests of the state" or might cause "discrimination" on the basis of tribe, sect, or region. Offenders face stiff prison penalties, bans on practicing journalism, and the closure of their newspapers. In some cases, courts have sentenced journalists to flogging.

In May, an appellate court sentenced editor Seif al-Hadheri of the weekly *Al-Shoumou* to a six-month suspended prison term and a fine of 1 million Yemeni riyals (about US$6,250) for articles he wrote in 2000 accusing the education minister of financial impropriety. The newspaper was also suspended for one month, and al-Hadheri was barred from practicing journalism for one year.

Two weeks later, the Supreme Court upheld a 1997 lower court decision suspending the opposition weekly *Al Shoura* for six months. The Supreme Court also upheld a sentence of 80 lashes against the paper's former editor, a punishment that he escaped only when the plaintiff dropped the suit.

Political Security officers and other state agents have earned a reputation over the years for harassing and intimidating journalists, and 2001 proved no different. *Yemen Times* correspondent Hassan al-Zaidi was detained and questioned three times in seven months over his reporting about the kidnappings of Europeans in Yemen.

In a country where the literacy rate is just over 50 percent, television is more influential than newspapers. The government, however, maintained tight control over the country's broadcast media, which provided—not surprisingly—one-dimensional, pro-government coverage.

Some foreign journalists who visited the country after the September 11 attacks on the United States encountered restrictions on their ability to travel outside the capital, Sanaa. Some foreign journalists were required to inform security agents of their destinations when leaving their hotels, while agents trailed other correspondents. ■

| CASES TABLE OF CONTENTS |

ALGERIA

Al-Ahram al-Arabi
CENSORED

Algerian authorities banned the distribution of the January 13 edition of the Egyptian weekly magazine *Al-Ahram al-Arabi*. That week's issue contained an article reporting on alleged conflicts between President Abdelaziz Bouteflika and the influential Algerian military.

The issue also included an interview with the Moroccan foreign minister, who spoke of deteriorating relations between Algeria and Morocco.

JUNE 14

Fadila Nejma, *Echourouk*
KILLED
Adel Zerrouk, *Al-Rai*
KILLED

Two Algerian journalists were killed while covering mass anti-government protests organized by Berber community leaders in the capital, Algiers.

Nejma, a reporter for the Arabic weekly *Echourouk*, died after being struck by a speeding bus during the protests. Nejma suffered severe chest and leg injuries and died later in the hospital.

Local journalists and press sources reported that the bus driver ran over Nejma while trying to escape demonstrators intent on torching his bus, or that one of the protesters had commandeered the vehicle and was trying to crash it into local security forces.

Also killed was Zerrouk, a reporter with the Arabic daily *Al-Rai*. Some CPJ sources and local press reports stated that Zerrouk died after a crowd of protesters trampled him. According to other reports, however, the journalist was hit by the same bus that killed Nejma.

JULY 11

Faouzia Ababsa, *L'Authentique*
LEGAL ACTION

Ababsa, managing editor of the French-language daily *L'Authentique*, was convicted in absentia of defaming Abdelkarim Mahmoudi, president of the Confederation of Finance Managers, a private trade association. The charge was based on a May 2000 article in which the journalist accused Mahmoudi of misusing the organization's funds.

Ababsa told CPJ that four months prior to the verdict, she had testified before a judge in connection with the defamation charges. But Ababsa only became aware of the trial on July 12, when she learned from an article in the newspaper *Echourouk* that she had received a suspended six-month prison sentence and a 1500 dinar (US$20) fine.

Rather than appeal the verdict, Ababsa rejected it altogether and wrote to the Ministry of Justice demanding an official investigation of the trial.

On July 25, CPJ issued an alert about the case.

BAHRAIN

NOVEMBER 11

Hafedh al-Shaikh Saleh, *Akhbar al-Khaleej*
LEGAL ACTION

Saleh, a writer for the Bahraini daily *Akhbar al-Khaleej* and a contributor to several Arab papers, faced charges of "harming national unity." The charges, filed by the Ministry of Information, were ostensibly based on unspecified articles that Saleh had published in *Akhbar al-Khaleej*. The journalist was released after posting bail of 50 dinars (US$133).

Saleh told CPJ that he suspects the charges actually stemmed from a November 4 article, published in the Lebanese newspaper *The Daily Star*, in which he criticized Bahrain's foreign policy toward the United States.

Officials reportedly told *Akhbar al Khaleej* not to publish Saleh's articles. According to the Bahrain Human Rights Society, the Information Ministry announced that it intended to contact other Gulf governments in an attempt to prevent regional media from publishing Saleh's work. Saleh appeared in court again after the Muslim fasting month of Ramadan, which ended around December 15.

The court ruled in Saleh's favor. In early January, state prosecutors dropped their appeal against the ruling.

EGYPT

JANUARY 18

Abdel Halim Qandil, *Al-Arabi*
LEGAL ACTION
Abdullah Sennawy, *Al-Arabi*
LEGAL ACTION
Al-Arabi
LEGAL ACTION

The family of former Egyptian president Anwar Sadat filed a US$1.3 million criminal defamation case against the Nasserist opposition weekly *Al-Arabi* and its editors, Qandil and Sennawy.

The case stemmed from a special issue of the paper, published December 31, 2000, under the title "Abdel Nasser: Hero of the Century. Sadat: the Greatest Traitor." The edition was a retrospective of Egypt in the 20th century.

In addition to the $1.3 million in damages, the case called for the imprisonment of Qandil and Sennawy and a three-month ban on the newspaper.

The Sadat family later agreed to drop the case after the newspaper published an apology on February 11, 2001.

SEPTEMBER 16

Mamdouh Mahran, *Al-Nabaa*
IMPRISONED

Mahran, editor of the controversial weekly newspaper *Al-Nabaa*, was sentenced to three years in prison and fined 200 Egyptian pounds (about US$50) for allegedly undermining public security, publishing scandalous photos, insulting religion, and causing civil turmoil.

The charges stemmed from a June 17 *Al-Nabaa* cover story alleging that a Coptic Christian monk had sex with several women in a Coptic monastery in southern Egypt and filmed the encounters to blackmail the women. The piece was accompanied by provocative photos.

The *Al-Nabaa* article led to demonstrations and riots among Egypt's Coptic minority, who viewed the story as an insult to their religion.

Coptic Church officials vehemently denied that sexual acts had taken place in the monastery and pointed out that the monk in question had been defrocked five years earlier, a fact omitted from *Al-Nabaa*'s account.

Mahran was not present in court for the verdict, but according to a legal expert quoted in the semiofficial Egyptian daily *Al-Ahram* on September 17, Mahran's sentence was enforceable immediately and could not be appealed.

The September 16 ruling also ordered the confiscation of the offending edition, as well as that of the daily *Akher Khabar*, also edited by Mahran. *Akher Khabar* ran an article about the alleged scandal one day after the *Al-Nabaa* cover story.

Previously, on July 4, an administrative court revoked *Al-Nabaa*'s and *Akher Khabar*'s publishing licenses over the articles.

In a September 20 press release, CPJ condemned Mahran's sentence, noting that, "While we understand that many Egyptians were offended by the *Al-Nabaa* article, CPJ believes that journalists should not face criminal prosecution for their work."

The day before he was to begin his sentence, Mahran reportedly suffered a heart attack. At press time he was under guard at a private heart trauma center in Cairo.

IRAN

January 17

Kiyan
LEGAL ACTION, CENSORED

Iranian state radio and television announced the closure of the monthly cultural and intellectual magazine *Kiyan*. Judge Saeed Mortazavi, head of Tehran's Press Court, ordered the magazine shut down, claiming it had "published lies, disturbed public opinion and insulted sacred law."

The closure was reportedly based on complaints filed by prosecutor general Abbassali Alizadeh. No specific offending articles were cited.

January 27

Naghi Afshari, *Hadis*
IMPRISONED
Hadis
CENSORED

Afshari, editor of the weekly *Hadis*, was arrested for publishing articles and cartoons deemed "insulting" and "critical" of the Iranian courts. The Tehran Press Court banned *Hadis* on January 28.

On January 29, Ashari was released on bail pending charges. CPJ was unable to obtain any further information about the case by press time.

February 11

Mohammad Bagher Vali-Beik,
Jameah-e-Ruz
IMPRISONED

Vali-Beik, director of the Jameah-e-Ruz publishing house, which has published several leading reformist newspapers since 1997, was arrested by order of the Tehran Press Court.

According to local press reports, Vali-Beik was accused of "supervising crimes committed by four newspapers." No details were provided.

Vali-Beik was released on bail on February 21 pending trial.

MARCH 8

Harim
LEGAL ACTION, CENSORED

Iran's Press Court suspended the conservative weekly newspaper *Harim* for allegedly defaming President Muhammad Khatami. The closure reportedly came after the newspaper published an article titled, "The Slogans of Mr. K," which criticized the president over his campaign promises to establish the rule of law and a civic society in Iran.

MARCH 18

Jameah Madani
LEGAL ACTION, CENSORED
Mobine
LEGAL ACTION, CENSORED
Doran-e-Emrooz
LEGAL ACTION, CENSORED
Payam-e-Emrooz
LEGAL ACTION, CENSORED

Tehran's Press Court ordered the closure of four pro-reform publications: the weeklies *Jameah Madani* and *Mobine*, the daily *Doran-e-Emrooz*, and the monthly *Payam-e-Emrooz*.

State-controlled television reported that the action was taken because the four publications committed "numerous and continuous violations of the law." No further details were provided.

APRIL 25

Amin-e-Zanjan
LEGAL ACTION, CENSORED

The state news agency IRNA reported that a local court had banned the weekly *Amin-e-Zanjan* for "sowing seeds of discord." The court also said

that the paper's content was likely "to provoke riots in the city."

The paper's director and other staff members were charged with "disrupting security and tranquility." It was not clear which articles prompted the ban.

MAY 9

Hamid Jafari Nasrabadi, *Kavir*
IMPRISONED
Mahmoud Mojdavi, *Kavir*
IMPRISONED

Nasrabadi, director of the Shahid Rajai University student magazine *Kavir*, and Mojdavi, a writer at the paper, were arrested by order of Tehran's Press Court in connection with an allegedly "indecent" article by Mojdavi. According to press reports, the seven-page article, titled "Trial of the Universal Creator," described fictitious proceedings in which God was put on trial. Officials said the article carried an "indecent tone and insulting interpretations."

Nasrabadi and Mojdavi were reportedly sentenced in December to five and three years respectively.

Nowsazi
LEGAL ACTION, CENSORED

Tehran's Press Court suspended the reformist daily *Nowsazi*, alleging that its editor, Hamid Reza Jalaiepour, was not competent to publish the paper. The court further alleged that Jalaiepour published other banned papers that printed so-called criminal material. No further details were provided.

Prior to the ban, *Nowsazi* had only published four editions. A staff member from the paper told Agence France-Presse that the publication received a fax from the Justice Department indicating that the paper's license had been withdrawn.

Abbas Dalvand, *Lorestan*
LEGAL ACTION

An Iranian Press Court in the province of Lorestan sentenced Dalvand, director of the weekly *Lorestan*, to nine months in prison and barred him from working as a journalist for three years. Dalvand was convicted of "slander, affront, libel, and spreading lies and publishing falsehoods," according to the conservative daily newspaper *Kayhan*.

The Press Court judge reduced Dalvand's sentence from 21 months and lifted an additional sentence of 90 lashes.

According to *Kayhan*, "the jury found the accused guilty of libel, slander and insult of the former head of the health network of Aligudarz, slander of a number of legal institutions and publishing satire in prose and printing falsehood against the Law Enforcement Force and the relief committee presumably the Imam Khomeyni Relief Committee."

Dalvand was arrested on February 14 and released on February 18 after posting bail. At press time he was free pending review of his appeal.

JUNE 10

John Simpson, BBC
ATTACKED

Simpson, a veteran BBC reporter, and a two-member camera crew were attacked by members of the extremist Ansar-e-Hezbollah militia while covering Iran's presidential elections.

According to Simpson, between eight and 10 Ansar-e-Hezbollah members surrounded him and his crew and tried to confiscate their camera equipment as they filmed crowds celebrating President Muhammad Khatami's June 8 reelection. When the crewmembers resisted, they were punched and kicked, Simpson said.

Police then intervened and pushed the journalists into a car, during which time one of the assailants poked Simpson in the eye. The journalists were taken to a police station and held for about three hours before an apologetic government official released them at 3:30 a.m.

JUNE 26

Arman
LEGAL ACTION, CENSORED

On or about June 26, Iranian judicial authorities ordered the Yazd University campus magazine *Arman* closed. The closure reportedly came after unspecified Islamic and cultural groups issued complaints about some of the publication's articles.

JUNE 30

Morteza Taghi Pour, *Faryad*
IMPRISONED
Ruzbeh Shafii, *Faryad*
IMPRISONED
Mohammad Reza Shirvand, *Faryad*
IMPRISONED

On or about June 30, Taghi Pour, director of the Khajeh-Nassir-Tussi Technical University campus magazine *Faryad*, and Shafii and Shirvand, writers for the magazine, were arrested by order of the Tehran Revolutionary Court. The arrests reportedly came in response to an allegedly offensive article the magazine published about the Twelfth Imam, an important figure in the Shi'a Islamic tradition.

The state news agency IRNA reported on July 30 that the case against the three journalists had originally been filed in a Public Court but was later transferred to a Revolutionary Court. The three journalists were released in late August 2001.

JULY 16

Akbar Ganji, *Sobh-e-Emrooz, Fat'h*
IMPRISONED, LEGAL ACTION

Ganji, a well-known investigative journalist whose reporting on the 1998 murders of several Iranian intellectuals and dissidents implicated senior government officials, was sentenced to six years in jail on charges of collecting confidential information that harmed national security and spreading propaganda against the Islamic system.

The charges stemmed from Ganji's participation in a controversial April 2000 conference in Berlin on the future of the Iranian reform movement. Ganji was arrested when he returned to Iran on April 22, 2000, and was charged with Press Law violations based on his published work. His public remarks during the Berlin conference were used to justify the charges of threatening national security and spreading propaganda against the Islamic regime.

In January 2001, the Revolutionary Court initially sentenced Ganji to 10 years in prison, followed by five years of internal exile. In May, an appellate

court reduced Ganji's punishment to six months in prison, though he had already served more than a year.

The Iranian Justice Department then appealed to the Supreme Court, arguing that the appellate court had committed errors in commuting the original 10-year sentence, IRNA, the Iranian news agency, reported.

The Supreme Court overturned the appellate court's decision and referred the case to a different appeals court, which sentenced Ganji to six years in prison on July 16. According to IRNA, the ruling was "definitive," meaning that it could not be appealed.

In a July 16 statement, CPJ condemned the new sentencing. "This judgment clearly shows that certain powers in Iran are intent on keeping Ganji and his colleagues behind bars at all costs," said CPJ executive director Ann Cooper.

AUGUST 4

Farday-e-Rochan
LEGAL ACTION, CENSORED

Judicial authorities revoked the license of *Farday-e-Rochan*, a weekly based in the western town of Zanjan, for allegedly publishing false and defamatory articles.

The state news agency IRNA reported that conservative organizations had filed several complaints against the publication but provided no further information.

AUGUST 8

Hambasteghi
CENSORED

Tehran's Press Court suspended the

moderate reformist daily *Hambasteghi* following an unspecified complaint from Iranian judicial authorities.

The closure came shortly after the paper published the comments of a pro-reform parliament member who accused the head of the judiciary, Mahmoud Hashemi Shahroudi, of "acting outside the interest of Iranians."

The closure, which took place the same day reformist president Muhammad Khatami delivered a speech about press freedom, was interpreted as a snub from the conservative judiciary.

On August 20, judicial authorities issued a statement saying that the ban on *Hambasteghi* was lifted after the paper's managing editor acknowledged having published "mistakes" and "insulting articles." Shahroudi reportedly approved the move.

SEPTEMBER 8

Mehr
LEGAL ACTION, CENSORED

On or about September 8, Iran's Special Court for Clergy, a conservative tribunal that operates independently of the regular Iranian court system, ordered the indefinite closure of the weekly cultural magazine *Mehr*, reportedly for "spreading lies to public opinion."

The precise reason for the closure was unclear. However, some press reports noted that the magazine had criticized the country's broadcast media, which are controlled by conservative forces, in a recent edition.

SEPTEMBER 20

Rahiyan-e-Feyziyeh
CENSORED

A court in the city of Qom closed the conservative local weekly *Rahiyan-e-Feyziyeh* for "insulting" government officials. The paper had accused President Muhammad Khatami, Interior Minister Abdolvahed Musavi-Lari, and former culture minister Ayatollah Mohajerani of "betraying religion."

OCTOBER 30

Omid-e-Zanjan
CENSORED

Publication of the reformist weekly *Omid-e-Zanjan* was suspended after a court in the northwest city of Zanjan found the paper guilty of printing stories that allegedly defamed Iranian government officials and the Islamic Republic, according to local sources.

In addition, the paper's editor, Ja'afar Karami, received a two-year suspended sentence. He was charged with "creating a schism among people's ranks." Karami was given 20 days to appeal the court's decision, but the case was still pending at press time.

NOVEMBER 29

Mellat
LEGAL ACTION, CENSORED

The Tehran Press Court closed the reformist daily *Mellat*, allegedly to prevent it from fomenting "crises and insecurity," according to the state news agency IRNA.

Court officials claimed that *Mellat* had ignored previous warnings, IRNA reported. It was not clear which particular articles provoked the closing.

ISRAEL AND THE OCCUPIED TERRITORIES

FEBRUARY 9

Laurent van der Stock, *Newsweek*
ATTACKED

Van der Stock, 36, a veteran photographer working for the GAMMA photo agency and *Newsweek* magazine, was struck in the left knee by a live bullet while covering clashes between Palestinian demonstrators and Israeli troops near the West Bank town of Ramallah. The bullet entered above his knee and exited through the back of his leg, severing an artery and causing nerve damage.

At the time of the incident, van der Stock and several other photojournalists had been covering clashes near the City Inn Hotel, along Ramallah's border with its sister city, Al-Bireh, for about two hours. An Israeli army position composed of soldiers in jeeps was located about 100 meters away from the hotel. According to journalists at the scene, armed Israeli troops were also stationed in buildings situated on the high ground behind the jeeps, some 500 meters (546 yards) from the journalists.

According to the journalists, Palestinian demonstrators had launched several attacks on the Israeli jeeps, using stones, pipes, and slingshots. The soldiers responded by exiting their jeeps and opening fire with rubber bullets, tear gas, and stun grenades. Palestinian gunmen in buildings along the main road also fired sporadically on the Israeli positions in the course of the afternoon.

At about 3:15 p.m., van der Stock ventured into the middle of the road during clashes in order to photograph Palestinian youths retreating from an Israel Defense Forces (IDF) counterattack. "I understood the demonstrators would run back, so I ran [out] about 20 seconds ahead of time and photographed people running [retreating] toward me," van der Stock told CPJ. "I was shot in the [left] knee."

Van der Stock described the situation just prior to the incident as chaotic but added that anyone firing live ammunition into the crowd should have known that he was a photographer, since he carried two cameras around his neck.

In a telephone interview, IDF spokesman Olivier Rafowicz told CPJ that IDF troops and Palestinian gunmen were engaged in a fierce gun battle at the time van der Stock was shot. Because of the general confusion and because the bullet that entered the photographer's leg was never retrieved, the army was unable to determine who fired the shot, Rafowicz claimed.

Nonetheless, van der Stock and eyewitnesses interviewed by CPJ maintained that the shot was likely fired by an Israeli soldier stationed either on the ground or in a nearby building. "The way the bullet came and hit him straight in the knee, there was no doubt it came from straight ahead [i.e., the Israeli positions]," one photographer at the scene told CPJ. "The Palestinian gunmen who were firing earlier were in the buildings...100 meters [109 yards] to the left and right but behind Laurent. His back would have been to the Palestinian gunmen...From what I saw...it would have to be a ballistic miracle for him to have been hit by Palestinian fire." Moreover, journalists on the scene added that gunfire from the Palestinian side had ceased for some time before van der Stock was shot.

On March 13, CPJ wrote the IDF spokesman's office to urge the IDF to launch a serious and thorough investigation to determine if one of its soldiers in fact fired the round that injured Laurent van der Stock, and for what reason. CPJ also requested that the IDF release the findings of this investigation, along with any additional information that might shed light on the incident. The IDF responded that it was looking into the incident and promised to reply in detail to CPJ's concerns.

On December 17, 2001, CPJ received a faxed document from Israel's Government Press Office, titled "Report on Injury of Foreign Journalists Covering the Violence in the West Bank and Gaza and Operational Procedures Implemented by the IDF."

The report claimed that it was impossible to establish that van der Stock was hit by IDF fire, adding that several attempts were made to have the photographer speak directly to the brigade commander so a more thorough investigation could be conducted, but that these attempts were unsuccessful.

FEBRUARY 11

Luay Abu Haikal, *Reuters*
`ATTACKED`
Hussam Abu Alan, Agence France-Presse
`ATTACKED, THREATENED`

Abu Haikal and Abu Alan, photographers for Reuters and Agence France-Presse, respectively, were attacked by two Jewish settlers while covering clashes between Palestinian youths and Israeli soldiers in the West Bank city of Hebron.

Abu Haikal told CPJ that when he tried to defend himself from attack by pushing the settlers back, an Israeli soldier struck him in the neck with a rifle butt.

The soldier then aimed the rifle at Abu Allan's head and threatened to shoot him, according to the journalists.

The soldier temporarily confiscated the journalists' identification cards, which were returned after their respective news agencies were contacted.

FEBRUARY 16

Al-Quds
`CENSORED`
Al-Hayat al-Jadida
`CENSORED`
Al-Ayyam
`CENSORED`

From February 16 to 20, Israeli authorities barred editions of three Palestinian daily newspapers from entering the Gaza Strip. The measure was part of a closure of the Gaza Strip imposed by Israel in response to an attack on Israeli soldiers by Palestinian militants.

MARCH 8

Christine Hauser, Reuters
`ATTACKED`
Ahmed Bahadou, Reuters
`ATTACKED`
Suhaib Salem, Reuters
`ATTACKED`

An Israel Defense Forces (IDF) soldier in an armored carrier opened fire in the direction of three Reuters journalists at the Netzarim Junction in the Gaza Strip. Reporter

Hauser, cameraman Bahadou, and free-lance photographer Salem were about 50 meters (160 feet) from the armored carrier when the soldier started firing a heavy machine gun in their direction. The journalists quickly took cover.

Reuters reported that when the shooting occurred, Bahadou and Salem were pointing their cameras in the opposite direction from the carrier, and that Hauser had taken out her notebook. The journalists believed they had made eye contact with the IDF soldiers in order to assure them that they were press. The Netzarim Junction was described as quiet at the time.

Army spokesman Olivier Rafowicz later characterized the gunfire as "warning shots," claiming the journalists had violating IDF policy by approaching the outpost. Due to the "tense security situation in Gaza," Rafowicz told Reuters, "civilians are not allowed to approach...outposts because of a present threat of terror activity." He added that the journalists failed to inform the IDF ahead of time of their presence in the area.

However, Reuters pointed out that the IDF requires no such notification from journalists working there. Hauser later said that contrary to what the Israeli army reported, the journalists were walking away from the IDF post when the shooting occurred.

In a March 13 letter to Prime Minister Ariel Sharon, CPJ urged him to ensure that the IDF launched an immediate and thorough investigation into the incident and made its findings public. CPJ received no response from the Israeli government or the IDF.

In a June 19 response to CPJ's

research, Israel's embassy in Washington, D.C., wrote that an "investigation was launched the day of the incident. The investigation found that the soldiers involved acted within IDF guidelines. An official statement from the IDF Spokesman was issued."

MARCH 10

Mazen Dana, Reuters
ATTACKED
Nael Shiyoukhi, Reuters
ATTACKED
Hussam Abu Alan, Agence France-Presse
ATTACKED

Reuters cameramen Dana and Shiyoukhi and Agence France-Presse photographer Abu Alan were attacked at around 4 p.m. by Jewish settlers in the West Bank town of Hebron.

The journalists were filming settlers throwing stones and empty bottles at local Palestinian residents near the Jewish settlement neighborhood of Tel Rumeida.

Dana was struck in the leg by a bottle and in the face by a stone, which cut his lip and broke three teeth. The settlers also threatened to smash the journalists' cameras. Shiyoukhi, meanwhile, was kicked in the leg and hit in the neck with a stone before fleeing.

Israeli soldiers finally intervened and escorted Dana and Abu Alan away from the scene of the attack. However, the journalists were again attacked by a separate group of Jewish settlers, who broke Abu Alan's camera. All three photographers were taken to a hospital for treatment.

CPJ protested the attacks in a March 13 letter to Israeli prime minister Ariel Sharon, urging that the settlers responsible for the assault be prosecuted to the fullest extent of the law.

MARCH 26

Amer al-Jaberi, ABC News
`ATTACKED`
Nael Shiyoukhi, Reuters
`ATTACKED`
Hussam Abu Alan, Agence France-Presse
`ATTACKED`

Israeli soldiers attacked Jabari, a cameraman for ABC News; Shiyoukhi, a cameraman for Reuters; and Abu Alan, a photographer for Agence France-Presse, while they were covering a Palestinian demonstration in the West Bank village of Halhoul.

According to Shiyoukhi, an officer approached the journalists and ordered them to evacuate the area in exactly one minute or face arrest. He gave no reason for the order.

When the journalists did not leave, soldiers began to push them, and one punched Jabari in the nose. Shiyoukhi was pushed against a military jeep. He also reported that an officer would have arrested him had a group of women not intervened.

Abu Alan, who was watching the incident, was struck with a rifle butt.

The Israeli army alleged that the cameramen were preventing the soldiers from performing their work, and that one had attacked a commander. The cameramen denied these allegations

APRIL 20

Layla Odeh, Abu Dhabi TV
`ATTACKED`

Odeh, a correspondent for the United Arab Emirates-based Abu Dhabi TV, was shot by Israeli troops at about 1 p.m. while she and two colleagues were interviewing residents in the town of Rafah whose homes had been destroyed by Israel Defense Forces (IDF), the journalist told CPJ.

Without warning, two shots were fired in the journalists' direction from a nearby IDF position. When the crew attempted to flee the scene, a third shot was fired, striking Odeh in the back of her thigh. She was taken to the Shifa hospital, where she underwent surgery to remove the bullet.

Odeh and her colleagues reported that no clashes were taking place in their vicinity at the time of the shooting. They also maintained they were clearly identifiable as journalists due to their conspicuous camera equipment. Video footage appeared to confirm their account.

IDF spokesman Olivier Rafowicz expressed regret for the incident and said that an IDF investigation was under way. He told CPJ that "there was no intention to hit the journalists" and added that the TV crew had been in a dangerous "area of violence."

On April 25, CPJ protested the attack in a letter to Prime Minister Ariel Sharon and urged him to ensure that Israeli authorities launched a thorough investigation into this incident, as well as other similar cases involving journalists wounded by Israeli gunfire.

In a June 7 letter to CPJ, Prime Minister Sharon's spokesman Raanan Gissin wrote that the Odeh incident was "under official IDF investigation," but said he "cannot release any of the findings yet." He added that "the Prime Minister and the IDF are serious about examining this matter thoroughly."

On June 11, a CPJ delegation met with the Israeli ambassador to the U.S., David Ivry, and presented him with the Odeh case and those of 15 other journalists wounded by live rounds or rubber-coated steel bullets since violence erupted in the occupied territories in late September 2001.

In response to CPJ's research, the embassy wrote on June 19: "There was an investigation into this incident. The investigation revealed that Ms. Odeh was hit by a rubber bullet fired from a raised lookout position. The severity of her injuries was due to the use of rubber bullets from this position. Because use of rubber bullets in this situation were found to be dangerous, their use has been forbidden in such cases."

The ambassador also promised to send a detailed report to the Foreign Ministry in Jerusalem and to the IDF asking for their immediate attention to the specific incidents highlighted by CPJ. In December, the IDF said the case was still under review.

MAY 15

Bertrand Aguirre, TF1
ATTACKED

Aguirre, a reporter for the French television channel TF1, was wounded in the chest by a live round while covering clashes between Israeli troops and Palestinian demonstrators near the West Bank city of Ramallah.

Aguirre had just finished a stand-up report when an Israeli border policeman opened fire from about 150 to 200 meters (218 yards) away. A single round struck the journalist in the chest. Aguirre's bulletproof vest most likely saved his life.

Aguirre was standing about 50 to 100 meters (54 to 109 yards) behind stone-throwing Palestinian demonstrators who were between him and the border policeman. The incident occurred during a lull in the clashes, according to eyewitnesses.

While it is uncertain whether the soldier was aiming at Aguirre, video footage shows the soldier opening fire in the direction of unarmed demonstrators and journalists. The footage shows that he was not in a life-threatening situation and had violated the IDF's rules of engagement.

"It's clear that the soldier opened fire with live ammunition on an unarmed crowd and that he was shooting to kill. Was he aiming at me or not? I can't tell that," Aguirre told CPJ. The journalist contended that he was easily recognizable as a reporter since he was holding a microphone and wearing a conspicuous white flak jacket as he stood alongside his camera crew.

On June 21, Danny Seaman, director of the Government Press Office's Foreign Press Department, told CPJ that an internal police investigation into Aguirre's shooting was under way. Investigators had received video footage of the incident, Seaman said, along with the bullet that wounded the journalist.

The investigation, Seaman said, was taking place under the jurisdiction of the Ministry of Justice. He reported that if any evidence of wrongdoing was found, the Justice Ministry might initiate a criminal prosecution. Seaman said the results of the investigation were expected to be released in late June.

In September, the Justice Ministry dismissed the case for what it said was lack of evidence. A report of the investigation dated November 20 contained a lengthy account of the Justice Ministry's investigation of the Aguirre case. After interviewing the Israeli soldier who fired the shot, other soldiers, and journalists on the scene, the investigator concluded that "it is impossible to make the connection with certainty between the shot fired by the suspect and the wounding of the journalist because the whole picture is not present.... In my opinion, it is appropriate to close the case due to lack of evidence."

JUNE 26

Hazem Bader, Associated Press Television News
ATTACKED

Bader, a free-lance cameraman working with The Associated Press Television News, came under heavy machine gun fire while riding in his car in the West Bank city of Hebron.

At around dusk, Bader was driving home from an assignment when his car was attacked in the Palestinian-controlled Bab al-Zawiyah section of the city. Bader said the gunfire came from an Israel Defense Forces (IDF) outpost near the Jewish settlement of Tel Rumeida, about 500 meters away.

The first round of shots hit a wall just a few meters from his car, forcing him to exit the vehicle and take cover. Ten seconds later, Bader said, another round struck a nearby streetlight. A few minutes later, five or six rounds were fired directly at his car, three of which struck the vehicle.

Bader told CPJ that the street where the attack occurred was empty and peaceful. "It was an open and clear

area," Bader said. "No one was moving in the area." He added that his car was plastered with Arabic, Hebrew, and English stickers that clearly identified it as a press vehicle.

IDF spokesman Olivier Rafowicz told CPJ that he had no information about the incident but added that the IDF had received a letter of inquiry from the AP and was "looking into it." Israeli authorities had taken no action on the case by year's end.

JULY 9

Hussam Abu Alan, Agence France-Presse
ATTACKED
Mazen Dana, Reuters
ATTACKED
Nael Shiyoukhi, Reuters
ATTACKED
Imad al-Said, Associated Press Television News
ATTACKED

Jewish settlers in the West Bank city of Hebron attacked Dana and Shiyoukhi, cameramen for Reuters; Abu Alan, a photographer for Agence France Presse; and al-Said, a cameraman for Associated Press Television News.

The journalists were covering settlers attacking a Palestinian wedding party in the Al-Raf section of the city, across from the large Jewish settlement of Kiryat Arba.

After they arrived at the scene, the photographers began filming the violence from 20 to 30 meters away, until Israeli border police ordered them to leave the area. They moved to a different location and resumed filming the settlers, who were throwing stones at cars and homes. Some of the settlers turned on the journalists and threw stones at them.

One settler pointed his machine gun at the cameras of Shyioukhi and al-Said. Abu Alan was beaten by another settler. None of the journalists were seriously injured, although Abu Alan sustained slight injuries to his face and neck.

According to the journalists, the soldiers and police who were present did nothing to stop the attacks.

JULY 29

Amar Awad, Reuters
`ATTACKED`
Mahfouz Abu Turk, Reuters
`ATTACKED`
Atta Oweisat, Zoom 77
`ATTACKED`
Mona Al-Kawatmi, free-lancer
`ATTACKED`
Rashid Safadi, Al Jazeera
`ATTACKED`

Israeli soldiers attacked a number of journalists in the compound of the Al-Aqsa mosque in Jerusalem, where the journalists were covering clashes between Israeli forces and Palestinian protesters.

Some 15 to 20 journalists were covering events in the Al-Aqsa compound. Among them were Awad and Abu Turk of Reuters, Oweisat of Zoom 77, free-lancer Al-Kawatmi, and Safadi of Al Jazeera. The journalists said they were standing together in a group and that because of their position and equipment, they could not have been mistaken for Palestinian demonstrators.

Abu Turk told CPJ that Israeli soldiers first tried to deny journalists entry to the compound by blocking all seven doors. He said that most of the journalists barred from entering the compound eventually gained access, including himself.

Once the clashes began, the journalists said, Israeli forces started firing rubber bullets and tear gas into the crowd. (The army denied using rubber bullets.) The journalists said that the attacks against journalists started during the "second wave" of Israeli attacks against demonstrators.

Individual journalists were abused, threatened, and forcefully removed from the compound. Awad sustained a broken tooth when he was kicked in the face by an Israeli soldier. Awad said that at about 3:15 p.m., as he was photographing the clashes, a soldier charged him and kicked him in the mouth.

Bleeding, Awad ran away. A few moments later he was again attacked by the same soldier, who kicked him several more times.

AUGUST 13

Tarek Abdel Jaber, Egyptian Television
`ATTACKED`
Abdel Nasser Abdoun, Egyptian Television
`ATTACKED`

Abdel Jaber and Abdoun, a reporter and cameraman, respectively, for the state-run Egyptian Television network, were assaulted by an unidentified Israeli soldier at the Qalandia checkpoint between Jerusalem and the West Bank city of Ramallah while they were filming in the area.

Abdoun told CPJ that the soldier

approached him and Abdel Jaber when they left their car to gather film footage. Abdoun said the soldier ordered him in English to move back, and that he obeyed. The soldier then tried to kick him in the shin.

He then approached Abdel Jaber and slapped him across the face. The soldier proceeded to kick Abdoun in the groin, and he fell to the ground.

According to Abdoun and Abdel Jaber, the other soldiers at the checkpoint did nothing to stop the attack. Abdoun captured the incident on video.

Abdoun was taken to Makased hospital in Jerusalem, where he was treated and released after three hours.

In an August 12 statement, the Israel Defense Forces (IDF) spokesman's office called the incident "wrong and completely unacceptable" but accused the journalists of refusing to leave the scene and of "provoking the soldiers guarding the checkpoint."

The IDF said that the soldier involved in the attack was "tried by the battalion commander and received a [suspended] 21-day prison sentence...and was suspended from commanding positions."

DECEMBER 6

Awad Awad, Agence France-Presse
HARASSED

Israeli authorities barred Awad, a photographer for Agence France-Presse (AFP), from entering Israeli prime minister Ariel Sharon's office. Awad, who had covered news events at the office on several previous occasions, was there to photograph a meeting between Sharon and the Norwegian foreign minister.

Awad was denied entry despite having the necessary Israeli Government Press Office press card, which grants journalists access to official events.

Israeli authorities later told AFP, without further explanation, that Awad would not be allowed in the prime minister's office for 15 days.

JORDAN

MARCH 26

Daniel Sobleman, *Haaretz*
EXPELLED
Smadar Perri, *Yedioth Ahronoth*
EXPELLED
Shaul Golan, *Yedioth Ahronoth*
EXPELLED
Bassam Jaber, *Panorama*
EXPELLED
Suleiman al-Shafie, Channel 2
EXPELLED
Munif Zahlaqa, Channel 2
EXPELLED

Jordanian security officials barred six Israeli journalists from covering the Arab Summit, in Amman, Jordan. Officials asked the journalists to leave the country because they claimed Jordan could not guarantee their safety in the face of alleged threats.

Sobleman, a reporter with the Israeli daily *Haaretz*, described the move as a polite and diplomatic expulsion.

Jordanian authorities maintain that their actions were not politically motivated, but Agence France-Presse quoted a senior Jordanian official as saying, "This is an Arab Summit and most [participants] do not wish to see Israelis." He added that Jordan's priority was to ensure the comfort of its guests.

MAY 11

Tareq Ayyoub, Al-Jazeera
HARASSED

Ayyoub, an Amman-based reporter for the Qatar-based satellite channel Al-Jazeera, was detained by Jordanian police in the capital, Amman, and transferred to intelligence headquarters, where he was interrogated for two and a half hours.

Jordanian authorities were apparently angered by Al-Jazeera's coverage of rallies and demonstrations that day in Amman, commemorating the upcoming 53rd anniversary of the Palestinian Nakba, or "catastrophe" (the term which Arabs use to refer to the creation of the State of Israel in 1948).

Protesters clashed with police, who dispersed them violently. Ayyoub was released the following day.

KUWAIT

MARCH 20

Hidaya Sultan al-Salem, Al-Majales
KILLED (MOTIVE UNCONFIRMED)

Al-Salem, a 66-year-old veteran journalist who owned and edited the weekly magazine Al-Majales, was killed on her way to work when an armed assailant opened fire on her chauffeur-driven car in Kuwait City.

The assailant, who was described as wearing a traditional long robe, apparently got out of a four-wheel drive car and fired several rounds into al-Salem's car while it was stopped in traffic. She died shortly thereafter.

According to Kuwaiti police and prosecutors, the main suspect, a police officer named Khaled al-Azmi,

confessed to killing al-Salem. However, he later recanted in court, saying police had forced him to confess. One Kuwaiti source who was monitoring the case told CPJ that al-Azmi recanted on the advice of his lawyer in order to avoid the death penalty. CPJ could not verify this claim. In February 2002, al-Azmi was convicted of the murder.

Early in the investigation, Kuwaiti authorities said that al-Azmi killed al-Salem in revenge for an earlier Al-Majales article that he found insulting to the women of his tribe. The article, however, was written some eight months earlier—a fact that struck some as peculiar.

There was considerable speculation about the reasons for the assassination, including alleged financial disputes within al-Salem's family and other alleged disputes with some of her employees. In the latest edition of Al-Majales, according to press reports, al-Salem published an open letter claiming she had been harassed by the police.

In November, a source in Kuwait said there was speculation that al-Azmi may have killed al-Salem because of a personal dispute between the two involving al-Azmi's sister.

LEBANON

MARCH 28

Samir Qassir, Al-Nahar
HARASSED

Lebanese security authorities confiscated the passport of Qassir, a journalist with the daily Al-Nahar, at the Beirut airport when he arrived from

Amman, Jordan, where he had been covering the Arab Summit.

Authorities told Qassir, a Lebanese citizen born of naturalized Lebanese parents, that they wanted to verify the passport's validity. Although Qassir's passport was returned on April 11, authorities warned that his case was still under investigation.

According to Qassir, the security officials who confiscated his passport mentioned an editorial he had written on March 16 that criticized the Lebanese armed forces and security services.

In an April 12 letter to Lebanese president Emile Lahoud, CPJ expressed its deep concern about the incident.

JUNE 1

Raghida Dergham, *Al-Hayat*
LEGAL ACTION

A Lebanese military court launched the criminal trial in absentia of Dergham, a New York-based Lebanese reporter who was charged with "dealing with the enemy" because she participated in a panel discussion with an Israeli official.

Dergham is the New York bureau chief for the London-based newspaper *Al-Hayat.* The charges, filed earlier in the year, stemmed from her participation in a May 19, 2000, panel discussion sponsored by the Washington Institute for Near East Policy in Washington, D.C. The panel included Uri Lubrani, formerly the Israeli government's coordinator of activities in southern Lebanon. The discussion focused on Middle Eastern politics, with special reference to Syria, Lebanon, and Israel. It was believed that the charges, along with previous harassment, was a

response to her critical coverage of Lebanon's dispute with the U.N. over the demarcation of border area between Lebanon and Israel in 2000.

On June 19, 2000, one month after the Washington panel, Lebanese authorities seized Dergham's Lebanese passport when she arrived at Beirut Airport with United Nations secretary-general Kofi Annan, who was touring several Middle Eastern countries. When the passport was returned it had been canceled. The cancellation stamp stated specifically that the passport could not be renewed without the approval of the General Directorate for Internal Security.

Security officials gave no reason for their actions at the time but later announced that Derghan had violated a Lebanese law prohibiting contacts between Lebanese citizens and Israelis.

The military indictment accused Dergham of being a "participant as a journalist in a debate that was arranged by the enemy at the Washington Institute for Near East Policy." It added that her actions "constituted a crime based on Article 278 of the Penal Code."

After opening the trial on June 1, 2001, the military court adjourned until November 30 to give Dergham an opportunity to appear before the court. On November 30, the court dismissed the charges altogether.

JUNE 19

Brent Sadler, CNN
THREATENED
Christian Streib, CNN
THREATENED
Nada Husseini, CNN
THREATENED

CNN Beirut bureau chief Sadler, cameraman Streib, producer Husseini, and their driver were fired on by cannabis growers while filming a story about the narcotics industry in the Bekaa Valley.

The crew was filming about 12 miles (20 kilometers) north of Hermel when several warning shots were fired in their direction as they left the area. "Several minutes later we were ambushed on a remote mountain road by about 10 gunmen in two cars, armed with assault rifles, pistols, and…a sniper rifle," Sadler told Agence France-Presse. "They pointed the gun at the driver and fired one shot. No one was shot."

The assailants then forced the CNN crew out of their car and fired several random shots. They took the crew's money, passports, cameras, and other equipment before leaving the scene.

AUGUST 9

Hussein al-Moulla, The Associated Press
`ATTACKED`
Sami Ayad, Al-Nahar
`ATTACKED`
Yehia Houjairi, Kuwait TV
`ATTACKED`

Al-Moulla and Ayad, photographers for The Associated Press and the Lebanese daily *Al-Nahar*, respectively, were beaten by men thought to be plainclothes agents while covering clashes between Lebanese security forces and anti-Syrian Christian groups.

Before al-Moulla was struck, a man in civilian clothes warned him not to take any photos. Al-Moulla agreed but later filmed and was struck in the back. It was unclear who attacked, but the journalist suspected the man who warned him.

Unidentified assailants struck Ayad after he refused to turn over his film.

According to journalists at the scene, security agents briefly detained Kuwaiti state television cameraman Houjairi, who was also filming the clashes.

MAURITANIA

APRIL 10

Mohammed Lemine Ould Bah, Radio Monte Carlo Middle East, Radio France International
`HARASSED`

Bah, a correspondent for two French radio stations, Radio Monte Carlo Middle East and Radio France International, was temporarily banned from practicing journalism after the minister of communications objected to his reports on the state of relations between Senegal and Mauritania.

MOROCCO

MARCH 1

Abou Bakr Jamai, *Le Journal Hebdomadaire*
`LEGAL ACTION`
Ali Ammar, *Le Journal Hebdomadaire*
`LEGAL ACTION`

Jamai, publications director of the weekly *Le Journal Hebdomadaire*, and Ammar, the newspaper's general director, were convicted of defaming Foreign Minister Muhammed Ben Aissa and sentenced to serve three months and two months in jail, respectively. They were also ordered to pay fines and damages totaling 2,020,000 dirhams (about US$200,000).

The charges stemmed from articles

published last year in *Le Journal Hebdomadaire's* now-defunct weekly predecessor, *Le Journal*, alleging that Ben Aissa profited from the purchase of an official residence during his tenure as Morocco's ambassador to the United States in the late 1990s.

The journalists appealed the ruling and also complained that procedural issues had been raised to deny their right to mount a defense. The court case was adjourned until late January 2002 but had not restarted as this book went to press.

In a March 1 letter to King Muhammad VI, CPJ condemned the criminal libel suit and called on the king to ensure that the harsh prison sentences were overturned.

JULY 6

Ali Lmrabet, *Demain Magazine*
HARASSED
Alain Chabod, France 3 Public Television
HARASSED
Demain Magazine
HARASSED

Moroccan secret service (DST) agents began following Chabod, deputy chief editor of France 3 Public Television, while he was in the country investigating recent revelations about the 1965 disappearance of dissident Mehdi Ben Barka.

The Ben Barka story broke on June 30, when a former DST agent named Ahmed Boukhari told Radio France Internationale that he had new evidence linking top Moroccan officials to the torture and killing of Ben Barka. In an interview with the station, Boukhari said he would cooperate with French authorities investigating the case.

After this interview, Chabod told CPJ, he and other French journalists flew to Morocco in hopes of talking to Boukhari. Chabod first noticed that he was being followed on June 6, after meeting with Ahmed Boukhari's son, Karim, in a public place in the capital, Rabat.

On July 6, two DST officials visited the offices of Safaprint, the printer that produces *Demain Magazine*. According to Lmrabet, the agents ordered the company to stop printing and then left the premises after confiscating several copies of the current issue.

Lmrabet told CPJ that the issue contained a handwritten letter from Ahmed Boukhari, dated December 2000, in which the agent claimed to have information about the Ben Barka case.

Seven hours later, the DST agents returned to Safaprint and announced that *Demain Magazine* could be printed after all.

On July 7 at about 11:00 a.m., Chabod and Lmrabet were driving in a Rabat suburb when two men approached their car. One of the men photographed Lmrabet and threatened him. Lmrabet told CPJ that he was able to note the license plate of the car. Chabod identified the two men as the DST agents who had followed him after his interview with Karim Boukhari.

CPJ issued an alert about these incidents on July 13.

NOVEMBER 17

Noureddine Darif, *Al-Amal al-Democrati*
IMPRISONED

Darif, a journalist for the leftist weekly *Al-Amal al-Democrati*, was detained by local authorities in Smara Province of Western Sahara, which is controlled by

Morocco. Darif was detained at a hospital where he was trying to interview individuals injured earlier in the day during demonstrations. He was taken to a police station and beaten, according to reports and CPJ sources. Darif is accused of "collusion with a foreign party" and of stirring up violent disturbances. He is in Ayoun Prison.

NOVEMBER 21

Ali Lmrabet, *Demain Magazine*
`LEGAL ACTION`

A Rabat court sentenced Lmrabet, director of *Demain Magazine*, to four months in prison and a 30,000 Dirham (US$3,000) fine for "distributing false information."

While the charges cited an October 20 *Demain Magazine* article claiming that a royal palace was for sale, Lmrabet pointed to his recent publication of excerpts from a French author's book about King Muhammed VI, along with an article about the king's cousin Moulay Hichem.

Lmrabet refused to appeal the sentence on the grounds that the charges were spurious and the court decision was politically motivated. After widespread coverage of his case in the regional press, the government filed an appeal on Lmrabet's behalf. The appeal was pending at year's end.

PALESTINIAN AUTHORITY TERRITORIES

JANUARY 16

Majdi al-Arbid, free-lancer
`LEGAL ACTION`

Al-Arbid, a free-lance cameraman and the owner of a private production company in the Gaza Strip, was detained by the Preventive Security Services of the Palestinian National Authority (PNA) in Gaza in connection with video footage of the PNA's execution of a Palestinian accused of collaborating with Israel.

The PNA was apparently angered that the execution had aired on Israel's Channel 2. Only a few PNA-sanctioned journalists were allowed to cover the execution, and al-Arbid was not among them. PNA officials suspected that whoever shot the footage then gave it to al-Arbid, who passed it to Channel 2.

Al-Arbid was released on January 23, after eight days in detention.

FEBRUARY 8

Al-Hayat al-Jadida
`ATTACKED`

The offices of the official Palestinian newspaper *Al-Hayat al-Jadida*, located in the West Bank town of Al-Bireh, were hit during a barrage of gunfire that lasted from about 9 a.m. to 2 p.m. No one was injured, but windows in the front of the building were heavily damaged. The staff took cover in the basement during the shooting.

According to staff, the shots came from the direction of the Israeli army base on Jabal al-Tawil, near the Jewish settlement of Pisgaout.

FEBRUARY 15

Nablus TV
`ATTACKED`

A transmission tower of the private television station Nablus TV was damaged by Israeli gunfire during clashes between Israeli troops and Palestinians in the West Bank city of Nablus. The tower was perched atop a residential building that was hit by the Israeli fire.

Ayman al-Nimer, technical director of the station, said that because of the destruction, about 40 percent of the station's viewers could not watch the channel. Israeli fire had also knocked out the station's transmission in January, stopping all broadcasts for 20 days.

Nimer told CPJ that he could not confirm that the station was targeted, but the fact that the transmission tower has been hit twice within a short period of time raises questions about the Israel Defense Forces' intentions.

MARCH 21

Al-Jazeera
CENSORED

Palestinian National Authority (PNA) security forces, acting on orders from President Yasser Arafat's office, closed the Ramallah bureau of the Qatar-based Al-Jazeera satellite channel and barred its staff from entering the premises. The move apparently resulted from an Al-Jazeera promotional trailer that advertised a forthcoming episode in a documentary series about the Lebanese civil war. The trailer showed a demonstrator holding a pair of shoes over a photo of Arafat.

On March 19, PNA security authorities contacted the bureau to demand that Al-Jazeera withdraw the trailer within two hours or else face closure. Shortly thereafter, security officials visited the bureau and told

staff that their office was closed indefinitely. On March 21, Palestinian security forces took up positions in front of the bureau and prevented staff from entering.

CPJ protested the incident in a March 22 letter to Arafat.

On March 23, following international condemnation and the intervention of several high-profile Palestinian figures, Arafat allowed Al-Jazeera's bureau to reopen.

MAY 29

Joshua Hammer, *Newsweek*
HARASSED
Gary Knight, *Newsweek*
HARASSED

Hammer, the Jerusalem bureau chief for *Newsweek* magazine, and Knight, a photographer on assignment with the publication, were detained by Palestinian militants in the Gaza Strip.

The two were interviewing Palestinian militants in the town of Rafah who claimed to be members of the Fatah Hawks, an organization that Palestinian National Authority officials claim no longer exists.

During the interview, the militants informed the two journalists that they were being detained "to protest unfair American and British press coverage of the Israeli-Palestinian conflict," according to *Newsweek*. The journalists' driver and translator were also detained.

In a statement, the militants said: "This operation comes as a message to the U.S. and British governments to reconsider their calculations and that all their citizens in Palestine and the Arab world will be subject to abduction and killing in case the full, biased and unjustified support continues to the government [of Israel]."

The journalists were allowed to leave unharmed after four and a half hours. They said they did not feel threatened, *Newsweek* reported. Meanwhile, Palestinian officials denied any involvement in the incident.

In a May 31 alert about the case, CPJ executive director Ann Cooper expressed relief that the two men were freed unharmed. Nonetheless, the incident was "a worrying threat to working journalists," she said.

She asked the Palestinian National Authority to "demonstrate that it will not tolerate abuses of press freedom in Palestinian territory."

JULY 29

Sakher Abu al-Aoun, Agence France-Presse
ATTACKED

Abu al-Aoun, a correspondent for Agence France-Presse (AFP) in the Gaza Strip, was beaten by five assailants armed with pipes as he made his way to AFP's offices. He suffered a concussion.

In a letter to Palestinian leader Yasser Arafat, AFP said the incident was "particularly alarming because the assailants...clearly said they knew Sakher was a journalist."

AFP quoted Palestinian Authority secretary general Ahmed Abdulrahman as saying that the attacks against Abu al-Aoun were probably connected with a report the journalist filed about bloody clashes involving two feuding families in the Khan Yunis refugee camp in Gaza.

JULY 31

Muhammad al-Bishawi, Najah Press Office, IslamOnline.net
KILLED

Al-Bishawi, a reporter for the Nablus-based Palestinian news service Najah Press Office and for IslamOnline.net, an Internet news service based in Qatar, was killed in an Israeli missile attack that had targeted Hamas leader Jamal Mansour. Israel had accused Mansour of masterminding several suicide bombings.

Various sources, including al-Bishawi's Cairo-based editor, reported that at the time of the attack, al-Bishawi was in the Palestinian Center for Studies and Media, a Hamas information office, to interview Mansour for an article he was writing for IslamOnline.net.

Al-Bishawi covered many topics for IslamOnline.net, ranging from Palestinian weddings to suicide bombers.

SEPTEMBER 11

Several journalists
THREATENED, HARASSED

According to international press reports, Palestinian police and armed gunmen prevented several news photographers and cameramen from documenting events in the West Bank city of Nablus, where groups of Palestinians celebrated the terrorist attacks on the United States by honking horns and firing live ammunition rounds into the air.

According to The Associated Press, Palestinian security authorities summoned a free-lance cameraman working for the AP that same day and warned him not to air his footage of the events. Members of the Tanzim militia, affiliated with the Fatah organization, also issued warnings that the AP cameraman interpreted as threatening.

Later, the AP quoted Palestinian National Authority (PNA) cabinet secretary Ahmed Abdel Rahman as saying that the PNA "[could] not guarantee the life" of the AP cameraman if the film were broadcast. In the end, the footage was not aired, apparently out of concern for the journalist's safety.

Three days later, on September 14, Palestinian police briefly detained several photographers and cameramen working with international news agencies in the Gaza Strip and confiscated their equipment. The journalists had been covering a rally to commemorate a Palestinian suicide bomber that the militant Islamic group Hamas staged in the Nusseirat refugee camp.

During the rally, one protester reportedly held up a portrait of Osama bin Laden, the exiled Saudi financier suspected by the United States of orchestrating the attacks on New York City and Washington, D.C. Palestinian police later stated that they "confiscated media material which documented illegal acts" at an illegal rally.

Although the PNA returned the journalists' camera equipment that weekend, some of their video footage had been erased. The AP reported that its video was missing 45 seconds of footage. Another photographer told CPJ that images stored on his digital camera had been erased.

CPJ protested the measures in a September 17 letter to Palestinian president Yasser Arafat.

SEPTEMBER 20

Al-Roa TV
CENSORED

At about 11:00 a.m., Palestinian police and security agents descended on the offices of the private television station Al-Roa TV and ordered the station to cease broadcasting immediately.

No reason was given for the suspension, and the officers failed to provide station staff with any official documentation to justify the raid. Station director Hamdi Faraj eventually received a document from the local police stating that the station had been closed by order of Hadj Ismail Jaber, general director of the Palestinian military and police forces in the West Bank.

Staff at Al-Roa told CPJ that they believe the closure came in reprisal for a news bulletin aired earlier in the day. The bulletin announced that Al-Roa had received a statement from the Al-Aqsa Brigades, a group affiliated with Yasser Arafat's Fatah organization, claiming responsibility for an attack on two Jewish settlers in the West bank, which resulted in the death of one settler.

The Palestinian National Authority (PNA) was evidently embarassed by Al-Roa's bulletin, which suggested that a group technically under Arafat's control might have violated the recently announced Palestinian cease-fire.

By Al Roa's own count, it was the 10th time PNA authorities had closed the station since it was founded in the early 1990s.

CPJ condemned the closure in a September 20 alert. Two days later, on September 22, authorities allowed the station to resume broadcasting.

OCTOBER 9

All media
HARASSED

Palestinian authorities barred foreign journalists from entering the Gaza Strip and prevented other reporters from reaching the scene of bloody clashes between Palestinian protesters and Palestinian police that resulted in the deaths of two protesters and the injuries of dozens more a day earlier. The ban remained in effect for one and a half days.

The demonstrators were protesting U.S. military strikes against Afghanistan. Some of the protesters expressed support for Osama bin Laden, the prime suspect in the September 11 terrorist attacks on New York City and Washington, D.C.

On October 8, Palestinian authorities banned some foreign reporters from entering Gaza and prevented others from reaching the scene of clashes. At least two journalists who did manage to cover the clashes were attacked by Palestinian police and later detained for several hours.

For security reasons, the journalists involved in this incident asked that their names and affiliations not be revealed to the public.

OCTOBER 12

All media
HARASSED

Palestinian security forces barred journalists from entering the Meghazi refugee camp in Gaza, where the militant Islamic Jihad organization was staging a memorial service for a group member who had been murdered.

Media outlets received the order via fax from Police Chief Ghazi Jabali.

OCTOBER 12

Alaa Saftawi, *Al-Istiqlal*
IMPRISONED

Palestinian security forces arrested Saftawi, publisher of the militant Islamic Jihad weekly *Al-Istiqlal*, over an article criticizing the Palestinian National Authority's crackdown on demonstrators in Gaza.

He was released without charge on November 16.

DECEMBER 13

Voice of Palestine
ATTACKED

Israeli missiles hit the Voice of Palestine radio station broadcasting headquarters in the West Bank city of Ramallah, according to international news reports. The building's main transmitter was destroyed, knocking the station off the air.

Later, bulldozers flattened the building while Israeli soldiers detonated explosives that toppled a 90-foot radio and television tower and destroyed the station's transmitter, which is also used by Palestine TV.

Voice of Palestine went back on the air using another frequency. Palestine TV reportedly broadcast with poor reception.

The attack came amid Israeli military strikes against Palestinian National Authority targets in what Israel described as reprisals for recent deadly suicide bombings and shootings carried out by radical Palestinian groups. Israel holds Palestinian leader Yasser Arafat responsible for the violence.

"We are appalled by Israel's military action against the Voice of Palestine," said CPJ's executive director Ann Cooper in a statement. "As civilian facilities, radio and television stations are protected from military attack under international humanitarian law. CPJ calls on Israeli authorities to cease attacking the media immediately."

QATAR

JUNE 6

Ahmed Ali, *Al-Watan*
ATTACKED

Three young men assaulted Ali, editor of the Qatari daily *Al-Watan*, in his office in the Qatari capital, Doha.

The assailants, relatives of Minister of Energy and Electricity Abdullah Hamad Al-Attia, were angered by Ali's article, which criticized the minister's proposal that citizens should pay for certain electric and water services that are currently available free of charge.

The men entered the paper's offices and demanded to speak to the editor. After Ali met them outside, the men followed him into his office and locked the door. There, they began beating him and eventually left, screaming threats at the other staff members who had gathered outside Ali's office.

Because staff members had noted the license plate number of the attackers' car, police were able to arrest the three men. They were then released after reaching an out-of-court settlement. Ali was taken to the hospital and treated for several bruises and a broken tooth.

SUDAN

FEBRUARY 3

Amal Abbas, *Al Rai al-Akher*
LEGAL ACTION
Ibrahim Hassan, *Al Rai al-Akher*
LEGAL ACTION

Abbas, editor of the daily *Al-Rai al-Akher*, and Hassan, a reporter for the paper, were ordered jailed for three months by a Khartoum court for failing to pay fines in a libel suit brought by the governor of Khartoum.

The two journalists were found guilty of libeling Governor Majzoub Khalifa by accusing him of corruption and nepotism in an August 2000 article. They were ordered to pay fines of 15 million pounds (US$5,900) each. The journalists were unable to pay the fines. Even though supporters offered to pay the fines on their behalf, they refused to accept this help, opting instead for prison.

Al-Rai al-Akher was also hit with a 1 billion pound fine (US$390,000), reportedly the largest sum ever handed down in a libel suit in Sudan. Both journalists were released on February 19 pending the outcome of their appeal.

SEPTEMBER 11

Khartoum Monitor
LEGAL ACTION

Khartoum Monitor, Sudan's main independent, English-language daily, was suspended and some staffers were detained over articles about the civil strife in southern Sudan and the influence of Western culture in the country.

The Press and Publications Council (PPC) imposed a three-day ban on the paper, claiming the articles had incited the country's Christian minority to violence and caused friction between the country's peoples. The PPC, which reports directly to the president, is responsible for enforcing Sudan's Press Law.

SYRIA

JUNE 17

Al-Domari
CENSORED

Syrian authorities censored pages from the privately owned satirical weekly *Al-Domari*. The offending pages featured an article and accompanying cartoon that mocked Prime Minister Muhammad Mustafa Miro.

According to the paper's publisher, Ali Farzat, the Ministry of Information and the prime minister's office threatened to ban the paper outright unless he agreed to excise two pages from the issue.

The two pages contained an article titled "Doctor Miro Is Depressed. He Has Lost His Enthusiasm," which attacked the government for failing to carry out economic reforms. An accompanying cartoon depicted a horse that had collapsed from exhaustion while pulling a cart whose driver is cracking his whip. The caption read: "Rumors of a change in government tie the minister's hands."

The paper was reportedly published with blank spaces where the censored articles had been.

TUNISIA

JANUARY 12

Al-Mawkif
LEGAL ACTION

Tunisian authorities seized issue 198 of the weekly newspaper *Al-Mawkif*, a publication of the small opposition Progressive Socialist Rally Party, at the paper's printing house.

Authorities gave no explanation for the seizure, but it was apparently triggered by articles dealing with human rights issues.

Al-Mawkif publishes irregularly due to its shaky financial situation, which it attributes to the government's refusal to give it the subsidies received by all other opposition papers. Sources at the paper add that public sector companies refuse to buy advertising space in its pages.

JUNE 26

Sihem Bensedrine, *Kalima*
IMPRISONED, LEGAL ACTION

Bensedrine is the spokeswoman for the nongovernmental National Council for Liberties in Tunisia (CNLT) and the editor of an Internet magazine called *Kalima*. On June 17, she took part in a television debate about Tunisian human rights on Al Mustaqilla, a London-based Arabic television station owned by émigré Tunisian dissident Mohammed El Hachimi Hamdi.

Tunisian police detained Bensedrine at the airport when she returned to the capital, Tunis, on June 26, 2001. That same day, according to her lawyer, Radhia Nasraoui, Bensedrine was charged with undermining the authority of the judiciary and spreading false information with the aim of undermining public authority. She was brought before an examining judge, who ordered her incarcerated.

Following her arrest, Nasraoui said, Bensedrine was missing for more than five hours before anyone knew what had happened to her.

Undermining the authority of the judiciary carries a penalty of up to six months' imprisonment and a 1000 dinar (US$660) fine. The false-information charge carries a prison sentence of up to three years and a fine of 1000 dinars.

Bensedrine was released on August 12, after spending six weeks in detention. Authorities provided no explanation for her release, and the charges against her were still pending at year's end.

CPJ published an alert about the case on June 28.

AUGUST 17

Sihem Bensedrine, *Kalima*
ATTACKED

Plainclothes police officers attacked Tunisian journalist and human rights activist Sihem Bensedrine and a group of supporters who had gathered to celebrate her recent release from prison.

Bensedrine, who edits the online news magazine *Kalima*, was jailed for six weeks after criticizing the Tunisian government during a June 17 television appearance in London.

As Bensedrine and some 150 to 200 supporters and friends gathered in front of an events hall in the afternoon, about 200 plainclothes police officers denied them entry. The police attacked the guests after they refused to disperse and sang the Tunisian national anthem.

One officer kicked Bensedrine in the side. Her husband and 13-year-old daughter were also beaten, along with several of her supporters.

Bensedrine was arrested on June 26 after returning from London, where she had taken part in a televised debate about Tunisian human rights on Al Mustaqilla, a London-based Arabic television station owned by émigré Tunisian dissident Mohammed El Hachimi Hamdi.

She was released from prison on August 12 but continued to face charges of "undermining the authority of the judiciary and spreading false information with the aim of undermining public authority."

CPJ published an alert about the attack on August 20.

TURKEY

JANUARY 18

Nese Duzel, *Radikal*
LEGAL ACTION

Duzel, a reporter for the mainstream liberal daily *Radikal*, was charged with inciting sectarian hatred or religious conflict, a crime under Article 312/2 of the Penal Code.

The case stemmed from a January 8, 2001, interview that Duzel conducted with the leader of Turkey's Alevi Muslim minority, Murteza Demir. In the interview, Demir complained about official discrimination against Alevis, claiming they are denied rights and a communal identity and are treated with contempt.

The interview was published shortly after prisoners staged jailhouse riots and hunger strikes in December. Many of those killed in the riots were Alevis.

Duzel's trial in the State Security Court in Istanbul began on June 27, 2001, but was subsequently postponed until February 2002. If convicted, Duzel faces two to six years in prison.

On October 23, Duzel was again

charged with inciting sectarian hatred or religious conflict. This time, the charge stemmed from her book, *The Hidden Face of Turkey*, a compilation of her articles and interviews published in several Turkish newspapers over the years.

In one interview, titled "Alevis Are Considered as Terrorists" and originally published in August 1996 in the now defunct daily *Yeni Yuzyil*, a minority Alevi leader discussed riots that had taken place in 1995 in an Alevi district in Istanbul.

Duzel was not charged when the article was originally published. This second trial was adjourned until March 6, 2002. If convicted, Duzel faces two to six years in prison.

JANUARY 23

Nese Duzel, *Radikal*
LEGAL ACTION

An Istanbul criminal court charged Duzel, a reporter for the liberal Turkish daily Radikal, with "insulting state institutions," an offense under Article 159 of the Penal Code.

The charge stemmed from a June 19, 2000, *Radikal* interview with a university professor who discussed drug trafficking in Turkey.

If convicted, Duzel faces up to six years in prison. Her case was adjourned until April 2002.

FEBRUARY 6

Metin Munir, free-lancer
LEGAL ACTION

Munir, a free-lance journalist who writes for the Turkish daily *Sabah* and the London-based *Financial Times*, was

charged with insulting the judiciary, a crime punishable by up to 6 years in prison.

The Ministry of Justice filed the charge over an article by Munir that appeared on May 10, 2000, in the now defunct daily *Yeni Binyil*. Munir's article harshly criticized the appointment of Oktar Cakir as chief prosecutor of the State Security Court.

Cakir was ultimately forced to step down after a traffic accident exposed the prosecutor's apparent relationship with a known criminal. But Munir suggested that Cakir's initial appointment raised troubling questions about the administration of justice in Turkey.

The journalist questioned how the Supreme Council of Judges and Prosecutors, the body responsible for appointing the chief prosecutor, could have chosen Cakir for the post when the council had been notified by the Ministry of Interior of Cakir's involvement in unspecified "malfeasance."

In a February 26 letter to Turkish prime minister Bulent Ecevit, CPJ protested the prosecution of Munir and urged him to examine all possible legal remedies to ensure that the charges were dropped.

The case has been adjourned until April 2002.

MARCH 21

Yeni Evrensel
CENSORED

The leftist daily *Yeni Evrensel* was suspended for seven days for violating Turkey's Anti-Terror Law. The suspension stemmed from a January 8, 2000, article titled "I Definitely Have to Cover It, Friends."

The piece recounted the brutal killing of *Yeni Evrensel* reporter Metin Goktepe, who was beaten to death by Turkish police in January 1996 while covering the funeral of two inmates who died in a prison riot. (The title quoted Goktepe's last words to his colleagues.)

A State Security Court in Istanbul ordered the closure on June 21, 2000. The newspaper lost an appeal on February 28, 2001, and began the suspension almost a month later.

APRIL 10

Zeynel Abidin Kizilyaprak, *Ozgur Bakis*
IMPRISONED, LEGAL ACTION

The Court of Appeals confirmed a 16-month sentence against Kizilyaprak, editor of a photo supplement for the now-defunct daily *Ozgur Bakis*. Kizilyaprak was supposed to go to jail on October 23, 2001, but apparently went underground instead.

On December 8, 2000, a State Security Court convicted Kizilyaprak of "separatist propaganda" under Article 8 of the Anti-Terror Law. The case stemmed from a book of photographs titled *From 1900 to 2000, the Kurds*. The book was confiscated on February 16, 2000, before it could be distributed.

APRIL 12

Fehmi Koru, *Yeni Safak*
LEGAL ACTION

Koru, an Ankara-based columnist for the Turkish daily *Yeni Safak* and a well-known commentator on political affairs, appeared at the No. 2 State Security Court in Besiktas, Istanbul, to face charges of disseminating information that "incites people to

enmity and hatred by pointing to class, racial, religious, confessional, or regional differences." He was charged under Article 312 of the Turkish Penal Code.

The prosecution stemmed from comments that Koru made in 1999 during an appearance on Turkey's Kanal 7 television station after the devastating August 1999 earthquake in northwestern Turkey. Certain religious Turks had described the quake as divine punishment against the country, a view that drew condemnation from secularist politicians and journalists. Koru, in turn, criticized the secularists for their intolerance.

"Everybody is entitled to their own beliefs," Koru said during his appearance. "Certain circles in Turkey...believe they have the right to tell people what they should believe in."

After an initial hearing, the trial was adjourned until June 2. In June, it was again postponed until March 5, 2002. If convicted, Koru faces up to four years in prison.

CPJ published an alert about the case on April 20.

JUNE 20

Ahmet Altan, *Aktuel*
LEGAL ACTION

A Turkish criminal court charged Altan, a popular columnist for the weekly *Aktuel*, with violating Article 159 of the Penal Code, which prohibits "insulting" state institutions, including the military.

The charge stemmed from a November 2000 article in which Altan urged the prosecution of Turkish military officers involved in a state-sponsored 1998 smear campaign against journalists and intellectuals viewed as sympathetic to Kurdish separatists.

In November 2000, military officials acknowledged having formulated such a plan but denied carrying it out. However, Mehmet Ali Birand, a liberal columnist for the daily *Sabah* and a talk show host, was reportedly victimized under the plan.

Birand was fired from *Sabah* in 1998 after the military allegedly leaked information that he was on the payroll of the Kurdistan Workers Party (PKK), a separatist rebel group. The information was said to have come from the confession of captured PKK military commander Semdin Sakik. A similar allegation was later leveled against Cengiz Candar, another columnist for *Sabah*, and also resulted in a dismissal.

Altan's trial was adjourned until February 15, 2002. If convicted, he faces up to six years in prison.

JUNE 29

Fikret Baskaya, *Ozgur Bakis*
IMPRISONED

Baskaya, an academic and writer for the now defunct, pro-Kurdish daily *Ozgur Bakis*, was jailed after a State Security Court sentenced him to 16 months in prison for "separatist propaganda," a violation of Article 8 of the Anti-Terror Law.

The case against Baskaya stemmed from a June 1, 1999, column he wrote in *Ozgur Bakis* titled "Is this a Historical Process?" The article decried Turkey's policy toward the country's Kurdish minority, saying: "Turkish leaders have always considered the Kurdish problem to be one of public order, when it is in fact a national

problem, and have thought they could resolve the problem through a chauvinist, racist and nationalist political agenda."

An Istanbul State Security Court convicted him on June 13, 2000. The sentence was confirmed by the Court of Appeals on January 15, 2001. He is jailed in Kalecik Prison near Ankara.

AUGUST 21

Celal Baslangic, *Radikal*
CENSORED

A Turkish criminal court banned the book *Temple of Fear*, written by journalist Celal Baslangic. The court claimed that the book insulted the Turkish army, a crime under Article 159 of the Penal Code. Police apparently seized copies of the book from shops in the country.

Temple of Fear, a collection of articles by Baslangic that originally appeared in the liberal Turkish daily *Radikal*, describes the violence of Turkey's long-running conflict with Kurdish rebels in southeastern Turkey. Some of the essays accuse Turkish authorities of committing human rights abuses against civilians, including alleged massacres by Turkish military forces and the disappearance of a pro-Kurdish politician.

Turkish authorities did not object to any of Baslangic's articles when they originally appeared in *Radikal*. The book, published in July 2000 by Iletisim Publishers, ran three editions before the ban.

Baslangic was expected to face criminal charges stemming from the book, but none had been filed at press time.

Erol Ozkoray, *Idea Politika*
LEGAL ACTION

Ozkoray, editor of the Istanbul-based quarterly magazine *Idea Politika*, was formally charged with two counts of "insulting" state institutions, a crime under Article 159 of the Penal Code.

The charges came after Ozkoray published an article in the March edition that strongly criticized the Turkish military's controversial role in Turkish politics and society. *Idea Politika* frequently published such articles.

Ozkoray faces between four and 12 years in prison if convicted, but no further developments in his case had been reported at press time.

NOVEMBER 12

Burak Bekdil, *Turkish Daily News*
LEGAL ACTION

A criminal court in Ankara charged Bekdil, a columnist for the English-language *Turkish Daily News*, with "insulting" the judiciary, a crime under Article 159 of the Penal Code.

The charge relates to an August 28 column in which Bekdil criticized alleged judicial corruption. Bekdil faces from two to six years in prison if convicted of the charge. No further developments had been reported at press time.

YEMEN

APRIL 24

Human Rights
CENSORED

Yemeni authorities confiscated the first issue of the new monthly newspaper *Human Rights* from newsstands.

The Yemeni Information Ministry ordered the confiscation, claiming that the newspaper had violated the press law but providing no further details.

Human Rights was the first Yemeni newspaper to deal specifically with human rights and democracy issues.

MAY 28

Seif al-Hadheri, *Al-Shoumou*
LEGAL ACTION

An appellate court in Sanaa upheld a lower court decision to ban al-Hadheri, editor of the weekly *Al-Shoumou*, from practicing journalism in Yemen for 10 months. The charges stemmed from allegedly libelous articles, published in *Al-Shoumou* in 2000, that accused the education minister of financial impropriety.

Al-Hadheri received a suspended six-month prison sentence and was ordered to pay a fine of 1 million riyals (about US$6,250). *Al-Shoumou* was ordered closed for one month, effective immediately. CPJ protested the case in a June 26 letter to Yemeni president Ali Abdullah Saleh.

JUNE 10

Hassan al-Zaidi, *Yemen Times*
IMPRISONED

State security agents arrested al-Zaidi, a reporter for the English-language weekly *Yemen Times*, at the paper's offices in Sanaa.

The journalist was apparently detained for interviewing a kidnapped German tourist whom security forces had not been able locate.

The agents told al-Zaidi that there were "supreme orders" for his arrest, according to a source at the newspaper. Al-Zaidi was released on June 25.

JUNE 11

Al-Shoura
LEGAL ACTION, CENSORED

Yemen's Supreme Court upheld a lower court decision to ban the opposition weekly *Al-Shoura* for six months.

The ban stemmed from a 1997 libel case brought against *Al-Shoura* and its former editors, the late Abdullah Saad and his brother Abdel Jabber Saad, by Islah Party leader Sheikh Abdel Majid al-Zindani.

The court also upheld Abdel Jabbar's sentence of 80 lashes and a ban on practicing journalism for one year. Abdel Jabbar was also ordered to pay damages of 100,000 riyals (about US$625) to Sheikh al-Zindani.

Al-Zindani later withdrew his case against the two brothers, according to *Al-Shoura*. It was unclear what effect this would have on the Supreme Court's ruling, which had not yet been delivered at press time.

SEPTEMBER 8

Hassan al-Zaidi, *Yemen Times*
IMPRISONED

Yemeni authorities detained al-Zaidi, a veteran reporter for the English-language weekly *Yemen Times*.

Al-Zaidi was apparently detained on the orders of Marib Province governor Naji Abdullah al-Sufi. The journalist was held incommunicado and his whereabouts were unknown.

Though officials gave no reason for the arrest, it was believed that al-Zaidi was detained in retaliation for his reporting on German diplomat Rainer Burns, who was kidnapped by armed gunmen on July 27 and was still a captive at the time.

According to local sources, al-Zaidi's articles embarrassed Governor al-Sufi because they contained accurate information on the location of Burns and his captors, suggesting that Yemeni authorities were incompetent.

In a September 21 letter to Yemeni president Ali Abdullah Saleh, CPJ protested al-Zaidi's detention and urged his immediate release. Al-Zaidi was released a few days later.

SEPTEMBER 16

Feras Farooq al-Yafai, *Al Haqiqah*
LEGAL ACTION

An Aden criminal court found al-Yafai, editor of the weekly *Al-Haqiqah*, guilty of insulting and humiliating a public official.

Al-Yafai was sentenced to three months in prison and ordered to pay a 5,000 riyal (US$30) fine.

The sentence came after an article by al-Yafai, published in the August 2 edition of *Al-Haqiqah*, falsely reported that the governor of Aden, Taha Ghanem, had resigned his post and fled the country. At press time, the case was under appeal.

DECEMBER 3

Hassan al-Zaidi, *Yemen Times*
HARASSED

Yemeni state security agents detained al-Zaidi, a reporter for

the English-language weekly *Yemen
Times*, in the early morning as he was
walking home.

Authorities gave no reason for the
arrest, but sources at the *Yemen Times*
said it was related to the recent
kidnapping of a German businessman
by members of al-Zaidi's tribe.

Al-Zaidi had already been arrested
twice in 2001 for his reporting on the
kidnappings of foreigners. Al-Zaidi's
work embarrassed local authorities
because it showed that he had more
information on the prisoners'
whereabouts than the government.

Al-Zaidi was arrested just as an
edition of the *Yemen Times* featuring a
story he wrote about the kidnapping
was being printed. He was released the
following day. ■

HOW CPJ INVESTIGATES AND CLASSIFIES ATTACKS ON THE PRESS

CPJ's RESEARCH STAFF INVESTIGATED AND VERIFIED THE CASES of press freedom violations described in this volume. Each account was corroborated by more than one source for factual accuracy, confirmation that the victims were journalists or news organizations, and verification that intimidation was the probable motive. CPJ defines journalists as people who cover news or write commentary. For additional information on individual cases, contact CPJ at (212) 465-1004. CPJ classifies the cases in this report according to the following categories:

Attacked In the case of journalists, wounded or assaulted. In the case of news facilities, damaged, raided, or searched; non-journalist employees attacked because of news coverage or commentary.

Censored Officially suppressed or banned; editions confiscated; news outlet closed.

Expelled Forced to leave a country because of news coverage or commentary.

Harassed Access denied or limited; materials confiscated or damaged; entry or exit denied; family members attacked or threatened; dismissed or demoted (when it is clearly the result of political or outside pressure); freedom of movement impeded.

Imprisoned Arrested or held against one's will; held for no less than 48 hours.

Killed Murdered, or missing and presumed dead, with evidence that the motive was retribution for news coverage or commentary. Includes journalists killed in cross fire while covering conflict.

Legal Action Credentials denied or suspended; fined; sentenced to prison; visas denied or canceled; passage of a restrictive law; libel suit intended to inhibit coverage.

Missing No group or government agency takes responsibility for the journalist's disappearance.

Threatened Menaced with physical harm or some other type of retribution.

CPJ DOCUMENTED THE CASES OF 37 JOURNALISTS who were killed for their work in 2001, the largest number since 1995. An analysis of this alarming death toll is included in the introduction to this book on page x.

The number of journalists killed in the line of duty each year is probably the world's most frequently cited press freedom statistic. CPJ thoroughly investigates each report of a journalist killed in order to determine whether the journalist was targeted because of his or her profession. Those caught in cross fire while covering conflict are included along with journalists singled out for assassination. We define journalists as those who cover the news or comment on public affairs in print, in photographs, on radio, on television, or online. Reporters, writers, editors, publishers, and directors of news organizations are all included. But we do not classify a case as confirmed until we are sure that death was related to the victim's journalistic work.

When the motive for a journalist's murder is unclear but there is reason to suspect that it was related to the journalist's profession, CPJ classifies that death as "motive unconfirmed" and maintains a separate listing of those cases. CPJ continues its research to identify the reasons for the crime. CPJ documented 17 "motive unconfirmed" cases in 2001. They are described beginning on page 553. With regard to both lists, CPJ continues pressure for official investigations of the killings, as well as the for the apprehension and punishment of the killers. ∎

AFGHANISTAN: 9

MARC BRUNEREAU,
free-lancer, September 5, 2001,
Tashkent, Uzbekistan

Brunereau, a free-lance reporter
who spent years covering the war in
Afghanistan for publications including
the Belgian daily *Le Soir*, died in
Tashkent of wounds sustained in a
1999 shelling incident in Taloqan,
Afghanistan.

Brunereau and others were arriving
by helicopter in the northern city of
Taloqan when the airfield came under
Taliban fire. Brunereau suffered severe
shrapnel wounds. Although he received
months of medical treatment, including
several operations, shrapnel that
remained in his body caused continuing
health problems and apparently
resulted in his death two years later.

JOHANNE SUTTON,
Radio France Internationale,
November 11, 2001, Takhar Province

PIERRE BILLAUD,
Radio Télévision Luxembourg,
November 11, 2001, Takhar Province

VOLKER HANDLOIK,
free-lance reporter, November 11, 2001,
Takhar Province

Sutton, a reporter for Radio France
Internationale; Billaud, a reporter for
Radio Télévision Luxembourg; and
Handloik, a free-lance reporter on
assignment for the German news
magazine *Stern*, were killed on the
evening of November 11 when
Taliban forces fired on a Northern
Alliance military convoy.

The reporters were among a group
of six journalists who were riding
with Northern Alliance soldiers in an
armored personnel carrier (APC). The
soldiers were advancing toward
Taliban positions near the city of
Taloqan, the capital of Takhar
Province and the alliance's former
headquarters.

Taliban forces opened fire on the
convoy and hit the APC carrying the
journalists with a rocket-propelled
grenade. The jolt from the grenade's
impact caused some people to fall off
the tank while others may have
jumped off. It was unclear whether the
journalists who died were killed in the
cross fire, or whether Taliban soldiers
later executed at least two of them.

Three journalists survived the
attack: Paul McGeough, a reporter for
the Australian newspaper *The Sydney
Morning Herald*; Véronique
Rebeyrotte, a reporter for France
Culture radio; and Levon Sevunts, a
reporter for the *Montreal Gazette*.

AZIZULLAH HAIDARI,
Reuters, November 19, 2001,
Nangarhar Province

HARRY BURTON,
Reuters Television, November 19, 2001,
Nangarhar Province

JULIO FUENTES,
El Mundo, November 19, 2001,
Nangarhar Province

MARIA GRAZIA CUTULI,
Corriere della Sera, November 19, 2001,
Nangarhar Province

❧

Haidari, an Afghan-born
photographer for the Reuters news
agency; Burton, an Australian
cameraman for Reuters; Fuentes, a
Spanish correspondent for the
Madrid-based newspaper *El Mundo*;
and Cutuli, an Italian correspondent
for the Milan-based daily *Corriere
della Sera,* were killed by a group of
gunmen who ambushed their convoy.

The journalists were traveling
through eastern Nangarhar Province
at the head of a convoy of about
eight vehicles when they were stopped
by a group of armed men near the
town of Sarobi, some 55 miles (90
kilometers) east of Kabul. Gunmen
dragged the four journalists out of
two of the front cars and executed
them using Kalashnikov rifles,
according to a driver and translator
who were allowed to flee and later
spoke to reporters.

On the morning of November 20,
the bodies were brought to Jalalabad,
where colleagues identified them.

Although an anti-Taliban coalition
in Jalalabad had chosen a new
governor for Nangarhar that
weekend, local authorities had not
secured full control over the province.

ULF STRÖMBERG,
TV4, November 26, 2001, Taloqan

❧

Strömberg, a cameraman for the
Swedish channel TV4, was murdered
in the early morning during a robbery
at the house in Taloqan where he and
several other journalists were staying.

At around 2 a.m., armed gunmen
broke into the house and entered the
room where two journalists from the
Swedish newspaper *Aftonbladet* were
sleeping. The intruders demanded
money, which they were given, and
also stole equipment including
cameras, computers, and a satellite
phone, according to *Aftonbladet.*

The robbers threatened to kill the
two journalists—Martin Adler, a
photographer, and Bo Liden, a
correspondent—but left the room
after an Afghan translator intervened
on their behalf, according to a Reuters
report. The gunmen then proceeded to
the room Strömberg was sharing with
his TV4 colleague Rolf Porseryd, a
correspondent. Porseryd told reporters
that Strömberg went to the door and
slammed it shut when he saw the
gunmen, who fired several shots
before fleeing.

Strömberg, 42, was apparently hit
in the chest by a bullet fired through
the door. Though colleagues rushed
him to a local hospital, his wounds
were fatal.

ALGERIA: 2

FADILA NEJMA,
Echourouk, June 14, 2001, Algiers

❧

ADEL ZERROUK,
Al-Rai, June 14, 2001, Algiers

❧

Two Algerian journalists were
killed while covering mass anti-
government protests organized by
Berber community leaders in the
capital, Algiers.

Nejma, a reporter for the Arabic weekly *Echourouk*, died after being struck by a speeding bus during the protests. Nejma suffered severe chest and leg injuries and died later in the hospital.

Local journalists and press sources reported that the bus driver ran over Nejma while trying to escape demonstrators intent on torching his bus, or that one of the protesters had commandeered the vehicle and was trying to crash it into local security forces.

Also killed was Zerrouk, a reporter with the Arabic daily *Al-Rai*. Some CPJ sources and local press reports stated that Zerrouk died after a crowd of protesters trampled him. According to other reports, however, the journalist was hit by the same bus that killed Nejma.

BANGLADESH: 1

NAHAR ALI,
Anirban, April 21, 2001, Khulna

Ali, a correspondent for the Khulna-based, Bengali-language daily *Anirban*, died shortly before midnight on April 21, while undergoing treatment at Khulna Medical College Hospital for injuries sustained in an attack days earlier. Late on the night of April 17, masked men kidnapped Ali from his home in the village of Shovna, according to local press reports. The assailants stabbed him, beat him severely, and broke his hands and legs before abandoning him on the outskirts of his village, according to police.

Ali was found unconscious and taken to the hospital in Khulna, a major city in southwestern Bangladesh. Doctors said he died due to major brain damage and profuse bleeding.

Police suggested that members of the outlawed Biplobi Communist Party may have killed Ali because of a dispute over ownership of a shrimp farm. However, journalists in Khulna said that the investigation lacked credibility because Ali's reporting had uncovered links between police and smuggling rings in the region. CPJ sources said that Ali, who worked as the Dumuria subdistrict correspondent for *Anirban*, was killed because "he knew too much" about the workings of local criminal syndicates and the complicity of some local authorities in their activities.

BOLIVIA: 1

JUAN CARLOS ENCINAS,
free-lancer, July 29, 2001, Catavi

Encinas, 39, a free-lance reporter in the small town of Catavi in La Paz Department, died of wounds sustained while he was covering a fight between two mining cooperatives that were vying for control of a limestone quarry outside Catavi.

On July 29, about 50 armed members of the mining cooperative Marmolera Comunitaria Ltda surrounded and attacked members of Cooperativa Multiactiva Catavi Ltda, which controlled the quarry.

The attackers fired at least seven shots, wounding a worker and Encinas, who was shot in the groin. Encinas was initially treated at a local medical post but died on the way to a hospital in the city of El Alto.

Encinas was carrying a camera and a tape recorder, and his credentials identified him as a journalist. Three days before Encinas' death, a small production company hired him to report on the story for La Paz-based TV channel Canal 21, according to the local press union Federación de Trabajadores de la Prensa de Bolivia.

Two days after Encinas' death, the El Alto police arrested eight men suspected of the killing. Though they were initially ordered released on bail, the Superior District Court of La Paz overturned that decision and the suspects remained in preventive detention.

CHINA: 1

FENG ZHAOXIA,
Gejie Daobao, January 15, 2001, Xi'an

Feng, a reporter for the Xi'an-based daily *Gejie Daobao*, was found in a ditch outside Xi'an with his throat cut, according to Chinese and international press reports.

Feng was an investigative reporter who wrote about criminal gangs and their links to corrupt local politicians. He had received repeated death threats, and his rented room had been broken into many times. In the days before his death, he told colleagues he was being followed and that he feared for his life, according to Reuters. On January 14, he moved to new lodgings as a safety precaution.

Soon after Feng's body was found, police ruled his death a suicide and banned the local press from writing about it. According to relatives who identified his body, there was a four-inch gash in his throat and no blood on his clothes, making it unlikely he could have killed himself. One relative told Reuters, "He had no reason to commit suicide. He had a happy, healthy family, a good job, and no psychological problems."

Feng's relatives and colleagues believe he was killed for his journalistic work. They have petitioned local authorities to reopen the case but have received no response.

Feng, a former farmer, began writing articles and sending them to local publications in the hope of becoming a journalist. After his first article was published in 1980, he won several awards for his writing before being hired by *Gejie Daobao* in 1996.

COLOMBIA: 3

FLAVIO BEDOYA,
Voz, April 27, 2001, Tumaco

Four unidentified gunmen on motorcycles shot and killed Bedoya, a regional correspondent for the Bogotá-based Communist Party newspaper *Voz*, as he stepped off a bus in the southwestern port city of Tumaco, police and colleagues said.

Bedoya, 52, had worked for *Voz* for about a year and a half, according to Álvaro Angarita, one of the weekly's senior correspondents.

Angarita linked the murder to a series of highly critical reports that Bedoya had published about collusion between security forces and right-wing paramilitary gangs in Nariño Department. Police confirmed the killing but gave no further details.

Southwestern Colombia, especially Nariño Department and neighboring Cauca Department, experienced a number of paramilitary attacks in the two months before the killing.

Colombia's small Communist Party has political links to the left-wing guerrilla organization Revolutionary Armed Forces of Colombia (FARC), but has traditionally advocated social change through grassroots mobilization and the ballot box rather than armed revolution.

JOSÉ DUVIEL VÁSQUEZ ARIAS,
La Voz de la Selva, July 6, 2001, Florencia
~

An unidentified gunman shot and killed Vásquez, director of the local radio station La Voz de la Selva (The Voice of the Jungle), and tried to kill his colleague Omar Orlando García Garzón, news director of the same station.

The two journalists, who had just finished the first broadcast of their twice-daily news program, were driving home from work in Florencia, a city in southern Caquetá Department that is a former stronghold of the Revolutionary Armed Forces of Colombia (FARC), the country's largest leftist guerrilla group. More recently, the town has become a power base for an anti-Communist paramilitary group linked to the right-wing United Self-Defense Forces of Colombia (AUC).

García told CPJ that the gunman first shot Vásquez and then aimed at García. Vásquez's slumped body intercepted the second bullet, which merely brushed García, who was able to give the authorities a detailed description of the killer. The next day, García began receiving threatening phone calls. On July 9, an anonymous caller warned him to leave Florencia on pain of death.

In addition to witnessing the killing, García had assisted Vásquez in documenting corruption implicating local government officials and members of the FARC, the journalist told CPJ.

The journalists had investigated Caquetá governor Pablo Adriano Muñoz, who was reportedly elected with support from the FARC, for allegedly embezzling public funds. Muñoz accused Vásquez of "persecuting" him, whereupon Vásquez filed a defamation suit against the governor. Vásquez's lawyer, Carlos Alberto Beltrán, had to flee Florencia after a failed attempt on his life, according to García.

Vásquez stated during one of his broadcasts that if anything happened to him or his family, it would be the governor's fault.

García reported that Vásquez's last broadcasts dealt with an AUC communiqué in which the organization announced changes in its local leadership and promised to refrain from kidnapping and extortion.

The journalist's murder followed those of the station's former director, Alfredo Abad López, whom Vásquez had replaced, and another colleague, Guillermo Léon Agudelo. García, his wife, and their two young daughters have since left the country.

JORGE ENRIQUE URBANO
SÁNCHEZ,
radio and television journalist, July 8, 2001,
Buenaventura

Two unidentified attackers shot Urbano four times at around 2 a.m. while he was celebrating his 55th birthday with friends in the coastal city of Buenaventura, family members and authorities said.

Urbano hosted a one-hour morning radio program broadcast on local station Mar Estéreo. He was also the administrator of the Néstor Urbano Tenorio Park.

Urbano apparently devoted his final radio broadcast to denouncing a local criminal gang called Tumba Puertas (Knock Down Doors). The gang was a frequent topic of discussion on Urbano's show; the broadcaster often blamed Tumba Puertas for rampant crime in the park and urged police to crack down on drug dealing there.

Urbano had also coordinated efforts to relocate street vendors and remove drug addicts from the park. Before his murder, he received death threats that he attributed to these public statements and actions.

COSTA RICA: 1

PARMENIO MEDINA PÉREZ,
"La Patada," July 7, 2001, San José

Medina, producer and host of the weekly radio program "La Patada" (The Kick), was murdered by unknown assailants who shot him three times at close range with a .38-caliber weapon, once in the back and twice in the head.

Medina's 28-year-old program often denounced official corruption and earned him numerous threats. On-air accusations he had made since 1999 about alleged fiscal improprieties at a local Catholic radio station led to its closure and an investigation of its former director.

Two months before his murder, Medina received death threats in connection with the accusations, and unknown attackers fired bullets at his house. Although Medina had been under police protection, he asked that it be lifted just before his death.

In a July 10 letter, CPJ praised President Miguel Ángel Rodríguez Echeverría for condemning the murder and encouraged the president to ensure that the perpetrators were caught. President Rodríguez responded with an e-mail message saying, "[M]y government is committed to cooperate as best as it can with the judicial authorities to clarify these facts until their ultimate consequences and will do all it can to discover the material and intellectual authors."

No substantial progress in the investigation had been reported at year's end, however.

GEORGIA: 1

GEORGY SANAYA,
Rustavi-2, July 26, 2001, Tbilisi

Sanaya, a popular 26-year-old Georgian journalist, was found dead in his Tbilisi apartment. He had been shot once in the head at close range with a 9 mm weapon. Sanaya anchored "Night Courier," a nightly political talk show in which he interviewed Georgia's leading politicians on the independent television station Rustavi-2.

Nika Tabatadze, news director of Rustavi-2, told CPJ that Sanaya's colleagues became concerned when he failed to report for work at the usual time on the afternoon of July 26 and did not answer his home or cellular telephones. That evening, a group of co-workers went to his apartment and knocked repeatedly on the door. When no one answered, they called the police, who entered the apartment and discovered Sanaya's body.

In a special television address, President Eduard Shevardnadze directed the minister of internal affairs, the prosecutor general, and the minister of state security to oversee the investigation personally. On July 27, President Shevardnadze met with U.S. chargé d'affaires Philip Remler and asked for the FBI's help in the investigation, according to Georgian and Russian press sources.

Although the police, assisted by a group of FBI agents, immediately launched an investigation, it failed to produce significant results. A suspect was detained in August but was later released due to lack of evidence, CPJ sources reported.

Sanaya's Rustavi-2 colleagues firmly believe that the murder resulted from his professional work. Erosi Kitsmarishvili, executive director of Rustavi-2, told CPJ that the murder could have been intended to intimidate the station, which is known for its investigative reporting on state

corruption and misuse of power in Georgia. The station has frequently been the target of government harassment in recent years.

While Sanaya's work was not generally controversial, he had recently hosted a segment on Georgia's Pankisi Gorge, a lawless area near the Chechen border that is known for drug smuggling and kidnapping. A former parliamentary deputy who appeared on the program speculated publicly that criminals from the Pankisi Gorge region may have been responsible for Sanaya's murder.

On December 6, police arrested former police officer Grigol Khurtsilava after a ballistic analysis traced the murder weapon to him, the Georgian news agency Black Sea Press reported. Acting on his confession, police found the murder weapon and keys to Sanaya's apartment. Khurtsilava was then officially charged with Sanaya's murder. In early February 2002, the Prosecutor General's Office announced that it will forward Khurtsilava's case to the courts and insisted that Sanaya's murder was not politically motivated, the Moscow-based Center for Journalism in Extreme situations reported. Sanaya's colleagues maintain he was killed because of his work.

GUATEMALA: 1

JORGE MYNOR ALEGRÍA
ARMENDÁRIZ,
Radio Amatique, September 5, 2001,
Puerto Barrios
❧

Alegría, host of the call-in show "Línea Directa," was shot at least five times outside his home in Puerto Barrios, a port city located on the Caribbean coast in Izabal Department.

Alegría, who also worked as a part-time correspondent for the national radio network Emisoras Unidas, had reportedly been threatened on three different occasions after broadcasting stories about corruption. In addition, one of his colleagues told the press that local officials had tried to bribe Alegría to keep him quiet about their activities.

Police detained two suspects in connection with Alegría's murder. One suspect had a 9 mm handgun whose bullets apparently matched those found at the crime scene. Preliminary investigations by the Puerto Barrios prosecutor's office revealed that the handgun had recently fired six shots.

On September 20, the Ombudsman's Office for Human Rights (PDH) released the results of its investigations. The report concluded that Alegría's murder was politically motivated and was probably masterminded by local officials in retaliation for the journalist's coverage of corruption in Puerto Barrios. The PDH added that the two suspects in police custody were scapegoats. A report with the PDH's findings was sent to the newly created Prosecutor's Office for Crimes against Journalists.

In early October, the two suspects were released after ballistics testing proved that the confiscated handgun was not the murder weapon.

At year's end, the Puerto Barrios prosecutor's office and police were investigating Alegría's murder as

either a crime of passion, a politically motivated crime, or a common crime. However, they have not offered any evidence to support their theories. According to the news agency CERIGUA, a local prosecutor declared that a political motivation could neither be ruled out nor confirmed.

HAITI: 1

BRIGNOLLE LINDOR,
Radio Echo 2000, December 3, 2001,
Petit-Goâve

A machete-wielding mob hacked to death Lindor, news director of the private station Radio Echo 2000 that is based in the coastal town of Petit-Goâve, some 40 miles west of Port-au-Prince.

At 11 a.m., Lindor and a colleague were driving to one of Lindor's other jobs, as a customs official. Their car was ambushed by supporters of President Jean-Bertrand Aristide's Lavalas Family party. Lindor's colleague fled, but Lindor was attacked and killed after he tried to take refuge in the nearby home of a local town counselor.

Lindor hosted the political talk show "Dialogue." He had received numerous threats from local authorities for inviting members of the 15-party opposition coalition Democratic Convergence to appear on his show.

After Aristide launched a "zero tolerance" anti-crime campaign in June, implying that street criminals caught red-handed could be summarily punished without trial,

Petit-Goâve deputy mayor Dumé Bony announced in public that the "zero tolerance" policy should be applied to Lindor. Opposition parties and human rights groups accused Aristide of issuing a carte blanche for extrajudicial executions.

Lindor's December 11 funeral turned violent when police used bludgeons and tear gas on mourners who were shouting anti-Aristide slogans, according to wire reports.

INDIA: 1

MOOLCHAND YADAV,
free-lancer, July 30, 2001, Jhansi

Yadav, a free-lance reporter who regularly contributed to Hindi-language dailies, including *Jansatta* and *Punjab Kesari*, was shot dead on the street in Jhansi, Uttar Pradesh. Colleagues said that Yadav had been murdered at the behest of two powerful landowners angered by his exposés about local corruption.

LATVIA: 1

GUNDARS MATISS,
Kurzeme Vards, November 28, Liepaja

Matiss, a crime reporter with the Liepaja-based daily *Kurzeme Vards*, was attacked on November 15 in the stairwell of his apartment building after he returned home from a shopping expedition. In a phone conversation from the hospital two hours after the attack, Matiss told the paper's editor-in-chief, Andzilss Remess, that someone followed him home and hit him from behind with a truncheon or club. He was struck several times on the head, arms, and legs. The assailant fled when neighbors interrupted the attack.

Matiss underwent three operations and fell into a coma. He died on November 28 from a brain hemorrhage. The reporter had most recently investigated the contraband alcohol trade in Liepaja, according to Remess.

Though the police cited robbery, personal revenge, and retaliation for his journalism as possible motives, Matiss had not been robbed, and does not seem to have been involved in any serious personal dispute. His editor told CPJ: "Matiss knew a lot about the criminal world. He was one of those reporters who went deep." At press time, the police investigation was still ongoing.

MEXICO: 1

JOSÉ LUIS ORTEGA MATA,
Semanario de Ojinaga, February 19, 2001, Ojinaga

Ortega Mata, 37, was the editor of the weekly *Semanario de Ojinaga*, based in Ojinaga, Chihuahua State. He was shot twice in the head at close range with a .22-caliber firearm on the evening of February 19, according to local press reports.

Friends and relatives of the journalist linked his murder to a front-page story in the February 15 issue of *Semanario de Ojinaga* reporting that the federal Attorney General's Office (PGR) was investigating drug trafficking activities in the town of Aldama, near the state capital, Chihuahua. *Semanario de Ojinaga* also claimed that local traffickers were moving drugs from safe houses in Aldama through Ojinaga to the United States.

It has also been reported that the paper was about to publish a story alleging that drug traffickers were funding the electoral campaigns of local politicians, and that Ortega Mata had received threats in connection with the story. In the past, the weekly has run articles criticizing local politicians and police.

On April 29, a businessman named Jesús Manuel Herrera was arrested by state police and charged with Ortega Mata's murder based on eyewitness testimony. However, jail records show that the alleged eyewitness who identified Herrera as the assailant was in jail at the time of Ortega Mata's death. In addition, the Chihuahua Attorney General's Office was unable to provide a motive and offered no other evidence. Despite these revelations, Herrera remained imprisoned pending further investigations.

On July 13, after several hearings and more than 70 days in prison, an appeals court judge ruled that the evidence against Herrera was insufficient, and he was released.

PALESTINIAN AUTHORITY TERRITORIES: 1

MUHAMMAD AL-BISHAWI,
Najah Press Office, IslamOnline.net,
July 31, 2001, Nablus, West Bank
⦈

Al-Bishawi, a reporter for the Nablus-based Palestinian news service Najah Press Office and for IslamOnline.net, an Internet news service based in Qatar, was killed in an Israeli missile attack that had targeted Hamas leader Jamal Mansour. Israel had accused Mansour of masterminding several suicide bombings.

Various sources, including al-Bishawi's Cairo-based editor, reported that at the time of the attack, al-Bishawi was in the Palestinian Center for Studies and Media, a Hamas information office, to interview Mansour for an article he was writing for IslamOnline.net.

Al-Bishawi covered many topics for IslamOnline.net, ranging from Palestinian weddings to suicide bombers.

PARAGUAY: 1

SALVADOR MEDINA VELÁZQUEZ,
FM Ñemity, January 5, 2001, Capiibary
⦈

Medina, 27, president of the board of community radio station FM Ñemity in the town of Capiibary in the San Pedro Department, about 250 km (150 miles) from Asunción, was ambushed and shot by an unidentified gunman.

The journalist was driving a motorcycle with his brother Gaspar when a masked attacker came out from behind some bushes and shot him in the left side at point-blank range. The attacker then fled into the bushes, according to local press reports. Medina lost control of his motorcycle, fell to the ground, and died immediately.

The journalist's family linked the

attack to his reports on timber smuggling in state-owned forest reservations in Capiibary, local sources told CPJ. In particular, Medina had singled out a gang of alleged smugglers with ties to the National Republican Association (ARN), also known as the Colorado Party.

One of those whom Medina had accused was arrested in March for timber smuggling. In addition, Medina had covered incidents of livestock theft, along with organized crime in a nearby town.

In January and February, the Paraguayan police arrested four men suspected of killing Medina, but at least four other suspects were still at large.

In a hearing on September 6, Public Prosecutor Ramón Trinidad Zelaya charged Milcíades Maylin, one of the four suspects in police custody, with Medina's murder. Judge Silvio Flores granted Trinidad's request that the charges against the three other suspects be dismissed.

On October 16, a three-judge sentencing tribunal found Maylin guilty of murdering Medina and sentenced him to a 25-year prison term. Medina's relatives, however, believe that the individuals who ordered the murder have not been brought to justice.

PHILIPPINES: 2

ROLAND URETA,
Radio DYKR, January 3, 2001,
Aklan Province
⋙

Radio journalist Ureta was gunned down on the night of January 3 when two motorcycle-riding men waylaid him en route from Kalibo, the capital of Aklan Province, to the town of Lezo.

Ureta was program director of the radio station DYKR, an affiliate of the Radio Mindanao Network. Police estimated that he was killed within an hour of leaving the radio station, where he had just hosted "Agong Nightwatch," his evening radio program.

Ureta was apparently murdered as a result of his radio commentaries, which included pieces about local government corruption and police involvement in the drug trade.

CANDELARIO CAYONA,
Radio DXLL, May 30, 2001,
Zamboanga City
⋙

At about 6 a.m. on May 30, three unidentified men ambushed Cayona, a radio commentator for the local station DXLL, as he left home on his motorcycle to host a morning broadcast. Cayona died on the spot from four gunshot wounds, including two to the face. The assailants, all identified as young males, fled the scene.

Cayona was an outspoken commentator who often criticized local politicians, the military, and Muslim separatist guerrillas. The journalist had recently received several death threats, including an on-air threat that was phoned in by Abu Sabaya, spokesman for the guerrilla group Abu Sayyaf. Although Cayona reported the threats to station officials, he was not escorted by a bodyguard on the morning of the attack.

Cayona is the second DXLL staffer to be murdered in recent years. In 1998, Rey Bancayrin, another outspoken commentator for the station, was actually killed on the air when two unidentified gunmen burst into the studio and shot him dead.

RUSSIA: 1

EDUARD MARKEVICH,
Novy Reft, September 18, Reftinsky,
Sverdlovsk Region

Markevich, 29, editor and publisher of *Novy Reft,* the local newspaper in the town of Reftinsky, Sverdlovsk Region, was found dead on September 18. He had been shot in the back.

Novy Reft often criticized local officials, and Markevich's colleagues told the Itar-Tass news service that he had received threatening telephone phone calls prior to the attack.

This was not the first attack on Markevich, the Region-Inform news agency reported. In 1998, two unknown assailants broke into his apartment and severely beat him in front of his pregnant wife. They were never caught.

Last year, Markevich was illegally detained for 10 days after the local prosecutor's office charged him with defamation over a *Novy Reft* article questioning the propriety of a lucrative government contract that gave a former deputy prosecutor the exclusive right to represent the Reftinsky administration in court.

In May 2001, federal prosecutor general Vladimir Ustinov reprimanded the local prosecutor for violating Markevich's constitutional rights.

Police have launched an investigation into Markevich's murder. Almost four months after the journalist's death, authorities have made no progress, the Moscow-based Center for Journalism in Extreme Situations has reported. Markevich's wife continues to publish *Novy Reft.*

THAILAND: 2

WITHAYUT SANGSOPIT,
free-lancer, April 10, 2001, Surat Thani

Withayut, a radio journalist and commentator, was gunned down on April 10 in the southern city of Surat Thani.

According to police, Withayut was approached by several gunmen and shot five times as he was about to enter his radio studio to begin his popular morning program, "Catch Up With the World." Withayut's program was carried on Fourth Army Radio, the regional affiliate of the Royal Thai Army Radio and Television network.

Surat Thani police believe Withayut, 56, was killed as a result of his reporting on irregularities involving a 50 million baht (US$1.1 million) real estate deal for a municipal garbage dump. The reports began in 1999 and eventually led the Interior Ministry to investigate and to order a portion of the money returned to the government.

Police arrested two men in connection with the shooting, one of them a municipal official implicated in the garbage dump scandal.

A well-known radio commentator in southern Thailand, Withayut was for many years a correspondent for the Bangkok-based, Thai-language *Daily News* before starting his radio program. Police said the journalist had received numerous death threats and was under police protection prior to the murder. However, Withayut's protection was lifted shortly before the killing, according to several Thai newspapers.

KASET PUENGPAK,
Thai Rath, May 2, 2001, Viset Chaichan

Kaset, a stringer for the Thai-language newspaper *Thai Rath*, was shot dead in Viset Chaichan District, Ang Thong Province. Kaset was known for his reporting on local drug gangs linked to powerful politicians and police officers, according to *Thai Rath* and several Thai journalists. The Thai Journalists Association issued a statement saying that Kaset was likely murdered for his journalistic work. After the killing, authorities interrogated a police corporal who had quarreled with Kaset over law enforcement issues in the area. No arrests have been reported in the case.

UKRAINE: 1

IGOR ALEKSANDROV,
Tor, July 7, 2001, Slavyansk

Aleksandrov, 44 and director of Tor, an independent television company based in Slavyansk, Donetsk Region, in eastern Ukraine, was attacked on the morning of July 3.

Unknown attackers assaulted Aleksandrov with baseball bats as he entered Tor's offices, according to local news reports. Tor deputy director Sergei Cherneta described the attack to the regional newspaper *Donbass*: "All of a sudden we heard...blows and screams, after that we heard a moan. I ran downstairs....Our manager was lying in the lobby in a pool of blood with his head cracked open. Two large baseball bats were left nearby."

Aleksandrov was rushed to the local city hospital, where he underwent surgery. The journalist never regained consciousness and died from the head injuries on the morning of July 7.

Aleksandrov's colleagues believe the murder was connected to his television program, "Bez Retushi" (Without Retouching), which featured investigative coverage of government corruption and organized crime. The program often criticized Slavyansk municipal authorities.

Soon after the attack, Donetsk regional prosecutor Viktor Pshonka launched an official investigation. The chief of the Donetsk Administration of Internal Affairs, Gen. Vladimir Malyshev, stated that revenge was the leading motive in the murder but did not elaborate.

Aleksandrov became well known in 1998, when prosecutors brought a criminal case against him for insulting the honor and dignity of a parliamentary deputy. The Slavyansk City Court initially found the journalist guilty but later reviewed its decision after criticism from Ukrainian journalists and international human rights organizations.

The deputy withdrew his defamation complaint against the journalist last year. That removed the immediate legal threat but did not clear Aleksandrov's name, since his conviction was still technically under review. Claiming damage to his professional reputation, Aleksandrov appealed to the European Court of Human Rights, where the case was pending at the time of his murder.

In late August, law enforcement officials arrested an unnamed suspect, according to local press reports. The officials claimed that Aleksandrov's murder was a case of mistaken identity and was not connected with his journalism.

A parliamentary investigative commission was established in September to examine Aleksandrov's murder. In December, the commission voiced its doubts about the validity of the "mistaken identity" theory and stated that it knew who had really killed Aleksandrov, according to local reports.

While the commission refused to forward this information to law enforcement officials, it accused the Ukrainian Security Service of falsifying evidence in the case.

In mid-December, the General Prosecutor's Office officially charged the suspect detained in August, Yuri Verdyuk, with Aleksandrov's murder, local and international sources reported. On December 27, the Donetsk Regional Court scheduled Verdyuk's trial for September 11, 2002. After public calls for an immediate trial, the court re-scheduled proceedings for January 2002; they were then postponed until March.

The journalist's colleagues and family maintain that he was killed for his work, local sources told CPJ.

UNITED KINGDOM: 1

MARTIN O'HAGAN,
Sunday World, September 28, 2001,
Lurgan, Northern Ireland

O'Hagan, a 51-year-old investigative journalist with the Dublin newspaper *Sunday World*, was shot dead outside his home in the Northern Ireland town of Lurgan.

O'Hagan was shot several times from a passing car while walking home from a pub with his wife, who was not hurt in the attack. The vehicle used in the attack was found on fire not far from the crime scene. O'Hagan, who worked in the Belfast office of the *Sunday World*, was an Irish Catholic journalist who had become well known for his coverage of both Catholic and Protestant paramilitary groups.

More than 20 years ago, before he became a journalist, O'Hagan was convicted of running guns for the Irish Republican Army and served five years in prison. But he later turned away from radical politics, studying sociology at the Open University and the University of Ulster and then entering journalism as a free-lancer for local newspapers. His connections in both Catholic Republican and Protestant Loyalist circles, as well as in the British security forces, gave him unusual insight into the conflict but also made him a target for paramilitary reprisals.

In 1989, he was kidnapped and interrogated by the Irish Republican

Army, which tried unsuccessfully to force him to divulge his sources, and in the early 1990s he was forced to flee to Dublin after receiving death threats from a top loyalist gunman. O'Hagan returned to Belfast in 1995 after most paramilitary groups had declared cease-fires.

While O'Hagan had received threats from Protestant militants in the past, it is not clear if he had been threatened prior to the shooting. The Red Hand Defenders, which police consider a cover name for Protestant militants from the Loyalist Volunteer Force (LVF) and the Ulster Defense Association, claimed responsibility for his murder.

Police initially identified the LVF as a primary suspect. Prior to his murder, O'Hagan had been working on several stories about the LVF, the BBC reported. Colleagues believe the LVF targeted O'Hagan for exposing the narcotics network they controlled, as well as assassinations and intimidation rackets they orchestrated. The police investigation continues, and at press time no one had been convicted for the killing.

UNITED STATES: 2

WILLIAM BIGGART,
free-lancer, September 11, New York City

Biggart, a free-lance news photographer, was killed in the terrorist attacks on the World Trade Center. The journalist's body was found on September 15 in the rubble at Ground Zero, near the bodies of several firefighters. Biggart had rushed to the scene with his camera shortly after hearing about the attacks.

ROBERT STEVENS,
The Sun, October 5, 2001, Boca Raton

Stevens, 63, a photo editor at the tabloid newspaper The Sun, died of inhalation anthrax in Boca Raton, Florida. Authorities opened a criminal investigation into the killing but have not determined where the anthrax came from. However, officials did confirm that the type of anthrax that killed Stevens is the same strain that was mailed to NBC Nightly News anchor Tom Brokaw.

YUGOSLAVIA: 2

KEREM LAWTON,
Associated Press Television News,
March 29, 2001, Krivenik, Kosovo

Lawton, 30, a British national and producer for Associated Press Television News, died from shrapnel wounds sustained when a shell struck his car. At least two other civilians were feared dead in the attack, and at least 10 others were injured.

On March 28, the Macedonian Army launched a mini-offensive against Albanian insurgents in the village of Gracani in northern Macedonia. Just across the border in Kosovo, NATO-led peacekeepers stepped up patrols to intercept Albanian guerrillas crossing into Macedonia.

At the time of his death, Lawton had just arrived in the village of Krivenik to cover the deployment of additional NATO-led peacekeeping forces. Both Macedonian military officials and ethnic Albanian insurgents denied responsibility for Lawton's death and the other civilian casualties.

MILAN PANTIC,
Vecernje Novosti, June 11, 2001,
Jagodina, Serbia

Pantic, a reporter for the Belgrade daily *Vecernje Novosti*, was killed shortly before 8 a.m. as he was entering his apartment building in the central Serbian town of Jagodina.

Pantic had gone to fetch a loaf of bread. As he entered the front door of his building, attackers grabbed him from behind, broke his neck, and then struck him several times on the head with a sharp object as he lay face down on the ground, according to *Vecernje Novosti*.

An eyewitness saw two attackers—both aged 20 to 30 and wearing masks and black shirts—running from the scene, sources at *Vecernje Novosti* said. Local authorities launched an investigation, but no progress was reported at year's end.

The 47-year-old journalist worked as the *Vecernje Novosti* correspondent for the Pomoravlje region of central Serbia. He reported extensively on criminal affairs, including financial malfeasance in local companies. His wife, Zivka Pantic, told *Vecernje Novosti* that Pantic had received numerous telephone threats in response to articles he had written.

JOURNALISTS KILLED: MOTIVE UNCONFIRMED

BANGLADESH: 1

AHSAN ALI,
free-lancer, July 20, 2001, Rupganj

Ali, a stringer for the daily newspaper *Jugantor*, was reported missing on July 20 and found dead on July 22 in an irrigation canal in Rupganj Village, where he lived. Assailants had bound the journalist's hands and legs, burned his face and chest with nitric acid, and stabbed him to death, according to police.

Ali had received death threats that same week from a local leader of the ruling Awami League's youth wing, according to his wife, Shahida Akhter. Akhter told journalists that the threats followed Ali's reporting months earlier that party activists were linked to incidents of highway robbery on the road from Dhaka to Chittagong. However, she also suggested that Ali might have been killed over a land dispute with some relatives.

BRAZIL: 1

MÁRIO COELHO
DE ALMEIDA FILHO,
A Verdade, August 16, 2001, Magé

An unidentified gunman killed Coelho, administrative editor and publisher of the local thrice-monthly newspaper *A Verdade*, outside his house with a .45-caliber handgun.

The journalist was murdered just one day before he was

scheduled to testify in a criminal defamation lawsuit.

Some local observers claimed that Coelho had persuaded local politicians to bankroll *A Verdade* in exchange for favorable coverage, according to the Brazilian media news Web site Comunique-se.com. Conversely, other sources claimed that Coelho had used the threat of negative coverage to extort money from politicians.

The suit against Coelho was brought by Magé mayor Narriman Zito and her husband, José Camilo Zito dos Santos, mayor of the local municipality of Duque de Caxias, after *A Verdade* printed the minutes of a state legislative assembly session during which a political rival of Zito accused her of having an affair with one of her security guards.

A Verdade often criticized local politicians for alleged corruption, and Coelho's father told the Brazilian daily *O Globo* that his son had received several phone threats five months before his death.

On September 14, acting on an anonymous tip, Magé police arrested retired Military Police sergeant Manoel Daniel de Abreu Filho as a suspect in the murder, according to *O Globo*. The person who tipped off the police also told them that de Abreu Filho had worked as a security guard for Rio de Janeiro state assemblywoman Andréia Zito, daughter of Duque de Caxias mayor Zito dos Santos.

At the time of his arrest, de Abreu Filho worked as a bodyguard for the wife of Waldir Zito, mayor of the city of Belford Roxo and brother of José Camilo Zito dos Santos.

After witnesses were shown a picture of de Abreu Filho and recognized him as the murderer, Judge Geraldo José Machado ordered that he be held in prison. The police seized two handguns from de Abreu Filho and said they would perform ballistic tests to determine if they were used in the crime. The police are also seeking to determine whether de Abreu Filho acted on his own or followed orders.

COLOMBIA: 5

PABLO EMILIO PARRA CASTAÑEDA, *Planadas Cultural Estéreo*, June 27, 2001, Bogotá

Leftist guerrillas shot Parra, 50, twice in the head after abducting him from his home in the Tolima Department township of Planadas. The body of Parra, who founded and directed the community radio station Planadas Cultural Estéreo, was found later that day along a rural road.

Col. Norberto Torres of the Planadas police said that after killing Parra, rebels from the Revolutionary Armed Forces of Colombia (FARC) attached a note to his body that read: "For being a spy." FARC rebels control the area, according to local authorities.

The FARC, the nation's largest leftist rebel group, later claimed responsibility for the assassination in a communiqué that accused Parra of being an informant for the army, Torres said.

When contacted by CPJ, a spokesman for the army's 6th Brigade denied that Parra was an informant. The spokesman, who asked to remain unidentified, said no one at the brigade had heard of him. Parra's 30-year-old daughter, Liliana Parra, also denied that her father was an informant. She told CPJ that her father broadcast popular music and community news on his radio program but never discussed political subjects.

The radio station was based in Parra's house. The journalist also worked with the local office of the Red Cross and had never received death threats, Liliana Parra said.

The departmental prosecutor's office was investigating the murder but had made no arrests by year's end. Special Prosecutor Jairo Francisco Leal Alvarado said evidence found so far suggested that Parra was not killed because of his work as a journalist. He would not elaborate.

ARQUÍMEDES ARIAS HENAO, *Fresno Estéreo,* July 4, 2001, Fresno

Arias, founder and director of the local radio station Fresno Estéreo, was killed during the evening when an assassin burst into his home in the Tolima Department township of Fresno and shot him three times in the head.

After shooting Arias, the gunman fled on a motorcycle driven by a man waiting outside, said José Parra, an investigator at the Tolima Department prosecutor's office.

Parra said no arrests have been made, and that the reasons for Arias' assassination remain unclear. Parra reported that the region is crawling with fighters from Colombia's two main leftist guerrilla groups and a rival right-wing paramilitary army.

Before moving to Fresno earlier in the year, Arias founded and directed several other radio stations that, along with Fresno Estéreo, broadcast popular music and nonpolitical community programs, said his brother, Eduardo Arias.

Eduardo Arias told CPJ that his brother operated the radio station from his home and had never received death threats.

There had been no progress in the investigation by year's end, Parra said.

EDUARDO ESTRADA GUTIÉRREZ, broadcaster, July 16, 2001, San Pablo

Estrada, a community leader and local broadcaster, was killed in the early morning of July 16 in the municipality of San Pablo, located in Bolívar Department.

Unidentified attackers shot the journalist as he was returning home with his wife after attending a family reunion.

Estrada was the president of the Asociación para el Desarrollo de la Comunicación y la Cultura de San Pablo, a community organization affiliated to a network of community radio stations. At the time of his death, the journalist was working to launch a community station for San Pablo.

Investigations have not revealed the identity of the attackers or the possible motive.

HERIBERTO CÁRDENAS ESCUDERO, retired radio and newspaper reporter, November 14, 2001, Buenaventura

Four armed assailants wearing hoods burst into the home of

Cárdenas, a retired journalist who lived in the western Colombian city of Buenaventura, killing him, his son, and his brother, police said.

Cárdenas was watching an evening soccer match on television when the attackers broke into the house and opened fire, said Col. Luis Alberto Ramírez of the Buenaventura Police.

Cárdenas, 51, died from gunshot wounds to his head and chest. His son and brother died two days later.

It was initially reported that Cárdenas' teenage nephew was killed in the attack. However, Colonel Ramírez said that the nephew was stabbed to death last year, and that the November 14 attack may have been related to his slaying.

Cárdenas had worked as a news announcer with radio Carcajal Stéreo in Buenaventura and as a local reporter for several newspapers, including *El Tiempo* and *El Espectador*, two of Colombia's most prominent national publications. In the past, journalists from both papers have been targeted by left-wing guerrillas and right-wing paramilitaries, as have provincial broadcast journalists all over the country.

During the last year, Cárdenas worked as a press officer at the local fire department.

At year's end, Colonel Ramírez said the investigation had turned up nothing new. Though no one had been captured, he still believed that Cárdenas was killed for personal reasons. The prosecutor handling the case in Buenaventura, Balmer Restrepo, refused to discuss the case over the phone.

ÁLVARO ALONSO ESCOBAR, *La Región,* December 23, 2001, Fundación

Escobar, the publisher of the monthly newspaper *La Región*, was shot and killed by a lone gunman after an argument, according to state police commander Luis Mesa. A visitor arrived at Escobar's home in the town of Fundación, Magdalena Department, at around 7 p.m. and shot the journalist three times in the head before fleeing on a motorcycle.

Magdalena Department is known as a violent area, with leftist guerillas and rightist paramilitary forces both active.

Mesa told CPJ that he believed Escobar had been murdered for personal reasons, but could provide no further details.

FRANCE: 1

NICOLAS GIUDICI, *Nice-Matin* and *Corse-Matin,* June 17, Corsica

Giudici's body was found in some bushes on the edge of a dirt track near the village of Piedriggio in northern Corsica on the morning of June 17. Giudici, 52, had been shot three times, in the left arm, chest and right hip, according to local reports. His torched car was found 50 kilometers (30 miles) away at the bottom of a ravine near the town of Cervione.

Guidici frequently covered the separatist movement on the French island of Corsica as a reporter for the regional weekly *Nice-Matin* and the daily *Corse-Matin*. He was also the author of *Le Crépuscule des Corses*

(Twilight of the Corsicans), a critical assessment of Corsican society that was published in 1997.

Local police launched an investigation into Giudici's murder, according to The Associated Press, but by year's end the inquiry was virtually at a standstill. Several possible motives, related both to Guidici's private life and his profession, were listed in local newspapers—including a possible connection to a local theft of rare paintings that concerned Guidici, who was a collector.

Political and criminal violence are part of life in Corsica. But Guidici's colleagues were unaware of any politically sensitive work that might have led to his murder.

KUWAIT: 1

HIDAYA SULTAN AL-SALEM,
Al-Majales, March 20, 2001, Kuwait City

Al-Salem, a 66-year-old veteran journalist who owned and edited the weekly magazine *Al-Majales,* was killed on her way to work when an armed assailant opened fire on her chauffeur-driven car in Kuwait City.

The assailant, who was described as wearing a traditional long robe, apparently got out of a four-wheel drive car and fired several rounds into al-Salem's car while it was stopped in traffic. She died shortly thereafter.

According to Kuwaiti police and prosecutors, the main suspect, a police officer named Khaled al-Azmi, confessed to killing al-Salem. However, he later recanted in court, saying police had forced him to confess. One Kuwaiti source who was monitoring the case told CPJ that al-Azmi recanted on the advice of his lawyer in order to avoid the death penalty. CPJ could not verify this claim. In February 2002, al-Azmi was convicted of the murder.

Early in the investigation, Kuwaiti authorities said that al-Azmi killed al-Salem in revenge for an earlier *Al-Majales* article that he found insulting to the women of his tribe. The article, however, was written some eight months earlier—a fact that struck some as peculiar.

There was considerable speculation about the reasons for the assassination, including alleged financial disputes within al-Salem's family and other alleged disputes with some of her employees. In the latest edition of *Al-Majales,* according to press reports, al-Salem published an open letter claiming she had been harassed by the police.

In November, a source in Kuwait said there was speculation that al-Azmi may have killed al-Salem because of a personal dispute between the two involving al-Azmi's sister.

PAKISTAN: 1

ASADULLAH,
free-lancer, September 1, 2001, Karachi

Asadullah, an occasional contributor to the news agency Kashmir Press International (KPI), was shot dead on the streets of Karachi by unidentified gunmen. KPI is run by the Jamaat-i-Islami, a conservative religious party. Local journalists said Asadullah was also an active member of the party, and that members of a rival political party may have killed him. The motive behind the shooting was unclear at year's end.

cooperatives she had organized in the region. However, police did not exclude the possibility that the murder was related to her journalism.

PHILIPPINES: 2

MOHAMMAD YUSOP,
Radio DXID, February 23, 2001,
Pagadian City

Yusop, a commentator for the radio station DXID in Pagadian City, was shot in the back of the head by two men on a motorcycle while he was riding in a three-wheel pedicab. He died on the spot.

Yusop hosted a religious program and was not known to have broadcast any controversial reports. The station manager at DXID, owned by the Islamic Radio Broadcasting Company, said that he was not aware of any threats against Yusop, and no group claimed responsibility for his murder.

JOY MORTEL,
Mindoro Guardian, May 31, 2001,
Occidental Mindoro

Mortel, a reporter for the *Mindoro Guardian*, was killed in her home in Barangay Talabanhan, Occidental Mindoro Province, according to local press reports. Two unidentified armed men reportedly shot Mortel after a heated argument. She died from multiple gunshot wounds.

The motive for Mortel's murder remained unclear at year's end. Local police told the *Manila Times* that communist rebels had targeted Mortel because of her allegedly questionable financial dealings relating to local

THAILAND: 3

SUCHART CHARNCHANAVIVAT,
Chao Mukdahan, Siam Rath,
November 18, 2001, Mukdahan

SETTHA SRIRIWAT,
Naew Na, Channel 3,
November 18, 2001, Mukdahan

CHUVIT CHUEHARN,
iTV, *The Nation, Krungthep Thurakij,*
November 18, 2001, Mukdahan

Paiboon Bunthos, a stringer for the daily *Thai Rath* in the provincial town of Mukdahan, near the Laotian border, opened fire on four of his colleagues during dinner on a floating restaurant, killing three, before committing suicide by turning his weapon on himself, according to police reports.

The reporters killed were Suchart, 62, editor of the newspaper *Chao Mukdahan* and a stringer for the daily *Siam Rath*; Settha, 38, a stringer for the daily *Naew Na* and Channel 3 television; and Chuvit, 38, a stringer for iTV, *The Nation* newspaper, and the daily *Krungthep Thurakij*. Also injured in the attack were Somboon Saenviset, a stringer for the *Daily News*, and Vichian Susonna, a lawyer.

The motive behind the attack remains unclear. At the time of the shooting, police reported that one of the victims, Suchart Charnchanavivat, had recently published articles in his local newspaper, *Chao Mukdahan,* accusing unidentified local journalists of bribe-taking and extortion. According to Thai journalists, there were other long-standing differences among the men, including allegations of theft lodged by the gunman against others in the group.

The dinner at the floating restaurant was supposedly organized so that the men could settle their differences.

Officials of the Thai Journalists Association say that the incident in Mukdahan might be related to the journalists' illegal business activities. It is not uncommon in Thailand for provincial newspaper stringers, who are notoriously underpaid, to use their positions to solicit bribes or to gain favors with local officials. Mukdahan is a center for a thriving border trade with neighboring Laos, which may also have played a role in the killing, according to Thai journalists. In the aftermath of the incident, the Press Council of Thailand issued a letter on December 10 calling on national newspapers to exercise more care in training and recruiting their provincial stringers in order to minimize corruption and unethical behavior.

The Thai Journalists Association did not consider the attack to be related directly to journalism, but the bizarre nature of the tragedy makes it very difficult to sort out the gunman's motive.

UKRAINE: 1

OLEH BREUS,
XXI Vek, June 24, 2001, Luhansk

Breus, publisher of the regional weekly *XXI Vek* in the provincial city of Luhansk, was shot dead at approximately 11 p.m. while driving up to his house accompanied by his wife and a friend.

As Breus exited his car, he was shot four or five times in the head and back at point-blank range. Neither passenger was harmed.

Eyewitnesses heard the shots and saw two men fleeing, one of them holding a pistol. The Luhansk weekly *Kuryer* reported that both perpetrators left in a car that was parked nearby.

The motive for the murder remains unclear. As publisher of *XXI Vek*, Breus was mainly responsible for financial matters. He had other business interests apart from the newspaper and also held a senior position in the regional Communist Party of Workers and Peasants.

XXI Vek editor Yuri Yurov told CPJ that the newspaper generally reflected Breus' political positions and business interests.

Local police have launched an investigation into Breus' murder. At year's end, a confidential source told CPJ that there is some evidence linking Breus' murder to both his business interests and to material published in *XXI Vek*.

YUGOSLAVIA: 1

BEKIM KASTRATI,
Bota Sot, October 19, Lausa, Kosovo

Kastrati, an ethnic Albanian journalist for the Albanian-language daily *Bota Sot*, was shot on October 19 at around 8 p.m. in the village of Lausa, west of the provincial capital,

Pristina, along with two other men who were riding in his car at the time. One of the passengers was killed, and the other was wounded.

Kastrati's employer, the Geneva-based *Bota Sot*, supports politician Ibrahim Rugova and his leading ethnic Albanian party, the Democratic Alliance of Kosovo.

A second man killed in the attack, Besim Dajaku, was reported to have been a current or former bodyguard of Rugova. The third man injured in the attack, Gani Geci, was a former member of the now-disbanded Kosovo Liberation Army. According to local sources, Geci was believed to be the true target of the shooting, but the murder investigation is still open. ■

JOURNALISTS IN PRISON IN 2001

118 journalists in prison on December 31, 2001

There were 118 journalists in prison around the world at the end of 2001 who were jailed for practicing their profession. The number is up significantly from the previous year, when 81 journalists were in jail, and represents a return to the level of 1998, when 118 were also imprisoned.

In January 2002, CPJ sent letters of inquiry to the head of state of every country on the list below, requesting information about each jailed journalist. Readers are encouraged to add their voices to CPJ's by writing directly to the heads of state, whose names and addresses can be found on CPJ's Web site (www.cpj.org).

Our census of imprisoned journalists represents a snapshot of all the journalists who were incarcerated when the clock struck midnight on December 31. It does not include the many journalists who were imprisoned and released during the year; accounts of those cases can be found in the regional sections of this book.

A word about how this list is compiled: In totalitarian societies where independent journalism is forbidden, CPJ often defends persecuted writers whose governments would view them as political dissidents rather than journalists. This category would embrace the samizdat publishers of the former Soviet Union and the wall-poster essayists of the pre-Tiananmen period in China. We also include political analysts, human rights activists, and others who were prosecuted because of their written or broadcast work.

CPJ uses a broad definition of the term "imprisoned." We consider all journalists held forcibly against their will by governments, guerrillas, or kidnappers to be imprisoned. For example, we include two Algerian journalists, Djamel Eddine Fahassi and Aziz Bouabdallah, who were apparently abducted by government agents in 1995 and 1997, respectively. While there is no information about their whereabouts, CPJ continues to hold the Algerian government responsible for their fate.

CPJ does not include "missing" journalists on this list, but we monitor all such cases. For example, we continue to demand that Belarus account for the disappearance of TV news cameraman Dmitry Zavadsky, who vanished in July 2000. ∎

ALGERIA: 2

Djamel Eddine Fahassi, Alger Chaîne III
Imprisoned: May 6, 1995

Fahassi, a reporter for the state-run radio station Alger Chaîne III and a contributor to several Algerian newspapers, including the now banned weekly of the Islamic Salvation Front *Al-Forqane*, was abducted near his home in the al-Harrache suburb of Algiers by four well-dressed men carrying walkie-talkies. According to eyewitnesses who later spoke with his wife, the men called out Fahassi's name and then pushed him into a waiting car. He has not been seen since, and Algerian authorities have denied any knowledge of his arrest.

Prior to Fahassi's "disappearance," Algerian authorities targeted him on at least two occasions because his writing criticized the government. In late 1991, he was arrested after an article in *Al-Forqane* criticized a raid conducted by security forces on an Algiers neighborhood. On January 1, 1992, the Blida Military Court convicted him of disseminating false information, attacking a state institution, and disseminating information that could harm national unity.

He received a one-year suspended sentence and was released after five months. On February 17, 1992, he was arrested a second time for allegedly attacking state institutions and spreading false information. He was transferred to the Ain Salah Detention Center in southern Algeria, where hundreds of Islamic suspects were detained in the months following the cancellation of the January 1992 elections.

In late January 2002, Algerian ambassador to the U.S. Idriss Jazairy responded to a CPJ query saying an investigation was launched and did not find those responsible. The ambassador added there was no evidence of state involvement.

Aziz Bouabdallah, *Al-Alam al-Siyassi*
Imprisoned: April 12, 1997

Three armed men abducted Bouabdallah, a 22-year-old reporter for the daily *Al-Alam al-Siyassi*, from his home in Algiers. According to Bouabdallah's family, the men stormed into their home and, after identifying the journalist, grabbed him, put his hands behind his back, and pushed him out the door and into a waiting car. An article published in the daily *El-Watan* a few days after his abduction reported that Bouabdallah was in police custody and was expected to be released imminently.

In July 1997, CPJ received credible information that Bouabdallah was being held at the Châteauneuf detention facility in Algiers, where he had been tortured. Bouabdallah's whereabouts are currently unknown. Authorities have denied any knowledge of his abduction.

In late January 2002, Algerian ambassador to the U.S. Idriss Jazairy responded to a CPJ query saying an investigation was launched and did not find those responsible. The ambassador added there was no evidence of state involvement.

BANGLADESH: 1

Shahriar Kabir, free-lancer
Imprisoned: November 22, 2001

On November 22, police at Dhaka's

Zia International Airport arrested Kabir when he returned to Bangladesh from India, where he had interviewed minority Bangladeshi Hindus who fled there following attacks against their community after Bangladesh's October 1 parliamentary elections. Kabir—a documentary filmmaker, regular contributor to the national Bengali-language daily *Janakantha*, and author of several books about Bangladesh's war for independence—was arrested for "anti-state activities on the basis of intelligence reports and at the instruction of higher authorities," according to a police report. Police seized his passport, five videotapes, 13 audiotapes, several rolls of unprocessed film, and his camera, according to news reports.

A November 25 statement issued by the Home Ministry alleged that Kabir was "involved in a heinous bid to tarnish the image of Bangladesh and its government," according to a report published by *The Daily Star*, a leading national paper. "Kabir had made a whirlwind tour across India with ulterior motives to shoot video films," it said, noting that the video footage and other materials seized from Kabir upon his arrest were "objectionable, misleading, instigating and provocative to destroy communal harmony." That same day, a district magistrate's court authorized the government to detain Kabir for up to 30 days under the provisions of Bangladesh's Special Powers Act. Authorities in Bangladesh frequently abuse this act, which allows for the arbitrary arrest and detention of any citizen suspected of engaging in activities that threaten national security.

On December 8, the government charged Kabir with treason. His detention was later extended by another three months.

On January 12, 2002, in response to a habeas corpus petition, a High Court bench declared the extension of Kabir's term of detention to be illegal and ordered the journalist's release. However, Kabir continued to be held on the treason charge. On January 19, a separate High Court bench ordered Kabir to be released on interim bail for six months, pending his treason trial. The High Court also issued a "show cause" notice to the government asking prosecutors to demonstrate why Kabir should not be granted permanent bail.

On January 20, authorities released Kabir from Dhaka Central Jail, where he was greeted by hundreds of colleagues, relatives, and other supporters. At press time, the government had not dropped the treason charge against Kabir, a charge that carries a maximum penalty of death.

BURMA: 12

U Win Tin, free-lancer
Imprisoned: July 4, 1989

U Win Tin, former editor-in-chief of the daily *Hanthawati* and vice chairman of Burma's Writers Association, was arrested and sentenced to three years of hard labor on the false charge of arranging a "forced abortion" for a member of the opposition National League for Democracy. A well-known and influential journalist, U Win Tin was active in establishing independent publications during the

1988 student democracy movement. He also worked closely with National League for Democracy leader Daw Aung San Suu Kyi and was one of her closest advisers.

In 1992, he was sentenced to an additional 10 years for "writing and publishing pamphlets to incite treason against the State" and "giving seditious talks," according to a report published in May 2000 by the Defense Ministry's Office of Strategic Studies. On March 28, 1996, prison authorities extended U Win Tin's sentence by another seven years after they convicted him, along with at least 22 others, of producing clandestine publications—including a report describing the horrific conditions of Rangoon's Insein Prison to Yozo Yokota, the United Nations special rapporteur for human rights in Burma.

U Win Tin was charged under Section 5(e) of the Emergency Provisions Act for having "secretly published anti-government propaganda to create riots in jail," according to the Defense Ministry report. His cumulative sentence is, therefore, 20 years of hard labor and imprisonment.

U Win Tin is said to be in extremely poor health after years of maltreatment in Burma's prisons—including a period when he was kept in solitary confinement in one of Insein Prison's notorious "dog cells," formerly used as a kennel for the facility's guard dogs. He has told international observers that he is suffering from spondylitis, a degenerative spine disease. A politician interviewed by the Oslo-

based Democratic Voice of Burma in August 2001 said that U Win Tin had suffered from a stroke and has heart problems, and that he had recently undergone emergency surgery for a hernia.

Ohn Kyaing, free-lancer
Thein Tan, free-lancer
Imprisoned: September 6, 1990

On September 7, 1990, Col. Than Tun, Burma's deputy chief of military intelligence, announced at a press conference that Ohn Kyaing and Thein Tan were among six leaders of the opposition National League for Democracy arrested on the previous day, according to international news reports.

On October 19, the Information Committee of the junta (then known as the State Law and Order Restoration Council and later renamed the State Peace and Development Council) announced at a press conference that Ohn Kyaing and Thein Tan "had been sentenced to seven years imprisonment by a military tribunal for inciting unrest by writing false reports about the unrest which occurred in Mandalay on 8 August 1990," according to the BBC's translation of a state radio broadcast.

The Mandalay "unrest" referred to by the committee involved the killing of four pro-democracy demonstrators by the military. Government troops had fired on demonstrators—who were commemorating the democracy rallies of August 8, 1988, when hundreds were shot dead—killing two monks and two students.

Ohn Kyaing, who also used the name Aung Wint, is the former

editor of the newspaper *Botahtaung* and one of Burma's most famous, well-respected journalists. He retired from *Botahtaung* in December 1988, according to the PEN American Center, to become more involved in the pro-democracy movement. In 1990, Ohn Kyaing was elected as a member of parliament for the National League for Democracy (NLD), representing a district in Mandalay. (The results of the elections, which the NLD won, were never honored by the military junta.) A leading intellectual, he continued to write as an extension of his political activities.

Thein Tan, whose name is sometimes written as Thein Dan, was also a free-lance writer and political activist associated with the NLD.

PEN reported that in mid-1991, Ohn Kyaing received an additional sentence of 10 years in prison under the 1950 Emergency Provisions Act for his involvement in drafting a pamphlet for the NLD titled "The Three Paths to Power." Thein Tan also received an additional 10-year sentence, according to Amnesty International, presumably for the same reason.

In a list of Burmese political prisoners published in April 2001, Amnesty International reported that the sentences of both men were reduced to 10 years on January 1, 1993. However, Ohn Kyaing and Thein Tan remained in prison at the end of 2001. Ohn Kyaing was jailed at Taungoo Prison, and Thein Tan was jailed at Thayet Prison, according to the Thailand-based Assistance Association for Political Prisoners in Burma.

Maung Maung Lay Ngwe, *Pe-Tin-Than*
Imprisoned: September 1990

Maung Maung Lay Ngwe was arrested and charged with writing and distributing publications that "make people lose respect for the government." The publications were titled, collectively, *Pe-Tin-Than* (Echoes). CPJ believes he may have been released but could not confirm his legal status or find records of his sentencing.

Myo Myint Nyein, *Pe-Phu-Hlwar*
Sein Hlaing, *Pe-Phu-Hlwar*
Imprisoned: September 1990

Myo Myint Nyein, editor of the magazine *Pe-Phu-Hlwar*, and Sein Hlaing, the magazine's publisher, were arrested for publishing a pamphlet featuring a satirical poem by Nyan Paw titled "Bar Dwae Phyit Kon Byi Lae" (What's Happening To Us?), which the Burmese junta claimed was anti-government propaganda. They were sentenced to seven years in prison. On March 28, 1996, they were among at least 22 other prisoners accused of contributing to clandestine publications, including a report describing prison conditions that was delivered to Yozo Yokota, the United Nations special rapporteur for human rights in Burma. After a summary trial inside Insein Prison, they each received sentences of an additional seven years. Myo Myint Nyein was granted an early release on February 13, 2002.

Sein Hla Oo, free-lancer
Imprisoned: August 5, 1994

Sein Hla Oo, a free-lance journalist and former editor of the newspaper *Botahtaung*, was arrested along with dissident writer San San Nwe on charges of contacting anti-government groups and spreading information damaging to the state. On October 6, 1994, Sein Hla Oo was sentenced to 10 years in prison. San San Nwe and three other dissidents, including a former UNICEF worker, received sentences of seven to 15 years in prison on similar charges.

Officials said the five had "fabricated and sent anti-government reports" to diplomats in foreign embassies, foreign radio stations, and foreign journalists. Sein Hla Oo, elected in 1990 as a member of parliament representing the National League for Democracy (NLD), had been imprisoned previously for his political activities.

Though San San Nwe was granted early release in July 2001 along with 10 other political prisoners associated with the NLD, Sein Hla Oo remained in jail at the end of 2001. He was held at Myitkyina Prison, according to the Thailand-based Assistance Association for Political Prisoners in Burma. The group reported that during his imprisonment, Sein Hla Oo received an additional 20-year sentence, but CPJ was unable to verify this information.

Aung Htun, author
Tha Ban, free-lancer
Imprisoned: February 1998

Aung Htun was arrested in February 1998 for writing a seven-volume book documenting the history of the Burmese student movement. A writer and activist with the All Burma Federation of Student Unions, Aung Htun was sentenced to a total of 17 years imprisonment, according to a

joint report published in December 2001 by the Thailand-based Assistance Association of Political Prisoners in Burma and the Burma Lawyers Council. He was sentenced to three years for allegedly violating the 1962 Printer and Publishers Registration Act, seven years under the 1950 Emergency Provisions Act, and another seven years under the 1908 Unlawful Associations Act. He was said to be jailed at Tharawaddy Prison.

In April 1998, the All Burma Students Democratic Front announced that five others were also prosecuted for contributing to the books, including journalist Tha Ban, a former reporter for the newspaper *Kyemon* and a prominent Arakanese activist. Tha Ban, whose name is sometimes written as Thar Ban, was sentenced to seven years imprisonment and is jailed at Kale Prison, according to the Thailand-based Assistance Association for Political Prisoners in Burma.

Yan Aung Soe, free-lancer
Imprisoned: September 1998

In a press conference broadcast by state television on October 7, 1998, a senior military intelligence officer accused Yan Aung Soe, a journalist, writer, and political activist, of being involved in a wide-ranging plot by the political opposition to "incite anarchy and uprising," as translated by the BBC. Air Force Col. Thein Swe, of the Defense Department's Office of Strategic Studies, identified "Yan Aung Soe, alias Ye Htut," as a "hardcore member" of the Democratic Party for a New Society. (Yan Aung Soe is also known as Ye Htut, but he is not the journalist Ye

Htut who was arrested in September 1995 on the charge of sending "fabricated news" to individuals and media organizations abroad. The latter Ye Htut was included in CPJ's previous records of imprisoned journalists in Burma but was released in 2001, according to Burmese journalists in Thailand.) The officer said that Yan Aung Soe was involved in writing, printing, and distributing anti-government pamphlets.

Yan Aung Soe, also known by his pen name Thurein Htet Linn, was arrested in September 1998 and sentenced to 52 years in prison, according to the Thailand-based Assistance Association for Political Prisoners in Burma. The group says he is jailed at Myaungmya Prison.

Aung Pwint, free-lancer
Thaung Tun, free-lancer
Imprisoned: October 1999

Aung Pwint, a videographer, editor, and poet, and Thaung Tun, an editor, reporter, and poet better known by his pen name Nyein Thit, were arrested separately in early October 1999. CPJ sources said they were arrested for making independent video documentaries that portrayed "real life" in Burma, including video of forced labor and hardship in rural areas. Aung Pwint worked at a private media company that produced videos for tourism and educational purposes, but he also worked with Thaung Tun on documentary-style projects. Their videotapes circulated through underground networks.

The military government had prohibited Aung Pwint from making videos in 1996 "because they were considered to show too negative a picture of Burmese society and living standards," according to Human Rights Watch, which awarded Aung Pwint a Hellman-Hammett grant in 2001. A notable poet, he also wrote under the name Maung Aung Pwint.

The two men were tried together and sentenced to eight years in prison, according to CPJ sources. Aung Pwint was initially jailed at Insein Prison but was later transferred to Tharawaddy Prison, according to CPJ sources. Thaung Tun was jailed at Moulmein Prison, according to the Thailand-based Assistance Association for Political Prisoners in Burma.

CHINA: 35

Chen Renjie, "Ziyou Bao"
Lin Youping, "Ziyou Bao"
Imprisoned: July 1983

In September 1982, Chen, Lin, and Chen Biling wrote and published a pamphlet titled "Ziyou Bao" (Freedom Report), distributing around 300 copies in Fuzhou, Fujian Province. Upon their arrest in July 1983, authorities accused the three men of making contact with Taiwanese spy organizations and publishing a counterrevolutionary pamphlet. According to official government records of the case, the men used "propaganda and incitement to encourage the overthrow of the people's democratic dictatorship and the socialist system." In August 1983, Chen Renjie was sentenced to life imprisonment, and Lin Youping was sentenced to death with reprieve. Chen Biling was sentenced to death and was later executed.

Hu Liping, *The Beijing Daily*
Imprisoned: April 7, 1990

Hu, a staff member of *The Beijing Daily*, was arrested and charged with "counterrevolutionary incitement and propaganda" and "trafficking in state secrets," according to a rare release of information on his case from the Chinese Ministry of Justice in 1998. The Beijing Intermediate People's Court sentenced him to 10 years in prison on August 15, 1990. Under the terms of his original sentence, Hu should have been released in 2000, but CPJ has been unable to obtain information about his legal status.

Zhang Yafei, *Tieliu*
Chen Yanbin, *Tieliu*
Imprisoned: September 1990

Zhang, a former student at Beifang Communications University, and Chen, also a former university student, were arrested and charged with counterrevolutionary incitement and propaganda for publishing *Tieliu* (Iron Currents), an underground publication about the 1989 crackdown at Tiananmen Square. Several hundred mimeographed copies of the publication were distributed. In March 1991, Zhang was sentenced to 11 years in prison and two years without political rights after his release. Chen was sentenced to 15 years in prison and four years without political rights after his release. In September 2000, the Justice Ministry announced that Chen's sentence was reduced by three months for good behavior. Under the terms of his original sentence, Zhang should have been released in September 2001, but CPJ has been unable to obtain information about his legal status.

Liu Jingsheng, *Tansuo*
Imprisoned: May 1992

Liu, a former writer and co-editor of the pro-democracy journal *Tansuo* (Explorations), was sentenced to 15 years in prison for "counterrevolutionary" activities after being tried secretly in July 1994. Liu was arrested in May 1992 and charged with belonging to labor and pro-democracy groups, including the Liberal Democratic Party of China, the Free Labor Union of China, and the Chinese Progressive Alliance.

Court documents stated that Liu was involved in organizing and leading anti-government and pro-democracy activities. Prosecutors also accused him and other dissidents who were tried on similar charges of writing and printing political leaflets that were distributed in June 1992, during the third anniversary of the Tiananmen Square demonstrations. Liu has had his sentence reduced twice, in May 2000 and in July 2001, by a total of 15 months.

Kang Yuchun, *Freedom Forum*
Imprisoned: May 1992

Kang disappeared on May 6, 1992, and was presumed arrested, according to the New York–based organization Human Rights Watch. In October 1993, in response to an inquiry from the United Nations Working Group on Disappearances, Chinese authorities said Kang was arrested on May 27, 1992. On July 14, 1994, he was one of 16 individuals tried in a Chinese court for their alleged involvement with underground pro-democracy groups.

Kang was accused, among other charges, of launching *Freedom Forum*, the magazine of the Chinese Progressive Alliance, and commissioning people to write articles for the magazine. On December 16, 1994, he was sentenced to 17 years in prison for "disseminating counterrevolutionary propaganda" and for "organizing and leading a counterrevolutionary group."

Wu Shishen, Xinhua News Agency
Ma Tao, *China Health Education News*
Imprisoned: November 6, 1992

Wu, an editor for China's state news agency Xinhua, was arrested for allegedly leaking an advance copy of President Jiang Zemin's 14th Party Congress address to a journalist from the Hong Kong newspaper *Kuai Bao* (Express). His wife, Ma, editor of *China Health Education News*, was also arrested on November 6, 1992, and accused of acting as Wu's accomplice. The Beijing Municipal Intermediate People's Court held a closed trial, and on August 30, 1993, sentenced Wu to life imprisonment for "illegally supplying state secrets to foreigners." Ma was sentenced to six years in prison.

According to the terms of her original sentence, Ma should have been released in November 1998, but CPJ has been unable to obtain information on her legal status.

Fan Yingshang, *Remen Huati*
Imprisoned: February 7, 1996

In 1994, Fan and Yang Jianguo printed more than 60,000 copies of a magazine called *Remen Huati*

(Popular Topics). The men had purchased fake printing authorizations from an editor of the *Journal of European Research* at the Chinese Academy of Social Sciences, according to official Chinese news sources. CPJ was unable to determine the date of Fan's arrest, but on February 7, 1996, the Chang'an District Court in Shijiazhuang City sentenced him to 15 years in prison for "engaging in speculation and profiteering." Authorities termed *Remen Huati* a "reactionary" publication. Yang escaped arrest and was not sentenced.

Hua Di, free-lancer
Imprisoned: January 5, 1998

Hua, a permanent resident of the United States, was arrested while visiting China and charged with revealing state secrets. The charge is believed to stem from articles that Hua, a scientist at Stanford University, had written about China's missile defense system.

On November 25, 1999, the Beijing No. 1 Intermediate People's Court tried Hua behind closed doors and sentenced him to 15 years in prison, according to the Hong Kong–based Information Center for Human Rights and Democracy. In March 2000, the Beijing High People's Court overturned Hua's conviction and ordered that the case be retried. This judicial reversal was extraordinary, particularly for a high-profile political case. Nevertheless, in April, the Beijing State Security Bureau rejected a request for Hua to be released on medical parole; he suffers from a rare form of male breast cancer.

On November 23, 2000, after a retrial, the Beijing No. 1 Intermediate People's Court issued a slightly modified verdict, sentencing Hua to 10 years in prison. News of Hua's sentencing broke in February 2001, when a relative gave the information to foreign correspondents based in Beijing. In late 2001, Hua was moved to Tilanqiao Prison in Shanghai, according to CPJ sources.

Gao Qinrong, Xinhua News Agency
Imprisoned: December 4, 1998

Gao, a reporter for the state news agency Xinhua, was jailed for reporting on a corrupt irrigation scheme in drought-plagued Yuncheng, Shanxi Province. Xinhua never carried Gao's article, which was finally published on May 27, 1998, in an internal reference edition of the official *People's Daily* that is distributed only among a select group of party leaders. But by fall 1998, the irrigation scandal had become national news, with reports appearing in the Guangzhou-based *Nanfang Zhoumo* (Southern Weekend) and on China Central Television. Gao's wife, Duan Maoying, said that local officials blamed Gao for the flurry of media interest and arranged for his prosecution on false charges.

Gao was arrested on December 4, 1998, and eventually charged with crimes including bribery, embezzlement, and pimping, according to Duan. On April 28, 1999, he was sentenced to 13 years in prison after a closed, one-day trial. He is being held in a prison in Qixian, Shanxi Province, according to CPJ sources.

In September 2001, Gao wrote to Mary Robinson, the United Nations High Commissioner for Human Rights, and asked her to intercede with the Chinese government on his behalf. Gao has received support from several members of the Chinese People's Political Consultative Conference of the National People's Congress, who issued a motion at the annual parliamentary meeting in March urging the Central Discipline Committee and Supreme People's Court to reopen his case. Yet by year's end, there was no change in his legal status.

Yue Tianxiang, *China Workers' Monitor*
Imprisoned: January 1999

The Tianshui People's Intermediate Court in Gansu Province sentenced Yue to 10 years in prison on July 5, 1999. The journalist was charged with "subverting state power," according to the Hong Kong–based Information Center for Human Rights and Democracy. Yue was arrested along with two other colleagues—Wang Fengshan and Guo Xinmin—both of whom were sentenced to two years imprisonment and have since been released. According to the Hong Kong–based daily *South China Morning Post*, Yue, Guo, and Wang were arrested in January 1999 for publishing *China Workers' Monitor*, a journal that campaigned for workers' rights.

With help from Wang, Yue and Guo started the journal after they were unable to get compensation from the Tianshui City Transport agency following their dismissal from the company in 1995. All three men were reportedly members of the outlawed China Democracy Party, a dissident group, and were forming an organization to protect the rights of laid-off workers. The first issue of *China Workers' Monitor* exposed extensive corruption among officials at the Tianshui City Transport agency. Only two issues were ever published.

Wang Yingzheng, free-lancer
Imprisoned: February 26, 1999

Police arrested Wang in the city of Xuzhou, in eastern Jiangsu Province, as he was photocopying an article he had written about political reform. The article was based on an open letter that the 19-year-old Wang had addressed to Chinese president Jiang Zemin. In the letter, Wang wrote—as translated by Agence France-Presse— "Many Chinese are discontented with the government's inability to squash corruption. This is largely due to a lack of opposition parties and a lack of press freedom."

Wang was imprisoned for two weeks in September 1998 and questioned about his association with Qin Yongmin, a key leader of the China Democracy Party, who received a 12-year prison sentence in December 1998.

On December 10, 1999, Wang was convicted of subversion and sentenced to three years in prison. His trial was closed to the public, but his family was notified by letter of the verdict, according to the Hong Kong–based Information Center for Human Rights and Democracy.

Wu Yilong, *Zaiye Dang*
Imprisoned: April 26, 1999

Mao Qingxiang, *Zaiye Dang*
Zhu Yufu, *Zaiye Dang*
Xu Guang, *Zaiye Dang*
Imprisoned: June 1999

Wu, an organizer for the banned China Democracy Party (CDP), was detained by police in Guangzhou on April 26, 1999, according to the New York–based organization Human Rights Watch. Mao, Zhu, and Xu, also leading CDP activists, were reportedly detained sometime around June 4, the 10th anniversary of the brutal crackdown on pro-democracy demonstrations in Tiananmen Square. The four were later charged with subversion for, among other things, establishing a magazine called *Zaiye Dang* (Opposition Party) and circulating pro-democracy articles and essays on the Internet.

On October 25, 1999, the Hangzhou Intermediate People's Court in Zhejiang Province conducted what *The New York Times* described as a "sham trial." On November 9, 1999, the Hong Kong- –based Information Center for Human Rights and Democracy reported that all four journalists had been convicted of subversion. Wu was sentenced to 11 years in prison, one of the most severe sentences imposed on a political prisoner in recent years. Mao was sentenced to eight years in prison; Zhu, to seven years; and Xu, to five years.

Liu Xianli, free-lancer
Imprisoned: May 11, 1999

The Beijing Intermediate Court found writer Liu Xianli guilty of subversion and sentenced him to four years in prison, according to a report by the Hong Kong–based Information Center for Human Rights and Democracy.

Liu's "crime" was attempting to publish a book on Chinese dissidents, including Xu Wenli, one of China's most prominent political prisoners and a leading figure in the China Democracy Party. In December 1998, Xu was himself convicted of subversion and sentenced to 13 years in prison.

Jiang Qisheng, free-lancer
Imprisoned: May 18, 1999

Police arrested Jiang late at night and searched his home, seizing his computer, several documents, and articles he had written for *Beijing zhi Chun* (Beijing Spring), a New York–based, pro-democracy publication. The arrest followed Jiang's publication of a series of essays and open letters related to the 10th anniversary of the government's violent suppression of student-led demonstrations in Tiananmen Square. One essay called for a candlelight vigil on June 4, 1999; another urged the government to conduct a full investigation into the massacre; and a third protested the police's brutal treatment of Cao Jiahe, an editor of *Dongfang* (Orient) magazine who was detained on May 10, 1999, and tortured while in police custody. Cao had been detained for allegedly circulating a petition to remember the hundreds killed by government troops during the Tiananmen crackdown.

During Jiang's two-and-a-half-hour trial, held on November 1, 1999, prosecutors cited an April essay calling for a protest vigil, "Light a Thousand Candles," as evidence of his anti-state activities. Prosecutors also accused him of circulating an article on political reform, though Jiang said he showed the piece to only three friends.

On December 27, 2000, 13 months after his trial, the Beijing No. 1 Intermediate People's Court sentenced Jiang to four years in prison.

An Jun, free-lancer
Imprisoned: July 1999

An, an anti-corruption campaigner, was sentenced to four years in prison on subversion charges. The Intermediate People's Court in Xinyang, Henan Province, announced the verdict on April 19, 2000, citing An's essays and articles on corruption as evidence of his anti-state activities.

A former manager of an export trading company, An founded the civic group China Corruption Monitor in 1998 and was arrested in July 1999. The group reportedly exposed more than 100 cases of corruption. During his November 1999 trial, An "said he was only trying to help the government end rampant corruption," according to Agence France-Presse.

In November 2001, An's family sent a letter to President Jiang Zemin appealing for the journalist's release for medical reasons. An suffers from heart problems and has not received adequate medical treatment while in prison, according to Agence France-Presse.

Qi Yanchen, free-lancer
Imprisoned: September 2, 1999

Police arrested Qi at his home in

Cangzhou, Hebei Province. His wife told reporters that officers confiscated his computer, printer, fax machine, and a number of documents.

Qi had published many articles in intellectual journals and was associated with the online magazine *Consultations*, a publication linked to the banned China Development Union. He also subscribed to the pro-democracy electronic newsletter *Dacankao* (VIP Reference), published by U.S.-based dissidents. Qi also worked as an economist with the local Agricultural Development Bank of China.

On May 30, 2000, Qi was prosecuted for subversion before the Cangzhou People's Court in a closed, half-day trial. He was sentenced to four years in prison on September 19.

Zhang Ji, free-lancer
Imprisoned: October 1999

Zhang Ji, a student at Qiqihar University in the northeastern province of Heilongjiang, was charged on November 8, 1999, with "disseminating reactionary documents via the Internet," according to the Hong Kong–based Information Center for Human Rights and Democracy.

Zhang had allegedly been distributing news and information about the banned spiritual movement Falun Gong. He was arrested sometime in October as part of the Chinese government's crackdown on the sect.

Using the Internet, Zhang reportedly transmitted news of the crackdown to Falun Gong members in the United States and Canada and also received reports from abroad,

which he then circulated among practitioners in China. Before Zhang's arrest, Chinese authorities had stepped up their surveillance of the Internet as part of their effort to crush Falun Gong.

Huang Qi, Tianwang Web site
Imprisoned: June 3, 2000

Huang Qi published the Tianwang Web site (www.6-4tianwang.com), which featured articles about pro-democracy activism in China, the independence movement in the Xinjiang Uighur Autonomous Region, and the banned spiritual group Falun Gong. He was arrested on June 3, 2000, and later charged with subversion.

The Chengdu Intermediate Court in Sichuan Province held a secret trial on August 14, 2001. Family members were not allowed to attend, and no verdict or sentencing date was released. However, in China, criminal cases brought to trial usually result in a guilty verdict. The charges against Huang Qi carry a punishment of up to 10 years in prison. Huang's trial was postponed several times throughout 2001 in an apparent effort to deflect international attention from China's human rights practices during the country's campaign to host the 2008 Olympic Games. Two of the trial delays—on February 23 and June 27—coincided with important dates in Beijing's Olympics bid.

Guo Qinghai, free-lancer
Imprisoned: September 15, 2000

Guo was arrested after posting several essays on overseas online bulletin boards calling for political reforms in China. In almost 40 essays posted under the pen name Qing Song, Guo covered a variety of topics, including political prisoners, environmental problems, and corruption. In one essay, Guo discussed the importance of a free press, saying, "Those who oppose lifting media censorship argue that it will negatively influence social stability. But according to what I have seen...countries that control speech may be able to maintain stability in the short term, but the end result is often violent upheaval, coup d'etats, or war."

Guo, who worked in a bank, also wrote articles for Taiwanese newspapers. He was a friend and classmate of writer Qi Yanchen, who was sentenced to four years in prison on subversion charges just four days after Guo's arrest. One of Guo's last online essays appealed for Qi's release.

On April 3, 2001, Guo was tried on subversion charges by a court in Cangzhou, Hebei Province. On April 26, he was sentenced to four years in prison.

Liu Weifang, free-lancer
Imprisoned: October 2000

Liu was arrested sometime after September 26, 2000, when security officials from the Ninth Agricultural Brigade District, in the Xinjiang Uighur Autonomous Region, came to his house, confiscated his computer, and announced that he was being officially investigated, according to an account that Liu posted on the Internet. Liu's most recent online essay was dated October 20, 2000.

Liu had recently posted a number of essays criticizing China's leaders and political system in Internet chat rooms. The essays, which the author signed either with his real name or with the initials "lgwf," covered topics such as official corruption, development policies in China's western regions, and environmental issues. At press time, the articles were available online at: http://liuweifang.ipfox.com.

"The reasons for my actions are all above-board," Liu wrote in one essay. "They are not aimed at any one person or any organization; rather, they are directed at any behavior in society that harms humanity. The goal is to speed up humanity's progress and development." The official *Xinjiang Daily* characterized Liu's work as "a major threat to national security."

According to a June 15, 2001, report in the *Xinjiang Daily*, Liu was sentenced to three years in prison by the Ninth Agricultural Brigade District's Intermediate People's Court. Liu's sentencing was announced amid government attempts to tighten control over the Internet.

Jiang Weiping, free-lancer
Imprisoned: December 5, 2000

Jiang, a free-lance reporter, was arrested on December 5, 2000, after publishing a number of articles in the Hong Kong magazine *Qianshao* (Frontline) that revealed corruption scandals in northeastern China. Jiang wrote the *Qianshao* articles, which were published between June and September 1999, under various pen names. His coverage exposed several major corruption scandals involving high-level officials. Notably, Jiang reported that Shenyang vice mayor Ma Xiangdong had lost nearly 30 million yuan (US$3.6 million) in public funds gambling in Macau casinos. Jiang also revealed that Daqing mayor Qian Dihua had used public funds to buy apartments for each of his 29 mistresses.

Soon after these cases were publicized in *Qianshao* and other Hong Kong media, central authorities detained Ma. He was accused of taking bribes, embezzling public funds, and gambling overseas. Ma was executed for these crimes in December 2001. After his arrest, Ma's case was widely reported in the domestic press and used as an example in the government's ongoing fight against corruption.

However, in May 2001, Jiang was indicted on the charge of "revealing state secrets."

An experienced journalist, Jiang had worked until May 2000 as the northeastern China bureau chief for the Hong Kong paper *Wen Hui Bao*. In the 1980s, he worked as a Dalian-based correspondent for Xinhua News Agency. He contributed free-lance articles to *Qianshao*, a monthly Chinese-language magazine focusing on mainland affairs.

The Dalian Intermediate Court sentenced Jiang to eight years in prison following a secret trial held on September 5, 2001. On November 20, 2001, CPJ honored Jiang with an International Press Freedom Award.

Lu Xinhua, free-lancer
Imprisoned: March 2001

Lu was arrested in mid-March in Wuhan, Hubei Province, after articles he had written about rural unrest and official corruption appeared on various Internet news sites based overseas. On April 20, he was charged with "inciting to subvert state power," a charge frequently used against journalists who write about politically sensitive subjects. Lu's trial began on September 18. On December 30, Lu was sentenced to four years in prison.

Yang Zili, free-lancer
Xu Wei, *Xiaofei Ribao*
Jin Haike, free-lancer
Zhang Honghai, free-lancer
Imprisoned: March 13, 2001

Yang, Xu, Jin, and Zhang were detained on March 13 and charged with subversion on April 20, according to the Hong Kong–based Information Center for Human Rights and Democracy. The four were active participants in the "Xin Qingnian Xuehui" (New Youth Study Group), an informal gathering of individuals who explored topics related to political and social reform and used the Internet to circulate relevant articles.

Yang and Xu were detained separately on March 13. Less is known about the circumstances under which Zhang and Jin were detained, but they were also taken into custody around mid-March, according to the Information Center.

Yang, the group's most prominent member, is well known in liberal academic circles for his technological expertise in evading government firewalls and creating e-mail accounts that cannot be monitored, according to a report in *The New York Times*. His Web site, "Yangzi de Sixiang

Jiayuan" (Yangzi's Garden of Ideas), featured poems, essays, and reports by various authors on subjects ranging from the shortcomings of rural elections to broad discussions of political theory.

Authorities shut down the site after Yang's arrest, according to a well-informed U.S.-based source who did not wish to be identified. The source created a mirror site (www.bringmenews.com/China/freeyzl/mirror/).

When Xu, a reporter with *Xiaofei Ribao* (Consumer Daily), was detained on March 13, authorities confiscated his computer, other professional equipment, and books, according to an account published online by his girlfriend, Wang Ying. Wang reported that public security officials also ordered the *Xiaofei Ribao* to fire Xu. The newspaper has refused to discuss Xu's case with reporters, according to The Associated Press.

All four were tried on September 28 by the Beijing Number One Intermediate People's Court, but no verdict had been announced by year's end.

Liu Haofeng, free-lancer
Imprisoned: March 2001

Liu was secretly arrested in Shanghai in mid-March while conducting research on social conditions in rural China for the dissident China Democracy Party (CDP). On May 16, Liu was sentenced to "reeducation through labor," a form of administrative detention that allows officials to send individuals to such camps for up to three years without trial or formal charges.

After Liu's arrest, friends and family members were not informed of his whereabouts, and CDP members say they only found out what had happened to him when they received news of his sentence in August.

Sentencing papers issued by the Shanghai Reeducation through Labor Committee cited several alleged offenses, including a policy paper and an essay written by Liu that were published under various pen names on the CDP's Web site. The essay focused on the current situation of China's peasants. The committee also accused Liu of trying to form an illegal organization, the "China Democracy Party Joint Headquarters, Second Front."

The journalist previously worked as an editor and reporter for various publications, including the magazine *Jishu Jingji Yu Guanli* (Technology Economy and Management), run by the Fujian Province Economic and Trade Committee, and *Zhongguo Shichang Jingji Bao* (China Market Economy News), run by the Central Party School in Beijing.

Beginning in 1999, he worked for Univillage, a research organization focusing on rural democratization, and managed their Web site. He was working as a free-lance journalist at the time of his arrest.

Zhu Ruixiang, free-lancer
Imprisoned: May 9, 2001

Zhu was arrested and charged with subversion after distributing articles via the Internet. Prosecutors accused him of distributing "hostile" materials, including copies of *Dacankao* (VIP Reference), a Chinese-language, pro-democracy electronic newsletter that Zhu had allegedly e-mailed to several friends, according to U.S.-based sources close to the case.

Dacankao, which is compiled in the United States and e-mailed to more than 1 million addresses in China every day, contains articles from various sources about social and political topics banned from China's tightly controlled domestic media.

Following his September 10 trial, the Shaoyang Municipal Intermediate People's Court signaled its intention to sentence Zhu to a nine-month jail term. However, the Political and Legal Committee of Shaoyang Municipality reviewed the case and insisted that the court impose a more severe sentence. On September 11, Zhu was sentenced to three years in prison.

Zhu, a respected lawyer in Shaoyang City, had previously worked as an editor at a local radio station. He was also the founder and editor-in-chief of the *Shaoyang City Radio and Television Journal*.

Wang Jinbo, free-lancer
Imprisoned: May 2001

Wang, a free-lance journalist, was arrested in early May 2001 for e-mailing essays to overseas organizations arguing that the government should change its official line that the 1989 protests in Tiananmen Square were "counterrevolutionary." In October, Wang was formally charged with "inciting to subvert state power." On November 14, the Junan County Court in Shandong Province conducted his closed trial; only the journalists' relatives were allowed to

attend. On December 13, Wang was sentenced to four years in prison.

Wang, a member of the banned China Democracy Party, had been detained several times in the past for his political activities. In February, days before the International Olympic Committee (IOC) visited Beijing, he was briefly taken into custody after signing an open letter calling on the IOC to pressure China to release political prisoners. A number of Wang's essays have been posted on various Internet sites. One, titled "My Account of Police Violations of Civil Rights," describes his January 2001 detention, when police interrogated him and held him for 20 hours with no food or heat after he signed an open letter calling for the release of political prisoners.

COMOROS: 1

Izdine Abdu Salam, Radio Karthala
Imprisoned: November 13, 2001

Salam, director of programming and a host for the private Radio Karthala, was detained and interrogated by police officers in the capital, Moroni. A journalist contacted by CPJ said the arrest came after participants in a call-in show hosted by Salam made statements that authorities claim defamed ruling officials.

The show, aired during the week of November 5, focused on a constitutional referendum planned for late December. Many callers harshly attacked provisions included in the proposed referendum text.

The charges against Salam are not known, but he remained in prison as of December 31, more than a month after his arrest. Police also seized tapes of the offending broadcast.

CUBA: 1

Bernardo Rogelio Arévalo Padrón,
Línea Sur Press
Imprisoned: November 18, 1997

Arévalo Padrón, founder of the Línea Sur Press news agency, continues to languish in prison despite being eligible for parole, and his health has suffered as a result of his prolonged imprisonment.

On October 31, 1997, a provincial court sentenced Arévalo Padrón to six years in prison for "lack of respect" for President Fidel Castro Ruz and Cuban State Council member Carlos Lage. The charges stemmed from a series of interviews Arévalo Padrón gave in late 1997 to Miami-based radio stations in which he alleged that while Cuban farmers starved, helicopters were taking fresh meat from the countryside to the dinner tables of President Castro, Lage, and other Communist Party officials in Havana.

The journalist began his sentence on November 18, 1997, in a maximum-security prison, where he shared a filthy cell with criminals. On April 11, 1998, State Security officers beat Arévalo Padrón and placed him in solitary confinement after accusing him of making anti-government posters. Later, another prisoner was found to have made the posters.

Arévalo Padrón also suffered bouts of bronchitis and was reportedly treated twice for high blood pressure in the prison infirmary. On January 8, 2000, the journalist was transferred to Labor Camp No. 20, where he served four months.

On April 6, 2000, the journalist was sent to the overcrowded and unsanitary San Marcos Labor Camp, where he worked chopping weeds with a machete in sugar cane fields. According to the independent news agency CubaPress, prison authorities constantly watched Arévalo Padrón, censored his incoming and outgoing mail, and threatened to send him to a maximum-security prison if he did not meet his production quota.

Because of his strenuous work at the labor camps, Arévalo Padrón developed lower back pain and coronary blockage. After ignoring Arévalo Padrón's pain for weeks, in September 2000 prison authorities allowed him to see a doctor, who determined that Arévalo Padrón's poor health disqualified him from physical work, and that he should permanently wear an orthopedic brace, CubaPress reported.

In October 2000, prison authorities informed Arévalo Padrón that his parole had been approved. Yet Arévalo Padrón remained in the labor camp, a violation of Cuban law.

Early in 2001, Arévalo Padrón was transferred to the El Diamante Labor Camp. According to the independent news agency HavanaPress, prison officers continued to harass him.

In February, the journalist's colleagues reported that he had again developed high blood pressure. In early March, Arévalo Padrón complained that officials refused to take him to a hospital outside the labor camp for treatment, according to CubaPress. On March 21, prison authorities relented after pressure from friends, family, and press freedom organizations. The journalist saw a heart specialist who recommended that Arévalo Padrón check his blood pressure daily, take medication, avoid tension, and stop smoking.

In May, CubaPress reported that prison officers routinely ignored the journalist's requests to have his blood pressure checked and often withheld his medication. During the same period, a court again denied him parole despite his poor health.

On June 30, the journalist was transferred to another labor camp. For the prison transfer, he had to walk several miles in the heat carrying his belongings, the journalist said in a letter to colleagues. In October, judges ignored Arévalo Padrón's request for parole, and the journalist continued to report constant harassment.

In November, the European Union requested that Arévalo Padrón be released and allowed to travel to Spain, but authorities did not respond. The journalist's request to attend a January appointment with the U.S. Interests Section Refugee Unit in Havana was also ignored.

Arévalo Padrón is currently jailed in a cubicle for chronically ill prisoners. While he is exempt from physical work, he lacks adequate medical attention and food and remains jailed in unsanitary conditions. Despite his legal right to be paroled, Arévalo Padrón's jailers tell him that he will serve his entire sentence.

DEMOCRATIC REPUBLIC OF THE CONGO: 1

Guy Kasongo Kilembwe, *Pot-Pourri*
Imprisoned: December 31, 2001
Kilembwe, editor-in-chief of the Kinshasa-based satirical newspaper *Pot-Pourri*, was arrested by Special Services agents and taken to the State Security Court in Kinshasa. He was charged with "threatening state security" and "insulting the person of the head of state" and was detained for 48 hours. Vicky Bolingola, the newsroom secretary, was also arrested and detained on the same charges.

The State Security Court's prosecutor released both on January 3, 2002. No official reason was given for their sudden release.

ERITREA: 11

Ghebrehiwet Keleta, *Tsigenay*
Imprisoned: July 2000
Keleta, a reporter with the weekly Tsigenay, was kidnapped by security agents on his way to work in July 2000 and has not been seen since.

Medhanie Haile, Keste Debena
Imprisoned: September 18, 2001
Yusuf Mohamed Ali, *Tsigenay*
Imprisoned: September 19, 2001
Mattewos Habteab, *Meqaleh,*
Imprisoned: September 19, 2001
Temesken Ghebreyesus, Keste Debena
Imprisoned: September 20, 2001
Amanuel Asrat, Zemen,
Imprisoned: September 2001
Fesshaye Yohannes, Setit
Imprisoned: September 27, 2001
Said Abdelkader, Admas
Imprisoned: September 20, 2001
Selamyinghes Beyene, Meqaleh,
Imprisoned: September 21, 2001
Dawit Habtemichael, Meqaleh,
Imprisoned: on or about September 21, 2001
Seyoum Fsehaye, free-lance photographer
Imprisoned: September 21, 2001

Beginning September 18, 2001, Eritrean security forces arrested at least 10 local journalists. Two others fled the country. The arrests came less than a week after authorities abruptly closed all privately owned newspapers, allegedly to safeguard national unity in the face of growing political turmoil in the tiny Horn of Africa nation.

International news reports quoted presidential adviser Yemane Gebremeskel as saying that the journalists could have been arrested for avoiding military service. Sources in Asmara, however, say that at least two of the detained journalists, free-lance photographer Fsehaye and Mohamed, editor of *Tsigenay*, were legally exempt from national service. Fsehaye is reportedly exempt since he is an independence war veteran; while Mohamed is apparently well over the maximum age for military service.

All these journalists remained in custody as of December 31.

CPJ sources in Asmara maintain that the suspension and subsequent arrests of independent journalists were part of a full-scale government effort to suppress political dissent in advance of December elections, which the government canceled without explanation.

ETHIOPIA: 1

Tamirate Zuma, *Atkurot*
Imprisoned: May 25, 2001

Zuma, former publisher and editor-in-chief of the defunct Amharic-language weekly *Atkurot*, was arrested and imprisoned on charges of failing to pay a publishing license fee, inciting violence or rebellion, and

defamation. All three are crimes under the Ethiopian Press Proclamation.

The first charge stemmed from a licensing requirement. Strapped for cash, Zuma was unable to pay the fee to renew his annual publishing license. In the second case, Zuma is accused of inciting people to violence or rebellion, a charge resulting from a recent *Atkurot* article that quoted an interview from the U.S.-based magazine *Ethiopian Review*. In it, a former official in dictator Mengistu Haile Mariam's Derg regime, Gen. Haile Meles, predicted the imminent overthrow of the current Ethiopian People's Revolutionary Democratic Front government.

The third case is a defamation charge resulting from an *Atkurot* article that reported on financial mismanagement at a government-owned leather factory. As of December 31, Zuma remained in jail. In October, a CPJ delegation visited the journalist during a fact-finding mission to Ethiopia.

IRAN: 5

Abdullah Nouri, *Khordad*
Imprisoned: November 28, 1999

In a trial that transfixed the nation, Iran's Special Court for Clergy convicted Nouri, publisher of the reformist daily *Khordad* and a former vice president and interior minister, of religious dissent on November 27. The conviction was widely viewed as an attempt by conservative forces within the regime to sideline Nouri, an influential ally of reformist president Muhammad Khatami, in advance of the country's February 2000 elections. Nouri was believed to be a frontrunner for the important position of speaker of Iran's Parliament.

The charges against him, which included defaming "the system," insulting religious leaders, and disseminating false information and propaganda against the state, were based on news articles published in *Khordad*. During the trial, Nouri sharply criticized the clerical establishment and called for greater freedoms in Iranian society.

He was sentenced to five years in prison and barred from practicing journalism for five years. *Khordad* was ordered to close. At year's end, Nouri was serving his sentence in Tehran's Evin Prison.

Akbar Ganji, *Sobh-e-Emrooz, Fath*
Imprisoned: April 22, 2000

Ganji, a leading investigative reporter for the reformist daily *Sobh-e-Emrooz* and a member of the editorial board of the pro-reform daily *Fath*, was arrested and prosecuted in both Iran's Press Court and Revolutionary Court.

The case in the Press Court stemmed from Ganji's investigative articles about the 1998 killings of several dissidents and intellectuals that implicated top intelligence officials and former president Hashemi Rafsanjani. In the Revolutionary Court, he was accused of making propaganda against the Islamic regime and threatening national security in comments he made at an April conference in Berlin on the future of the reform movement in Iran.

The Press Court case is still pending, but on January 13, 2001, the Revolutionary Court sentenced Ganji

to 10 years in prison, followed by five years of internal exile. In May, after Ganji had already served more than a year in prison, an appellate court reduced his punishment to six months.

The Iranian Justice Department then appealed that ruling to the Supreme Court, arguing that the appellate court had committed errors in commuting the original 10-year sentence. The Supreme Court overturned the appellate court's decision and referred the case to a different appeals court. On July 16, that court sentenced Ganji to six years in jail. According to the state news agency IRNA, the ruling was "definitive," meaning that it cannot be appealed.

The legal situation was not clear, however. IRNA quoted an official with the Tehran-based Society for Defending Press Freedom in August 2001 as saying, "No one as yet knows which judge or which officials of the judiciary have made this latest decision."

Emadeddin Baghi, *Fath, Neshat*
Imprisoned: May 29, 2000

Baghi, a contributor to the banned daily *Neshat* who was on the editorial board of another outlawed daily, *Fath*, was detained during a closed-door trial. On July 17, Tehran's Press Court sentenced him to five and a half years in prison.

According to the state news agency IRNA, Baghi was charged with publishing articles that "questioned the validity of...Islamic law," with "threatening national security, and... spreading unsubstantiated news stories" about the role of "agents of the Intelligence Ministry in the serial murder of intellectuals and dissidents in 1998."

The charges were based on complaints that a number of government agencies had lodged, including the Intelligence Ministry, the conservative-controlled Islamic Republic of Iran Broadcasting, and former security officials.

The charges also mentioned a 1999 piece Baghi published in *Neshat* responding to another article criticizing the death penalty that had itself landed *Neshat* editor Mashallah Shamsolvaezin in jail. The closed-door trial began on May 1. In late October, an appeals court reduced the sentence to three years. Baghi remains in Tehran's Evin Prison.

Hamid Jafari Nasrabadi, *Kavir*
Imprisoned: May 9, 2001
Mahmoud Mojdavi, *Kavir*
Imprisoned: May 9, 2001

Nasrabadi, director of the Shahid Rajai University student magazine *Kavir*, and Mojdavi, a writer at the paper, were arrested by order of Tehran's Press Court in connection with an allegedly "indecent" article by Mojdavi. According to press reports, the seven-page article, titled "Trial of the Universal Creator," described fictitious proceedings in which God was put on trial. Officials said the article carried an "indecent tone and insulting interpretations."

Nasrabadi and Mojdavi were reportedly sentenced in December to five and three years respectively.

KUWAIT: 2

Ibtisam Berto Sulaiman al-Dakhil,
Al-Nida'
Imprisoned: June 1991

Fawwaz Muhammad al-Awadi Bessisso, *Al-Nida'*
Imprisoned: June 1991

Bessisso and al-Dakhil were sentenced to life in prison for their work with *Al-Nida'*, a newspaper Iraqi authorities launched during Iraq's occupation of Kuwait in 1990. At year's end, they were the last remaining journalists in prison in Kuwait, which jailed 17 reporters and editors for their work with *Al-Nida'* following the Gulf War and charged them with collaboration.

The defendants were reportedly tortured during their interrogations. Their trial, which began on May 19, 1991, in a martial-law court, failed to meet international standards of justice. In particular, prosecutors failed to rebut the journalists' defense that they had been forced to work for the Iraqi newspaper.

On June 16, 1991, the journalists were sentenced to death. Ten days later, following international protests, all martial-law death sentences were commuted to life imprisonment. The other 15 journalists were freed gradually starting in 1996, most on the occasion of the emir's annual prisoner amnesty in February.

MOROCCO (WESTERN SAHARA): 1

Noureddine Darif, *Al-Amal al-Democrati*
Imprisoned: November 17, 2001

Darif, a journalist for the leftist weekly *Al-Amal al-Democrati*, was detained by local authorities in Smara Province of Western Sahara, which is controlled by Morocco. Darif was detained at a hospital where he was trying to interview individuals injured earlier in the day during demonstrations. He was taken to a police station and beaten, according to reports and CPJ sources. Darif is accused of "collusion with a foreign party" and of stirring up violent disturbances. He is in Ayoun Prison.

NEPAL: 17

Om Sharma, *Janadisha*
Dipendra Rokaya, *Janadisha*
Govinda Acharya, *Janadesh*
Khil Bahadur Bhandari, *Janadesh*
Deepak Sapkota, *Janadesh*
Manarishi Dhital, *Dishabodh*
Ishwarchandra Gyawali, *Dishabodh*
Imprisoned: November 26, 2001

On November 26, police raided the offices of three publications closely associated with Nepal's Maoist movement: the daily *Janadisha,* the weekly *Janadesh*, and the monthly *Dishabodh*. The police arrested nine staff members, including seven journalists, and also confiscated equipment and written materials. The arrested journalists included Sharma, an editor for *Janadisha*; Rokaya, whose position at *Janadisha* was not known; Archarya, an editor of *Janadesh*; Bhandari, executive editor of *Janadesh*; Sapkota, a reporter for *Janadesh*; Dhital, a reporter for *Dishabodh*; and Gyawali, executive editor of *Dishabodh*.

All were arrested about two hours before the government declared a state of emergency and enacted the Terrorist and Destructive Activities (Control and Punishment) ordinance, which named the Communist Party of Nepal-Maoist (CPN-M) a terrorist organization and therefore illegal. The government announcement also stipulated that any organizations or individuals supporting the CPN-M and its activities would be considered terrorists, according to local news reports. Under the new regulations, terrorism carries a life sentence.

On January 9, 2002, lawyers for the journalists filed a habeas corpus petition to the Supreme Court, which then issued a show cause notice to the government. The government responded that six of the journalists were charged under the terrorism ordinance for engaging in activities supporting the Maoist movement, according to a lawyer for the journalists. At press time, the government had not yet issued a response for Om Sharma's case, and the hearing date for all the cases would not be set until it did. The defense lawyers argue that the journalists' detention is illegal because they were arrested before the terrorist ordinance was officially declared.

In the aftermath of the state of emergency declaration on November 26, dozens of journalists were rounded up for interrogation or arrest, although most were released after a short period of time. CPJ confirmed that the following journalists remained in prison on December 31, 2001. By year's end, the government had not released information about the reasons behind these journalists' arrests. Local journalists and human rights organizations were unable to determine whether any of the following had been officially charged.

Dev Kumar Yadav, *Janadesh*
Imprisoned: November 28, 2001

Yadav, a reporter for the weekly *Janadesh*, was arrested in Siraha. Although the circumstances surrounding his detention were unclear, at year's end he was being held in Siraha, according to the Informal Sector Service Center (INSEC), a Kathmandu-based human rights organization.

Ganga Bista, Nepal Television, *Chautari Times*
Shankar Khanal, Radio Nepal, *Spacetime Daily*
Imprisoned: December 2, 2001

Bista, a reporter for Nepal Television and *Chautari Times*, and Khanal, a reporter for Radio Nepal and *Spacetime Daily*, were arrested by the army along with *Nepal Samacharpatra* reporter Indira Giri, according to INSEC. Giri was released on December 6.

Sama Thapa, *Yugayan*
Imprisoned: December 6, 2001

After his arrest in Kailali District, Thapa, publisher of *Yugayan*, was brought to the local police station in Tikapur, according to the Federation of Nepalese Journalists (FNJ) and INSEC. He was then shifted to the Regional Police Unit Office in Dhangadhi, where he was being held at year's end.

Chitra Choudhary, *Nawa Paricharcha*
Imprisoned: December 6, 2001

Choudhary is an adviser-editor of *Nawa Paricharcha* weekly in Tikapur and the former editor-in-chief of *Yugayan*. He was also the principal of the National Lower Secondary School in Patharaiya. School

personnel arrested him on the morning of December 6. He was brought with Sama Thapa to police stations in Tikapur and Dhangadhi. At year's end, he was being held in Army Barracks, Dhangadhi, according to INSEC.

Komal Nath Baral, *Swaviman*
Imprisoned: December 21, 2001

Baral, an editor at *Swaviman* weekly, was arrested at his home in Kaski district, Pokhara, according to FNJ and INSEC.

Prem Bahadur Diyali, *Blast Daily*
Imprisoned: December 21, 2001

Diyali, a reporter at *Blast Daily*, was arrested by police at his residence in Sunsari District, according to FNJ and INSEC. He was put under preventive detention on December 23. Local journalists have said *Blast*, based in Dharan, was targeted because it had published reports criticizing local leaders.

Badri Prasad Sharma, *Baglung Weekly*
Imprisoned: December 25, 2001

Sharma, editor and publisher of *Baglung Weekly*, was arrested by security personnel from his house in Baglung, according to FNJ and INSEC.

Chandra Man Shrestha, *Janadisha*
Imprisoned: December 27, 2001

Shrestha, a managing director at the daily *Janadisha*, was arrested in Kathmandu. His whereabouts were unknown at year's end.

Janardan Biyogi, *Swaviman*
Imprisoned: December 31, 2001

Biyogi, a subeditor of *Swaviman* weekly, was arrested by the army in Kaski District, Pokhara, according to FNJ.

Munawwar Mohsin, *The Frontier Post*
Imprisoned: January 29, 2001

Police in Peshawar arrested Mohsin and four colleagues from *The Frontier Post* on the evening of January 29, after the newspaper published a letter to the editor titled "Why Muslims Hate Jews," which included derogatory references to the Prophet Muhammad. Although senior management at the newspaper claimed the letter was inserted into the copy by mistake and apologized for failing to stop its publication, district officials responded to complaints from local religious leaders by shutting down the paper and ordering the immediate arrest of seven staff members on charges of blasphemy. In Pakistan, anyone accused of blasphemy is subject to immediate arrest without due process safeguards; those found guilty may be sentenced to death.

At the end of 2001, the blasphemy case was ongoing, and Mohsin was the only journalist from *The Frontier Post* remaining in prison. (Two of the journalists charged in the case immediately went into hiding and were never arrested. The other four were eventually released on bail.) Mohsin, who was working as the newspaper's subeditor, admitted responsibility for publishing the letter, which he says he had not read carefully. He told *The New York Times* that he "could never think of abusing our Holy Prophet" but confessed that, having only recently completed a drug rehabilitation program, his mind may have been slightly addled. Mohsin was imprisoned in Peshawar Central Jail.

Grigory Pasko, *Boyevaya Vakhta*
Imprisoned: December 25, 2001

Pasko, an investigative reporter with *Boyevaya Vakhta* (Battle Watch), a newspaper published by the Pacific Fleet, was convicted of treason on December 25 and sentenced to four years in prison by the Military Court of the Pacific Fleet in Vladivostok. The ruling also stripped Pasko of his military rank and state decorations.

The journalist was taken into custody in the courtroom and then jailed. Pasko's attorney, Anatoly Pyshkin, filed an appeal with the Military Collegium of the Russian Supreme Court seeking full acquittal.

Pasko was arrested in November 1997 and charged with passing classified documents to Japanese news outlets. He had been reporting on environmental damage caused by the Russian navy. Pasko spent 20 months in prison while awaiting trial.

In July 1999, he was acquitted of treason but found guilty of abusing his authority as an officer. He was immediately amnestied, but four months later the Military Collegium of the Russian Supreme Court canceled the Vladivostok court's verdict and ordered a new trial.

Pasko's second trial began on July 11, 2001, after having been postponed three times since March.

During the trial, Pasko's defense

demonstrated that the proceedings lacked a basis in Russian law. Article 7 of the Federal Law on State Secrets, which stipulates that information about environmental dangers cannot be classified, protects Pasko's work on sensitive issues, such as unlawful dumping of radioactive waste. The prosecution relied on a secret Ministry of Defense decree (No. 055) even though the Russian Constitution bars the use of secret legislation in criminal cases.

The defense also challenged the veracity of many of the witnesses, several of whom acknowledged that the Federal Security Service (FSB) falsified their statements or tried to persuade them to give false testimony. An FSB investigator was reprimanded for falsifying evidence in the first trial, and the signatures of two people who witnessed a search of the reporter's apartment were forged.

Throughout the year, CPJ issued numerous statements calling attention to Pasko's ordeal, and in early June, a CPJ delegation traveled to Vladivostok before Pasko's trial to publicize concerns over the charges.

RWANDA: 1
Amiel Nkuliza, *Le Partisan*
Imprisoned: December 31, 2001

Police detained Nkuliza, a journalist with *Le Partisan* newspaper, and questioned him about his reporting on the murder of Gratien Munyarubuga, a founder of the opposition Democratic Party for Renewal-Ubuyanja, and his stories about the Democratic Republican Movement party. He was released on January 3, 2002.

SOUTH KOREA: 3
Lee Chang Gi, *Jajuminbo*
Park Joon Young, *Jajuminbo*
Baek Oon Jong, *Jajuminbo*
Imprisoned: October 23, 2001

Agents from South Korea's National Intelligence Service arrested Lee, chief editor of the monthly *Jajuminbo*, and Park and Baek, both reporters for the magazine. The journalists were charged with violating South Korea's National Security Law, which has been used to punish those who publish or broadcast views deemed anti-state, especially material seen as supportive of North Korea or of communism generally.

Jajuminbo, which also produces an online publication at www.jajuminbo.com, is a small-circulation, private magazine that promotes the reunification of North and South Korea.

During the trial, prosecutors accused *Jajuminbo* of publishing articles that promoted North Korea's vision of reunification. The three journalists were also accused of maintaining contact with "pro-North Korean" activists in Japan.

The district attorney asked that each of the journalists be sentenced to four years in prison. The court was scheduled to announce its verdict on February 9, 2002. As this book went to press, all three journalists were being held at the Seoul Detention Center.

TUNISIA: 2
Hamadi Jebali, *Al-Fajr*
Imprisoned: January 1991

On August 28, 1992, a military

court sentenced Jebali, editor of *Al-Fajr*, the weekly newspaper of the banned Islamic Al-Nahda Party, to 16 years in prison. He was tried along with 279 other individuals accused of belonging to Al-Nahda. Jebali was convicted of "aggression with the intention of changing the nature of the state" and "membership in an illegal organization."

During his testimony, Jebali denied the charges and displayed evidence that he had been tortured while in custody. Jebali has been in jail since January 1991, when he was sentenced to one year in prison after *Al-Fajr* published an article calling for the abolition of military courts in Tunisia. International human rights groups monitoring the mass trial concluded that the proceedings fell far below international standards of justice.

Abdellah Zouari, *Al-Fajr*
Imprisoned: February 1991

On August 28, 1992, a military court sentenced Zouari, a contributor to *Al-Fajr*, the weekly newspaper of the banned Islamic Al-Nahda Party, to 11 years in prison. Zouari was tried along with 279 other individuals accused of belonging to Al-Nahda. He has been in jail since February 1991, when he was charged with "association with an unrecognized organization." International human rights groups monitoring the trial concluded it fell far short of meeting international standards of justice.

TURKEY: 13

Huseyin Solak, *Mucadele*
Imprisoned: October 27, 1993

Solak, the Gaziantep bureau chief

of the socialist magazine *Mucadele,* was arrested and charged under Article 168/2 of the Penal Code with membership in Devrimci Sol (also known as Dev Sol), an outlawed underground leftist organization responsible for numerous terrorist operations in Turkey. Solak was convicted on the strength of statements from a witness who said he had seen the journalist distributing copies of *Mucadele.*

According to the trial transcript, the prosecution witness also testified that Solak had hung unspecified banners in public and served as a lookout while members of Devrimci Sol threw a Molotov cocktail at a bank in the town of Gaziantep. The prosecution also cited "illegal" documents found after searches of Solak's home and office. Solak confessed to the charges while in police custody but recanted in court.

On November 24, 1994, Solak was sentenced to 12 years and six months in prison. At year's end, he was being held in Sincan F-type Prison.

Hasan Ozgun, Ozgur Gundem
Imprisoned: December 9, 1993

Ozgun, a Diyarbakir correspondent for the now defunct pro-Kurdish daily *Ozgur Gundem,* was arrested during a December 9, 1993, police raid on the paper's Diyarbakir bureau. He was charged with being a member of the outlawed Kurdistan Workers' Party (PKK), under Article 168 of the Penal Code.

Trial transcripts show that the prosecution based its case on what it described as *Ozgur Gundem*'s pro-PKK slant, following a Turkish-government pattern of harassing journalists affiliated with the publication. The prosecution also submitted copies of the banned PKK publications *Serkhabun* and *Berxehun*, found in Ozgun's possession, as well as photographs and biographical sketches of PKK members from the newspaper's archive. The state also cited Ozgun's possession of an unlicensed handgun as evidence of his membership in the PKK.

In his defense, Ozgun maintained that the PKK publications were used as sources of information for newspaper articles and that the photos of PKK members were in the archive because of interviews the newspaper had conducted in the past. Ozgun admitted to having purchased the gun on the black market but denied all other charges.

At year's end, Ozgun was being held in Aydin Prison.

Serdar Gelir, *Mucadele*
Imprisoned: April 25, 1994

Gelir, Ankara bureau chief for the weekly socialist magazine *Mucadele*, was detained on April 16, 1994. He was formally arrested and imprisoned 10 days later on the charge of belonging to an illegal organization.

The Ministry of Justice informed CPJ that Gelir was charged and convicted under Article 168/2 of the Penal Code and Article 5 of the Anti-Terror Law 3713 and sentenced to 15 years' imprisonment by the Ankara State Security Court for being a member of an armed, illegal leftist organization (Devrimci Sol, also known as Dev Sol). Court records,

however, indicate that he was sentenced to 12 years and six months. At year's end, Gelir was being held in Sincan F-type Prison.

Utku Deniz Sirkeci, *Tavir*
Imprisoned: August 6, 1994

Sirkeci, the Ankara bureau chief of the leftist cultural magazine *Tavir*, was arrested and charged with belonging to the outlawed organization Devrimci Sol (also known as Dev Sol), under Article 168/2 of the Penal Code.

Court records from Sirkeci's trial show that the state accused him of throwing a Molotov cocktail at a bank in Ankara, but the documents do not state what evidence was introduced to support the allegation. Prosecutors also cited Sirkeci's attendance at the funeral of a Devrimci Sol activist to support the charge that he was a member of the organization.

In his defense, Sirkeci said he had attended the funeral in his capacity as a journalist. He provided detailed testimony of his torture by police, who, he alleged, coerced him to confess.

He was convicted and sentenced to 12 years and six months in prison and is currently jailed in Sincan F-type Prison.

Aysel Bolucek, *Mucadele*
Imprisoned: October 11, 1994

Bolucek, an Ankara correspondent for the weekly socialist magazine *Mucadele*, was arrested at her home and charged with belonging to an outlawed organization under Article 168/2 of the Penal Code, partly on the basis of a handwritten document that allegedly linked her to the banned leftist group Devrimci Sol (also known as Dev Sol). She has been in prison since her arrest.

Court documents from her trial show that the state also cited the October 8, 1994, issue of *Mucadele* to support its argument that the magazine was a Devrimci Sol publication. The prosecutor claimed that the October 8 issue insulted security forces and state officials and praised Devrimci Sol guerrillas who had been killed in clashes with security forces.

The defense argued that it was illegal for the defendant to be tried twice for the same crime. (Earlier in 1994, Bolucek had been acquitted of the same charges.) The defense accepted the prosecution's claim that Bolucek had written the document but said that the police forced her to write it under torture while she was in custody. The defense also argued that a legal publication could not be used as evidence, and that the individuals who made incriminating statements about Bolucek to the police had done so under torture and had subsequently recanted. But on December 23, 1994, Bolucek was convicted and sentenced to 12 years and six months in jail.

At year's end, she was being held in Kutahya Prison.

Ozlem Turk, *Mucadele*
Imprisoned: January 17, 1995

Turk, a reporter in the town of Samsun for the weekly socialist magazine *Mucadele*, was arrested at a relative's home and charged with belonging to the outlawed

Revolutionary People's Liberation Party-Front, under Article 169 of the Penal Code. Court documents from her trial state that the prosecution's evidence included the fact that Turk collected money for *Mucadele*, along with a handwritten autobiography allegedly found in the home of a party member. Two people testified that she belonged to the group.

Turk maintained that the money she had collected came from selling copies of *Mucadele*. She also claimed that she was forced to confess to the charges under torture. The only material evidence presented at the trial was copies of legal publications found at her home and copies of her alleged autobiography. Police provided expert testimony to authenticate the allegedly incriminating documents.

According to court documents, Turk was convicted under Article 168/2 of the Penal Code and sentenced to 15 years in prison. At year's end, she was being held in Kutahya Prison.

Burhan Gardas, *Mucadele*
Imprisoned: March 23, 1995

Gardas, the Ankara bureau chief for the weekly socialist magazine *Mucadele*, was prosecuted several times beginning in 1994. Court records state that Gardas was arrested on January 12, 1994, at his office and charged with violating Article 168/2 of the Penal Code. During a search of the premises, the police reportedly found four copies of "news bulletins" of the outlawed organization Devrimci Sol (also known as Dev Sol). During the trial, the prosecution claimed that police also found banners with left-wing slogans, along with photographs of Devrimci Sol militants who had been killed in clashes with security forces. The prosecution also claimed that Gardas shouted anti-state slogans during his arrest and that he was using *Mucadele*'s office for Devrimci Sol activities.

Gardas denied all the charges. His attorney argued that the illegal publications were part of the magazine's archive and that Gardas had been tortured in prison. The lawyer submitted a medical report to prove the torture allegation. On May 14, 1994, Gardas was released pending the outcome of his trial.

While awaiting the verdict in the 1994 prosecution, Gardas was arrested on March 23, 1995, when police raided the office of the successor to *Mucadele*, the weekly socialist magazine *Kurtulus*, of which he was also the Ankara bureau chief. Officials said he had violated Article 168/2 of the Penal Code because of his alleged membership in the banned organization Devrimci Sol. During the raid, police seized three copies of *Kurtulus* "news bulletins" and six *Kurtulus* articles that discussed illegal rallies.

Court documents from his second trial, held at the Number 2 State Security Court of Ankara, reveal that the prosecution's evidence against Gardas consisted of his refusal to talk during a police interrogation—allegedly a Devrimci Sol policy—and his possession of publications that the prosecution contended were the mouthpieces of outlawed organizations. The state also

introduced the testimony of Ali Han, an employee at *Kurtulus*' Ankara bureau, that Gardas was a Devrimci Sol member. Gardas denied the claim, and his lawyer argued that his client had the constitutional right to remain silent during police interrogation.

On July 4, 1995, the Number 1 State Security Court of Ankara sentenced Gardas to 15 years in prison on the 1994 charge. In 1996, he was convicted and sentenced to an additional 15 years for the second set of charges. At year's end, Gardas was serving his term at Kirsehir Prison.

Ozgur Gudenoglu, *Mucadele*
Imprisoned: May 24, 1995

Gudenoglu, Konya bureau chief of the socialist weekly magazine *Mucadele*, was arrested, charged, tried, and convicted under Article 168 of the Penal Code for belonging to an illegal organization. He was sentenced to 12 years and six months in prison for alleged membership in the outlawed leftist organization Devrimci Sol (also known as Dev Sol). His prosecution is part of the state's long-standing pattern of harassing *Mucadele* and its employees.

Gudenoglu was reportedly jailed in Konya Prison.

Fatma Harman, *Atilim*
Imprisoned: July 10, 1995

Harman, a reporter for the now defunct weekly socialist newspaper *Atilim*, was taken into custody during a June 15, 1995, police raid on the newspaper's Mersin bureau. Her colleague Bulent Oner was also detained.

On June 24, 1995, Harman was

formally arrested and charged under Article 168 of the Penal Code for allegedly belonging to the outlawed Marxist-Leninist Communist Party (MLKP). *Atilim*'s lawyer reports that the prosecution based its case on the argument that the MKLP published *Atilim*. The prosecution introduced copies of *Atilim* found in Harman's possession as evidence of her affiliation with the MLKP and claimed that several unspecified "banners" were found in the *Atilim* office. The prosecution also alleged that Harman and Oner both lived in a house belonging to the MLKP. On January 26, 1996, Harman was sentenced to 12 years and six months in prison and jailed in Adana Prison.

Erdal Dogan, *Alinteri*
Imprisoned: July 10, 1995

Dogan, an Ankara reporter for the now defunct socialist weekly *Alinteri*, was arrested on July 10, 1995. He was later charged under Article 168/2 of the Penal Code for allegedly belonging to the outlawed Turkish Revolutionary Communist Union (TIKB).

According to the trial transcript, the prosecution argued that the TIKB published *Alinteri*. The case against Dogan was based on the following evidence: (1) a photograph of Dogan, taken at a 1992 May Day parade, allegedly showing him standing underneath a United Revolutionary Trade Union banner; (2) a photograph of Dogan taken on the anniversary of a TIKB militant's death; (3) a photograph alleged to show Dogan attending an illegal demonstration in Ankara; (4) a

statement of an alleged member of the TIKB, who claimed that Dogan belonged to the organization.

The defense argued that the allegedly incriminating statement was invalid because it had been extracted under torture. Dogan's lawyer told CPJ that the photograph from the militant's memorial was blurry, and Dogan testified in court that he had attended the May Day parade as a journalist. He was convicted, sentenced to 12 years and six months in prison, and jailed in Bursa Prison. At year's end, he was being held in Gebze Prison.

Sadik Celik, *Kurtulus*
Imprisoned: December 23, 1995

Celik, Zonguldak bureau chief for the leftist weekly *Kurtulus*, was detained and charged with violating Article 168/2 of the Penal Code for allegedly belonging to the outlawed Revolutionary People's Liberation Party-Front (DHKP-C).

The prosecution claimed that the DHKP-C published *Kurtulus* and that Celik's position with the magazine proved he was a member of the group. Celik was accused of conducting "seminars" for the DHKP-C at the magazine's office, propagandizing for the organization, transporting copies of the magazine from Istanbul to Zonguldak by bus, and organizing the magazine's distribution in Zonguldak. The prosecution also stated that Celik's name appeared in a document written by a DHKP-C leader. (It is not clear whether the document was introduced as material evidence.)

The prosecution claimed that

Celik's refusal to speak while in police custody proved his guilt. The defense argued that the prosecution could not substantiate any of its claims. Celik acknowledged having distributed the magazine in his capacity as *Kurtulus'* bureau chief. He said that he held meetings in the office to discuss the magazine's affairs. The defense presented the statements of two *Kurtulus* reporters to corroborate Celik's statements.

On October 17, 1996, Celik was sentenced to 12 years and six months in prison.

Mustafa Benli, *Hedef*
Imprisoned: February 24, 1998

Benli, the owner and editor of the leftist weekly *Hedef*, was arrested and later charged with "membership in an illegal organization"—a crime under article 168 of the Penal Code. According to court documents, the prosecution charged that *Hedef* was the mouthpiece of the Turkish Revolutionary Party (TDP), and that authorities had found copies of illegal magazines in Benli's possession. That, along with articles published in *Hedef*, was cited as partial proof of Benli's membership in the organization.

He was sentenced to 12 years and six months in prison.

Fikret Baskaya, *Ozgur Bakis*
Imprisoned: June 29, 2001

Baskaya, an academic and writer for the now defunct, pro-Kurdish daily *Ozgur Bakis*, was jailed after a State Security Court sentenced him to 16 months in prison for "separatist propaganda," a violation of Article 8 of the Anti-Terror Law.

The case against Baskaya stemmed from a June 1, 1999, column he wrote in *Ozgur Bakis* titled "Is this a Historical Process?" The article decried Turkey's policy toward the country's Kurdish minority, saying: "Turkish leaders have always considered the Kurdish problem to be one of public order, when it is in fact a national problem, and have thought they could resolve the problem through a chauvinist, racist and nationalist political agenda"

An Istanbul State Security Court convicted him of the charge on June 13, 2000. The sentence was confirmed by the Court of Appeals on January 15, 2001. He is jailed in Kalecik Prison near Ankara.

UNITED STATES: 1

Vanessa Leggett, free-lancer
Imprisoned: July 20, 2001

Leggett, a Houston-based free-lancer, was jailed without bail after refusing to hand over research for a book she was writing about the 1997 murder of Houston socialite Doris Angleton. Leggett, who is believed to have served in prison longer than any journalist in U.S. history, was released on January 4.

The journalist, 33, was asked to give her research materials to a federal grand jury. These materials include tapes of interviews she conducted with murder suspect Roger Angleton, the victim's brother-in-law, shortly before he committed suicide.

Since the Watergate era, federal prosecutors have needed permission from the U.S. attorney general before ordering a journalist to reveal his or her sources. The last federal jailing of journalists was in 1991, when four journalists were briefly detained for refusing to testify in a corruption trial.

Justice Department spokeswoman Mindy Tucker was quoted in the fall issue of *The News Media & The Law* as saying, "She was not handled as a member of the media, so [the department] would not have followed the procedure that we have laid out for subpoenas of members of the media."

Leggett, who was clearly investigating a news story for public dissemination, refused to comply with the subpoena, citing confidentiality of her sources. In a closed hearing on July 19, District Judge Melinda Harmon found Leggett in contempt of court and gave her a one-day grace period to surrender to authorities. Leggett turned herself in on July 20.

Leggett's lawyer, Mike DeGeurin, filed an appeal with the U.S. Court of Appeals for the Fifth Circuit asking that bail be granted immediately and that the appeal be handled in an expedited manner. The court refused bail but granted the request for an expedited appeal hearing, which was held on August 15.

The Appeals Court denied requests by news organizations to argue on Leggett's behalf during the hearing. Initially, the court had closed the hearing to the public, but after the news organizations filed an emergency motion, the courtroom was opened on August 14.

During the August 15 hearing

before a three-judge panel, Justice Department attorney Paula Offenhauser acknowledged, under questioning, that prosecutors were not sure what they were after.

But on August 17, the panel of the Appeals Court upheld Judge Harmon's ruling, saying, "The district court did not abuse its discretion in ordering Leggett incarcerated for contempt." DeGeurin told CPJ that the Appeals Court panel assumed Leggett to be a journalist but contended that reporter's privilege carries less weight in a federal grand jury investigation.

DeGeurin appealed to the full court, but his request for a rehearing was denied in November. The Appeals Court also denied DeGeurin's motion to release Leggett during the appeals process.

DeGeurin then filed a petition for a writ of certiorari with the U.S. Supreme Court on December 31 asking for a review of the appeals court decision.

Leggett was released on January 4, 2002, the day the grand jury's term expired. "I'm very grateful to be free. I don't think anyone realizes how precious freedom is until it's threatened or taken away from them," Leggett told CPJ shortly after her release.

The appeal before the Supreme Court, however, remained important because Leggett could still be summoned as a witness in any future trial related to the Angleton murder. She could also face criminal contempt charges.

At press time, the Supreme Court was still reviewing the case.

UZBEKISTAN: 4

Shodi Mardiev, Samarkand Radio
Imprisoned: June 11, 1998

Mardiev, a 63-year-old reporter with the state-run Samarkand Radio, was sentenced to 11 years in prison. The journalist, who is known for his criticism of government officials and for his satirical writings in the journal *Mushtum*, was found guilty of slandering an official in a program satirizing the alleged corruption of the Samarkand deputy prosecutor, and of attempting to extort money from him.

CPJ believes the prosecution and prison term were in reprisal for the journalist's critical stance toward government officials. His sentence was later cut in half under President Islam Karimov's decrees of April 30, 1999, and August 28, 2000.

Mardiev was held in Penal Colony 64/47 in the town of Kizil-tepa in the Navoi Region. Local human rights groups say many political prisoners are sent to this particular correctional facility. Prisoners are allowed only one visit every three months and may receive only one package every four months from outside the prison. The prison is also notorious for its poor medical facilities and food services.

Mardiev's physical and mental health deteriorated as a result of these poor conditions. Shortly after his arrest in November 1997, the journalist suffered two cerebral hemorrhages while in a pretrial detention center. He was hospitalized twice last year for a heart condition and did not receive the medical attention he urgently needed.

On January 5, 2002, Mardiev was released under an August 22, 2001, presidential amnesty marking the 10th anniversary of the country's independence from the former Soviet republic. Human rights advocates in the capital, Tashkent, say an estimated 18,000 ordinary prisoners were released under the decree, along with 700 religious and political detainees. Mardiev was eligible for early release because he is over 60 and had already served a portion of his sentence.

Muhammad Bekjanov, *Erk*
Imprisoned: March 15, 1999
Iusuf Ruzimuradov, *Erk*
Imprisoned: March 15, 1999

Bekjanov, editor of *Erk*, a newspaper published by the banned opposition Erk party, and Ruzimuradov, an employee of the paper, were sentenced to 14 years and 15 years in prison, respectively, at an August 1999 trial in the capital, Tashkent. They were convicted for distributing a banned newspaper containing slanderous criticism of President Islam Karimov, participating in a banned political protest, and attempting to overthrow the regime. In addition, the court found them guilty of illegally leaving the country and damaging their Uzbek passports.

Both men were tortured during their six-month pretrial detention in the Tashkent City Prison. Their health is deteriorating as a result of conditions in the prison camp where they are currently held.

According to human-rights activists in Tashkent, Bekjanov was transferred on November 27 to "strict-regime" Penal Colony 64/46 in the city of Navoi in central Uzbekistan. He has lost considerable weight and, like many prisoners in Uzbek camps, suffers from malnutrition. Local sources have informed CPJ that Ruzimuradov is being held in "strict regime" Penal Colony 64/33 in the village of Shakhali near the town of Karshi.

Madzhid Abduraimov, *Yangi Asr*
Imprisoned: August 1, 2001

Abduraimov, a correspondent with the national weekly *Yangi Asr*, was convicted of extortion and sentenced to 13 years in prison.

In a January 15 article in *Yangi Asr*, Abduraimov charged that Nusrat Radzhabov, head of the Boysunsky District grain production company Zagotzerno, had misappropriated state funds and falsified documents.

Abduraimov also accused the businessman of killing a 12-year-old in a car accident and alleged that Radzhabov's teenage son was part of a group that had beaten and raped a 13-year-old boy.

Radzhabov claims that Abduraimov asked him for money and threatened to publish more accusations unless he was paid. According to the Institute for War and Peace Reporting (IWPR), Radzhabov tried to sue Abduraimov for slander, but dropped the suit after a local prosecutor's investigation confirmed the facts in the article.

Authorities arrested Abduraimov and accused him of receiving a US$6,000 bribe. He and a witness quoted by the IWPR claimed that a man threw the money into the back seat of his car immediately before police stopped his vehicle, searched it, and arrested him.

Abduraimov was held in Termez Regional Police Department jail until his trial began in Termez City Court on July 4.

According to Abduraimov, the court proceedings were influenced by local officials who objected to his reporting on corruption in the oil business. His request for a change of venue was not granted. He refused to attend the hearings and was sentenced in absentia.

Abduraimov is known for his investigative reporting and critical stance toward local law enforcement bodies and authorities. The journalist and his family have been persecuted for several years with threatening phone calls, and his son was reportedly beaten by police and sentenced to four months in jail for disorderly conduct.

Supporters say Abduraimov was most likely framed, and it is not known where he is being held. His family plans to appeal the sentence to the Supreme Court.

VIETNAM: 2

Nguyen Thanh Giang, free-lancer
Imprisoned: March 4, 1999

Giang, a prominent writer and geophysicist, was arrested by police in Hanoi for allegedly possessing "antisocialist propaganda."

Vietnamese authorities had frequently harassed Giang for his published writings about corruption within the Communist Party. Giang's political essays—which dealt with such issues as peaceful reform, multiparty democracy, and human rights—regularly appeared on Internet sites and in newspapers published by Vietnamese living in exile. His arrest followed a series of articles in the government-controlled press arguing that dissidents posed a threat to the state.

On May 10, 1999, Giang was released on bail after an international campaign on his behalf. However, he remained under house arrest in 2001, with his activities closely monitored.

Ha Sy Phu, free-lancer
Imprisoned: May 12, 2000

Nguyen Xuan Tu, a scientist and political essayist better known by his pen name, Ha Sy Phu, was placed under house arrest and charged with treason, a crime punishable by death. The arrest came after an April 28 raid on Ha's home in Dalat, Lam Dong Province, during which police confiscated a computer, a printer, and several diskettes. They returned on May 12 with orders for his arrest signed by Col. Nguyen Van Do, police chief of Lam Dong Province.

The case began when officials suspected that Ha had helped draft a pro-democracy declaration, according to CPJ sources, and it continued with the government's long-term harassment of the writer. Ha was held under Administrative Detention Directive 31/CP, which provides for indefinite house arrest without due process, and was required to report daily to the Dalat police for interrogation.

Though the treason charge against Ha Sy Phu was withdrawn in January 2001, he remained under house arrest at year's end. ∎

ENEMIES OF THE PRESS 2001

EACH YEAR ON WORLD PRESS FREEDOM DAY (MAY 3), CPJ names the Ten Worst Enemies of the Press. The list focuses attention on individual leaders who are responsible for the world's worst abuses against the media. This year, repeat offenders Supreme Leader Ayatollah Ali Khamenei of Iran and President Jiang Zemin of China are joined by Liberian president Charles Taylor at the top of CPJ's annual accounting of press tyrants.

Khamenei, the religious leader who exercises enormous influence over key institutions in Iran, is the instigator of a relentless campaign that has shuttered the country's vibrant reformist press by closing dozens of newspapers and jailing outspoken journalists. China's Jiang appears on CPJ's list for a fifth straight year for maintaining the Communist Party's obsessive control over information, enforced in part via harsh prison sentences that have made China the world's leading jailer of journalists. In Liberia, Taylor has used censorship, prison, and threats of violence to silence virtually all independent media.

In addition to Taylor, three other press offenders, each using very different methods to intimidate media in their countries, are also new to CPJ's list this year: President Robert Mugabe of Zimbabwe, President Vladimir Putin of Russia, and Colombian paramilitary leader Carlos Castaño. CPJ put Ukrainian president Leonid Kuchma back on the list (he last appeared in 1999) and once more named perennial press freedom offenders President Fidel Castro of Cuba (a seven-year veteran of the press enemies list), President Zine Al-Abdine Ben Ali of Tunisia (listed for four years), and Malaysian prime minister Mahathir Mohamad (listed for three years).

"Although three of last year's worst press enemies—Sierra Leonean rebel leader Foday Sankoh, Peru's Alberto K. Fujimori, and Slobodan Milosevic of Yugoslavia—were ousted from power, there was no shortage of candidates to replace them," said CPJ executive director Ann Cooper. "Whether they are sly or blatant, the goal of each of these leaders is to hold on to political power by controlling information and muffling criticism."

"President Putin, for example, pays lip service to press freedom in Russia but then maneuvers in the shadows to centralize control of the media, stifle criticism, and destroy the independent press. Others, like Mahathir in Malaysia, don't even bother to try to hide their abuses behind a screen of empty rhetoric," said Cooper. "We hope that by naming these 10 press tyrants, we can focus world attention on their deeds and, by exposing them, bring about change."

Ayatollah Ali Khamenei, Supreme Leader of the Islamic Republic of Iran.

Ayatollah Ali Khamenei's fiery April 2000 sermon against the press inspired an unsparing campaign of repression against Iran's reformist media. To date, the conservative courts have banned at least 47 newspapers and publications since April 2000 and have jailed the country's best-known liberal journalists. When parliament debated reversing harsh provisions of Iran's notorious press law in 2000, Khamenei stopped things cold, declaring that any easing of the rules was not "in the interests of the system and the revolution." Today, the press law remains untouched, and at least five journalists languish in jail.

Charles Taylor, President of Liberia.

Since he became president of this war-plagued nation in 1997, Charles Taylor has been single-minded in clamping down on the independent press. He has jailed outspoken journalists on trumped-up charges, censored some media outfits at will, and forced others out of business through abusive tax audits. The popular Star Radio was effectively banned in March 2000. Since August 2000, at least eight journalists have been jailed in Liberia on baseless charges of espionage. In September 2000, Taylor, known for his erratic and bloody tactics, pledged to become "ferocious" with local media that did not toe his line. Several papers immediately closed, and their staffs fled the country en masse. Beginning July 2001, Taylor also banned all national radio stations except for those he personally controls.

Jiang Zemin, President of The People's Republic of China.

Jiang Zemin presides over the world's most elaborate system of media control. Thirty-five journalists were jailed for their work in China at the end of 2001, more than in any other country. Wary of the Internet's potential power to break the state's information monopoly, Jiang has poured huge resources into policing online content. His campaign to strengthen "ideological conformity" led to closings or reorganizations at several media outlets that had begun to assert some editorial independence.

Robert Mugabe, President of Zimbabwe.

Robert Mugabe's government has launched an all-out war against independent media, using weapons that range from lawsuits to physical violence. Since January 1999, two local journalists have been tortured and two foreign correspondents expelled, while the secret service screens e-mail and Internet communications to preserve "national security." Bomb attacks twice damaged the premises of the independent *Daily News*; the second bombing followed close on the heels of a call from Mugabe's information minister to silence that paper "once and for all." Meanwhile, Mugabe makes liberal use of his courts to prosecute independent journalists for criminal defamation. In January 2002, the government passed harsh legislation authorizing the state to register journalists and decide what can and cannot be published. Journalists who violate the new law face huge fines and lengthy prison terms.

Vladimir Putin, President of Russia.

Since his election in March 2000, Vladimir Putin has presided over an alarming assault on press freedom in Russia. The Kremlin imposed censorship in Chechnya, orchestrated legal harassment against private media outlets, and granted sweeping powers of surveillance to the security services. Despite Putin's professed goal of imposing the rule of law, numerous violent attacks on journalists have been carried out with impunity across Russia. In an ominous and dramatic move in April 2001, the government-dominated Gazprom corporation took over the company that controls NTV, the country's most prominent independent national television network. Within days, Gazprom also shut down a leading Moscow daily and ousted the journalists in charge of the country's most prestigious newsweekly. Despite Gazprom's insistence that the changes were strictly business, the main beneficiary was Putin himself, whose primary critics were silenced. A four-year prison sentence imposed on Russian military journalist Grigory Pasko in December 2001, as well as a January 2002 court ruling to liquidate the parent company of TV-6, an independent national television network that has criticized the Kremlin, indicate that Putin's campaign against the media has intensified.

Carlos Castaño, Leader of The United Self-Defense Forces of Colombia (AUC).

Even against the violent backdrop of Colombia's escalating civil war, in which all sides have targeted journalists, Carlos Castaño stands out as a ruthless enemy of the press. As founder of the United Self-Defense Forces of Colombia (AUC), the ultra-violent right-wing paramilitary organization, Castaño has been formally charged with ordering the 1999 murder of commentator and political satirist Jaime Garzón. His AUC has been implicated in the murders of at least three other journalists. Castaño's vicious public relations strategy is to grant frequent interviews to journalists who defend his actions, while using violence and threats of violence to terrorize those whose coverage he dislikes.

Leonid Kuchma, President of Ukraine.

Leonid Kuchma's government has stepped up its habitual censorship of opposition newspapers and increased attacks and threats against independent journalists. The disappearance and presumed murder of Internet editor Georgy Gongadze in late 2000 brought the plight of Ukrainian journalists into sharp focus. Allegations that Kuchma himself may have directed the elimination of Gongadze sparked a political crisis that threatened to bring down his government, and police security services made numerous attempts to muzzle publications that carried coverage critical of the Gongadze scandal. The July 2001 murder of Igor Aleksandrov, director of the independent television company Tor, and the unsolved Gongadze case highlight a pattern where police obstruct investigations and claim, despite evidence, that journalists are not targeted for their work. As a result, perpetrators continue to attack media workers with impunity.

Fidel Castro Ruz, President of Cuba.

Fidel Castro Ruz's government continues its scorched-earth assault on independent Cuban journalists by interrogating and detaining reporters, monitoring and interrupting their telephone calls, restricting their travel, and routinely putting them under house arrest to prevent coverage of certain events. A new tactic of intimidation involves arresting journalists and releasing them hundreds of miles from their homes. Meanwhile, foreign journalists who write critically about Cuba are routinely denied visas. In early 2001, Castro threatened some international news bureaus with expulsion from Cuba for "transmitting insults and lies."

Zine al-Abdine Ben Ali, President of Tunisia.

For more than a decade, Zine al-Abdine Ben Ali has brought Tunisia's press to almost total submission through censorship and crude intimidation. Newspapers have been closed. Journalists have been dismissed from their jobs, denied accreditation, put under police surveillance, and prevented from leaving the country. Some have been subjected to physical abuse. With the exception of a few courageous journalists, the totalitarian tactics of Ben Ali's police state have produced one of the most heavily self-censored presses in the region, while his propaganda machine churns out endless paeans to the dictator's supposed achievements in democracy and human rights. Incredibly, Ben Ali often chides local journalists for self-censorship. "Do write on any subject you choose," he said in a May interview. "There are no taboos except what is prohibited by law and press ethics."

Mahathir Mohamad, Prime Minister of Malaysia.

Openly contemptuous of press freedom, Mahathir Mohamad and his ruling National Front coalition further tightened the political establishment's control over the mainstream media through coercion, ownership changes, and staff purges. With traditional media outlets held firmly in check, the Internet was one of the few remaining forums for independent news and opinion. Notoriously thin-skinned, the prime minister regularly demonizes the foreign media for reporting he considers unfair. In 2001, his administration repeatedly blocked the circulation of international news magazines that featured articles about Malaysia. ■

CPJ's INTERNATIONAL PRESS FREEDOM AWARDS FOR THE YEAR 2001

Honored for Extraordinary Courage

EVERY YEAR, CPJ HONORS SEVERAL JOURNALISTS from around the world with its International Press Freedom Awards. Recipients have shown extraordinary courage in the face of enormous risks, bravely standing up to tyrants who refuse to allow free discussion in order to hide corruption or keep the world from witnessing their deeds. These journalists have endured terrible difficulties, including jail or physical violence, simply for working to uncover and report the truth, or because they have expressed opinions that the leaders of their countries deem to be dangerous.

Three winners of the **11th Annual International Press Freedom Awards** were honored on November 20 at a ceremony in New York City. The fourth, Chinese journalist **Jiang Weiping**, was in prison. Jiang is a veteran journalist currently jailed on charges of "revealing state secrets" after pushing the boundaries of censorship and aggressively reporting on the taboo subject of official graft in China's industrial northeast region. He is the former Dalian bureau chief for the newspaper *Wen Hui Bao* and a reporter for the state news agency Xinhua. Jiang was detained in December 2000 after writing a series of articles exposing government corruption for the Hong Kong magazine *Qianshao* (Frontline). Jiang was sentenced to eight years in prison following a secret trial held on September 5, 2001.

Jiang's reporting uncovered several corruption scandals involving high-level officials, including such well-connected leaders as Bo Xilai, governor of Liaoning Province and son of Communist Party elder Bo Yibo. Jiang also revealed that the vice mayor of Shenyang gambled away 30 million yuan (US$3.6 million) of public funds, and he reported that the mayor of Daqing used state money to buy apartments for each of his 29 mistresses.

Though Chinese government leaders have urged journalists to help fight corruption, few legal protections exist for reporters who do so. Courageous investigative journalists like Jiang who work independently to expose official impropriety risk harassment and imprisonment. According to CPJ records, 35 journalists were imprisoned in China at the end of 2001, more than in any other country in the world.

Geoff Nyarota is the editor of *The Daily News*, Zimbabwe's only independent daily newspaper. Launched less than two years ago, the Harare-based paper has managed to become Zimbabwe's most influential voice despite repeated attempts by President Robert Mugabe's government to silence it.

Nyarota's office still bears the scars of the homemade bomb that was thrown at the front door from a passing car in April 2000. And in January 2001, unknown assailants blew up the paper's printing presses. Police investigations have languished and no arrests have been made, although credible sources have attributed these attacks to the Zimbabwean military.

Most recently, on August 16, 2001, Nyarota and three other journalists from *The Daily News* were arrested and charged with publishing "rumor or false information likely to discredit security forces" after a front-page article reported that police vehicles had been used to support violent raids on some white-owned commercial farms. A judge invalidated the charges and the journalists were freed days later.

Mazen Dana is a Palestinian cameraman for the Reuters news agency covering one of the most dangerous beats in the world, the West Bank city of Hebron, where journalists are routinely targets of violence. Dana has been wounded repeatedly during the seven years he has documented the clashes in his hometown for Reuters.

Despite the great physical risk, Dana's commitment to his work keeps powerful images of Hebron's clashes in the public eye. Hebron is a cauldron of religious and political tension. In a city of 150,000 Palestinians, some 400 Jewish settlers live in the center of town, protected by hundreds of Israeli soldiers.

In May 2000, Dana was shot in the leg with a rubber-coated bullet while filming Palestinian youths throwing rocks at Israeli soldiers. Two months later, Jewish settlers beat him unconscious while he tried to film a conflict. The next day, an Israeli police officer slammed Dana's head in the rear door of an ambulance while he was filming the evacuation of a Palestinian youth wounded in clashes. In October 2000, Dana was shot in the same leg, two days in a row.

Horacio Verbitsky is one of Argentina's leading investigative journalists, as well as a columnist and press freedom activist. He has built his distinguished career by fearlessly exposing government corruption and battling restrictive press laws. A working journalist since 1960, Verbitsky's relentless pursuit of a story has earned him his nickname *el perro*, or "the dog."

In January 1991, Verbitsky was thrust into the national spotlight after writing an article alleging that former Argentine president Carlos Saúl Menem's brother-in-law had demanded a bribe from a company in return for a tax exemption. The scandal became known as "Swiftgate." Menem called Verbitsky "a journalistic delinquent," but the affair forced the president to purge half his cabinet and put corruption on the national agenda.

His best-selling book *The Flight* contained the first public confessions of an official involved in Argentina's "dirty war" and related how hundreds of prisoners of the military regime from 1976 to 1983 were thrown to their deaths from airplanes. Verbitsky has played a front-line role in strengthening democracy and safeguarding press freedom in Argentina and Latin America.

CPJ also honored **Joseph Lelyveld** with the Burton Benjamin Memorial Award. During nearly four decades at *The New York Times*, Lelyveld helped define the highest principles of American journalism. He began at *The Times* as a copy boy in 1962. His distinguished reporting included years as a foreign correspondent in London, New Delhi, Hong Kong, and Johannesburg. His 1985 book, *Move Your Shadow*, based on his reporting on South Africa under apartheid, won several major awards, including the Pulitzer Prize. Other honors for his reporting have included the George Polk Memorial Award and a Guggenheim fellowship.

Lelyveld moved from foreign correspondent to foreign editor in 1987, then he became managing editor and finally executive editor of *The Times* in 1994.

The Burton Benjamin Memorial Award, given for a lifetime of distinguished achievement for the cause of press freedom, honors the late CBS News senior producer and former CPJ chairman, who died in 1988. ■

CONTRIBUTORS

THE COMMITTEE TO PROTECT JOURNALISTS IS EXTREMELY GRATEFUL to the following foundations, corporations, and individuals for their invaluable support during 2001:

EXECUTIVE LEADERSHIP
$100,000 and above
The Ford Foundation
The Freedom Forum
John S. and James L. Knight Foundation
Lexis-Nexis
The Robert R. McCormick Tribune Foundation
Open Society Institute
Pittman Family Foundation
Ruben and Elisabeth Rausing Trust

LEADERSHIP
$50,000–$99,999
Advance Publications

UNDERWRITERS
$25,000–$49,999
A. H. Belo Foundation
AOL Time Warner Inc.
Bloomberg
Meredith and Tom Brokaw
The Coca-Cola Company
Phil Donahue and Marlo Thomas
Katharine Graham
Los Angeles Times
Merrill Lynch & Co., Inc.
The New York Times Company
The New York Times Company Foundation
S. I. Newhouse Foundation, Inc.
Dan and Jean Rather
Reuters
St. Petersburg Times
Scripps Howard Foundation
The Tinker Foundation
Vivendi Universal

SPONSORS
$15,000–$24,999
Terry Anderson
BP America, Inc.
Citigroup
Continental Airlines
Crowell & Moring LLP
Ford Motor Company
Harper's Magazine
HBO
Johnson & Johnson
The Miami Herald/Knight Ridder
The News Corporation
Ken and Marianne Novack
Viacom/CBS News

PATRONS
$10,000–$14,999
ABC, Inc.
Boston Ventures
Cisneros Group
CNN
Condé Nast Publications
Dow Jones & Company, Inc.
Dubin and Swieca
The Glaser Family Foundation
James C. and Toni K. Goodale
Heinz Endowments
The Mack Company
NBC
The Joan Shorenstein Center on the Press, Politics, and Public Policy
Sony Corporation of America
Time Inc.
TIME Magazine
The Washington Post Company

FRIENDS
$5,000–$9,999
Allen & Company Incorporated
Franz and Marcia Allina
The Baltimore Sun
Cablevision Systems Corporation
Columbia Journalism Review
Community Counselling Services
Court TV
Daedalus Foundation
Daily News/US News & World Report
Debevoise & Plimpton
Drue Heinz Trust
Fortune
Fox News Channel
Gannett Foundation
Gateway, Inc.
The JKW Foundation
Henry R. Kravis Foundation, Inc.
Matt Lauer
The MCJ Foundation
Geraldine Fabrikant Metz and Robert T. Metz
The Nation
National Hockey League
Newsday
Newsweek
Nieman Foundation for Journalism
Petroleum Argus

We also extend our deepest gratitude to the many individuals and organizations that supported the Committee to Protect Journalists with gifts below $1,000 and cannot be recognized in this list because of space limitations.

Some of the vital resources that help make the work of CPJ possible are in-kind services and contributions. We thank the following for their support during the past year:

ABC   IDT
The Associated Press   David Marash
CNN   Reuters
Freedom Forum

CPJ is grateful to Lexis-Nexis for its continued in-kind contribution of information technology services.   **LEXIS·NEXIS** ℞ A member of the Reed Elsevier plc group

Continental Airlines is the Preferred Airline for the Committee to Protect Journalists.   **Continental Airlines**

CPJ AT A GLANCE

FACTS ABOUT THE ORGANIZATION AND ITS ACTIVITIES

The Committee to Protect Journalists is a nonpartisan, nonprofit organization founded in 1981. We promote freedom of the press throughout the world by defending the right of journalists to report the news without fear of reprisal.

HOW DID CPJ GET STARTED?

A group of U.S. foreign correspondents created CPJ in 1981 in response to the often brutal treatment of their foreign colleagues by authoritarian governments and other enemies of independent journalism.

WHO RUNS CPJ?

CPJ has a full-time staff of 23 at its New York headquarters, including area specialists for each major world region. CPJ also has a Washington, D.C., representative, an Asia program consultant based in Bangkok, Thailand, and a Europe and Central Asia consultant based in the United Kingdom. CPJ's activities are directed by a 35-member board of prominent U.S. journalists.

HOW IS CPJ FUNDED?

CPJ is funded solely by contributions from individuals, corporations, and foundations. CPJ does not accept government funding.

WHY IS PRESS FREEDOM IMPORTANT?

Without a free press, few other human rights are attainable. A strong press freedom environment encourages the growth of a robust civil society, which itself leads to stable, sustainable democracies and healthy social, political, and economic development.

CPJ works in more than 130 countries, many of which suffer under repressive regimes, debilitating civil war, or other problems that are detrimental to press freedom and democracy.

HOW DOES CPJ PROTECT JOURNALISTS?

By publicly revealing abuses against the press and by acting on behalf of imprisoned and threatened journalists, CPJ effectively warns journalists and news organizations where attacks on press freedom are occurring. CPJ organizes vigorous protest at all levels—ranging from local governments to the United Nations—and, when necessary, works behind the scenes through other diplomatic channels to effect change. CPJ also publishes articles and news releases, special reports, a biannual magazine, and the most comprehensive annual report on attacks against the press around the world.

WHERE DOES CPJ GET ITS INFORMATION?

CPJ has full-time program coordinators monitoring the press in Africa, the Americas, Asia, Europe, and the Middle East. They track developments through their own independent research, fact-finding missions, and firsthand contacts in the field, including reports from other journalists. CPJ shares information on breaking cases with other press freedom organizations worldwide through the International Freedom of Expression Exchange (IFEX), a global e-mail network.

WHEN WOULD A JOURNALIST CALL UPON CPJ?

- *In an emergency.* Using local and foreign contacts, CPJ can intervene whenever foreign correspondents are in trouble. CPJ is also prepared to immediately notify news organizations, government officials, and human rights organizations of press freedom violations.
- *When traveling on assignment.* CPJ maintains a database of journalist contacts around the world and can advise journalists covering dangerous assignments.
- *When covering the news.* Attacks against the press are news, and they often serve as the first signal of a crackdown on all freedoms. CPJ is uniquely situated to provide journalists with information and insight into press conditions around the world.
- *When becoming a member.* A basic membership costs only US$45, and each donation helps CPJ defend journalists if the need arises. Members receive CPJ's magazine, *Dangerous Assignments*; its annual book, *Attacks on the Press*; and its e-newsletter, *CPJ Update*.

WAYS TO PARTICIPATE IN CPJ

WHEN YOU GIVE YOUR DOLLARS OR SERVICES TO CPJ, you sustain our ability to protect journalists in danger, defend the rights of journalists and news organizations against the censorship of repressive regimes, and create a climate of improved press freedom in all regions of the world. To maintain the independence necessary to carry out this mission, we accept no government funding and depend solely on the support of foundations, corporations, and individuals. Thus, your various contributions are of vital importance to us; please consider participating in CPJ through the method that best suits your needs.

Individual Membership
Whether you're a journalist, media executive, or concerned person, by becoming a member of CPJ you can show your support for freedom of the press and stay informed about press conditions. All members of CPJ, even at the basic level of US$45 per year, receive a subscription to CPJ's biannual news magazine, *Dangerous Assignments,* as well as its e-newsletter, *CPJ Update,* and a 50 percent discount on all other CPJ publications. In addition, all members receive a complimentary copy of *Attacks on the Press,* CPJ's comprehensive annual report on press freedom conditions around the world. Gift memberships are also available. A membership form can be found on CPJ's Web site, www.cpj.org.

Institutional Membership (US$1,000 and above)
CPJ works on behalf of journalists everywhere. If you represent a news organization, your membership commitment will send a powerful message that journalists throughout the globe are looking out for the rights of their colleagues. Demonstrate your organization's commitment to the profession and to your colleagues' safety by joining CPJ. For corporations, the free flow of information is vitally important to business in the global marketplace. Private sector institutions in the communications, legal, and financial services industries have become increasingly involved in supporting the freedom of the press to report on political and economic conditions. Show your company's support for CPJ's critical analyses and actions by becoming an institutional member.

Educational institutions are invited to take advantage of CPJ's academic membership category, available at the discounted rate of US$500 per year. At this special level, schools may enjoy all the benefits offered to organizations subscribing to a traditional institutional membership. A membership form can be found on CPJ's Web site, www.cpj.org.

Support our Membership and Fundraising Campaigns
2002 marks our 21st year of protecting journalists under siege and furthering the cause of press freedom throughout the world. Demonstrate your support for our continued efforts by participating in our membership and fundraising campaigns. Encourage your colleagues to become members of CPJ. Contact your public/corporate affairs office and find out if your company will match your contribution to CPJ. In-kind donations and services can also make a significant difference to CPJ. Consider donating a broad range of products and services, including: research; technology; advertising; publicity; printing; graphic design; photography; video; computer equipment; and even office space.

Support the 12th Annual International Press Freedom Awards Dinner, Fall 2002, New York City

The International Press Freedom Awards Dinner honors the struggle of journalists who risk their lives to report the news. Award recipients from around the world are the guests of honor for a very special evening that demonstrates the unity of media in the fight for press freedom. The gala is a major media industry gathering of journalists, publishers, and communications professionals, as well as leaders in the entertainment, finance, and legal spheres. Held each fall in New York City, the dinner historically has raised nearly half of CPJ's annual operating funds. Show your support for freedom of the press by attending the 12th Annual International Press Freedom Awards Dinner—the key media event of 2002. Corporations can demonstrate their commitment to CPJ by becoming corporate sponsors of the gala program and of the awardees.

Provide Information on Cases and Support CPJ's Efforts on Behalf of Journalists in Danger

Whenever a journalist or news organization is threatened, harassed, or attacked, CPJ needs accurate and reliable information immediately from as many sources as possible. Letters, petitions, and various communiqués from journalists in support of colleagues under attack or in prison do make a difference. Stay on top of late-breaking developments by visiting CPJ's Web site at www.cpj.org.

BECOMING A MEMBER OF CPJ

I wish to join as an individual member:

❏ Participant $45
❏ Contributor $100
❏ Supporter $500
❏ Benefactor $1000 and above
❏ Student $20

My company is subscribing to an institutional membership:

❏ Activist $1000
❏ Champion $2500
❏ Advocate $5000
❏ Catalyst $10,000
❏ Corporate Supporter $15,000
❏ Corporate Leader $20,000
❏ Academic Supporter $500

Member Name   Mr./Miss/Mrs./Ms. (as you wish to be listed for acknowledgment)

Institution

(Please indicate preferred mailing address)
❏ Home   ❏ Business

Title

Company   Street address

City   State   Zip/Postal   Country

Home Phone   Business Phone

Fax   E-mail

PAYMENT INFORMATION

My corporation will match my gift to CPJ: ❏ Yes (Enclosed is the relevant matching gift form.)   ❏ No
Enclosed, please find my tax-deductible contribution of US$_____ or charge my gift of
US$_____.

❏ Visa   ❏ MasterCard   ❏ American Express   ❏ Check enclosed

Card Number   Expiration Date

Name on Card (please print)   Signature

Please write checks or money orders to **Committee to Protect
Journalists** (funds must be drawn in U.S. dollars and on a U.S. bank
or U.S. resident branch), or indicate charge information, and send to:

**The Development Department ■ CPJ ■ 330 Seventh Avenue, 12th Floor
New York, N.Y. 10001, USA
Phone: (212) 465-1004 ■ Fax: (212) 465-9568 ■ E-mail: development@cpj.org**

HOW TO REPORT AN ATTACK
ON THE PRESS

CPJ needs accurate, detailed information in order to document abuses of press freedom and help journalists in trouble. CPJ corroborates the information and takes appropriate action on behalf of the journalists and news organizations involved.

What to report:
Journalists who are:
- Arrested
- Assaulted
- Censored
- Denied credentials
- Harassed
- Kidnapped
- Killed
- Missing
- Threatened

- Wounded
- Wrongfully expelled
- Wrongfully sued for libel or defamation

News organizations that are:
- Attacked or illegally searched
- Censored
- Closed by force
- Editions confiscated or transmissions jammed
- Materials confiscated or damaged
- Wrongfully sued for libel or defamation

Information needed:
CPJ needs accurate, detailed information about:
- Journalists and news organizations involved
- Date and circumstances of incident
- Background information

Anyone with information about an attack on the press should call CPJ.
Call collect if necessary: (212) 465-1004, or send us a fax at (212) 465-9568.

Contact information for regional programs:
Africa: (212) 465-9344, ext. 112
E-mail: africa@cpj.org
Americas: (212) 465-9344, ext. 120
E-mail: americas@cpj.org
Asia: (212) 465-9344, ext. 140
E-mail: asia@cpj.org
Europe and Central Asia: (212) 465-9344, ext. 101
E-mail: europe@cpj.org
Middle East and North Africa: (212) 465-9344, ext. 104
E-mail: mideast@cpj.org

What happens next:
Depending on the case, CPJ will:
- Investigate and confirm the report.
- Pressure authorities to respond.
- Notify human rights groups and press organizations around the world, including IFEX, Article 19, Amnesty International, Reporters sans frontières, PEN, International Federation of Journalists, and Human Rights Watch.
- Increase public awareness through the press.
- Publish advisories to warn other journalists about potential dangers.
- Send a fact-finding mission to investigate.

SAVE ON *ATTACKS ON THE PRESS IN 2001*
LIBRARIES • SCHOOLS • TEACHERS
Save 50% on orders of five copies or more
US$15.00 per copy (cover price: US$30.00)

Please send me _____ **copies of** *ATTACKS ON THE PRESS IN 2001*
_____ **at US$15.00 each (discount)**   _____ **at US$30.00 (regular price)**

_____   _____
Mr./Miss/Mrs./Ms. First Name   Last Name

_____
Title

_____
Institution

_____
Street address

_____   _____ _____
City   State   Zip/Postal   Country

_____   _____
Home Phone   Business Phone

_____   _____
Fax   E-mail

PAYMENT INFORMATION

Enclosed, please find my check or money order in the amount of US$_____ or
charge my credit card in the amount of US$_____.

❏ Visa   ❏ MasterCard   ❏ American Express   ❏ Check enclosed

_____   _____
Card Number   Expiration Date

_____   _____
Name on Card (please print)   Signature

Please write checks or money orders to **Committee to Protect
Journalists** (funds must be drawn in U.S. dollars and on a U.S. bank
or U.S. resident branch), or indicate charge information, and send to:

**Director of Development ■ CPJ ■ 330 Seventh Avenue, 12th Floor
New York, N.Y. 10001, USA
Phone: (212) 465-9344, ext. 144 ■ Fax: (212) 465-9568
E-mail: development@cpj.org**

CPJ STAFF

Executive Director, Ann Cooper
(212) 465-9344, ext. 102
acooper@cpj.org

Deputy Director, Joel Simon
(212) 465-9344, ext. 116
jsimon@cpj.org

Editorial and Program Director,
Richard McGill Murphy
(212) 465-9344, ext. 108
rmurphy@cpj.org

Director of Development, Vesna Neskow
(212) 465-9344, ext. 113
vneskow@cpj.org

Financial Director, Lade Kadejo
(212) 465-9344, ext. 110
lkadejo@cpj.org

Journalist Assistance Coordinator,
Elisabeth Witchel
(212) 465-9344, ext. 146
ewitchel@cpj.org

Communications Coordinator, Abi Wright
(212) 465-9344, ext. 105
awright@cpj.org

Washington, D.C., Representative,
Frank Smyth
(202) 244-2948
franksmyth@compuserve.com

Deputy Editor, Amanda Watson-Boles
(212) 465-9344, ext. 147
awatsonboles@cpj.org

Webmaster and Systems Administrator,
Michael Stern
(212) 465-9344, ext. 119
mstern@cpj.org

Development Associate, Julia Parshall
(212) 465-9344, ext. 109
jparshall@cpj.org

Development Assistant, Jesse Heiwa
(212) 465-9344, ext. 144
jheiwa@cpj.org

Office Manager, Q-Tesha Lee
(212) 465-1004
qlee@cpj.org

REGIONAL PROGRAMS

AFRICA
Program Coordinator, Yves Sorokobi
(212) 465-9344, ext. 112
ysorokobi@cpj.org
Research Associate, Wacuka Mungai
(212) 465-9344, ext. 106
wmungai@cpj.org
Research Associate, Adam Posluns
(212) 465-9344, ext. 107
aposluns@cpj.org

THE AMERICAS
Program Coordinator, Marylene Smeets
(212) 465-9344, ext. 120
msmeets@cpj.org
Research Associate,
Sauro González Rodríguez
(212) 465-9344, ext. 118
sgonzalez@cpj.org

ASIA
Program Coordinator, Kavita Menon
(212) 465-9344, ext. 140
kmenon@cpj.org
Program Consultant, A. Lin Neumann
(011) 66-2-279-9610
lin_neumann@csi.com
Research Associate, Sophie Beach
(212) 465-9344, ext. 117
sbeach@cpj.org

EUROPE AND CENTRAL ASIA
Program Coordinator, Alexander Lupis
(212) 465-9344, ext. 101
alupis@cpj.org
Program Consultant, Emma Gray
egray@cpj.org
Research Associate, Olga Tarasov
(212) 465-9344, ext. 115
otarasov@cpj.org

MIDDLE EAST AND NORTH AFRICA
Program Coordinator, Joel Campagna
(240) 426-1810
jcampagna@cpj.org
Research Associate, Hani Sabra
(212) 465-9344, ext. 104
hsabra@cpj.org

| INDEX OF COUNTRIES |